# THE ASHGATE RESEARCH COMPANION TO WORLD METHODISM

The *Ashgate Research Companions* are designed to offer scholars and graduate students a comprehensive and authoritative state-of-the-art review of current research in a particular area. The companions' editors bring together a team of respected and experienced experts to write chapters on the key issues in their speciality, providing a comprehensive reference to the field.

# Ashgate Methodist Studies Series

*Editorial Board*

Dr Ted Campbell, Associate Professor, Perkins School of Theology, Southern Methodist University, Texas, USA.
Professor William Gibson, Director of the Oxford Centre for Methodism and Church History, Oxford Brookes University, UK.
Professor David Hempton, Dean, Harvard Divinity School, Harvard University, USA.
Dr Jason Vickers, Associate Professor of Theology and Wesleyan Studies; Director of the Center for Evangelical United Brethren Heritage at the United Theological Seminary, Dayton, Ohio, USA
Dr Martin Wellings, Superintendent Minister of Oxford Methodist Circuit and Past President of the World Methodist Historical Society.

Methodism remains one of the largest denominations in the USA and is growing in South America, Africa and Asia (especially in Korea and China). This series spans Methodist history and theology, exploring its success as a movement historically and in its global expansion. Books in the series will look particularly at features within Methodism which attract wide interest, including: the unique position of the Wesleys; the prominent role of women and minorities in Methodism; the interaction between Methodism and politics; the 'Methodist conscience' and its motivation for temperance and pacifist movements; the wide range of Pentecostal, holiness and evangelical movements, and the interaction of Methodism with different cultures.

# The Ashgate Research Companion to World Methodism

*Edited by*

WILLIAM GIBSON
*Oxford Brookes University, UK*

PETER FORSAITH
*Oxford Brookes University, UK*

MARTIN WELLINGS
*Oxford Methodist Circuit, UK*

ASHGATE

© William Gibson, Peter Forsaith, Martin Wellings and the contributors 2013

All rights reserved. No part of this publication may be reproduced, stored in a retrieval system or transmitted in any form or by any means, electronic, mechanical, photocopying, recording or otherwise without the prior permission of the publisher.

William Gibson, Peter Forsaith and Martin Wellings have asserted their right under the Copyright, Designs and Patents Act, 1988, to be identified as the editors of this work.

Published by
Ashgate Publishing Limited
Wey Court East
Union Road
Farnham
Surrey, GU9 7PT
England

Ashgate Publishing Company
110 Cherry Street
Suite 3-1
Burlington, VT 05401-3818
USA

www.ashgate.com

**British Library Cataloguing in Publication Data**
The Ashgate Research Companion on World Methodism. – (Ashgate Methodist Studies Series)
1. Methodism. 2. Methodism – History. 3. Methodist Church. 4. Methodist Church – History. I. Series II. World Methodism III. Gibson, William, 1959- . IV. Forsaith, Peter S. V. Wellings, Martin.
287–dc23

**Library of Congress Cataloging-in-Publication Data**
The Ashgate Research Companion to World Methodism / edited by William Gibson, Peter Forsaith and Martin Wellings.
    pages   cm – (Ashgate Methodist Studies Series)
Includes bibliographical references and index.
1. Methodism. I. Gibson, William, 1959– editor of compilation. II. Forsaith, Peter S., editor of compilation. III. Wellings, Martin, editor of compilation.
BX8332.A84 2013
287–dc23                                                                                                    2012026628

ISBN   9781409401384 (hbk)
ISBN   9781409462149 (ebk-PDF)
ISBN   9781472405142 (ebk-ePUB)

Printed and bound in Great Britain by MPG Books Group, UK

# Contents

| | | |
|---|---|---|
| *List of Tables* | | *vii* |
| *Notes on Contributors* | | *ix* |

## PART I: INTRODUCTION

| 1 | Introduction<br>William Gibson | 3 |
|---|---|---|

## PART II: HISTORICAL CONTEXT

| 2 | The Origins and Early Growth of Methodism, 1730–91<br>Ted A. Campbell | 13 |
|---|---|---|
| 3 | The Price of Respectability: Methodism in Britain and the United States, 1791–1865<br>Kevin Watson | 33 |
| 4 | Methodism: Consolidation and Reunion, 1865–1939<br>Morris L. Davis | 51 |
| 5 | Methodism: Shifting Balances, 1939–2010<br>Brian Beck | 65 |

## PART III: WORLD METHODISM

| 6 | Church Statistics and the Growth of Global Methodism: Some Preliminary Descriptive Statistics<br>David J. Jeremy | 87 |
|---|---|---|
| 7 | The Wesleys' Role in World Methodism<br>Jason E. Vickers | 109 |
| 8 | Methodism, Ecumenism and Interfaith Relations<br>David M. Chapman | 121 |

| 9 | Holiness and Pentecostal Movements Within Methodism<br>*Priscilla Pope-Levison* | 141 |
|---|---|---|
| 10 | Methodism and Women<br>*Margaret Jones* | 157 |
| 11 | Methodism and Liberation Theology<br>*Joerg Rieger* | 175 |
| 12 | Methodism, Globalisation and John Wesley<br>*Keith Robbins* | 199 |

## PART IV: BELIEF AND PRACTICE

| 13 | Methodism and the Bible<br>*Peter Phillips* | 217 |
|---|---|---|
| 14 | Music, Hymnody and the Culture of Methodism in Britain<br>*J. R. Watson* | 233 |
| 15 | Episkopé and Connexionalism: Ecclesiology and Church Government in Methodism<br>*Russell E. Richey* | 251 |
| 16 | Methodist Liturgy and Worship<br>*Karen B. Westerfield Tucker* | 269 |
| 17 | Methodist Spirituality<br>*Ian M. Randall* | 289 |
| 18 | Methodism and the Evangelical Tradition<br>*Martin Wellings* | 307 |
| 19 | A Historical Survey of Methodist Preaching<br>*John Munsey Turner* | 325 |

## PART V: CULTURE AND SOCIETY

| 20 | Methodism and Politics: Mapping the Political on the Methodist Genome<br>*Stephen J. Plant* | 345 |
|---|---|---|
| 21 | The Methodist Conscience: Slavery, Temperance and Pacifism<br>*Jennifer L. Woodruff Tait* | 365 |

| 22 | Material and Cultural Aspects of Methodism: Architecture, Artefacts and Art<br>*Peter Forsaith* | 387 |
|---|---|---|
| 23 | Methodism and Education<br>*John T. Smith* | 407 |
| 24 | Methodists and Business, 1860–1960<br>*David J. Jeremy* | 431 |
| 25 | Methodism in Literature<br>*Laura Davies* | 461 |
| 26 | Methodism and Social Justice<br>*Jonathan Rodell* | 477 |

*Select Bibliography and Further Reading* — 501

*Index* — 515

# List of Tables

| | | |
|---|---|---|
| 6.1 | Divergencies in British Methodist statistics of members: EMC and WMC compared with Currie et al. for 1880, 1910 and 1955. | 97 |
| 6.2 | Official global Methodist statistics of members, 1880–2006 | 99 |
| 6.3 | The global presence of Methodists, 1880–2006 | 102 |
| 6.4 | Average percentage and numerical growth rates in global Methodist membership for selected available periods, | 103 |
| 6.5 | National Methodist densities ranked by size, 1880–2006 | 104 |
| 24.1 | Occupational composition of UK Methodist lay leaders, 1872–2000 (percentages) | 436 |
| 24.2 | Methodist adult affiliations among business leaders in Britain in the *DBB* and the *DSBB* (1,561 individuals) compared with members in 1907 | 438 |
| A.1 | Methodists among British business leaders, nineteenth and twentieth centuries | 454 |
| A.2 | Methodists among American business leaders, nineteenth and twentieth centuries | 457 |

# Notes on Contributors

**Brian Beck** is a Past President and former Secretary of the British Methodist Conference in the UK.

**Ted A. Campbell** is Associate Professor of Church History in the Perkins School of Theology at Southern Methodist University, Dallas, Texas.

**David M. Chapman** is Co-leader of the Central Sussex United Area of the Methodist Church and the United Reformed Church, UK.

**Laura Davies** is Research Fellow at the Centre for Christianity and Culture, Regent's Park College University of Oxford, UK.

**Morris L. Davis** is Associate Dean for Academic Affairs, and Associate Professor of the History of Christianity and Wesleyan Methodist Studies, Drew University, New Jersey.

**Peter Forsaith** is Research Fellow in the Oxford Centre for Methodism and Church History, Oxford Brookes University, UK.

**William Gibson** is Professor of Ecclesiastical History and Director of the Oxford Centre for Methodism and Church History, Oxford Brookes University, UK.

**David J. Jeremy** is Emeritus Professor of Business History, Manchester Metropolitan University, UK.

**Margaret Jones** is a Supernumerary Minister and former Team Leader in the Formation in Ministry Office in the Methodist Church of Great Britain.

**Peter Phillips** is Director, Centre for Biblical Literacy and Communication at St John's College, University of Durham, UK.

**Stephen J. Plant** is Dean of Trinity Hall, Cambridge, UK.

**Priscilla Pope-Levison** is Professor of Theology at Seattle Pacific University, Washington.

**Ian M. Randall** is Senior Research Fellow of Spurgeon's College, London, UK.

**Russell E. Richey** is Dean Emeritus of the Candler School of Theology, Emory University, Atlanta, Georgia.

**Joerg Rieger** is Wendland-Cook Professor of Constructive Theology at the Perkins School of Theology, Southern Methodist University, Dallas, Texas.

**Keith Robbins** is former Vice-Chancellor of the University of Wales Lampeter, UK.

**Jonathan Rodell** teaches in the Institute of Continuing Education at the University of Cambridge, UK.

**John T. Smith** is Senior Lecturer in Education, University of Hull, UK.

**John Munsey Turner** is a Supernumerary Minister and former Tutor at the Queen's College, Birmingham, UK.

**Jason E. Vickers** is Associate Professor of Theology and Wesleyan Studies and Director of the Center for Evangelical United Brethren Heritage at the United Theological Seminary, Dayton, Ohio.

**J. R. Watson** is Professor in the Department of English and Fellow of St Chad's College, University of Durham, UK.

**Kevin Watson** was Director of Englesea Brook Chapel and Museum and currently works at the University of Chester, UK.

**Martin Wellings** is Superintendent Minister of the Oxford Circuit, UK and Past President of the World Methodist Historical Society.

**Karen B. Westerfield Tucker** is Professor of Worship at Boston University School of Theology, Massachusetts.

**Jennifer L. Woodruff Tait** is Managing Editor of *Christian History Magazine* and Affiliate Professor of Church History at Asbury Theological Seminary, Kentucky.

# PART I
# Introduction

# Introduction

## William Gibson

### The Complexity of Methodism

The publication of a research companion to world Methodism invites some explanation. This collection of essays seeks to capture some of the complexity of the phenomenon of Methodism, and does so by harnessing the talents of scholars from diverse disciplinary backgrounds. Historians, theologians, liturgists, scholars of business, material culture, literature and music provide insights into the character and development of world Methodism. The complex interdisciplinary picture that emerges from these essays is entirely appropriate, for Methodism, like many other churches and denominations, is itself complicated and multi-layered, and suffers from the reductionist urge to simplify and uncomplicate. Accounts of Methodism could be supplied which concentrate solely on its narrative history from a society within the Church of England in Oxford in the 1730s to a worldwide church with millions of adherents in 2011. Its theology could be reduced to a version of the Bebbington 'quadrilateral' – though perhaps in the case of Methodism that quadrilateral would consist of a present-centred Wesleyan rhombus of calling, conversion, conscience and cross. Methodist popular culture could be condensed into the hagiography of John Wesley and an emphasis on souvenirs and commemorative crockery. Local studies, biographies, sociology and the plethora of fashionable disciplinary 'studies' can all lend a hand in reducing Methodism to a two-dimensional form of religion. But this is not what this volume seeks to provide.

It is important at the outset to be clear about what is meant here by 'Methodism' and, equally, what is not. In at least what is now regarded as the movement's first half century, dating its genesis from around 1730, 'Methodist' was a term of mild ridicule used of those whose religious behaviour, usually termed 'enthusiasm', seemed excessive. If this was a popular usage, it had specific reference to individuals and groups linked to a number of leading personalities, most notably George Whitefield, the Countess of Huntingdon and the brothers John and Charles Wesley. Moreover, during this time the Methodists were essentially (although not universally) part of the national Church of England and any sense of forming separate denominations was generally denied. It should also be recognised that

'Methodist' was a term coined and applied by others, which was only reluctantly accepted by participants.

The Calvinistic Methodism of Whitefield, Howell Harris (in Wales) and Lady Huntingdon did not develop the sort of social and theological adaptability that David Hempton has so clearly demonstrated was a feature of Wesleyan Methodism.[1] Nor, despite its strongly evangelical roots, did it sustain a sense of missionary urgency in the way Wesleyan Methodism did. Its identity remained closely focused on the communities in which it had thrived in the eighteenth and nineteenth centuries and in which it saw revivals and revivalism as a continuous process rather than as a prelude to global evangelism. The separateness of Calvinistic Methodism from Wesleyanism should not be surprising given that its roots lay more firmly in the soil of Reformed theological traditions than the Arminian principles of the Wesleys. The editors therefore have seen Calvinistic Methodism as much more akin to the Reformed tradition and best considered as such.

The Methodism which concerns this volume, then, is that which traces its roots back to the activities of the Wesleys in what has also become known as the evangelical movement, but which through the nineteenth century developed into a global phenomenon. From the start Methodism was untidy and ambiguous. It sought to exist within an established church which had settled parish boundaries, episcopal authority and a range of legal and doctrinal constraints. For such an emotive, enthusiastic and earnest endeavour Anglican constraints were unlikely to do other than chafe and snap. They did in the 1780s and 1790s, leaving Methodism to complete the process of forming itself into a discrete church. Methodism in varying degrees sought lay involvement in its organisation and worship which elevated 'heart religion' above articles of faith and a settled liturgy. Consequently it carried untidiness and ambiguity into the world of independence from Anglicanism. Was it radical or conservative in its political as well as its social and spiritual gospel? Was it ecumenical in outlook or competitive and antagonistic towards other churches? Was it a force for the freeing of women, slaves, ethnic and other minorities from the shackles that society had made for them? Was it emotionally indulgent or demanding? Was it a force for godly discipline or spiritual excess? Did it promote 'respectable' values of hard work and aspiration or was it sympathetic to those who lacked such values? These, and many other questions, have concerned scholars of Methodism. But for the most part there is no single answer to such questions and Methodism and its scholars have had to accommodate a 'both/and' response to them, rather than 'either/or'. This makes for complexity, but it also gives world Methodism a rich interior which defies reduction to simplicities and platitudes.

The expansion of Methodism was not a matter of physics; it did not result in spiritual entropy – rather the opposite. As Methodism expanded to North America and then to Asia, Latin America, Africa and beyond, it became more variegated and diverse. This is perhaps a feature of religious expansion which Methodism shares with Catholicism, Anglicanism and other churches. Yet a founding feature of

---

[1] D. Hempton, *Methodism: Empire of the Spirit* (New Haven, CT and London: Yale University Press, 2005).

## Introduction

Methodism, its syncretic spiritual and ecclesiological inflection, was a particularly attractive quality. While Methodism had central truths, they were comprehensive in character and allowed Methodism to accommodate the different cultural settings into which it expanded. The same features that made Methodism accessible in the late eighteenth and early nineteenth centuries in the industrial towns in the North of England, and later in the expanding states of America, made it equally so in the plains of Asia and the plateaus of Africa. Of course as a human endeavour it employed and exploited opportunism and determination as much as, if not more than, other churches, but it did so from a fortified position of conviction and certainty which fuelled its missionary enterprise. This evangelicalism was at the heart of Methodism and a key element in Methodist identity. And it determined the character of much Methodist activity; there were few, if any, Methodist meetings which did not – in good times and adversity – set themselves the goal of spreading the word of God beyond the confines of its immediate society and country. The experience of conversion felt by so many Methodists, as well as the intensity of the emotional pull of its worship, were feelings that had to be shared alongside the spiritual call of its teachings about God, Christ and salvation.

A factor in the success of Methodism has been the forms and movements in which it has popularly spread across the developing world, particularly holiness and pentecostalism. The rudimentary class distinction identified by some scholars that middle classes were attracted to 'traditional' Methodism and working classes to holiness and pentecostalism resulted in an enormous growth of the latter in the developing world. Pentecostalism became a religious form for the poor partly because it required little formal education, relying instead on vital piety.[2] In contrast, in Europe, and perhaps North America, Methodism has become a religiously normative institution which increasingly resembles other Christian denominations, and it has shared in the decline that has affected such groups. In the developing world it has retained its freshness and emotional intensity through the incorporation of holiness and pentecostalism. In these places John Wesley's experience in Aldersgate provides a potent model for inner spirituality and Methodist hymns give a harmonious setting. The processes of urbanisation and industrialisation in the developing world emulate those in Britain and America in which Methodism achieved its greatest successes, and it is unsurprising that the same population shifts and transformations see a similar desire to lay down spiritual roots. But the multivalent character of Methodism has given fresh impetus from the adoption of holiness and pentecostalism into indigenous forms of Methodism. The fragmentation of Methodism has happened in Latin America and elsewhere as much as it did in early nineteenth century Britain. There are more than fifteen separate denominations in Brazil which are Wesleyan in origin.

---

[2] L. E. Wethington, 'The Impact of *Orbas de Wesley* in the Hispanic World', in C. Yrigoyen (ed.), *The Global Impact of the Wesleyan Traditions and Their Related Movements* (Lanham, MD: Scarecrow Press, 2002), 275–84

## The Primacy of John Wesley

The hold of John Wesley over the organisation he founded is a remarkable feature of world Methodism. The desire to read Wesley's words has meant that his works are available in – among other languages – Spanish and Chinese, and the Aldersgate renewal conferences, which grew up in the USA, have found as much success in Manila as in Michigan. Wesley was taken to the developing world by missionaries who used the 'twice-told tales' of Wesley's conversion and extraordinary work in the eighteenth century – and of course this happened before the emergence of analytical Wesley scholarship in the UK and USA.[3] Consequently the Methodism of the developing world and that of Britain -and increasingly North America- have diverged. In Britain and North America the John Wesley of scholarly history has become different from the John Wesley of faith. The forensic attention to which John Wesley has been subjected has meant that the hagiographic treatment of him can no longer prevail in scholarly circles. But this revisionism has not spread much beyond scholarly circles and remains surprising to many in the USA as well as in the developing world. In the same way that Horace Walpole told William Mason in 1781 that he did not want to unlearn all the myths of his youth about the Whig heroes of the Glorious Revolution, many Methodists do not want to unlearn the foundational myths of John Wesley.[4] This tension between myth, history and faith is a theme of some of the essays in this volume which try to understand how the Wesley of history and the Wesley of faith can coexist.

Consequently world Methodism accommodates an uncomfortable dual view of John Wesley as human, flawed and problematic as well as Wesley as a model of spiritual values, authentic conversion, evangelical zeal and passion to achieve the salvation of others. Thomas Carlyle might have been right that, in another church, Wesley would have been made a saint for founding a unique preaching order. But in Methodism his beatification is a source of division and controversy. Nevertheless the ingredients of Wesley's success, stripped of negative features, have been a vital force in the formation of Methodist identity across the world and are features that all Methodisms can claim in common. When Methodist missionaries were struggling to make headway in Latin America their cry was 'what we need is Wesley himself preaching the Gospel and teaching the Methodist discipline.'[5] He is the equivalent of the throne of Peter for Catholicism and that of Augustine for Anglicanism. And in the same way, the idealisation of Wesley has developed a character independent of

---

[3] See in particular Jason Vickers's essay in this volume.

[4] W. S. Lewis. (ed.), *Horace Walpole's Correspondence* (New Haven, CT: Yale University Press, 1935–1982), 42 vols, XXIX: 135.

[5] Wethington, 'The Impact of *Orbas de Wesley*', 280. At the conference launching the translation of Wesley into Spanish, Bishop Mortimer Arias of Bolivia said that 'we can hope that for the next century Wesley may become a fertile source of inspiration, doctrinal formation and pastoral orientation for pastors, lay leaders, students, teachers and academic researchers of the always expanding Wesleyan family.' M. Arias, 'Wesley, Our Heritage and the Global Holiness Movement', Methodist World Council meeting, Rio De Janeiro, August 1996.

the historical reality. The question is, should this be troubling and problematic? In the sense that the idealised Wesley has *become* a historical reality in the way in which he has been adopted and embraced by Methodism across the world this may not be troubling. In this respect Methodism is no different from other denominations and religions which idealise their saints and heroes. Such idealised figures can express the truths of religion and can establish and communicate the identity of a church. However the idealisation of Wesley is perturbing when his work is stripped of its eighteenth century context and twenty first century assumptions and values are projected back onto it.[6] Writing of the challenge of introducing the works of John Wesley in Latin America, L. E. Wethington wrote:

> One of the greatest challenges of introducing Wesley himself is how 'the essential Wesley' can be lifted out of his 18$^{th}$C [sic] context, pruned and replanted in 21$^{st}$C Latin America? Some Methodists have rejected Wesley because he did not project in his own 18$^{th}$C a model of social ethics for the 21$^{st}$ C. Dare we suggest that no Wesley scholar is likely to develop a Wesleyan social ethics for the 21$^{st}$ C unless it is deeply rooted in John Wesley's essential theology.[7]

It is a serious problem when the words people want Wesley to have said are put into his mouth and thoughts he did not express are credited to him. When the Wesley of faith trumps the Wesley of history both are damaged and diminished. So the treatment of Wesley as a model of *sociological* concern for the poor and as a liberation theologian – in the modern sense of that term – are unlikely to contribute to the health and vitality of world Methodism; indeed they are more likely over time to sap it. It is no wonder therefore that one of the authors in this volume asks 'will the real John Wesley please stand up?'[8]

The centrality of John Wesley in the minds of many Methodists presents two related problems. First it has the tendency to exclude, or at least marginalise, the role of other key leaders in Methodism. Among his contemporaries the wattage of the spotlight on John Wesley impairs our view of Charles Wesley, John Fletcher and others.[9] The contribution of such early Methodists to the formation of the identity of the tradition is significant and under-represented both in scholarship and in popular Methodisms. The second problem is that John Wesley's voice drowns out those of the non-Wesleyan Methodist traditions and those groups which split from

---

[6] A model of the ways in which a leading scholar has appropriately contextualised Wesley's attitude to property and poverty without anachronism is John Walsh's outstanding article 'John Wesley and the Community of Goods', in K. Robbins (ed.), *Protestant Evangelicalism: Britain, Ireland, Germany and America c 1750–c 1950: Essays in Honour of W. R. Ward* (Oxford: Blackwell, 1990).

[7] Wethington, 'The Impact of *Orbas de Wesley*', 281.

[8] See T. A. Campbell's essay in this volume.

[9] Fletcher has at last obtained greater recognition in the light of the recent collection, G. Hammond and P. S. Forsaith (eds), *Religion, Gender and Industry: Exploring Methodism in a Local Setting* (Eugene, OR: Pickwick, 2011).

Wesleyan Methodism. In these categories lie Calvinistic Methodism, Primitive Methodism, Bible Christians and various Free Methodist groups. Such groups and churches are responsible for some of the vigour and power of the radical agenda of Methodism in the nineteenth and twentieth centuries. They were often in the forefront of championing the role of women in worship and they also contributed some of the distinctive theology of Methodism.[10] It was principally from the non-Wesleyan traditions that the working class leadership of Methodism was most strongly represented.[11] And non-Wesleyan Methodism was responsible for some of the missions which spread Methodism across the world. Moreover the interaction between Wesleyan and non-Wesleyan strands can be distorted if the distinctive character of non-Wesleyan Methodism and traditions is not recognised.[12] How can the debt owed by Methodists to non-Wesleyan influences be fully acknowledged and understood if there is no room in Methodism for such strands? An elegant call for such recognition was made in Martin Wellings's Fernley Hartley Lecture, 2003, in which he said:

We know that John Wesley made a very limited impact in Wales and Scotland, and even in England there were plenty of non-Wesleyan 'Methodists': a 'Methodist' in the mid-eighteenth century meant anyone who supported the revival and who stressed the core evangelical doctrine of justification by grace through faith and claimed the defining evangelical experience of conversion. The societies founded by the Wesley brothers or assimilated into their 'connexion' were part of a much wider movement including the Moravians and Calvinistic evangelicals inside and outside the Church of England.[13] While the Salvation Army owes its foundation to Wesleyan Methodism it also regards itself as a non-Wesleyan institution.[14] In short, Methodist emphasis on John Wesley can help to define the character and identity of Methodism but it can also prevent Methodism from appreciating some of the wider and more diverse influences and inspirations which moulded the tradition.

---

[10] B. Holland, *The Doctrine of Infant Baptism in Non-Wesleyan Methodism* (Wesley Historical Society, 1970).

[11] D. Hempton, 'Wesleyan Methodism and Educational Politics in Early Nineteenth-Century England' *History of Education*, 8:3 (1979).

[12] Non-Wesleyan pentecostal scholars acknowledge the Wesleyan influence upon the early development of the Pentecostal movement: E. L. Blumhofer, 'Purity and Preparation', in S. M. Burgess (ed.), *Reaching Beyond: Chapters in the History of Perfectionism* (Peabody, MA: Hendrickson, 1986), 275 and W. M. Menzies, 'The Non-Wesleyan Origins of the Pentecostal Movement', in V. Synan (ed.), *Aspects of Pentecostal Charismatic Origins* (Plainfield, NJ: Logos, 1975), 97.

[13] M. Wellings, 'Evangelicals in Methodism: Mainstream, Marginal or Misunderstood?', Fernley Hartley Lecture, 2003 at www.methodist.org.uk/index.cfm?fuseaction=opentogod. content&cmid=693 (accessed 10 December 2011).

[14] See for example the themed volume of *Word and Deed: A Journal of Salvation Army Theology and Ministry* for May 2004 (vol. 6, no. 2) on the connections and distinctions between Wesleyan and Salvationist theology.

*INTRODUCTION*

# Many Methodisms

In the eighteenth century 'Methodist' might apply to a considerable range of people, from Church of England clergy to political radicals. It had a looseness we might today recognise in terms such as 'extremist' or 'fundamentalist'; its use served to mock those it described. Wesley's 1780 hymnbook 'for the use of the people called Methodists', was mainly, albeit not exclusively, aimed at those 'in connexion' with himself. Only towards the end of that century did the groupings become clearly demarcated and start to form denominations. In eighteenth century Britain many 'Methodist' clergy remained as evangelical Anglicans, Whitefield's societies largely became 'Independent' congregations, while the Countess of Huntingdon's and John Wesley's followers became denominations – in America this was only applicable to the Whitefieldites and Wesleyans.

From its earliest days there was a bifurcation between those who adhered to a Reformed, Calvinistic understanding of doctrine and those who embraced an 'Arminian' framework. Yet this was not a clear divide, and there was a general consensus to 'agree to disagree' since the spread of an evangelistic message had greater priority. It was only after Whitefield's death in 1770 that this fault-line became contested, but for many the message and the mission still mattered more than destructive dogmatics. The Calvinists were probably in the majority – certainly from the 1770s the Wesleys found themselves under siege; a position which probably strengthened a distinctive identity and in turn an organisational coherence which led to denominational resilience.

The landscape of nineteenth century Methodism was in significant contrast to that of its bedrock. The cause of religious liberty was strengthened by the impact of the American and French revolutions; other factors fostered the development of organisational identity. Religious choice became a matter of right, and the Methodist movement started to fragment into a bewildering variety of groups large and small, each with its own structure and emphases. There were many Methodisms of the Wesleyan tradition – some of which forswore allegiance to their founding figure. If the nineteenth century was generally characterised by fissiparousness, the agenda of the twentieth was that of reunification. The first Methodist Oecumenical Conference took place in 1881, although its aim was not initially towards any kind of organic reconfiguration.

This throws into relief the question, what constitutes Methodism? From the perspective of the eighteenth century the answer would probably be framed in terms of conversion, connexionalism, Anglicanism and Arminianism. From the nineteenth century viewpoint the character of its conscience and spirituality, giving rise to social and political movements, and also traditions of holiness and Pentecostalism might be uppermost. In the twentieth century Methodist ecumenism, theological pluralism and innovation in worship and liturgy could represent an answer. Such responses suggest that Methodist identity is not – and perhaps never was – tightly knit. Methodism is a ship whose planks and rigging have enough pliability and 'give' to enable its back not to be broken in the storms and swells that it has encountered in becoming a global denomination. Underpinning Methodism, in all its forms, are perhaps three features: its Bible-centred teaching, its sense of belonging to a Wesleyan tradition, and its shared history and heritage.

The authors in this volume develop and explore key issues of the identity of Methodism as a global denomination. The structure of the volume seeks to enable the reader to consider Methodism from various different perspectives. The essays on 'Historical Context' show how the germ of Methodism developed and spread across Britain and North America and especially how, despite the fragmentation of the Wesleyan movement, its essence was able to survive and flourish in periods of inner and external turbulence. The section on 'World Methodism' adopts the perspective of those aspects of Methodism which have influenced its emergence as a global denomination. These essays particularly examine the phenomenon of Methodism's transformation and metamorphosis despite, and perhaps because of, its Wesleyan heritage. The essays on 'Belief and Practice' consider those aspects of global Methodism which are broadly shared across its many forms and expressions: preaching, scripture, hymnody, worship, spirituality and evangelism. The final section on 'Culture and Society' considers some aspects of Methodism that can be overlooked if it is considered solely as a religious organisation and examines its essential human ingredients. Many of these ingredients are culturally specific but nevertheless stand as examples of the diversity and breadth of the Methodist experience and culture.

# PART II
# Historical Context

# The Origins and Early Growth of Methodism, 1730–91

Ted A. Campbell

## Introduction

As the introduction to this volume indicates, the term 'Methodism' can be understood in a variety of ways. This chapter offers a summary and assessment of scholarship on the origins and early growth of Methodism understood in the specific sense of the Wesleyan branch of the Evangelical Revival. The dates 1730–91 refer to specific events in the life of John Wesley: his initial engagement with an Oxford religious society between 1729 and 1730, and his death in 1791. In this period Methodism functioned primarily as a religious movement and not as a separate church or denomination, though by 1784 John Wesley had authorised the formation of a Methodist church in the United States and he had taken measures in the British Isles that, as Frank Baker explained it, had separated the Methodist societies from the Church of England in fact if not in name.[1]

Because of the huge range of scholarship on early Methodism, this chapter follows a historiographical and topical structure rather than the chronological framework that other chapters follow. Readers who want a chronological survey are encouraged to utilise the biographical studies of John Wesley and his role in early Methodism by Henry D. Rack and Richard P. Heitzenrater referred to below.

---

[1] This is the argument of Frank Baker's *John Wesley and the Church of England* (Nashville, TN: Abingdon Press, 1970). Baker details, chapter by chapter, the series of events that led Methodist groups under John Wesley's leadership farther and farther from the Church of England, culminating in his ordinations and other actions of 1784.

## Background: The Church of England in the Eighteenth Century and Pietistic Movements of the Age

In the first place, we have to take account of important developments in the understanding of two intersecting contexts of the early Methodist movement, namely the Church of England in the eighteenth century and Protestant pietistic movements in the same period. How one represents these contexts deeply affects how one tells the narrative of Methodism in this period.

The last three decades have witnessed a transformation of our understanding of the Church of England in the age of John and Charles Wesley, and this transformed understanding of the eighteenth-century Church has critical implications for understanding the Methodist movement in that era. Conventional accounts of the origins of Methodism consistently claimed that the immediate context out of which the Methodist movement emerged was the dysfunctional state of the eighteenth-century Church. Despite John and Charles Wesley's own reticence to criticise the Established Church publicly, Methodist literature as early as Thomas Coke's and Henry Moore's *Life of the Rev. John Wesley, A.M.* (1793) offered a decidedly negative image of eighteenth-century Anglicanism that became a standard trope in Methodist literature. Coke and Moore represented the state of the British nation as well as the Church as being thoroughly corrupted by 'practical atheism', 'looseness of morals' and a failure on the part of clergy to preach 'the great leading truths of the Gospel', namely justification by faith alone, communion with God (the quest for Christian holiness), the assurance of pardon and the doctrine of original sin.[2]

This image of the Church in the Wesleys' time evolved in the nineteenth century into an appalling image of the Establishment complete with fox-hunting, port-drinking vicars neglecting their pastoral duties to spend their days in pursuit of lucrative benefices. The bizarre truth is that Anglicans themselves largely accepted this account of their own history, especially after the time of the Oxford or Tractarian movement of the nineteenth century, whose advocates utilised the image of a corrupt church establishment in the prior age as a foil to their own vision of reform.

One of the earliest signs of changing attitudes towards eighteenth-century Anglicanism came in the work of J. C. D. Clark. Reacting against the Whig interpretation of history and especially the Marxist historiography that grew out of it, Clark refuted the notion that English society in the period after the Glorious Revolution had become thoroughly capitalist with respect to its economic basis and internally atheistic or at least deistic with respect to its religious views. Clark likewise rejected the concomitant idea that the *ancien régime* was a mere shell in this period, and this obliged Clark to argue that the Church of England was a vibrant institution in the eighteenth century. He seemed almost surprised to find strong

---

[2] [Thomas] Coke and [Henry] Moore, *The Life of the Rev. John Wesley, A.M.: Including an Account of the Great Revival of Religion, in Europe and America, of which He was the First and Chief Instrument* (London: G. Paramore, 1793), 1–8, quotations on p. 7.

evidence of this in his study of *English Society, 1688–1832* (1985, significantly revised and expanded in 2000). Church leaders, he pointed out, responded vigorously to such challenges as that of Unitarianism, and they revised their political theology in a way that accommodated the mutations of monarchy and divine right that had come about as a result of the Revolution of 1688–89.[3] Even such movements as Methodism and the growth of Dissenting Protestantism, Clark argued, showed the vitality of the Church and traditional religious ideas rather than their weakness.[4]

The trajectory initiated by Clark continued in a collection of essays edited by John Walsh, Colin Haydon and Stephen Taylor. Like Clark's work, this volume entitled *The Church of England, c. 1689– c. 1833* (1993) examined 'the long eighteenth century', that is, the period extending from the Glorious Revolution (1688) and the Act of Toleration (1689) through the first stirrings of the Oxford or Tractarian Movement in the early 1830s. An introductory essay by John Walsh and Stephen Taylor gave an account of the earlier dysfunctional view of the eighteenth-century Church and offered correctives in a number of areas explored in subsequent chapters of the book. Countering the conventional view of Anglican clergy, for example, they found evidence of vigorous pastoral activity throughout the eighteenth-century Church. Countering the conventional claim of low attendance at Anglican services, they pointed out that the earlier figures were based on numbers of communicants, noting that abstention from communion was a common practice and could be a sign of piety in that age. They found evidence, moreover, of consistent efforts at reform in the Church, in efforts for the reform of public morality, in missionary enterprises, and in instruction on the part of clergy and others.[5]

These changing perceptions of eighteenth-century Anglicanism have been followed by a trajectory of scholarship as yet unfolding, including works by William Gibson, Jeremy Gregory and others.[6] To be sure, there remains plenty of evidence – as there would be in any age – of ecclesial corruption and dysfunction, but this trajectory of recent scholarship has fundamentally changed the way in which scholars think about the eighteenth-century context in which Methodism arose. It suggests that eighteenth-century Methodism should be seen as one of a number of responses on the part of Anglicans and Protestants more broadly to the crises of that age.

An intersecting element of the cultural background to the rise of Methodism was the rise of Pietism and other religious movements for affective piety beginning

---

[3] J. C. D. Clark, *English Society, 1688–1832* (Cambridge: Cambridge University Press, 1985), 216–35.

[4] Ibid., 235–47.

[5] J. Walsh, C. Haydon and S. Taylor (eds), *The Church of England, c. 1689–c. 1833* (Cambridge: Cambridge University Press, 1993). The introductory essay by Walsh and Taylor is on 1–64.

[6] W. Gibson, *The Church of England, 1688–1832: Unity and Accord* (London: Routledge, 2001) emphasises the strong cohesion of the national Church in the eighteenth century and its consistently Protestant identity. J. Gregory, *Restoration, Reformation, and Reform, 1660–1828: The Archbishops of Canterbury and Their Diocese* (Oxford: Oxford University Press, 2000) points to evidence of ecclesial vitality in the diocese of Canterbury in the long eighteenth century.

in the seventeenth century and continuing into the eighteenth century. My study of *The Religion of the Heart* (1991) examined a variety of parallel European religious movements that emphasised affective piety as the centre of religious life, including the Jansenist and Quietist movements in seventeenth-century French and Spanish Catholicism, Precisianism and Pietism in seventeenth- and eighteenth-century Reformed and Lutheran churches and in the renewed Moravian *Unitas Fratrum* in the eighteenth century. I suggested that the Wesleyan movement and the Evangelical Revival more broadly could be seen as an Anglican expression of similar trends towards affective piety in European culture.[7] W. R. Ward's study of *The Protestant Evangelical Awakening* (1992), written almost simultaneously with my book, focused specifically on the Evangelical Revival in English-speaking contexts, but also pointed to Continental cultural ties, in particular, with European Protestant pietistic movements. Ward also tied the early emergence of the Methodist movement to its precedents in Continental Protestant forms of piety.[8]

One can locate the Wesleyan revival of the eighteenth century at the intersection of eighteenth-century Anglicanism and the crosscurrents of affective Christian piety originating in European pietistic movements. One study that examines this intersection in the era just prior to the Wesleyan movement is Scott Thomas Kisker's *Foundation for Revival: Anthony Horneck, the Religious Societies, and the Construction of an Anglican Pietism* (2008). Kisker examined the career of Anthony (Anton) Horneck (1641–97), a Rhineland Lutheran pastor who emigrated to Britain around 1661 and became an influential Anglican clergyman from the 1670s, producing a voluminous bibliography of works cultivating heartfelt piety, and also organising 'religious societies' in which believers could pursue such a vision of Christian piety within the context of Anglican parishes.[9] John Wesley read Horneck's works in his formative period in Oxford and would later include a selection from Horneck in his *Christian Library*.[10]

---

[7] T. A. Campbell, *The Religion of the Heart: A Study of European Religious Life in the Seventeenth and Eighteenth Centuries* (Columbia, SC: University of South Carolina Press, 1991), and specifically 115–28 on connections between earlier expressions of affective piety and the Wesleyan movement.

[8] W. R. Ward, *The Protestant Evangelical Awakening* (Cambridge: Cambridge University Press, 1992), cf. 339–52.

[9] S. T. Kisker, *Foundation for Revival: Anthony Horneck, the Religious Societies, and the Construction of an Anglican Pietism* (Pietist and Wesley Studies series; Lanham, MD: Scarecrow Press, 2008).

[10] R. P. Heitzenrater, 'John Wesley and the Oxford Methodists, 1725–1735' (PhD dissertation, Duke University, 1972; reprint edition, Ann Arbor, MI: University Microfilms International, 1973), 270–71 and 508.

## Sources

Critical for the development of Wesleyan and Methodist studies in recent decades has been the publication of a number of sources in critical, unexpurgated editions. One of the central historiographical problems for the study of early Methodism is that, despite the apparent plethora of published sources, most of the sources published within the eighteenth century and even in the early nineteenth century were published by John Wesley himself or by subsequent Methodist church publishing houses which had a vested interest in maintaining a particular image of the Wesleys and of the early Methodist movement. One who studies only the sources authorised by Wesley and by Methodist churches is more or less bound to offer a conventional image of John and Charles Wesley along the lines begun by Coke and Moore and continued through Methodist interpreters in the nineteenth century.

The late nineteenth century and the early twentieth century witnessed the publication of four series of works – one of poetry by John and Charles Wesley, and three of the works of John Wesley – and these series offered readers a small number of sources beyond those authorised by the Wesleys or later Methodist churches. In the 1860s the Wesleyan Conference Office in London published George Osborn's edition of *The Poetical Works of John and Charles Wesley*, including many previously unpublished works.[11] Nehemiah Curnock's edition of the *Journal of the Reverend John Wesley* (eight volumes, 1909–16) included the published *Journal* and some interpretations of material coded and in shorthand from John Wesley's private diaries.[12] E. H. Sugden's edition of *The Standard Sermons* of John Wesley (two volumes, 1920) offered only the 53 authorised 'standard' sermons, although Sugden did add historical comments to the preface of the sermons.[13] John Telford's edition of *The Letters of the Reverend John Wesley* (eight volumes, 1931) offered more than 2,600 letters in contrast to the 900 letters that had appeared in Thomas Jackson's edition of the *Works of the Reverend John Wesley* in the 1820s.[14]

These editions have been superseded in recent decades by a comprehensive and critical edition of the works of John Wesley that began publication in 1976 as 'The Oxford Edition of the Works of John Wesley' and has continued since 1984 as 'The Bicentennial Edition of the Works of John Wesley', published by the United Methodist Publishing House in the USA. These include the complete range of the *Journal* with accompanying interpretations of the private diary.[15] A separate

---

[11] G. Osborn (ed.), *The Poetical Works of John and Charles Wesley* (13 vols; London: Wesleyan Conference Office, 1868).

[12] N. Curnock (ed.), *The Journal of the Rev. John Wesley, A.M., Sometime Fellow of Lincoln College, Oxford* ('Standard Edition' of the Works of John Wesley; 8 vols; London: Epworth Press, 1909–16).

[13] E. H. Sugden (ed.), *Wesley's Standard Sermons* ('Standard Edition' of the Works of John Wesley; 2 vols; London: Epworth Press, 3rd edition, 1951).

[14] J. Telford (ed.), *Letters of the Rev. John Wesley, A.M.* ('Standard Edition' of the Works of John Wesley; 8 vols; London: Epworth Press, 1931).

[15] The Oxford/Bicentennial volumes include A. C. Outler (ed.), *Sermons* (vols 1–4; Nash-ville, TN: Abingdon Press, 1984–87); F. Hildebrandt and O. O. Beckerlegge (eds), *A*

volume will give an interpretation of the Oxford diaries, for which there are no corresponding *Journal* entries. Scholars also need to be aware of the fact, though, that there is a 41 year period (1742–83) for which the diaries are entirely missing and were probably destroyed. For this long period, one can only rely on the *Journal*. The Bicentennial Edition also includes the full range of John Wesley's sermons (151 of them), and a number of other critical works. It will eventually include more of these as well as seven or eight volumes of letters, though only two volumes of letters (for the period 1721–55) are currently available.

In addition to the works of John Wesley in progress, editions have also been appearing of works by persons associated with eighteenth-century Methodism. The Charles Wesley Society, organised in 1990, has sponsored a number of facsimile publications of Charles Wesley's works, and has also sponsored contemporary editions of many of Charles Wesley's works, including *The Manuscript Journal of the Reverend Charles Wesley, M.A.* (2 vols, 2007–8),[16] *The Sermons of Charles Wesley* (2001)[17] and *The Unpublished Poetry of Charles Wesley* (3 vols, 1988–92).[18] Other publications of texts by eighteenth-century Methodist leaders include *Susanna Wesley: The Complete Writings* (1997),[19] *Diary of an Oxford Methodist: Benjamin Ingham, 1733–1734* (1985)[20] and *The Journals of Dr. Thomas Coke* (2005).[21]

# Biographical Surveys

Although a number of biographical studies of John and Charles Wesley have appeared in recent decades, three stand out as highly influential, critical historical studies that make extensive use of manuscript sources. Henry D. Rack's *Reasonable Enthusiast: John Wesley and the Rise of Methodism* (1989) is a well-written biographical study of John Wesley and Wesley's role in the origins of the Methodist movement.[22]

---

*Collection of Hymns for the Use of the People Called Methodists* (vol. 7; Nashville, TN: Abingdon Press, 1983); R. Davies (ed.), *The Methodist Societies: History, Nature, and Design* (vol. 9; Nashville, TN: Abingdon Press, 1989); H. D. Rack (ed.), *The Methodist Societies: The Minutes of the Conference* (vol. 10; Nashville, TN: Abingdon Press, 2011); G. R. Cragg (ed.), *The Appeals to Men of Reason and Religion and Certain Related Open Letters* (vol. 11; Oxford: Oxford University Press, 1975); W. R. Ward and R. P. Heitzenrater (eds), *Journal and Diaries* (vols 18–24; Nashville, TN: Abingdon Press, 1988–2003); F. Baker (ed.), *Letters* (vols 25–6; as yet incomplete).

[16] Edited by ST Kimbrough, Jr. and K. G. C. Newport; Nashville, TN: Kingswood Books, 2007–8.
[17] Edited by K. G. C. Newport; Oxford and New York: Oxford University Press, 2001.
[18] Edited by ST Kimbrough, Jr. and O. A. Beckerlegge; Nashville, TN: Kingswood Books, 1988–92.
[19] Edited by C. Wallace, Jr.; Oxford and New York: Oxford University Press, 1997.
[20] Edited by R. P. Heitzenrater; Durham, NC: Duke University Press, 1985.
[21] Edited by J. A. Vickers; Nashville, TN: Kingswood Books, 2005.
[22] Philadelphia: Trinity Press International, 1989.

As the title suggests, Rack was concerned to locate Wesley within the eighteenth-century British social and cultural context, emphasising the 'enthusiastic' aspects of the Wesleyan movement but also the many ways in which Wesley reflected the culture of the Enlightenment including, for example, Wesley's use of Lockean terms in explicating the role of religious experience as a source of knowledge. Rack's work shied away from the more complex theological controversies associated with Wesley, and it appeared just ahead of some of the important developments in eighteenth-century British history noted above, but his work was cognisant of the newly developing understanding of eighteenth-century British culture and society that was appearing in the 1980s and 1990s.

Richard P. Heitzenrater's study of *Wesley and the People Called Methodists* (1995) addressed a subject matter delimited very much like that of Rack, that is, a biographical study of John Wesley and his role in fostering the nascent Methodist movement.[23] Heitzenrater's work is about half of the overall length of Rack's, though Heitzenrater wrote in a highly compressed style. Heitzenrater's work was designed more as a textbook and does not offer a single consistent argument in the way that Rack's study does, though Heitzenrater did summarise major themes in the conclusion of his work. His study pays less attention to contemporary studies of eighteenth-century British culture and society, but shows more concern than Rack's book for the development of Wesleyan theological categories. Speaking generally, British studies of the Wesleyan movement in recent decades have tended to be more concerned with social and cultural contexts, whereas American studies of the Wesleyan movement in the same period have focused more consistently on theological developments and developments in the structures of Methodist communities. The biographies by Rack and Heitzenrater illustrate these tendencies.

One further biographical study warrants consideration here, and that is Gareth Lloyd's study of *Charles Wesley and the Struggle for Methodist Identity* (2007).[24] Although not as comprehensive a biographical study as those of Rack and Heitzenrater, it utilised manuscript sources extensively and brought to light a number of aspects of the early Wesleyan movement that escaped the attention of earlier interpreters. Most critically, Lloyd showed how deep the rift between John and Charles Wesley actually was from the 1750s forward, a rift that conventional Methodist historiography had consistently and, Lloyd demonstrates, deliberately minimised in its stress on the brothers' unity in their evangelistic mission. Lloyd's was the first work to document the distinct existence of a continuing 'Church Methodist' party associated with Charles Wesley, a group that inculcated Evangelical 'heart religion' and practised Wesleyan class, band and society meetings, but which did not practise itinerancy and chose to remain in canonical conformity with the Church of England. Lloyd's study has caused us to recognise, by contrast, some of John Wesley's independent and more separatist tendencies.

---

[23] Nashville, TN: Abingdon Press, 1995.
[24] Oxford: Oxford University Press, 2007.

## John Wesley and the Xes

One of the characteristic trajectories of Wesleyan scholarship in the late nineteenth century and into the twentieth century was the examination of specific aspects of John Wesley's life and especially his thought in comparison with specific sources in eighteenth-century or earlier Christian culture. Sometimes cast as studies of the influence of various Christian cultures on Wesley, many of these studies originated as dissertations, though some have survived revision into critically important books on a range of topics comparing John Wesley and a range of particular theological and ethical movements. I have referred to such studies under the heading 'John Wesley and the Xes,' where X is a variable that can be replaced by the name of a specific movement in Christian culture.

This trajectory of study originated in the Victorian era by an Anglican barrister and legal scholar, Richard Denny Urlin, in his study of *John Wesley's Place in Church History: Determined with the Aid of Facts and Documents Unknown to, Or Unnoticed by, His Biographers* (1870).[25] Urlin argued that Wesley displayed many traits of 'high church' Anglicanism.

Urlin's work was answered by Methodist scholar James H. Rigg in a pamphlet entitled *Was John Wesley A High Churchman? A Dialogue for the Times* (1882).[26] Rigg argued that the meaning of 'high church' had changed between the eighteenth and nineteenth centuries: 'a clergyman might have steadily held the opinions and profession of a High Churchman all his life in the last century [the eighteenth century] and yet not hold one of the characteristic opinions of a Ritualising High Churchman of to-day.'[27]

The dialogue between Urlin and Rigg over 'high churchmanship' set the pattern for studies of John Wesley in relationship to particular strands of Christian tradition. The early and mid-twentieth century saw studies of John Wesley in relationship to Protestant Reformers (George Croft Cell),[28] to Catholic reformers and Catholic culture in general (Maximin Piette and John Murray Todd),[29] to Puritanism (Robert Monk),[30] and to Pietism and Moravianism (Martin Schmidt).[31]

---

[25] London, Oxford and Cambridge: Rivingtons, 1870.

[26] London: The Wesleyan Methodist Book Room, 1882.

[27] Ibid., 7; Rigg's pamphlet refers to C. J. Abbey and J. H. Overton's *The English Church in the Eighteenth Century* (London: Longman & Co, 1887) on this point about the meaning of 'High Church' in the eighteenth century.

[28] G. Croft Cell, *The Rediscovery of John Wesley* (New York: Holt, 1935).

[29] M. Piette, *John Wesley in the Evolution of Protestantism* (New York: Sheed and Ward, 1937; originally published in 1925 as *John Wesley: Sa Réaction dans l'Evolution du Protestantisme*). J. Murray Todd, *John Wesley and the Catholic Church* (London: Hodder and Stoughton, 1958).

[30] R. C. Monk, *John Wesley: His Puritan Heritage* (Nashville, TN and New York: Abingdon Press, 1966).

[31] M. Schmidt, *John Wesley: A Theological Biography* (trans. Norman Goldhawk and Denis Inman; 2 vols; Nashville, TN: Abingdon Press, 1973).

## Theology of the Wesleyan Movement

The various studies of 'John Wesley and the Xes' led in the decades after the Second World War to a flourishing of studies of John Wesley's theology, especially in the United States. The earliest of these studies – those of Colin W. Williams and Albert C. Outler – were undertaken as a result of ecumenical contacts and the desire to 'place' Wesleyan and Methodist theologies in dialogue with a variety of other Christian theological and doctrinal traditions. Wesleyan and Methodist churches have historically taken the theology of John Wesley as normative for their communities,[32] and many of these studies were undertaken by adherents of these communities as essays in systematic theology, combining criteria of theological validity along with historical study.

Within the scope of numerous accounts of Wesley's theology in the last half-century, I shall focus here on a series of single-volume studies of John Wesley's theology. The first of these was offered by the Australian Methodist theologian Colin W. Williams (1921–2000), who later served as dean of Yale Divinity School (1969–79). Williams had worked with the ecumenical movement, and recounted his experience of attending ecumenical meetings in which Methodists seemed hard-pressed to state what their churches believed.[33] His study of *John Wesley's Theology Today* (1960) was an attempt to help Methodists relate to the ecumenical movement by offering an overview of Wesley's theology.[34] Williams set some important precedents in this work. An early chapter on religious authority had five sections, two of which were devoted to the authority of scripture, and the others to experience, reason and tradition.[35] This would set up discussions of the so-called 'Wesleyan Quadrilateral' in the 1970s and beyond. Moreover, Williams followed a scheme through his book that roughly reflects what subsequent Wesleyan theologians would refer to as the *ordo salutis*, the 'order of salvation' or 'way of salvation', as an organising motif for Wesley's most distinctive theological beliefs.[36] He also attempted to discern which of Wesley's teachings were 'essential' doctrines and which were considered to be opinions on which differences could be generously allowed.[37]

---

[32] The specific senses in which Wesley's thought is normative for Wesleyan communities has been much disputed, and differs between the various Wesleyan denominations, but all Wesleyan communities take at least the Wesleyan teachings on the 'way of salvation' to be normative for their communities.

[33] C. W. Williams, *John Wesley's Theology Today* (Nashville, TN: Abingdon Press, 1960), 5.

[34] Ibid., 7–9.

[35] Ibid., 23–38.

[36] Ibid., the sequence of chapters 3 (prevenient grace), 4 (original sin), 5 (repentance and justification), 7 (new birth and assurance), 8 (repentance in believers) and 10 (entire sanctification).

[37] Ibid., 15–21. I have followed this trajectory, though with slightly different results, in *Wesleyan Beliefs: Formal and Popular Expressions of the Core Beliefs of Wesleyan Communities* (Nashville, TN: Kingswood Books, 2010), 17–62.

Williams's work had viewed Wesley in the light of the Lutheran and Reformed theologies that were consistent foci of the Protestant Neo-Orthodoxy that had shaped theological debate in the mid-twentieth century. Another interpreter of John Wesley's theology who also worked from experience in the ecumenical movement was Albert C. Outler of Southern Methodist University. But Outler expanded the backdrop for theological comparison with Wesley to reflect his substantial knowledge of Anglican, Catholic and Eastern Orthodox Christian cultures. Outler's 1973 Fondren Lectures, published in 1975 as *Theology in the Wesleyan Spirit*, followed the recognisable pattern of the 'way of salvation', with chapters on the human condition, the 'gist of the Gospel' (including justification) and Christian holiness. The book raised questions about whether Wesley's doctrine of sin followed more a Catholic pattern than typically Protestant teachings about original sin, and also asked if Wesley's understanding of sanctification did not follow Catholic as well as Orthodox models of teaching about Christian holiness.[38]

Randy Maddox's *Responsible Grace: John Wesley's Practical Theology* (1994) represented a new generation in single-volume studies of John Wesley's theology, though Maddox built upon many of Outler's insights, including his notion of John Wesley as a 'practical theologian' and on Wesley's convergences with Anglican, Catholic and Eastern-Christian thought. Maddox showed an awareness of many private texts beyond the published texts on which accounts of Wesley's theology have often relied. For example, on the doctrine of original sin, he cited a letter of John Wesley to Dr. Mason in which Wesley expressed doubts that any person would ever be condemned on the basis of original sin alone.[39] Maddox also pointed to crucial transitions in Wesley's thought, for example Wesley's growing sense of the cosmic scope of redemption reflected in his sermon on 'The New Creation'.[40]

The same John Wesley sermon on 'The New Creation' became the basis of another single-volume study offered by Maddox's mentor at Emory University, Theodore Runyon, whose book, *The New Creation: John Wesley's Theology Today*, appeared in 1998. The subtitle of Runyon's work indicates that in some sense he saw his work as an extension of Colin W. Williams's earlier study of *John Wesley's Theology Today*, but Runyon was much more attuned to concerns coming from contemporary Christian theologians concerned with issues of human liberation, issues that had been explored in meetings of the Oxford Institute of Methodist Theological Studies, and which had also been the subject of a book-length study by one of Runyon's doctoral students, Theodore W. Jennings, Jr., in *Good News to the Poor: John Wesley's Evangelical Economics* (1990).[41] Another area to which Runyon's

---

[38] A. C. Outler, *Theology in the Wesleyan Spirit* (Nashville, TN: Tidings, 1975), 34–9 on Wesley's 'essentially catholic' (34) view of original sin, and 72–3 on his understanding of Christian perfection as *teleiosis*.

[39] R. L. Maddox, *Responsible Grace: John Wesley's Practical Theology* (Nashville, TN: Kingswood Books, 1994), 74–5 and footnote 76.

[40] Ibid., 235–53, esp. 252–3.

[41] T. Runyon, *The New Creation: John Wesley's Theology Today* (Nashville, TN: Abingdon Press, 1998). T. W. Jennings, Jr., *Good News to the Poor: John Wesley's Evangelical Economics*

work paid sustained attention was the issue of human religious experience and the cultivation of the 'religious affections', a subject that had been explored by yet another of Runyon's doctoral students, Gregory S. Clapper, in *John Wesley on Religious Affections: His Views on Experience and Emotion and Their Role in the Christian Life and Theology* (1989).[42]

The most recent work in this series of single-volume explorations of John Wesley's theology is that of Kenneth J. Collins, *The Theology of John Wesley: Holy Love and the Shape of Grace* (2007). Collins's work offers a constructionist account of John Wesley's thought in the sense in which legal scholars describe accounts of legal texts that adhere closely to original meanings as 'constructionist' readings of the texts. The book utilises the thematic conception of 'holy love' as a consistent motif through which Wesley's theology is interpreted, paying close attention to consistent meanings of terms and expressions used in John Wesley's writings.[43] This is important because John Wesley often made rather fine distinctions, for example when he distinguished one sense or 'extent' of the term 'salvation' in which the term includes preventing grace, and another more 'proper' or restricted sense in which it includes only justification and sanctification.[44] Collins's work utilised charts to illustrate the distinctions that he found in Wesley's thought. For example, it showed how the expressions 'full assurance of faith' and 'full assurance of hope', which one might take as referring to the same phenomenon, are in fact used consistently to refer to subtly different ranges denoted by the term 'assurance': the former ('full assurance of faith') is consistently associated with entire sanctification, whereas the latter ('full assurance of hope') could be used to refer either to an assurance that accompanies entire sanctification or to an assurance that follows from regeneration.[45]

These five single-volume studies represent only a shadow of the voluminous output on John Wesley's theology since 1960. Adding a substantial body of work on the theology of his brother Charles would expand this bibliography even further. These include studies of specific theological topics (original sin, justification, sanctification, sacramental theology and moral theology),[46] studies of the Wesleys'

---

(Nashville, TN: Abingdon Press, 1990).

[42] Runyon, *The New Creation*, 146–67; G. S. Clapper, *John Wesley on Religious Affections: His Views on Experience and Emotion and Their Role in the Christian Life and Theology* (Metuchen, NJ: Scarecrow Press: 1989).

[43] K. J. Collins, *The Theology of John Wesley: Holy Love and the Shape of Grace* (Nashville, TN: Abingdon Press, 2007), esp. 6–12 where Collins lays out the 'axial theme' of holy love.

[44] John Wesley, sermon on 'The Scripture Way of Salvation', I:2 and I:3; in A. C. Outler (ed.), *Sermons* (Bicentennial Edition of the Works of John Wesley; Nashville, TN: Abingdon Press, 1984–87), 2:156–8.

[45] Collins, 140–42.

[46] Only a sample of these can be listed as follows and in the next two notes. B. E. Bryant, 'John Wesley's Doctrine of Sin' (PhD dissertation, King's College, University of London, 1992). W. R. Cannon, *The Theology of John Wesley, With Special Reference to the Doctrine of Justification* (New York and Nashville, TN: Abingdon-Cokesbury Press, 1946). H. Lindström, *Wesley and Sanctification: A Study in the Doctrine of Salvation* (London: Epworth Press, 1950). J.

uses of scripture and other sources such as early Christian writings and the works of Catholic mystical theologians,[47] and comparisons of the Wesleys' theologies with those of other prominent Christian thinkers.[48]

## Structures of the Wesleyan Movement

A number of studies since the 1960s have focused on the distinctive institutions or structures of the Wesleyan movement. One of the earliest of these was motivated by the Anglican–Methodist negotiations that were underway in the UK in the late 1960s. Frank Baker's study of *John Wesley and the Church of England* (1970) examined the sequence of events that led the Methodist people to a *de facto* separation from the Church of England by the time of John Wesley's death in 1791.[49] The study focused on the development of separate Methodist structures, including the classes, bands and societies, the conference of preachers (both lay as well as ordained preachers), the Model Deed and subsequent legal steps that gave the Methodist people a distinct legal identity, and eventually the ordinations John Wesley performed in the 1780s and his production of an alternative to the Book of Common Prayer, *The Sunday Service of the Methodists In North America* (1784) which, despite the title, was also published and used in Britain.

Baker's study was followed by a more focused study by his doctoral student at Duke University, David Lowes Watson, in *The Early Methodist Class Meeting* (1985). Watson's work pointed to the regular agenda of the Methodist class meetings, focused on accountability for the specific items listed in the 'General Rules of the United Societies' (1743). Watson's work points out that these groups did not function primarily for Bible study, prayer or sharing of personal experiences. Some of those elements were present, but the focus of the groups was on accountability to the very specific commitments encoded in the 'General Rules'.[50] Watson's work on

---

R. Tyson, *Charles Wesley on Sanctification: A Biographical and Theological Study* (Grand Rapids, MI: Francis Asbury Press, 1986). O. E. Borgen, *John Wesley on the Sacraments: A Theological Study* (Nashville, TN: Abingdon Press, 1972). D. S. Long, *John Wesley's Moral Theology: The Quest for God and Goodness* (Nashville, TN: Kingswood Books, 2005).

[47] S. J. Jones, *John Wesley's Conception and Use of Scripture* (Nashville, TN: Kingswood Books, 1995). T. A. Campbell, *John Wesley and Christian Antiquity: Religious Vision and Cultural Change* (Nashville, TN: Kingswood Books, 1991). R. G. Tuttle, *John Wesley: His Life and Theology* (Paternoster Press, 1979; reprint edition, Grand Rapids, MI: Zondervan, 1984), which focuses on Wesley's use of Catholic mystical sources.

[48] R. S. Brightman, 'Gregory of Nyssa and John Wesley in Theological Dialogue on the Christian Life' (PhD dissertation, Boston University, 1969). E. Colón-Emeric, *Wesley, Aquinas, and Christian Perfection: An Ecumenical Dialogue* (Waco, TX: Baylor University Press, 2009).

[49] Baker, *passim*.

[50] D. L. Watson, *The Early Methodist Class Meeting* (Nashville, TN: Discipleship Resources, 1985), 93–123, 134–45.

the Methodist class meetings became the basis for a renewal of the practice of small-group accountability that Watson advocated under the title 'Covenant Discipleship'.

A recently completed doctoral dissertation at Southern Methodist University extends this trajectory of scholarship. In this work, Kevin M. Watson has studied the early Methodist band meetings.[51] The band meetings seem to have originated earlier than the Methodist class meetings, and were based on Moravian models as well as the model of English 'religious societies'. They involved groups of adherents who professed a conversion experience and who were seeking the goal of perfect love: entire sanctification. The bands were separated by gender and marital status to enable more intimate sharing within the groups. Watson's work utilises manuscript sources from participants in the band meetings in addition to the writings of the Wesleys, and his research shows how the bands were able to foster communities with intense personal relationships that served as core groups for the larger Methodist societies. His work also suggests that the distinct identity of the Methodist bands was difficult to maintain through the eighteenth century, and they seem to have evolved into the gender-segregated 'prayer meetings' of American Methodism by the early nineteenth century.

## The Wesleyan Movement, the Enlightenment and the Early Romantic Culture of the Eighteenth Century

Scholarship on the eighteenth-century Wesleyan revival has very often focused on the movement's central emphases on religious experience and the 'religious affections' that the Wesleys took to be signs of divine grace. Early twentieth-century Methodist interpreters Herbert Brook Workman and Umphrey Lee both understood the Wesleys' emphasis on religious experience to be a key element in the culture of the revival.[52] The Wesleyan teaching on religious experience and religious affections has received attention in recent theological studies by Gregory S. Clapper, Theodore Runyon and, most recently, William J. Abraham.[53] Clapper, in particular, pointed to Wesley's use of Lockean concepts and Lockean terminology

---

[51] K. M. Watson, 'The Early Methodist Band Meeting: Its Origin, Development, and Significance' (PhD dissertation, Southern Methodist University, 2012). K. M. Watson is no relation to D. L. Watson.

[52] H. B. Workman, *The Place of Methodism in the Catholic Church* (London: Epworth Press, revised and enlarged edition of 1921; first edition was 1909), 16. U. Lee, *John Wesley and Modern Religion* (Nashville, TN: Cokesbury Press, 1936), 17, 302–3, and the conclusion on 321.

[53] Clapper, *passim*. Runyon, *The New Creation*, 146–67. W. J. Abraham, *Aldersgate and Athens: John Wesley and the Foundations of Christian Belief* (Waco, TX: Baylor University Press, 2010), 23–40.

('simple ideas') to make sense of Wesley's emphasis on religious experience in the light of the epistemological concerns of the Enlightenment.[54]

In recent decades, the Wesleyan culture regarding religious experience and the religious affections has come to be considered in relation to the cultures of the Enlightenment and the early Romanticism of the eighteenth century. Richard Brantley's study of *Locke, Wesley, and the Method of English Romanticism* (1984) argued that John Wesley's modification of Locke's epistemology, by which Wesley allowed for religious experience and certain religious affections as genuine sources of human knowledge, laid an intellectual foundation for the work of the English Romantic poets.[55] Brantley had focused on Wesley and leading poets of the Romantic period. A more recent study by Phyllis Mack, *Heart Religion in the British Enlightenment* (2008), views the phenomenon of Methodist 'heart religion' as a function of popular religious culture, utilising hymns, pamphlets, tracts and other literature as indications of the spirituality of common people. Her work focuses on the tension between the exuberant religious experiences of the Methodists, on the one hand, and the Methodist insistence on self-discipline, on the other.[56] In their own ways, both Mack and Brantley reflect a growing consensus among interpreters of the eighteenth century that early Romanticism does not need to be seen in opposition to the Enlightenment; the various expressions of 'heart religion' could be understood as popular analogues to the empirical epistemology of more sophisticated Enlightenment *philosophes*.

## The Wesleyan Movement in Relation to Social Issues and Social Change

A final area of intense scholarly research is concerned with the relationship between the early Methodist movement in relation to the Industrial Revolution and the social transformations that came about as a result of the move towards industrialisation concurrent with the evolution of the Methodist movement from the 1730s. Enormously influential on twentieth-century scholarship in this area was the French social historian Élie Halévy, whose study of *England in 1815* (1913) and earlier articles advocated the view that Methodism functioned for England as an

---

[54] Clapper, 55–7. Similarly, cf. F. Dreyer, 'Faith and Experience in the Thought of John Wesley', *American Historical Review*, 88 (1983), 12–30, and Rack, *Reasonable Enthusiast*, 384–6.

[55] R. Brantley, *Locke, Wesley, and the Method of English Romanticism* (Gainesville, FL: University of Florida Press, 1984), *passim*, and see his explanations of this thesis in his introduction, pp. 1 and 2, then 201–13. He continued this trajectory of scholarship with *Coordinates of Anglo-American Romanticism: Wesley, Edwards, Carlyle, and Emerson* (Gainesville, FL: University of Florida Press, 1993).

[56] P. Mack, *Heart Religion in the British Enlightenment: Gender and Emotion in Early Methodism* (Cambridge: Cambridge University Press, 2008).

'antidote' to the Jacobin fervour that fuelled the French Revolution.[57] Methodism was seen, then, despite its challenges to British culture, as an essentially conservative and anti-revolutionary phenomenon. Wesley's own political conservatism has often been cited in favour of such a view.

Among British historians, E. P. Thompson's study of *The Making of the English Working Class* (1963) was widely acclaimed as substantiating Halévy's argument about the conservative role that Methodism played in eighteenth-century British society.[58] This view became a standard trope in British historiography, at least in non-Methodist circles, in the twentieth century. Thus J. H. Plumb's volume on *England in the Eighteenth Century* in The Pelican History of England series described Wesley as 'absolutely and completely conservative' and his Methodist movement as being 'not a religion *of* the poor but *for* the poor'. In Methodism, Plumb explained, 'The puritan ideal was reborn shorn of its political radicalism.' Methodism worked against movements for popular education, he claimed, and 'The successful Methodist could regard his overworked children with a complacent heart.' The movement 'encouraged violent hatred of Papists and did all it could to maintain laws against them'. 'Jews were the murderers of Christ', according to Plumb's view of Methodism, and Methodist leaders vehemently rejected 'any work which tended to cast doubt on the literal interpretation of the Bible'.[59]

An early criticism of these perspectives was offered by Methodist historian Robert F. Wearmouth in his 1945 study of *Methodism and the Common People of the Eighteenth Century*. Wearmouth argued that Wesley and the eighteenth-century Methodists had consistently sought to empower poor and working-class people by recognising their gifts and offering education and organisation as well as religious formation.[60] Wearmouth highlighted the practical as well as spiritual concerns of John Wesley and early Methodists for the common people of the eighteenth century. In this way he reinterpreted the Wesleyan movement as a movement in support of 'the depressed classes'.[61] In doing so, he set in motion a thread of interpretation that would be favoured within Wesleyan churches, quite contrary to the views of Halévy and the later views expressed by Thompson and Plumb.

Many subsequent interpretations of John Wesley by Methodists and non-Methodists alike have emphasised the socially progressive works of the Methodist

---

[57] É. Halévy, *Histoire de peuple anglais aux dix-neuvième siècle* (in English: *Halévy's History of the English People in the Nineteenth Century*; E. I. Watkin, tr.; 6 vols; London: Ernest Benn Ltd, 1931–32). An earlier article of Halévy on 'La naissance du Méthodisme en Angleterre' appeared in the *Revue de Paris* (1906) and was subsequently translated into English by Bernard Semmel as *The Birth of Methodism in England* (Chicago, IL: University of Chicago Press, 1971).

[58] E. P. Thompson, *The Making of the English Working Class* (London: V. Gollancz, 1963).

[59] J. H. Plumb, *England in the Eighteenth Century* (The Pelican History of England series; Harmondsworth: Penguin Books, 1950; revised edition of 1963), 91–7; the quotations are from 94, 95 and 96.

[60] R. F. Wearmouth, *Methodism and the Common People of the Eighteenth Century* (London: Epworth Press, 1945), 263–8, which is the concluding argument of the book as a whole.

[61] Ibid., 267.

movement. Bernard Semmel's book on *The Methodist Revolution* (1973) had pointed to ways in which Methodism brought about a quiet 'revolution' that had positive consequences for common people in the eighteenth century.[62] Semmel was an academic historian who had translated Halévy's work on *The Birth of Methodism in England* into English, and had no personal ties to Wesleyan or Methodist communities. Semmel emphasised progressive elements of the theology of the Wesleyan movement, especially its Arminian theological stance in opposition to Calvinist teaching of limited atonement, which Semmel saw as a theological analogue to the rise of democratic political ideas. The Wesleyan revival should be understood, Semmel wrote, 'as both a spiritual Revolution of a progressive and liberal character and as a counter to revolutionary violence'.[63] Parallel to Semmel, the Methodist theologian and social ethicist Manfred Marquardt's study, *John Wesley's Social Ethics: Praxis and Principles* (originally published in German in 1975) pointed to many of the same phenomena as Semmel had described, calling attention to Wesley's encouragement of social work on behalf of the poor, his work in establishing schools for working-class people, his involvement in the cause of the abolition of slavery and his work on behalf of prison reform.[64] Although Wesley's emphasis on diligence and hard work could be construed as favouring 'the spirit of capitalism', Marquardt explained, Wesley's warnings about the dangers of wealth, his opposition to surplus accumulation and his severe qualifications as to what should count as appropriate labour for Christians ran contrary to the advocacy of unrestrained capitalism.[65]

This chapter has had reference above to the work of Theodore Runyon (*The New Creation*, 1998) and Theodore Jennings (*Good News to the Poor: John Wesley's Evangelical Economics*, 1990). These works represent the high-water mark of a politically and economically radical reading of John Wesley. The authors were well aware of Wesley's professed political conservatism. Nevertheless, they argued, Wesley's actions in regard to the poor, his condemnation of surplus accumulation, his warnings about the dangers of wealth and his occasional analyses of economic conditions (for example, in his 'Thoughts upon the Present Scarcity of Provisions') offered a critical opening for the critique of Western capitalism and consumerism and the possibility of radical political alternatives. Jennings went so far as to claim that 'Wesley's understanding of stewardship is a frontal attack on the principles of capitalism and the ethos of accumulation and consumption of wealth.'[66] The trajectory of interpretation suggested by Runyon and Jennings has continued

---

[62] B. Semmel, *The Methodist Revolution* (New York: Basic Books, 1973).
[63] Ibid., 4–5.
[64] M. Marquardt, *John Wesley's Social Ethics: Praxis and Principles* (English translation by John E. Steely and W. Stephen Gunter; Nashville, TN: Abingdon Press, 1992). These are the topics of chapters 1–2 (social work and aid to the poor, 19–34), 4 (educational work, 49–66), 5 (abolitionism, 67–75) and 6 (work for prison reform, 77–86).
[65] Ibid., chapter 3 (35–48, and esp. 41–3).
[66] Jennings, *Good News to the Poor*, 116; cf. Runyon *The New Creation*, 168–93.

most recently in a collection of essays entitled *Methodist and Radical: Rejuvenating a Tradition* (2003).[67]

So did John Wesley and Methodist societies associated with him represent the conservative and repressive movement depicted by Plumb and Thompson and others, opposed to education and modern ideas in general and complacently unconcerned about the plight of the poor? Or was it a progressive movement identifying with the plight of the poor against the rich and bearing a 'frontal attack on the principles of capitalism' suggested by Jennings, Runyon and others? We might well ask, in the words of an American television game show from the 1950s, 'Will the real John Wesley please stand up?' Fortunately, there are some interpretations of John Wesley and early Methodism that have drawn more historically contextualised and nuanced understandings of the relationship between the Methodist movement and the social situation of eighteenth-century Britain.

Theodore R. Weber's study of *Politics in the Order of Salvation: Transforming Wesleyan Political Ethics* (2001) offered a well-contextualised account of the evolution of John Wesley's political thought. More than any other preceding book, Weber's narrative took seriously the context of the Revolution of 1688–89 and its implications for the political thought of John Wesley. What Weber recognised was that the option of old-style Toryism conjoined with a belief in the divine right of monarchs was simply untenable after the events of 1688–89 when Parliament *de facto* deposed the reigning monarch and invited a foreign prince to rule Britain. Untenable, that is, except in the case of the most radical Jacobites who after 1688–89 were forced into the position of a minority political group excluded from participation in the political process and service in civil and ecclesiastical roles because of their refusal to swear allegiance to monarchs appointed by Parliament. John Wesley's views, Weber showed, involved not only a concern for 'natural rights' but a consistent concern for constitutional rights grounded in British customary law.[68] Thus Wesley's politically conservative views can be seen as grounded in his general acceptance of the principle of parliamentary constraint of the monarchy.

A similar trajectory has been pursued by Jason E. Vickers in *Wesley: A Guide for the Perplexed* (2009). Vickers had come to similar conclusions to those of Weber before realising that his conclusions had been anticipated by Weber. I would add that Bernard Semmel had expressed such an understanding well ahead of Weber and Vickers. Vickers described Wesley's political persuasion as 'Tory constitutionalism' where Weber had used the expression 'organic constitutionalism'. Vickers showed that Wesley, while affirming the legitimacy of the House of Orange and the Hanoverian monarchs and thus the principle of restraint enshrined in the Glorious Revolution, continued to lean towards the conservative affirmation of passive obedience to the Crown. Vickers's work went beyond Weber in its use of more

---

[67] J. Rieger and J. Vincent (eds), *Methodist and Radical: Rejuvenating a Tradition* (Nashville, TN: Kingswood Books, 2003).

[68] T. R. Weber, *Politics in the Order of Salvation: Transforming Wesleyan Political Ethics* (Nashville, TN: Kingswood Books, 2001), *passim*, and on the specific point about constitutional rights, see chapter 10, 303–52.

recent scholarship on eighteenth-century British political and cultural life (such as that of J. C. D. Clark) that provided the context for his reading of Wesley's political thought.[69] Such an understanding of Wesley's political views seems consistent with Wesley's practices. In a Bristol by-election in the spring of 1756, for example, John Wesley publicly supported the moderate Whig candidate, John Spencer, against the Tory candidate, Jarrit Smyth, because he feared that Smyth was a Jacobite.[70]

Wesley's support for a moderate Whig like Spencer would hardly qualify him as a political radical intent on shaking the foundations of British political and economic life. It remains true, however, that theologians and ethicists can find grounds in Wesley's principles and in Wesley's actions for more progressive political and economic moves, acknowledging Wesley's own conservative application of those principles. It also remains true that many of Wesley's followers, unlike Wesley himself, may have shunned education and modern thought, and may have ignored the plight of the poor and the working class in their age. But the interpretations of Wesley and the early Methodist movement offered by Semmel, Weber and Vickers have the considerable advantage of understanding the political situation on the ground in John Wesley's time, a situation against which Wesley's views make consistent sense.

## Conclusion

This brings us back around to the first section of this chapter, in which we considered changing understandings of the Church of England in John Wesley's age. One of the consistent marks of credible scholarship on the early Methodist movement is the level of its cognisance of the political, social and cultural conditions of the age in which the Methodist movement first emerged. Another such mark must be the use of manuscript sources in addition to the printed sources available for the study of the view of Wesley and early Methodist leaders. Theologians and ethicists concerned with the interpretation of Wesleyan thought might appropriately plead that their study should be limited to what the Wesleys were willing to say publicly (in print) about theological or moral issues, but manuscript sources often

---

[69] J. E. Vickers, *Wesley: A Guide for the Perplexed* (London and New York: T&T Clark International, 2009).

[70] John Wesley, letter to Ebenezer Blackwell, 4 March 1756; a manuscript in the Methodist Archives of the John Rylands University Library of Manchester identified as 'JW 1.62'. Note that 'Spencer' is sometimes written 'Spenser' and 'Smyth' is sometimes written 'Smith'. Smyth was a member of the Steadfast Society of Bristol, a group sometimes represented as harbouring Jacobite tendencies, though the Steadfast Society was the main Tory group in Bristol; on this, see W. E. Minchinton (ed.), *Politics and the Port of Bristol in the Eighteenth Century: The Petitions of the Society of Merchant Venturers, 1698–1803* (Bristol Record Society Publications, vol. 23; Bristol: Bristol Record Society, 1963), 78, n. 2 and 80, n. 1. On Spencer, cf. *The Oxford Dictionary of National Biography* (2003), 51: 864–5.

illuminate these issues as well as the general history of the Methodist movement in the eighteenth century.

Another set of issues has to do with the study of popular expressions of the Methodist movement in addition to studies of its better-known and better-documented leaders. The works of Kevin M. Watson and Phyllis Mack discussed above and of other historians such as David Hempton have shown that the public reception of Wesleyan teachings and practices often stood in tension with the expressed views of Methodist figureheads such as the Wesleys.[71] But whereas the Wesleyan sources (including works of Charles and Susannah Wesley) have received careful attention from editors and historians in recent decades, popular sources have not been as well preserved or catalogued, and the acquisition and publication of such popular sources will have to become a high priority in the near future.

---

[71] D. Hempton, *Methodism: Empire of the Spirit* (New Haven, CT and London: Yale University Press, 2005).

# The Price of Respectability: Methodism in Britain and the United States, 1791–1865

### Kevin Watson

## Introduction

Situated in a pleasant Cheshire hamlet, Englesea Brook Chapel and Museum tells the story of the Primitive Methodists, one of several splinter groups in British Methodism that emerged in the early part of the nineteenth century. Not everyone in British Methodism was pleased at the prospect of a museum telling this story when it became a possibility in the 1980s. To some it appeared to run against the spirit of Methodist unity that had existed since the establishment of the Methodist Church in 1932. The fear was that the museum would encourage people to live in the past and open up old wounds.

A visitor to the museum recalled an occasion in the Staffordshire town where she grew up when the local Wesleyan congregation planned to hold a garden party. Hearing about it, several Primitive Methodist women met specifically to pray for rain. This is clearly not an inspirational story. Indeed, it is not even a respectable story and as such it is indicative of the problem of Methodist heritage beyond 1791. It is not as respectable as it ought to be.

In existing Methodist historiography no one did more to undermine the impression of respectability than E. P. Thompson. Thompson's parents were Methodist missionaries, though it is clear from his writing that the experience of growing up within the denomination was not a happy one. An entire chapter of *The Making of the English Working Class* is devoted to religion, and it makes for memorable reading as Thompson abandoned objectivity so that his full ire could be directed at the pernicious influence in history and his own life that was Methodism:

> It is difficult to conceive of a more essential disorganisation of human life, a pollution of the sources of spontaneity bound to reflect itself in every aspect of personality. Since joy was associated with sin and guilt,

> and pain (Christ's wounds) with goodness and love, so every impulse became twisted into the reverse, and it became natural to suppose that man or child only found grace in God's eyes when performing painful, laborious or self-denying tasks. To labour and to sorrow was to find pleasure, and masochism was 'Love'. It is inconceivable that men could actually live like this; but many Methodists did their best.[1]

Almost fifty years after it was first published, Thompson's writing on Methodism still has the capacity to impress and appall in equal measure. As a result of his work the predominant theme in Methodist historiography for the next thirty years was class and whether Methodism might be seen as politically revolutionary or counter-revolutionary. In this chapter class is one theme among several but the broader scope of analysis is the relationship between Methodism and respectability that Thompson undermined so effectively.

Much of what follows revisits the familiar terrain of Methodist history from below, exploring the contribution of ordinary, working people including women and African Americans, who until relatively recently were sidelined or overly-compartmentalised from the main narrative. In exploring these themes, a particular area of concern for British Methodist historiography is that in recent years it has become increasingly marginalised from the main narrative of the nineteenth century. In the post-Christian era of British life, the nineteenth century is in danger of being secularised, with few historians focusing on the interplay between religion and society. A new generation of scholars of British Methodism has yet to emerge to continue the work of people like David Hempton, David Bebbington and W. R. Ward.

Whilst objectivity is the goal and intention of every historian, this essay is offered with the sense that, partly as a reaction to the excesses of Thompson's prose, the tone of scholarship on Methodist history in the past few decades has tended a little too much towards the reverential. In the nineteenth century Methodism expanded at a phenomenal rate; it provided working people with new skills and raised self-esteem, and its adherents enjoyed a sense of community that many, if not most, in modern society have cause to envy. However, the movement also provided a platform from which racism was rendered respectable, and women's expectations of their expanding role in society were raised but then trampled upon. Between 1791 and 1865 Methodists around the world rejoiced in increasing numbers and increasing respectability but that respectability came at a price.

By the second decade of the nineteenth century, Methodism was spreading around the world at an impressive rate. In this chapter a transatlantic comparative analysis will explore Methodism's movement from fringe sect to an establishment of several denominations. It will examine Methodist worship and politics (internal and external) and demonstrate how a growing need for wider acceptance and respectability moved sinners from the mourning benches of the camp meeting to the grand galleried chapels of the Victorian era.

---

[1] E. P. Thompson, *The Making of the English Working Class* (London: Penguin, 1980), 409.

## Fear versus Respectability in Revival Worship

Drawing together an impressive range of statistics, Mark Noll has noted that whilst the United States had just 20 Methodist churches in 1770, this number had risen to 19,883 by 1860. In the tumult of the impending war of Independence in 1776 only 17 per cent of the population were active in any church but by 1850 34 per cent of Americans belonged to churches, many of them converts of an extraordinary era of revival that eventually became known as the Second Great Awakening.[2]

For many years the terms 'Second Great Awakening' and 'camp meeting' were regarded as practically synonymous, and generalised accounts of Methodism as the embodiment of new and fresh 'frontier' religion became the official version of events. More recently, such a perspective has been increasingly called into question. Ruth Lester has demonstrated that much of what has been regarded as new and fresh in 'camp meetings' was already happening in Methodist quarterly meetings, field meetings and, in Virginia, a sixteen day 'siege' before camp meetings became popular.[3] Taking the story even further back, Paul Conkin asserts that 'little if anything that happened … was new, without precedents that stretched back through two centuries, to Carolina, to Virginia, to Pennsylvania, and ultimately to Ulster and Scotland'.[4] Nevertheless, stripped of its frontier associations the camp meeting is worthy of brief consideration for the insight it offers into a style of Methodist worship that attracted a million people in 1811 alone.[5]

The archetypal image of an early camp meeting is J. Maze Burbank's 1839 watercolour entitled 'Religious Camp Meeting'.[6] In the painting an evangelist with wild hair is gesturing violently on a platform but none of his listeners can bear to look at him as they are in various states of distress on the mourning benches below. Some are praying, some have their arms outstretched and some have collapsed. Most are visibly distressed. With such dramatic 'manifestations of the spirit' as the 'jerks', 'holy laughter' and 'holy barking', camp meetings were occasions for sinners to endure a dark night of the soul in the hope of rising with a knowledge of their sins forgiven.

One of the most popular camp meeting evangelists of this era was Lorenzo Dow. With a fashion sense that appears to have been modelled on John the Baptist, Dow based many important life decisions on dreams he had.[7] In his reliance on

---

[2] Mark A. Noll, *America's God: From Jonathan Edwards to Abraham Lincoln* (Oxford: Oxford University Press, 2002), 166.

[3] Lester Ruth, 'Reconsidering the Emergence of the Second Great Awakening and Camp Meetings Among Early Methodists', *Worship*, 75:4 (2001), 242.

[4] Paul K. Conkin, *Cane Ridge: America's Pentecost* (Madison, WI: University of Wisconsin Press, 1990), 63.

[5] Ruth, 'Reconsidering the Emergence of the Second Great Awakening', 337.

[6] J. Maze Burbank, 'Religious Camp Meeting' [watercolour] (1839), housed in New Bedford Whaling Museum, New Bedford, Connecticut.

[7] Lorenzo Dow, *History of Cosmopolite; or the Four Volumes of Lorenzo's Journal, Concentrated in One: Containing His Experiences and Travels, from Childhood to 1815, Being Upward of Thirty-Seven Years. Also His Polemical Writings; Consisting Of His Chain, with Five*

dreams as a means of Divine communication, Dow was no different from many other Methodists of the era. In England, the Magic Methodists of Delamere Forest went so far as to make dreams and trances a central aspect of their devotional life and many Methodist memoirs of the time devote serious space and attention to revelations of the spirit experienced in sleep. As Methodism on both sides of the Atlantic became more respectable, representations of dreams and visions became less common but their function in shaping the experiences and worship style of early Methodists is worthy of serious academic attention.

Whether through dreams or other events, it is clear that fear of damnation was important in shaping Lorenzo Dow's Christian conviction and he was anxious to share in this gospel of fear with others. This he did to remarkable, theatrical effect, for example by hiring a small boy to hide in a tree and sound a horn at the moment when the evangelist was talking about the Day of Judgment and the arrival of the Angel Gabriel.[8]

Whilst fear remained part of the spiritual armoury of Methodism, the lack of emotional restraint it encouraged at camp meetings and other revival events came to be regarded by some as bad for business. In the marketplace of American religion, it was essential that the denomination attracted not only ordinary, working people but the affluent as well. However, the respectably well-off tended to regard camp meetings with a certain amount of disdain, for these were vulgar gatherings of common people expressing themselves in unsophisticated music and embarrassing emotional displays. In trying to appeal to a broader cross-section of society, much of Methodism retreated indoors and camp meetings were rendered respectable. As Winthrop Hudson has noted, 'By the 1830's, even among Methodists, camp meetings had become occasions when the faithful gathered to combine an annual outing with an opportunity to listen to an inspirational address.'[9]

It was not only the camp meeting that underwent significant change and decline in the period of this study. In a study of Methodism in New York City, Philip Hardy drew attention to the importance of the class meeting not only as a means of renewal, support and discipline for members but as a method of conversion for those not yet full members of the church. Indeed, the class meeting is described as the primary evangelistic mechanism of Methodism in the city in the opening decades of the century during which time the denomination deliberately established classes in areas without a Methodist presence to bring about conversions. However, by the early 1820s these class meetings were in decline. It was felt that prayer meetings

---

*Links, Two Hooks and a Swivel. Reflections on Matrimony. Hints on the Fulfilment of Prophecy. Dialogue between the Curious and the Singular. Analects Upon the Rights of Man. A Journey from Babylon to Jerusalem &c.* (Philadelphia, 1815) 25, 8.

[8]   Charles Coleman Sellers, *Lorenzo Dow: The Bearer of the Word* (New York: Minton, Balch & Co., 1928), 147.

[9]   Winthrop S. Hudson, *Religion in America: An Historical Account of the Development of American Religious Life* [4th Edition] (New York: Pearson, 1989).

effected conversions more quickly.[10] It may also have been the case that Methodists welcomed some level of release from the tight discipline of the class meeting in which other lay people had authority over them. In his comments on British Methodism, E. P. Thompson labelled class meetings as a form of espionage, though most other scholars have regarded them in a less sinister light.[11] Class meetings had a disciplinary aspect to them but they were also an effective means of binding the Methodist community together in sacred devotion, mutual respect and love. Love feasts served a similar purpose, though these were open to members only and, as a consequence, proved very popular among non-members whose imaginations reeled at the possibilities of what such a gathering might involve.

That camp meetings, class meetings and love feasts declined in popularity throughout the nineteenth century is undoubtedly attributable to some of the factors that informed Liston Pope's flawed but useful selection of indices of change from sect to denomination which he based on the typology of Max Weber.[12] For example, in both the United States and England the movement began to move from cultural periphery to centre, from fervent, active religious expression to a more restrained form of worship and, to an extent, from constant emphasis on evangelism and conversion to religious education and fellowship.[13] To some degree this was a natural reaction to the changing environment in which Methodism operated. In the United States, as communities became more settled so too did churches, but in England many felt that the appearance of respectability was essential to the survival of the movement, and that perception was to trigger a half-century of controversy.

An illustration of this point is to be found within the export of the Second Great Awakening's religious excitement to working-class communities in England. In Nathan Hatch's seminal text on American religion he argues that at a deep level evangelical religion in the United States mirrored the political values of the new nation.[14] It was religion of the people, by the people and for the people. Camp meetings gave a voice to everyone irrespective of class, gender, age and sometimes race. Whilst such respectable Methodist leaders as Francis Asbury expressed approval of camp meetings in the United States they were an altogether more controversial prospect in Great Britain largely because of their perceived potential to incite political radicalism among working people.

Matters were not helped by the fact that the man who initiated the idea of camp meetings in England was Lorenzo Dow whose fusion of evangelical and republican values made him a dangerous proposition. These were tense times in

---

[10] Philip F. Hardy, 'The Evangelistic and Catechetical Role of the Class Meeting in Early New York City Methodism', *Methodist History*, 38:1 (1999), 14–26.

[11] Thompson, *Making of the English Working Class*, 388.

[12] Liston Pope, *Millhands and Preachers: A Study of Gastonia* (New Haven, CT and London: Yale University Press, 1965).

[13] John Munsey Turner, *Conflict and Reconciliation: Studies in Methodism and Ecumenism in England 1740–1982* (London, 1985), 59.

[14] Nathan O. Hatch, *The Democratization of American Christianity* (New Haven, CT: Yale University Press, 1989).

which the perceived threat of revolution was heavy in the air so it is little wonder that Dow found many Methodist pulpits closed to him. The controversy deepened when Dow's preaching triggered a camp meeting movement in Staffordshire, led by Hugh Bourne, a wheelwright and carpenter. The first English camp meeting took place on a hill called Mow Cop in May of 1807 and attracted many working people from surrounding villages. Whilst it was a much more restrained affair than its American counterparts, its occurrence prompted the Wesleyan Conference to officially announce that 'even supposing such meetings to be allowable in America, we find them highly improper'.[15] For the leaders of Wesleyanism, the preservation of a respectable image was of paramount importance, for this was an era in which the denomination was not yet fully protected by law and in which charges of sedition and revolution might derail the progress that had been made since Wesley's death in 1791.

The camp meeting controversy went on for several years and was the main factor in the emergence of what was to become the second largest Methodist denomination in the United Kingdom – the Primitive Methodists.[16] However, the chief founder of the movement complained that, as early as 1816, Primitive Methodists were losing their impact, especially with regard to the way camp meetings were run. He argued that preaching was too long, that there was not enough prayer, resources were badly directed and that the meetings had lost their converting power.[17] To his mind Primitive Methodism was swiftly evolving into something that lacked the raw emotional and spiritual power that characterised its birth, and Bourne was committed to resisting Primitive Methodism's rise to respectability.

Methodist worship in the early nineteenth century was well organised, drew effectively on popular culture (for example in the use of contemporary folk tunes for revival singing) and was adaptable to change. In both Britain and the United States, Methodist worship developed significantly in the period from 1791 to 1865, spurred on by opportunities for growth, the desire to include a wider range of people and the variety of spaces in which worship took place. Whilst deviance from the central doctrines was not tolerated, ordinary men, women and children found that in various modes of Methodist worship they had a voice and what they said mattered. In finding their voices such people consciously or subconsciously raised questions about where authority in Methodism lay and how it related to the wider political world.

---

[15] Quoted in Hugh Bourne, *History of the Primitive Methodists, Giving an Account of their Rise and Progress up to the Year 1823* (Bemersley: Primitive Methodist Connexion, 1823), 14.

[16] For a detailed analysis of the origins of Primitive Methodism see Julia Stewart Werner, *The Primitive Methodist Connexion: Its Background and Early History* (Madison, WI: University of Wisconsin Press, 1984).

[17] John Walford, *Memoirs of the Life and Labours of the Late Venerable Hugh Bourne, Founder of the English Camp Meetings, and the Originator, and for Twenty-Two Years Editor, of the Primitive Methodist Magazines* (Stoke-on-Trent: Berith, 1999 [reprint of 1856]), 59–62.

## Methodism Goes Forth and Multiplies

One of the reasons why many modern Methodists shy away from exploring their nineteenth-century heritage is the perception that it was a spectacularly unecumenical age. In the sixty years from Wesley's death in 1791 new Methodist denominations in England frequently arose out of disputes within Wesleyanism. These included the Methodist New Connexion, Primitive Methodists, Tent Methodists and Bible Christians. Whilst the political context was rather different in the United States, some strikingly similar issues led to the formation of a range of new denominations including the Republican Methodists, Methodist Protestants and African Methodist Episcopalians. Most serious of all was the eventual sectional split in the Methodist Episcopal Church that even at the time was regarded as a grim foretaste of the conflict faced by the nation in years to come.

In theological terms there was very little difference between most of these groups. Exceptions to the rule include the Methodist Unitarians in England, who might better be understood as part of Unitarian history rather than Methodist, and the Evangelical Alliance in the United States, who drew from Lutheran theology and culture as much as Methodist.[18] For the most part, however, the different Methodist groups had very similar patterns of organisation and discipline, similar styles of worship and similar theological emphases. What separated these groups was not theology but arguments about who should be in control. In struggles over lay representation at conferences, the rights of black American Methodists to organise their own societies and worship, or the struggle in England to make camp meetings an acceptable part of Methodist practice, there is a common theme of ordinary people demanding a greater involvement in the running of their religious societies and as such the story of Methodism contributes significantly to the history of democracy.

That said, in the parallel narratives of the two countries, differences can be detected. Mark Noll portrays American evangelicals of the time as having a much more affirming view of human nature than their British counterparts. Life was a staging ground for personal and social transformation and churches were nurturing communities in which God could put his people to work. In Britain, by contrast, there was a stronger emphasis on the sovereignty of God and the inability of human beings to really reform the institutions of society. The overwhelmingly hierarchical nature of British society was echoed in theology that portrayed life as a transitory time of moral trial.[19] Such an analysis resonates convincingly when applied to the elite clergy who strove to keep Wesleyans under control in the period but, as scholars of the movement on both sides of the Atlantic have made clear, issues of denominational government were no less difficult to resolve in the new republic than they were in Britain.

---

[18] Methodist Unitarianism has not been given a great deal of serious academic attention but for an overview of the movement see H. McLachlan, *The Methodist Unitarian Movement* (Manchester: Manchester University Press, 1919).

[19] Noll, *America's God*, 193.

In 1968, Robert Currie published a provocative study of the causes and consequences of the divisions and reunions that were a large part of the British Methodist story. He engaged with the idea of Methodism as a training ground for democracy, observing that 'if all the offices in Methodism had been held singly, every other member could have been an office holder. In the event, one member in twelve was a local preacher or steward, one in ten a trustee, one in four a Sunday School officer or teacher.'[20] However, a clear theme in Currie's work was that at a national and district level Wesleyan Methodism in the first half of the nineteenth century was run as an autocracy. For example, when the impressive Leeds Brunswick church was opened in 1825, the local trustees felt that an organ would be desirable whilst the leaders and Local Preachers believed that worship was purer when kept simple so they opposed it. The District then endorsed this view only to have it overturned by Conference. Ultimately, the Conference decision was upheld but such was the strength of feeling that some Methodists left the movement to form the Protestant Methodists. Further controversy erupted between 1849 and 1852 after the publication of a series of fly-sheets criticising the way that Wesleyan Methodism was run. At the centre of it all was Jabez Bunting, the four times President of the Wesleyan Conference whose leadership style is epitomised in his famous declaration that Methodism was as opposed to democracy as sin.[21] The fly-sheet situation was not handled well, as Bunting's supporters published increasingly intemperate counter-attacks on their critics. In an era in which Methodism was gaining a greater sense of respectability within society, this was an extraordinarily degrading time for those who led the movement. Currie paints a picture of a Tory elite attempting to over-manage a membership made up of people of largely liberal sympathies.

A more nuanced and less judgemental view is offered by David Hempton, who provides the events of the half-century from Wesley's death with some important political context. Issues around the distribution of sacraments in Wesleyan chapels in the 1790s were not mere details of how worship was conducted but had important political implications connected with the relationship between Methodism and the Church of England and the perceived loyalty of Methodists to the king. Hempton considers it quite an achievement that there was only one British Methodist secession in the decade. Alexander Kilham led 5 per cent of existing Wesleyan Methodists into the Methodist New Connexion after being expelled from the mother connexion for failing to retract the radical beliefs he expressed in *The Progress of Liberty among the People Called Methodists* (1795). In targeting the ministerial elite he felt were exploiting ordinary Methodists and calling for lay representation in the government of Methodism, Kilham mirrored the ongoing radical critique of the British constitution.[22] Hempton goes on to place the controversy that brought about the Primitive Methodists in the context of the ongoing threats of revolution and

---

[20] Robert Currie, *Methodism Divided: A Study in the Sociology of Ecumenicalism* (London: Faber and Faber, 1968), 46.

[21] Ibid., 43.

[22] David Hempton, *Methodism and Politics in British Society 1750–1850* (Stanford, CA: Stanford University Press, 1984), 68.

Lord Sidmouth's bill, which threatened to severely curtail Methodist activity. As Hempton notes, Sidmouth felt the need to limit the number of preachers' licences being issued as among those who had been granted them in recent years were 'cobblers, tailors, pig-drovers, and chimney sweeps'.[23]

The political context of Methodism in the United States was quite different and, it might be assumed, more favourable to the democratisation of the denomination. As Louis Billington has noted, Methodists in America did not live with the same sense of impending threat as some of their British cousins did, where job loss and persecution were a real possibility for the ordinary Methodist in the wrong place.[24] However, this actually encouraged participants in the Methodist drama in the United States to voice their objections even more vociferously than was the case in Great Britain.

One obvious problem that American Methodist leaders faced was geography. Methodism quickly expanded throughout a vast area and whilst Francis Asbury tried to keep up with this it swiftly became apparent that organising the movement into a single conference would not be an effective or practical way forward. Thus the work was split into several conferences with a General Conference meeting every four years to consider issues of national importance.

The political context of the United States was also problematic as in its early days in the country Methodism was still noticeably Anglican. Freed from the fetters of Church of England associations, American Methodists even had bishops, a move that was ill-received among those who believed in a more democratic future for the church and/or had not been made bishops themselves.

Standing on the cusp of all this was Francis Asbury, a man who scholars have portrayed as sympathetic to the idea of the need for Methodism in America to reflect republican values but also someone who gained his understanding of the rules, language and discipline of the movement in England.[25] Drawing on sources relating to American Methodism's first schismatic controversy (which brought about the Republican Methodists and ultimately the Christian Church), J. Timothy Allen has demonstrated that, consciously or not, Asbury reacted to the taunting of James O'Kelly's fierce, patriotic, republican expression with language that reflected English, Wesleyan and even Anglican sensibilities.[26] Whilst American politicians continued to disagree quite vociferously on what shape the United States government should take, similar disagreements were generated within Methodism as Asbury unquestionably created an ecclesiastical aristocracy of people invited by him to participate in the governance of Methodism. As Allen

---

[23] Cited in ibid., 100.

[24] Louis Billington, 'British and American Methodisms Grow Apart', in R. A. Burchell (ed.), *The End of Anglo-America: Historical Essays in the Study of Cultural Divergence* (Manchester: Manchester University Press, 1991), 117.

[25] For an excellent study of the life of Asbury and the broader issues with which he was involved see John Wigger, *American Saint: Francis Asbury and the Methodists* (Oxford: Oxford University Press, 2009).

[26] J. Timothy Allen, 'Religion and Politics: James O'Kelly's Republicanism and Francis Asbury's Federalism', *Methodist History*, 44:3 (2006), 154.

notes, 'Since Anglicanism was gaining a stronghold in the North and Asbury was acting more like an Anglican bishop, it was only natural for O'Kelly to assume that he was recreating the very British government the Americans had fought so hard to eradicate.'[27]

By the early part of the nineteenth century republicanism had become to some within the denomination as sacred a cause as Methodism itself and the first line of defence in any disagreements about authority in the church. Thus debates ranging from obviously important matters such as the possible election of elders to the installation of church carpets contributed to an increasingly furious debate in which the patriotism of Methodist Episcopal leaders was called into question. Writing in 1827, Alexander McCaine made a direct connection between what he perceived to be the shortcomings of Methodist leadership and the future security of the country:

> It is believed that a community living under the influence of such a form of government as that of the Methodist Episcopal Church, where the members are not permitted to participate in legislation, will sooner or later prefer a monarchical form of civil government to the pure republican institutions of our happy country.[28]

This controversy ultimately resulted in the formation of the Methodist Protestant denomination, one of several non-episcopal groups that used their political distance from the Methodist mainstream as an indicator of their enhanced American political values. However, even the Methodist Protestants failed to adequately include black people in their vision of what the future church would look like.

## Revivalists and Race

From the beginning, the Methodist movement in the United States included black people in both north and south. J. Gordon Melton has observed that Methodism was the only denomination that systematically approached African Americans and invited them into membership.[29] Whilst Donald Mathews once argued that embracing Christian evangelicalism amounted to a rejection of African American heritage, contemporary scholars have demonstrated ways in which blacks imbued Methodist worship with a distinctly African style of music and expression.[30] Ample evidence can be found to portray Methodism both as a tool of control of black

---

[27] Ibid.,161.
[28] Alexander McCaine, *The History and Mystery of Methodist Episcopacy or A Glance at the Institutions of the Church, as we received them from our Fathers* (Baltimore: R. J. Matchett, 1827), v.
[29] J. Gordon Melton, *A Will to Choose: The Origins of African American Methodism* (Lanham, MD: Rowman & Littlefield, 2007), 126.
[30] Donald G. Mathews, *Religion in the Old South* (Chicago, IL: University of Chicago Press, 1977), 67.

Methodists and a means of liberating self-expression. Frederick Douglass, the former slave who became the most famous black activist in the United States, had a tense relationship with the Methodist movement throughout his life. Unimpressed by the effects of his former master's involvement with the Methodist movement, Douglass nevertheless recalled that religious expression could simultaneously give the impression of submission while being an act of resistance:

> We were at times, remarkably buoyant, singing hymns and making joyous exclamations, almost as triumphant in their tone as if we had reached a land of freedom and safety. A keen observer might have detected in our singing of
>
> 'O Canaan, sweet Canaan,
>
> I am bound for the land of Canaan,'
>
> something more than a hope of reaching heaven. We meant to reach the *north* – and the north was our Canaan.[31]

Years after his liberation from slavery, Douglass almost became a member of a Methodist church in New Bedford, Massachusetts, but was appalled to discover that blacks were expected to wait until all the whites had received communion before they could receive theirs.[32] This anecdote gets to the heart of why Methodism was simultaneously such a blessing and a frustration to American blacks. Methodist slaves saw in their church a hope of future freedom and present dignity. The church provided blacks in both the north and south with a sense of self-esteem and purpose that was often denied them but that dignity was easily undermined by the paternalistic racism of those whites who saw no corollary between the ideas of equality before the throne of grace and equality at Methodist conferences or church councils.

One of the weaknesses of Methodist historiography is a tendency to construct narratives from a top-down, denominational approach, in the case of African Americans defining their contribution almost entirely by the disputes that led to the formation of new and exclusively black Methodist denominations. Even scholars working specifically in black history have tended towards narrowing their focus to a particular Methodist group rather than the black Methodist experience more broadly. In 2007, J. Gordon Melton provided an effective challenge to the assumptions that accompany such approaches with the publication of a book providing an overview of African American Methodism. Instead of segregating blacks into the churches that some of them formed, Melton used a sophisticated

---

[31] Cited in James H. Cone, 'Black Spirituals: A Theological Interpretation', in Cornell West and Eddie S. Glaude Jr (eds), *African American Religious Thought: An Anthology* (Louisville, KY: Westminster John Knox Press, 2003), 787.

[32] David Hempton, *Methodism: Empire of the Spirit* (Newhaven, CT and London: Yale University Press, 2005), 25.

array of sources not only to demonstrate the interrelationship of different black Methodist churches and organisations but also to highlight the black contribution to the Methodist mainstream.[33]

Whether or not it has been overstated, the tragedy of black American Methodism in the nineteenth century was that the racism they endured often did necessitate separation from white Methodists, and the thirty years from 1790 are notable for the establishment of several exclusively black American Methodist denominations. Usually this began with an affront to the dignity of African Americans in the congregation that brought a period of integrated worship to an end. For example, the story of the African Methodist Episcopal Church can be traced to the Sunday when black members of St George's Methodist Episcopal Church in Philadelphia were removed from a 'whites only' section of the church. In protest, they walked out of the church intent on forming a community in which they could be respected as equals.[34] For a while they worshipped as a black community within the Methodist Episcopal Church but ultimately their lack of representation within the church government demanded separation, a process that involved complex legal battles.[35] Unfortunately, the drama that was to lead to the formation of the African Methodist Episcopal Church involved a great deal of indignity on both sides, with white Methodist authorities attempting to stop black ministers from administering the sacraments and black Methodists blocking the pulpit to white preachers.[36] Made in the image of God as they may have been, many black and white Methodists felt the call to love their neighbours but balked at the idea of doing it in the same room.

## From Slavery to Freedom and Back to Slavery: White Methodists and the Peculiar Institution

In Wesley's day, Methodism was a great source of hope for those who opposed slavery. Opposition to slavery was the official Methodist position from the publication of the first *General Rules* in 1743 and in his famous last letter to William Wilberforce, Wesley labelled American slavery 'the vilest that ever saw the sun'.[37] In 1784 an anti-slavery stance became the official American Methodist position and strict rules were drawn up requiring that people freed their slaves within one

---

[33] Melton, *A Will to Choose*.
[34] Hatch, *The Democratization of American Christianity*, 109.
[35] Frederick A. Norwood, *The Story of American Methodism: A History of the United Methodists and Their Relations* (Nashville, TN: Abingdon, 1974), 169.
[36] Hatch, *The Democratization of American Christianity*, 110.
[37] Robert H. Craig, 'Liberative History and Liberation Ethics: A Case Study of American Methodism and Popular Struggle', in D. M. Yeager (ed.), *The Annual of the Society of Christian Ethics* (Washington, DC: Georgetown University Press, 1987), 142.

year of becoming a Methodist. Six months later, this rule had already proved to be completely ineffective.

Opposition to slavery within white Methodism was sporadic and largely ineffective in the nineteenth century. Most white Methodists in the 1830s and 1840s saw abolitionism as a much greater evil than slavery for it disparaged the reputations of slaveholders who had joined the church and threatened opportunities for evangelism. As one southern minister proclaimed in a passionate anti-abolitionist speech at the General Methodist Episcopal Conference of 1844:

> If you really wish to do us good, and be a blessing to the black man, I will tell you how to accomplish it … Go with me to the cabin of the slave and wipe the tear from the sorrowing face of affliction. Stand by his dying couch, and tell him Jesus died that he might live. Exalt before the admiring gaze of slave and master the consecrated cross, and let both come and weep beneath its shadow![38]

It was a powerful argument that was made many times. Indeed, the only effective predominantly white abolitionist Methodist denomination, the Wesleyan Methodist, came into being largely because the Methodist Episcopal Church from 1824 onwards proved more effective at enforcing discipline against those considered abolitionist extremists than expressing unease at the existence of slavery.[39]

Free from the shackles of the mother church the Wesleyans were able to oppose the peculiar institution in a way that drew strong praise from the likes of Frederick Douglass and William Lloyd Garrison. However, as Mark Noll has demonstrated, those who argued in favour of slavery had the upper hand with biblical literalists for the institution of slavery is mentioned but not criticised several times in the Bible. The abolitionist perspective demanded an appeal to the spirit rather than the letter of scripture; there were arguments about whether modern slavery and biblical slavery could be treated separately, and William Lloyd Garrison made the controversial claim that since scripture appeared to sanction slavery, scripture must be wrong.[40]

The General Conference of 1844 was the moment when the mainstream of American Methodism split in two. Controversy erupted over a series of actions taken against southern ministers who owned slaves, the best remembered being Bishop James O. Andrew, of Georgia, who became a slave-owner through marriage. The majority of delegates at that Conference have been described by historians of the last few decades as 'moderates', an ill-fitting label for those who were not pro-slavery but were anti-abolitionist, clinging to the racist assumptions of the

---

[38] *The Debates of the General Conference of the M.E. Church, May 1844 to which is added a review of the proceedings of said conference, by Rev. Luther Lee and Rev. E. Smith* (New York: Wesleyan Methodist Connection of America, 1845), 46.

[39] Chris Padgett, 'Hearing the Antislavery Rank-and-File: The Wesleyan Methodist Schism of 1843', *Journal of the Early Republic*, 12 (Spring 1992), 70.

[40] Noll, *America's God*, 387–90.

middle ground in the hope of preserving the status quo. They sought to pacify both extremes in the debate by arguing that whilst the institution of slavery was a great societal evil, the owning of slaves was not an individual sin.[41] To them, slavery was bad but offending southern honour was worse and liable to lead to schism. The schism of 1844 was a tragedy for the Methodist Episcopal Church and for race relations in the United States. Furthermore, it was a foretaste of the horrors that were to come. As the Reverend H. Splicer warned during the debates about Bishop Andrew, 'I say, when we must part and dissolve our ecclesiastical connection, the death-knell of the Union is certainly given; for I am well persuaded that no power has more to do with binding the remote parts of our country together, than the itinerancy and general superintendency of the M. E. Church.'[42]

## The Political Impact of Methodism

The sad story of Methodism and slavery in the United States demonstrates the impossibility of keeping religion out of politics. For historians of British Methodism in the twenty years following the publication of *The Making of the English Working Class*, class was the defining issue. Robert Moore, for example, argued that one influence of Methodism was to inhibit the development of a class consciousness and reduce class conflict.[43] Sometimes, however, Methodism provided people of a radical persuasion with the skills and the platform to express their ideas. For example, on 21 March 1849 Joseph Heslop used a meeting at Swinhope Primitive Methodist Chapel in the North Pennines to incite a miners' strike. After the singing of a hymn and a period of prayer, Heslop delivered a speech that drew heavily on biblical references and the conventions of revival preaching. Those who refused to join in the strike action were encouraged towards eternal hellfire. 'Let them be like Cain, deserted by God and forsaken of men,' Heslop warned the congregation. 'Let them be like Judas, only fit for taking their own lives if none of you can do it for them.'[44] Read in the twenty-first century Heslop's speech still has the power to shock and it is easy to understand why such voices were challenged and suppressed in nineteenth-century Methodism. Just as opposition to slavery was curtailed in the United States because of its capacity to cause offence and undermine opportunities for evangelism, so was labour radicalism discouraged in Britain. In his work on Primitive Methodism Geoffrey Milburn drew attention to a number of trade union leaders who held prominent lay positions within the denomination but also demonstrated that political radicalism and Methodism were uneasy bedfellows. Tommy Hepburn,

---

[41] *Debates of the General Conference, 1844*, 41.
[42] Ibid., 32.
[43] Robert Moore, *Pit-Men, Preachers and Politics: The Effects of Methodism in a Durham Mining Community* (London: Cambridge University Press, 1974), 13.
[44] Quoted in C. J. Hunt, *The Lead Miners of the Northern Pennines in the Eighteenth and Nineteenth Centuries* (Manchester: Manchester University Press, 1984), 132–3.

for example, was a Primitive Methodist local preacher and strike leader in 1831 but the denomination 'felt obliged to disown him' because of his trade union activities.[45] Methodists may have been offended at the activities of labour radicals at the connexional level but, as Robert Colls has demonstrated, locally the situation was quite different. In the Durham coalfields, for example, Methodists felt called to a mission of community and the result was something radical enough to deeply challenge Thompsonian assumptions.[46]

British Methodism has been credited with bolstering the Tolpuddle Martyrs, providing Chartists with a form of worship that could be put to very effective political use (the camp meeting) and ensuring that the revolutionary change that took place in the country during the first half of the nineteenth century was largely non-violent. For half a century debates have focused on Methodism and class but the challenge for the next generation of historians is to move the debate on from this whilst avoiding the risk of sidelining the movement to a position of political irrelevance.

Inspiration can be drawn from the United States where similar debates about evangelicalism and class took place in the 1960s and 1970s. However, historians of American Methodism have been careful to ensure that class has not completely consumed the political agenda. In the 1990s Richard Carwardine waded into the political and theological currents of antebellum America and showed how Methodists helped to steer the political course of the nation. Early in the century Methodists saw involvement in politics as an unnecessary distraction from the work of evangelism but by the end of the Civil War the situation had changed so dramatically that Ulysses Grant claimed the three great parties in the United States were the Republican, the Democratic and the Methodist Church.[47] Carwardine explored how engagement with Wesley's idea of Christian Perfection encouraged an optimistic view of the political future of the country. In the 1840s, Methodists may have had their own increasingly fragmented position in mind when they opposed the two-party system because it made conflict the default position of politics. In an era of paranoia that mirrored the Communist scare a century later, the 1840s and 1850s were a time when many Methodists were actively committed to controlling the enemy within. Roman Catholics were regarded as that enemy and a papal takeover of the United States the threat to be faced. Whilst the Democratic Party gained Roman Catholic votes through its opposition to religious tyranny, many Methodists supported the Whigs who championed the legislation of morality, opposing political corruption and Sunday mailings among other issues, before being swallowed up in the tumultuous events of the 1850s. The decade before the Civil War was a time of radicalisation for Methodists with many in the north finally adopting an abolitionist stance. However, it was also a fiercely anti-Catholic period

---

[45] Geoffrey Milburn, *Primitive Methodism* (Peterborough: Epworth Press, 2002), 55.

[46] Robert Colls, *The Pitmen of the Northern Coalfields: Work, Culture and Protest, 1790–1850* (Manchester: Manchester University Press, 1987), 118–203. See also Hempton, *Methodism and Politics*, 215–16.

[47] Richard Carwardine, 'Methodists, Politics, and the Coming of the American Civil War', *Church History*, 69:3 (September 2000), 578.

that saw the advent of the nativist Know-Nothing Party. Carwardine notes that the Know-Nothings certainly appealed to many Methodists but ultimately failed to attract the support they needed because of their emphasis on secrecy, vitriolic hatred of foreigners and failure to properly address the slavery issue.[48]

An area that Carwardine mentions but does not develop is the contribution of evangelical women to the political landscape of antebellum America. The contention that women had a feminising influence on the Whig Party is an alluring perspective though difficult to prove. It is arguably dependent on the kind of stereotypes of women as the moral and spiritual superiors of men that were current in the opening decades of the nineteenth century and allowed women to enjoy positions of responsibility that they would later be denied.[49] Nevertheless, Carwardine's perceptive analysis invites further exploration on both sides of the Atlantic. Whilst the evangelical basis of women's opposition to issues like temperance, Sabbath observance and poor relief is easily demonstrable, the more subtle influences that Carwardine refers to deserve more detailed investigation and application to the broader story of Methodism's intersection with the wider political world.

Carwardine's comments can be placed in the context of thirty years in which the women who made up the majority of Methodist membership on both sides of the Atlantic have been reinstated into the main internal narrative of the movement's history. Particular attention has been given to the role of women preachers. In the opening decades of the nineteenth century, as religious revival swept across the United States, the number of women preachers increased. Catherine Brekus emphasises that the women preachers of this revivalist age tended to have imminent millennial expectations that overrode any consideration of whether what they were doing was proper and were usually working class.[50]

Although the religious landscape of Great Britain was more conservative than that of the United States in the early nineteenth century, women preachers played an integral part in the early history of Primitive Methodism in England. R. W. Ambler places women preachers in the context of the Industrial Revolution in England, claiming that they provided a refuge from the harshness of a fast-changing world by offering a gospel based in traditional homeliness.[51] Deborah Valenze takes up this theme, noting how hymns of the time portrayed heaven as a place of idealised domesticity but also emphasising that through religion women found 'ideological support and inspiration for their campaign against economic defeat'.[52]

---

[48] Richard Carwardine, *Evangelicals and Politics in Antebellum America* (New Haven, CT and London: Yale University Press, 2000).

[49] Richard Carwardine, 'Religious Revival and Political Renewal in Antebellum America', in J. Garnett and H. G. C. Matthew (eds), *Revivals and Religion Since 1700: Essays for John Walsh* (London: Hambledon, 1993), 129.

[50] Catherine A. Brekus, *Strangers and Pilgrims: Female Preaching in America 1740–1845* (Chapel Hill, NC and London: University of North Carolina Press, 1998), 6, 120.

[51] R. W. Ambler, *Ranters, Revivalists and Reformers: Primitive Methodism and Rural Society in South Lincolnshire 1817–1875* (Hull Academic Press, 1989), 47.

[52] Deborah Valenze, *Prophetic Sons and Daughters: Female Preaching and Popular Religion in Industrial England* (Princeton: Princeton University Press, 1985), 30, 40.

In Britain, the phenomenon of women preaching was particularly strong among the Primitive Methodists. Dorothy Graham's research reveals that 125 different women served as travelling preachers in the Primitive Methodist Connexion.[53] However, few of these women lasted more than a few years in the role since their mission was undermined by restrictions on married women preaching and oppressive working conditions. For example, in 1836 the maximum salary for a male single preacher was four pounds per quarter while for women it was two pounds and ten shillings.[54] The assumption that women could survive on so much less than men was a blow to their dignity and well-being. Ruth Watkins was a travelling preacher who served the British denomination in its short-lived mission to the United States. In 1835, she wrote to the British Conference complaining that she had not been paid in four years, a situation that had caused her intense physical and emotional hardship and was about to force her departure from the denomination. On the back of the letter, a representative of the British Conference wrote, 'From Ruth Watkins in America dated March /35. To the Conference as it could not be officially answered, no answer was sent.'[55] Anne Wearing was another Primitive Methodist missionary in America although her work mainly involved family visiting. She covered a very large area that forced her to rely on the hospitality of many people including 'an old gentleman, a Methodist Episcopal', a 'Quaker lady' and 'a gentleman of French extraction'.[56] These small details reveal that the reputations of female preachers were extremely fragile. Little wonder that most ultimately sought the respectability and security of marriage.

By midcentury, women preachers were increasingly rare on both sides of the Atlantic. They were victims of Methodism's rise to respectability. In an era in which Methodism had moved from open fields to increasingly decorative and impressive buildings and the role of the travelling preacher had become professionalised, women were no longer regarded as suited to the role. There is a certain irony in the fact that in 1848, when the popularity and acceptability of women preaching was fading away, the radical Wesleyan Methodist Church in Seneca Falls, New York played host to the first Women's Rights Convention. Even as this historic event was taking place Methodism's women preachers were becoming a thing of the past, sacrificed on the altar of respectability.

---

[53] Quoted in Milburn, *Primitive Methodism*, 15.

[54] *Various Regulations Made by the Conferences of the Primitive Methodist Connexion and Consolidated at and by the Conference held at Lynn-Regis in Norfolk, May 20–25, 1836* (London: M. R. Publications, 1836), 2–3.

[55] Ruth Watkins to William Clowes and John Flesher, March 1835 (Methodist Collection: John Rylands Library, University of Manchester).

[56] *Primitive Methodist Magazine*, 1831, 206–9; 184–7.

## Conclusion

In the first half of the nineteenth century, Methodists on both sides of the Atlantic made the difficult transition from childhood to adolescence. Whilst growth was rapid and impressive, it often came with shocking consequences. Like most adolescents, many Methodists found it difficult to get along with family members, resulting in numerous bitter arguments that echoed the political divisions of the day.

For the traditionalist elites who attempted to dominate the story on both sides of the Atlantic, respectability was of central importance but the pursuit of respectability sometimes undermined the dignity of those who saw in Methodism their great hope of liberation. Consequently much of American Methodism suffered the blemish of a missed opportunity in race relations and the women who made up the majority of Methodists were often reduced to standing on the sidelines, like cheerleaders at a football game.

There is much to inspire people in the story of Methodism in the early part of the nineteenth century but there is also an awkwardness, emotional intensity and naivety that is more embarrassing to the contemporary church than the literary outpourings of a teenager's diary rediscovered after thirty years. Methodism provided many early nineteenth-century adherents and members with a sense of purpose, confidence and belonging that no other institution could match. By midcentury, the movement was still fresh and idealistic but it was also fragmented and damaged. For many contemporary Methodists this is a period of repressed historical memory, when our forbears, so often remembered as dignified and restrained, struggled towards the day when they could call themselves grown-ups.

# Methodism: Consolidation and Reunion, 1865–1939

## Morris L. Davis

Western historians considerably overstate the amount, kind, and quality of change experienced by societies in the North Atlantic, between 1865 and 1939. Perhaps because historians often associate the increase in the speed of technological change and the creation of vast private wealth with the latter half of the nineteenth century, and because it is the era of the rise of the United States as a global power, contemporary observers tend to favor it as a possible story of origin for the twenty-first century and our current predicaments and optimistic self-regard. Among scholars of Wesleyan Methodist traditions, however, there seems to be a low level of interest, especially in relation to the amount of work produced on eighteenth-century Methodism. Again, historians' fascination with narratives and moments of origin can help explain this, as competing desires for the contemporary state of Wesleyan Methodist institutions lead those with interest and stake to lay claim to founders and their times. The late nineteenth and early twentieth centuries, though, offer fewer examples of solid ground on which such narratives, used in the service of contemporary constructive interest, can find purchase. Several aspects of this time period present themselves as obstacles to more conventional forms of denominational history—such as narratives of origins or founders, narratives of growth and success, or morality tales. The earlier part of the nineteenth century, for instance, while obviously a dark chapter in Methodist self-narratives in which Methodists in the U.S. still owned slaves or condoned the slave system, remains the source for histories of inspiration. Slaves who found and held onto their faith in the midst of unimaginable suffering, and abolitionists who fought against overwhelming odds, offer material that lends itself to satisfying endings, recognizable causes, and fodder for the continuing myths of progress that permeate Western historiography. Some of this is available in the time period of this chapter as well: missionary heroes, strong and activist women, self-supporting churches in former colonized nations, and churches that turned their attention to helping the poor and systemic social problems. There are endlessly fascinating stories to be told from this era: world-traveling adventurers, strong women, brilliant, culture-savvy converts in non-Western lands who adapt to the bewildering array of options and changes that confronted them as they navigated with a new religion ensconced in a menacing and strange new array of powerful appendages of empire. But perhaps what holds additional robust scholarly work at bay are the more difficult features of this time period. How do we understand the relationships between missions, colonialism, and empire? How can historians of this topic move beyond the entrenched framing of missions as either imperialistic or not? What were the causes of the leveling and then decline in numbers of the North Atlantic Methodist bodies? Why were the fissures among Methodists caused by race, region, and gender so enduring? How do we understand what changes were wrought by the exponential increases in wealth in the churches and among many of their members? How did national influence and cultural prominence change the Methodist denominations in the North Atlantic? What is the nature of those Methodisms that remain from missionary endeavors, and how do they tell their histories?

The general contours and the basic events and figures in this period are well known, yet these questions, and many more, remain open to scholars of this era. A considerable number of local studies have been done, especially on specific aspects and locations of mission, though there remains plenty of subject matter that has not seen enough attention. The history of missions more generally has seen resurgence in the last few decades, but it remains isolated as a field from histories of English, Canadian, or U.S. Methodism. History of Methodist women has been an active and very fruitful field, but yet the full gender implications of this work have not yet been completely realized.[1] In those North Atlantic contexts in this time period, however, very little work has been done, and certainly the field stands wide open when it comes to historical treatments that integrate the mission work of Methodist bodies with the histories of the churches at "home." What we will attempt in this chapter is to survey very briefly the general institutional narratives of global Methodism, particularly the dynamics of institutional consolidation, denominational reunion, and continued mission expansion. In order to attend to the global concerns of this collection, this chapter will attempt to sketch larger patterns that affected the shape and quality of dispersal of the established Methodist bodies in the North Atlantic.[2] Space does not permit much attention to the scholarly work done on individual

---

[1] David Hempton makes this point in the introduction to his *Methodism: Empire of the Spirit* (New Haven, CT and London: Yale University Press, 2005). Anne Braude put this question to the field of American religious history in the 1990s in her essay "Women's History is American Religious History," in Thomas Tweed (ed.), *Retelling U.S. Religious History* (Berkeley, CA and London: University of California Press, 1997), 87–107.

[2] Much of the detail for this time period has already been covered in previous reference publications, especially Manfred Marquardt's essay "Methodism in the Nineteenth and Twentieth Centuries," in W. J. Abraham and J. E. Kirby (eds), *The Oxford Handbook Of Methodist Studies* (Oxford and New York: Oxford University Press, 2009), 85–103. Marquardt surveys the geographic spread of Methodism and the subsequent reunions and mergers comprehensively, and so we will not repeat that here, but rather try and draw out larger patterns and point to areas in need of further study. As in Marquardt's essay, K. Cracknell and S. J. White also survey the spread of Methodism by geographic region in this time period, following them to late-twentieth-century arrangements. See Chapter Four, "World Methodism at the beginning

Methodist figures and each area of mission, but we will deal with historiographical issues surrounding the study of Methodist missions.

The central problem in this task is, of course, to find a way to conceptualize global Methodism coherently and with enough precision. Global Methodism is almost incomprehensibly complex and multivalent. A few scholars, in attempting a similar task, have chosen to put a signpost at the divergence of British and North American streams of Methodists, and thus at least sharpen the focus a little. And indeed, these two streams are different enough that it is productive to make the distinction. In the Preface to *An Introduction to World Methodism*, Kenneth Cracknell and Susan White call these two streams "distinct traditions."[3] For the purposes of this essay, however, we will favor those aspects that can be found in common, and assume as our subject matter not those Methodists who look the most alike, but rather those who claim some stake in the Wesleyan Methodist tradition. The commonality will be that Wesleyan Methodism is the common thread for Christian identity in our subjects. Thus, the way that identity is contested and fought for and put into practice is the history we are observing.

## Consolidation and Reunion

In the societies of Canada, Britain, and the United States in the last half of the nineteenth century, the trajectories and sources of sweeping change, well documented in historical literature more generally, affected the Methodist churches profoundly. Not only did Methodists begin to respond differently to a wider array of new problems but—and most importantly for this essay—Methodists also began to rethink the design, governance, and style of their denominational structures. Several of the most important of these changes bear marking here as we begin to think about the ways Methodists reshaped themselves. Industrialization was a primary cause of most of these sweeping social rearrangements. Populations shifting to urban areas in search of work, both immigrant and emigrant; the changing nature of labor and laborers' relation to capital; the growth of large poor neighborhoods in industrial cities and the attendant change in the character of poverty; the parallel increase in extreme wealth and the numbers of the wealthy; the rise of a relatively wealthy middle class; the creation of new professions and the

---

of the 20th Century," in K. Cracknell and S. J. White (eds), *An Introduction to World Methodism* (Cambridge and New York: Cambridge University Press, 2005), 66–91.

[3] Cracknell and White, *An Introduction to World Methodism*, vii. R. E. Richey, K. E. Rowe and J. MillerSchmidt make the same point in the "Preface" to *The Methodist Experience in America: A History*, vol. I (Nashville, TN: Abingdon Press, 2010), xvii. The primary difference between the two branches is that British Methodist mission churches became and remain separate denominations (this includes Canadian missions), while most of those who trace their history back to U.S. missions are part of the present United Methodist Church. South Korea, Mexico, and Brazil are exceptions to this development.

increase in numbers of new universities—many built by Methodist denominations; the growing women's movement and the influential organizations associated with it; and a strong and focused post-slavery racialism, particularly in the United States, including a consolidation of whiteness as a legal and cultural category.

Methodist denominations began to turn their energies to social problems of the industrial age with great force and commitment, while at the same time embracing the spirit of the age and the optimism for progress that fueled it.[4] Not all Methodists agreed, of course, and it was these very issues that contributed to some of the schisms that continued, running counter to the trend of consolidation. Participants in the Holiness movement in North America, and the Higher Life movement in England,[5] while also deeply concerned for the poor and for identifying an appropriate Christian response to the problems of the industrial revolution, generally maintained more distance from and skepticism toward the optimism about the progress of human civilization.[6] A few schisms and many individuals of the holiness persuasion contributed to the reversal of steady growth in Methodist churches, but space does not allow us to follow that part of the global Methodist story.[7] The conviction among Methodists that Christians are called to serve the broader society and address its ills led to some spectacularly successful organizing, both within and without denominational structures.[8] Within the churches, home mission societies, often led by women, became a primary avenue to channel assistance. These denominational bodies addressed urban poverty, the plight of children, built outreach to immigrant workers, founded schools and clinics. Methodists worked for improvement in factory work conditions and fought against child labor. In fighting for the prohibition of alcohol, Methodist teetotalers

---

[4] For an overview of the situation in the U.S., see H. F. May, *Protestant Churches and Industrial America* (New York: Harper and Brothers, 1949).

[5] For overviews of the Holiness movement, see D. W. Bebbington, *Holiness in Nineteenth-Century England* (Carlisle: Paternoster Press, 2000); and for the U.S., M. Dieter, *The Holiness Revival of the Nineteenth Century* (Methuchen, NJ: Scarecrow Press, 1980).

[6] One good example of this would be Henry Clay Morrison, founder of Asbury College and Seminary in Kentucky. Morrison never left his denomination but he did provide a strong voice for a return to Wesleyan holiness doctrine, as well as resistance to many of the changes in the Methodist denominations that he considered worldly conformity. See Chapter One of K. C. Kinghorn, *The Story of Asbury Seminary* (Lexington, KY: Emeth Press, 2010).

[7] This chapter will not follow those denominational debates that led to schisms, but we certainly could take that path, even to trace the influence of Methodism and Methodist peoples on the rise of Pentecostalism. The defining work on the connections between Methodist theology and Pentecostalism remains D. Dayton's *Theological Roots of Pentecostalism* (Grand Rapids, MI: Francis Asbury Press of Zondervan Publishing House, 1987).

[8] The trans-Atlantic work of the Women's Christian Temperance Union, led by Methodist Francis Willard, is perhaps the best known example of organizing outside denominational structures. See R. B. Anderson Bordin, *Frances Willard: A Biography* (Chapel Hill, NC: University of North Carolina Press, 1986).

were also addressing what they considered the degradation of Christian families, and thus Christian societies.[9]

Beyond responses to perceptions of need, though, Methodist churches were also caught up in the optimism of the age. Human creativity, hard work, use of new technologies for communication and travel, and corporate-style planning were considered keys to continuing Methodist growth. Methodists found that their fellow citizens no longer assumed them to be culturally marginal. In the United States perhaps most especially, Methodists came to hold significant cultural capital, which in turn became tangible political influence. Methodist Episcopal Church (MEC) bishop Matthew Simpson illustrates this point for us well, as he became a nationally known figure, an informal advisor to President Abraham Lincoln, and an active leader in rallying support for the Union side in the U.S. Civil War.[10] While they certainly continued to identify with the poor in society, many Methodists grew wealthy, and this wealth made its way into church coffers.[11] So great was the influence of the new wealth and those who brought it, that the very complexion of the General Conferences began to change. Lay members were allowed to be delegates, first in the MEC in the U.S. in 1872 and quickly followed by the Wesleyan Methodists in the United Kingdom in 1878.[12] This influx of a new kind of delegate had profound effects on the way Methodist denominations conducted business and consolidated in various ways over the next few decades. These lay men brought with them their business thinking, corporate or governmental theory, and different sense of calling as ministers in the church. It is in this era that Methodist denominations on both sides of the Atlantic, alongside many other Protestant denominations, began vigorous renovation of their structures. This included both attempts at consolidation and (re)unification, as well as expansion of programs and projects in new corporate-style arrangements. Methodists across the Atlantic world pulled together data on congregations and mission work and analyzed it to

---

[9] The literature on these topics is perhaps the most abundant for this era. Space does not permit a full bibliography, but current Methodist bibliographies can point researchers in the right direction.

[10] Simpson is well known for a speech he gave as he traveled around the northern U.S. during the war, drumming up support for the cause by declaring that the Union was divinely destined to win the war and achieve its place at the pinnacle of human civilization. See M. L. Davis, "From the Gospel Circuit to the War Circuit: Bishop Matthew Simpson and Upwardly Mobile Methodism," *Methodist History*, 37:3 (April 2000), 199–209.

[11] See especially D. B. Marti, "Rich Methodists: The Rise and Consequences of Lay Philanthropy in the Mid-Nineteenth Century," in R. E. Richey and K. E. Rowe (eds), *Rethinking Methodism* (Nashville, TN: Kingswood Books, 1985), 159–66; also in R. E. Richey, K. E. Rowe and J. Miller Schmidt (eds), *Perspectives on American Methodism: Interpretive Essays* (Nashville, TN: Kingswood Books, 1993), 265–76.

[12] In the MEC, a quick look at the first lay delegates to the 1872 General Conference is instructive. The group included three U.S. Senators, two state governors, and four wealthy industrialists.

address inefficiencies and redundancies.[13] Their confidence in these methods was not without merit. Canadian Methodists, for instance, put together a successful merger in 1884 only a few short years after the British North America Act in 1867, and saw their numbers grow steadily over the next four decades, while other Methodists were seeing a leveling off or decline in growth rates.[14] This apparent success was encouraging to other Methodist denominations, even as they struggled to settle their differences. Most significantly for the character of Methodism, however, was that the shift of the congregational or annual conference benevolent institutions to centralized boards and agencies constituted a reordering of the basic understanding of Methodist ministry.[15] The grand vision for the Methodists was that new modern methods and focused, centralized organizing would mean less waste, less chance for financial mismanagement, the ability to engage in larger-scale projects, and—perhaps just as importantly—the new style and substance of the improved denominations would provide a greater and more homogenous sense of identity for Methodists.

The furious pace of Methodist expansion in the early nineteenth century, especially in North America, meant that Methodist identity was diffuse. As the revivals waned, and with them the central feature that brought new converts into the fold, Methodists needed something else to provide coherent narratives and excitement for the laity. While many Methodists looked back to a "golden age" of simple faith and powerful revivals, they concurrently felt pride and were energized by the idea of their denomination representing the best of the modern world, made sacred by faith, and continuing to "reform the nation" in a new way that kept with the times.[16] The new denominational structures were seen by those who supported them as a reflection of a larger spirit of optimism around technology, corporate processes, and increased education more generally. With a ready narrative of more primitive origins, the new age of denominationalism flowed perfectly with the progress narrative in place from the revivals. As the energy of revivals waned, the

---

[13] For broader treatments on this topic, see Ben Primer, *Protestants and American Business Methods* (Ann Arbor, MI: UMI Research Press, 1979).

[14] Hempton, *Methodism: Empire of the Spirit*, 183.

[15] W. McGuire King covers this aspect of the history using the MEC as a case study, in "Denominational Modernization and Religious Identity: The Case of the Methodist Episcopal Church," in Richey, Rowe and Miller Schmidt(eds), *Perspectives on American Methodism*, 343–55. John Kent presents a very similar picture of both motivations for and effects of bureaucratic consolidation in Great Britain. See *The Age of Disunity* (London: Epworth Press, 1966).

[16] W. McGuire King makes a similar point, arguing that, unlike the way many scholars describe the process of centralization and bureaucratization in this time period, this process was a point of pride for many Methodists at the time, and that it only could have happened with the support and excitement of the laity: "This process succeeded to the degree that it related organizational consolidation to the desiderata of modern democratic culture and yoked organizational ideals to the aspirations of an ascendant middle-class culture." King, "Denominational Modernization", 343–5.

energy of consolidation would pick it up and focus it in new and improved ways for continued growth.

For many Methodists, reunions or mergers with other Methodist denominations seemed the most obvious place to begin a full-scale consolidation of Methodist resources and prepare for a thorough modernization of its institutional practices. All over the globe, even in very young Methodist churches which were still objects of missionary attention, Methodist denominations began to work for reunion or mergers.[17] Many pulled themselves together, or at least began to work out better relationships that would address redundant work and foster greater cooperation. In this endeavor, Methodists were participating in the larger Protestant trend of ecumenical dialogue.[18] The conversation moved along a spectrum of openness to different levels of ecumenicity. A few Methodists dreamt of post-denominational global Christianity, while some were content to begin with one or two Methodist denominations with which they had once been joined, or which were at least geographically close. The first Ecumenical Methodist Conference met in London in 1881, and was repeated every decade until the interruption of the Second World War, which was the moment of the largest of the reunions, the creation of the Methodist Church in the United States. We should mark the difference, though, in ecumenical dialogue as an essentially theological conversation, and the processes of consolidation and reunion as the result of many different impulses and desires among Methodists, which can only be understood within the larger social and cultural contexts we outlined above. While the burgeoning ecumenical movement certainly provided energy and movement for Methodist reunions and mergers, they should not be confused as synonymous. We will return to this point in our discussion of the Methodist Church, which provides an illustration.

In Ireland reunion came fairly quickly after the Canadian merger, as the Primitive Wesleyan Connexion (which was within the Church of Ireland at the time) and the Wesleyan Methodists formed the Methodist Church of Ireland in 1878. The Methodist Church of Australasia was formed from several denominations of mixed missional origins, including British soldiers who started Methodist congregations, a phenomenon that occurred in southern Africa as well. The Methodist Church of Japan, or Kyodan, was formed in 1907 as a merger between Methodist congregations from several different Methodist missions in North America. In the U.S., German immigrant churches in the Evangelical Association—which had already consolidated their mission congregations in Germany in 1882—and the United Evangelical Church reunited in 1922 to form the Evangelical Church, a foreshadowing of later mergers with United Brethren in 1946, and their final merger (or a reuniting, if we recall Phillip Otterbein was at the Christmas Conference with Francis Asbury), as a part of the creation of the United Methodist Church in 1968. Over the next two

---

[17] Much of the detail and listing of these reunions and mergers can be found in Marquardt, "Methodism in the Nineteenth and Twentieth Centuries."

[18] For an overview see Geoffrey Wainwright, "Methodism and the Ecumenical Movement," in C. Yrigoyen, Jr. (ed.), *T&T Clark Companion to Methodism* (London and New York: T&T Clark, 2010), 329–49.

decades reunions came quickly. Bishops from the African Methodist Episcopal (AME), African Methodist Episcopal Zion (AMEZ), and Christian Methodist Episcopal (CME) churches in the United States engaged in serious talks about a merger up until 1918, when they reached an impasse.[19] In Korea, amid the turmoil of the Japanese occupation, congregations formed by separate MEC and Methodist Episcopal Church, South (MECS) missions merged to form the Korean Methodist Church in 1930, a church that stood, symbolically as well as literally, resistant to Japanese political and cultural oppression, and celebrated most of its missionaries as sharing in that resistance to a colonial power. The Methodist Church of Canada and the Methodist Episcopal Church of Canada took one extra ecumenical step by merging with each other and other Protestant bodies in Canada to form the United Church of Canada, a church that represented a strong sense of national spirit, modernist sensibilities, and high-level ecumenical commitments. In 1932, the Primitive Methodists, the Wesleyans, and the United Methodists reunited to form the Methodist Church in Great Britain, a reunion that was accompanied by high expectations for renewed growth and influence in England.

The final reunion of the period covered in this chapter—the reunion of three Methodist denominations in the U.S. in 1939 that formed the Methodist Church—created the largest and wealthiest Methodist church in the world with over 7 million members.[20] The merger was only possible, however, through the creation of institutional racial division and separation. The new church constructed a jurisdictional system defined by race, with white Methodists in separate annual conferences in regional jurisdictions, and black Methodists in their own conferences within one sprawling Central Jurisdiction. What is striking and illustrative for the larger global trends in consolidation and reunion is that the merger was made possible through the language of efficiency, expediency, and even unity. Ecumenical theology was an assumed value and resource for the desire for merger, but in the end institutional unity was of a far greater significance than unity of human difference. The desire for institutional unity and all the expected benefits, in other words, overcame other values held in tandem. This final reunion does not mark the end of Methodist consolidations and reunions—the trend would continue throughout the twentieth century, along with a greater focus on ecumenical dialogue and cooperation—but it does mark the end of a kind of denominational consolidation in both the major streams of Methodism that was reflective of that particular context of Western optimism. What the example of the Methodist Church unification provides is a window into just what it meant for the Methodist denominations to begin to think differently and creatively and, indeed, ecumenically. What were the possible unintended consequences of the consolidation of denominational identity, for instance? What do all the other Methodist reunions and mergers have in common

---

[19] R. W. Trueblood, "Union Negotiations between Black Methodists in America," *Methodist History*, 8: 4 (July 1970), 18–29.

[20] For analysis of the debates leading to the merger, see M. L. Davis, *The Methodist Unification: Christianity and the Politics of Race in the Jim Crow Era* (New York: New York University Press, 2008).

with this larger, more dramatic example? This is illustrated by the great ironies and disappointments in the details of this merger.

Despite the optimism and continued general support for modernization efforts in bureaucratic organization, professionalization of ministry, extension of church concerns to include hospitals, elder care, educational institutions, and centralization of finances, the eventual decline in growth and actual numbers for Methodists began in this era.[21] There were a few exceptions, such as the Canadian Methodists after their initial merger, and the AME and AMEZ churches for a few decades as they gained members from the ranks of freed slaves, but the general trend as the revivals waned throughout the North Atlantic world, and especially after the Second World War, was that Methodists would not see a similar phenomenon again. The debates about why this happened and what it meant and means now remain a deeply contested issue in the field, but one that has not had the advantage of scholarly attention that we have seen for the eighteenth century.

The numbers themselves are not contested too hotly, but the explanations for the numbers are.[22] Much about general assumptions by observers of this phenomenon can be gleaned by the choices in language. In much of the literature the growth in numbers is described as "success," and the slowing of growth and eventual drop in numbers are described as "decline."[23] While in important ways the "rise and decline of Methodism" narrative holds true, it also inhibits a wider variety of analysis because it offers scholars a polarized set of outcomes: growth is good; slow growth, no growth, or shrinking numbers is bad. If we eliminate this framing, there are far more possibilities and, frankly, far more interesting questions that can be asked. It will also help move scholars away from the easy association

---

[21] For Methodists and hospitals, see K. E. Rowe, "Temples of Healing: The Founding Era of Methodist Hospitals, 1880–1900," *Methodist History*, 46:1 (Oct. 2007), 47–57.

[22] Hempton's survey of the numbers in *Methodism: Empire of the Spirit* seems the best and most thorough survey of the data. Significant gaps remain in raw data, unfortunately, for African American Methodist denominations, as well as for many mission stations. But Hempton's clear-eyed analysis of the three prevailing explanations of the "growth and decline" narrative in *Empire of the Spirit* is helpful to scholars wishing to sort out the disagreements. Hempton, *Methodism: Empire of the Spirit*, Chapter Eight, "Consolidation and Decline", 178–201.

[23] The framework of "decline" in the literature is inherited not only from Methodists themselves (who, like other denominations, have tended to write their own histories), but from the multidisciplinary scholarly debates about secularization. Participant-observers tend to use the secularization thesis to prove that moving away from church tradition is unhealthy for their churches. Non-participating "secular" observers have used the secularization thesis to prove that the rise (read progress) of modernity has been the doom of religion. I will only note this literature here, because the "secularization thesis," which held sway for decades in the twentieth century, has been shown to be misleading, and the larger scholarly debate is now a bit dated. However, the echoes of the debate remain in the current framing of the questions, which have not changed significantly in the study of Methodism. A helpful overview of the debates can be found in S. Bruce (ed.), *Religion and Modernization: Sociologists and Historians Debate the Secularization Thesis* (Oxford: Clarendon Press, 1992).

between the rise of denominationalism and the decline in membership. If scholars ask different questions about change, what do we learn about who stayed in the denominations as member numbers decreased? Who left? Who stayed? What new kinds of members were gained? What connections might there be to the global expansion of Methodism and the simultaneous shrinking of members in the North Atlantic sending churches?

## Mission Expansion and the End of the Era of Growth

This last question leads us to more rethinking of global Methodist history. While there is a general dearth of scholarship on Methodism in this era in the sending churches of the North Atlantic, the same cannot be said for the study of missions. The study of missions more generally has been flourishing over the last few decades, and the study of Methodist missions history has benefited. Yet, there is much more to be done, and much more to be done differently as well. In particular, the field is in need of new general scholarly monographs of missions from all branches of world Methodism.[24] What could be done differently is for scholars to find ways to integrate the history of missions with the study of sending churches in the North Atlantic. For the most part, the history of missions has remained a separate field. Finding ways to pull the two together will produce not only a more accurate view of the time period, but it will yield different and exciting insights, as has occurred in other related fields for this time period. Using an approach often referred to as "transnational studies," historians in related fields are beginning to understand the benefits of fitting the history of one nation in global contexts, rather than studying, for instance, the history of Methodist missions from Britain isolated from the study of Methodism in Britain. As Ian Tyrrell has shown convincingly in his monograph *Reforming the World: The Creation of America's Moral Empire*, the work of missionaries

---

[24] The only recent surveys were published by the General Board of Global Ministries of the United Methodist Church, covering its predecessor denominations, but the series does not have a history of the largest and most influential of the churches, the MEC. See R. A. Daugherty, *The Missionary Spirit: The History of Mission of the Methodist Protestant Church, 1830–1939* (New York, NY: General Board of Global Ministries of the UMC, 2004); R. W. Sledge, *Five Dollars and Myself: The History of Mission of the Methodist Episcopal Church, South, 1845–1939* (New York, NY: General Board of Global Ministries of the UMC, 2005); L. Gesling, *Mirror and Beacon: The History of Mission of the Methodist Church, 1939–1968* (New York, NY: General Board of Global Ministries of the UMC, 2005); J. S. O'Malley, *On the Journey Home: The History of Mission of the Evangelical United Brethren Church 1946–1968* (New York, NY: General Board of Global Ministries of the UMC, 2003); R. J. Harman, *From Missions to Mission: The History of Mission of the United Methodist Church, 1968–2000* (New York, NY: General Board of Global Ministries of the UMC, 2005). The best overall history for the twentieth century is J. Tremayne Copplestone, continuing Wade Crawford Barclay's History of Methodist Missions series, vol. IV, *Twentieth Century Perspectives* (New York, NY: The Board of Global Ministries, the United Methodist Church, 1973).

and the ensuing development of indigenous responses afterward had significant impact on the sending societies. Work conceptualized in a similar way would yield a history of missions which is more accurately a narrative of reciprocity and exchange, than it is simply one of imposition and isolated response.[25] The study of Methodism in this time period could benefit from more of this kind of framing.

What has perhaps been the most difficult hurdle for the history of Methodist missions, however, is the complexity of articulating a satisfying description of the relationship between British and American colonialism and imperialism and the work of missionaries within those contexts. The contours of the debates are well known, as are the historiographical trends of the last few decades. Mission historians had largely retreated from conversations with historians who dismissed missionaries and their work as complicit or actively engaged in Western oppression. Mission historians continued to document in great detail the spread of Christianity across the globe, often without significant analysis of the relationship to the Western political and economic power that made their work possible. Often the tone was simply defensive about these relationships. Excellent work has emerged over the last twenty years, however, to remedy this problem, though we do not yet have a corresponding resurgence in the history of Methodist mission work specifically. Even among historians of empire, perspectives on the role of missionaries have changed, as we find in the addition of a fifth volume of the Oxford History of the British Empire Companion Series, *Missions and Empire*.[26] The series "Studies in the History of Christian Missions," edited by Robert E. Frykenberg and Brian Stanley, stands out as a signal contribution to the field.[27] Dana L. Robert's *Christian*

---

[25] I. Tyrrell, *Reforming the World: The Creation of America's Moral Empire* (Princeton, NJ: Princeton University Press, 2010). A significant collection of essays on North American missions that takes a similar approach is D. Bays and G. Wacker (eds), *The Foreign Missionary Enterprise at Home: Explorations in North American Cultural History* (Tuscaloosa, AL and London: University of Alabama Press, 2003). R. E. Richey's essay in this collection stands out for historians of Methodism: "Organizing for Missions: A Methodist Case Study," 75–94. For a recent case study that focuses on the effects of mission work back "home," see M. L. Davis, "Early Twentieth-Century Methodist Missions Photography: The Problems of 'Home,'" *Methodist Review*, 2 (2010), 33–67.

[26] N. Etherington (ed.), *Missions and Empire*, vol. vi of the Oxford History of the British Empire Companion Series (Oxford and New York: Oxford University Press, 2005). This final volume was necessary because the previous five volumes almost completely ignored the role of missions and missionaries. Etherington's Introduction to the volume is useful in this historiographical discussion, especially "Placing Missions and Empire in a Global Context," 13–18.

[27] Several books in the series might be particularly helpful to Methodist historians: B. Stanley, *The World Missionary Conference, 1910* (Grand Rapids, MI: Eerdmans, 2009); D. L. Robert, *Converting Colonialism: Visions and Realities in Mission History 1706–1914* (Grand Rapids, MI: Eerdmans, 2008); B. Stanley and A. Low (eds), *Missions, Nationalism, and the End of Empire* (Grand Rapids, MI: Eerdmans, 2003).

*Mission: How Christianity Became a World Religion* provides an excellent framework for thinking globally about Methodist mission history.[28]

While this recent work has transformed the field of mission studies in exciting ways, there is more to be done. Occasionally, echoes of the older binary structures can still be heard. In the Introduction to the *Converting Colonialism* collection, Robert suggests that rather than assuming all missionaries in all times and places "supported colonialism, it is more accurate to speak in ambiguous terms of missionary efforts to 'convert' it." This is a helpful formulation, but she goes on to say that "[f]orced to operate within a political framework of European expansionism that lay outside their power to control, missionaries and early converts variously attempted to co-opt aspects of colonialism deemed compatible with missionary goals, and to change what seemed prejudicial to gospel values." This is a sensible approach, except that it still places missionaries and converts outside of "colonialism," likely unsatisfactory for many scholars. To say that missionaries were "forced" is to overstate their separation from, and understate their participation in and dependence on, the structures of various colonial enterprises. Robert rightly recommends speaking in "ambiguous" terms about the efforts of missionaries and converts, but yet I think the framing of "outside colonialism" is not ambiguous enough.[29]

Scholars of global Methodism in this time period might look to Jeffrey Cox and his helpful historiographical essay "Master Narratives of Imperial Missions."[30] Cox offers an excellent overview of the competing "master narratives" of missions, as they are used by contemporary historians and were used by missionaries and converts themselves. These various narratives compete with each other and produce an irresolvable interpretive conflict. What Cox suggests historians might do, rather than advocate for one master narrative over another, is to focus on those "contact zones" where the personal experience of the subject—missionary or convert—clashes with the multiple master narratives that are supposed to make sense of that experience. These "contact zones" are "social spaces" in which different cultures meet, often in inequitable relations of power, and produce "mixed messages."[31] Western missionaries, Cox argues, while certainly caught in the webs of imperialism, are also quite different in intention from other agents of colonial enterprises, and thus must be understood differently. So understanding and writing about the missions in this era is not to pick a master narrative, but rather to embrace the full complexity of the "mixed messages" created by the contests between personal experience and the larger narratives that vied for influence in the missionary/convert/potential convert encounters. This approach might help alleviate the tensions that have caused scholars of Methodist history

---

[28] D. L. Robert, *Christian Mission: How Christianity Became a World Religion* (Malden, MA: Wiley-Blackwell, 2009).

[29] Ibid., passim.

[30] J. Cox, "Master Narratives of Imperial Missions," Introduction to J. S. Scott and G. Griffiths (eds), *Mixed Messages: Materiality, Textuality, Missions* (New York, NY: Palgrave Macmillan, 2005), 3–18.

[31] Ibid., 14.

to avoid the topic of missions altogether (or simply take a defensive stance), by offering a constructive framing in which the assumption is one of complexity and ambiguity, insisting, even, that mission history cannot be understood as imperial or not, or good or bad, victorious or unsuccessful, but that it can be assumed to be all of these held in tension.

## Conclusions

While there are numerous local studies of Methodist history in this time period, particularly an abundance of focused mission histories and histories of women, there remains a tremendous amount of exciting study to be done. More work needs to be done to integrate insights from Methodist women's history, particularly studies that ask questions about gender and Methodism. We still do not have adequate research into the converts of missionary endeavors. Nor do we yet adequately understand the ways that the mission enterprise changed the sending churches, or the ways that mission work was a deep cross-cultural exchange in which the cultures of the societies to which missionaries were sent effected deep change "back home." The sending churches of the North Atlantic and the former missions churches (now also sending churches) all need continued attention. More importantly, though, is the need for integrated research and writing that works from the recognition that mission history should not be isolated from the rest of Methodist history. To write the history of Methodism as a constantly expanding and evolving movement, abandoning the notion of stasis and even "home," is to more accurately reflect its nature and thus open up our understanding to the constant human cultural interplay that is the reality of mission work. I might suggest that the word "mission" itself is misleading. Are there other ways to name the effort that Methodists have made to spread their faith that more accurately describe the exchanges that take place whenever they have done so? And when have Methodists not engaged in some effort to enlarge their work?[32] Would it not serve our understanding better to note the character of that expansion in different eras, and ask what caused the changes in rationale, in effort, in level of resources expended, in the way that it was named and described? What has it meant, for instance, for Methodists to begin to talk of "home missions"? What does it help us understand about Methodism when we understand why those seen to be in need were no longer considered neighbors? If we begin to see how missionaries and converts themselves were fractured by contradictory experiences and imposed grand narratives that both condemned and blessed their work, how does this change our contemporary disposition toward the churches in the colonial

---

[32] Indeed, Wade Crawford Barclay, like Abel Stevens before him, argued that Methodism has always been at its core a missionary movement, and cannot be understood without that insight. See W. Crawford Barclay, *The History of Methodist Missions*, vol. 1 (New York, NY: Board of Missions and Church Extension of the Methodist Church, 1949).

era? What happens to our historical understanding if we begin to recognize that both missionaries and converts were just as aware of the difficulties of colonial relationships as we are now? That we are not in possession of special insights about the complex power dynamics of that era that were unavailable to the historical actors themselves?[33]

Finally, the history of Methodism in this era needs more synthetic survey work. David Hempton's *Methodism: Empire of the Spirit* stands alone in this category, and, because of this, remains more of an invitation to additional work than any kind of final word. Hempton's book provides an abundance of possible analytical categories around which new work can be built. His emphasis on tension and dialectic presents historians of Methodism a rich set of theses which can be tested and pressed from multiple angles. The book sets a tone of conversation and provides a beautifully articulated point of reference for further work, particularly for the time period covered in this chapter. In its very title, we are presented with a suggestion on which Hempton does not elaborate. In what way has Methodism been an "empire"? What connotations of empire does Hempton have in mind? Other than very large numbers and global scope, what other characteristics of empire has Methodism exhibited? What kind of spiritual power constitutes an empire? What does this mean for current Methodist bodies in former colonies? Is he suggesting that because Methodism was born in an empire, there remains a permanent imperial genetic remnant?

---

[33] We would do well to remember the critique of Western power and racism from Methodist missionary to India, E. S. Jones, in his transformative book *The Christ of the Indian Road* (New York, NY and Cincinnati, OH: Abingdon Press, 1925).

# Methodism: Shifting Balances, 1939–2010

*Brian Beck*

The historian who attempts a survey of the seven decades that comprise our period knows that any assessment must be provisional. Time needs to elapse before events can be properly evaluated or patterns observed. What is more, the second half of the twentieth century must be seen as the period in which world Methodism came of age. The story can no longer be adequately told, as the story of earlier periods largely has been told, from the perspective of the major missionary churches of Europe and North America. The demise of empire and the maturing of newly independent nations have been reflected in church relations. The full story of Methodism world-wide from 1939 to 2010 will depend on local histories, many of which have yet to be written, but for which much of the archival evidence, ironically, lies in the vaults of missionary agencies in Europe and North America. All that can be attempted in this chapter therefore is a broad overview through the eyes of a British observer of some of the ways in which Methodism has changed.[1]

To turn back to 1939 is to be reminded how much the world itself has undergone change. The period has witnessed a world war, a cold war that lasted an entire generation, a series of localised international conflicts, many civil wars, and most recently the rise of international terrorism. The political map has changed, with the end of the Third Reich and, more recently, the Soviet Union, and the long and often painful process of decolonisation. The United Nations, founded in 1945 with fifty-

---

[1] Invaluable resources for the period are: Russell E. Richey, Kenneth E. Rowe and Jean Miller Schmidt, *The Methodist Experience in America* (Nashville, TN: Abingdon, vol. 1 *A History* 2010, vol. 2 *A Sourcebook* 2000), and, on a smaller scale, John Munsey Turner, *Modern Methodism in England 1932–1998* (Peterborough: Epworth, 1998). Chapters by R. E. Davies in his *Methodism* (London: Epworth, 2nd rev. ed. 1985) and in Rupert Davies, A. Raymond George and Gordon Rupp (eds), *A History of the Methodist Church in Great Britain*, vol. 3 (London: Epworth, 1983) take the story to the date of publication. See also Kenneth Cracknell and Susan J. White, *An Introduction to World Methodism* (Cambridge: Cambridge University Press, 2005), Rex D. Matthews, *Timetables of History for Students of Methodism* (Nashville, TN: Abingdon, 2007), and Charles Yrigoyen Jr. (ed), *T&T Clark Companion to Methodism* (London and New York, NY: T&T Clark, 2010).

one members now has one hundred and ninety-two. There have been immense technological advances, especially in communications, making a huge quantity of information instantly available to anyone anywhere with the required equipment, and enabling news to be shared widely across the globe. The growth of powerful multinational corporations has been one of the results. It has been an age of large-scale migration, as the result of the partition of India in 1947 and the creation of the State of Israel in 1948, but also with the opening of borders as a result of the European Union and with the movement of many thousands fleeing conflict or persecution in many places or seeking a more prosperous way of life, thereby transforming the character of previously monochrome communities and creating new tensions. The balance of economic power is shifting from west to east, the gap between rich and poor in the world grows wider and is more apparent because visible by television, the AIDS pandemic has devastated an entire generation in Africa and parts of Asia, and there is now serious concern about whether the planet can be conserved as a viable environment for future generations. Perhaps most significant of all for the churches has been widespread reaction against traditional attitudes and values, resulting, especially in the global north, in increasing indifference to religion and widespread tolerance of alternative lifestyles, particularly in sexual relations. It is against such a background that the churches have to live out their lives and bear their witness, while also experiencing the effects of such changes within their own life.

## Methodist Union

In April 1939 in Kansas City USA the Methodist Episcopal Church, the Methodist Episcopal Church South and the Methodist Protestant Church united to become the Methodist Church. Seven years earlier in Britain the Wesleyan Methodist, Primitive Methodist and United Methodist Churches had united to form the Methodist Church. Our period begins therefore with Methodists both in the United States and in Britain getting used to new identities. Elsewhere, except where more than one of the uniting churches had been working in the same country, as in Sierra Leone and China, the impact was limited and little felt. Both unions brought together churches that in an earlier period had separated on matters of principle. In the United States the issues were episcopacy, the powers of the General Conference, participation of the laity in church government and, supremely, racial segregation. In Britain, too, the powers of the conference and the role of the laity had been factors in separation. Unions became possible over time as positions became less rigid. In Britain lay participation had been common to the uniting churches since 1878. In the United States the Methodist Protestants were largely ready by 1939 to accept episcopacy, and lay participation in conferences had been introduced in all three traditions. Even so the 1939 union succeeded in part because some members of the uniting churches refused to enter it and continued as separate denominations: the Southern Methodist Church, the Methodist Protestant Church and the Bible Protestant Church, holding to a strongly conservative theological position.

Both unions left a legacy of unfinished business. In the United States the most obvious evidence was the existence of the Central Jurisdiction. At union the church was divided into six jurisdictional conferences in the States and a number of central conferences in other parts of the world as an intermediate governmental stage between the local annual conference and the four-yearly General Conference. In response to southern resistance to racial integration, all the African-American annual conferences, regardless of geographical location, were gathered into a separate jurisdiction. While this provided for a stronger African-American voice in the General Conference and connexional boards, it hardened the boundaries between black and white Methodists throughout the country. Bitterly opposed from the beginning, it was the price of union between north and south, but against the background of the Civil Rights protests in America could not be sustained and was dropped when the Methodist Church united with the Evangelical United Brethren in 1968.

In Britain the unfinished business of union was rather different. While it was quickly achieved in connexional and district structures it was assumed that local churches would rapidly follow suit. This proved not to be the case. The three uniting churches continued to exist side by side in hundreds of towns and villages across the country, and local attitudes and loyalties proved resistant to change. It was only in the 1970s that the real fruits of agreements reached forty years earlier began to be seen. There remains a less obvious legacy. The Primitive and United Methodist traditions preserved a strong emphasis on lay ministry and lay participation in government, and while valuing the ordained ministry as a preaching and pastoral office did not accord it the same prerogatives in church government as had been the case in Wesleyan Methodism and, with some modification, has continued to be the case in the united church. Issues of lay participation in leadership and lay presidency at Holy Communion continue to be raised from time to time by people who may not be able to name the tradition they represent but have nevertheless inherited its emphases.

Union in the United States in 1939 was followed by others. In 1946 the Evangelical Church and the United Brethren, both with earlier Methodist connections, united to become the Evangelical United Brethren Church, which in 1968 joined with the Methodist Church to form the current United Methodist Church (hereafter UMC). Again the impact of these changes was greater within the United States than outside (in Germany the Methodist Church had already united with the United Brethren in 1908). But this union also left unfinished business in the need for a common doctrinal statement.[2]

None of these unions embraced the other Methodist denominations in the United States, in particular the three major African-American churches, the African Methodist Episcopal Church (AME), the African Methodist Episcopal Church Zion (AMEZ) and the Christian Methodist Episcopal Church (CME).[3] In

---

[2] For the period following the union see Charles Yrigoyen Jr., John G. McEllhenney and Kenneth E. Rowe, *United Methodism at Forty* (Nashville, TN: Abingdon, 2008).

[3] Until 1954 the Colored Methodist Episcopal Church.

1985 a Commission on Pan-Methodist Co-operation was created with a view to producing a Plan of Union including these and two smaller churches, the African Union Methodist Protestant and the Union American Methodist Episcopal Church. There was a service of reconciliation in 2000 and some cross-representation at board level, and conversations continue. In Britain similarly the Independent Methodist Connexion and the Wesleyan Reform Union did not participate in the union of 1932.[4]

## Inclusiveness

As we have just seen a major issue for the United Methodist Church was the inclusion of African-Americans on a full participatory basis, but a comparison of photographs of annual conferences of 1939 with those of 2010 anywhere in the world is likely to illustrate how the composition of such gatherings has changed in other respects, particularly in the proportion of women present and in the ages of those taking part. Our period has witnessed growing sensitivity to the importance of inclusiveness in the life of the church and particularly in its leadership. In this the churches are reflecting changing attitudes in society generally, although what is true of Europe and North America would not necessarily be true where other cultures prevail. It is not confined to issues of gender and ethnic balance in conferences and committees or in leadership positions. Provision in church buildings for those with disabilities, not considered in 1939, would in many countries be considered normal for new buildings in 2010 and many older buildings have been adapted.

The ordination of women to the ministry of word and sacrament was an unresolved issue in both British and American traditions. In Britain it had been agreed as early as 1933 that there was no objection in principle to the ordination of women, but no ordinations took place for forty years. In addition to general cultural prejudice much of the hesitation focussed on availability for stationing. It was widely assumed that marriage and consequent domestic duties would be a bar to continuing. An additional cause of delay from the 1950s onwards was the proposed unity scheme with the Church of England discussed below, as it was assumed that it could not proceed if women were ordained by the Methodist Church. By 1968, however, it was accepted that it would not initially be an obstacle and the first women candidates for ordination were accepted in 1973, by which time the unity scheme had already been rejected, and the first ordinations took place in 1974.

In the American tradition the picture is complicated by the distinction between ordination and full membership of a conference. The earlier practice of ordaining

---

[4] It needs to be remembered that 'Methodism' embraces a large family. Beside churches in the Holiness and Pentecostal traditions that trace their origins to Methodism without retaining the name, the *World Methodist Handbook 2007–2011* lists thirteen Methodist bodies in the USA alone in addition to those mentioned here, some with extensive overseas work.

women in the Methodist Protestant Church and the Evangelical United Brethren ceased at the unions of 1939 and 1946. It was not until 1956 that the Methodist Church granted ordination with full conference membership to women, while the Evangelical United Brethren waited until the union of 1968. Korean Methodism, by contrast, had been ordaining women since 1930. Progress in other parts of the world has been much slower, influenced by cultural differences.

There was yet longer to wait before ordained women were appointed to senior positions. In Britain the first woman District Chair was appointed in 1987 and the first President of the Conference in 1992 (Kathleen Richardson in both cases). In the United Methodist Church the first woman bishop (Marjorie Matthews) was consecrated in 1980. It remains universally true, however, that the leadership of Methodist churches across the world is predominantly male. At the time of writing there are six women out of thirty-three District Chairs in Britain and fifteen out of sixty-nine active United Methodist bishops worldwide, thirteen of whom are serving in the United States.[5]

For women in many parts of the world the main opportunity for the exercise of their gifts continues to be the women's organisation. Any visitor to Southern Africa for example will be struck by the sight of the women in the congregation in their uniforms of red, black and white. In America union in 1939 led to the combination of women's organisations for home and overseas mission work and in 1968 to the formation of United Methodist Women. In Britain the emphasis was initially entirely on overseas mission through Women's Work, founded in 1858. In 1942 Women's Fellowship was founded to develop women's leadership in the home church and in 1987 the two combined to form Network, to be joined in 2011 by the British Section of the World Federation of Methodist and Uniting Church Women to form Methodist Women in Britain. The Federation was first organised in 1939 and became an affiliated organisation of the World Methodist Council in 1956. It is registered at the United Nations as a Non-Governmental Organisation.

Inclusiveness, however, has been found to have its downside, as the continuing strength of women's organisations illustrates. Institutions are slow to change. Both in the United States and in Britain various ethnic groups – Black, Asian, Hispanic, Native American – have found it desirable to organise, both to affirm a common identity and to make their distinctive voices heard. In New Zealand Maori Methodism has been largely autonomous since 1973 in a covenant relationship with the rest of the church.

---

[5] Figures supplied by the UMC Council of Bishops. AME, AMEZ and the CME also have a small number of women bishops.

## World Mission

Methodist churches tend to see themselves in the light of John Wesley's often misquoted dictum 'The world is my parish'.[6] Not only the British Methodist Church and the UMC and their respective predecessors but other Methodist churches have engaged in mission beyond their national borders. From the beginning the Irish Conference has collaborated with the British in the Methodist Missionary Society. The AME has extensive work in Africa, the Caribbean and India, the AMEZ in Africa and the Caribbean, and the CME on a lesser scale in Ghana, Liberia, Nigeria and Haiti. The Free Methodists and the Wesleyans are represented, in some parts strongly, in Africa, Asia, South America, the Caribbean, New Zealand and elsewhere. The Free Methodists also have work in Egypt, and the Wesleyans in parts of mainland Europe. The Korean Methodist Church is present in some forty-three countries, in some places serving expatriate churches, in others, as in Tanzania, opening work among indigenous populations. Some of this extension work inevitably suffered during World War II and under Communist rule. Foreign workers were expelled from China in 1951 and all communications ceased. Contacts have been resumed in recent years since the ban on public worship was lifted in 1979 but on a different footing. Since the end of the Soviet Union Methodist work in the Baltic States, Russia and parts of the Commonwealth of Independent States has revived and been extended.[7]

Nowhere is the changing scene in world Methodism more evident than in a comparison of membership figures. In 1956 over 81 per cent of the recorded membership of world Methodism was in Europe and North America; by 2006 it had fallen to 35 per cent. The proportion in Africa and Asia had risen from just under 15 per cent to over 57 per cent. There were almost as many Methodists in Africa as in North America. In 1940 Methodist membership represented 6.5 per cent of the population of the United States; by 1990 it had fallen to 3.6 per cent. In Britain over the same period it fell from 1.67 per cent to 0.74 per cent.

These broad figures deserve examination in more detail. Reliable membership figures, however, are hard to come by. Churches differ in the importance they attach to accurate recording and in the precise meaning of membership. Different sources offer conflicting results. Where churches have entered into unions, comparisons over time become impossible. Some broad observations can however be made.[8]

---

[6] The correct version is 'I look upon all the world as my parish'. See the *Journal* entry for 11 June 1739.

[7] See Yrigoyen, *Companion to Methodism*, 188 ff.; ST Kimbrough (ed.), *Methodism in Russia and the Baltic States* (Nashville, TN: Abingdon, 1995).

[8] The figures quoted are based on data in the *World Methodist Handbooks* for 1957 and 2007, but they do not closely tally with other sources. Comparisons are also difficult because of the changing status and groupings of churches over the period, particularly in the Caribbean, and because some churches have entered into wider unions. I was not able to consult the on-line *World Christian Database* which is available only to institutional subscribers, but suspect the same limitations would apply. Some statistics from the 1950s are now beyond retrieval.

The major growth areas over the period were clearly Africa, parts of Asia, the Caribbean and the Pacific. But the pattern is not uniform. While Cote d'Ivoire, Nigeria and Sierra Leone are recorded as having grown each by some 2,000 per cent and Kenya by nearly 13,000 per cent, The Gambia has been virtually static. While Korea has grown by more than 2,000 per cent, Sri Lanka's growth is only 113 per cent. While many Caribbean regions have grown by 1,000 per cent or more, Puerto Rico has recorded growth of only 8 per cent. In South America the picture is more mixed, with Peru gaining by over 400 per cent while Uruguay is recorded as showing a slight decline. The contrasting picture is to be seen in Western Europe, North America and Australasia. Aside from the recent developments in the Baltic States and Russia no European church has shown growth; losses range from 5 per cent to 79 per cent. In the USA growth overall among churches in the Methodist tradition was down to 2 per cent. New Zealand showed a decrease of 49 per cent.

What these comparisons illustrate, broad-brush as they are, is the weakening hold, often commented on, of traditional expressions of Christianity on western society. The phenomenon is not confined to Methodism and many reasons can be offered for it. Secularism is often invoked, though less easily defined, and may be no more than an alternative term for the decline of religion.[9] Relative prosperity, creating a sense of relative security, and the spread of scientific knowledge, putting in question any invocation of the supernatural, may be factors. If true, that bodes ill for the future in areas where Methodism at present flourishes but where scientific education and relative prosperity may become more widespread. On the other hand such explanations do not wholly account for the difference in rates of decline between Europe and North America. What is clear is that environment plays a significant part. A strong Islamic presence, as in The Gambia, or the dominance of Roman Catholicism, as in Portugal, Italy or parts of South America, or a vacuum created by the demise of Communism may in particular cases be factors, but each area requires separate analysis.

Relationships also have changed. In 1939 the British Conference had oversight of 34 overseas districts; by 2010 there were none. As former colonies became independent Methodist districts were granted autonomy or entered into union churches, as in India and Zambia. Even churches formerly considered too small to stand on their own, as in the case of Portugal and The Gambia, have now become autonomous. But autonomy has not led to a complete severing of relationships. There continues to be cross-representation between conferences and regular consultations on matters of common concern, with continued financial assistance and the sharing of personnel.

In this policy the British Conference has followed a pattern long set, beginning with the United States in 1784, and followed later in the 'old colonies' such as Australia and South Africa. The desire has been to protect former missionary districts from accusations of being continuing outposts of the colonial power and to give greater freedom for indigenous expressions of church life. The Methodist Church

---

[9] See the discussion in David Hempton, *Methodism: Empire of the Spirit* (New Haven, CT and London: Yale University Press, 2005), 189 ff.

in Australasia has followed a similar policy in relation to former mission fields in the Pacific. Autonomy has not been a mere formality. In various ways the new churches have shown themselves ready to develop new relationships and patterns of working. Côte d'Ivoire, formerly a British District which became autonomous in 1985, became part of the West Africa Central Conference of the United Methodist Church in 2003. More widely, some have abandoned the British pattern of a president as the church's chief officer in favour of a bishop. In some cases this has been prompted by political pressure to avoid appearing to rival the head of state. Another factor has been the desire to reflect more closely traditional patterns of leadership in the surrounding culture. In Nigeria this led in 1976 to the creation of the office of patriarch with other officers and symbols of office, influenced not only by local custom but by the traditions of the church in Ethiopia, widely seen in Africa as a model of indigenisation.[10] The changes ran into difficulty, however, as not all the tribal traditions included the idea of chieftaincy, and a division in the church occurred which was not healed until 1992 as a result of modifications made to the constitution in 1989 when the patriarchate was replaced by the office of prelate.

In the United States the UMC has followed a different pattern. In 1968 some twenty-eight churches in Latin America became autonomous, but elsewhere many have continued as central conferences connected to the quadrennial General Conference meeting in the United States, while exercising a measure of autonomy in having power to adapt the *Discipline* to local circumstances. The arrangement gives expression to the concept of connexion on a global scale but has also proved to have disadvantages. The American representation in the General Conference massively outweighs that of the rest of the world, and its agenda tends to be dominated by United States concerns. In the last decade there have been attempts to formulate a different pattern, creating a regional conference for the United States in parallel with the central conferences elsewhere, all alike answerable to the General Conference, but so far without approval.

Britain and America have thus pursued different expressions of the ideal of being churches 'in connexion'. From time to time the idea of one global Methodist connexion has been mooted but it has been generally resisted, both because of differences in ethos and because the numerical weight of the churches in the United States would create an unmanageable imbalance. A formal overture from the American side did however lead in 1968 to a concordat agreement between the General Conference and the British Conference with the exchange of voting representatives.[11]

Evidence of the new order in both British and American traditions has been the growth in indigenous leadership. In 1939, for example, the British Conference was supporting 319 ordained and 330 lay missionaries. With adjustments to take account of different criteria a comparable figure in 2010 would be ten and thirty-

---

[10] For the ideas behind the development see Bolaji Idowu, *Towards an Indigenous Church* (London and Ibadan: Oxford University Press, 1965).

[11] Mexico, Brazil, Puerto Rico and the Methodist Church in the Caribbean and the Americas are also concordat churches.

two, hardly any in senior positions.[12] Life-long missionary service has become the exception, with single- or two-term commitments the norm. The sharing of personnel has become a two-way process, with ministers and lay people from overseas churches serving in British circuits or in other autonomous conferences than their own. Expressive of such changes has been the shift in terminology from 'missionary' to 'mission partner'. Some such partnerships are ecumenical. A similar picture could be drawn of the UMC, although there are still some five hundred personnel serving outside the United States.[13]

These developments represent a significant shift from the nineteenth-century understanding of world mission as the planting of overseas churches towards the ideal of working with overseas churches in their own local missionary outreach. They also mark a broadening of the traditional missionary agenda of evangelism, education and medicine to include other aspects of community development, especially in support of the economically and socially disadvantaged, women, ethnic minorities and the poor generally. Parallel to it has been the growth, born out of efforts to repair the devastation of World War II, of both denominational and ecumenical agencies (such as Christian Aid). The Methodist (now United Methodist) Committee on Relief was founded in 1940 and the British Methodist Relief and Development Fund was formed in 1985 out of two earlier post-war funds: Methodist Relief and World Development.

These developments have not been universally welcome. The Mission Society for United Methodists was founded in 1984 specifically to continue the pattern of sending missionaries overseas to reach the unevangelised in the conviction that this aspect of the church's mission was being neglected. The disagreement was part of a wider debate about the proper nature of Christian mission in a post-colonial era, prompted in part by awareness of the extent to which earlier efforts to communicate the gospel had in the process transplanted many features of Western culture. As conflict to end colonial rule intensified, especially in Africa, there were calls for the churches to identify with liberation movements and give them humanitarian aid. The World Council of Churches' Programme to Combat Racism and its Special Fund were launched, and at a conference on 'Salvation Today' in Bangkok in 1973 there was a call for a moratorium on the sending of missionaries and financial aid so that hitherto dependent churches might establish their own identity. This was countered at the International Congress on World Evangelisation in Lausanne in 1974 by a reaffirmation of the need for world evangelism. The debate has continued but both sides have modified their positions as circumstances have changed, acknowledging the need for engagement in social and political issues and the relief of need, and for the communication of the Christian message and securing converts.[14]

---

[12] Exact comparisons are difficult; in 1939 spouses were not separately counted, even if actively engaged in mission work.
[13] See Yrigoyen, *United Methodism at Forty*, 111; Dana L. Robert, *Joy to the World! Mission in the Age of Global Christianity* (New York, NY: General Board of Global Ministries, 2010).
[14] See Yrigoyen, *Companion to Methodism*, 232 ff.

## The World Methodist Council

The nearest Methodist churches come to a global connexion is in their membership of the World Methodist Council. Founded in 1881 as the Oecumenical Methodist Conference meeting every ten years, it was reorganised in 1951 as a quinquennial meeting of a council, with elected representatives from all the member churches, together with a conference open without limit to all who are able to secure accreditation from their home church. The Council is deliberative only, and has no authority over the member churches. The meetings of the conference provide opportunities for education and inspiration and for world-wide fellowship.

The oldest of the world confessional bodies, the World Methodist Council can be said to have matured over the years. A significant development was noted in the *Proceedings* of the 1976 Council as being the first occasion at which the Council felt able to debate contentious issues and pass resolutions critical of governmental policies. Some efforts at mediation in divided churches have been made and a delegation met the white-led government of South Africa following the 1986 Council. The Council has adopted a statement of Wesleyan Essentials of Christian Faith (1996) and a Social Affirmation (1986). But there is a chronic shortage of funds which hampers full development of the Council's potential and there is an unresolved tension between conflicting concepts of representation, on the one hand to provide for every member church, however small, to have voice and vote in the Council's deliberations, and on the other to give due weight to the numerical strength and financial contribution made by a few larger churches. At the time of writing there are proposals to revise the constitution to create a smaller Council meeting more frequently. They are expected to be debated at the Council in 2011.

The Council sponsors a number of significant activities. In addition to the ecumenical dialogues and the Oxford Institute referred to below there have been initiatives in evangelism across the world with an Institute in Atlanta, Georgia, for training evangelistic workers, with an emphasis now on indigenous expressions of evangelism. The Council has regularly made a Peace Award since 1976 to various public and some lesser-known figures, and administers a scheme for short-term exchanges of preachers. The World Federation of Methodist and Uniting Church Women, the World Fellowship of Methodist and Uniting Church Men, and the World Methodist Historical Society are affiliated organisations.Note should also be taken of a number of regional bodies, such as CIEMAL (Council of Evangelical Methodist Churches of Latin America) for Latin America and the Caribbean, founded in 1969, and the European Methodist Council founded in its present form in 1993, although these are not formally related to the World Council.

## Wider Ecumenical Relations

It is natural to move on to a discussion of wider ecumenical relations in our period. In doing so we need to be aware that 'ecumenical' in US usage still has for many the meaning it held in 1881: 'ecumenical Methodist'. Here we are using it in the wider sense of relations between churches of differing traditions.

Ecumenical co-operation through councils of churches has developed extensively over our period. The World Council of Churches held its first Assembly in Amsterdam in 1948, bringing together the earlier movements of Life and Work, and Faith and Order and, in 1961, the International Missionary Council. Methodist churches have been members from the beginning and Methodist individuals have played a leading part, including the veteran John R. Mott, who chaired one of the sessions at Amsterdam, and three General Secretaries: Philip Potter, Emilio Castro and Samuel Kobia. The same can be said of regional councils. The British Council of Churches (now replaced by Churches Together in Britain and Ireland and parallel bodies for each of the nations, England, Scotland, Wales and Ireland) was founded in 1942, and the National Council of Churches of Christ in the USA in 1950, taking up the work of earlier bodies. The East Asia Christian Conference (since 1973 the Christian Conference of Asia) was formed in 1957 and the All-Africa Conference of Churches in 1963. There have been similar developments elsewhere.

Our period has also seen a number of church unions in which Methodist churches have been involved: the Church of South India (1947), the Church of North India, in which Methodists in the British and Australian, but not the American, connexions joined (1970), the United Church of Zambia (1965), and the Uniting Church in Australia, including Methodist, Presbyterian and Congregationalist churches (1977). In 1979 the Methodist Church in Italy entered a federation with the Waldensian Church. The first two of these unions included Anglican churches and retained the historic episcopate. Other unions were proposed (Ghana, Nigeria, Sri Lanka, East Africa) but did not come to fruition.

In England, following an appeal by the Archbishop of Canterbury, Geoffrey Fisher, in 1946 to the Free Churches to 'take episcopacy into their system', conversations were begun between the Methodist Church and the Church of England. This led in 1956 to proposals for a union in two stages, which in 1972 failed to secure the level of support required for adoption by the Church of England. This was followed by an attempt to initiate a covenant between the Methodist Church, the Church of England, the Moravian Church, the Churches of Christ and the United Reformed Church which in 1982 similarly failed to secure the necessary Anglican support. Key factors have been the reconciliation of episcopal and non-episcopal ministries and the ordination of women. More recently, in 2003 Anglicans and Methodists in England signed a covenant of mutual recognition committing both churches to work together where possible and to pursue the goal of visible unity. Conversations are also proceeding with the United Reformed Church. In Wales a covenant involving the (Anglican) Church in Wales and the Presbyterian, Methodist, United Reformed and Covenanted Baptist Churches was signed in 1975 and in Scotland the most recent development has been a Statement of Partnership signed in 2010 involving the Episcopal, Methodist and United Reformed Churches, but not the (Presbyterian) Church of Scotland. All these involve the British Conference but different Anglican jurisdictions. A distinctive feature of the British scene has also been the growth of local sharing agreements under which buildings, worship and sometimes pastoral oversight are shared between different denominations, although nationally the churches remain separate. Methodism has shared in these with a variety of partners.

In the United States the Consultation on Church Union (since 2002 Churches Uniting in Christ), ultimately involving ten member churches (including the UMC, AME, AMEZ and CME), was initiated in 1962 and produced a plan for union in 1969 which failed to secure approval; it has, however, continued to facilitate dialogue and co-operation between the churches. Meanwhile the United Methodist Church and the Evangelical Lutheran Church in America entered into full communion with each other in 2010 and discussions are proceeding between the United Methodist and the Episcopal churches.

There has also been a series of significant international bilateral dialogues under the auspices of the World Methodist Council designed to address the theological issues underlying the separation of churches. The series with the Roman Catholic Church produced its first report in 1971 and continues.[15] There have also been dialogues with the World Lutheran Federation (reporting in 1984), the World Alliance of Reformed Churches (1987) and the Anglican Communion (1996). Dialogue with the Salvation Army began in 2003 and initial contacts have been made with the Ecumenical Patriarch of the Orthodox Church. These have been mirrored by local dialogues in many countries. The Lutheran dialogue led to intercommunion in Germany, Austria, Sweden and Norway in the 1990s. Another development has been the adoption by the Leuenberg Churches (Lutheran and Reformed in Europe) and by the European Methodist Council, its member churches and the Methodist Church in Argentina of a Joint Declaration of Church Fellowship drawn up in 1993, setting out points of agreement and difference and providing for fellowship of word and sacrament.

This bare summary does not do justice to two seismic shifts which have occurred since 1939. One is the general thaw in relations between the Roman Catholic and Protestant churches following the Second Vatican Council (1962–65). While the effect on local attitudes and relationships varies widely from region to region, and is influenced by local history, political power structures and relative size, there is a new climate of expectation and a readiness to think more inclusively about ecumenical relations than was the case before the Council, when it was Vatican policy to forbid even saying the Lord's Prayer in common. In 2006 the World Methodist Council formally associated itself with the significant 1999 Joint Declaration on the Doctrine of Justification between the Lutheran World Federation and the Roman Catholic Church.

The second shift has been a progressive questioning of the assumption of the 1920s and 1930s, continuing into the 1960s, that Christian unity implies the dissolution of current church structures in favour of a single organisation, in more secular terms 'merger' or 'amalgamation'. The failure of so many schemes designed to achieve

---

[15] Reports of these dialogues have been published at five-year intervals by the World Methodist Council, Lake Junaluska, NC, as have the reports of other dialogues. See also Geoffrey Wainwright, *Methodists in Dialog* (Nashville, TN: Kingswood Books, 1995).

this has been a factor in the development. A further factor has been the influence of cultural change in society generally and reaction in many churches against inherited styles of worship and church life, which has meant that in all denominations, including Methodism, there is greater diversity. All this has affected the nature of the ecumenical vision. It is now much more common to speak in terms of 'reconciled diversity' and 'being in communion', where the aim is to secure collaboration in mission, interchangeability of ministers and open access to Holy Communion while leaving organisational patterns and worship styles unchanged.[16]

A further development since the 1950s has been in the field of shared theological education. Driven in many cases by the need to pool resources, mission agencies created united colleges for the training of local ministers. Kenya, Nigeria, Sri Lanka and Fiji are among the examples. In Britain The Queen's Foundation in Birmingham and in the United States the Interdenominational Theological Center in Atlanta, Georgia, a consortium of six colleges, should be mentioned, although in both countries many other separate colleges are linked in associations of various kinds with cross-accreditation for courses. This must in time affect wider relationships between the churches.

Attention also needs to be drawn briefly to a growing interest in inter-faith dialogue, which by its nature calls for ecumenical rather than denominational engagement. It has been driven in part by the problems of community relations created by migration and the presence in considerable numbers of Muslims, Hindus, Sikhs and Buddhists in countries hitherto exclusively if only nominally Christian. Additional impetus has been given by the memory of what was done to the Jews under the Nazi regime and in the last decade by the desire to counter Islamic terrorism. As yet, however, inter-faith dialogue does not feature prominently on the agendas of most Methodist churches.

Finally under this head, attention needs to be drawn to the influence of ecumenical debate upon the development in both the United Methodist and British Methodist traditions of a permanent ordained diaconate. Although both traditions had been familiar with diaconal ministry and United Methodism has retained its order of deaconesses, the British Conference in 1993 and the UMC General Conference in 1996 both voted to introduce, in slightly different forms, the order of deacon in full connexion, open to both men and women, as a ministry in its own right rather than as a step towards the presbyterate.

---

[16] For discussion of the issues see Jeremy Morris and Nicholas Sagovsky (eds), *The Unity We Have and the Unity We Seek* (London and New York, NY: T&T Clark, 2003); Colin Podmore (ed.), *Community – Unity – Communion* (London: Church House Publishing, 1998).

## Worship

An aspect of the ecumenical movement has been the liturgical convergence that has taken place in the last fifty years affecting a wide range of Christian traditions.[17] The worship books in use in Methodism on both sides of the Atlantic in 1939 (and used or adapted in dependent missionary churches in many other parts) still largely reflected the language and structure of Thomas Cranmer's Book of Common Prayer. Those in use in 2010 reveal the influence of more ancient liturgical traditions. Greater prominence has been given to baptism and confirmation. The eucharist is celebrated more frequently as a complete act of worship rather than as a separate addition to a preaching service and with an emphasis on thanksgiving in a prayer which follows ancient patterns. A common lectionary is in use following the Christian year more fully and there are ecumenically agreed English translations of standard texts such as the Nicene Creed. Along with this has come fuller congregational participation, greater use of candles and other visual symbols and in architecture the pulpit yielding its traditional central place in Methodist churches to the communion table.

But any discussion of worship must take account of the widespread disparity which Methodism has always permitted between published liturgies and actual practice. The extent to which authorised forms of worship are used faithfully, or with ad lib adaptations, or not at all is unrecorded beyond the general knowledge that all three occur. Nevertheless, in English-speaking Methodism over our period there has been a general decline in the use of genuinely extempore prayer in public worship in favour of prepared material of one kind or another, the exception being those congregations where the charismatic movement is strong and the use of contemporary music styles and extempore preaching and prayer remain the norm.

Alongside the growing use of formal orders of service, therefore, must be noted trends towards experimentation and adaptation to local culture across the world, as the mould set by the nineteenth century has gradually been broken. In East Africa, for example, in the 1960s the use of traditional instruments, rhythms and dance in worship was still largely taboo. By the mid1980s it had become widespread. But the general picture in most places would still appear to be one of conservatism, whether the pattern is formal or extempore.

In fact nowhere are the changes, and the tensions between old and new, more apparent than in hymnody. Methodism has a long tradition, back to the eighteenth century, of using popular music to accompany hymns. What has frequently happened, however, has been that yesterday's popular has become today's traditional. The last seventy years have witnessed a major shift in Western popular culture and the gap between the traditional and the contemporary in music styles is probably greater than it has ever been. It is a divisive issue for many congregations

---

[17] For a survey of Methodist worship in various cultures see Karen B. Westerfield Tucker (ed.), *The Sunday Service of the Methodists: Twentieth-Century Worship in Worldwide Methodism* (Nashville, TN: Kingswood, 1996).

although the difference in tastes cannot be described, as it sometimes is, simply as one between different age-groups.

A notable feature of our period has been a recovery of interest in Charles Wesley's hymns, which have been recognised as having had a formative influence on Methodist spirituality. It has been encouraged by the publication of a number of studies, particularly by J. E. Rattenbury in the 1940s,[18] and the foundation of the Charles Wesley Society in 1990. Paradoxically, however, over the same period the number of his hymns in authorised hymn books has diminished. In the UMC it fell from 77 in 1964 to 51 in 1992 while in Britain it fell from 254 in 1933 to 156 in 1983 and has fallen further to 79 with the latest publication. Elsewhere the currency of Wesley hymns is limited by the constraints of translation.

## Theology

The second half of the twentieth century must surely rank as one of the more unsettled periods in theological history. In 1939 it could be widely assumed that the task of theologians was to address a received agenda: the existence and nature of God, the person of Jesus Christ, sin, redemption and atonement, the Holy Spirit, church, ministry and sacraments, the last things. There would be variations in treatment, and in Methodist hands a particular emphasis upon personal experience, assurance and the pursuit of holiness, but an agreed framework. In the post-war period that came increasingly to be challenged. In part this was driven by a desire to come to terms with the increasing secularism of Western society. As wider society reacted against traditional mores and authority patterns in the 'swinging sixties', voices in the church also sought a radical re-statement of the faith. Bonhoeffer's phrases 'man come of age' and 'religionless Christianity' suggested a new agenda 'written by the world', and some explored the implications of 'the death of God'. 'The Ground of Being' and 'the Man for Others' became new catchphrases.

Others took as their starting point the collective experience of particular groups: the poor in Latin America, African-Americans in the United States, Africans under apartheid in South Africa and women in society generally. Liberation became a common theme and the biblical story of the exodus its inspiration. The focus was on changing society and the transformation of attitudes, rather than, as in much traditional Methodist theology, the experience of the individual before God. The ministry of Jesus and his proclamation of the Kingdom of God took precedence over the theology of St Paul. Some of it was influenced by Marxist ideas and to emphasise personal salvation in the traditional Methodist manner was seen as escapism. On another front theologians in Africa and Asia were questioning the long integration of Christian theology with the Greco-Roman philosophical tradition and seeking to relate it to other cultural traditions. While the Bible remained an inspiration for

---

[18] *The Eucharistic Hymns of John and Charles Wesley* (London: Epworth, 1948) and *The Evangelical Doctrines of Charles Wesley's Hymns* (London: Epworth, 1954 [3rd edn.]).

these developments it too came under scrutiny by the same criteria. At the same time there were other movements originating in Europe which were in contention there and in America: the strongly biblically based conservative reaction of Karl Barth, and the existentialism which found its Christian exponents particularly in Rudolf Bultmann and Paul Tillich.

These were general trends to which Methodist theologians contributed. Much of the debate was in published work; how much percolated to the pulpits it is hard to say. One way in which liberationist ideas have had a wide impact, however, has been in the trend towards more inclusive language, particularly in worship. While the elimination of gender-specific language in relation to God and extensive editing of traditional hymns to eliminate exclusive language remain a contentious issue, greater care is certainly taken in general discourse to make it inclusive of both women and men.

It is not surprising that these developments have provoked reaction. In Britain in the 1960s and 1970s there was considerable debate and protest at the content of some of the study material officially issued for lay preacher training. It has been most marked in the United States, where the Good News movement, founded in 1967 and conservative theologically, ethically and politically, commands a considerable following and has given rise to the Mission Society for United Methodism mentioned above. There was widespread anxiety prior to the 1986 General Conference as to whether a projected revision of the United Methodist doctrinal statement following the 1968 union could be achieved.[19] Although that task was in the end accomplished and the statement incorporated in the *Discipline*, there remains a degree of polarisation in American Methodism which is not paralleled elsewhere, either because churches are more generally conservative and less affected by developments elsewhere or because, as in Britain, those holding opposing views have largely come to respect each other's integrity. A significant step in this direction was the adoption by the British Conference in 1985 of the report *Sharing in God's Mission*, which brought together evangelism, social caring and action for social change as equally important aspects of the one mission of God in which the church is called to share.[20]

A different form of reaction has been the rise of the charismatic movement within Methodism. Strongly influenced by the ideas and practice of the established Pentecostal churches and emphasising experience of the Holy Spirit and the exercise of spiritual gifts, particularly speaking in tongues, the movement has touched most churches, both Protestant and Roman Catholic, and Methodist churches have been no exception. Provoking most debate in the 1970s and 1980s, it has influenced worship styles in many congregations and has served to re-focus theological attention on the third Person of the Trinity. But it has not led, as in the nineteenth century, to any significant separatist movements.

---

[19] See Thomas A. Langford (ed.), *Doctrine and Theology in the United Methodist Church* (Nashville, TN: Abingdon, 1991).

[20] See also page 73 above, and the UMC statement *Grace Upon Grace* (1990), grounding all missional outreach in the nature of the loving God.

An important forum for the exchange of ideas among Methodists has been the Oxford Institute of Methodist Theological Studies, founded in 1958 under the auspices of the World Methodist Council and meeting (in Oxford) every three to five years. Ranging in membership between one and two hundred theologians and pastors from an increasingly wide range of churches claiming their origins in the work of the Wesleys, it has witnessed many confrontations between advocates of the new theologies and conservative defenders of the traditional agenda. In more recent decades it has concentrated on exploring the distinctively Wesleyan contribution to current theological debates.[21] In the process it has given impetus to one of the notable developments since 1939: the study, in the United States and Britain especially, of John Wesley as a theologian. There is now an extensive literature on the subject and an imprint of the Abingdon Press (Kingswood Books) dedicated to it and related subjects. As a result, a new critical edition of John Wesley's works is in course of publication[22] and a Spanish translation of the Jackson edition was begun in 1996 and is now complete.

The development has not been without its critics, who feared that emphasising John Wesley would make Methodism inward-looking and be in conflict with attempts to bridge wider ecumenical divisions, but as the ecumenical movement itself has moved to an emphasis on embracing diversity this has been seen less as an obstacle and more as a particular offering Methodism could bring to the table. How far the preoccupation with John Wesley extends across the Methodist world is hard to judge. An obvious difficulty is language, as illustrated by the need for a Spanish version to make him accessible. In some parts of the world, one suspects, the pressing issue is simply to gain a hearing for any form of Christian witness, and Methodist specifics would take second place. In others, where there is a plurality of Christian traditions, distinctiveness becomes more important.

## Social, Political and Moral Issues

The engagement of Methodism with wider society over public issues in our period has been affected by several factors. It has been easier in the open democracies of Britain, Ireland and the United States than under regimes intolerant of political dissent; easier too for churches representing a significant proportion of the voting population than for small minority churches whose voice, if raised, could easily be ignored. In some areas, as in continental Europe, the pietistic tradition has not encouraged such engagement. Often, as was the case with slavery in the early

---

[21] For a history of the Institute up to 2002 with details of its meetings and publications see Brian E. Beck, *Exploring Methodism's Heritage: The Story of the Oxford Institute of Methodist Theological Studies* (Nashville, TN: General Board of Higher Education and Ministry of the United Methodist Church, 2004).

[22] Vols 7 and 9 by Oxford University Press, 1983 and 1989, the remainder as the Bicentennial Edition by Abingdon Press.

nineteenth century, the churches themselves have been divided, on some issues such as human sexuality quite sharply, on others such as the use of nuclear weapons and pacifism generally with a greater willingness to accept conscientious differences. It is impossible in a short survey to offer a detailed examination, or even a full list, of the questions that have concerned the churches over the period. Many have been regional. But some trends can be observed.

One such trend has been an increasing willingness to go beyond questions of personal conduct to comment on broader issues of public policy. A small token of this has been the successive changes in the title of the agency responsible in British Methodism, from 'Temperance and Social Welfare' in 1939, through 'Christian Citizenship' and 'Social Responsibility' to 'Public Issues' in 2010. Another instance has been the increasing readiness of the Council of Bishops of the UMC to publish considered statements on public issues, such as nuclear weapons (*In Defense of Creation* 1986) and *Children and Poverty* (1996), both to inform and guide Methodist opinion and to speak prophetically to the nation. In some cases conferences have issued official statements, in others it has been a matter of prominent individuals involved in wider movements, as over Civil Rights in the United States or apartheid in South Africa. Mention should be made in this context of the contribution, in the person of leading figures and by published statements, of the Methodist Church in Ireland to community reconciliation since 1968.

In questions of personal morality the task of sketching developments is complicated by wide cultural differences across the world, and even within churches of different traditions in the same country. In Britain and America, however, it is noticeable how the churches have responded to changes in wider society. Official pronouncements on questions of marriage and sexuality now have to address issues of serial divorce, cohabitation, single-parent families, homosexuality and abortion in a way unthinkable in 1939. As society has become more manifestly multi-cultural, churches have become less inclined to assume that Christian values can be imposed by legislation on wider society. In some quarters there has been an evident desire to escape from a negative image of Methodism as preoccupied with opposition to alcohol, gambling and dancing and with promoting sabbath observance. Within many congregations divorce, cohabitation and premarital sex are tacitly accepted. While it is impossible to generalise, there has been a movement, in Europe and America at least, to a more liberal attitude to lifestyle and less willingness to see Christianity in terms of a counter-culture, although there remains strong resistance to it in some quarters. Homosexual practice remains a deeply divisive issue, although in Britain, since the conference debated the matter in 1993 and adopted resolutions which on the one hand reaffirmed traditional teaching about sexual morality and on the other affirmed and celebrated the participation and ministry of lesbians and gay men in the church, there has not been the degree of militant confrontation still evident in the United States, where a clause banning the ordination of practising homosexuals was introduced into the *Discipline* in 1984.

## Conclusion

Methodism has changed much since its beginnings in the eighteenth century but never more so than in the last seventy years. The preceding pages have attempted to sketch some of the developments. How far do they live up to the title of the chapter: 'shifting balances'? Such a description might imply an equilibrium to which Methodism will eventually arrive, on the analogy of a perfectly balanced pair of scales. But there is no ideal equilibrium – only an ongoing process of adjustment to changing circumstances, surrounding cultures and contending perceptions within of what it means to be faithful to the traditions received. Nevertheless, two of the changes we have noted, the demographic shift from global north to global south and the increasing contribution of women to leadership, are unlikely to be reversed.

Methodism across the world is more diverse now than it has ever been, reflecting in each place the culture in which it is set, even when in many respects critical of it. Except in Western Europe, North America and Australasia it is still expanding. David Hempton, in his important study of the rise and relative decline of Methodism in its first century and a half, *Methodism: Empire of the Spirit*,[23] has pointed to the tensions and contradictions in its character. A product both of enthusiasm and eighteenth-century enlightenment, it was a popular, egalitarian movement with a tradition of authoritarian control; it preached a religion of the heart subject to discipline, a gospel both of free grace and of works of righteousness; it sought personal holiness and reform of the nation; it appealed to the unlearned yet promoted education. It grew nourished by its environment but also in reaction to it. In the strains caused by its expansion were the seeds of its decline. It will be important in future work to discover how far that analysis also applies to the growing churches of the late twentieth and early twenty-first centuries.

What 'shifting balances' points to, then, is the existence of tensions or dualities within the movement, with emphasis shifting from one to the other. Methodism seeks the stability of being a church and the constant adaptability of being a mission movement. It holds to Scripture and Creeds and claims its place in the one, holy, catholic and apostolic Church, yet by its stress on a particular version of personal spirituality and constant references to John Wesley sometimes courts the danger of becoming a sect. It claims an ordained ministry of word and sacrament in line with Christian tradition and at the same time affirms the ministry of the laity and depends for its life upon it. It prizes leadership yet is often restive under authority, seeks to affirm global connectedness while respecting regional integrity and independence, looks for unity while affirming diversity. What is it that holds the movement together? Perhaps only a shared history and what traces that history has left of itself in the different communities claiming the name. In theology it is broadly Arminian; ecclesiologically it values its connectedness, more closely structured for some members of the family than for others; it holds to no defining practice as churches in the Baptist tradition do; it sees itself as a movement in mission. But the Oxford Institute of 1987, when it addressed the question, 'What

---

[23] See note 9 above.

should Methodists teach?' refused to accept any prescriptive definition of what is Methodist doctrine, insisting that each community must determine for itself what constitutes an authentic Methodist identity.[24]

One cannot forecast what the movement will become in the next seventy years. Perhaps in some areas Methodist churches will enter into unions with churches of other traditions to mutual enrichment, in others it may dwindle away, in yet others grow and flourish. One reading of Hempton's final page is that the future lies not with Methodism but with its fast-growing offspring, Pentecostalism. Whether that is to be welcomed depends upon a theological assessment of what it offers. Whatever the future, one can only pray and hope that John Wesley's vision of individuals and societies transformed by the gospel will continue to inspire God's people even if the original structures that preserved that vision have given place to something new.

---

[24] M. Douglas Meeks (ed.), *What Should Methodists Teach?* (Nashville, TN: Abingdon Press, 1990), 131 ff.

# PART III
# World Methodism

# Church Statistics and the Growth of Global Methodism: Some Preliminary Descriptive Statistics

David J. Jeremy[1]

## Global Church Statistics

Historical statistics can be slippery, and meta-historical religious statistics more so than most. In contrast to the conducting of an opinion survey, the collection of basic church statistics, such as numbers of church congregations, members, ministers and buildings, sounds relatively easy. However, variability and uncertainty arise, especially in 'younger churches', in regard to the collection, communication and collation of national church statistics, to say nothing of national and denominational variations in matters such as the definition and meaning of membership.[2] Unsurprisingly, in contrast to the long-run series of data on churches and churchgoing in Britain by Robert Currie et al.,[3] little serious effort has yet been made to produce anything comparable across all Christian communions and all countries.

---

[1]  Besides the editors of this volume for accommodating this essay (especially Dr Peter Forsaith, who has added several useful references), I am grateful to Rebecca Mon Williams for reading an earlier draft. Without the interlibrary loan support of the Manchester Metropolitan University Library, the printed resources of the John Rylands University Library of Manchester, and the electronic library of the Manchester Central Library, the research for this essay could not have been completed. I am indebted to them all but of course take responsibility for the end result.

[2]  See Frank Wilson Price, 'World Christian Statistics: Some Warnings, and Discussion on their Future Collection', in H. Wakelin Coxill and Sir Kenneth Grubb (eds), *World Christian Handbook, 1968* (London: Lutterworth, 1967), 48–52.

[3]  Robert Currie, Alan Gilbert and Lee Horsley, *Churches and Churchgoers: Patterns of Church Growth in the British Isles since 1700* (Oxford: Clarendon Press, 1977).

The collection of global religious statistics may be traced back to the seventeenth and eighteenth centuries.[4] The 'Compton census' of 1676, for England and Wales, was an early attempt to quantify church affiliation, but was subject to pitfalls which have plagued religious counting ever since.[5] A fresh impetus came when trade, colonial expansion and religion intersected in the late eighteenth and early nineteenth centuries. Adam Smith, progenitor of classical economics, in the 1760s and 1770s pronounced that societies pass through progressive stages of civilising development, the ultimate being a Christian civilisation based on commerce. In his *Wealth of Nations* (1776) Smith emphasised that the real wealth of a country consisted not in its silver mines but in the produce of its land and people's labour, and that manufacturing was more profitable than agriculture.[6] Smith's disciples, interested in both civilisation and commerce, kept a statistical eye on the natural and human resources and civilising progress of Britain's colonies.[7] Initially 'counting the people' contravened the Old Testament taboo on censuses motivated by pride.[8] Clerics from both Church and Nonconformity participated on all sides of the population controversy, which protagonists won without disastrous effect after the first British Census of population was conducted in 1801.[9] Additional interest in the collection of statistics grew in the early nineteenth century with the emergence of modern Christian missions and the associated concern to measure missionary progress.[10]

---

[4] Karl Pearson, *The History of Statistics in the 17th and 18th Centuries against the Changing Background of Intellectual, Scientific and Religious Thought*, ed. Egon S. Pearson (London: Griffin, 1978).

[5] Anne Whiteman (ed.), *The Compton Census of 1676: A Critical Edition* (London: Oxford University Press, 1986).

[6] Andrew Porter, *Religion versus Empire? British Protestant Missionaries and Overseas Expansion, 1700–1914* (Manchester: Manchester University Press, 2004), 92; Adam Smith, *An Inquiry into the Nature and Causes of the Wealth of Nations* (1776; Canaan edition, New York: Modern Library, 1937), lx, 3–21, 357–60.

[7] John Ramsey McCulloch, *A Statistical Account of the British Empire, Exhibiting Its Extent, Physical Capacities, Population, Industry, and Civil and Religious Institutions* (1st edn, 2 vols; London: Society for the Diffusion of Useful Knowledge, 1837; 4th edn, 1854).

[8] David Glass, *Numbering the People: The Eighteenth Century Population Controversy and the Development of Census and Vital Statistics in Britain* (Farnborough: D. C. Heath, 1973), chapter 1, especially 19. See Exodus 30: 11–16, I Samuel 24 and I Chronicles 21 for the prohibition. For explicit Church opposition to the idea of a national census see *Royal Folly: or, David's Sin in Numbering of the People: A Sermon Preached at St Mary's in Oxford, on Sunday, April 1. Occasioned by a Design on Foot of Registering the People of Great Britain, by a Fellow of St John's* (London: M. Cooper, W. Reeve and C. Sympson, 1753). For a popular eighteenth-century Nonconformist understanding of these passages see Matthew Henry, *Exposition of the Old and New Testaments, or Complete Commentary*, 6 vols (London: Thomas Bunce, 1708–10).

[9] Glass, *Numbering the People*.

[10] An early example was Andrew Stirling, *An Account, Geographical, Statistical and Historical, of Orissa Proper or Cuttack* (1822). It was re-issued as Andrew Stirling, *Orissa: Its Geography, Statistics, History, Religion and Antiquities, to which Is Added, a History of the General Baptist Mission Established in the Province, by James Peggs* (London: John Snow, 1846).

In 1851, Britain conducted the only full, national religious census of 'Accommodation and Attendance at Worship' it has ever attempted. On 30 March all places of worship were required to count attendance – this extended beyond Christian churches to synagogues. The decennial population census, carried out at the same time, did not include questions about religious affiliation, which might have provided very different figures. The results of the 1851 religious census have been dissected and disputed ever since. The census, for instance, could not differentiate between those who attended more than one service, sometimes in different churches. The date chosen was also Mothering Sunday, which may have resulted in higher attendance by children and parents. To the raw data a complex formula was applied to estimate church membership figures for England and Wales.[11]

Setting aside collections of religious statistics for urban centres, such as those for London by Charles Booth and Richard Mudie Smith,[12] attempts to cover authoritatively all church denominations, even for one country, generally waited until the watershed World Missionary Conference held in Edinburgh in 1910. In preparation for this the World Missionary Conference Commission produced a *Statistical Atlas of Christian Missions* (Edinburgh: World Missionary Conference, 1910). A second edition, with maps by the cartographic publisher Bartholomew, came the following year. Under the auspices of its Continuation Committee and inspired by the missionary strategist J. H. Oldham, an *International Review of Missions*, edited by Oldham, was launched in 1912. Missionary statistics were included in contributions to the *IRM*.[13] The next major effort to make a comprehensive global record of missionary statistics was the *World Missionary Atlas* edited by Harlan Page Beach and Charles Harvey Fahs and published by Edinburgh House Press in 1925.[14] Essentially it was the third edition of the *Statistical Atlas of Christian Missions*, but much enlarged, and still a Protestant atlas in which the Roman Catholic or Eastern Churches did not participate. More highly rated was the *Interpretative Statistical Survey of the World Mission of the Christian Church* edited by Joseph Parker (New York and London: International Missionary Council, 1938).

First moves towards a systematic compilation of global church statistics came from outside the mainline missionary movement, with the founding of the World Dominion Press funded by the Survey Application Trust. This had been set up and funded in 1918 by Sidney James Wells Clark (1862–1930) whose successful management for William Bradley of a Chester-based drapery chain had made

---

[11] For an analysis of Methodist data, see R. E. Davies, A. R. George and G. Rupp, (eds), *A History of the Methodist Church in Great Britain*, vol. 4 (London: Epworth, 1988), 497–505. For Nonconformity as a whole see Michael R. Watts, *The Dissenters: Vol. II, The Expansion of Evangelical Nonconformity* (Oxford: Clarendon Press, 1995).

[12] Charles Booth, *Life and Labour of the People in London* (London: Macmillan & Co., 1902–03), series 3, *Religious Influences* (7 vols). Richard Mudie Smith, *The Religious Life of London* (London: Hodder & Stoughton, 1904).

[13] Keith Clements, *Faith on the Frontier: A Life of J. H. Oldham* (Edinburgh: T&T Clark, 1999), 105–8.

[14] Edinburgh House, London, was the headquarters of the Continuation Committee of the World Missionary Conference.

him a rich man.[15] On business tours abroad he 'began to visit overseas missions, particularly in China'. Initially a benefactor of the London Missionary Society, he became critical of some of its work. Inspired by what might be, yet constrained by ill-health, in 1907 he retired at the early age of forty-five and dedicated the rest of his life to promoting overseas missions in a different way. As Sir Kenneth Grubb, who worked with the Survey Application Trust in the 1930s, recalled, 'The Trust also attached importance to ascertaining via research the real facts about the distribution of churches, missions and Christians throughout the world. Unless one knew what had been done, how could one know what there was to do?' A Survey Department was established under the Rev. Alexander McLeish of the Church of Scotland.[16] At first McLeish and his collaborators studied single countries across all Christian denominations. After the Second World War, they widened their scope and intermittently published the *World Christian Handbook* (London: World Dominion Press, 1949, 1952, 1957, 1962, 1968). This proved to be the final colonial-period endeavour to assemble a global statistical picture of the universal church.

Since 1945 the World Council of Churches (WCC) has infrequently collected such data but as yet no one has attempted to collate and publish what is available. In the experience of the Rev. Dr Simon Oxley, formerly Executive Secretary for Education at the WCC in Geneva,

> membership statistics are notoriously difficult to pin down, even in the UK context. Denominations have different understandings of membership, with some restricting that category to those active in the life of the local church with others including all the baptised and/or adherents. Figures also vary depending on why membership figures are needed. If it is so that denominations or parishes can be assessed for' membership fees' on a per capita basis the figures are often much lower than, say, for the purposes of claiming influence in society!
>
> This issue is writ large at the global level. Although member churches are expected to contribute to the WCC's funding according to broad size bands, where churches are located within those bands has proved contentious. I'm not sure whether the WCC has ever tried to collect membership statistics but it certainly has not done so in any serious way for many years. The Report of the Central Committee to each Assembly and the Assembly Handbook have not contained membership statistics for the member churches.

---

[15] Kenneth G. Grubb, 'The Story of the Survey Application Trust', in David M. Paton (ed.), *Reform of the Ministry* (London: Lutterworth, 1968), 61–84; Sidney James Wells Clark entries in UK Censuses, 1871–1901, searched via www.ancestry.co.uk (accessed 8 September 2012).

[16] Sir Kenneth Grubb, *Crypts of Power: An Autobiography* (London: Hodder and Stoughton, 1971), 91–2.

However, in 2006 (just before the Porto Alegre Assemby) the WCC published *A Handbook of Churches and Councils* (Geneva, WCC, 2006). This replaced a similar publication of some 20 years before. Membership figures are given for each church. These were obtained from the churches themselves or from other sources.[17]

Today the WCC (which has 349 member churches 'seeking unity, common witness and Christian service') maintains a valuable website compiled from national church returns.[18] It offers limited access to the general public. For each country and each church communion the site records national-level data: the church family to which the denomination belongs; the denomination's base; membership; pastors; diaconal workers; congregations; and wider church affiliations. The data are presumably compiled from WCC member church returns. The website would be an indispensable statistical starting point for any serious study of the recent global expansion of Christianity.

The Center for the Study of Global Christianity at Gordon-Conwell Theological Seminary, South Hamilton, Massachusetts, USA, produces the *World Christian Encyclopedia: A Comparative Survey of Churches and Religion in the Modern World* (2 vols, New York: Oxford University Press). The same research group generates another source of global church statistics: the World Christian Database website. However, this makes no mention of the nature of the statistics – whether any are based on historical evidence and, if so, whether they are short term or long term; nor whether they have been accepted at their face value or subjected to rigorous scrutiny and testing. Furthermore, the bald figures of raw data are poorly presented and their accuracy may be suspect. The size of the Methodist Church UK for 2010 is given as 950,000 (the Isle of Man is listed separately as 5,700, although neither the Channel Isles nor Scotland are differentiated). Yet by the Methodist Church's own computation: 'At the last count in 2007 the British Methodist Church had 267,257 members. There are over 800,000 people in Britain who have an active connection with the Methodist Church.'[19]

## Global Methodist Statistics

Fearing no danger of pride, Methodists rejoiced in numbers as a biblical sign of divine approval of their witness.[20] Under John Wesley's direction, from the

---

[17] Rev. Dr Simon Oxley to author, e-mail of 8 February 2011. I am grateful to him for these observations.
[18] http://www.oikoumene.org/en/resources/documents.html (accessed 8 September 2012) with full access to members.
[19] www.methodist.org.uk (accessed 5 September 2011).
[20] See for example Numbers 26; Acts 1: 15; 2: 41; 11: 21; 16: 5. Late-nineteenth-century Methodists were nevertheless mindful of the hazard: the Rev. James M. Buckley DD,

beginning they were vigorous in their recording, collecting and publishing of church statistics. Complete membership returns were first published in 1767. To these the Wesleyans added members on trial (1855 onwards), Sunday school scholars (1863 onwards), deaths of members (1864 onwards), new members (1875 onwards), junior members, lapsed members and membership transfers between circuits (all 1881 onwards), losses through emigration (1888 onwards), and transfers to and from other churches (1906 onwards).[21] Other branches of UK Methodism published membership numbers almost from their inception: the Methodist New Connexion from 1797, the Primitive Methodists from 1820, the Bible Christians from 1826, the Wesleyan Methodists Association from 1837 and the United Methodist Free Churches (which absorbed the WMA) in 1857.[22] The Wesleyans even published their own atlas in 1873.[23]

In an environment of intense competition between Nonconformist denominations, both locally and nationally, measures of growth served to spur or encourage the efforts of ministers and members, and to advertise to civic and political authorities relative weights of the respective constituencies.

The decennial publication of global statistics began in 1881 under the sponsorship of the first Ecumenical Methodist Conference (EMC), which promoted considerable transatlantic exchanges of personnel and information. Annual tables of global Methodist statistics first appeared in 1900 in the *Minutes of Conference* of the main British branches of Methodism. They were continued after 1932 in the *Minutes of Conference* of the newly united Methodist Church, but were ended after 1939 with the coming of the Second World War.

The value of Methodist global statistics was soon put to the test. Speaking at a public meeting in the early 1880s chaired by Mark Pattison, the distinguished scholar and theological radical,[24] Hugh Price Hughes, then superintendent Wesleyan minister in Oxford, mentioned that there was no adequate memorial in the university to John Wesley, one of its greatest sons. Pattison, Rector [Head] of Lincoln College, Oxford, where Wesley had been a Fellow, audibly demurred. Hughes (according to his daughter) pointed to 'the worldwide work and influence of Wesley' as 'the founder of a Church which numbers twenty five millions'. Pattison tried to correct Hughes: 'twenty five thousand, you mean, not twenty five millions'.

---

Methodist Episcopal delegate at the First Ecumenical Methodist Conference, from New York City, warned: 'Numbering Israel in the ancient times was a snare. Numbering Israel in all times requires much caution.' *Proceedings of the [First] Oecumenical Methodist Conference Held in City Road Chapel, London, September, 1881* (Cincinnati, OH and New York, NY: Walden & Stowe, 1882), 64.

[21] Currie et al., *Churches and Churchgoers*, 12–13; Henry Rack, *Reasonable Enthusiast: John Wesley and the Rise of Methodism* (London: Epworth Press, 3rd edn, 2002), 236–7.

[22] Currie et al., *Churches and Churchgoers*, 139–46.

[23] Edwin H. Tindall, *The Wesleyan Methodist Atlas of England and Wales* (London: Bemrose & Sons, 1873).

[24] H. S. Jones, 'Mark Pattison' *ODNB*.

Whereupon Hughes 'dived into his coat pocket and produced a pocketbook, from which he proceeded to verify his statement'.[25]

The statistic used by Hughes, however, was not the five million Methodist members worldwide given in the *Proceedings of the First Ecumenical Methodist Conference* of 1881 but the intensely disputed number of adherents. Modern sociologists of religion have validated the concept of adherents and explained its mechanism.[26] But where did Hughes's multiplier come from? At the EMC in September 1881, several alternative estimates of the world's Methodist population were bandied about. These ranged from 14 million (the *London Almanack* for 1879) to 17 million, 23 million (Tyerman's *Life of Wesley*) or 25 million (one of the morning papers in September 1881).[27] The Rev. W. Crook DD of the Irish Methodist Church, who cited these figures, favoured 14 million. *The Times* of 22 August 1881 reported a worldwide Methodist population of 18 million.[28] Hughes, a delegate to the Conference, was well aware of the unsettled definition of 'adherent' and evidently picked the highest figure available.

The debate about the definition and calculation of adherents was resumed in the Second Ecumenical Methodist Conference in Washington, DC in October 1891. For Ireland, Canada and Australasia government censuses provided numbers of adherents. Other bases for calculation included numbers of sittings. The Rev. William Arthur strongly objected to that and observed that adherents ought to include members, Sunday school scholars, children and persons in families of members who are not yet members, families of other attenders and 'looser adherents'. The Conference's Committee on Statistics defined adherents everywhere as including ministers, members and Sunday School scholars. In addition local variables were used: number of sittings (British Wesleyans); government censuses (Ireland, Canada, Australasia); missionaries' reports (Asiatic and African missions); while other British Methodist branches were assigned a multiplier of four without further justification. United States Methodists employed a ratio proposed by the Rev. Dr Dorchester and Henry K. Carroll, again without elaboration but equivalent to about three times for membership but with the membership figure then added.[29]

Discussants at the Ecumenical Conference in 1891 were very anxious to demonstrate a rational basis for their estimate of adherents because their statistics would be printed and come under public scrutiny. Their fears that their figure

---

[25] Dorothea Price Hughes, *The Life of Hugh Price Hughes* (London: Hodder & Stoughton, 1904), 161–2. Quoted in David Hempton, *Methodism: Empire of the Spirit* (New Haven, CT and London: Yale University Press, 2005), 1.
[26] Currie et al., *Churches and Churchgoers*, 6–7, 42–4.
[27] *Proceedings of the [First] Oecumenical Methodist Conference, 1881*, 61–8.
[28] *The Times*, 22 August 1881, 8.
[29] *Proceedings of the Second Ecumenical Methodist Conference Held in the Metropolitan Methodist Episcopal Church, Washington, October, 1891* (New York: Hunt & Eaton, 1892), 542–52. Carroll was a journalist from Plainfield, New Jersey in 1880; Dorchester was possibly the Rev. Dr Daniel Dorchester (1827–1907), a leading Methodist clergyman. See United States Census for 1880, accessed via www.ancestry.com (accessed 16 September 2012); and *Dictionary of American Biography*.

would be doubted were realised. In 1900 *Whitaker's Almanack* noted, 'At Washington in October, 1891 it was reported that there were more than 30,000,000 Methodists. This statement has been recently repeated by leading Wesleyans; but no evidence is forthcoming to establish its accuracy, which is more than doubtful.'[30] In fact the number of adherents given in the tables of the *Proceedings* of the 1891 Conference totalled 24,899,416.[31] It is unclear where *Whitaker's* other 5 million came from. At any rate the Conference of 1901 responded by choosing more conservative ratios: the Eastern Section (Britain, mainland Europe, South Africa and Australasia), now based on some sampling, became four to one members; and the Western Section (the USA and Canada), three-and-a-half to one members.[32]

In 1911, the EMC preserved the Western Section multiplier for adherents of three-and-a-half to one members but increased the Eastern Section ratio to 'four adherents to each member, the number of members being multiplied by five'.[33]

As seen in this discussion on adherents, the international EMC met every ten years after 1881, with the exception of 1941, when the Conference was postponed until after the war, convening again in 1947. At the EMC meetings in Oxford in 1951 the name was changed to the World Methodist Council (WMC) and it was decided to meet every five years.[34] No statistics were published in the 1951 Conference *Proceedings*. Statistics resumed in the *Handbook of Information* of the WMC.

Both the published series of global Methodist statistics of members (excluding adherents, for the purposes of the rest of this essay) issued by the EMC pre-1947, and that by the WMC after 1950, present problems to users. The EMC series were assembled in an age of Empire when Methodist congregations in the non-white British colonies were administered from England. This was apparent in the EMC division of the world into Eastern and Western sections of Methodism, as noted above. Under this aggregation, in 1881 Eastern memberships were divided between Wesleyan and non-Wesleyan. Only the Wesleyans were shown as having members beyond England – in Ireland, Australia and France. By 1910 the Irish, French, South African and Australasian numbers were shown separately and described simply as Methodist. The Western Section in 1880 was split between Episcopal (ten branche) and non-Episcopal (nine), all in the USA apart from three in Canada. In 1910, nineteen Methodist branches were recorded in the USA and one in Canada. Japan's Methodists then appeared in the Western Section.

---

[30]  *Whitaker's Almanack*, 1900, 244.

[31]  *Proceedings of the Second Ecumenical Methodist Conference, 1891*, 547–8.

[32]  *Proceedings of the Third Ecumenical Methodist Conference Held in City Road Chapel, London, September, 1901* (London: Wesleyan Methodist Book Room, 1901), 273, 561–2.

[33]  *Proceedings of the Fourth Ecumenical Methodist Conference Held in the Metropolitan Methodist Church, Toronto, Canada, October 4–17, 1911* (London: Methodist Publishing House, 1911), 754.

[34]  World Methodist Council, *Handbook of Information 1971–1976*, 3. My thanks to Dr George Freeman, General Secretary, World Methodist Council, Lake Junaluska, North Carolina, USA, for bringing this source to my attention and for supplying a copy of the Statistics section in the *Handbook of Information 2007–2011* which, he confirms, was compiled and published in 2006–07.

The submerging of non-European Methodist Districts in these aggregated figures cannot have been due solely to the size of the numbers involved. France had fewer Methodist members than many African, Indian or Chinese Districts. The *Conference Minutes* of the Wesleyan Methodist Church for 1906 (one of British Methodism's absolute peak years) shows that there were separate Irish, French and South African Conferences but all other overseas circuits served by Wesleyan Methodist missionaries were clumped together as 'Foreign Missions'. Admittedly it would be possible to work from the disaggregated foreign District returns found in this volume,[35] but even that would not be possible for the South African Conference because its disaggregated District returns were not shown.

In the 'General Statistics of Methodism', annually published in the *Conference Minutes* of the smaller Methodist branches, the Primitive Methodist Connexion, United Methodist Free Churches, Methodist New Connexion and the Bible Christians' membership data were simply split between Home and Foreign statistics. The Wesleyan Reform Union and the Independent Methodist Church submitted no overseas statistics for this Table.[36] In addition, members 'on trial' were also counted by the Wesleyans and when aggregated for the Methodist branches in the 'General Statistics of Methodism' appear as 'Church members and probationers'.[37]

Statistics for Methodist branches in the United States were published in the 'General Statistics of Methodism' accompanying the annual *Conference Minutes* of the British Wesleyan Methodists, the Primitive Methodists and the Methodist New Connexion/United Methodist Church after 1907 (and possibly the *Minutes* of other Methodist Conferences), as noted above, between 1900 and 1932; and in the Methodist Church *Minutes of Conference*, 1932–39. The identity of the Methodist denominational publications in the United States from which they were taken is presently unknown.

The WMC series suffers from two obvious statistical difficulties. Each *Handbook of Information* spans five years but there is no indication when in the five-year cycle each *Handbook* was published. Consequently retrospective users cannot pin the data down to a particular year for comparative purposes. Secondly, the editors of each *Handbook* rarely set out their sources or any criteria which they might have been following.

The one exception to the latter handicap was the *Handbook of Information 1956–1961*. It was noted that the Secretaries of the WMC had contacted all Methodist groups for figures of 'actual members and also the highest claim as to the total Methodist community' but that, '[figures] must be regarded as approximate only'.[38] In some countries approximation would be a reasonable expectation. Problems

---

[35] Wesleyan Methodist Church, *Conference Minutes*, 1906, 299–305, 539.

[36] See, for example, the *Conference Minutes for 1906* of the Wesleyan Methodist Church, 539; the Methodist New Connexion, 144–5; or the Primitive Methodist Church, 208 (which reported that they were 'not to hand as we go to press, and hence are omitted in the tabular form in which they have appeared in our Connexional "Minutes" in previous years').

[37] Wesleyan Methodist Church, *Conference Minutes*, 1906, 305, 539.

[38] World Methodist Council, *Handbook of Information 1956–1961*, 68.

with time or distance, literacy or education, membership qualifications, or even a religious revival, might prevent national church leaders from making more than an informed guess at the size of their constituencies. The appearance of rounded figures, particularly when recorded by the thousand, sometimes, but not always, indicated the absence of exact enumeration.

The *Handbook of Information 1956–1961* also provided the sources from which its membership and 'community' figures were obtained. Members were actual members, 'taken from the latest reports and in nearly every case official'. This sounds impeccable. However, there was considerable diversity between cultures. 'The British policy is conservative and tends to confine membership within rather strict limits. In the United States the policy is more liberal and the figures include many persons who were formerly classed as "inactive members". These differ from the "constituency" or "community" in that they are actual members who voluntarily joined the church after reaching "years of accountability" and remain on the church rolls.'[39] Here was a fresh attempt to grapple with the old problem of adherents.

The community figures were evidently an attempt to capture the numbers of those who had been raised as Methodists but had lapsed. Firm figures came from national population censuses recording such information, as was the case in Australia and Jamaica. Otherwise community figures were estimates derived from five sources: two published volumes, the *World Christian Handbook*, 1952[40] and the *Yearbook of American Churches*, 1959;[41] reports of missionary boards of societies; reports directly submitted by representatives of the churches; and WMC estimates.[42]

Verifying editions produces one important conclusion for the global Methodist statistics in the WMC *Handbook of Information 1956–1961*: between the years 1952 and 1959, and perhaps earlier and later, their origins were widely spread. The implications of this are disturbing for the Methodist statistician. No common baseline for Methodist memberships in all countries in the 1950s is known. This vitiates all growth measures using a 1950s benchmark.

One way round the difficulty might be to try to reconstruct the data, using the *World Christian Handbook* and the *Yearbook of American and Canadian Churches*, checking and amplifying them with the *Conference Minutes* of the various Methodist branches in the United States and Canada for a particular date in the 1950s. For the United States, where 70 per cent of Methodists then lived, the data could also be tested against the Federal census of church members: *Religious Bodies: 1936: Selected Statistics for the United States by Denominations and Geographic Divisions* published by the US Government Printing Office in 1941. None of this has been attempted here.

---

[39] Ibid., pp. 68–73.

[40] H. Coxill, H. Wakelin and K. Grubb, *World Christian Handbook, 1952* (London: World Dominion Press, 1953).

[41] *Yearbook of American and Canadian Churches* (New York: Round Table Press, Inc., 1933–72) (biennial to 1952, thence annual).

[42] This and the previous paragraph derive from World Methodist Council, *Handbook of Information 1956–1961*, 68.

For Britain, the EMC and WMC statistics can be tested against the standard source for the UK's measures of churchgoing: Currie et al., *Churches and Churchgoers* (1977)[43]– see Table 6.1.

Table 6.1  Divergencies in British Methodist statistics of members: EMC and WMC compared with Currie et al. for 1880, 1910 and 1955.

|  |  | EMC |  | Currie et al., pp. 142–3 |
|---|---|---|---|---|
| 1880 | Wesleyan | 501,300 |  | 345,332 |
|  | Methodist New Connexion | 31,652 |  | 25,241 |
|  | Bible Christian | 31,542 |  | 20,664 |
|  | Primitive Methodist | 185,316 |  | 166,108 |
|  | United Methodist Free Churches | 79,756 |  | 64,712 |
|  | Wales |  |  | 26,324 |
|  | Scotland |  |  | 5,022 |
|  | Ireland | 24,237 |  | 24,463 |
|  | Reform Union | 7,745 |  |  |
|  |  | 861,548 |  | 677,866 |
|  | EMC – Currie discrepancy |  | 183,682 |  |
| 1910 | Wesleyan | 664,958 |  | 439,230 |
|  | Primitive Methodist | 211,691 |  | 206,016 |
|  | United Methodist Church | 165,722 |  | 146,715 |
|  | Wales |  |  | 39,563 |
|  | Scotland |  |  | 9,770 |
|  | Ireland | 29,648 |  | 29,357 |
|  | Wesleyan Reform Union | 8,366 |  |  |
|  | Independent Methodist | 8,769 |  |  |

---

[43] After 1932 the Methodist Church received its statistical returns each December and attributed them to the following calendar year. Currie et al., in contrast, attribute them to the December calendar year.

|  |  |  | 1,690 |  |
|---|---|---|---|---|
|  | French |  |  |  |
|  | South African |  | 117,146 |  |
|  | Australasian |  | 150,890 |  |
|  | EMC–Currie discrepancy | 1,089,154 | 218,503 | 870,651 |
|  |  | WMC *Hdbk of Info.* 1956–61, p. 72 |  | Currie et al., p. 144 |
| 1955 guess | Methodist Church in Great Britain | 750,000 |  | 744,321 |
|  | Methodist Church in Ireland | 49,000 |  | 32,724 |
|  | Wesleyan Reform Union | 6,300 |  |  |
|  | Independent Methodist churches | 9,500 |  |  |
|  | WMC–Currie discrepancy | 814,800 | 37,755 | 777,045 |

In Table 6.1 it can be seen that the EMC figures are 180,000 to 210,000 more than those in Currie et al., which is strictly based on membership numbers given in the published annual *Minutes of Conference* of the respective Methodist branches. The EMC *Proceedings* for 1910 make it clear that the British figures amalgamate members with probationer members, as was done in the Wesleyan *Minutes of Conference*. Numbers of members on trial or probationer members are not provided by Currie et al. but the discrepancies in 1880 and 1910 seem too great for that to explain the gap. In 1955 those on trial (8,180) plus members of junior society classes (25,676) still leave a shortfall of nearly 4,000.

## Some Estimates of Global Growth of Methodist Membership, 1880–2006

Table 6.2 presents a number of official (published by Methodist Conferences) global statistics, together with those published in several of the United States Federal censuses of religious bodies (1906, 1916, 1926 and 1938). It is noticeable that there is still no perfect agreement between the Ecumenical Methodist Conference figures and those published by the British Wesleyan and Methodist Church Conferences.

Table 6.2   Official global Methodist statistics of members, 1880–2006

| Date of statistic | | Ecumenical Methodist Conference/ World Methodist Council | EMC/WMC | Methodist branches and Methodist Church, Minutes of Conference | United States Federal censuses of religious bodies |
|---|---|---|---|---|---|
| | No. | Location and date of Conference | Global members | Global members | USA only |
| 1880 | 1st | London, City Road Chapel, 1881 | 4,999,541 | | |
| 1890 | 2nd | Washington DC, Metropolitan Methodist Episcopal Church, 1891 | 6,503,959 | | |
| 1900 | 3rd | London, City Road Chapel, 1881 | 7,659,285 | 7,382,146 | |
| 1906 | | | | 7,870,730 | 5,749,838 |
| 1910 | 4th | Toronto, Metropolitan Methodist Church, 1911 | 8,768,616 | 8,885,052 | |
| 1916 | | | | | 7,166,471 |

| Date of statistic | | Ecumenical Methodist Conference/ World Methodist Council | EMC/WMC | Methodist branches and Methodist Church, Minutes of Conference | United States Federal censuses of religious bodies |
|---|---|---|---|---|---|
| 1920 | 5th | London, Central Hall, Westminster, 1921 | 10,153,821 | 10,138,861 | |
| 1926 | | | | | 8,070,619 |
| 1930 | 6th | Atlanta, GA, Wesley Memorial Church, 1931 | | 12,309,755 | |
| 1935 | | | | 11,747,663 | |
| 1936 | | | | | 7,001,631 |
| 1939 | | | | 11,652,837 | |
| 1947 | 7th | Springfield, MA | | | |
| 1950 | 8th | Oxford, England Wesley Memorial Church, 1951 | No statistic published | | |
| 1955 | | Lake Junaluska, NC, 1956 | 19,086,426 | | |
| 1960 | | Oslo, Norway, 1961 | | | |
| 1970 | | Denver, CO, 1971 | 20,091,829 | | |

| Date of statistic | Ecumenical Methodist Conference/ World Methodist Council | EMC/WMC | Methodist branches and Methodist Church, Minutes of Conference | United States Federal censuses of religious bodies |
|---|---|---|---|---|
| 1975 | Dublin, Ireland, 1976 | 20,772,825 | | |
| | Honolulu, Hawaii, 1981 | | | |
| | Nairobi, Kenya, 1986 | | | |
| | Singapore, 1991 | | | |
| | Rio de Janeiro, Brazil, 1996 | | | |
| | Brighton, England, 2001 | | | |
| 2006 | Seoul, South Korea, 2006 | 42,828,400 | | |
| | Durban, South Africa, 2011 | | | |

*Sources*:

*Proceedings of the First Oecumenical Methodist Conference*, 1881;
*Proceedings of the Fourth Ecumenical Methodist Conference*, 1911;
*Proceedings of the Fifth Ecumenical Methodist Conference*, 1921;
Wesleyan Methodist Church, *Minutes of Conference*, 1930, 1939;
World Methodist Council, *Handbook of Information* for years
1956–61, 1971–76, 1976–81, 2007–11 (it is assumed that they were
compiled in each of the previous years);

US Census Bureau, *Historical Estimates of World Population*, http://www.census.gov/population/international/data/mapping/ (accessed 2 October 2012).
United States Department of Commerce, Bureau of the Census, *Religious Bodies: 1926* (2 vols, Washington, DC: United States Government Printing Office, 1929), II, 916–17; United States Department of Commerce, Bureau of the Census, *Religious Bodies: 1936: Selected Statistics* (Washington, DC: United States Government Printing Office, 1941), 18.

Global Methodist membership statistics compared with global population provide an approximate idea of relative spurts of growth between 1880 and 2006, as seen in Table 6.3.

Table 6.3 The global presence of Methodists, 1880–2006

|      | World population | Global Methodist members Number | Percentage of world population |
|------|------------------|---------------------------------|-------------------------------|
| 1880 | 1,260,000,000 *  | 4,999,541                       | 0.40                          |
| 1900 | 1,550,000,000    | 7,659,285                       | 0.49                          |
| 1910 | 1,750,000,000    | 8,768,616                       | 0.50                          |
| 1920 | 1,860,000,000    | 10,153,821                      | 0.55                          |
| 1930 | 2,070,000,000    | 12,309,755                      | 0.59                          |
| 1955 | 2,781,208,671    | 19,086,426**                    | 0.69                          |
| 1970 | 3,712,963,247    | 20,091,829                      | 0.54                          |
| 1975 | 4,090,414,797    | 20,772,825                      | 0.51                          |
| 2006 | 6,546,299,902    | 42,828,400                      | 0.65                          |

*Notes*:
\* *Ave*rage of 1850 and 1900 estimates of world populations.
\*\* This figure, as discussed in the text, is not based on one particular year.

*Sources*
*Proceedings of the First Oecumenical Methodist Conference*, 1881;
*Proceedings of the Fourth Ecumenical Methodist Conference*, 1911;
*Proceedings of the Fifth Ecumenical Methodist Conference*, 1921;
Wesleyan Methodist Church, *Minutes of Conference*, 1930, 1939;
World Methodist Council, *Handbook of Information* for years 1956–61, 1971–76, 1976–81, 2007–11 (it is assumed that they were *compi*led in each of the previous years);

US Census Bureau, *Historical Estimates of World Population*, http://www.census.gov/population/international/data/mapping/ (accessed t2 october 2012).

The table shows three features. In absolute figures, the global Methodist presence expanded eight-fold between 1880 and 2006. Secondly, Methodists never reached 1 per cent of the global population. Thirdly, there appear to be two peaks in Methodist shares of world population: one in the mid-1950s and one in the early twenty-first century.

The third of these conclusions rests on an imprecisely dated estimate of global Methodist membership in the 1950s (as seen above). In Table 6.3 it is assumed that the 1950s global Methodist membership figure pertained to 1955 and therefore a world population at that date has been used. The extreme alternative assumptions for a 1950s date, namely 1950 and 1960, were checked. This gave Methodist shares of world population of 0.75 per cent in 1950 and 0.63 per cent in 1960: still leaving the mid-century decade as a peak.

Table 6.4 attempts to examine growth rates, but unrelated to changing demographics. The first half of the twentieth century apparently had a lower growth rate than the last quarter of the century. However, these long-term trends must conceal bursts of expansion. These are evident in the right-hand part of Table 6.4.

Table 6.4    Average percentage and numerical growth rates in global Methodist membership for selected available periods, 1880–2006

| Period | Average growth rates per cent per annum | Period | Years | Period's numerical increase | Average annual numerical increase in each period |
|---|---|---|---|---|---|
| 1880–1910 (30 years, base 1880) | 2.5 | 1880–1900 | 20 | 2,659,744* | 132,987 |
|  |  | 1900–1910 | 10 | 1,109,331 | 110,933 |
| 1900–1955 (55 years, base 1900) | 2.7 | 1910–1955 | 45 | 10,317,810 | 229,285 |
| 1955–2006 (51 years, base 1955) | 2.4 | 1955–1970 | 15 | 1,005,403 | 67,027 |
|  |  | 1970–1975 | 5 | 680,996 | 136,199 |
| 1975–2006 (31 years, base 1975) | 3.4 | 1975–2006 | 31 | 22,055,575 | 711,470 |

*Note*: *1880 world population is the average of 1850 and 1900 estimates.
*Sources*: As for Table 6.3.

Again the table is marred by the lack of a reliable figure for global Methodist membership at a particular date in the 1950s. Assuming world populations for 1950 and for 1960 gives different results: a 3 per cent annual growth rate for 1900–1950 and a 2.2 growth rate for 1950–2006; as opposed to a 2.5 per cent annual growth rate for 1900–1960 and a 2.7 per cent growth rate for 1960–2006. Under all assumptions the late-twentieth-century expansion is unprecedented. Surprisingly, the late-nineteenth- century growth rate in absolute membership numbers (far right column), coincident with the height of European imperial domination and missionary enterprise, was but a fifth of the late-twentieth-century growth in global Methodism.

Table 6.5 indicates whereabouts global enlargement of Methodism has occurred. This time no attempt has been made to test for different dates of national populations. Instead, the population dates are given in their own column.

Table 6.5  National Methodist densities ranked by size, 1880–2006

|  | Methodist members | Country population | Density | Pop'n date | No. of Methodist branches |
| --- | --- | --- | --- | --- | --- |
| 1880 |  |  | % |  |  |
| USA | 3,875,030 | 50,156,000 | 7.73 | 1880 | 16 |
| Canada | 159,320 | 4,325,000 | 3.68 | 1881 | 3 |
| Australasia | 69,147 | 2,250,000 | 3.07 | 1881 | 1 |
| UK | 861,548 | 34,623,000 | 2.49 | 1881 | 6 |
|  |  |  |  |  |  |
| 1910 |  |  |  |  |  |
| USA | 7,057,323 | 91,972,000 | 7.67 | 1910 | 19 |
| Canada | 340,091 | 7,207,000 | 4.72 | 1911 | 1 |
| Australasia | 150,890 | 5,513,000 | 2.74 | 1911 | 1 |
| UK | 1,089,154 | 44,916,000 | 2.42 | 1910 | 6 |
| South Africa | 117,146 | 5,973,000 | 1.96 | 1911 | 1 |
|  |  |  |  |  |  |
| 1955 |  |  |  |  |  |
| USA | 13,611,336 | 179,323,000 | 7.59 | 1955 | 26 |
| Australia | 350,000 | 8,987,000 | 3.89 | 1954 | 1 |
| South Africa | 617,200 | 16,003,000 | 3.86 | 1960 | 4 |
| Chile | 137,000 | 7,374,000 | 1.86 | 1960 | 2 |
| UK | 814,800 | 50,947,000 | 1.60 | 1955 | 4 |

|  | Methodist members | Country population | Density | Pop'n date | No. of Methodist branches |
|---|---|---|---|---|---|
| Gold Coast/Ghana | 95,000 | 6,727,000 | 1.41 | 1960 | 2 |
| Jamaica | 17,550 | 1,487,000 | 1.18 | 1953 | 2 |
| Philippines | 155,060 | 27,088,000 | 0.57 | 1960 | 3 |
| Nigeria | 94,500 | 30,418,000 | 0.31 | 1952 | 3 |
| Belgian Congo | 39,800 | 14,140,000 | 0.28 | 1960 | 2 |
| South Korea | 60,000 | 24,989,000 | 0.24 | 1960 | 1 |
| Ceylon/Sri Lanka | 15,000 | 8,098,000 | 0.19 | 1953 | 1 |
| Brazil | 45,350 | 70,119,000 | 0.06 | 1960 | 2 |
|  |  |  |  |  |  |
| 2006 |  |  |  |  |  |
| Swaziland | 163,194 | 1,100,000 | 14.84 |  | 6 |
| South Africa | 3,269,215 | 47,300,000 | 6.91 |  | 9 |
| Sierra Leone | 302,082 | 5,700,000 | 5.30 |  | 5 |
| Chile | 825,760 | 16,400,000 | 5.04 |  | 7 |
| Liberia | 159,902 | 3,400,000 | 4.70 |  | 6 |
| USA | 13,894,621 | 299,100,000 | 4.65 |  | 20 |
| Gold Coast/Ghana | 913,712 | 22,600,000 | 4.04 |  | 6 |
| South Korea | 1,883,851 | 48,500,000 | 3.88 |  | 6 |
| Dominican Republic | 214,050 | 9,000,000 | 2.38 |  | 5 |
| Dem. Rep. of Congo | 1,401,742 | 62,700,000 | 2.24 |  | 8 |
| Nigeria | 2,565,674 | 134,500,000 | 1.91 |  | 9 |
| Zimbabwe | 248,628 | 13,100,000 | 1.90 |  | 10 |
| Benin | 136,382 | 8,700,000 | 1.57 |  | 6 |
| Jamaica | 31,473 | 2,700,000 | 1.17 |  | 7 |
| UK | 325,695 | 60,500,000 | 0.54 |  | 11 |
| Ceylon/Sri Lanka | 32,000 | 19,900,000 | 0.16 |  | 4 |
| Brazil | 234,749 | 186,800,000 | 0.13 |  | 4 |

*Notes*

1. The densities are crude because age structures of Methodist members and country populations differ.
2. Countries with small Methodist memberships have not been tested for density.
3. For the UK in 2006, Ireland has been included.
4. The figures for 2006 include memberships of the Church of the Nazarene
5. Australia, Canada, India, New Guinea Papua, the Philippines and Zambia are omitted because the largest Methodist churches in these countries united with other church bodies to form ecumenical mergers

*Sources*

Methodist membership figures, as for Table 6.3.

Population figures for 1955 are mostly from Brian R. Mitchell, *International Historical Statistics* (3 vols, Basingstoke: Palgrave Macmillan, 2003).

UK population figures from Brian R. Mitchell, *British Historical Statistics* (Cambridge: Cambridge University Press, 1988).

United States population figures from US Department of Commerce, Bureau of the Census, *Historical Statistics of the United States: Colonial Times to 1970* (2 vols, Washington, DC: US Government Printing Office, 1975), I, 8, ser. A6.

All the 2006 population statistics are from the Population Reference Bureau, 2006 World Population Data Sheet, http://www.prb.org/pdf06/06WorldDataSheet.pdf (accessed 2 October 2012)

Several trends appear in this table, though it must be emphasised that Methodist members were mostly over the age of fourteen while country populations were persons of all ages. First, the late nineteenth century saw rapid growth in North America. Before the First World War, the vast majority, four-fifths, of the globe's Methodists lived in the USA. Both in absolute numbers and as shares of the global total, American Methodist churches were expanding at a faster rate than those in Britain. By the measure of religious density in the population, British Methodist churches were in decline before 1914. North American and colonial Methodist membership changes before 1914 are partly explained by immigration and, in the case of South Africa, the redrawing of political boundaries. By the middle of the twentieth century, Methodist membership in Britain was still second in absolute size, behind the USA, but by the measure of religious density it had been overtaken by Australia, South Africa and Chile. At the beginning of the twenty-first century, with about 14 million members, the USA hosted the largest number of Methodists. They appeared in 20 varieties, determined by theology, ethnicity, location, liturgy and governance. However, by the religious density measure, the United States no longer had the greatest concentration of Methodists. Well ahead now were Swaziland, South Africa, Sierra Leone, Chile and Liberia. Not far behind were Ghana and South Korea.

All this demonstrates the well-known phenomenon of the remarkable expansion of Christianity during the second half of the twentieth century in the developing world, particularly Africa. Behind these seemingly tedious statistics lie a myriad of individual and collective faith stories. One task for church historians in these church growth countries will be to compare their churches' experiences with those of the developed West, where a much higher standard of living and secularism have challenged or eroded churchgoing and allegiance to the Christian faith.

Another implication of these statistics is suggested by the numbers of separate Methodist branches, shown in the far right column of Table 6.5. Was church growth in the late nineteenth century and in the late twentieth century signalled by proliferating connexions and, conversely, was church decline evident in denominational mergers, as Robert Currie[44] suggested? Managing the polar tendencies of evangelistic expansion and church consolidation, between charismatic and traditional churchmanship, has represented a significant challenge for the ecumenical movement since it emerged in the 1930s.

---

[44] Robert Currie, *Methodism Divided: A Study in the Sociology of Ecumenicalism* (London: Faber & Faber, 1968), 293–316.

# The Wesleys' Role in World Methodism

## Jason E. Vickers

Broadly conceived, the field of Wesley Studies goes all the way back to the early nineteenth century. Today many scholars regard most of the early works about John and Charles Wesley and about the rise and spread of Methodism in eighteenth century England as a mixture of history and hagiography.[1] This way of characterizing early Wesley Studies is understandable insofar as Methodist clergy were responsible for much of this work.[2] On the one hand, Methodist clergy were sincere in their desire to provide an accurate account of their own history. They took care to provide as much factual information as was readily available to them. On the other hand, they readily and unapologetically focused on and even embellished the most inspiring and theologically potent aspects of the story that they were attempting to tell. For example, they routinely played up things like the providential rescuing of John Wesley during his childhood from the Epworth Rectory fire; Wesley's doubting whether he really had faith in God in the face of a violent storm on the high seas during his missionary journey to Georgia; Wesley's heart-warming conversion experience on Aldersgate Street;and Wesley's calm assurance and peacefulness in his last days on earth. Written through and for the eyes of faith, these stories and others like them became familiar among Methodists, providing them with a deep sense that Methodism was a matter of special divine providence and that Wesley's spiritual pilgrimage was something of a blueprint for the Christian life. Thus not a few Methodists across the centuries, having internalized these stories, have undertaken similar journeys from the spiritual

---

[1] The distinction between history and hagiography often turns on modernist or positivist conceptions of historical inquiry and criticism.

[2] For more on the ecclesial orientation of early Wesley Studies, see J. Gregory, "Wesley's tercentenary and the state of Wesley Studies," *Bulletin of the John Rylands University Library of Manchester*, 85:2–3 (2003), 17–29.

darkness of doubt and uncertainty to the warm light of assurance and of grace and peace in the face of death.[3]

Whatever function these early works on the Wesleys and the rise of Methodism may have had in the religious lives of Methodists, historians in the mid twentieth century increasingly questioned the value of these works for historical inquiry and knowledge. By the 1960s, scholars were calling for and working to develop a more "critical" account of the life of John Wesley and the rise and spread of Methodism in eighteenth century England.[4] Today, Wesley Studies experts often trace the emergence of this more critical perspective to the publication of Albert C. Outler's *John Wesley* in Oxford University Press's Library of Protestant Thought in 1964. Less frequently noted but no less important is the fact that, in the 1960s, scholars outside Methodism began paying more attention to John Wesley and to the rise and spread of Methodism.[5] In the 1970s, Outler, and Frank Baker, took another crucial step in the advancement of critical Wesley Studies when they began publishing a scholarly edition of Wesley's works.[6] In the 1980s, Richard P. Heitzenrater's two-volume *The Elusive Mr. Wesley*, a work designed in part to identify the hagiographic and mythological elements in early lives of Wesley, also helped to solidify a critical consciousness in Wesley Studies.[7]

Most recently, four developments within critical Wesley Studies are especially worth noting. First, Wesley Studies has become a highly sophisticated domain of inquiry that exemplifies the highest critical standards in numerous scholarly disciplines, including intellectual, social, political and material history, as well as sociology, theology and even relatively new disciplines such as rhetorical criticism and cultural studies.[8] Secondly, in Henry Rack's *Reasonable Enthusiast*, there is now a first rate critical biography of John Wesley.[9] Thirdly, Charles Wesley has at

---

[3] In recent years, scholars have begun to focus on Wesley's role as a saint. For example, see W. J. Abraham, "The End of Wesleyan Theology," *Wesleyan Theological Journal*, 40:1 (2005), 7–25; P. S. Forsaith, *John Wesley — Religious Hero?: 'A Brand Plucked as from the Burning'* (Oxford: Applied Theology Press, 2004); and R. L. Maddox, "Celebrating Wesley — When?" *Methodist History*, 29 (1991), 63–75.

[4] For a recent survey of the history of Wesley Studies, see H. D. Rack, "Some Recent Trends in Wesley Scholarship," *Wesleyan Theological Journal*, 41:2 (2006), 182–99.

[5] On this front, see especially the work of the Oxford historian V. H. H. Green, most notably *The Young Mr. Wesley: A Study of John Wesley and Oxford* (London: Edward Arnold, 1963).

[6] As of 2011, seventeen of the projected thirty-five volumes have been published.

[7] See R. P. Heitzenrater, *The Elusive Mr. Wesley* (Nashville, TN: Abingdon Press, 1984).

[8] R. L. Maddox and J. E. Vickers (eds), *The Cambridge Companion to John Wesley* (Cambridge: Cambridge University Press, 2010) exemplifies the multi-disciplinary nature of Wesley Studies today. For an intriguing study of Wesley and early Methodism from the standpoint of rhetorical and cultural disciplines, see V. Tolar Burton, *Spiritual Literacy in John Wesley's Methodism: Reading, Writing, and Speaking to Believe* (Waco, TX: Baylor University Press, 2008).

[9] H. D. Rack, *Reasonable Enthusiast: John Wesley and the Rise of Methodism*, 3rd edition (Peterborough: Epworth Press, 2002). Also see R. P. Heitzenrater, *Wesley and the People Called*

long last begun to receive the attention from scholars that he deserves.[10] Fourthly, a growing number of scholars have begun to contextualize the critical study of the Wesleys and of early Methodism within the political and social framework of the so-called "long-eighteenth century" and within the wider parameters of trans-Atlantic revivalism.[11]

Despite the phenomenal work of the last fifty years, there remains a significant gap in the literature. Few, if any, scholarly works deal with the reception history of the Wesleys outside their native eighteenth century Anglican context. In other words, there is a lack of good critical studies of how the Wesleys have functioned and continue to function in world Methodism. For better or worse, scholars have been so preoccupied with the quest for the real historical Wesleys that they have failed to develop any sustained inquiry about the roles the Wesleys have played across the centuries in world Methodism.

A good test case for this claim is the scholarly literature on American Methodism.[12] The last twenty-five years constitute something of a golden age in the scholarly study of American Methodism.[13] Indeed, there is now a fast-growing scholarly literature on a wide range of topics, including the relationship between American Methodism and American culture, the involvement of American Methodists in American politics, American Methodists and race, American Methodists and gender, and the like.[14] And yet, with two very important exceptions, there is a

---

*Methodists* (Nashville, TN: Abingdon Press, 1995).

[10] As with the critical study of John Wesley, the critical study of Charles Wesley is presently being aided by the production of critical editions of his works. For example, see K. G. C. Newport, *The Sermons of Charles Wesley: A Critical Edition with Introduction and Notes* (Oxford: Oxford University Press, 2001); and ST Kimbrough and K. G. C. Newport (eds), *The Manuscript Journal of the Reverend Charles Wesley, M.A.* (Nashville, TN: Kingswood Books, 2008). Recent secondary works on Charles Wesley that are especially worth noting include G. Best, *Charles Wesley: A Biography* (Peterborough: Epworth Press, 2006); G. Lloyd, *Charles Wesley and the Struggle for Methodist Identity* (Oxford: Oxford University Press, 2007); and K. G. C. Newport and T. A. Campbell (eds), *Charles Wesley: Life, Literature and Legacy* (Peterborough: Epworth Press, 2007).

[11] For example, see J. C. D. Clark, "The Eighteenth Century Context," in W. J. Abraham and J. E. Kirby (eds), *The Oxford Handbook of Methodist Studies* (Oxford: Oxford University Press, 2009), 3–29; J. Gregory, "The Long Eighteenth Century," in *The Cambridge Companion to John Wesley*, 13–42; D. Hempton, "Wesley in Context," in *The Cambridge Companion to John Wesley*, 60–77; and J. E. Vickers, *Wesley: A Guide for the Perplexed* (London: T&T Clark, 2009).

[12] If Methodism is understood first and foremost as a renewal movement within the Church of England in the eighteenth century, then American Methodism is by definition a part of global or world Methodism.

[13] For two of the most important works in this area, see N. O. Hatch, *The Democratization of American Christianity* (New Haven, CT: Yale University Press, 1989); and R. Richey, *Early American Methodism* (Bloomington, IN: Indiana University Press, 1991).

[14] For recent works on these and other topics, see D. Andrews, *The Methodists and Revolutionary America: The Shaping of an Evangelical Culture* (Princeton, NJ: Princeton University Press, 2000); M. L. Davis, *The Methodist Unification: Christianity and the Politics of Race in the Jim Crow Era* (New York, NY: New York University Press, 2008); N. O. Hatch and J.

lack of serious scholarly studies of the ways in which the Wesleys have functioned across the centuries in American Methodism.[15]

Turning from American Methodism to other global areas, the problem is even greater, owing mainly to the fact that the scholarly study of Methodism in other world areas is just now getting underway. One reason for this is that scholars of American Methodism have concentrated most of their attention on the early period, which is to say, from the founding of American Methodism in the late eighteenth century to the end of the Civil War. As a result, the energy in the scholarly study of American Methodism has, until very recently, dropped off at precisely the time when the global transmission of Methodism via American Methodist missions really begins to accelerate.[16]

Fortunately, there is now a nascent but fast-growing body of scholarship that is pushing the scholarly study of Methodism beyond the boundaries of eighteenth century England and early America.[17] Generally speaking, this body of scholarship

---

H. Wigger (eds), *Methodism and the Shaping of American Culture*, (Nashville, TN: Kingswood Books, 2001); Peter Murray, *Methodists and the Crucible of Race, 1930–1975* (Columbia, MO: University of Missouri Press, 2004); B. Barton Schweiger, *The Gospel Working Up: Progress and the Pulpit in Nineteenth Century Virginia* (New York, NY: Oxford University Press, 2000); and D. Strong, *Perfectionist Politics: Abolitionism and the Religious Tensions of American Democracy* (Syracuse, NY: Syracuse University Press, 1999). Also see J. E. Vickers (ed.), *The Cambridge Companion to American Methodism*(forthcoming from Cambridge University Press).

[15] See D. C. Dickerson, "Liberation, Wesleyan Theology and Early African Methodism, 1766–1840," *Wesley and Methodist Studies*, 3 (2011), 109–20; and R. L. Maddox, "Respected Founder/Neglected Guide: The Role of Wesley in American Methodist Theology," *Methodist History*, 37 (1999), 71–88. As the title suggests, Maddox's concern has strictly to do with John Wesley's role in American Methodist theology.

[16] An exception that must be noted here is the four volume History of Methodist Missions series commissioned by the Methodist Church's Board of Mission in 1949. The volumes are as follows: W. Crawford Barclay, *Early American Methodism, 1769–1844: Missionary Motivation and Expansion* (New York, NY: The Board of Missions and Church Extension of the Methodist Church, 1949); W. Crawford Barclay, *Early American Methodism, 1769–1844: To Reform the Nation* (New York, NY, BMCE-MC, 1950); W. Crawford Barclay, *The Methodist Episcopal Church, 1845–1939: Widening Horizons, 1845–95* (New York, NY: Board of Missions of the Methodist Church, 1957); and J. Tremayne Copplestone, *Twentieth- Century Perspectives: The Methodist Episcopal Church, 1896–1939* (New York, NY: Board of Global Ministries, 1973).

[17] It should be noted, however, that virtually all of this literature is shot through with lament over the sorry state of the resources and research related to world Methodism and with repeated calls for more work to be done. For example, with respect to the state of research on Wesleyanism in Africa, Robert Kipkemoi Lang'at concludes his otherwise very helpful essay this way: "More work needs to be done using all the possible research apparatus to ascertain the historical, theological, as well as contextual underpinnings of the experience of sanctification in Africa." See R. Kipkemoi Lang'at, "The Impact of Wesleyanism on Africa: Toward an Understanding of Divine Grace in a Changing Continent," in Charles Yrigoyen, Jr. (ed.), *The Global Impact of the Wesleyan Traditions and Their Related Movements* (Lanham, MD: Scarecrow Press, 2002), 101.

subdivides into four types of works, though there is some overlap among the four types. First, there are works that provide an overview of world Methodism. These works tend to focus on statistical data, including the number of Methodist churches, members and clergy in various world areas. They also provide minimal historical data related to the beginning of Methodism in various world areas, including the names of the earliest missionaries and indigenous leaders.[18] Secondly, there is a small but growing literature on Methodism in particular countries or particular parts of the world.[19] Thirdly, there is also a small but growing number of scholarly works devoted to Methodist missions, among which the seven volume United Methodist History of Mission series sponsored by the United Methodist General Board of Global Ministries is especially worth mentioning.[20] Finally, there are recent works by Methodist theologians who are seeking to articulate a Wesleyan theological vision *on behalf of* the Methodist movement or churches in the areas or countries that they represent.[21]

These works notwithstanding, the scholarly study of world Methodism is still very much in its infancy. If the scholarly study of world Methodism is to reach its full potential, then it will require a massive, multi-generational research program. Even now, it is easy to envision dozens of Ph.D. dissertation topics that will help to fill out this project. For example, there is a need for a careful study of how Methodist missionaries explained Methodism and thereby sought to inculcate Methodist identity around the world. Moving in the other direction, there is a need for a close examination of how indigenous peoples came to understand and to interpret Methodism for themselves, and how their understandings and interpretations of Methodism have changed across several generations.

---

[18] See K. Cracknell and S. White, *An Introduction to World Methodism* (Cambridge: Cambridge University Press, 2005). Also see K. Cracknell, "Spread of Wesleyan Methodism," *The Cambridge Companion to John Wesley*, 245–61.

[19] See the relevant chapters in the recently published *T&T Clark Companion to Methodism* (London: T&T Clark, 2010) and Abraham and Kirby (eds), *The Oxford Handbook of Methodist Studies*.

[20] See R. A. Daugherty, *The Missionary Spirit: The History of Mission of the Methodist Protestant Church, 1830–1939* (New York, NY: GBGM Books, 2004); R. W. Sledge, *Five Dollars and Myself: The History of Mission of the Methodist Episcopal Church, South, 1845–1939* (New York, NY: GBGM Books, 2005); L. Gesling, *Mirror and Beacon: The History of Mission of the Methodist Church, 1939–1968* (New York, NY: GBGM Books, 2005); J. S. O'Malley, *On the Journey Home: The History of Mission of the Evangelical United Brethren Church, 1946–1968* (New York, NY: GBGM Books, 2003); R. J. Harman, *From Missions to Mission: The History of Mission of the United Methodist Church, 1968–2000* (New York, NY: GBGM Books, 2005); and C. E. Cole, ed., *Initiatives for Mission, 1980–2002* (New York: GBGM Books, 2003); C. E. Cole (ed.), *Christian Mission in the Third Millennium* (New York, NY: GBGM Books, 2004).

[21] One of the first volumes to do this was Yrigoyen, Jr(ed.), *The Global Impact of the Wesleyan Traditions and Their Related Movements*Another good example of this type of literature is A. Sung Park, "Holiness and Healing: An Asian American Voice Shaping the Methodist Tradition," in J. Vincent and J. Rieger (eds), *Methodist and Radical: Rejuvenating a Tradition* (Nashville, TN: Kingswood Books, 2004), 95–106.

Given the present state of the literature, it is not surprising that few, if any, scholars have given sustained attention to the Wesleys' roles in world Methodism. As with the wider research program, it is easy to envision not one, but numerous Ph.D. dissertations related to this topic. For example, one of the first orders of business has to do with the translation, production and distribution patterns of primary and secondary sources. On this front, there is a need for a thorough study of which of John and Charles Wesley's works have been translated and of how many different languages they have been translated into.[22] Moreover, someone needs to provide an account of distribution patterns. For instance, someone needs to undertake a study of where Spanish translations of the Wesleys' works have been distributed. Similarly, someone needs to provide an account of when translation and distribution began in various parts of the world, as well as where translation and distribution is ongoing today. The same holds for secondary works on the Wesleys and/or Wesleyan theology.[23] Finally, there is a need for a study of where translation work is being done and by whom. Along these lines, it would be particularly helpful to know how much unofficial or unauthorized translation work happens in various parts of the world, especially as this pertains to Wesley hymns, over against, say, how much official translation work takes place in denominational publishing houses in the United States of America.

More projects of this type are easy to imagine, but at this stage I want to interrupt my comments about future projects that need to be undertaken in order to provide a *preliminary* account of the Wesleys' role(s) in world Methodism. In doing so, I must begin with a candid confession. The account that I will give is under-determined by the evidence. The account is not altogether lacking evidence, but it does need to be confirmed or disconfirmed by more extensive global field research. In other words, what follows is my scholarly hunch about what, upon closer examination, scholars who undertake a study of the Wesleys' role in world Methodism are likely to find.

Here is my thesis. Historically speaking, the majority of the global transmission of Methodism took place within two horizons simultaneously. On the one hand, the global transmission of Methodism took place within the horizon of the modern missionary movement. On the other hand, it occurred within the horizon of trans-

---

[22] For instance, in 1998, Jose Miguez Bonino reported that "only the fifty-two 'standard' sermons and a few scattered writings [of John Wesley] have been translated into Spanish." See J. Miguez Bonino, "Wesley in Latin America: A Theological and Historical Reflection," in R. Maddox (ed.), *Rethinking Wesley's Theology for Contemporary Methodism* (Nashville, TN: Kingswood Books, 1998), 172. Just four years later, the situation changed dramatically with the decision to publish a fourteen volume edition of Wesley's works in Spanish. For more on this, see L. E. Wethington, "The Impact of *Orbas de Wesley* in the Hispanic World," in Yrigoyen (ed.), *The Global Impact of the Wesleyan Traditions*, 275–84.

[23] R. P. Heitzenrater's *Wesley and the People Called Methodists* (Nashville, TN: Abingdon Press, 1995), Michael Lodahl's *The Story of God* (Kansas City, MO: Beacon Hill Press, 2008) and T. Runyon's *The New Creation* (Nashville, TN: Abingdon Press, 1998) have all been translated into numerous languages, including Spanish, Portuguese, German and Russian, to name just a few.

Atlantic revivalism, the second Great Awakening, and the holiness and Pentecostal movements. Thus, insofar as the Wesleys have been influential in world Methodism, their influence has been *mediated* by the complex cultures of these two horizons.[24]

What does this entail? Let me now put the point sharply. To the extent that Methodist missionaries introduced the Wesleys in various world areas (here is another research project that needs to be undertaken), the Wesleys that they are most likely to have introduced are precisely the Wesleys that Wesley scholars in the latter third of the twentieth century have worked diligently to deconstruct, namely the Wesleys of the early hagiographic period in Wesley Studies. In other words, the stories about the Wesleys that Methodist missionaries are most likely to have known and passed along are precisely the stories that were most beloved (and often embellished) by early Methodist clergy-scholars. The simple fact is that the majority of the global transmission of Methodism occurred prior to the rise of critical Wesley Studies detailed above. Consequently, the hagiographic Wesleys were the only Wesleys that the vast majority of Methodist missionaries would have known.

For historians whose work revolves around discovering the real historical Wesleys, this may be a lamentable situation. Indeed, it may even serve as a deterrent to the ongoing research that is so desperately needed. Why would anyone want to study the global dissemination of the hagiographic Wesleys in lieu of joining the quest for the *real* historical Wesleys? Or, to put it another way, why should scholars spend time studying the Wesleys of faith when they can continue to unearth the Wesleys of history?

While the temptation to limit critical Wesley Studies to the study of the Wesleys in eighteenth century England is a strong one, my own sense is that there may be

---

[24] This is precisely Jose Miguez Bonino's judgment with respect to the transmission of Methodism in Latin America. According to Bonino, all that Latin America received with respect to Wesley and Methodism "was *filtered through the American* [i.e., North American] *experience*. More precisely, the Methodism introduced into Latin America was that shaped by the North American 'second great awakening' and holiness movement." "Wesley in Latin America," 172. For more on the mediation of Methodism in Latin America, see Bonino's "Catholic and Protestant, but Missionary," in Yrigoyen (ed.), *The Global Impact of the Wesleyan Traditions*, 69–79. Michel Weyer makes a similar point about the transmission of Methodism in Germany. See M. Weyer, "The Impact of Wesleyanism on Continental Europe: The Case of the Germans," in Yrigoyen (ed.), *The Global Impact of the Wesleyan Traditions*, 231–43. Robert Kipkemoi Lang'at insists that, in Africa, Methodism was introduced within the horizons of the holiness and missionary movements, which is to say, within a form of "Pietistic Christianity." See R. Kipkemoi Lang'at, "The Doctrine of Holiness and Missions: A Pietistic Foundation of African Evangelical Christianity," in Yrigoyen (ed.), *The Global Impact of the Wesleyan Traditions*, 91–104. John Cho describes the Wesleys' impact in Korea in ways that suggest mediation by the cultures of these two horizons. See Chongnahm (John) Cho, "The Impact of John Wesley's Ministry and Theology on the Korean Church: A Model for Church Renewal," in Yrigoyen (ed.), *The Global Impact of the Wesleyan Traditions*, 157–70. For a similar argument with respect to the spread of Methodism in Japan, see Kiyoshi Nathanael Kunishige, "Alternate Wesleyan Influence: The Impact of 18th Century British Methodism and 19th Century American Revivalism on a Japanese Indigineous Holiness Church," in Yrigoyen (ed.), *The Global Impact of the Wesleyan Traditions*, 143–56.

another kind of history waiting to be written here. The quest for the real historical Wesleys—the quest that has been the primary concern of critical Wesley Studies for the last fifty years—has focused scholars' attention almost exclusively on Methodism in eighteenth century England. As a result, there is now an abundance of scholarship related to the Wesleys in their eighteenth century context, but there is not nearly enough about the Wesleys' careers in world Methodism, which is to say, about their careers in the history of Methodist missions. Scholars have spent an enormous amount of time and energy showing how twice told tales have obscured the past. They have not spent nearly enough time inquiring after how those tales might have been instrumental in opening a future.[25]

In the event that scholars begin seriously to explore the role of the Wesleys in world Methodism, my own hunch is that they will discover that the Wesleys have functioned (and in many quarters continue to function) primarily not as great theologians but as saints of the church. Scholars will find that, when Methodist missionaries spoke of the Wesleys, they held them up as exemplars of the Christian life and of Christian living. More specifically, if they recall that, in the global transmission of Methodism, the lives of the Wesleys have been mediated by the complex cultures of the modern missionary movement, revivalism and the holiness and Pentecostal movements, then they should not be surprised to discover that Methodist missionaries held up the Wesleys as exemplars of evangelistic and missionary zeal—as tireless in their efforts to spread the Gospel. Similarly, scholars should not be surprised if they discover that Methodist missionaries promoted the Wesleys as masters of organization for the sake of mission.[26] And they should not be surprised to learn that Methodist missionaries held up the Wesleys as exemplars of a particular pattern of the Christian life—a pattern that progresses from sincere repentance to the new birth, assurance, the sanctifying work of the Holy Spirit, a longing for holiness and ultimately to Christian perfection.[27] Last, but certainly not least, they should not be surprised if the story about John being rescued from the Epworth Rectory fire turns out to be a favorite in some quarters, conveying as it does a robust sense of special divine providence that can be readily extended to the Methodist movement today.[28]

---

[25] Dana Robert, an expert on Methodist missions at Boston University, shares this judgment. In a personal telephone conversation, she suggested that this is precisely the direction that Wesley Studies needs to go.

[26] D. K. Yemba clearly sees organization/connectionalism as one of the main ways that the Wesleys influenced the transmission of Methodism in Africa. See his "The Impact of Wesleyanism on Africa: Toward an Understanding of Divine Grace in a Changing Continent," in Yrigoyen (ed.), *The Global Impact of the Wesleyan Traditions*, 81–90.

[27] Bonino suggests that the Wesleys functioned this way in Latin America. Yemba and Lang'at suggest the same for Africa.

[28] My own sense is that one of the crucial differences between British and American Methodism on the one hand and world Methodism on the other is precisely that adherents of the former forms of Methodism are less certain than adherents of the latter that they are the object of special divine providence.

The point that I want to make here is that, while there is a sense in which twice told tales make for bad history, there is also a sense in which they can help *to make* history by shaping religious identities. Thus I suspect that the Wesleys' role in world Methodism both historically and presently has above all to do with the ways in which twice-told tales about their lives have helped to shape an understanding of the Christian life and Christian living—an understanding in which three things are paradigmatic, namely conversion, evangelistic and missionary zeal, and a life of humble and joyful obedience before God. Indeed, if I am right, then the twice-told tales about the lives of the Wesleys may actually help to account for the rapid spread of Methodism in many world areas. Within the complex cultures of the modern missionary movement, revivalism and the holiness and Pentecostal movements, the Wesleys have functioned and in many quarters continue to function primarily as exemplars of a form of Christian piety that demands replication.

At this stage, a word of clarification is in order. I am not suggesting that scholars should cease to think critically when they are working on the Wesleys' role in world Methodism. On the contrary, when future scholars undertake to examine the Wesleys' role in world Methodism, they will have to be on guard against a very different set of twice told tales, most notably twice told tales having to do with empire and eschatology. Given the prevalence of empire in recent discussions of the global transmission of Christianity and of eschatology in recent discussions of revivalism and the holiness and Pentecostal movements, I should take a moment to say a little more about this.[29]

Twice told tales about empire and eschatology invariably surface in scholarly discussions of the modern missionary movement, revivalism, and of the holiness and Pentecostal movements. For example, because the modern missionary movement occurred more or less simultaneously with the spread of European (and later American) political and economic hegemony, scholars have often assumed that missionaries were, at the very least, unwitting agents of imperialism and empire, spreading political and economic doctrines alongside the Gospel. Yet recent studies have begun to question this assumption, inquiring about whether missionaries were entirely lacking in self-critical awareness with respect to the political and economic aspirations of the empires to which they belonged and which they therefore represented.[30] Along these lines, there is a growing need to investigate whether

---

[29] For recent works on empire and the global transmission of Christianity, see Wes Avram (ed.), *Anxious About Empire: Theological Essays on the New Global Realities* (Grand Rapids, MI: Brazos Press, 2004); L. Gregorson and S. Juster (eds), *Empires of God: Religious Encounters in the Early Modern Atlantic* (Philadelphia, PA: University of Pennsylvania Press, 2010); and C. Pestana, *Protestant Empire: Religion and the Making of the British Atlantic World* (Philadelphia, PA: University of Pennsylvania Press, 2010). For a recent work that examines the role of eschatology in the holiness and Pentecostal movements, see R. Stephens, *The Fire Spreads: Holiness and Pentecostalism in the American South* (Cambridge, MA: Harvard University Press, 2010).

[30] David Yemba calls attention to this old scholarly saw in "The Impact of Wesleyanism on Africa," 88–90. For a work that calls the standard assumptions about the relationship between the modern missionary movement and colonial expansion into question, see N.

the vision of the Christian life and of Christian living that Methodist missionaries transmitted globally might actually have contained within it crucial resources for resisting the trappings of empires and whether Methodist missionaries recognized these resources and appropriated them in self-critical ways.[31]

With respect to revivalism and the holiness and Pentecostal movements, there is a need for a fresh critical examination of twice told tales about eschatology. Fortunately, this work is already underway, as scholars are rediscovering the intense political and social activism of people who were neck deep in revivalism, awakening, and the holiness and Pentecostal movements.[32] For example, people who embraced pre-millennialism also advocated for prohibition, and they did so for political and social reasons. In other words, there are good reasons to question whether pre-millennialism actually led to a form of Christianity in which the expectation of the imminent return of Christ left Christians tone-deaf to social concerns.

In conclusion, I want to call attention to some anecdotal evidence for my thesis about the Wesleys' role in world Methodism both historically and presently. For many years now, Methodists in Singapore have held an annual Aldersgate Convention and Hymn Festival.[33] The name of the convention is, of course, a reference to John Wesley's heart-warming conversion experience which took place on Aldersgate Street, on May 24, 1738. As I have already noted, stories about Wesley's Aldersgate experience were among the most beloved (and most heavily embellished) in early lives of Wesley, and they were therefore among the most likely to be known and shared by Methodist missionaries. The important thing to notice here is the prevalence of Aldersgate-themed conferences and celebrations in world Methodism today. Indeed, Aldersgate conferences and celebrations occur in a wide variety of places around the globe, including South Africa, Brazil, Costa Rica and Korea, to name just a few.[34] Also telling is the fact that conference

---

Etherington (ed.), *Missions and Empire* (Oxford: Oxford University Press, 2008). Also see A. Porter, *Religion versus Empire? British Protestant Missionaries and Overseas Expansion, 1700–1914* (Manchester: Manchester University Press, 2004).

[31] Methodist theologian Joerg Rieger, who is deeply invested in current discussions around empire, acknowledges this point. For example, in his *Christ and Empire: From Paul to Postcolonial Times* (Minneapolis, MN: Fortress Press, 2007), Rieger is mostly concerned to discuss the ways in which the early councils and creedal statements became instruments of empire. Yet he also acknowledges that there are ways in which Nicea and Chalcedon can also be instruments for resisting empire.

[32] The standard works here are T. Smith, *Revivalism and Social Reform* (Eugene, OR: Wipf & Stock, 2004) and D. Dayton, *Discovering an Evangelical Heritage* (New York, NY: Hendrickson Publishers, 1988). For more recent works, see especially B. L. Hartley, *Evangelicals at a Crossroads: Revivalism and Social Reform in Boston, 1860–1910* (Durham, NH: University of New Hampshire Press, 2011) and W. Kotslevy, *Holy Jumpers: Evangelicals and Radicals in Progressive Era America* (Oxford: Oxford University Press, 2010).

[33] For more on this, see http://www.methodist.org.sg/index.php, the official website of The Methodist Church in Singapore (accessed March 17, 2011).

[34] For more on this, see R. Maddox, "Aldersgate: A Tradition History," in Maddox (ed.), *Aldersgate Reconsidered* (Nashville, TN: Kingswood Books, 1990), 133–46.

organizers routinely pick themes that reflect the cultures of the modern missionary movement, revivalism, and the holiness and Pentecostal movements. For example, for its 2011 Aldersgate Convention and Hymn Festival theme, the Methodist Church in Singapore selected "Go & Tell: Proclaiming the Gospel Today." Moreover, the conference itself revolves around a "key event" known as the "Evangelistic Rally."

All of this raises a series of questions about what role the Wesleys *should* play in world Methodism today. Should scholars and church leaders work to introduce Methodists around the world to the real historical Wesleys unearthed by critical Wesley Studies? Should Methodists around the world be disabused of the notion that the Wesleys are exemplars of Christian faith and Christian living in favor of a more critical account that depicts the Wesleys as failed missionaries, priests and lovers? Should scholars work to divest world Methodism of twice-told tales about the Wesleys and of the trappings of empire that purportedly accompany those tales? Should they seek to remove the Pietistic, revivalistic and holiness–Pentecostal overlay, as so many layers of dross that presently cover up the real historical Wesleys?

Rather than answering these questions directly, I want to issue a warning and make a suggestion. First, the warning: Before scholars point out the speck in the eyes of Methodists in other parts of the world, they should take a moment to check for a plank in their own. For example, before they point out the purported trappings of empire latent in the version of Methodism and of the lives of the Wesleys that have been globally transmitted over the last two hundred years, they should take a moment to ask whether there might be trappings of empire latent in the more critical accounts of Methodism and of the lives of the Wesleys that have emerged in England and America over the last fifty years. From a *theological* point of view, many critical accounts of Methodism and of the lives of the Wesleys reflect a crucial aspect of empire in the late modern West insofar as they are refracted through the lenses of radical skepticism, secularism and a thoroughgoing naturalism. Thus many "critical" accounts of Wesley and of Methodism reduce both phenomena to sociological and psychological categories, studiously avoiding explanatory reference to direct divine action. Before chastening others for embracing and celebrating a vision of the Wesleys and of Methodism that obscures the truth about the past by reading the past through theological lenses, scholars should ask themselves what sort of future their more critical visions of the Wesleys and of Methodism is likely to open. Shorn of the robust conviction that the Wesleys and Methodism were the objects of special divine providence and action, one can only wonder what Methodists around the world will sing about at their Aldersgate conventions and hymn festivals.

Secondly, a suggestion: if scholars are to understand the Wesleys' role in world Methodism, then they may have to set aside, at least temporarily, their worries about differences between the Wesleys of history and the Wesleys of faith. In many quarters of world Methodism, scholars must recognize and accept that the Wesleys of faith are no less historical than the Wesleys of history insofar as the Wesleys of faith made a real difference in how Methodist identity was constructed and understood. Along these lines, scholars need to think anew and afresh about whether they really can establish a neat boundary between the missions of history and the missions of faith. I am not suggesting that the pursuit of the Wesleys of faith should put an end to the scholarly pursuit of the Wesleys of history. On the contrary, scholars must have the Wesleys of history if they are to see clearly the Wesleys of faith. Rather, my suggestion is that scholars need also to think about the Wesleys of history from the standpoint of the Wesleys of faith, which is to say, from the standpoint of the *ongoing* global transmission of Methodism. In other words, the time has come to inquire after what contributions critical Wesley Studies might now make to the future of global Methodism beyond simply getting the story straight about what happened in the past. Having done their historical spade work, scholars must press forward, asking questions about how the past that they have labored to unearth might inspire and sustain Methodists around the world today. If they have not asked and answered these questions, then they should think twice before setting out to disabuse Methodists around the world of the Wesleys that they have come to know and to love, and yes, even to celebrate.

For what it is worth, I believe that scholars can ask and answer these questions. For example, I believe that a critical account of Wesley's conversion experience at Aldersgate can provide spiritual nourishment for those who, following a conversion experience, find themselves once again doubting whether or not it is well with their souls.[35] I believe this is possible because the spiritual wasteland that was modernity is finally beginning to fade. And in the wake of this fading, a certain freedom is at long last beginning to emerge. The freedom that I have in mind is a freedom that presents scholars with a rare opportunity to rethink the very work that they do. There may even be an opportunity to invent new scholarly genres—scholarly genres that transgress old boundaries and thereby provide fresh angles of vision from which to see and to think about both the Wesleys and world Methodism. Indeed, for those with eyes to see, strange-sounding things like Methodist Dogmatics and critical hagiography are already on the horizon.[36] In the meantime, serious and sustained study of the Wesleys' role in world Methodism may serve to awaken scholars still beholden to modernity from their Kantian slumbers.

---

[35] Traditional accounts often claim that, following his conversion at Aldersgate, John Wesley never again had any doubts about whether he was a true Christian, a Child of God, born again, saved, and so on. Critical accounts have provided evidence from Wesley's own journals and diaries that Wesley did have lingering doubts *after* Aldersgate. Indeed, this is the point of what is, in my judgment, one of the most important essays in Wesley Studies from the last fifty years, namely, R. P. Heitzenrater's "Great Expectations: Aldersgate and the Evidences of Genuine Christianity," in *Mirror and Memory: Reflections on Early Methodism* (Nashville, TN: Kingswood Books, 1989), 106–49.

[36] I have personally taken preliminary steps toward the invention of Methodist Dogmatics. We already have a wonderful example of critical hagiography in J. Wigger's *American Saint: Francis Asbury and the Methodists* (Oxford: Oxford University Press, 2009).

# Methodism, Ecumenism and Interfaith Relations

David M. Chapman

This chapter investigates the theological state of Methodism's ecumenical and interfaith relations before outlining suggested areas for further research. Since inter-Christian and interfaith relations are of a different order theologically, they are treated separately.

## Inter-Christian Relations

### Missiological and Ecclesiological Foundations of Ecumenism

The ecumenical ideals of Methodism were succinctly stated as long ago as 1820 when the Wesleyan Methodist Conference of Great Britain declared:

> Let us [...] maintain towards all denominations of Christians, who 'hold the Head', the kind and catholic spirit of primitive Methodism; and, according to the noble maxim of our Fathers in the Gospel, 'be the friends of all, the enemies of none'.[1]

Although they have not always lived up to this noble aspiration, Methodists still consider ecumenical friendship to be an integral feature of their denominational identity.

The origin of Methodism's openness to other ecclesial communities lies in John Wesley's evangelical Arminianism, which led him to recognise in them the presence of authentic Christian faith and holy living, irrespective of denominational

---

[1] 'Liverpool Minutes' (1820); Rupert Davies, A. Raymond George and Gordon Rupp (eds), *A History of the Methodist Church in Great Britain* (4 vols, London: Epworth Press, 1965–1988), vol. 4, 369.

allegiance. His *Letter to a Roman Catholic* (1745), penned in the wake of rioting between Catholics and Methodists in Dublin, famously pleads for mutual forbearance on the basis of shared Christian faith.

Wesley addressed this same theme in his sermon on 'catholic spirit'. According to Wesley, those possessed of 'catholic spirit' adhere to the 'essentials' of Christian faith while tolerating diverse theological 'opinions'. They:

> [love] as friends, as brethren in the Lord, as members of Christ and children of God, as joint partakers now of the present kingdom of God, and fellow-heirs of his eternal Kingdom, all of whatever opinion or worship or congregation who believe in the Lord Jesus Christ; who love God and man; who, rejoicing to please and fearing to offend God, are careful to abstain from evil and zealous of good works.[2]

For Methodists, then, 'catholic spirit' entails ecumenical friendship towards all who manifest the 'essentials' of Christian faith.

Early Methodist interest in what would now be termed ecumenism was directed towards internal reunification in the wake of the schisms that fractured the movement in the half-century following the death of John Wesley in 1791. Methodism in Britain split over issues concerning the authority of the Wesleyan Conference and the status of the itinerant preachers. In the United States issues relating to race and slavery caused deep and lasting divisions. Following a series of mergers, British Methodism was finally reunited in 1932, and in the United States reunions took place in 1939 and 1968 to form the present United Methodist Church (UMC).

Given the fissiparous tendencies of Methodism in the nineteenth century, the redirection of energy towards internal reunification in the twentieth requires a more satisfactory explanation than the tendentious accounts hitherto supplied by denominational historians. Revisionist history of the reunification of Methodism must take into account two significant trends: one theological; the other practical. In the latter part of the nineteenth century, Methodist theologians, led by Benjamin Gregory, began to reflect on the catholicity of Methodism and thus to reaffirm its 'connexionalism'.[3] Also, as the spiritual ardour of Methodism cooled and the expansionist era gave way to contraction, denominational leaders came to regard reunification as the most promising means of stimulating a new phase of expansion – an outcome achieved only on paper as institutional mergers disguised long-term decline. Of course, Methodists were not alone in finding it increasingly difficult to sustain the momentum of Christian mission in the face of resistance and unrealistic expectations. By the beginning of the twentieth century, widespread concern about the future prospects for 'overseas missions' inspired Protestants of all shades to seek the reunification of the Church.

---

[2] Albert Outler (ed.), *The Works of John Wesley* (Nashville, TN: Abingdon, 1984), vol. 2, 94.
[3] Benjamin Gregory, *The Holy Catholic Church: The Communion of Saints* (London: Wesleyan Conference, 1873).

The Edinburgh World Missionary Conference of 1910, convened as a working forum for Western practitioners 'To Consider Missionary Problems in relation to the Non-Christian World', provided the catalyst for the modern ecumenical movement. The conference chairman was John R. Mott, an American Methodist layman and leading evangelical entrepreneur of broad sympathies. To like-minded Christians, Mott's slogan for the conference, initially devised for his Student Volunteer Movement for Foreign Missions, still seemed a realistic prospect in 1910: 'The Evangelisation of the World in this Generation.' However, Protestants increasingly recognised that achieving this ambitious goal would require the divided churches to settle their differences in the interest of more effective Christian mission.

If Methodists have generally proved receptive to missiological arguments in favour of ecumenism, it is because, in tension with their denominational status, they tend also to think of themselves as constituting a disciplined movement at the service of Christian mission, interpreted as the proclamation of the evangelical faith and the spread of scriptural holiness. An ecumenical method that seeks to develop unity-in-mission, as distinct from an ecumenism of return to an historic ecclesial institution, reflects Methodism's missiological priorities.

While the missionary horizons of Christianity in the West have shifted decisively from 'the non-Christian World' to the more immediate challenges of secularisation and the collapse of Christendom as a viable theological concept, Methodists continue to justify ecumenism principally on missiological, rather than on ecclesiological, grounds. As in many other aspects of Methodism, however, ecumenical method is based on theological suppositions that have yet to be systematised or even fully stated.

The theological suppositions underlying Methodism's ecumenical method derive from a unique blend of Lutheran, Anglican and Puritan ecclesiology. In the Methodist tradition:

> The Church is a community of all true believers under the Lordship of Christ. It is the redeemed and redeeming fellowship in which the Word of God is preached by persons divinely called, and the Sacraments are duly administered according to Christ's own appointment.[4]

This minimalist doctrine of the Church as a 'redeemed and redeeming fellowship' is ontological and teleological: the Church is *for* mission. It assumes no specific ecclesial structures and leaves unstated the criteria by which a particular Christian community may be identified as 'the Church'. Indeed, it is debatable whether, on this definition, the sacraments belong to the *esse* of the Church.

Adopting a reductionist approach to ecclesiology has led Methodists to suppose that the mutual *recognition* of ecclesial communities as containing the means of salvation is a sufficient basis for identifying the presence of the Church and thus for establishing unity. Granted that the purpose of the Church is to save souls, ecclesial structures are subservient to this end and as such fall within the competence of

---

[4] United Methodist Church, *Book of Discipline* (2008), Preamble.

ecclesial communities to adapt for the sake of more effective mission in changing circumstances. While Methodists accept that structural reforms could be beneficial for the sake of unity-in-mission, they are generally reluctant to adopt any that would imply deficiencies in their existing structures.

The problem for Methodists so far as ecumenism is concerned is that their principal dialogue partners among the major world communions do not approach inter-Christian relations with the same missiological priorities or ecclesiological flexibility as Methodism. At times, Methodists have become frustrated when dialogue partners adhere to more rigid ecclesiological positions that suggest Methodism lacks a number of essential ecclesial elements. Methodists have had to learn, sometimes painfully, that ecumenical friendship and goodwill alone are insufficient to overcome theological obstacles to unity.

## World Methodist Council and World Council of Churches

Despite their mixed experience of ecumenism, Methodists have long been committed to participating in ecumenical structures. An 'Oecumenical Methodist Conference' first met in London in 1881 at the instigation of American Methodism in order to strengthen links among Methodist denominations around the world. Thereafter an informal 'World Methodist Conference' met every ten years until 1931. Since 1951 a similar conference has assembled every five years, most recently in Durban (2011). Continuing the aim of the first such conference, attendees gathered from 76 member churches in 132 countries, representing a global community of 75 million Methodists, in order to celebrate and affirm Methodist identity.

The World Methodist Council (WMC), which meets more frequently, is a smaller body comprising representatives appointed by autonomous Methodist churches. The WMC, like the World Methodist Conference, has no executive powers but it constitutes a standing structure of communion and an institutional presence at the level of world communions, thereby providing a means for global Methodism to engage in dialogue with other communions. Despite internal tensions – some of which relate to the dominant position of the UMC – member churches of the WMC remain bound to one another by a common, albeit largely undefined, Wesleyan/Methodist ethos and heritage.

The definitive history of the WMC has yet to be written. From the outset there have been divergent views concerning its purpose and value. Today, some Methodists envisage a more authoritative role for the WMC as an instrument of communion uniting the global Methodist family; others assert the right of autonomous Methodist churches to pursue their own ecumenical agenda as opportunities arise.

For various reasons that remain to be investigated the WMC has not been greatly affected by the kind of controversies that currently threaten to divide the Anglican Communion. Nevertheless, a common Wesleyan/Methodist ethos and heritage may no longer be sufficient to safeguard the present degree of communion among member churches in the face of growing doctrinal pluralism. Strengthening the

WMC as a structure of communion will almost certainly require member churches to adhere to a statement of doctrine and ethics based on an agreed summary of what constitute the Wesleyan 'essentials' of the faith.

One notable achievement of the WMC has been to associate world Methodism with the Joint Declaration on the Doctrine of Justification between the Catholic Church and the Lutheran World Federation (JDDJ, 1999). With strong support from member churches of the WMC, all three parties signed the Official Common Affirmation of the Methodist Statement of Association with the JDDJ at the WMC meeting in Seoul in 2006. Methodists, Catholics and Lutherans affirm together their fundamental doctrinal agreement with the teaching expressed in the JDDJ, thereby committing them to deepen their common understanding of justification in teaching, study and preaching as a step towards common mission and eventual full communion. The signatories affirm that any remaining differences on justification are not sufficient cause for continuing separation.

Methodism's contribution to the World Council of Churches (WCC) has been disproportionate to its size among world communions. Methodists have been among the most committed supporters of the WCC since an elderly John Mott was invited to preach at its inaugural meeting in Amsterdam (1948) in recognition of his outstanding contribution to global ecumenism. Earlier, Robert Newton Flew (Great Britain) was a leading figure in the interwar Faith and Order movement, which led to the founding of the WCC. Remarkably, since 1948 Methodism has provided three WCC general secretaries: Philip Potter (1972–84), Emilio Castro (1985–92) and Samuel Kobia (2004–10). Geoffrey Wainwright, world Methodism's leading ecumenist, served with distinction on the WCC Faith and Order Commission (1977–91) and was principal editor at Lima, Peru, of the landmark convergence statement *Baptism, Eucharist and Ministry* (*BEM*) (1982).

While Methodists have generally responded positively to *BEM*, they have yet to embrace fully its principal recommendations, though some of its central theological ideas, such as *koinonia*, have been incorporated piecemeal into Methodist ecclesiology. An analysis of Methodist responses to the subsequent WCC convergence statement on *The Nature and Mission of the Church* (2007) would reveal the extent to which the *BEM* process has been absorbed into Methodist ecclesiology and ecumenical method in the intervening twenty-five years.

## Survey of Ecumenical Relations

Besides participating in ecumenical structures, Methodists have been actively involved in unity schemes. In some territories Methodists have joined united or uniting churches: Canada (1925); South India (1947); Zambia (1965); Pakistan (1970); North India (1970); and Australia (1977). In 1996 seven European Methodist churches signed a Joint Declaration of Church Fellowship establishing inter-communion with the Community of Protestant Churches in Europe.

After failed unity schemes in the 1960s and 1980s, Methodists and Anglicans in Britain have been in a covenant relationship since 2003. The Anglican–Methodist

Covenant commits the two churches to work together to overcome the remaining obstacles to full visible unity.[5] Addressing Methodist sensibilities, the Covenant declares: 'We affirm one another's churches as true churches belonging to the One, Holy, Catholic and Apostolic Church of Jesus Christ and as truly participating in the apostolic mission of the whole people of God' (§194).

The UMC has developed strong links with the Evangelical Lutheran Church of America (ELCA) and Lutheran churches in Europe. A state of communion exists between United Methodists and Lutherans in Germany (1990), Austria (1991), Sweden (1993) and Norway (1997). The UMC and ELCA have been in 'full communion' since 2008, though arguably it would be more accurate to describe this as 'inter-communion' since each retains its complete ecclesial independence.

## Theological Dialogue

Methodists are, or have been, involved in bilateral conversations co-sponsored by the WMC and the following world communions: the Catholic Church (1967–); Lutheran World Federation (1977–84); World Alliance of Reformed Churches (1985–87); Anglican Communion (1992–96); Orthodox (1992–95); and Salvation Army (2003–2011).[6]

The most notable absentees from this list are Baptists and Pentecostals. Though Pentecostals increasingly participate in theological and ecumenical networks, their informal structures and theology make them elusive dialogue partners. Nevertheless, historical parallels between the rapid expansion of Methodism in the late eighteenth and early nineteenth centuries from a network of religious societies within the Church of England into a global 'empire of the Spirit',[7] and the growth of classical Pentecostalism a century later, suggest a dialogue between Methodists and Pentecostals would be worthwhile.

The fact that there has been no dialogue between the WMC and the Baptist World Alliance can be attributed in part to historic sensitivities stemming from the paradoxical nature of Methodism as a renewal movement that remains committed to infant baptism. Also, Methodism's 'connexionalism' runs counter to the congregationalism of Baptist churches. The prospects for a productive dialogue between Methodists and Baptists will depend largely upon whether they can agree together that Christian initiation is a process (not an event) in which infant baptism/confirmation and believer-baptism constitute equivalent trajectories.

---

[5] British Methodist Conference, *An Anglican-Methodist Covenant: Common Statement of the Formal Conversations between the Methodist Church of Great Britain and the Church of England* (London: Church House Publishing and Methodist Publishing House, 2001).

[6] The text of these reports can be accessed via denominational websites and is published in the WCC series *Growth in Agreement*. For an introduction to Methodist bilateral conversations see Geoffrey Wainwright, *Methodists in Dialog* (Nashville, TN: Abingdon, 1995).

[7] Cf. David Hempton, *Methodism: Empire of the Spirit* (New Haven, CT and London: Yale University Press, 2005).

As each of the WMC's bilateral dialogues has its own character, we now consider them separately in turn.

*Methodist–Catholic Dialogue*

WMC–Catholic dialogue, which began as a consequence of the Second Vatican Council, ranks among the most industrious of the Western dialogues.[8] A fixed reporting period of five years (coinciding with the WMC cycle) instils focus and realistic goals. The WMC formally receives the reports of the joint commission and commends them for study by member churches; the Vatican appoints a Catholic theologian to write a commentary.

Briefly, the initial phase of dialogue (1967–76) produced two preliminary reports registering broad agreement in a range of topics. Succeeding conversations have addressed aspects of core Christian doctrines: the Holy Spirit (1981); the Church (1986); the apostolic tradition (1991); revelation and faith (1996); and teaching authority (2001).

The two most recent reports, focussing on ecclesiology, are theologically the most mature and ecumenically the most significant to emerge from the dialogue. *The Grace Given You in Christ: Catholics and Methodists Reflect Further on the Church* (2006) breaks fresh ground in ecumenical method. Building on John Paul II's assertion that inter-church dialogue involves not only an exchange of ideas but also an 'exchange of gifts', the report explores eirenically what Catholics and Methodists might receive from each other.[9] This method anticipates the receptive ecumenism agenda.[10] The report also sets out general principles for developing relations between Methodists and Catholics.

The most recent report, *Encountering Christ the Saviour: Church and Sacraments* (2011, hereafter *ECS*), revisits some of the central topics addressed in *BEM* in order to extend and deepen existing areas of agreement between Methodists and Catholics concerning aspects of baptism, Eucharist and ministry.

Notably, *ECS* investigates the Eucharist as the sacramental 'memorial' of Christ's saving death and resurrection, and his real presence in the sacrament. The theological framework for this study is the participation of the baptised in the Paschal Mystery of the death and resurrection of Christ and his self-offering to the Father. Creatively, the report draws on the Eucharistic hymns of John and Charles Wesley, long neglected by Methodists as a theological resource, as the basis for suggesting that 'Catholic language of a eucharistic "offering" of Christ's sacrifice and Methodist language of "pleading" that sacrifice can be reconciled' (§132).

Questions remain, however. Granted that the once-for-all historical sacrifice of Christ is made sacramentally present at the Eucharist, it is effective with all its

---

[8] David M. Chapman, *In search of the Catholic Spirit: Methodists and Roman Catholics in Dialogue* (Peterborough: Epworth Press, 2004).
[9] *Ut Unum Sint*, §28; cf. *Lumen Gentium*, §13.
[10] Paul Murray (ed.), *Receptive Ecumenism and the Call to Catholic Learning: Exploring a Way for Contemporary Ecumenism* (Oxford: Oxford University Press, 2006).

power for the salvation of humankind. This provides theological underpinning for the Catholic intention to offer the Eucharistic sacrifice on behalf of the whole communion of saints, living and departed. For Methodists, such an intention raises questions about Catholic beliefs concerning the efficacy of prayer for the departed, purgatory and indulgences.

The treatment of ordained ministry in *ECS* is among its most far-reaching aspects. Neglecting the theological subtleties of their Wesleyan heritage, Methodists have long espoused the Protestant idea of 'the priesthood of all believers' in reaction to Catholic teaching concerning the ordained ministry as a sacrificing priesthood. Based on a more nuanced understanding that Christ continues to exercise his priestly ministry in the Church by means of the ministerial priesthood, together with the common priesthood of the faithful, *ECS* reaches a number of closely argued conclusions (§189):

1. all ministry in the Church is ultimately that of Christ and is only ever exercised by individuals as his representatives;
2. the ordained ministry is both sign and instrument of Christ's ministry;
3. a rite of Ordination (involving the imposition of ministerial hands and the invocation of the Holy Spirit for the appropriate gifts for ministry) is itself sacramental in nature;
4. by virtue of their Ordination, individuals are enabled to represent Christ to the Church and to represent the Church before God;
5. the ministerial priesthood and the common priesthood of the faithful participate in distinct but related ways in the priesthood of Christ;
6. in the celebration of the Eucharist, the ordained bishop or presbyter represents Christ the priest in the midst of the priestly people of God;
7. the orderly transmission of the ordained ministry is a sign and instrument of the apostolicity of the Church.

How the member churches of the WMC will receive this latest report of the WMC–Catholic dialogue is difficult to predict since, despite their Wesleyan heritage, Methodists hold a variety of views concerning the Eucharist and ordained ministry. The idea that the Eucharist is a sacrifice offered by the Church in union with Christ's eternal sacrifice is contentious, as is the view that ordained ministers possess spiritual gifts beyond those ordinarily conferred upon the faithful by virtue of their baptism and call to serve Christ.

Since 1986 the goal of WMC–Catholic dialogue has been 'full communion in faith, mission and sacramental life', a description of Christian unity that includes the possibility of Methodism retaining its ecclesial identity in communion with the Catholic Church. Establishing full communion between Methodists and Catholics is not simply a matter of mutual recognition but 'will also depend upon a fresh creative act of reconciliation which acknowledges the manifold yet unified activity of the Holy Spirit throughout the ages. It will involve a joint act of obedience to the sovereign Word of God' (*The Apostolic Tradition* (1991), §117).

In addition to the international conversations co-sponsored by the WMC there are Methodist–Catholic dialogue commissions in Britain, the United States and New Zealand. These have produced a number of convergence statements, notably *Mary: Mother of the Lord* (Great Britain, 1995) and *Through Divine Love: The Church in Each Place and All Places* (USA, 2006). In Australia Methodist–Catholic conversations began in the early 1970s, focussing on common beliefs and pastoral concerns relating to baptism. Since 1977 the Uniting Church in Australia (a member church of the WMC) has extended this exploratory dialogue into fresh areas of shared pastoral concern. The most recent reports to emerge from this dialogue investigate *Interchurch Marriages* (1999) and *The Mission of the Church* (2008).

*Methodist–Anglican Dialogue*
Dialogue between the WMC and the Anglican Communion began at the initiative of the 1988 Lambeth Conference, quickly focussing on the ordained ministry as the main point of contention. Acknowledging the extensive agreement between Anglicans and Methodists in faith and doctrine, and believing there to be sufficient convergence in understanding ordained ministry and mission, *Sharing in the Apostolic Communion* (1996) invited the WMC and the Lambeth Conference to recognise and affirm that:

> Both Anglicans and Methodists belong to the one, holy, catholic and apostolic church of Jesus Christ and participate in the apostolic mission of the whole people of God;
>
> In the churches of our two communions the word of God is authentically preached and the sacraments instituted by Christ are duly administered;
>
> Our churches share in the common confession and heritage of the apostolic faith. (§95)

A second resolution called for the establishment of a joint working group to prepare guidelines for procedures whereby national and regional authorities would be able to implement the mutual recognition of members, Eucharistic communion, the mutual recognition and inter-changeability of ministries and rites, and structures of common decision-making.

Whereas the WMC unhesitatingly endorsed these resolutions, the 1998 Lambeth Conference declined to adopt them as presented in the report. Member churches of the Anglican Communion were invited instead to study the report and, where judged appropriate, to develop local agreements of *acknowledgement* – an imprecise and less theologically loaded term than *recognition*. Cautiously, the conference envisaged the joint working group would prepare 'guidelines for moving beyond acknowledgement to the reconciliation of churches and, within that, the reconciliation of ordained ministries and structures for common decisionmaking'.[11] Reference here to the *reconciliation* of ministries signalled unwillingness formally to recognise Methodist ordination as such.

Officially, this remains the position of the Anglican Communion as a whole, though the substance of the first resolution is enshrined in the mutual affirmations contained within the Anglican–Methodist Covenant in Great Britain, whereby both churches recognise each other as true churches. Questions concerning the status and structure of the ordained ministry remain the most sensitive aspect of relations between Methodists and Anglicans.

The recently established Anglican–Methodist International Commission for Unity in Mission (AMICUM) is intended to monitor and promote regional and national initiatives involving the two communions. A significant challenge facing AMICUM is the fact that relations between Methodists and Anglicans vary considerably around the world. Moreover, when seen from a global perspective, the plethora of multilateral and bilateral agreements involving either Methodists or Anglicans creates a complex and confusing patchwork of regional and national ecumenical relationships.

*Methodist–Lutheran Dialogue*

WMC–Lutheran dialogue has produced a common statement on *The Church: A Community of Grace* (1984). Behind the different theological expressions and forms of Christian life represented by Methodism and by Lutheranism, the conversations discovered shared basic convictions and sufficient agreement about (1) the authority of the Scriptures, (2) salvation by grace through faith, (3) the Church, (4) means of grace and (5) the mission of the Church, to be able to recommend that 'our churches take steps to declare and establish full fellowship of word and sacrament' (§91). Unresolved issues meriting further discussion were identified as 'providence and two kingdoms, aspects of anthropology, and forms of unity' (§88). Publication of this common statement on the Church encouraged developments in Methodist–Lutheran dialogue in the United States.

Methodist–Lutheran relations in the United States have progressed considerably since preliminary conversations covering baptism (1977–79) and episcopacy (1985–87). In 2004 proposals for Eucharistic sharing were adopted by both communities as an interim measure in anticipation of further convergence. *Confessing our Faith Together* (2005) is a common statement setting out the basis for full communion between the UMC and ELCA in terms of: (1) a common confession of the Christian faith; (2) mutual recognition of baptism and sharing of the Eucharist; (3) mutual recognition of ordained ministries; (4) common commitment to evangelism, witness and service; and (5) 'a means of common decision making on critical common issues of faith and life'. In 2008 the UMC General Conference and ELCA Assembly approved proposals to implement 'full communion', though what constitutes visible unity remains unresolved.

---

[11] http://justus.anglican.org/resources/Lambeth1998/LC98res/sec4.html (accessed 16 September 2012).

## Methodist–Reformed Dialogue

WMC–Reformed dialogue has produced a short statement, *Together in God's Grace* (1987). Noting the extensive agreement between Methodists and Reformed across a range of theological topics, the statement considers five contentious areas (the Tradition and traditions, grace, the Church as covenant community, Church and state, and perfect salvation), before concluding that 'Historic differences of theological perspective and practice still maintain their influence, but are not of sufficient weight to divide us'.[12]

Hitherto, theological differences between Wesley and Calvin concerning freedom and grace had been regarded as an obstacle to unity. In Calvinist understanding it is the elect who come to faith and thus receive saving grace, whereas in Arminian Methodism it is those who in freedom desire to be saved. However, according to *Together in God's Grace*, 'that Wesley and Calvin advocated conflicting ways of holding together what they affirm in common should not constitute a barrier between our traditions'.[13] In general, 'the classical doctrinal issues … ought not to be seen as obstacles to unity between Methodists and Reformed'.[14]

The statement invites Methodists and Reformed to consider closer co-operation and whether there are territories in which union negotiations might be initiated. However, in contrast to the way in which WMC–Lutheran dialogue has contributed to developing bilateral relations in North America and Europe, WMC–Reformed dialogue has so far failed to exert a corresponding influence. This may suggest that theological differences between Methodists and Reformed are more significant than is currently supposed. Despite the findings of *Together in God's Grace*, the question remains whether soteriological differences between Methodists and Reformed are an obstacle to a common theology of mission and thus a disincentive to unity-in-mission.

## Orthodox and Salvation Army

A preparatory commission appointed by the WMC and the Ecumenical Patriarch of Constantinople recommended the inauguration of a bilateral dialogue between Methodists and Orthodox. Its report, *Orthodox and Methodists* (1995), contains a self-description by both traditions, an appreciation of each other's principal features, and suggestions for future dialogue. After a long delay, WMC–Orthodox dialogue is finally due to get underway in 2013.

In the United States there have been a series of informal conversations between United Methodist and Orthodox theologians on the subject of Wesleyan and

---

[12] Jeffrey Gros, Harding Meyer and William G. Rusch (eds), *Growth in Agreement II: Reports and Agreed Statements of Ecumenical Conversations on a World Level 1982–1998* (Geneva: WCC, 2000), 270.
[13] Ibid., 272.
[14] Ibid., 274.

Orthodox spirituality and ecclesiology.[15] A particular challenge for dialogue between Methodists and Orthodox is to develop a methodology that takes account of their respective and very different historical, theological and liturgical contexts.

That the origins of the Salvation Army lie in Methodism makes the two communions natural dialogue partners, though relations at an institutional level have sometimes been strained because of lingering mutual distrust. Formal conversations co-sponsored by the WMC began as recently as 2003, the intention being 'to explore our common heritage as Wesleyan Christians, examining the historical/doctrinal moorings of the Salvation Army and "Methodist essentials"'.[16] For the WMC, dialogue with the Salvation Army fulfils the original intention of the 1881 Oecumenical Methodist Conference in bringing together Christians with a common Wesleyan/Methodist heritage.

WMC–Salvation Army dialogue thus far has focussed on ecclesiology. Since both communities originated as renewal movements within larger ecclesial bodies, their understanding of the Church has been shaped by similar concerns. Yet, despite the minimalist perspective of Methodist ecclesiology, there are limits to Methodism's flexibility in identifying the concrete location of the Church (as distinct from its effective presence). The Salvation Army has no sacraments; whereas Methodists regard baptism and the Eucharist as essential ecclesial elements. In tension with their reluctance to 'unchurch' others, Methodists find it difficult theologically to accept non-sacramental communities as 'the Church' in the fullest sense of the term.

## Theological Issues for Future Study

There are a number of ways in which Methodists might usefully contribute to the future development of ecumenism and ecumenical theology. The following paragraphs explore a few of these.

### Ecumenical Method and the Nature of Agreement

The precise nature of ecumenical 'agreement' remains elusive, despite a growing library of ecumenically 'agreed' texts. The idea of 'consensus' is especially slippery: reference to 'basic consensus' or 'consensus in basic truths' raises questions about the depth and extent of such agreement and whether it constitutes a secure foundation for incremental expansion.

Moreover, it would be misleading to suppose that ecumenical agreement means simply the joint acceptance of doctrinal propositions that involve a common vocabulary and interpretive framework. For ecclesial communities express and hand on their faith in different ways. In the course of time they develop a vocabulary

---

[15] See the edited collections: ST Kimbrough, (ed.), *Orthodox and Wesleyan Spirituality* (Crestwood, NY: St Vladimir Seminary Press, 2002); ST Kimbrough, (ed.), *Orthodox and Wesleyan Ecclesiology* (Crestwood, NY: St Vladimir Seminary Press, 2007).

[16] WMC, *God in Christ Reconciling* (2006), 206.

and interpretive framework involving a complex combination of language, sacred signs and actions, normative way of life and inherited patterns of behaviour. In the case of Methodism, doctrinal consensus is carried by its authorised hymnody, connexional polity, discipline and official liturgies, in addition to its doctrinal standards, which anyway do not claim to articulate the full content of the Christian faith as Methodists have received it. So far as most ecumenical dialogues are concerned, securing agreement is likely to be a multi-faceted process that involves more than the comparison of doctrine.

The implications of this for ecumenical method have yet to be fully determined. Methodists might usefully investigate with dialogue partners what would constitute a sufficiently close correspondence between their respective vocabularies and interpretive frameworks such that agreement can be said to exist which is not contradicted by any remaining differences.

We have already observed that whereas Methodists tend to regard Christian unity as the culmination of a process of mutual *recognition*, unity with Anglicans and Catholics will necessarily involve ecclesial *reconciliation*. Methodists will continue to be frustrated in ecumenical dialogue unless these contrasting methodologies can be combined in such a way as to safeguard their respective ecclesiological priorities.

## *Marks of the Church*

Methodists interpret the creedal marks of the Church to reflect their missiological priorities: apostolicity denotes continuity in the apostolic mission; catholicity refers to the universality of the Christian community. This interpretation assumes there is a sufficient consensus among Christians concerning the content of the apostolic mission (the 'essentials' of the faith) to constitute a basis for the Church's unity. However, such a consensus can no longer be taken for granted in the midst of the current crisis in teaching authority. Methodists must therefore develop objective criteria for discerning whether the communities that result from Christian mission are apostolic in the sense of preserving the faith of the apostles, and catholic in the sense of preserving the whole of Christ's ministry. Methodists have much to gain from continuing dialogue concerning the proper role of the ordained ministry among the criteria for identifying that a particular Christian community bears the marks of the Church.

## *Nature of Oversight*

The ministry of oversight or *episkope* in Methodism raises a number of issues that have yet to be addressed in ecumenical dialogue. Idealistically, *BEM* suggests that 'The ordained ministry should be exercised in a personal, collegial and communal way' (Ministry, §26). In Methodism *episkope* has mostly been exercised communally, even in those Methodist churches endowed with bishops. While nowadays Methodists are more committed than ever before to the exercise of *episkope* in communal, collegial and personal ways, they have yet to determine the theological and practical relationship among these aspects of oversight. Nevertheless, the

Methodist experience of *episkope* has much to contribute to continuing ecumenical dialogue concerning the exercise of oversight in the Church.

*Theological Coherence and Ecumenical Consistency*
The doctrinal standards of Methodist churches are based on the New Testament, the historic creeds, Reformation theology and the sermons of John Wesley. However, it is debatable in what way and to what extent these doctrinal standards retain authoritative status among Methodists today. The actual status and contemporary interpretation of the Methodist doctrinal standards by clergy and laity have implications for dialogue partners, who naturally want to be confident that they are in conversation with those who truly represent the faith of Methodists. The uninterested reception commonly given to dialogue reports in Methodism may reflect a theological gap between its representatives in ecumenical dialogue and the bulk of the community.

Even where experienced practitioners are involved, maintaining theological coherence across ecumenical dialogues and over the course of time is a major challenge. In the worst case, churches in their desire to agree with diverse dialogue partners may subscribe to ecumenical statements that are theologically incompatible or contradictory. A detailed survey of the WMC dialogue reports would reveal the extent to which they are theologically coherent.

The complex and asymmetrical web of global ecumenical relationships gives rise to situations in which two churches, each in communion with a third, are not in communion with each other. Drawing on a mathematical analogy, this is referred to as 'intransitivity'. Though not unique to Methodism, the problem of intransitivity in ecumenical relations might usefully be investigated with dialogue partners with the intention of resolving inconsistencies and anomalies in ecumenical relationships. Strengthening the WMC as an instrument of communion might facilitate the rationalisation of Methodism's ecumenical relations, though this would appear a distant prospect at the present time.

## Towards a Global Methodist Ecumenical Perspective

The varied experience of Methodists in South and Central America, Africa and Asia suggests the need for a more integrated ecumenical perspective within the WMC, where voices from the global South are under-represented in ecumenical dialogue. Methodism in Singapore, for example, is vibrant and actively engaged in mission in several countries of south-east Asia where Christianity is a minority religion. The developing Methodist theological tradition in Asia has much to contribute to global Methodism and the future of ecumenism. Elsewhere, the Pentecostal flavour of Methodism in South America brings yet another set of concerns and emphases into the ecumenical equation. Present tensions with Orthodox in Eastern Europe and with Roman Catholics in Central and South America stand in marked contrast to ecumenism in the West, and are a salutary reminder that the fruits of theological dialogue have yet to be fully received in the churches. The theological and non-theological factors that inhibit the ecclesial reception of ecumenical agreement have yet to be fully investigated. Ecclesial tensions also indicate a need to rediscover the Wesleyan theological tradition as the foundation for Methodist attitudes to other Christians.

Regrettably, the experience of those Methodists who have formed united churches with other traditions has mostly been lost from Methodism's ecumenical perspective. Thus the imaginative way in which, for instance, the Uniting Church in Australia has embraced Methodists, Presbyterians and Congregationalists (together with their different polities) has yet to contribute meaningfully to Methodism's ecumenical agenda. The experience of united churches that have adopted 'the historic episcopate' (generally from Anglican sources), such as the Church of South India, hardly impinges on Methodism's ecumenical perspective. Further research into united and uniting churches has significant potential for shaping Methodism's future ecumenical agenda.

# Interfaith Relations

## Methodist Relations with Non-Christian Religions

The fact of religious pluralism as a result of global demographic trends makes interfaith relations integral to the Christian life. Moreover, shifting strategic priorities for Christians in the twenty-first century suggest a need for greater investment in interfaith dialogue in order to reduce interreligious tensions. Fuelled by fears arising from terrorism and perceived religious imperialism, such tensions coalesce around the location of sacred buildings, the status of religious and secular law, and sectarianism.

Despite global interreligious tensions, Methodists generally seek to cultivate good relations with non-Christian communities and are active in interreligious structures, such as the Congress of World Faiths, though Methodist sponsorship of interfaith dialogue is rare. For various reasons the WMC has yet to initiate interfaith dialogue.

Relations between Methodists and Jews are complicated by political issues relating to the state of Israel. The UMC General Conference has declared its opposition to anti-Semitism in the strongest terms.[17] United Methodists are encouraged to observe Holocaust Memorial Day and to avoid targeting Jews for conversion. However, Jewish groups have condemned a recent UMC report, *Israel–Palestine* (2007), which is critical of Israel's policy towards Palestinians. Similarly,

---

[17] UMC, *Building New Bridges in Hope: Statement of the United Methodist Church on Christian–Jewish Relations* (General Board of Global Ministries, General Commission on Christian Unity and Interreligious Concerns, 1996).

Jewish groups have strongly criticised the British Methodist Conference for adopting a report, *Justice for Palestine and Israel* (2010), which calls for a boycott of Israeli goods emanating from illegal settlements.

Relations between Methodists and Muslims vary regionally. The UMC Council of Bishops and the Methodist Church of New Zealand responded positively to the open letter *A Common Word Between Us and You* (2007), signed by 138 leading Muslim scholars and clerics. However, beyond expressing their desire for interfaith dialogue, United Methodists have yet to commence any specific initiatives. In Africa, Methodist attitudes towards Muslims have mostly changed from aggressive evangelisation to the cultivation of peaceable relations, though an intention to gain converts from Islam remains central to the mission of Methodists in many African countries.[18]

## Historical Origins of Interfaith Relations in Overseas Missions

As a Church of England missionary in Georgia, employed by the Society for the Propagation of the Gospel, John Wesley expected to convert Native Americans to Christianity. A lack of success, however, compounded his abject failure as a missionary among European settlers. Following his return to England in 1738, Wesley confined subsequent overseas visits to Christian Europe.

A lack of firsthand experience did not deter the mature Wesley from expressing singular views on non-Christian religions. He dismissed a favourable assessment of Chinese virtues as 'a mere pious fraud', even though (or possibly because) it was based on reports from Jesuit missionaries (*Journal*, 17 January 1787). Likewise, he disdained an enthusiastic account of Turkish people and culture by a celebrated travel writer and wife of the English ambassador to the Turkish Porte.[19] His few positive references to non-Christian religions cannot be construed as sympathetic since they occur in the context of pastoral rebukes intended to shame Methodists.[20]

The global expansion of Methodist overseas missions in the nineteenth century led to the first serious encounters between Methodism and non-Christian religions. Methodist missionaries in Asia, like others, were surprised to discover a degree of religious sophistication at odds with conventional Western perceptions of 'heathenish' people. Missionaries with scholarly gifts translated the sacred writings of non-Christian religions for the benefit of Western audiences, though remoteness from academia hindered theological reflection on the interreligious encounter. Only in Africa did the oral traditions and cosmology of tribal religions appear to conform to expectations.

---

[18] For example, Martha T. Frederiks, 'Methodists and Muslims in the Gambia', *Islam and Muslim–Christian Relations*, 20 (2009), 61–72.

[19] Outler, *Works*, vol. 2, 486.

[20] Rebekah L. Miles, 'John Wesley as Interreligious Resource', in Martin Forward, Stephen Plant and Susan White (eds), *A Great Commission: Christian Hope and Religious Diversity* (Frankfurt: Peter Lang, 2000), 61–75.

If the first Parliament of Religions (1893) marked the start of institutional interfaith relations, a comparable achievement of the Edinburgh World Missionary Conference was to survey the collective experience among Protestant missions of the interaction between Christianity and other religions over the previous fifty years as a stimulus to developing that encounter in theologically constructive ways.

## Methodist Pioneers in Interfaith Relations

Methodists were among the most active pioneers in interfaith relations in the early years of the twentieth century. James Hope Moulton made comparative religion the subject of his 1913 Fernley lecture to the Wesleyan Methodist Conference in Britain.[21] E. Stanley Jones, an American Methodist missionary in India, organised a series of interreligious conferences that formed the basis of his influential book on interfaith relations.[22]

Several Methodist missionaries subsequently became acknowledged experts in non-Christian religions and culture, including W. E. Soothill (1861–1935), who was appointed Professor of Chinese Language and Literature at Oxford. A generation later, Homer Dubs (1892–1969), renowned Sinologist and son of American Methodist missionaries, occupied the same chair. After serving as a missionary in Africa, Geoffrey Parrinder (1910–2005) became an academic and leading authority on African religions.

Foremost among contemporary Methodist practitioners in interfaith relations is Kenneth Cracknell, whose experience as a British Methodist missionary in Nigeria in the 1960s led him to reject the received wisdom that traditional African religion knows nothing of God. Later Cracknell served influentially as director of the WCC sub-unit on interfaith dialogue. His historical survey of Christian attitudes towards non-Christian religions and interfaith dialogue argues for a new relationship between Christians and people of 'other faith'.[23]

Other prominent Methodist practitioners in interfaith relations include: Martin Forward (US, Christian–Islam); Lynn de Silva (Sri Lanka, Christian–Buddhist); and Elizabeth Harris (Britain, Christian–Buddhist). Wesley Ariarajah served as staff member of the WCC sub-unit on interfaith dialogue and was a participant in the controversial debate on the subject at the 1975 WCC assembly in Nairobi. His experience of Christian–Hindu relations in Sri Lanka informs his WCC study on interfaith relations.[24]

---

[21] James Hope Moulton, *Religions and Religion* (London: Kelly, 1913).
[22] E. Stanley Jones, *Christ at the Round Table* (London: Hodder and Stoughton, 1928).
[23] Kenneth Cracknell, *Towards a New Relationship: Christians and People of Other Faith* (London: Epworth Press, 1986).
[24] S. Wesley Ariarajah, *Not Without My Neighbour: Issues in Interfaith Relations* (Geneva: WCC, 1999).

## Towards a Methodist Theology of Religions and Interfaith Dialogue

The absence of a tradition of systematic theology in Methodism has been a limiting factor in the development of a robust theology of religions and interfaith dialogue. Methodist theological reflection on non-Christian religions has mostly been undertaken by missionaries and other interfaith practitioners as a branch of missiological studies. The work of Wilfred Cantwell Smith on faith development has particularly influenced Methodist theological reflection on non-Christian religions.[25]

John Wesley's limited contribution to a Methodist theology of religions lies chiefly in his evangelical Arminianism, which stresses the pure universal love of God. While there have been various attempts to articulate an inclusive Wesleyan theology of religions, the safest conclusion is that Wesley himself envisaged the possibility of saving grace beyond the Christian economy in spite (and not because) of non-Christian religious beliefs.[26] The status of non-Christian religions as salvific structures is a systematic issue that simply did not occur to him.

Cracknell proposes a Word/Spirit/Logos Christology as the basis for an inclusive theology of religions in salvation history.[27] According to Cracknell, that Christ fills all things (Ephesians 4.7–10) means he is present everywhere. The object of Christian mission, then, properly understood, is not to take Christ to situations where he is supposedly absent but rather to discover, through dialogue with people of non-Christian faith, his presence beyond the boundaries of the Church. This understanding of the nature and method of interfaith dialogue invites comment from a systematic perspective.

First, the presence–absence dichotomy takes no account of differences in the *mode* of Christ's presence in the sacraments, in the proclamation of the Gospel, in the poor and in the world. Christians discern the presence of Christ in the poor (Matthew 25) because they already know him, not because the poor reveal him. Systematically, Christ's presence in the Church provides the theological framework for discerning and interpreting his universal presence, not vice versa. The truths present in non-Christian religions can only ever be those found in Jesus Christ, 'the way, the truth and the life' (John 14.6). Christian dialogue with non-Christian religions is therefore dialectical (both 'yes' and 'no') since these contain a mixture of truth and error.

Secondly, Christology requires an ecclesiological dimension because Christ is always united with his body, the Church. Whatever the Holy Spirit achieves in the history of peoples is therefore not an alternative to the Church but in some way

---

[25] *Religionswissenschaft als Welt-Theologie: Wilfred Cantwell Smiths interreligiose Hermeneutik* (Berlin: Vandenhoeck & Ruprecht, 1994).

[26] Lynne Price, *Interfaith Encounter and Dialogue: A Methodist Pilgrimage* (Frankfurt: Peter Lang, 1991); Elizabeth J. Harris, 'Wesleyan Witness in an Interreligious Context', in Philip R. Meadows (ed.), *Windows on Wesley: Wesleyan Theology in Today's World* (Oxford: Applied Theology Press, 1997).

[27] Kenneth Cracknell, *In Good and Generous Faith: Christian Responses to Religious Pluralism* (Peterborough: Epworth Press, 2005).

serves as a preparation for the Gospel and can only be understood and fulfilled in relation to the Church. At the same time, without implying any deficiency in its *esse*, the Church, too, is fulfilled in receiving the gifts of God that the non-Christian partner, consciously or otherwise, brings to interfaith dialogue. As practitioners like Cracknell rightly assert, the experiential aspect of interfaith relations has a proper contribution to make towards a Methodist theology of religions and interfaith dialogue.

## Theological Issues for Future Study

The Methodist contribution to interfaith relations and to a theology of religions and interfaith dialogue remains under-recognised, even among Methodists. A recent major survey of Methodist studies fails even to mention the subject.[28] Although of legitimate interest to Christians, interfaith dialogue is a controversial subject that will doubtless continue to raise spiritual and theological concerns among Methodists.

Methodist interfaith practitioners have tended to neglect the Catholic origins and intention behind John Wesley's inherited doctrine as a possible resource for a theology of religions and interfaith dialogue. Methodist research in this field would benefit from engagement with post-Vatican II Catholic scholarship, including the theo-dramatic method of Hans Urs von Balthasar.[29] The traditional Catholic teaching that *extra ecclesia nulla salus* was never formulated or applied with regard to non-Christian religions. On the contrary, Catholic doctrine affirms that non-Christians may be saved. Systematically, the status of non-Christian religions as salvific structures hinges on the relationship between nature and grace.

Methodists have yet to address methodological issues of interfaith dialogue. An uncritical appeal to the *missio Dei* leads some to regard interfaith dialogue as the 'wider ecumenism' and thus to adopt the method and principles of inter-church dialogue.[30] Despite claims to the contrary, this compromises the uniqueness of the Incarnation and Pentecost in the divine economy. Approaching interfaith dialogue in a spirit of 'good and generous faith' should not be at the expense of addressing questions of truth, knowledge and judgement from the perspective of Christian revelation.

It would also be misleading to assume that the content of Christian revelation can be separated from its inherited form so as to be assimilated into different cultures and interpretive frameworks. Despite current theological trends in Methodism and beyond, the historical particularity of the Incarnation does not lend itself to the development of a universal 'incarnational principle' that supposes all cultures to be

---

[28] William J. Abraham and James E. Kirby (eds), *The Oxford Handbook of Methodist Studies* (Oxford: Oxford University Press, 2009).

[29] Hans Urs von Balthasar, *Theo-drama: Theological Dramatic Theory*, (5 vols, San Francisco, CA: Ignatius Press, 1988–98).

[30] Cracknell, *Towards a New Relationship*, 57.

equally viable hosts for interpreting the Gospel. Granted that the form and content of the Gospel are to a certain degree inseparable, Christian discourse concerning the person of Christ cannot simply be extracted from the interpretive framework supplied by Greek philosophy in the formative period of Church history in order now to find expression in categories that belong to Hindu or Muslim thought. The viability of interfaith dialogue thus depends upon finding a theological basis and method for a process of correlation between religious and philosophical universes.

The solution cannot be to posit a Christian religion without doctrine. While Christian faith is not reducible to giving cognitive assent to doctrinal propositions, nor is it devoid of objective content within a particular account of truth and knowledge. The tendency among some Methodist interfaith practitioners to treat Christian faith as if it were a particular form of a universal religious faith (in classical Christian terms, 'the faith by which we believe') needs to be corrected by an equal concern for its content ('the faith that is believed'). For such content gives Christian faith a foundation and structure beyond a vague intuition of trust in some unnamed supernatural being.

Still, methodological issues relating to dialogue, while important, constitute only one aspect of interfaith relations. Since interreligious tensions are unlikely to diminish in the foreseeable future, Methodists might usefully re-vision for a religiously plural age their historical aspiration to 'be the friends of all, the enemies of none'. The proper foundation for such a strategy is neither an unwarranted optimism concerning human nature nor an inclination to religious pluralism but evangelical Arminianism and God's pure universal love.

# 9

# Holiness and Pentecostal Movements Within Methodism

## Priscilla Pope-Levison

The revival which commenced in 1905 and lasted well over a year at Mukti Mission in Kedagon near Pune, India, marked a significant, global confluence of Holiness and Pentecostal movements within Methodism. The Mukti Mission was founded by Pandita Ramabai (1858–1922), from a Hindu Brahmin family who was baptised as a Christian while studying in England. Upon her return to India in 1889, she launched Mukti, whose name means 'salvation', as a refuge, skill-training and evangelistic centre for young Indian women widowed or orphaned. In 1894, Ramabai herself experienced a marked infusion of the Holy Spirit which sparked a close association with the global holiness network. She became friends, for instance, with B. T. Roberts, founder of the Free Methodist Church, and her daughter, Manoramabai, studied in New York at the precursor institution to Roberts Wesleyan University. This network helped to fund her mission and sponsored her speaking tours in Great Britain and the United States. In addition, Ramabai's experienced assistant from 1898 on, Minnie Abrams (1859–1912), a Methodist Episcopal Church (MEC) deaconess missionary who testified to sanctification in 1896, had already been working in India for more than a decade, including four years as a conference evangelist appointed under MEC Bishop James Thoburn.

In January 1905, Ramabai scheduled an early morning meeting devoted to seeking 'a special outpouring of the Holy Spirit on all Christians of every land'.[1] A revival soon poured over Mukti Mission prompting more than 1,000 baptisms, 500 attendees at morning prayer and numerous outward manifestations of the Holy Spirit. Reports of the revival made headlines in the Pentecostal press, including Azusa Street's *The Apostolic Faith*, and Pentecostal leaders claimed Mukti as a precedent to the Azusa Street revival. International visitors travelled to Mukti, like Thomas Ball Barratt, a holiness Methodist who launched Pentecostalism in Norway. Chilean Pentecostalism also traces its beginning to Mukti through Minnie Abrams' booklet, *The Baptism of the Holy Ghost and Fire*, a report of the revival

---

[1] Allan Anderson, *Spreading Fires: The Missionary Nature of Early Pentecostalism* (Maryknoll, NY: Orbis, 2007), 79.

interspersed with 'Wesleyan Holiness and Higher Life themes of purification and empowerment'.[2] Abrams mailed the booklet to her Methodist missionary friends in Chile, May and Willis Hoover, who would also then pray for a revival which, when it happened, led to the formation of the Methodist Pentecostal Church in Chile. Thus, the Mukti Mission exemplifies two themes to be developed in this essay, themes that concomitantly portend current, noteworthy research trajectories: the centrality of women and the global interconnectedness of the Holiness and Pentecostal movements within Methodism.

The Methodist revival of the eighteenth century brought to prominence the doctrine of sanctification as a second moment of grace through the abiding power of the Holy Spirit that removes the bent towards sinning, thus perfecting the will in its ability to triumph over sinful desires and selfish motives. As Methodist holiness evangelist Iva Durham Vennard (1871–1945) explained about sanctification, it 'reinforces the power implanted in our souls at conversion, so that we need not sin'.

> No recognized teacher of Christian perfection claims that we get beyond the power to sin. Look at these two sentences. Notice the position of the negative. *I am not able to sin*. That is inability. *I am able not to sin*. That is ability, power, deliverance, victory. Christ by His Atonement does not hamper my will. He does not take from me the power to sin, but praise His name, He puts His power within me, by the abiding presence of the Holy Ghost, thus enabling me to keep from sin.[3]

The result is not sinless perfection, but the perfection of love, specifically perfect love towards God and neighbour. Perfect love, then, is not perfection in knowledge, memory or judgement. In these areas of human infirmities, there is always room for improvement. Rather, it is perfection of heart motive.

John Wesley (1703–91) understood entire sanctification as a gradual goal for the Christian life that believers attained with a high level of maturity and experience. At the same time, he allowed for the possibility, particularly later in his life, of an instantaneous sanctification even in the midst of this maturation process. A contemporary of Wesley, John Fletcher (1729–85), popularised this latter view by connecting sanctification to an instantaneous experience such as happened at Pentecost, what he referred to as the 'baptism of the Holy Spirit'. Rather than sanctification as the terminus of the Christian life, as Wesley seemed to prefer, Fletcher moved it closer in proximity to justification in order to impart power for overcoming infirmities throughout the Christian life. Further, Fletcher's doctrine

---

[2] Gary McGee, 'Minnie F. Abrams: Another Context, Another Founder', in James R. Goff and Grant Wacker (eds), *Portraits of a Generation: Early Pentecostal Leaders* (Fayetteville, AR: University of Arkansas, 2002), 94.

[3] Iva Durham Vennard, *Upper Room Messages* (Chicago, IL: Chicago Evangelistic Institute, 1916), 114–15.

of 'Pentecostal sanctification' highlighted the crisis event character of entire sanctification subsequently adopted by the Holiness and Pentecostal movements.[4]

## The Holiness Movement: Wesleyan

The Wesleyan branch of the Holiness movement emerged in the 1830s, primarily within American Methodism, which was enjoying phenomenal growth upwards to a million members. Several events catalysed an emphasis on entire sanctification or its more popular synonym, holiness. The Tuesday Meetings for the Promotion of Holiness commenced in 1835 in the New York City home of Sarah Worrall Lankford shortly after she experienced entire sanctification. Her sister, Phoebe Palmer, eventually assumed leadership of the weekly meetings and extended their influence to a national and international level. In 1839, Timothy Merritt founded the premier journal on holiness in the United States, *The Guide to Christian Perfection*, later known as *The Guide to Holiness* under the editorial pen of Phoebe Palmer. Merritt's influential book, *The Christian's Manual; A Treatise on Christian Perfection, with Directions for Achieving that State*, published in 1825, consisted of excerpts from Wesley and Fletcher on entire sanctification.

The Wesleyan Holiness movement was institutionalised in the National Camp Meeting Association for the Promotion of Holiness, founded in 1867 to glorify God in building up the church by holiness and saving sinners. That year, thousands of people gathered for a ten-day camp meeting in Vineland, New Jersey to listen to sermons and exhortations on the theme of holiness. Due to the overwhelmingly enthusiastic response, holiness leaders established the organisation as a national conduit for the Holiness movement, initially through annual camp meetings held at such locations as Camp Sychar in Ohio and Mountain Lake Campground in Maryland. The participation in these camp meetings of Methodist bishops, presiding elders and large numbers of laity demonstrated a growing acceptance of the Holiness movement within Methodism. Within a decade, the national association directly or indirectly sponsored an extensive network of national, regional and local holiness associations, periodicals, national and international missions, schools, camps, conferences and weekly prayer meetings. By the mid-1870s, however, serious opposition to the Holiness movement surfaced in American Methodism over what detractors considered an overemphasis and misinterpretation of entire sanctification and a flouting of ecclesiastical authority. For the next decade, leaders

---

[4] Donald Dayton, 'Methodism and Pentecostalism', in William J. Abraham and James E. Kirby (eds), *The Oxford Handbook of Methodist Studies* (Oxford: Oxford University Press, 2009), 174. This topic is debated among Methodist scholars; for example see Laurence W. Wood, *The Meaning of Pentecost in Early Methodism: Rediscovering John Fletcher as John Wesley's Vindicator and Designated Successor* (Nashville, TN: Abingdon, 2002) and Randy Maddox, 'Wesley's Understanding of Christian Perfection: In What Sense Pentecostal?', *Wesleyan Theological Journal*, 34:2 (1999), 78–83.

of the national holiness association struggled to keep the movement within Methodism but to no avail. Between 1880 and1905, some 100,000 'come-outers' as they were called, left Methodism to form their own holiness denominations, such as the Church of the Nazarene, the Pilgrim Holiness Church (which eventually merged with the Wesleyan Methodist Church to form the Wesleyan Church) and the Church of God (Anderson, Indiana). These and other denominations around the world hold current membership in the Christian Holiness Partnership, the successor of the National Camp Meeting Association.

Methodist holiness evangelist Phoebe Palmer (1807–74), arguably the leading figure in the Wesleyan Holiness movement, experienced entire sanctification on her 'day of days', 26 July 1837, after an intense time of searching, working and waiting. Based upon this experience, she promoted a 'shorter way' to sanctification, grounded not in sustained spiritual struggle but in the entire consecration of self offered upon the altar. Highlighting the phrase from Matthew 23:19, 'the altar sanctifieth the gift', Palmer taught that one need only trust in God's promise to sanctify what was placed on the altar. 'I now say that I had *obtained* this blessing, by *laying all upon the altar*. … So long as the offering was *kept upon the altar*, I saw it to be not only a privilege, but a *duty*, to believe.'[5] In keeping with her gravitation towards Fletcher's views, she would come to adopt his phrase, 'baptism of the Holy Spirit' as the descriptor for entire sanctification. Palmer promoted her teaching on sanctification through her national and transatlantic revivals, her editorial leadership of *The Guide to Holiness*, her several bestselling books, including *The Way of Holiness*, and her leadership of the Tuesday Meetings.

Palmer applied her now infamous phrase, 'Holiness is power', to women's preaching. She declared that Jesus' promise in Luke 24:49 – to be clothed with power from on high – found fulfilment at Pentecost when the Holy Spirit fell in 'tongues of fire' on those gathered. This endowment of power fell on both men and women: 'This is what was spoken through the prophet Joel: In the last days it will be, God declares, that I will pour out my Spirit upon all flesh, and your sons and your daughters shall prophesy' (Acts 2:16–18; Joel 2:28–32). This was the paradigmatic verse, according to Palmer, because it encapsulated the 'promise of the Father' to impart to women, in the last days of this present age, the power to bear witness to the saving and sanctifying gospel of Jesus Christ.[6] In other words, she believed that the power of the Holy Spirit, given at Pentecost, was not restricted to New Testament times; it was still available through entire sanctification to women and men.

Central to her teaching on entire sanctification was the necessity to testify to it lest it be squandered. As a result, many women spoke aloud and in public about their sanctification who otherwise would have remained silent in the church.

---

[5] Phoebe Palmer, *The Way of Holiness, with Notes by the Way: Being a Narrative of Religious Experience, Resulting from a Determination to be a Bible Christian* (New York, NY: Piercy and Reed, 1843), 53.

[6] Phoebe Palmer, *Promise of the Father; or A Neglected Speciality of the Last Days* (Boston, MA: Henry V. Degen, 1859).

Sanctification imparted to women a 'holy boldness' for preaching.[7] Mary Lee Cagle (1864–1955), a minister in the Church of the Nazarene, appeared quite timid when she first spoke in public, so she prayed for God's loosening.

> [God] absolutely broke every fetter. ... It was the first time in her life that she could turn the pulpit loose – she ran from one end of the large platform to the other and shouted and praised God, and preached with the Holy Ghost sent down from above. ... It was a permanent loosing from that day, and she has never been bound again. Although of a shrinking, backward disposition, she has never seen a crowd since that day large enough to make her knees tremble, and she has preached to thousands.[8]

Similarly, Sarah Smith (1822–1908), Church of God (Anderson, Indiana) evangelist, declared: 'When God sanctified me He took all the shrink and fear of men and devils out of me.' She claimed victory over the 'man-fearing spirit', which 'was taken away, and my heart was overflowing with perfect love that was so unspeakable and full of glory'.[9]

The Wesleyan Holiness movement spread globally through transatlantic revivalism by women, like Amanda Berry Smith (1837–1915), a former slave who became a celebrity as a singer and preacher on the holiness camp meeting circuit. Her sanctification happened on a September Sunday morning in 1868. She walked nearly a mile to hear John Inskip, first president of the National Camp Meeting Association, preach on sanctification at the Green Street Methodist Episcopal Church in New York City. During his preaching, she was sanctified with an electric jolt that prompted an audible shout from her lips, 'Glory to Jesus.' Then she felt a palpable touch:

> I seemed to feel a hand, the touch of which I cannot describe. It seemed to press me gently on the top of my head, and I felt something part and roll down and cover me like a great cloak! I felt it distinctly; it was done in a moment, and O what a mighty peace and power took possession of me![10]

In 1878, she turned her attention to transatlantic revivalism and preached the holiness and temperance message for several years in Great Britain, at the initial

---

[7] Susie Stanley, *Holy Boldness: Women Preachers' Autobiographies and the Sanctified Self* (Knoxville, TN: University of Tennessee, 2002).

[8] Mary Lee Cagle, *The Life and Work of Mary Lee Cagle: An Autobiography* (Kansas City, MO: Nazarene Publishing House, 1928), 29.

[9] Sarah Smith, *Life Sketches of Mother Sarah Smith: 'A Mother in Israel'* (Anderson, IN: Gospel Trumpet, 1902), 9, 11, 26; quoted in Stanley, *Holy Boldness*, 78.

[10] Amanda Smith, *An Autobiography: The Story of the Lord's Dealings with Mrs. Amanda Smith, The Colored Evangelist* (Chicago, IL: Christian Witness Co., 1921), 42.

invitation of Lady Henry Somerset, and in India. She then travelled to West Africa, where she helped Bishop William Taylor establish mission work in Liberia; in 1886 alone, they opened sixteen mission stations.

While preaching in the British Isles during a four-year span, Phoebe and Walter Palmer spurred transatlantic holiness revivalism through their profound influence on William and Catherine Booth, cofounders of the Salvation Army. In the wake of criticism against Phoebe's preaching in particular and women preachers in general, Catherine (1829–90) published her supportive views in a substantive pamphlet, *Female Ministry; or Women's Right to Preach the Gospel*. She then preached her first sermon in 1860 when William was ill and unable to hold services in his churches, and she preached for the next thirty years to overflowing crowds. As Evangeline Booth, the fourth General of the Salvation Army, commented about her mother's legacy on women's preaching, 'She led the way for the host of women who have followed her into the pulpit.'[11]

The Palmers' influence also extended to the Booths' decision to incorporate entire sanctification into the heart of the Army's doctrine. The Army began to spread the holiness message around the globe when, in 1880, eight workers travelled to the United States; within several months, they had twelve corps up and running. That same year, meetings were held for the first time in Australia, then in Canada the next year. Within the decade, Army work opened in India, Sweden, France and Norway, when in 1887 William Booth (1829–1912) preached for the initial Army meeting on Norwegian soil. Thomas Ball Barratt (1862–1940), who emigrated to Norway with his Wesleyan Methodists parents worked closely with the Salvation Army as he pastored several Methodist churches. From 1892–98, Barratt served as Presiding Elder of the Oslo District. He remained in Oslo to found a city mission for evangelism and social work among the poor and working classes. Barratt transitioned into Pentecostalism when, in his mid-forties, he experienced glossalalia while in the United States; he then returned to Norway with the Pentecostal message.[12] His personal contacts with Pentecostal leaders in many countries – Sweden, Finland, Poland, Estonia, Iceland, Denmark and India – promoted the establishment and growth of indigenous Pentecostal churches. When his Methodist clergy credentials were terminated, he founded and pastored the Filadelfia Church in Oslo.

Another factor in the global Holiness movement was the work of missionaries like William Taylor (1821–1902), the quintessential holiness missionary who laboured on six continents. Taylor was converted in a Methodist camp meeting, ordained a Methodist minister, experienced sanctification through Palmer's influence, and became active in the National Camp Meeting Association for the Promotion of Holiness. As a missionary, he focused on developing indigenous self-governing, self-supporting and self-propagating churches. Armed with this three-self

---

[11] The Salvation Army National Archives and Research Center, Alexandria, VA, Evangeline Booth, 'A Woman's Place – World'.

[12] David Bundy, 'The Holiness Movements in World Christianity: Historiographical Questions', *Wesleyan Theological Journal*, 38 (Spring 2003), 33–4.

strategy and an itinerant fervour, his mission work spawned Methodist churches in 'Panama, Belize, Ecuador, Bolivia, Peru, Chile, Brazil, Angola, Mozambique, Congo, and South India'. In addition, he worked alongside 'Wesleyan Methodists in Australia, South Africa and the Caribbean'.[13] Through his worldwide connections, he developed relationships not only with holiness leaders, like Pandita Ramabai in India, but also with first generation Pentecostal leaders, such as Thomas Ball Barratt, Minnie Abrams and the Hoovers.

## The Holiness Movement: Keswick

Simultaneous with the emergence of the Wesleyan Holiness movement, perfectionist tendencies existed in the 1830s beyond Methodism. In the United States, these became associated with Oberlin College. Both Asa Mahan, first president of Oberlin, and Charles G. Finney, first Professor of Theology and Mahan's successor as president, experienced entire sanctification and became promoters of Oberlin perfectionism, as it became known. In 1839, Mahan authored *The Scriptural Doctrine of Christian Perfection* in which he outlined his views on sanctification. When he retired to England, he connected with the British Holiness movement and the Keswick movement, which takes its name from a town in the Lake District. An annual holiness conference has met in Keswick since 1875. The Keswick movement, launched at the Union Meeting for the Promotion of Scripture Holiness at Oxford in 1874, gathered together holiness figures from Great Britain, Europe and the United States.

For the Keswick movement, there are three steps to spiritual fulfilment and power, the first being a full surrender or consecration to Christ, in which the individual relinquishes her will to be replaced by the Spirit's. This is the decisive crisis experience after conversion which launches the Christian into a 'higher life'. The second step is being filled with the Spirit, also known as the baptism of the Holy Spirit. Similar to Palmer's teaching, the individual claims this by faith, irrespective of his feelings. In the third step, the individual receives power for service, a step which cemented a close connection between the Keswick movement and global mission at the turn of the twentieth century. A missionary speaker, like Pandita Ramabai, always headlined the Keswick annual meeting to underscore a 'higher life' made manifest through service to others, particularly as a missionary.

Also, the Keswick movement developed a close connection between sanctification and divine healing, as this statement by Captain R. Kelso Carter exemplified:

> It is a remarkable fact, that no one has been known to seek the healing power for the body, without receiving a distinct spiritual baptism; and further, that everyone known to the writer (a very large number),

---

[13] David Bundy, *Visions of Apostolic Mission: Scandinavian Pentecostal Mission to 1935* (Uppsala: Uppsala Universitet, 2009), 57.

who has been *entirely healed* in body, is or has become a believer in and professor of entire sanctification of soul.[14]

His mentor, A. B. Simpson (1843–1919), believed in divine healing through faith alone, without the interference of any medicine or medical expertise. Simpson promoted this teaching in conjunction with his sanctification in 1874, after reading W. E. Boardman's *The Higher Christian Life*, and his healing, seven years later, under the ministry of Charles Cullis. According to Simpson, for those who are a new creation, having died to self and been raised to new life in Jesus Christ, there is imparted to them a 'higher life' adding power and strength to the body and soul. This attendant power comes from God's free grace alone, not from any kind of works; thus he dismissed reliance on all human means for healing – one need only to believe. Further, because this power and strength were not a permanent endowment, he exhorted believers to depend constantly on Jesus Christ through the power of the Holy Spirit. Simpson, who founded the Christian and Missionary Alliance denomination, summarised his teaching as the four-fold gospel: Jesus Christ as Saviour, Sanctifier, Healer and Coming King. Several decades later, Aimee Semple McPherson (18901944), the leading Pentecostal woman preacher, incorporated the four-fold gospel as the doctrinal foundation for her denomination, the International Church of the Foursquare Gospel.

## The Pentecostal Movement

The closing decades of the nineteenth century highlighted significant influence and overlap between the Holiness and Pentecostal movements due to shared emphasis on the Holy Spirit. As historian Grant Wacker explains,' the whole nineteenth-century evangelical movement, Wesleyan as well as Reformed, might well be defined as historic Protestant orthodoxy spiced with a tingling expectation that the power of the Holy Spirit, lost since the days of the apostles, was about to be restored.'[15] This confluence of attention on the Holy Spirit from varying perspectives, people and publications complicated the meaning of language about Spirit-related matters, such as the phrase 'baptism of the Holy Spirit', central to the Holiness movement and then adopted as the watchword of Pentecostalism. For instance, in the autobiography of Emma Ray (1859–1930), a former slave who became a Free Methodist evangelist, she referred several times to sanctification as the baptism of the Holy Spirit. However, when she used this phrase in her 1926 autobiography, it also meant glossalalia, or speaking in tongues, in the Pentecostal

---

[14] Donald Dayton, *Theological Roots of Pentecostalism* (Peabody, MA: Hendrickson, 1987), 130.

[15] Grant Wacker, 'The Holy Spirit and the Spirit of the Age in American Protestantism, 1880–1910', in Martin Marty (ed.), *New and Intense Movements*, vol. 11: *Modern American Protestantism and Its World* (New York, NY: K. G. Saur, 1993), 190.

movement. Lest her readers misunderstand, Ray clarified that her experience of sanctification did *not* include glossalalia: 'Neither did we speak in tongues, but He gave us a new tongue to testify and tell the glad tidings.'[16] The same confusion was evident, according to historian Donald Dayton, with the term 'sanctification', because it could be understood as cleansing and perfecting, or with the more Pentecostal motif of power. 'Often the "power" themes merely overwhelmed the "holiness" themes ... The mainstream Holiness movement tried valiantly to preserve the classical themes in the midst of the new changes in vocabulary and rhetoric.'[17]

Maria Woodworth-Etter (1844–1924), evangelist and faith healer, exemplified the shift in vocabulary from holiness to power. In her autobiography, she described a spiritual experience that utilised holiness vocabulary, though she incorporated neither the term 'holiness' nor sanctification. In the first edition of her autobiography in 1885, she conveyed the experience with these words:

> ... then I began to seek a better experience, and pray for an anointing of power. I made a full conversion and asked for a baptism of fire to take everything out of my heart and cleanse it with the blood of Christ, and fill it with the Holy Ghost. I promised to let nothing but sickness or death come between me and the work. God accepted the offering, and the blessing and power came, and I went about praising God from morning till night. My heart was full of his love and praise. It was as natural for me to say, 'Praise God,' as it was to breathe. The Bible was a new book. All desires to sin were gone. ... With these words would come such power that I gained the victory every time.[18]

The holiness theme appeared particularly in phrases such as 'full conversion' and 'all desires to sin were gone'. Yet the power theme was even stronger. Not only was the word itself repeated multiple times, but also she explained that power was what she sought. With power, she 'gained the victory every time', and power prevailed throughout her evangelistic ministry. After several revised editions of her autobiography, by 1912, her language about this same experience exhibited even more Pentecostal power motifs and fire:

> I was baptized with the Holy Ghost, and fire, and power which has never left me. Oh, Praise the Lord! There was liquid fire, and the angels were all around in the fire and glory. It is through the Lord Jesus Christ,

---

[16] Emma Ray, *Twice Sold, Twice Ransomed: Autobiography of Mr. and Mrs. L. P. Ray* (Chicago, IL: Free Methodist Publishing, 1926), 65.
[17] Dayton, *Theological Roots of Pentecostalism*, 94.
[18] Maria B. Woodworth, *The Life and Experience of Maria B. Woodworth* (Dayton, OH: United Brethren Publishing, 1885), 35.

and by this power, that I have stood before hundreds of thousands of
men and women, proclaiming the unsearchable riches of Christ.[19]

By the mid-1880s at her meetings, Woodworth-Etter reported Pentecostal-like signs and wonders. These occurrences predated similar events listed as precursors to Pentecostalism, such as the watch night service at Bethel Bible School (1900), the Welsh Revival (1904), the Mukti Mission revival (1905) and the Azusa Street revival (1906). In 1885, trances first occurred during her meeting in Hartford City, Indiana, and from then on they were commonplace. Woodworth-Etter herself often fell into a trance while preaching and remained rigid in a semi-conscious state for an extended period. 'Mrs. Woodworth's face is working strangely and its color has changed to a grayish white. Suddenly she drops into a chair. Her face is turned upwards, her eyes open, staring, the pupils dilated.' For forty-five minutes, she held her right arm raised above her head, waving it slowly back and forth, while the index finger pointed upward and pulsated. A worker at the meeting explained the significance of these physical gestures: 'the rigid evangelist was pointing heavenward with one finger and toward hell with the other, and "Oh, dear friends, which way will you go?"'[20] Trances even happened to people in other parts of the city far from the meeting venue, according to accounts in her autobiography. 'Men, women and children were struck down in their homes, in their places of business, on the highways, and lay as dead.'[21]

Several months after Hartford City, Woodworth-Etter believed God had given her 'the gift of healing, and of laying on of hands for the recovery of the sick'.[22] Healings happened sporadically at first, but eventually they became the primary manifestation of signs and wonders when she preached. Nearly half of the 1922 edition of her autobiography, *Marvels and Miracles*, was devoted to published accounts by individuals healed at her meetings. In addition, glossalalia emerged prominently at her 1904 St. Louis meetings, again a date that preceded the Azusa Street revival, which she noted in her 1916 autobiography: 'One sister spake in unknown tongues all night. This was before the Holy Ghost fell at Los Angeles, California.'[23] Even earlier in her 1885 autobiography, she mentioned tongues in conjunction with her husband's conversion. 'About this time my husband was converted in the Methodist Church ... He was very bright and seemed to speak with other tongues.'[24] She repeated the phrase in her description of a post-conversion

---

[19] Maria Woodworth-Etter, *Signs and Wonders*, rev. edn (New Kensington, PA: Whitaker House, 1997), 32.
[20] 'Mrs. Woodworth In Trance', *The Indianapolis Journal* (31 May 1885), 5; Flower Pentecostal Heritage Center, Springfield, Missouri.
[21] Maria B. Woodworth, *The Life, Work and Experience of Maria Beulah Woodworth, Evangelist*, rev. edn (St. Louis, MO: Commercial Printing, 1894), 174.
[22] Woodworth, *Life, Work and Experience*, 189.
[23] Maria Woodworth-Etter, *Acts of the Holy Ghost, or The Life, Work, and Experience of Mrs. M. B. Woodworth-Etter, Evangelist* (Dallas, TX: John F. Worley Printing, 1916), 84.
[24] Woodworth, *Life and Experience* (1885), 28.

celebration in December 1883, when a man was on his feet, 'speaking as if it were with other tongues, exhorting sinners to come to Christ'.[25]

Woodworth-Etter believed her revivals with their ecstatic expressions awakened dead churches, and she likened herself in that regard to earlier revivalists, such as when 'Wesley, Whitfield and Cartwright preached'.[26] This same conclusion found resonance with her supporters:

> And to you, Christians of the Methodist and Quaker order, who have been praying so long and loud for the fullness of that religion of which you have been permited (sic) to have a little taste, let me say that this woman only has that fullness for which your souls have long panted; so be careful how you treat her when she comes among you.[27]

At the same time, she faced unrelenting criticism from newspaper reporters as well as leaders in her denomination, the Churches of God, General Conference (Winebrenner), because they found her style too exuberant and the churches she planted too unwieldy. Nevertheless, her services with plentiful ecstatic phenomena – trances, visions, healings and speaking in tongues – attracted crowds who overflowed her 8,000-seat tent. By 1912, she had made her way into Pentecostal circles, with F. F. Bosworth, a prominent Pentecostal minister, inviting her to hold meetings for six months in his Dallas church. From then on, she regularly preached on Pentecostal platforms across the country.

Another transitional figure from the Holiness movement to the fledgling Pentecostal movement prior to Azusa Street was Charles Parham (1873–1929), who formulated the initial evidence concept of glossalalia as marking the baptism of the Holy Spirit. He had experienced sanctification and preached it first as a Methodist minister in Kansas for two years, then as an independent holiness evangelist. In 1900, he founded Bethel Bible School in Topeka, Kansas, and forty students enrolled for the one and only year of the school's existence. During a watch night service on 31 December 1900, a Methodist student, Agnes Ozman, asked Parham to lay hands on her and pray for the baptism of the Holy Spirit. She experienced glossalalia and the ability to speak Chinese. Not long after, many other students and Parham himself experienced glossalalia. This event catalysed for Parham the confirmation of glossalalia as the initial evidence of Spirit baptism and the import of xenoglossia, the ability to speak in foreign languages. His teachings on these manifestations provided pivotal doctrinal and missiological foundations for the global Pentecostal

---

[25] Woodworth, *Life, Work and Experience*, 97.

[26] 'She Has No Fears', *St. Louis Post Dispatch* (2 September 1890); quoted in Joshua J. McMullen, 'Maria B. Woodworth-Etter: Bridging the Wesleyan–Pentecostal Divide', in Henry H. Knight (ed.), *From Aldersgate to Azusa Street: Wesleyan, Holiness, and Pentecostal Visions of the New Creation* (Eugene, OR: Pickwick, 2010), 191.

[27] Dr T. V. Gifford, 'Conversion By Trance', *Kokomo Dispatch* (7 May 1885), 5; Flower Pentecostal Heritage Center, Springfield, Missouri.

movement. Parham relocated to Houston, Texas, where he planted several churches and began another Bible school as part of the Apostolic Faith movement.

Parham in turn influenced William J. Seymour (1870–1922), leader of the Azusa Street revival. Seymour, already conversant with holiness teachings, came to Houston to learn from Parham. Even though Seymour had to sit outside in the school's hallway because integrated classrooms were against the law in Texas, he spent six weeks at Parham's school. From there, he accepted a pastoral call from a holiness church in Los Angeles; however, when he preached 'the Pentecostal message, taking Acts 2:4 as a text, even though he himself had not received "the blessing"', he found himself literally locked out from the church.[28] He first convened a prayer meeting in a private home during which he and others experienced glossalalia, then he moved the meetings to a former African Methodist Episcopal Church located at 312 Azusa Street. From the outset, Seymour's interracial, intercultural Apostolic Faith Mission attracted attention because of the unusual features of its worship services. Men and women experienced ecstatic occurrences, such as speaking in tongues, interpreting tongues, healings and prophesying. Thousands of people made the pilgrimage to Azusa Street, and the revival itself lasted for three years with three services every day of the week. 'Those who were convinced that this was a "latter rain" paralleling the first Pentecost left Azusa Street to carry the message across America and throughout the world, sometimes sparking Azusa-type revivals and sometimes making connections with indigenous revivals already underway.'[29]

Communication about the revival immediately crossed continents. To inform people around the world about events at Azusa Street, Seymour and Clara E. Lum co-edited a free paper, *The Apostolic Faith*. They initially printed 5,000 copies of the September 1906 first edition; by 1907 the press run had reached 40,000. Also by 1907, an international mail correspondence among Pentecostal groups had flourished to such an extent that Azusa Street received fifty letters a day from around the world.[30] In addition, global communication passed by word of mouth through Pentecostal missionaries taking news of the revival to other countries and Pentecostal leaders itinerating internationally on revival tours, such as Thomas Ball Barratt who visited Azusa Street in 1906 and then travelled throughout Europe and to India.

The Pentecostal movement spread rapidly around the world, including among holiness folk like Willis C. Hoover (1858–1936), an American Methodist pastoring the largest MEC in Chile and serving simultaneously as district superintendent. He learned about the Mukti revival through Minnie Abrams' booklet, which she

---

[28] Steven J. Land, 'William J. Seymour: The Father of the Holiness–Pentecostal Message', in Knight (ed.), *From Aldersgate to Azusa Street*, 221.

[29] 'The Twentieth Century: The Emergence of Pentecostalism, Introduction', in Knight (ed.) *From Aldersgate to Azusa Street*, , 202.

[30] Michael Bergunder, 'Constructing Indian Pentecostalism: On Issues of Methodology and Representation', in Allan Anderson and Edmond Tang (eds), *Asian and Pentecostal: The Charismatic Face of Christianity in Asia* (Oxford: Regnum Books International, 2005), 184.

mailed to his wife, May Louise Hoover, Abrams' former classmate at Lucy Rider Meyer's Chicago Training School. Hearing of the Pentecostal revival stirred Hoover and his congregation 'to pray for and expect such a "Holy Ghost revival" and daily prayer meetings "for the outpouring of the Holy Spirit upon our church"'.[31] The revival commenced in 1909 with hundreds of conversions and Spirit-filled manifestations, including glossalalia. In the midst of the revival, A. B. Simpson visited Chile and preached in Hoover's church to a thousand people. Meanwhile, Methodist leaders removed Hoover as district superintendent and pressured him either to return to the States or leave Methodism altogether. Instead, he founded the Methodist Pentecostal Church, the first entirely self-supporting church in Latin America, which maintains Methodist doctrines and practices today. 'The closeness to Methodism differentiates Chilean Pentecostalism from North American classical Pentecostalism. Significantly, this Chilean movement with origins in the Mukti revival in India was not connected to American Pentecostal churches and Hoover was founder of an autochthonous Chilean church.'[32] Currently, Chilean Pentecostals comprise nearly 20 per cent of the country's population.[33]

Sanctification remained a catalysing doctrine within the African American Pentecostal community, spawning sanctified churches, described by historian Cheryl Townsend Gilkes as maintaining a twin focus on sanctification and 'ritual practices emphasizing the work of the Holy Ghost (or Holy Spirit) through such activities as "shouting," the "holy dance," speaking in tongues, healing and other spiritual gifts'.[34] Sanctified churches include the Church of God in Christ, the United Holy Church of America and the Mount Sinai Holy Church of America, founded by Ida Robinson (1891–1946). Robinson was ordained in 1919 in the United Holy Church of America and appointed to her own small mission church. However, she perceived a decline in prospects for women within the denomination that conflicted with a promise from God given to her, 'that He would do a great work through the women as time passed on'.[35] In January 1924, as she spent ten days in prayer and fasting, she believed that God called her to 'Come out on Mount Sinai' and 'I will use you to loose the women.' Immediately she chartered a new denomination, the Mount Sinai Holy Church of America, which continues today.

Sanctification forms a central part of the denomination's doctrine and its hymnody, as epitomised in stanzas from a favourite hymn at Mount Sinai services, 'The Standard of Mount Sinai is Good Enough for Me':

---

[31] Anderson, *Spreading Fires*, 202.
[32] Ibid., 203.
[33] Allan Anderson, 'Revising Pentecostal History in Global Perspective', in Anderson and Tang (eds), *Asian and Pentecostal*, 156.
[34] Rosemary Skinner Keller, Rosemary Radford Ruether and Marie Cantlon (eds), *Encyclopedia of Women and Religion in North America*, I:430 (3 vols, Bloomington IN: Indiana University Press, 2006).
[35] 'Brief History of Mount Sinai', pamphlet prepared for the sixty-fifth anniversary, 3; given to the author by Elder Minerva Bell, denominational historian.

> We don't use tobacco over here; don't smoke or drink or chew,
> We don't make Moonshine, don't drink it, and won't sell it to you,
> Mount Sinai's standard reaches so high, no adulterer may abide,
> But woman to one husband, man to one wife, no sweethearts on the side.
>
> One beauty of Mount Sinai is the way the people dress,
> Which is as becometh Holiness, but they always look the best,
> Don't think its people look like bums, as you can plainly see,
> You'll find they're very up-to-date, and it's good enough for me.[36]

Another hymn, sung at every Easter Sunday Sunrise Service, displayed the denomination's commitment to women. Robinson would take up her tambourine and lead congregants in this song about Jesus' female disciples who first announced the good news of his resurrection:

> Didn't those women run,
> Didn't those women run,
> They ran the good news to spread.
> The angel told them to go
> For Jesus had gone on before.
> 'He is risen just as He said.'[37]

As founder and bishop of the Pentecostal denomination, Robinson ensured that women in the Mount Sinai Holy Church enjoyed unlimited opportunities from the outset when six of nine members of the Board of Elders and the top four officers were women. Numerically women far outnumbered men as ministers, as in 1946, the year of Robinson's death, when the ratio was 125 women to 38 men serving in a denomination consisting of 84 churches, an accredited school in Philadelphia, mission work in Cuba and Guyana, and a farm in South Jersey for members to escape for a vacation from crowded city neighbourhoods.[38]

## Conclusion

In terms of future research trajectories, Donald Dayton predicts that 'it will become clear that Pentecostalism is a very natural outgrowth of the currents that took shape in the late nineteenth century under the influence of the Holiness Movement'.[39] His

---

[36] Dean Trulear, 'Reshaping Black Pastoral Theology: The Vision of Bishop Ida B. Robinson', *Journal of Religious Thought*, 46 (1989), 27.

[37] Dean Trulear, 'Reshaping Black Pastoral Theology: The Vision of Bishop Ida B. Robinson', *Journal of Religious Thought*, 46 (1989), 31.

[38] Ibid., 23–4.

[39] Dayton, 'Methodism and Pentecostalism', 181.

words corroborate the interconnectedness between the two movements developed in his book, *Theological Roots of Pentecostalism* and Vinson Synan's *The Holiness–Pentecostal Tradition: Charismatic Movements in the Twentieth Century*, to name but two. As this essay demonstrates the next step for this research trajectory is to shift the focus from a largely intra-national concern – within the North American historical context – to an international venture, analysing the interconnections between Holiness and Pentecostal leaders and labours across countries and continents. Vital in this regard is the ongoing work of historian David Bundy, who traces both the Holiness and Pentecostal movements in a variety of countries, such as Brazil, China, India, Japan, Norway, Russia and Sweden. Of particular import as a model of global interconnectedness is his monograph, *Visions of Apostolic Mission: Scandinavian Pentecostal Mission to 1935*. A key to developing this trajectory will be international collaboration among researchers in conferences and edited monographs.

Research on women in these movements is well underway. Studies continue to pour out on individual women leaders, such as Phoebe Palmer, Amanda Berry Smith, Aimee Semple McPherson and Maria Woodworth-Etter, as well as groups of women – Wesleyan/Holiness women preachers, Salvation Army women, and women in African American sanctified churches. Further, historians of these movements routinely include a section or even a chapter specifically devoted to women. While these resources have been and will continue to be necessary for recovering women's ground-breaking contributions to these movements, they are not the finished product, because they segregate gender into a separate category, like race or class. Women are not yet fully integrated alongside men as co-creators of these movements. Therefore, future histories of these movements must reflect the full spectrum of gendered leadership and participation of both women and men as theologians, scribes, preachers, missionaries, fundraisers, educators, leaders, administrators and members.

# Methodism and Women

*Margaret Jones*

## Methodology

### 'Methodism and Women': What Kind of Topic?

This chapter began life under two possible headings: 'Methodism and Women' or 'Women in Methodism'. Without refining too much on the nuances of word order, the difference between them usefully indicates some of the theoretical issues raised by the topic.

'Women in Methodism' has always featured in the story that Methodism has told about itself, and thus of the history that has been constructed about it. Women's stories have always formed part of a movement whose faith and spirituality have been grounded in and validated by experience from the very beginning. It must be noted, however, that post-modern and cross-cultural[1] insights have prompted recent re-examinations[2] of the meaning of the term 'experience'.

In the early years of the evangelical revival 'Lives' and 'Accounts' of individuals' journey of faith, building on well-established Puritan tradition,[3] soon acquired a conventional Methodist format and a ready audience. The preponderance of

---

[1]   Christina Landman, 'Mercy Amba Ewudziwa Oduyoye, Mother of our Stories', *Studia Historiae Ecclesiasticae*, 33:1 (2009), 92.

[2]   Gregory S. Clapper, *John Wesley on Religious Affections: His Views on Experience and Emotion and their Role in Christian Life and Theology* (Metuchen, NJ: Scarecrow Press, 1989); Randy L. Maddox, *Responsible Grace: John Wesley's Practical Theology* (Nashville, TN: Kingswood Books, 1994); Randy L. Maddox, 'A Change of Affections: The Development, Dynamics and Dethronement of John Wesley's Heart Religion', in Richard B. Steele (ed.), *'Heart Religion' in the Methodist Tradition and Related Movements* (Lanham, MD: Scarecrow Press, 2001); Clive Marsh, 'Appealing to "Experience": What Does It Mean?', in C. Marsh, B. Beck, A. Shier-Jones and H. Wareing (eds), *Unmasking Methodist Theology* (London: Continuum, 2004).

[3]   Bruce Hindmarsh, *The Evangelical Conversion Narrative: Spiritual Autobiography in Early Modern England* (Oxford: Oxford University Press, 2005).

women within British Methodism (and, for the early period, John Wesley's close relationships with his women correspondents and his willingness to publish their writings[4]) gave their stories prominence in published media, albeit not in proportion to their actual numbers within the movement.[5] In the course of the nineteenth century such stories became formalised and less common, but as new roles for women developed so new stories – of women missionaries,[6] deaconesses[7] and Friends of the Poor[8] – were told. The tradition of using women's life-stories as a resource to 'help us understand the dynamics of Christian authenticity and renewal more fully'[9] persists to this day alongside the more self-consciously feminist perspectives outlined below.

Without stretching the point too far, the title 'Methodism and Women' suggests a different kind of relationship. There is a linguistic space allowing 'Women' to be placed in an over–against category in relation to 'Methodism' as well as being part of it. They are presented as a differentiated group with their own special place *as women* within Methodism. This understanding has clear links with feminist theory developed since the 1960s[10] but its Methodist roots lie much deeper. It may be traced to Zechariah Taft's publication of *Biographical Sketches of the Lives and Public Ministry of Various Holy Women* in 1825. This was a work with a polemical as well as an 'improving' and didactic purpose, using women preachers' biographies as ammunition in the contemporary controversy about women's preaching in British Wesleyan Methodism. It positioned women as a group with a particular (and problematic) relationship to the structures of Methodism and as potential subjects of collective history. It both reflected and established an awareness of 'Methodism and Women' in the terms outlined above.

From the second quarter of the nineteenth century, therefore, awareness of women as (in a structural sense) a special group both persisted and changed, reflecting developments both within and outside the churches. Twentieth-century feminist theory identifies this awareness as part of 'first wave' feminism, concerned with the achievement of equal rights. Feminist historiography locates it within

---

[4] Margaret Jones, 'From "The State of my Soul" to "Exalted Piety": Women's Voices in the *Arminian/Methodist* Magazine, 1778–1821', in R. N. Swanson (ed.), *Gender and Religion* (*SCH* 34) (Woodbridge: Boydell and Brewer, 1998).

[5] E.g. William Bramwell, *A Short Account of the Life and Death of Ann Cutler* (Sheffield: John Smith, 1796); Henry Moore, *The Life of Mrs Mary Fletcher* (London: J. Kershaw, 1818); Richard Rogers, *The Experience and Spiritual Letters of Mrs Hester Ann Rogers* (London: William Milner, 1854).

[6] E.g. Alfred Barrett, *Holy Living: Exemplified in the Life of Mrs Mary Cryer* (London: John Mason, 1849); Benjamin Clough, *Extracts from the Journal and Correspondence of the Late Mrs M.M. Clough* (London: J. Mason, 1829).

[7] Especially in periodicals of deaconess orders such as the Wesleyan *Flying Leaves*.

[8] E.g. James Tollefree Parr, *The Angel of Blackfriars; or, the Sister with the Shining Face* (London: W. A. Hammond, 1914).

[9] Paul W. Chilcote (ed.), *Her Own Story: Autobiographical Portraits of Early Methodist Women* (Nashville, TN: Kingswood Books, 2001), 36.

[10] See p. 160 below.

'traditional' women's history, which is identified as making women visible, compensating for their absence from the mainstream historical narrative.[11] George Coles's *Heroines of Methodism*,[12] for example, published at the relatively early date of 1857, and Abel Stevens's *Women of Methodism*[13] of 1876 (the latter produced in response to a specific request from the 'American Methodist Ladies' Centenary Committee') reflect the emergence of a defined feminist consciousness in the United States, conventionally dated to the Seneca Falls Anti-Slavery Convention of 1836. The establishment by women of the (British) Wesleyan Methodist Missionary Society's Ladies Committee in 1858, to enable women to work in women's education overseas, led to the publication through denominational channels of accounts of missionary work specifically by and for women. Annie Keeling's *Eminent Methodist Women* of 1889 deliberately aimed to publicise the stories of less-well-known 'holy women'[14] and indirectly acknowledged that women might be silenced in the historical record.[15] Writing in this tradition continued throughout the first half of the twentieth century, sometimes explicitly with the aim of providing inspiration and role-models for girls.[16] It might sometimes be linked with 'that emancipation of women, which during the past century has so radically changed the pattern of our own community' noted by Pauline Webb in 1958.[17]

'Second wave' feminism from the 1960s onwards, identifying the need to move beyond equality to the affirmation of difference, brought a different set of questions and a different methodology to the history of women as women. David Hempton[18] charts the way in which writing influenced by the *Annales* school gave a rationale for historians to consider women as a distinct though internally diverse group.[19] An alternative account might place more emphasis on the insights generated by the thinking of women-only feminist groups.[20] Whatever the history of these changes, their impact has been dramatic.

---

[11] E.g. Gerda Lerner, *The Creation of Patriarchy* (Oxford: Oxford University Press, 1986); Joan Wallach Scott, 'Gender: A Useful Category of Historical Analysis', *American Historical Review*, 91:5 (1986).

[12] George Coles, *Heroines of Methodism* (New York, NY: Carlton & Porter, 1857).

[13] Abel Stevens, *Women of Methodism* (New York, NY: Carlton & Porter, 1876), vi.

[14] Annie Keeling, *Eminent Methodist Women* (London, Charles H. Kelly, 1889), 5.

[15] Ibid., 6.

[16] See for example Thomas M. Morrow, *Early Methodist Women* (Altrincham: Epworth, 1967); Pauline M. Webb, *Women of Our Company* (London: Cargate Press, 1958).

[17] Ibid., 9.

[18] David Hempton, *Methodism: Empire of the Spirit* (New Haven, CT and London: Yale University Press, 2005), 145.

[19] Ibid.

[20] Scott, 'Gender'; Sandra Harding (ed.), *Feminism and Methodology* (Bloomington, IN: Indiana University Press, 1987); K. Kearns, *Psychoanalysis, Historiography and Feminist Theory* (Cambridge: Cambridge University Press, 1997); Judith M. Bennett, *History Matters: Patriarchy and the Challenge of Feminism* (Philadelphia, PA: University of Pennsylvania Press, 2006).

Descriptions of feminist methodology may be differently nuanced[21] but its main outlines are well established. First, gender is understood as a defining analytical category: women may intelligibly be dealt with as a group. Women's roles, and the way those roles are created and maintained, are scrutinised. The historian consciously searches for possible conflicts between roles and expectations created by society as a whole (the power to create such roles and expectations having historically lain with men), and those generated by women by and for themselves. Secondly, the historian must question assumptions about whose history should be studied. The majority of women have been regarded as 'ordinary': their stories must be discovered and told despite all the difficulties of obscurity and lack of sources. Post-modern approaches to texts highlight the power-relationships, exclusions and silences that lie behind the creation of the historical record. Thirdly, the historian searches for women's own points of view rather than writings about women. Fourthly, the historian is wary of generalised assumptions about what periods, movements, individuals or characterisations are 'important'.[22]

Third-wave feminism, however, from the 1980s onward, challenged the very notion of 'women's' identity. The post-modern insights which were so important in identifying 'women' as a group in the interpretation of history led to the category of 'women' itself being seen as a social construct. 'Women' may have gender in common, but gender itself is a varied and shifting category. World-view and self-understanding are not the same for all women everywhere. Womanist theology, insisting that an overall category of 'feminist theology' could not take account of black women's experience, was highly significant here. Writing about 'women' as a group could involve the same power issues as those identified by earlier feminist criticism in respect of writing about ostensibly non-gendered 'mankind'.

Such post-structuralist approaches can lead the philosopher to the complete deconstruction of the notion of a 'self' and the historian to a total inability to make any generalisations at all. Fortunately this catastrophe has not overtaken writing about 'Methodism and Women': what has become evident is, in some quarters, a greater degree of differentiation between various contexts of women's experience and a reintegration of the history of religious experience for men and women. Bruce Hindmarsh, for example, uses examples of conversion narratives from both men and women, while paying attention to the means by which the various denominational genres were constructed and the extent to which they did or did not give women a voice.[23] Hempton discusses the place of gender in his account

---

[21] See note 15 above: a helpful summary is given in Gloria N. Redekop, *The Work of Their Hands: Mennonite Women's Societies in Canada* (Waterloo, Ontario: Wilfred Laurier University Press, 1996), 15–19.

[22] For an early exploration of these issues in relation to Methodist history, see Donald G. Matthews, 'Women's History/Everyone's History', in H. F. Thomas, R. Keller and L. Queen (eds), *Women in New Worlds: Historical Perspectives on the Wesleyan Tradition* (Nashville, TN: Abingdon, 1982).

[23] Hindmarsh, *Evangelical Conversion Narrative*, 173–83, 235–8.

of Methodism as a faith tradition[24] and indicates possible directions for future research in describing it as 'comprehensively shaped by women in ways that we still do not fully understand'.[25] Phyllis Mack goes further and uses gender as a category of analysis throughout her work on 'heart religion' and is thus able to present men's spiritual experience as gendered rather than normative.[26]

## Women's History: The Problem of Sources

Would-be researchers into women's history are immediately confronted with problems created by the nature of the subject. The creation and preservation of source material are subject to selection according to the judgements and opinions of those who control such resources. Historically these have largely been men. The possibility of evidence of roles and ways of being unique to women being preserved is therefore greatly lessened. The same holds true for the preservation of women's authentic voices and points of view, and for records of 'ordinary' women.

The process of making judgements about what is 'important' also affects the categorisation and ordering of records and therefore the ease of the historian's access to them. Records tend to be grouped according to topics suggested by public history or well-known personalities, or because the papers deposited have collected around an 'important' figure. Mary Fletcher proves to be exceptional not only because of her leadership role and her quasi-public functions, but because in the Fletcher-Tooth papers deposited at the Methodist Archives Centre we have a collection of women's papers and correspondence between women, gathered round leading women. In general, church structures and office-holding, and therefore the creation of records, have tended to be the province of men. Women's groups have, broadly speaking, often been more informal and sometimes affected by a lower standard of literacy and a different attitude to record-keeping.

These 'problems', however, may also indicate opportunities. Women's history may often be best discovered by a 'bottom-up' approach – the kind of historical investigation that focuses on a geographical or social area in all its variety, rather than a church-based structured grouping whose use and choice of records have already self-selected the writing of its history. Recent works referenced in this chapter illustrate how detailed work at a local level has the potential to generate new insights into women's history.[27]

---

[24] Hempton, *Methodism: Empire of the Spirit*, 137–50.
[25] Ibid., 149.
[26] Phyllis Mack, *Heart Religion in the British Enlightenment: Gender and Emotion in Early Methodism* (Cambridge: Cambridge University Press, 2008).
[27] See the bibliographies of, for example, Linda Wilson, *Constrained by Zeal: Female Spirituality Amongst Nonconformists 1825–1875* (Carlisle: Paternoster, 2000), Hindmarsh, *Evangelical Conversion Narrative*; and Mack, *Heart Religion*.

## Methodism and Women: Some Themes

### Why 'Themes'?

Despite the plethora of published material about 'Women in Methodism' from the earliest days, therefore, the creation of a history of 'Methodism and Women', while traceable in embryo from 1825, dates in the main only from around 1980.[28] Even so, despite the widespread acceptance since that date of 'women' as a discrete area of historical study, not all writing on 'Methodism and Women' takes account of feminist critical perspectives. In this chapter I therefore adopt a framework built around a series of themes that have been important in the area to date, aiming to survey recent historical writing.[29] At the same time I hope to be able to use the themes as vantage points, looking beyond them for possible further lines of enquiry. The methodology outlined above suggests that all such themes should be treated with caution, with the fundamental power issue in mind: on what basis is this area defined as 'important' (or even as 'an area')?

### The Eighteenth Century and Early Methodism: The Women (Not) Around Wesley

Writing the history of Methodism and women has remained largely (though not exclusively) an Anglo-Saxon pursuit and has been particularly prominent in the United States. Given the significance of John Wesley as a focus and norm for Methodist theology and ecclesiology in the US context, and the strength of the Methodist academy there, it is not surprising that considerable attention has been given to the women who were his confidantes and correspondents.

Annie Keeling in 1889 introduced her selection of 'Eminent Methodist Women' by suggesting that enough had been heard of Susanna Wesley, Mary Fletcher and Hester Anne Rogers. With the lapse of time her choice of less-well-known women has been overtaken by events: the two from John Wesley's lifetime are Elizabeth Mortimer and Barbara Heck, who would surely feature near the top of any list of well-known Methodist women being drawn up today. Her further observations, however, offer a commentary on the problems of writing women's history which has stood the test of time rather better – the difficulty of obtaining information about the details of 'ordinary' life which (in her way of thinking) are important because they bring the subject to life by giving the personal touch. This of course identifies

---

[28] An earlier example is Olive Anderson, 'Women Preachers in Mid-Victorian Britain: Some Reflexions on Feminism, Popular Religion and Social Change', *Historical Journal*, 12:3 (1969).

[29] See also Margaret Jones, '"Her Claim to Public Notice": Reflections on the Historiography of Women in British Methodism', in Richard Sykes (ed.), *God's Own Story? Some Trends in Methodist Historiography* (Oxford: Applied Theology Press, 2003).

one of the main reasons why women connected with John and Charles[30] Wesley have continued to be such prominent subjects of study – the sheer availability and accessibility of source material through their correspondence and, in the case of John, his work in publishing their 'Lives' and letters.[31] But the range has broadened out of all recognition as large numbers of women's 'Lives', both autobiographical and (more commonly) biographical, have been subjects of study. All the major works in this area referenced in this chapter include extensive bibliographies of primary sources. Nearly all of those sources are located in collections in the United Kingdom or North America.

A range of publications in the field in the 1980s reflected the realisation that there were significant women's stories as yet untold. Writers such as Earl Kent Brown and, most notably, Paul Chilcote, placed women's role within the overall framework of Methodist theology and spirituality and extensively described it.[32] Methodism's experiential basis was interpreted as an important factor in giving a voice to those, including women, who were excluded from the traditional routes to power and influence such as office-holding and education. This work made it clear that the contribution of 'ordinary' women to the early Methodist movement had been overlooked. As already noted, the re-presentation of these women's stories can be seen as sitting within the tradition of 'holy lives'; that is, with the overt aim of offering a spiritual resource to readers. Researchers working further along these lines will need to pay careful attention to the nature of any parallels they may wish to draw between present-day and eighteenth-century faith and discipleship. Henry Abelove, by contrast, offered a particularly sharp critical examination of the relationship between Wesley and his women supporters and his work may be ripe for revisiting.[33]

The history of women in eighteenth-century Methodism has however moved away from its 'Wesley-centric' beginnings. The kind of analysis deployed by Mack,[34] for example, rather than beginning from the standpoint of Methodist theology and practice, looks for those features of religious experience and expression that were distinctively important to women. Her examination of women's religiosity through the lenses of love, suffering and dreaming sheds light on women and men alike, given the importance of 'feeling' (in its eighteenth-century sense) and of the transformation of 'the affections' in early Methodist spirituality.[35] Hindmarsh's

---

[30] Hindmarsh, *Evangelical Conversion Narrative*, 130.

[31] Jones, 'Women's Voices'.

[32] E.g. Earl Kent Brown, *Women of Mr Wesley's Methodism* (New York, NY: Mellen, 1983); Paul W. Chilcote, *John Wesley and the Women Preachers of Early Methodism* (Metuchen, NJ: Scarecrow Press, 1991); Paul W. Chilcote Paul W. Chilcote , *She Offered Them Christ: The Legacy of Women Preachers in Early Methodism* (Nashville, TN: Abingdon, 1993).

[33] Henry Abelove, *Evangelist of Desire: John Wesley and the Methodists* (Stanford, CA: Stanford University Press, 1990).

[34] Mack, *Heart Religion*.

[35] See for example Clapper, *John Wesley on Religious Affections*; Richard Steele, *'Gracious Affections' and 'True Virtue' according to Jonathan Edwards and John Wesley* (Metuchen, NJ: Scarecrow Press, 1994); Maddox, *Responsible Grace* and 'A Change of Affections'.

examination of evangelical conversion narratives across a wider constituency offers a salutary reminder that eighteenth-century Methodism was part of a larger movement.[36] Both of these writers challenge historians of Methodism to move away from preoccupation either with the Wesley circle or with Methodism *per se* and to draw wider comparisons. Earlier emphases by historians such as W. R. Ward on the international and particularly the transatlantic dimensions of the evangelical revival also have important implications for the further reading and interpretation of women's stories.[37]

Sensitivity to context is not of course a recent phenomenon among historians. John Newton's work on Susanna Wesley places her within the Puritan tradition that was so influential in developing a private spirituality particularly accessible and practicable for women.[38] Tim Macquiban's very recent brief comparison of her spirituality with that of her contemporary, Elizabeth Burnet, however, shows the impact of subsequent work on the history of women's spirituality.[39] The work of G. J. Barker-Benfield has been particularly significant in this field.[40] And Mack's chapter 'Women in Love', for example,[41] sets the Methodist emphasis on 'feeling', with all its nuances of meaning, in an even broader context of eighteenth-century language and sensibility.

Another intriguing area for future research within the broader social context may be connected with the place of hospitality within early Methodism. The significance of women's role in ensuring the well-being of preachers (well-aired sheets being a particular concern) diminished as preachers' lives became more settled, just as the building of preaching-houses undermined cottage religion (as charted by Deborah Valenze[42]). There would seem to be room for dialogue with the research and reflection on the home and its changing role in eighteenth-century society that is particularly associated with the work of Amanda Vickery.[43]

---

[36] Hindmarsh, *Evangelical Conversion Narrative*.

[37] W. R. Ward, *The Protestant Evangelical Awakening* (Cambridge: Cambridge University Press, 1992); W. R. Ward, *Early Evangelicalism: A Global Intellectual History, 1670–1789* (Cambridge: Cambridge University Press, 2006).

[38] John A. Newton, *Susanna Wesley and the Puritan Tradition in Methodism* (London: Epworth, 1968).

[39] Timothy S. Macquiban, 'Proto-Methodists of Anglican Piety in Post-Revolution England', in Mervyn Davies (ed.), *A Thankful Heart and a Discerning Mind: Essays in Honour of John Newton* (Dursley: Lonely Scribe, 2010).

[40] G. J. Barker-Benfield, *The Culture of Sensibility: Sex and Society in Eighteenth-Century Britain* (Chicago, IL: University of Chicago Press, 1992).

[41] Mack, *Heart Religion*, 127–70.

[42] Deborah Valenze, *Prophetic Sons and Daughters: Female Preaching and Popular Religion in Industrial England* (Princeton, NJ: Princeton University Press, 1985).

[43] Amanda Vickery, *The Gentleman's Daughter: Women's Lives in Georgian England* (New Haven, CT: Yale University Press, 1998); Amanda Vickery, *Behind Closed Doors: At Home in Georgian England* (New Haven, CT: Yale University Press, 2009). See also Gail Malmgreen, 'Domestic Discords – Women and the Family in East Cheshire Methodism, 1750–1830', in

The 'Wesley' period is therefore far from exhausted as a field for research into women's history: a sophisticated awareness of broader historical contexts will have much to contribute to familiar territory, as well as to 'bottom-up' research on 'unimportant' individuals.

## Preachers and Non-preachers

Much work has been done on women as preachers in early Methodism.[44] This may to some extent reflect the sheer excitement of rediscovering their life and work, as Methodist historians from the 1980s onward began more generally to look for women in the sources. It also reflects the availability of sources about women preachers: they were not only the kind of people who would have had leadership roles and thus be more thoroughly memorialised, but were also controversial and thus generated a very particular kind of record.[45] The danger for the researcher is precisely that identified by Gerda Lerner et al.: the category of 'preacher' was one identified by a male-dominated movement as 'important', so that the circularity of that movement's generation of records ensured that historians would perceive it as important. Other areas of women's experience and activism, less thoroughly documented, may not have carried the same perceptions of 'importance'. Historical writing of the last twenty years has taken account of this and offers a broader picture.[46]

Reading the story of women's preaching through the eyes of 'official' British Methodism led to the conclusion that the Wesleyan Conference ruling of 1803 (forbidding women to preach except in their own circuit with the permission of their Superintendent, and only to other women) saw an end to their activity as preachers in that Connexion, and this assertion is still sometimes made. Meticulous work among local sources of the kind exemplified by John Lenton has produced a revisionist account which not only discovers women preachers where none were

---

James Obelkevich (ed.), *Disciplines of Faith: Studies in Religion, Politics and Patriarchy* (London: Routledge and Kegan Paul, 1987).

[44] E.g. Oliver A. Beckerlegge, 'Women Itinerant Preachers', *Proceedings of the Wesley Historical Society (PWHS)*, 30:4 (1956); Chilcote, *John Wesley and the Women Preachers*; E. Dorothy Graham, *Chosen by God: A List of the Female Travelling Preachers of Early Primitive Methodism* (Banbury: Bankhead Press, 1989); E. Dorothy Graham , 'Female Preachers of Primitive Methodism', *PWHS*, 47 (1994), 68; E. Dorothy Graham , 'Women Local Preachers', in Geoffrey E. Milburn and Margaret Batty (eds), *Workaday Preachers* (Peterborough: MPH, 1995); E. Dorothy Graham , 'Two Primitive Methodist Women Preachers', *PWHS*, 56:2 (2007); Gareth Lloyd, 'Repression and Resistance: Wesleyan Female Public Ministry in the Generation after 1791', in Norma Virgoe (ed.), *Angels and Impudent Women* (Loughborough: WHS, 2007); Susie C. Stanley, *Holy Boldness: Women Preachers' Autobiographies and the Sanctified Self* (Knoxville, TN: University of Tennessee Press, 2004).

[45] E.g. Hugh Bourne, *Remarks on the Ministry of Women* (Bemersley: Primitive Methodist Connexion, 1808); Zechariah Taft, *Biographical Sketches of the Lives and Public Ministry of Various Holy Women* (London, Kershaw, 1825).

[46] E.g. Chilcote, *Her Own Story*; cf. Chilcote, *John Wesley and the Women Preachers*.

known before, but explores the terminology of 'preaching' and other genres of women's exposition of faith and spirituality and the overlap between them.[47] A brief section in Lenton's work on John Wesley's itinerant preachers indicates both the current state of work on women preachers of the Wesley period and the kind of methodology that will help researchers to discover them.[48]

The field of women's preaching, not only in the eighteenth century but right up to the present day, is still full of possibility for original research. The distinctiveness of women's preaching did not end when its existence ceased to be the subject of open controversy: its positioning within Methodist structures and its 'voice' could be historically investigated right up to the present day.[49] Topics such as women preachers at ordination services or women as professors and teachers of liturgy and homiletics come to mind. Jennifer Lloyd offers an excellent model in her exploration of the content and tone of women revivalists' preaching in the later nineteenth century.[50]

## Separate Spheres? Women and the Institutionalisation of Methodism

It could be argued that the history of Methodism and women is only now beginning to find its own periodisation as it breaks away from over-dependence on the John Wesley era and seeks to investigate the less accessible and, to some modern sensibilities, less attractive nineteenth century. The clustering of world-changing events in the years immediately before, and for some forty years after, John Wesley's death in 1791 seems to create a 'natural break' in the historical narrative: the methodology of women's history demands a critical examination of such a perception based on public events and important figures. Nevertheless work such as Hempton's[51] digs deeply into the impact of social, economic, industrial, geographical and political change on every aspect of Methodism in Britain and America at this time and affirms the early nineteenth century as a crucial turning point for the movement on both sides of the Atlantic (though not all the reasons are the same).

The same pattern is traced in the writing and interpretation of the history of women in Great Britain. The terms of debate for some time to come were set by

---

[47] John H. Lenton, 'Labouring for the Lord: Women Preachers in Wesleyan Methodism 1802–1932. A Revisionist View', in R. Sykes (ed.), *Beyond the Boundaries: Preaching in the Wesleyan Tradition* (Oxford: Applied Theology Press, 1998).

[48] John H. Lenton, *John Wesley's Preachers: A Social and Statistical Analysis of the British and Irish Preachers who Entered the Methodist Itinerancy before 1791* (Milton Keynes: Paternoster, 2009), 33–5.

[49] E.g. Jane Craske, *A Woman's Perspective on Preaching* (Peterborough: Foundery Press, 2001).

[50] Jennifer M. Lloyd, *Women and the Shaping of British Methodism* (Manchester: Manchester University Press, 2009), 167–205.

[51] David Hempton, *The Religion of the People: Methodism and Popular Religion c. 1750–1900* (London: Routledge, 1996); Hempton, *Methodism: Empire of the Spirit*.

Leonore Davidoff and Catherine Hall in 1987.[52] They contended that women in this period were increasingly excluded from public roles and confined to the private realm by an ideology of 'the angel in the house'. Their argument has influenced the interpretation of both secular and religious history for the first half of the nineteenth century. It has been critically examined and nuanced in the secular sphere, for instance by Vickery,[53] and most notably in the religious sphere by Linda Wilson.[54] Wilson gives a detailed analysis of obituary evidence for women's faith and religious practice across a range of evangelical traditions (both Methodist and Reformed) and concludes that, while Davidoff and Hall's basic model holds good, evangelical spirituality was important in giving women the opportunity to push the boundaries and inhabit more active roles.[55] John Wolffe also sets Methodism within the wider evangelical frame in this respect.[56]

The 'separate spheres' framework continues to offer a useful perspective for further work. Studies such as Margaret Batty's which focus on 'leadership' roles as defined by contemporaries will by definition exclude women.[57] But was the role of women as leaders of women's classes an exclusion from power and influence by restrictive confinement to a women-only environment? Was their involvement in the support of foreign missions through Auxiliary Societies a retreat from the active faith-sharing mission of the evangelical revival?[58] Could activities such as these have functioned as the seedbed for the development of an autonomous spirituality and the capacity for leadership and administrative roles? Despite Wilson's pioneering work, much remains to be discovered about the nature of women's interaction in such groups and their spiritual and practical support of one another.

These observations hold even more true for the second half of the nineteenth century. Jennifer Lloyd's recent work places the religious activities of British Methodist women in the wider framework of social change in a way that remains all too uncommon. Because of the focus of her work, originally sparked off by her interest in the Bible Christians, she deals only with them and the other non-Wesleyan 'branches' of British Methodism after 1807. She takes account of some of the factors which significantly changed the social context of many women's lives between 1850 and 1914 – for example increasing literacy, access to further and higher education, the possibility of professional and other non-domestic employment, greater ease of travel and the movement for women's suffrage. She

---

[52] Leonore Davidoff and Catherine Hall, *Family Fortunes: Men and Women of the English Middle Class, 1780–1850* (London: Routledge, 1987[second ed. 2002]).
[53] Vickery, *The Gentleman's Daughter*.
[54] Wilson, *Constrained by Zeal*.
[55] Ibid., 224–5.
[56] John Wolffe, *The Expansion of Evangelicalism: The Age of Wilberforce, More, Chalmers and Finney* (Nottingham: IVP, 2006), 121–50.
[57] Margaret Batty, *Stages in the Development and Control of Methodist Lay Leadership, 1791–1878* (Peterborough: MPH, 1988).
[58] David J. Bosch, *Transforming Mission and Paradigm Shifts in the Theology of Mission* (New York, NY: Orbis, 1991), 262–345.

also pays attention to the continuing worldwide nature of Methodism due, in the case of the groups she studies, to emigration from the British Isles.

It is clear, therefore, that many areas remain to be opened up in the field of 'Methodism and Women' in the long (Methodist) nineteenth century of 1791–1914. This is particularly, though not only, true of work by British historians on British Methodism. Such areas might include: Wesleyan Methodism in general, women's involvement in and support of foreign missionary activity both at home and abroad, city missions and their associated support activities, the role of religion (and Methodism in particular) for emigrant women, and education for girls and women. The most worthwhile contributions, I would contend, will understand the relationship between Methodism and women as part of the wider story linking women and their religious lives with their place in society at large. Until this work has been done for women there is little possibility of a unified account of religious experience for women and men such as is beginning to emerge for the eighteenth century.

## The Twentieth Century: The British Dark Ages

'Work remaining to be done' constitutes the dominant motif in the history of Methodism and women in the twentieth century. Deaconess orders[59] and missionary activity (both 'in the field' and in auxiliary work 'at home') have been charted in somewhat traditional mode[60] and from a more gender-aware perspective.[61] Jacqueline Field-Bibb gives a theological and historical account of the movement for women's ordination across the major denominations.[62] Further studies of women's faith, spirituality and religious practice, and of women's groupings and their significance, would be of practical value to the church in understanding the continuing changes in women's lives and roles, as well as being of interest in themselves.

---

[59] Constance M. Oosthuizen, *Conquerors Through Christ; the Untold Story of the Methodist Deaconess in South Africa* (Port Shepstone, S.A.: Deaconess Order of the Methodist Church of Southern Africa, 1990); Bethany Hancock, *A History of the Methodist Deaconess Order in South Australia* (Malvern: Uniting Church Historical Society, 1995); Mary Agnes Dougherty, *My Calling to Fulfill: Deaconesses in the United Methodist Tradition* (New York, NY: GBGM, 1997); E. Dorothy Graham, *Saved to Serve: The Story of the Wesley Deaconess Order, 1890–1978* (Peterborough: MPH, 2002).

[60] Webb, *Women of Our Company*; Cyril Davey and Hugh Thomas, *Together Travel On: A History of Women's Work* (London: Cargate, 1984).

[61] Joy Fox, 'Excellent Women, 1870–1970: The Female Role in Missionary Service', in Virgoe (ed.), *Angels and Impudent Women*.

[62] Jacqueline Field-Bibb, *Women Towards Priesthood* (Cambridge: Cambridge University Press, 1991).

## Beyond Euro-centrism

The story of 'Methodism and Women' up to the early years of the nineteenth century inevitably largely concerns Great Britain. As already noted, historians in the United States have also given a great deal of attention to British Methodist history in this period: the possible reasons for such a strong emphasis on continuity lie outside the scope of this chapter. The history of Methodism, and of women in Methodism, in other parts of the world was first constructed from the point of view of the nations which supplied either emigrants or missionaries (largely Great Britain and the United States). A Euro-centric, or at least North-Atlantic-centred, bias was thus inevitable. Distinctive local voices have however emerged, and are emerging. It must be borne in mind also that the scope of this chapter is exclusively Anglophone. This section offers some pointers to a few areas of research around the world but does not claim to be comprehensive.

The feminist issues around the construction of women's historical identity that have been emphasised in preceding paragraphs have on the whole been more prominent in the Anglo-Saxon context than elsewhere. It is important at this point to emphasise that other approaches, such as first-wave feminism's concern with equal rights, or those kinds of writing characterised as 'traditional',[63] 'compensatory'[64] or 'contribution'[65] history, are in no way inferior to work informed by second- or third-wave feminism.[66] All historical writing is the product of its own context, and must be judged by its degree of accuracy, thoroughness, insight and integrity within that context. The structures and institutions within which women's religious lives have been played out must be identified and their history related by means of whatever historical method is appropriate for the writer. But nevertheless the historian in any context in the early twenty-first century may reasonably be expected to take account of women's particular identity (however understood) and the special issues pertaining to their lives, given the worldwide awareness of these issues.[67]

### *The United States*

The situation of women in American Methodism was at first strongly linked with and broadly comparable with that in Britain – not least because traffic across the Atlantic was two-way – but its social and political setting became increasingly differentiated even before Independence. The United States stands at the head of the countries that have generated their own self-reflexive women's history: it may

---

[63] Carroll Smith-Rosenberg, *Disorderly Conduct: Visions of Gender in Victorian America* (New York, NY: A. A. Knopf, 1985), 11–19.
[64] Scott, 'Gender'.
[65] Lerner, *Creation of Patriarchy*.
[66] All these terms are used to describe the kind of women's history that seeks to emphasise women's activity in past events but does not engage with the problems of having that history structured around male-defined norms.
[67] The UN designated 1975 (!) as International Women's Year.

even be held to have invented the genre. The historiography of women wears a different face in the United States in part because of the stronger and earlier impact of feminism on the academy. Susan Warrick's invaluable bibliography,[68] which includes works published up to 2001, highlights the immense range of historical writing about 'Methodism and women' connected with the United Methodist Church and its constituent predecessor churches. Its content is described thus:

> The bibliography's primary focus is The United Methodist Church and its predecessors. Secondarily, we have included titles from the British tradition, particularly from the time of the Wesleyan revival. Some related Methodist groups are included, with special attention given to African American Methodist denominations, along with reference to Free Methodists, Primitive Methodists, and Wesleyans. More general titles have been included that help place these women's activities in a broader historical and social context.

The sheer volume of material listed under the headings 'Missions and Missionaries' and 'Social Reform and Reformers'[69] indicates areas of particular research interest up to the date of compilation. The treatment particularly of the latter shows a greater degree of linkage with the social context than is generally the case with British work. This may not be entirely due to academic structures or the conventions of scholarship: a comparison of the different nature of religiosity in the two contexts and possible differences in the links between religious life and social reform, especially in terms of women's faith, organisation and motivation, would make a fascinating study. In addition (like feminism) organised religion in general and Methodism in particular has a much higher profile in academic circles in the United States than in Britain – as well of course as the sheer scale of the enterprise. It should therefore be expected that more writers will attain a greater degree of academic rigour and breadth. Given these facts, however, it is worth noting how many US historians (and even more markedly, theologians) have continued to devote themselves to the study of John Wesley and his age.

Given the plethora of American resources and secondary writing, a research guide on the scale of the present can do little more than indicate some themes and questions. On-line guides, such as that from Middle Tennessee State University at www.mtsu.edu/~kmiddlet/history/women/wh-rel.html or the blog at http://scholaristas.wordpress.com/women-in-american-religious-history-a-research-guide/, provide well-developed resources for the researcher.

The history of women's organisations in the United Methodist Church is a study area in itself. To take only one example, Theressa Hoover, author of a history

---

[68] Susan E. Warrick, *Women in the Wesleyan and United Methodist Traditions: A Bibliography* (Madison, WI: GCAH, 2003).
[69] Ibid., 3.

of the Women's Division of the General Board of Global Ministries,[70] was head of the Division, an executive member of the National Council of Negro Women, a board member of the Bossey Ecumenical Institute and a Commission member for the World Council of Churches. The Women's Division and its local expression, United Methodist Women, continue to take a highly proactive stance in advocating women's issues within the United Methodist Church.

The reintegration of women's history with that of other groups, and its integration within the broader social context, is once again worth noting as a feature of recent work in the field.[71] Harvard University's Pluralism Project, set up in 1990 to engage with religious diversity in America, began work on 'Women's Networks in Multi-religious America' in 2001 and in 2005 set up the Women's Initiative which 'explores the varied expressions of women's religious leadership, and provides opportunities for collaboration with secular women's organizations'.[72] United Methodist Women is of course included in the project field. Investigation of women's situation in the present calls for a nuanced understanding of the past; while history does not have to justify itself by its 'relevance', a present-day context may usefully suggest questions for the historian to pursue.

## Canada
Studies in the area of 'Methodism and Women' in Canada have particularly focused on the late nineteenth and early twentieth centuries, showing a considerable degree of engagement with the particular contexts of emigration and the development of new social structures and networks. Major works by Nancy Christie,[73] Rosemary Gagan[74] and Marilyn Färdig Whiteley,[75] all with extensive bibliographies, relate to similar concerns to those already outlined.

## Australia and New Zealand/Aotearoa
Writing in the field in Australia also reflects particular contextual factors: the relationship between women, religion and the construction of white identity,[76]

---

[70] Theressa Hoover, *With Unveiled Face: Centennial Reflections on Women and Men in the Community of the Church* (New York, NY: GBGM, 1983).

[71] E.g. Anne Braude, *Women and American Religion* (Oxford: Oxford University Press, 2000) and Catherine A. Brekus, *The Religious History of American Women* (Chapel Hill, NC: University of North Carolina Press, 2007).

[72] http://pluralism.org/about/history (accessed 16 September 2012)..

[73] Nancy F. Christie (ed.), *Households of Faith: Family, Gender and Community in Canada, 1760–1969* (Montreal: McGill-Queen's University Press, 2002).

[74] Rosemary Gagan, *A Sensitive Independence: Canadian Methodist Women Missionaries in Canada and the Orient, 1881–1925* (Montreal: McGill-Queen's University Press, 1992).

[75] Marilyn Fardig Whiteley, *Canadian Methodist Women, 1766–1925: Marys, Marthas* (Waterloo, Ontario: Wilfred Laurier University Press, 2005).

[76] Jane Carey and Claire McLisky, *Creating White Australia* (Sydney: Sydney University Press, 2009).

the role of women in social care and particularly in children's homes[77] and the importance of women in building civil society.[78] The history of Methodist women in Australia, as in other 'white dominions', also impinges on the British story: Lloyd notes the preaching career of Serena Thorne in South Australia and the way that female preaching in Australia was closely linked with the suffrage and temperance movements, in clear distinction from the situation in Britain.[79] The treatment of Methodism and women in New Zealand/Aotearoa also reflects the issues of nation-building and national identity.[80] In both cases it might be expected that current views and controversies on matters such as the treatment of indigenous peoples and of orphaned and emigrant children will contribute to generating lines of historical enquiry of particular relevance to women's history.

*Ghana*

Ghana has produced a Methodist scholar of international standing in Mercy Amba Oduyoye. Her work and that of her colleagues on the intersection between religion, economics and culture in the life of African women has been informed by the theoretical insights of the international academic and theological community where she has held office at the highest level, and also by her practical concern for the situation of African women. The union of these two areas of motivation in her work provides a fascinating case-study of theological method in a specific cultural context. Her major work, *Daughters of Anowa: African Women and Patriarchy*,[81] is identified by Christina Landman as 'retriev[ing] sources from an African heritage to put African religious historiography on track'.[82]

Ghanaian *diaspora* communities in Canada are producing work such as the Ghanaian Immigrants Religious Transnationalism (GIRT) Project, whose research remit 'seeks to understand how Ghanaians in Toronto live their religious lives across borders'.[83] Given the importance of the Methodist Women's Fellowship in Ghanaian Methodism, and the research interests of participating scholars, this project has interesting implications for women's history. The British Ghanaian Methodist Susanna Wesley Mission Auxiliary is the subject of feminist analysis by Mattiah Fumanti.[84] These studies serve as a useful reminder to historians of the

---

[77] Renate Howe and Shurlee Swain, *All God's Children* (Kambah, ACT: Acorn Press, 1989).

[78] Dorothy Kate O'Neill, *Fanny Kate Boadicea Cocks, MBE, 1875–1954:Tthe Story of a Woman with Purpose* (Henley Beach, S.A.: Seaview Press, 2005).

[79] Lloyd, *Women and the Shaping of British Methodism*, 167–71.

[80] Ruth Fry, *Out of the Silence: Methodist Women of Aotearoa 1822–1985* (Christchurch: Methodist Publishing, 1987).

[81] Mercy Amba Oduyoye, *Daughters of Anowa: African Women and Patriarchy* (Maryknoll, NY: Orbis, 1995).

[82] Landman, 'Mercy Amba Ewudziwa Oduyoye'.

[83] http://www.yorku.ca/girt/index.html (accessed 16 September 2012).

[84] Mattiah Fumanti, '"A Light-Hearted Bunch of Ladies": Gendered Power and Irreverent Piety in the Ghanaian Methodist Diaspora', *Africa: The Journal of the International*

relevance of work whose research focus places it technically in the field of sociology rather than history.

## South Africa

The post-apartheid context in South Africa is generating research work into women's spirituality and in particular their support groups and networks. Deborah Gaitskell undertook foundational work in this area[85] and is continuing to research South African ecumenical leadership.[86] Uta Theilen looks at a range of Methodist women's organisations and considers the place of African traditional religion in the spirituality and faith of their members.[87] Anne Preston undertakes a smaller-scale study in the same area, while Lyn Holness focuses exclusively on the Women's Manyano movement.[88]

## Korea

Once again a part of the worldwide Methodist family whose history was at one time seen as part of the history of missionary movements, most notably that of the United Methodist Church, Korea is now generating its own historical writing and is responding to trends of thought and interpretation as part of the global academic community. Nam-Soon Kang reflects on the particular nature of feminist theology in the Asian context, and its necessary relationship with history because of its grounding in women's experience.[89] Mi-Soon Im deals with the role of missionaries from the Methodist Episcopal Church, South, in Korea in the first half of the nineteenth century.[90]

---

*African Institute*, 80:2 (2010).

[85] Deborah Gaitskell, 'Female Mission Initiatives: Black and White Women in Three Witwatersrand Churches, 1903–1939', PhD thesis, University of London, 1981.

[86] http://www.methodistheritage.org.uk/heritagecommittee.htm (accessed 16 September 2012).

[87] Uta Theilen, 'Gender, Race, Power and Religion: Women in the Methodist Church of Southern Africa in Post-apartheid Society,' PhD thesis, Phillipps University, Marburg, 2003.

[88] Anne Preston, 'An Appraisal of the Spirituality of Methodist Women in Post-Apartheid South Africa', MTh thesis, University of South Africa, 2007; Lyn Holness, 'An Observer's Understanding of the Methodist Women's Manyano Movement', *Journal of Theology for Southern Africa*, 98 (July 1997) 21–31.

[89] Nam-Soon Kang, 'Creating "Dangerous Memory": Challenges for Asian and Korean Feminist Theology', *Ecumenical Review*, 47:1, (1995).

[90] Mi-Soon Im, 'The Role of Single Women Missionaries of the Methodist Episcopal Church, South, in Korea, 1897–1940', PhD thesis, Boston University School of Theology, 2008.

## Conclusion

This inevitably highly selective survey will have served its purpose if it reminds would-be researchers into the topics of 'Methodism and Women' of the contours of the subject in today's world of scholarship, if it provides sufficient starting-places for the gathering of resources and if it indicates some as yet unexamined areas or fresh approaches to those that might seem more familiar. Above all, it will have done this and more if further researchers come to share the joy and delight of giving a place to the marginalised and a voice to the silent.

# Methodism and Liberation Theology

## Joerg Rieger

It is one of the historic misunderstandings of liberation theology that it is a Roman Catholic phenomenon which had its exclusive beginnings in Latin America. Part of this misunderstanding is the common assumption that liberation theology spread because others copied and imitated the Roman Catholic Latin American fathers. Liberation theology, in this perspective, would be just like any other theology, devised by a few prominent theologians in the realm of ideas and promoted via academic networks. However, liberation theology cannot be understood in these terms. Its beginnings are found simultaneously in different contexts, on different continents and in different denominations of the Christian churches.[1] Even the terms "liberation theology" or "theology of liberation" were used simultaneously and independently. The different authors who proposed these terms did not know that others were using them at the same time in other parts of the world and even within the same country. Methodists were involved from the very beginning. When James Cone, a Methodist African American theologian in the United States, devised the term "liberation theology," he was not aware that Gustavo Gutiérrez, a Roman Catholic priest in Peru, used this term in Latin America. Likewise, Gutiérrez was not aware that Cone was using the same term. And Frederick Herzog, a white theologian writing at Methodist-related Duke Divinity School in the South of the United States, was not aware that either Cone or Gutiérrez were working with the notion when he published the first English-language article on liberation theology in the United States.[2]

---

[1] Note that there are also Islamic, Jewish and Buddhist liberation theologies.
[2] See J. Cone, *A Black Theology of Liberation*, 2nd edition (Maryknoll, NY: Orbis Books, 1986); G. Gutiérrez, *A Theology of Liberation: History, Politics, and Salvation*, revised 15th anniversary edition, trans. Sister Caridad Inda and John Eagleson (Maryknoll, NY: Orbis, 1988); F. Herzog, "Theology of Liberation," *Continuum*, 7:4 (Winter 1970), 515–24. Herzog, a member of the United Church of Christ, taught at Duke Divinity School from 1960 until his death in 1995. His affinity to Methodism can also be seen in his participation in the Oxford Institute in Methodist Theology Studies in the 1980s, on topics of liberation theology.

From the Asian perspective, Korean Minjung theologians have noted the same issue, pointing out that Minjung theology is neither a copy of Latin American liberation theology nor an imitation of European political theology.[3] For Great Britain, Methodist theologian John Vincent noted in 1995 that "British liberation theology has been happening in the cracks and crevices of the land more or less for a decade. Its practitioners are not people with much time for reading and research, much less reflection and writing."[4] This sort of liberation theology continues to be practiced at the grassroots, and the practitioners include many who have worked at the grassroots level all their lives, like the Methodist theologian Gil Dawes, who ministered to churches in rural areas of the United States, in Iowa. Dawes was able to involve established fundamentalist Methodist churches in the practice of liberation theology by taking them up on their intention to take the Bible as seriously as possible and by reading the Bible with them.[5]

This history has implications not only for our understanding of liberation theology but for our understanding of theology as a whole. The history of liberation theology shows that theology does not have to be an elitist and idealist discipline, devised by individuals in exclusive conversations with ideas found in books, or with their own personal experience of God that is subsequently universalized. Theology, in this context, is related to communities of faith as they seek to identify the work of God in the midst of particular tensions of life, which are often matters of life and death. This is what is frequently missing in mainline theologies and churches.

If God is sought in the midst of the tensions of life, rather than on the religious mountaintops or in the artificial calm of studies and sanctuaries, theology shapes up differently. It can no longer be systematized as easily, for instance. This theology cannot pretend easy command of universality, nor can it be done abstractly and at a safe distance. Nevertheless, what may sound shocking to the guild of professional theologians today was a common way of doing theology in the past. The apostle Paul, for instance, did not write theological treatises; he instead wrote letters to churches that were struggling to identify God in the midst of the pressures of the Roman Empire. Neither did Martin Luther write systematic treatises when he pursued a large-scale reformation of the church in the sixteenth century.

Theologies written in the midst of the tensions of life have a long tradition, and it is in light of these traditions that John Wesley's theology must be understood as well. When seen in this context, it is no longer necessary to respond defensively to those who refuse to consider Wesley as a theologian of value because he failed to produce a

---

[3] See D. Kwang-sun Suh, "A Biographical Sketch of an Asian Theological Consultation," in K. Yong Bock (ed.), *Minjung Theology: People as the Subjects of History* (Singapore: The Commission on Theological Concerns, The Christian Conference of Asia, 1981), 17–40.

[4] J. Vincent, "Liberation Theology in Britain, 1970–1995," in Chris Rowland and John Vincent (eds.), *Liberation Theology UK*, British Liberation Theology 1 (Sheffield: Urban Theology Unit, 1995), 29.

[5] See the report in G. Dawes, "Working People and the Church: Profile of a Liberated Church in Reactionary Territory," in W. K. Tabb (ed.), *Churches in Struggle: Liberation Theologies and Social Change in North America* (New York, NY: Monthly Review Press, 1986).

textbook of systematic theology and because he developed his theology in the form of sermons instead. During the past decades, Methodist theologians like Albert Outler and others have rediscovered that Wesley's lack of theological systematization does not have to prevent us from taking him seriously as a theologian. But there is more to this lack of systematization than has commonly been realized.

Similar to the various liberation theologies, Wesley's theology can be understood as an effort to identify the work of God in the midst of the tensions of life. It is widely acknowledged that Wesley was not only aware of the grave tensions of life in his time but that he was involved in efforts to alleviate them. This sets him apart from the professional systematic theologian who may well be aware of some of these tensions, but who considers them either a nuisance or of little relevance for the discipline. Wesley, as I have argued elsewhere, not only acknowledges and addresses the tensions of life and death but does theology in light of these tensions, seeking to understand the work of God in this context. Wesley's theology of grace, a theme that has been strongly emphasized by recent studies of Wesleyan theology,[6] is thus a theology of "grace under pressure."[7] In the Methodist traditions, divine grace is more authentically and forcefully experienced in the midst of the tensions of life than on the mountaintops.

These insights change everything. Methodist theology as a whole now needs to be rethought from the perspective of the tensions of life, "from the bottom up," as it were. While Albert Outler was right to call Wesley a "folk theologian,"[8] Outler and subsequent Methodist theology considered only half of the story. Outler's concern was with a Wesley who was able to communicate difficult theological issues to simple people. But what are the theological insights that Wesley might have picked up from the people? I have posed this question for years in Methodist theological circles, but we have yet to see a study of this subject by a historical theologian.[9]

Likewise, liberation theologies can now be seen in a different light. One of the most common misunderstandings that has been lingering for decades is that liberation theologies are mostly concerned with matters of social ethics.[10] But liberation theologies were never merely interested in the ethical implications of

---

[6] See, for instance T. Langford, *Methodist Theology* (Peterborough, England: Epworth Press, 1998), and R. Maddox, *Responsible Grace: John Wesley's Practical Theology* (Nashville, TN: Kingswood Books, 1994).

[7] See J. Rieger, *Grace under Pressure: Renegotiating the Heart of the Methodist Traditions* (Nashville, TN: The General Board of Higher Education and Ministry, 2011).

[8] See A. Outler, "John Wesley: Folk Theologian," *Theology Today*, 34 (July 1977), 150–60.

[9] One brief answer is given by J. González, "Can Wesley be Read in Spanish?" in R. Maddox (ed.), *Rethinking Wesley's Theology for Contemporary Methodism* (Nashville, TN: Kingswood Books, 1998), 161–8, when he seeks to show the impact that Spanish thinkers like Miguel de Molinos (a Spanish mystic) and Gregorio Lopez (a mysterious author, born in Madrid in 1542 and dying in Mexico in 1596) made on Wesley, who was able to read Spanish. Of course, these authors are not necessarily the representatives of the people either.

[10] K. Cracknell and S. J. White (eds.), *An Introduction to World Methodism* (Cambridge: Cambridge University Press, 2005), chapter 9, discusses the Methodist efforts related to liberation theology under this heading.

the Christian faith. Liberation theologies were devised to deal with the core issues of the faith, including our understanding of God, Jesus Christ, the Holy Spirit, humanity, the church and the nature of salvation itself. Doing so in the midst of the tensions and pressures of life parallels the theological method of many of the biblical authors. In the words of James Cone: "When theologians and preachers experience contradictions in life that shake the foundation of the accepted faith of the community, they are forced by faith itself to return to its source so as to interpret faith in a new light and thereby be empowered to struggle against the forces of evil that seek to destroy its credibility."[11]

In sum, liberation theology throws new light on how we understand Methodist theology. We shall see whether the reverse is true as well, that Methodist theology can help us understand liberation theology. In this exploration, we need to keep in mind various things: While the liberation theologies to be discussed here have their beginnings in the 1960s and 1970s, the concerns are much older; they are at the heart of the core of the Judeo-Christian traditions and have been at work throughout the history of the church, often unnoticed. Due to the limitations of space, we will mostly focus on the various liberation theologies that emerged beginning in the late 1960s.

Moreover, liberation theologies and their concerns continue to be devised and written by new generations in ways that push beyond and challenge the mothers and fathers of these approaches, and liberation theologies are unlikely to end until the various tensions and pressures of life to which they refer have ended.[12] Finally, none of the theologians who will be discussed in what follows should be considered as individuals who came up with great ideas in the privacy of their studies. Liberation theologians are aware of their indebtedness to communities and they need to be understood in relation to these communities. Only when this is grasped can we understand their broader implications and a certain universal relevance that differs from the sort of universality that is imposed from the top down, and which usually mirrors the unreflected context of the conventional theologian. Theology and the identity of the theologian will have to be conceived in entirely new terms. In the following, I will trace the developments of Methodist liberation theologies based on major theological topics. Having been engaged in the development of recent generations of liberation theology from a Methodist perspective myself, it is my intention to let others speak as much as possible.

---

[11] J. Cone, *For My People: Black Theology and the Black Church* (Maryknoll, NY: Orbis Books, 1984), 41.

[12] For one example of contemporary liberation theology, which brings together the Americas, see N. Míguez, J. Rieger and J. Mo Sung, *Beyond the Spirit of Empire: Theology and Politics in a New Key* (London: SCM Press, 2009). Míguez and Rieger are Methodist theologians from Argentina and the United States, and Sung is a Roman Catholic theologian from Brazil, teaching at a Methodist University in Sao Paulo.

## Sin

Perhaps the most important concern that is shared by the various theologies of liberation is the concern for the theological topic of sin. This topic distinguishes liberation theologies from both liberal and conservative variations of theology. Liberal theologies tend to share in optimistic attitudes about sin that consider sin as malleable and limited, to be overcome by human freedom and zeal. Conservative theologies emphasize the gravity of sin, often siding with Augustine on the notion of original sin, but they define sin in abstract terms, and thus it is remedied in equally abstract terms. What does the classical definition of sin as pride entail, for instance? Is this simply a matter of individual attitudes, as liberal theologians would hold, or is it a matter of a fundamental distortion that can be overcome with a prayer for forgiveness, as conservative theologians would argue? Liberation theologies, by contrast, wonder about the actual forms that pride takes and they seek to address the structures that undergird it, in search for God's grace.

John Wesley, as is well known, asserted an Augustinian view of the "total depravity" of the human being. This was one of the few points where he found himself in agreement with the Calvinism of his time.[13] Wesley also understood that the fallen state of humanity had implications not only for individuals but for social relationships and for the world as a whole. Where others blamed the sinfulness of the poor for their lack of resources, Wesley pointed out the role of the wealthy landowners in pushing the poor off their lands.[14] Since nothing was excluded from sinfulness, nothing was excluded from the need for salvation. Wesley's hope is for nothing less than a salvation, which ushers in a new creation by the grace of God.

It is often overlooked that feminist theologies, for instance, side with Wesley on this issue in principle when they depart from liberal theologies on matters of sin. As I have shown elsewhere, feminist theologies start out not with a religious experience that grants them immediate connection to God, but with a sense that things are not the way they are supposed to be.[15] U.S. Methodist feminist theologian Rebecca Chopp, for instance, laments the lack of a deeper understanding of sin in mainline theology, especially where it is still defined in bourgeois existentialist or analytical philosophical terms and develops a bigger picture: "I have a vision that one of the great gifts that the weaving together of liberation theology and Wesleyan theology can contribute to hegemonic cultures is a discourse of sin that names the reality of

---

[13] See J. Wesley, *Works,* "Minutes of Some Late Conversations Between the Rev. Mr. Wesleys [sic] and Others," in T. Jackson( ed.), *The Works of the Rev. John Wesley*, 3rd edn (London: Wesleyan Methodist Book Room, 1872; repr. Peabody, MA: Hendrickson, 1986), viii, 285: "Q. 23. Wherein may we come to the very edge of Calvinism? A. (1.) In ascribing all good to the free grace of God. (2.) In denying all natural free-will and all power antecedent to grace. And, (3.) In excluding all merit from man; even for what he has or does by the grace of God."

[14] See J. Wesley, "Thoughts on the Present Scarcity of Provisions," in Jackson (ed.), *Works*, xi, 56–7.

[15] See J. Rieger, *God and the Excluded: Vision and Blindspots in Contemporary Theology* (Minneapolis, MN: Fortress Press, 2001), chapter 4.

suffering and destruction, that criticizes unjust systems in need of correction, and that analyzes basic idolatrous forms of life in need of radical transformation."[16] Liberation and Wesleyan theologies are well positioned to develop such deeper understandings of sin.

From the perspectives of the Gay, Lesbian, Bisexual, Transgender communities, a deeper understanding of sin is required as well. According to Theodore Jennings, a U.S. liberation theologian, the problem is that sin has been narrowed to sexual issues, blocking the biblical concern for sin in terms of oppression, injustice and the biblical concern for the poor.[17] Moreover, where sex involves sin in its most blatant forms in our context, like in the abuse of the weak and the defenseless or domestic abuse, the mainline church remains silent. In this way, it overlooks that the Jesus of the gospels challenges what we call "family values."[18] Jennings reminds us—and this is a common thread in all liberation theologies—that what is at stake here is not just ethics; what is at stake is nothing less than "the identity of Christ."[19] In this context, the deeper theological issue becomes clear: homophobia becomes destructive of the church because it lacks a deeper understanding of sin. The issue at stake is not about liberal tolerance or an effort to be more civil to those who are different.

In the context of liberation theological debates around race and ethnicity, another set of deep theological reflections on sin emerges. Hispanic Methodist theologian Justo González, in conversation with feminist theologians, has pointed out that sin is not just a matter of pride. Sin, especially where the oppressed are concerned, can also manifest itself as false humility, putting oneself down and not trusting our God-given powers.[20]

From the perspective of African American theology, Methodist theologian Josiah Young has observed that the problem of sin, as it is tied to racism and the abuse of African Americans, is a deeply theological matter. Wesley himself, Young notes, understood that the abuse of slaves was not simply an offense against moral decency; rather, it constituted an offense against Godself.[21]

Asian American Methodist theologians Andrew Sung Park and the late Jung Young Lee add two important aspects to a broadening understanding of sin. Park notes that we have been so focused on the salvation of sinners that we have often not considered those who are sinned against. Rather than the classical call to repentance, victims need healing. A typical call to repentance makes the situation

---

[16] R. S. Chopp, "Anointed to Preach: Speaking of Sin in the Midst of Grace," in M. D. Meeks, (ed.), *The Portion of the Poor: Good News to the Poor in the Wesleyan Tradition* (Nashville, TN: Kingswood Books, 1995), 99.

[17] T. W. Jennings Jr., "Breaking Down the Walls of Division: Challenges Facing the People Called Methodist," in J. Rieger and J. Vincent (eds.), *Methodist and Radical* (Nashville, TN: Kingswood Books, 2003), 60.

[18] Ibid., 61.

[19] Ibid., 65.

[20] J. González, *Mañana: Christian Theology from a Hispanic Perspective* (Nashville, TN: Abingdon Press, 1990), 137.

[21] J. U. Young III, "Distinguishing Sterility from Fecundity in the Wesleyan Tradition," in Rieger and Vincent (eds.), *Methodist and Radical*, 71.

of victims worse because it encourages self-hatred.[22] The definition of sin as pride is not necessarily helpful here. It is from the perspectives of the victims, Park argues, that "we can see the mode of sin more holistically."[23] Lee looks at the same problem from the other side, when he notes that the fundamental Christian problem that needs resolution is what he calls the cardinal sin of centrality. Lee states: "The church is deeply embedded in centralist motivation. Most are based on a centralist ideology and a hierarchical structure of belief, which both exclude and control the poor, minorities, and the powerless. This is contrary to the essence of Jesus Christ's intent. As Jesus Christ was a marginal person, the norm of the church should be marginality."[24] We might think of centrality as one of the forms that pride takes in our time. This matches to some degree the critique of empire put forth by contemporary theologians, including several Methodists.[25]

Native American theologians in the United States have made their own contributions to the topic of sin. Methodist theologian Homer Noley, collaborating with two other Native American theologians, George Tinker and Clara Sue Kidwell, on a Native American theology, defines sin in the following way: "Sin from an Indian perspective can be defined as failure to live up to one's responsibility, sometimes deliberately but more likely as a result of impulsive or unthinking behavior, a mistake. In Christianity, sin has become privatized as a personal matter. For Indian people it is a matter of responsibility to community."[26] Writing in a culture of individualism, where sin is often psychologized or treated as a matter of individual therapy, the rediscovery of a communal and structural understanding of the nature and gravity of sin is no small accomplishment in North American theology.

Latin American liberation theologians have perhaps been most prominent in their reinterpretation of the doctrine of sin in terms of economic structures. Victorio Araya-Guillén, a Methodist theologian from Costa Rica, notes the problem in stark terms: "The dawn of the third millennium confronts us with a painful historical reality of sinfulness: the holocaust of the majority of human beings—the poor of the earth."[27] Here, sin is experienced in terms of its ultimate consequence: death. While the world has changed rapidly since Araya wrote these lines in the 1990s,

---

[22] A. Sung Park, "Holiness and Healing: An Asian American Voice Shaping the Methodist Traditions," in Rieger and Vincent (eds.), *Methodist and Radical*, 100.

[23] Ibid., 96.

[24] J. Young Lee, *Marginality: The Key to Multicultural Theology* (Minneapolis, MN: Fortress Press, 1995), 123.

[25] See J. Rieger, *Christ and Empire: From Paul to Postcolonial Times* (Minneapolis, MN: Fortress Press, 2007); Míguez, Rieger and Sung, *Beyond the Spirit of Empire*; see also Theodore W. Jennings, "John Wesley," in K. Pui-lan, D. Compier and J. Rieger (eds.), *Empire and the Christian Tradition* (Minneapolis, MN: Fortress Press, 2007).

[26] C. S. Kidwell, H. Noley and G. E. Tinker, *A Native American Theology* (Maryknoll, NY: Orbis Books, 2001), 110.

[27] V. Araya-Guillén, "The 500th Anniversary of the European Invasion of Abya-Yala: An Ethical and Pastoral Reflection from the Third World," in Meeks, (ed.), *The Portion of the Poor*, 135.

the situation that he addresses has not changed but worsened. Unfortunately, this situation is still greeted with silence by much of theology.

The trademark of Latin American liberation theologians has, of course, been the critique of Western ideas of development and a theology that went by that same name, the "theology of development." Argentinean Methodist theologian José Míguez Bonino, in a book that has become one of the all-time classics of liberation theology, frames the problem in these words: "Development and underdevelopment are not two independent realities, nor two stages in a continuum but two mutually related processes: … Northern development is built on third-world underdevelopment. The basic categories for understanding our history are not development and underdevelopment but domination and dependence."[28] This critique is related to the so-called dependency theory, but the underlying problem is a theological one. We are confronted with a distortion of human relationships that has reached epidemic proportions. What liberal theology has missed is the stark reality of sin, which is manifest in problems like underdevelopment: it is for this reason that liberals could call for economic development. While liberalism has helped end feudalism and conquest in Latin America, it has become part of a modern colonization in the service of the so-called developed countries.

Sin, in this context, is theologically defined as idolatry. As Araya-Guillén points out, capitalism is a "system of economic idolatry. Idolatry occurs when humankind deposits its faith and life in something that is not God, but a creation of its own hands, the idol."[29] In other words, the laws of the market have become God. Sin, in this context, means to put something in the place of God that is not God. This is a crucial theme in Latin American liberation theology, and Methodist theologians have helped to develop it. Here is a parallel to an aspect of the theology of Karl Barth that is often neglected in so called First World theology: the core of theological struggle is not between faith and atheism, or between faith and the absence of faith. The theological struggle needs to be waged between good faith and bad faith, between faith and idolatry. Orthodoxy is thus very much an issue, despite many claims that Latin American liberation theology would be only concerned about orthopraxis.

From a Cuban perspective, Methodist theologian Israel Batista Guerra points out the deceptive qualities of this idolatry, since "the economic influence of the capitalist model [sic] of production is so intrinsically present in Protestantism that it has become a factor of which we are hardly aware."[30] This relation still haunts the

---

[28] J. Míguez Bonino, *Doing Theology in a Revolutionary Situation* (Philadelphia, PA: Fortress Press, 1975), 16.

[29] Araya-Guillén, "The 500th Anniversary," 139.

[30] I. B. Guerra, "The Missionary Heritage of the Cuban Churches," in D. Kirkpatrick, (ed.), trans. L. McCoy, *Faith Born in the Struggle for Life: A Rereading of Protestant Faith in Latin America Today* (Grand Rapids, MI: W. B. Eerdmans, 1988), 246.

Cuban Methodist churches, and it would be worthwhile to examine the churches in the First World in this light as well.[31]

Despite a clear sense of sin in its economic form, Latin American theologians are also aware of sin in a broader framework. Miguez Bonino, for instance, notes that, "while oppression may appear *dominantly* as economic exploitation, or racial discrimination, or political domination, and so on, the other dimensions are also normally put at the service of this dominant organizer of oppression."[32] Such oppression includes personal issues, including psychological structures and people's emotional make-up.

South African Methodist theologian Basil Moore, a past general secretary of the University Christian Movement who was exiled to London and who popularized Black Theology in South Africa already in the early 1970s, notes that while South Africans use the title "Black Theology," based on James Cone's term, "the content of American Black Theology has not been imported."[33] According to Moore, Black Theology in South Africa brings together issues of sin along the lines of race and class, as it deals with black people "facing the strangling problems of oppression, fear, hunger, and dehumanization."[34] Note again that we are not dealing merely with ethical issues here but with the heart of the gospel.

Cedric Mayson, another white South African theologian who spent time in prison and many years in exile due to his involvement in the liberation struggle, also notes the relation of race and class in terms of sin. Quoting a friend, he says: "Because our poor are mostly black and our rich are mostly white it seems to be a problem of race, but the heart of the problem is the question of wealth and poverty."[35] According to Mayson, the major black liberation organizations agree that "the central factor of oppression is economic and people use race as a tool of capitalist oppression and manipulation."[36] Racism, in this context, is a useful tool for economic ends, as it allows the employers to reject black Africans, "whom the white economy does not require."[37]

Moreover, sin alone does not account for the behavior of South African business leaders and politicians. The churches have proven to be especially troublesome in this regard. In Mayson's words: "I have strong feelings about the Security Branch and the Government, but I do not blame them for being hypocrites. It is the leaders of the churches who condone and support this hypocrisy, who recognized the

---

[31] For a broader study of the structures of theology along the lines of economics as religion see J. Rieger, *No Rising Tide: Theology, Economics, and the Future* (Minneapolis, MN: Fortress Press, 2009).

[32] J. Míguez Bonino, "Methodism and Latin American Liberation Movements," in Rieger and Vincent (eds.), *Methodist and Radical*, 194.

[33] B. Moore, "What is Black Theology?" in B. Moore(ed.), *The Challenge of Black Theology in Africa* (Atlanta, GA: John Knox Press, 1974), 1.

[34] Ibid., 6.

[35] C. Mayson, *A Certain Sound: The Struggle for Liberation in South Africa* (Maryknoll, NY: Orbis Books, 1985), 38.

[36] Ibid., 38.

[37] Ibid., 46.

heretical beliefs and continue to accept them, that must bear full responsibility."[38] In addition, those who look in from the outside, enlightened people in the North in particular, are not off the hook either. Again Mayson: "People in the West do not know that they are oppressors or part of an oppressive society: they think that they are Liberals and Reformers and do not recognize that these are the garments worn by oppressors."[39]

Elsewhere in the world, similar observations of the all-pervasiveness of sin have been made. Methodist theologian Jong Chun Park, for instance, working in relation to Minjung theology, has noted the perpetual struggle in which Koreans and other East Asians find themselves: "In East Asia there has never been a time of genuine peace and justice. The Korean *minjung* has suffered Chinese domination in the old past, Japanese imperialism in the recent past, and American hegemony in the present."[40] This is the weight of sin that must be dealt with.

When examined in this context, theology in the First World has produced comparatively weak accounts of sin. Nevertheless, a strong understanding of sin can also be found in the work of male Methodist liberation theologians in the United States and England. John Vincent, for instance, has pointed out the Methodists' temptation to conform to the cultural establishment and its "embourgeoisement."[41] The problem is not, of course, that Methodists might be middle or upper class, but whether they have become so narcissistic that they are unable to see anything else—whether the neighbor or God. Already John Wesley was concerned that the Methodists had advanced up the social ladder without looking back to where they came from. Sin here is the old problem of the *"homo incurvatus in se,"* the human being turned in on itself.

After the end of state communism in the East, much was made of the sinfulness of that system. Unfortunately, however, the self-critical attitude that is required for detecting one's own sinful state is often neglected in theological studies. If a certain form of communism has collapsed, capitalism is not therefore off the hook. The theological work required in this regard has been done by various Methodist theologians, including Douglas Meeks, Theodore Jennings and myself.[42]

In the United States, theological critiques of capitalism in terms of sin have been devised by Methodism, beginning with the Social Creed during the early twentieth century. Walter Muelder, Methodist ethicist and former dean of Boston University School of Theology, notes, for instance, how in 1932 the Social Creed of the Methodist Episcopal Church "radically moved from single-interest reforms to a

---

[38] Ibid., 109.

[39] Ibid., 138.

[40] J. Chun Park, "Interliving Theology as a Wesleyan Minjung Theology," in Rieger and Vincent (eds.), *Methodist and Radical*, 176.

[41] J. Vincent, "Basics of Radical Methodism: Challenges for Today," in Rieger and Vincent (eds.), *Methodist and Radical*, 31.

[42] See M. D. Meeks, *God the Economist: The Doctrine of God and Political Economy* (Minneapolis, MN: Fortress Press, 1989); T. W. Jennings, Jr., *Good News to the Poor: John Wesley's Evangelical Economics* (Nashville, TN: Abingdon Press, 1990); and Rieger, *No Rising Tide*.

more systematic examination of the social-economic system." In this context, "the whole capitalistic profit system was addressed. In large numbers church persons and the General Conference asked whether there was not something basically amiss in the industrial and financial order." This intuition, which is rooted in a notion of sinfulness, was not located merely at the corporate level of the church but was brought into everyday ministry: "A direct responsibility was laid on the local church to investigate local moral and economic conditions as well as to know world needs."[43]

In 1932, the General Conference of the Methodist Episcopal Church declared that "the present industrial order is unchristian, unethical, and antisocial." In those years the Northeast Ohio Conference talked about capitalism as a "pagan economic order," and the Pittsburgh Conference stated that the real problem is capitalism, and its "enormous waste…its undemocratic control…its concentration of wealth."[44] In the aftermath of the Great Depression of 1929, sin was concretely named and pointed out by many. In the aftermath of what has been called the "Great Recession" in 2007 and 2008, there has not been a comparable outcry in the churches.

In all these ways, Methodist liberation theologies have deepened the understanding of sin. Liberation theologians' rejoinders to their colleagues remind us of Anselm's famous rejoinder to his student Boso: "You have not yet considered the weight of sin."[45] In this context, it is important to see these various descriptions as competing but as pieces of a bigger puzzle. As several of the male theologians have observed, for instance, women often had a better sense for sinfulness than men. This is probably due to the fact that women, even if they hold more privileged social positions, are more prone to experiencing oppression than men of similar positions.[46]

---

[43] W. G. Muelder, "The Methodist Social Creed and Ecumenical Ethics," in T. Runyon, (ed.), *Wesleyan Theology Today: A Bicentennial Theological Consultation* (Nashville, TN: Kingswood Books, 1985), 353.

[44] All quoted from G. D. McClain, "Pioneering Social Gospel Radicalism: An Overview of the History of the Methodist Federation for Social Action," in R. E. Richey, K. E. Rowe and J. Miller Schmidt (eds.), *Perspectives on American Methodism: Interpretive Essays* (Nashville, TN: Kingswood Books, 1993), 375. In 1934, a survey among 5,000 Methodists reported that 39 percent favored replacing capitalism with socialism, and 56 percent argued for a "drastically reformed capitalism." Ibid., 379.

[45] Anselm of Canterbury, *Cur Deus Homo*, trans. J. Fairweather, in B. Davies and G. R. Evans (eds.), *Anselm of Canterbury: The Major Works* (Oxford: Oxford University Press, 1998), 305.

[46] Vincent, "Liberation Theology in Britain, 1970–1995," 31, also notes the role of women in developing a sense for oppressive situations; Muelder, "The Methodist Social Creed," 355, also notes how the female members of the church were often ahead of the white male members in social matters.

## Grace and Salvation

When considered in the context of a substantive notion of sin, the notions of grace and salvation have to be rethought. Wesley's own approach to salvation is much broader than has commonly been realized, and it is being broadened further by the various liberation traditions. As I have argued elsewhere: "If grace is what happens in our relationships with God and other people, there is little sense in rehearsing the old question of whether we are talking about an 'otherworldly' or a 'this-worldly' process."[47] Such a notion of grace is reflected in Wesley's doctrine of salvation. In his sermon "The Scripture Way of Salvation" (based on Eph. 2:8: "ye have been saved" [KJV]), he points out that salvation is not primarily to be understood as going to heaven or eternal happiness. Rather, Wesley argues that salvation is what takes place here and now: "ye are saved" or "ye have been saved" is how Wesley translates the passage from Ephesians.[48] Our concern for how we relate to God and to others here and now, and for what God is doing in these relationships, does not diminish our expectations for the future but focuses them in such a way that they shape up as a critique of the powers of sin, from which we need to be saved not only after death but here and now.

Wesley's optimism has often been described as an optimism of grace. Míguez Bonino talks about "a christo-soteriologically founded anthropological optimism."[49] In his earlier writings, Míguez Bonino noted the limitations of Wesley's notion of sanctification as being focused too much on the individual and a related failure to critique the status quo, which led the Methodists "to accept their role in society and to improve their lot without challenging the rules of the game."[50] Nevertheless, Míguez Bonino later on acknowledges that there are other ways to read Wesley's doctrine of sanctification that are more communally oriented, and another Latin American Methodist theologian, Elsa Tamez, concludes that Wesley's notion of sanctification can be described as "the struggle for life." She even identifies a parallel to Ernesto Cardenal's notion of the "holiness of revolution."[51]

Theodore Runyon, a Methodist theologian in the United States, summarizes a consensus of many presenters in his introduction to the lectures presented at the Oxford Institute on Methodist Theological Studies in 1977 on the topic of "Sanctification and Liberation," noting that "there is a peculiar affinity between Wesleyan theology—especially Wesley's doctrine of sanctification—and movements for social change. When *Christian perfection* becomes the goal of the individual, a fundamental hope is engendered that the future can surpass

---

[47] Rieger, *Grace under Pressure*, 53.

[48] J. Wesley, "The Scripture Way of Salvation," in A. Outler (ed.), *The Bicentennial Edition of the Works of John Wesley* (Nashville, TN: Abingdon, 1987), ii, 156.

[49] J. Míguez Bonino, "Wesley's Doctrine of Sanctification from a Liberation Perspective," in T. Runyon (ed.), *Sanctification and Liberation* (Nashville, TN: Abingdon Books, 1981), 61.

[50] Ibid., 59.

[51] E. Tamez, "Wesley as Read by the Poor," in M. D. Meeks (ed.), *The Future of the Methodist Theological Traditions* (Nashville, TN: Abingdon, 1985), 82.

the present. Concomitantly, a holy dissatisfaction is aroused with regard to any present state of affairs—a dissatisfaction that supplies the critical edge necessary to keep the process of individual transformation moving."[52] This dissatisfaction works both on the personal and on the social levels, since Wesley does not see the kingdom of God as referring merely to an individual's life after death.

Feminist theologians agree with Wesley that a theological discussion of salvation needs to discuss a transformation that takes place here and now. From the perspective of women in the United States, Rebecca Chopp notes that "a Wesleyan feminist theology can offer a way of Christianity by combining the feminist insistence on Christian praxis of emancipatory transformation with Wesley's notion of Christianity as a way of love of God and neighbor."[53] The transformation towards which feminists work is not merely a political issue: it is deeply woven into the salvific ways of God in the world. Put the other way around, feminist theology notes that there can be no salvation without God. In Chopp's words: "It is only through hearing the word of God and neighbor that radical transformation, including the emancipatory transformation of changing oppressive social systems and unjust economic systems, occurs."[54]

This theocentric perspective is common in other liberation theologies as well. Black theology in the United States, for instance, has given expression to it in the words of renowned Methodist theologian James Cone. Reconciliation, according to Cone, "is a divine action that embraces the whole world, changing our relationship with God and making us new creatures."[55] This theocentric perspective has consequences, because it focuses not on the preferences of Christians but about the preferences of God. This is the context in which we need to understand the following statement by Cone: "The Christian view of reconciliation has nothing to do with black people being nice to white people as if the gospel demands that we ignore their insults and their humiliating presence. It does not mean discussing with whites what it means to be black or going to white gatherings and displaying what whites call an understanding attitude."[56] There can be no reconciliation without liberation. Cone sums it up: "Christ is the Reconciler because he is first the Liberator."[57]

From a KoreanAmerican perspective, Andrew Sung Park follows up on his assessment that the doctrine of sin needs to take into account the wounded in this way: "God achieves the healing of the sinned-against and the sanctification of the sinner in the process of synergetic healing. By setting the wounded free from their

---

[52] T. Runyon, "Introduction: Wesley and the Theologies of Liberation," in Runyon (ed.), *Sanctification and Liberation*, 10.

[53] R. S. Chopp, "Hearing, Holiness, and Happiness: Listening to God and Neighbor," in Rieger and Vincent (eds.), *Methodist and Radical*, 112.

[54] Ibid., 119.

[55] J. Cone, *God of the Oppressed* (New York, NY: The Seabury Press, 1975), 228.

[56] Ibid., 226–7.

[57] Ibid., 239. "White people must be made to realize that reconciliation is a costly experience. It is not holding hands and singing 'Black and white together' and 'We shall overcome.' Reconciliation means *death*, and only those who are prepared to die in the struggle for freedom will experience new life with God."

oppression, the Spirit heals their wounds." As God initiates a healing process, the victims of sin are empowered to collaborate with God. Here, the theocentric perspective opens out to a perspective that includes the work of the redeemed human being: "Graced by the Holy Spirit, the wounded can confront and transform the *han* of the world with their own wounds."[58]

Native Americans in the United States, including Methodist Homer Noley, note the communal aspect of salvation that has often been lost in the history of Western theology. For them, "salvation can be defined as the ability of an individual or a community to return to a state of communitas that has been disrupted."[59] While Noley and his colleagues do not state this in that context, the relation of salvation to the community is a thoroughly biblical concept as well. Particularly in the Old Testament salvation was never considered "private property" but was aimed at the well-being of the whole community.

No matter what our theologies say about salvation, it cannot ultimately be confined to individual and personal issues alone. Even those theologies which tried to confine salvation in this way have consequences for the bigger picture. Those who defined salvation as individual life after death, for instance, often endorsed the ecclesial, political and economic status quo. Those who defined salvation as individual holiness often fell into the same traps. From the Latin American perspective, Míguez Bonino has raised the following question that has deep implications for the doctrine of salvation: "Can Methodism be understood as an attempt to 'reform the nation,' or is it to be seen as a religious accompanying music to the introduction of industrial capital?"[60] The latter option was, of course, the fate of the early Methodist beginnings in Latin America, although Methodists were mostly unaware of it. For Míguez Bonino, the question is whether Methodists can participate in a "genuine Latin American project of social transformation."[61]

Salvation, in this context, needs to be understood in concrete terms. Míguez Bonino, for instance, discusses the notion of reconciliation in this way, starting with the biblical concept: "Reconciliation is not achieved by some sort of compromise between the new and the old but through the defeat of the old and the victory of the new age. The ideological appropriation of the Christian doctrine of reconciliation by the liberal capitalist system in order to conceal the brutal fact of class and imperialist exploitation and conflict is one—if not *the*—major heresy of our time."[62] Jesus' love does not mean tolerance or compromise with evil; after all, he also loved the Pharisees and Herod, whom he denounced.[63]

---

[58] Park, "Holiness and Healing," 106.
[59] Tinker, Noley and Kidwell, *A Native American Theology*, 110.
[60] J. Míguez Bonino, "Salvation as the Work of the Trinity: An Attempt at a Holistic Understanding from a Latin American Perspective," in M. D. Meeks (ed.), *Trinity, Community and Power* (Nashville, TN: Abingdon Books, 2000), 69.
[61] Ibid.
[62] Míguez Bonino, *Doing Theology in a Revolutionary Situation*, 121.
[63] See ibid., 121–2.

Pursuing an understanding of salvation that includes the cross, the Uruguayan Methodist theologian Julio de Santa Ana puts the challenge of love in this way: "Living in the practice of love means adopting a theological perspective which, while not forgetting the resurrection, understands that human life must pass *via* the cross. Only thus, without triumphalism, and recognizing that we cannot avoid either suffering or pain, can we confront the powers of this world, the true counterpowers of Jesus Christ."[64] The believers need to know that the strength to do this comes from Christ.

One caveat on which many Methodist liberation theologians agree has to do with the notion of the unity of history, which is a key concept in Roman Catholic liberation theology in Latin America, designed to overcome conservative attempts at splitting history in two parts. Míguez Bonino speaks for others when he cautions not to take the unity of history too far. The split, which this notion addresses, is clearly problematic: we cannot separate the history of the world and the history of the church, a move that results in withdrawal or ecclesiocratic attitudes. Nevertheless, Míguez Bonino explains, "for us Gentile Christians to confess the Kingdom is not only to enter into the meaning of our own history but also to take distance from it and to be grafted into another history."[65] The unity of history has its limits. Also, the radical nature of sin needs to be remembered, reminding us that God's actions in history cannot be equated directly with human actions. By the same token, the encounter with Christ cannot be equated directly with the encounter with the poor.[66]

In the South African situation, the broader understanding of salvation had to be rethought after the fall of Apartheid. Charles Villa-Vicencio, a Methodist South African theologian who held key leadership positions in the South African Truth and Reconciliation Commission after the fall of Apartheid, has given an account of the different theological challenges during and after Apartheid in South Africa. One of the challenges that he notes is that a socio-economic order inherited from the past must also be overcome. Talking about a "realism committed to the liberation process," the goal must be the "transformation of the existing order to the benefit of the poor."[67] This clashes with the realism of the status quo. Villa-Vicencio sees a parallel to Latin American liberation theology, which also has shifted "from the systematic resistance of the past to nuanced reconstruction in the present."[68] After

---

[64] J. de Santa Ana, *Good News to the Poor: The Challenge of the Poor in the History of the Church*, trans. Helen Whittle (Maryknoll, NY: Orbis Books, 1979), 108.

[65] Míguez Bonino, "Salvation as the Work of the Trinity, 77.

[66] Ibid., 78. This is an important concern for Methodist liberation theologians. I have dealt with this problem in my book *Remember the Poor: The Challenge to Theology in the Twenty-First Century* (London: T&T Clark, 1998).

[67] C. Villa-Vicencio, "Freedom is Forever Unfinished: The Incomplete Theological Agenda," in B. N. Pityana and C. Villa-Vicencio (eds.), *Being the Church in South Africa Today: Papers Delivered at the Consultation on "South Africa in Regional and Global Context: Being the Church Today"* (Johannesburg: South African Council of Churches, 1995), 59.

[68] Ibid., 62.

all, the cause of the poor is promoted not by the clash of ideas but in actual labor struggles.[69]

Issues of reconciliation are, of course, especially problematic in situations where systems of great injustice have collapsed. In South Africa, for instance, after Apartheid ended there was a large demand for reconciliation. Unfortunately, reconciliation has too often been used to tell the oppressed to forgive and forget, while those who benefited from systems of oppression continue with business as usual. In the contemporary situation, former South African Methodist presiding bishop Mvume Dandala notes the problem with such a shallow notion of reconciliation and poses a deeper challenge for the doctrine of salvation: "The crucial question is whether the developed world can be persuaded to harness its appetite for the resources of the developing world in order to allow processes to emerge that enable all to benefit from these resources without eroding our ecology and environment. ... This may be our evangelical challenge."[70] There can be no reconciliation without transformation.

North American Methodist theologian Mary Elizabeth Moore talks about repentance and reparation, notions which have deep implications for our understanding of reconciliation. Moore begins by noting that repentance includes a "special privilege of voice granted to the oppressed, underrepresented, or marginalized." Reparation, in this context, includes "the concrete repairing of injuries and relationships." What comes to mind, though not mentioned by Moore, is the story of Zaccheus, who restores fourfold that which he had taken (Luke 19:1–10). No easy reconciliation is possible here, notes Moore, "because reconciliation is not a place to rest."[71]

In the Methodist traditions, salvation—the work of God in the lives of humans and of the world—is inextricably tied together with working alongside God. As Korean Minjung theologian Jong Chun Park has pointed out: "The famous Wesleyan doctrine of assurance in relation to the witness of the Spirit tends to become enthusiastic if it is disconnected from another Wesleyan doctrine, that of faith working through love."[72]

In the British context, John Vincent notes the importance of following Christ in the context of the doctrine of salvation: "The heart of religion was the imitation of Christ. To be perfect was to be perfectly like Christ, filled with 'love divine.'"[73] What needs to be kept in mind here is that from the perspective of liberation theologies

---

[69] Ibid., 63–4. Villa-Vicencio seeks to push beyond capitalism and socialism—but perhaps at the time he underestimated the power of capitalism, although he notes the importance to build alternatives to exploitative capitalism which is the place where the old and the new agendas of liberation are connected. Ibid., 69.

[70] H. Mvume Dandala, "Methodist Mission to Ecological Challenges in Africa," in M. D. Meeks (ed.), *Wesleyan Perspectives on the New Creation* (Nashville, TN: Kingswood Books, 2003), 113–16.

[71] M. E. Mullino Moore, "New Creation: Repentance, Reparation, and Reconciliation," in Meeks (ed.), *Wesleyan Perspectives on the New Creation*, 113–16.

[72] Park, "Interliving Theology," 172.

[73] Vincent, "Basics of Radical Methodism," 36.

there is a close relation between the work of God and the work of Christians. In Wesley's own theology, God's work is not conceived in narrowly religious terms, and so he noted the parallel of works of piety and the works of mercy, pointing out that the latter are real means of grace.[74] If works of mercy are indeed means of grace, the point is not that those who act mercifully earn salvation. The opposite is true: works of mercy, like reading the Bible, praying and taking Holy Communion, are the channels through which we invite and receive God's grace into our lives, and through which we are empowered to follow God's work in the world.

Thus, what has often been considered "social action," or the ethical application of Christianity, becomes an essential part of salvation. Salvation, understood as God's gracious action in the lives of humanity and the world, focuses on what God is doing, rather than on the performance of our individual piety. This reversal is crucial, and it seems that so far only liberation theologians have fully understood it. Wesley himself had an inkling, it seems, when he noted that even Methodists who performed all the works of piety were falling from grace if they did not realize that works of piety were also means of grace.[75] In the words of North American theologian Ted Jennings: "In visiting the marginalized we invite them to transform us, to transform our hearts, to transform our understanding, to transform us into instruments of the divine mercy and justice."[76]

## God, Church and the Bible

### God

While matters of sin and salvation are crucial in liberation theology, the core concern has to do with the doctrine of God. After all, it is God who saves us from sin and who liberates. It is in this context of the primacy of the divine that the doctrine of the church and the role of the Bible must be considered. As John Vincent and I have stated in an edited volume titled *Methodist and Radical*: "None of this will mean anything unless God in Christ through the Holy Spirit is the first radical."[77]

Jennings notes the deeper reasons for Wesley's work, which are often neglected in mainline Methodism: "We often recall that Wesley directed himself to the poor of England and away from the prosperous and prestigious. ... Whatever else it was, however, it was the rigorous application in the field of proclamation

---

[74] On this topic see Rieger, *Grace under Pressure*, chapter 2.
[75] See J. Wesley, "On Visiting the Sick," in *Works* (Bicentennial Edition), 3:385.
[76] Jennings, *Good News to the Poor*, 57–8.
[77] J. Rieger and J. Vincent, "Conclusion," in Rieger and Vincent (eds.), *Methodist and Radical*, 207–8.

and community formation of the biblical revelation of the being of God."[78] This is absolutely fundamental to Wesley and to any subsequent Methodist liberation theology. Meeks agrees in his own way: "The concentration of Wesley's view of stewardship on the poor is not an ideological quirk. It derives from the character of the God of Israel."[79] The core issue for liberation theologies remains the doctrine of God.

When contemporary liberation theologians talk about God taking sides, mainline theology is shaken up. Cone has been known to make strong claims like the following: "From God's side, reconciliation between blacks and whites means that God is unquestionably on the side of the oppressed blacks struggling for justice."[80] This claim, which appears harsh at first sight, matches the logic of the gospel, which Wesley sought to make his own. Cone notes that "when Paul said, 'God was in Christ reconciling the world unto himself,' he was not making a sentimental comment on race relations. God's reconciling act is centered on the cross, and it reveals the depths of divine suffering for the reconciliation of enslaved humanity. God encounters evil and suffering, the principalities and the powers that hold people in captivity; and the resurrection is the sign that these powers have been decisively defeated, even though they are still very active in the world."[81] A God who makes a difference is a God who takes sides against sin and evil, as the ministry of Jesus demonstrates.

North American Latino Methodist theologian Harold Recinos reports that in his work with Salvadoran immigrants he discovered that "radical discipleship ... included nothing less than confronting the established church's theological view of God ruling in almighty power and trampling the poor." Here, he also learned about the alternative, "a genuine surrender to the God of compassion who favors trampled people."[82] God's power is not disputed here, but it is relocated in acts of compassion and of resistance against sin and evil. Those who uphold the status quo are not neglected here, but the priorities are reordered: "The last will be the first, and the first will be last" (Matt. 20:16).

When Latin American liberation theology formulated its famous "preferential option for the poor," the theological reason was never the goodness of the poor but the goodness of God, who cares about the "least of these" (Matt. 25:45). At stake is nothing less than the character of God, which is love. What is at the heart of Latin American liberation theology is precisely this love; as Míguez Bonino

---

[78] T. Jennings, "Transcendence, Justice, and Mercy: Toward a (Wesleyan) Reconceptualization of God," in Maddox (ed.), 82. Jennings, ibid., 65, reflecting on Psalm 82 and Exodus 3, states even more strongly: "The being of God is constituted as a relationship to the violated and humiliated"; this is what "distinguishes the God of the Bible from all other gods."

[79] M. D. Meeks, "Sanctification and Economy: A Wesleyan Perspective on Stewardship," in Maddox (ed.), *Rethinking Wesley's Theology*, 87.

[80] Cone, *God of the Oppressed*, 235.

[81] Ibid., 236.

[82] H. J. Recinos, "Barrio Christianity and American Methodism," in Rieger and Vincent (eds.), *Methodist and Radical*, 79, 80.

notes: "The 'option for the poor' is simply the concrete sign of the universality and intentionality of love."[83] This universal love is rooted in the love of God. This issue has deep roots in the Methodist traditions, as Jennings has identified a preferential option for the poor in Wesley's own work.[84]

Néstor Míguez, a Methodist theologian and biblical scholar from Argentina and a liberation theologian of the second generation, describes the horizon of liberation theology in the non-revolutionary situation of contemporary empire (note that his father, Míguez Bonino, has written about theology in a revolutionary situation). The new creation, Míguez proclaims, still has to do with "God's saving judgment for the poor, the despised, and the excluded," pointing to an alternative way. Today, however, we are clearer than ever before that this creation is God's and not ours.[85] It is this insight that gives hope to contemporary liberation theologians that the cause of the marginalized is not lost.

## Church

Liberation theologies are not the products of individuals but grow out of close relations with the church and feed back into close relations with the church. The famous Latin American Bishop's Conferences in Medellín and Puebla, in the years 1968 and 1979, exemplify this dynamic for the Roman Catholic world. At these conferences, the church embraced the preferential option for the poor. In South Africa, the Kairos document exemplifies a similar dynamic, where ecumenical church groups affirmed central concerns of liberation. Methodist theologians were an integral part and played important roles in the production of this document. Liberation theology is what the Kairos document calls "prophetic theology" in its best sense: growing out of community, for the benefit of the world. Such theology has to take sides, as God "does not attempt to reconcile Moses and Pharaoh," but "takes side with the oppressed," because "oppression is sin and cannot be compromised with."[86] There are many other statements made by Methodist churches along those lines. In the United States, for instance, the African Methodist Episcopal Church published a statement titled: "Liberation Movements: A Critical

---

[83] J. Míguez Bonino, "Wesley in Latin America: A Theological and Historical Reflection," in Maddox (ed.), *Rethinking Wesley's Theology*, 179.

[84] Jennings, *Good News to the Poor*, chapter 3.

[85] N. Míguez, "The Old Creation in the New, the New Creation in the Old," in Meeks (ed.), *Wesleyan Perspectives on the New Creation*, 69. Míguez describes the challenge of the empire thus: under the conditions of empire, public matters are subordinated to private interests, "the democratic republican political *ethos* of the nation-state is substituted by the power of private benefit through corporate action." Ibid., 57.

[86] The Kairos document, in C. Villa-Vicencio, *Between Christ and Caesar: Classic and Contemporary Texts on Church and State* (Cape Town: David Philip, 1986), 263.

Assessment and a Reaffirmation," noting the inextricable relation of the church and liberation.[87]

Unfortunately, these traditions are often overlooked in mainline Methodism today. One reason is that, in the United Methodist Church, so-called Social Principles are not considered binding, unlike doctrinal statements like the Wesleyan Articles of Religion or the Confession of Faith. One must, of course, wonder whether this sharp distinction between social creeds and religious creeds is not a faulty one. Such a sharp distinction certainly does not exist in Wesley's own thinking as expressed, for instance, in the General Rules, which are also part of the constitutional documents for United Methodism. Wesley considered as binding for Methodists all three parts of the General Rules: "doing no harm," "doing good," and "attending upon all the ordinances of God."[88]

In the more recent history of Methodism, the 1996 United Methodist Bishops' Initiative on Children and Poverty stands out. In this initiative, the bishops of the global United Methodist Church examine the dire situation of children in poverty from a theological perspective. Their surprising conclusion is that the church does not need more programs: "The crisis among children and the impoverished and our theological and historical mandates demand more than additional programs or emphases. Nothing less than the reshaping of The United Methodist Church in response to the God who is among 'the least of these' is required."[89] Meeks notes the theological challenge: "Who is God in the face of children in poverty? Who are we *coram Deo* (before God) in the face of children in poverty?" This is the Wesleyan way of doing theology, says Meeks, wondering: "Why is there no Methodist revival for the survival of children?"[90]

The deeper problem of the church is best seen from outside the power centers of the mainline church. Methodist theologian Mercy Amba Oduyoye, from Ghana, formulates it thus: "A cultural and religious domination continues to exist in the relationship between the Northern churches and their Southern counterparts that thwarts any hope for mutuality and partnership."[91] This domination is mirrored in the relation of men and women in African communities, and it applies not only to education, as religion can be an even more powerful form of control. Oduyoye's

---

[87] J. Cone and G. Wilmore (eds.), *Position Paper of the AME Church*, in *Black Theology: A Documentary History*, Volume 1: *1966–1979*, 2nd rev. ed. (Maryknoll, NY: Orbis Books, 1993), 254: "The liberation movement had its origin in the formation of the Black Church. Much of the post-Emancipation leadership for the liberation movement came from the Black Church."

[88] J. Wesley, "The Nature, Design, and General Rules of Our United Societies," in *The Book of Discipline of the United Methodist Church 2008* (Nashville, TN: The United Methodist Publishing House, 2008), 72–4.

[89] The Council of Bishops of the United Methodist Church, *Children and Poverty: An Episcopal Initiative* (Nashville, TN: The United Methodist Publishing House, 1996), 7.

[90] M. D. Meeks, "Trinity, Community, and Power," in Meeks (ed.), *Trinity, Community and Power*, 18.

[91] M. Amba Oduyoye, "The Challenges of Partnership and Mutuality in the Task of Evangelizing Ghana," in Rieger and Vincent (eds.), *Methodist and Radical*, 156.

observation applies also to the relation between the status quo and the margins in the Northern churches. The alternative is a partnership in mission and mutuality in service, which grows out of an awareness of what Oduyoye calls the "hazards of life." She concludes with an important question to the church that remains to be answered: "What is the African contribution to the North?"[92] The answer might be found in Oduyoye's description of how Methodists in Ghana have embraced both Methodist concerns for healing and deliverance of individuals from evil, as well as a deep concern for the social evils of our time. Liberation theologies encourage rethinking and rebuilding the church from the margins, where God is at work.

Mortimer Arias, a former bishop of the Evangelical Methodist Church in Bolivia, and his wife Esther remind us of the importance of evangelization in Latin America liberation theology: "When Puebla elaborates on evangelization, we Protestants—who are so committed to evangelization and consider it our fundamental vocation—would do well to listen. The Puebla interpretation of evangelization is thoroughly holistic, in the context of the Gospel, in the scope of evangelization (to evangelize the poor, the elite, youth, the family, the church, culture, popular religiosity, etc.) and in the methodology of evangelization."[93] It is too often forgotten that Roman Catholic liberation theologians like Gustavo Gutiérrez have declared evangelization the primary purpose of liberation theology. In the words of Míguez Bonino, the fundamental question of evangelization is the fundamental question of the Christian life: "In very simple terms, evangelization ought to deal with the question: What does it mean concretely and specifically to follow Christ in thought and action in today's world?"[94]

In liberation theology, moreover, evangelization cuts both ways. Vincent talks about being evangelized by the poor: "The practitioner theologian does not 'bring' the Gospel, but is rather brought into the Gospel, or aspects of it, through the experiences of the poor, and the experiences of working with them."[95] This changes everything, and it can be argued that John Wesley himself experienced this evangelization from the bottom up, what Vincent calls being "brought into the Gospel."

Asian Methodist theologians who have suggested the importance of interreligious dialogue have picked up an important Wesleyan theme without naming it. As Wesley collaborated with other Christians on the basis of a common cause,[96] a common cause might further interreligious encounters. J. C. Park has

---

[92] Oduyoye, "The Challenges of Partnership and Mutuality," 157, 162.

[93] E. and M. Arias, *The Cry of My People: Out of Captivity in Latin America* (New York, NY: Friendship Press, 1980), 119.

[94] J. Míguez Bonino, "Sanctification: A Latin American Rereading," in Kirkpatrick, (ed.), trans. McCoy, *Born in the Struggle for Life*, 13.

[95] J. Vincent, "A New Theology and Spirituality," in J. Vincent and C. Rowland (eds..), *Liberation Spirituality*, British Liberation Theology 2 (Sheffield: Urban Theology Unit, 1999), 100.

[96] J. Wesley, "Letter to A Roman Catholic," in Jackson, *Works*, x, 85: "If we cannot as yet think alike in all things, at least we may love alike. Herein we cannot possibly do amiss. For of one point none can doubt a moment,—God is love; and he that dwelleth in love, dwelleth in God, and God in him."

argued that the place interreligious dialogue happens is in the crises of life. In the context of a Christian–Confucian dialogue, both of which have patriarchal components, Park lifts up "the groans and moans of the most oppressed and marginalized in East Asia, such as women, migrant workers, children, and the so-called lesser in society, as well as all suffering sentient beings in one of the most polluted regions of the world."[97]

## Bible

For the most part, liberation theologies have their origins in the biblical texts. Black theology in the United States, for instance, derives from a reading of the Bible in light of the African American experience. The theologian, according to Cone, is *"before all else* an exegete, simultaneously of Scripture and of existence." In this context, the Bible is "the primary source of theological discourse."[98] To be sure, Methodist liberation theologians have been more pronounced about the primacy of Scripture than many other Methodist theologians. This emphasis on the primacy of Scripture is not merely an idea of Cone and other theologians. The primacy of Scripture as affirmed by Black theology, for instance, is rooted in slave religion. The slaves understood the liberating powers of the gospel based on their own encounters with the biblical texts, as liberation was not preached to them by their white masters or by the established churches.

In the South African situation, Methodist biblical scholar Itumeleng Mosala has picked up on the importance of the Bible in his own way, noting the tensions within Scripture itself as supporting various different projects. "A black biblical hermeneutics of liberation must battle to recover precisely that history and those origins of struggle in the text and engage them anew in the service of ongoing human struggles."[99] The Bible plays its most important role not when it is put on a pedestal but when it is read in the midst of the tensions of life.

Elsa Tamez notes that throughout history some Methodists have continued in the Wesleyan practice of reading the Bible from the perspective of the poor.[100] This is what Tamez has done in her own ways throughout her career, producing important insights into fundamental topics, including a significant reinterpretation of Paul's notion of justification from the perspectives of the struggles of Latin America that goes deep into the logic of Paul.[101] It is well known that in Latin American

---

[97] Park, "Interliving Theology," 124.
[98] Cone, *God of the Oppressed*, 8.
[99] I. J. Mosala, *Biblical Hermeneutics and Black Theology in South Africa* (Grand Rapids, MI: W. B. Eerdmans, 1989), 20.
[100] Tamez, "Wesley as Read by the Poor," 72.
[101] E. Tamez, trans. S. Ringe, *The Amnesty of Grace: Justification by Faith from a Latin American Perspective* (Nashville, TN: Abingdon, 1993). One of her key insights is that "insofar as it is by faith and not by law that one is justified, the excluded person becomes aware of being a historical subject and not an object." Ibid., 166.

liberation theology, the primacy of Scripture is rooted in the practice of Ecclesial Base Communities, who read the Bible in light of their everyday struggles. Here are the roots of Latin American liberation theology. For good reasons, Gustavo Gutiérrez has talked about the fact that Christians are not only reading the Bible; the Bible also "reads us."[102] In Hispanic theology in the United States, Methodist theologian Justo González has made similar comments, noting that "the [biblical] text that we address addresses us in return."[103]

From the South African perspective Basil Moore sums up what is at stake: Scripture and tradition are read in the real-life situation of struggling people in South Africa. Moore notes, however, that this does not mean that liberation theologians can do with the sources whatever they want. Through these readings, they have come closer to the original issues addressed, including the fact that Jesus' ministry was located under the conditions of the Roman Empire and that Jesus himself "was one of the poor, the colonized, the oppressed."[104] Reading the Bible in contexts of tension that resemble the tensions of the times when these texts were written and of the events to which they refer, leads to deeper exegetical insights than the ones produced in the ivory towers.

Oduyoye notes the irony that is implied in these struggles: Methodism in Ghana began with a few young men reading the Bible, but when "the Bible study group called for Bibles" they "got missionaries in addition."[105] The readings of the people have too often been policed by mainline theology and its beholdenness to the status quo. Where liberation theologians have been successful at reversing these dynamics, the readings of the Bible from the perspective of the people have not only led to new theological insights but have made a tremendous difference in the life of the church.

## Conclusions

Liberation theologies are not copying the theological methods of the recent past, whether they come under liberal or conservative banners. While a difference to conservative models has been taken for granted, there are also significant differences that separate liberation theologies and liberal theologies, especially in Latin America, where liberalism took over in the nineteenth century after independence of various countries was declared from Spain and its more conservative ways.

When challenged from the margins, liberals and conservatives often find themselves on the side of the status quo and join forces. Míguez Bonino describes

---

[102] G. Gutiérrez, *We Drink from Our Own Wells: The Spiritual Journey of a People*, foreword by H. Nouwen, trans. M. J. O'Connell (Maryknoll, NY: Orbis, and Melbourne: Dove, 1984), 34.
[103] González, *Mañana*, 86.
[104] Moore, "What is Black Theology?," 8.
[105] Oduyoye, "The Challenges of Partnership and Mutuality," 153.

the Latin American situation in these words: "When, since the end of World War I, the masses entered public life, conservatives and liberals became more and more unified around the defense of the capitalist order." As a result, "Roman Catholicism and Protestantism could, after a long war, join hands in the support of a democratic, enlightened, liberal society in Latin America."[106] Whenever the poor and marginalized appeared on the map, old theological differences were quickly settled. Similar dynamics can be observed in many other contexts as well, including contemporary academic and ecclesial settings in Europe and the United States.

In this context, liberation theology has little choice but to continue its call for "a total overhaul of Christian piety, ecclesiastical institutions, discipline, and theological reflection," as Míguez Bonino put it in the 1970s.[107]

Perhaps the most pernicious of all misunderstandings of liberation theology is that liberation theologies are special interest theologies, geared towards the interest of particular groups, with no relevance for others. While I have addressed this reproach in detail in other places, a few words need to be said in conclusion.[108] Theology, whether it is aware of it or not, has always been contextual. Once this is clear, a certain relativity is unavoidable in any theological enterprise. Nevertheless, acknowledging this relativity does not have to lead to relativism, where "anything goes." Relativity needs to be dealt with by acknowledging it, rather than by denying it.

Liberation theologies are the only true common interest theologies, because common interest cannot be built from the top by claiming a generic context for humanity.[109] Liberation theologies are aware that the various contexts, while different and diverse, are related. The context of the poor, for instance, is inextricably related to the context of the wealthy. The context of women is inextricably related to the context of men, the context of Asians is related to the context of Europeans, Americans, and so on. The challenge before us, therefore, is to go to the bottom of our contexts, where we can see the various relationships that exist between us, both in their positive and negative shapes. The apostle Paul knew this well: "If one member suffers, all suffer together with it; if one member is honored, all rejoice together with it" (1 Cor. 12:26). And since Paul spoke these words about the body of Christ, theologians could do worse than look for God in these places of common struggle and joy.

---

[106] Míguez Bonino, *Doing Theology*, 13.

[107] Ibid., xxiv. In Latin America, this was especially important in Protestant contexts. Míguez Bonino notes that among Protestants in Latin America, theological reflection is a new effort. For the longest time, they used translations and adapted European or North American theology. Ibid., 73.

[108] See, for instance, J. Rieger, "Developing a Common Interest Theology from the Underside," in J. Rieger (ed.), *Liberating the Future: God, Mammon, and Theology* (Minneapolis, MN: Fortress Press, 1998), 124–41.

[109] This has, of course, been attempted by theologians like Rudolf Bultmann and Paul Tillich, as well as by some early feminist theologians who claimed a generic "women's experience."

# 12

# Methodism, Globalisation and John Wesley[1]

## Keith Robbins[2]

In 1883, Mark Pattison, Rector of Lincoln College, Oxford, chaired a meeting in the city at which the speaker was Hugh Price Hughes, then a local Wesleyan Methodist minister. Hughes took it upon himself to remark upon the fact that 'no adequate memorial of John Wesley existed in a university, of whose sons he was one of the greatest'. The Rector stirred. 'Not one of the *greatest*', he audibly remarked. The speaker heard this comment and repeated his observation, adding, 'nothing has caused me greater astonishment since I came to Oxford, than the ignorance of the University with regard to the world-wide work and influence of Wesley. The founder of a Church which numbers twenty-five millions…' 'No, no, Mr Hughes', interrupted the Rector; 'twenty-five thousand, you mean, not twenty-five millions'. The audience waited in breathless silence while Hughes dived into his coat-pocket and produced a pocket-book from which he proceeded to verify his statement. Subsequently, a correspondence ensued in which Hughes argued that if a man who had had so palpable an effect on history as Wesley was not great, who was? It is not clear what rejoinder Pattison made.[3]

The task of the historian, to put it disarmingly simply, is somehow to relate the past to the present – hence, in my title, the grouping of words which are not often found together. There is, first, the remarkable man who 'felt his heart strangely warmed' on 24 May 1738. John Wesley, whose life spanned almost its entire length, was of course an Englishman of the eighteenth century. 'Dating' him will also

---

[1] This chapter (as 'John Wesley, Methodism and Globalization') was originally given as the inaugural John Wesley lecture at Lincoln College, Oxford in May 2006. An edited version was subsequently published in *The Epworth Review*, 34:4 (October 2007), 23–37.

[2] See Keith Robbins, *England, Ireland, Scotland, Wales: The Christian Church 1900–2000* (Oxford: Oxford University Press, 2008); Keith Robbins (ed.), *The Dynamics of Religious Reform in Northern Europe 1780–1920: Political and Legal Perspectives* (Leuven: Leuven University Press, 2010); Keith Robbins and John Fisher (eds), *Religion and British Foreign Policy 1815 to 1941* (Dordrecht: Republic of Letters, 2010).

[3] Dorothy Hughes, *The Life of Hugh Price Hughes* (London: Hodder and Stoughton, 1904), 161–2.

mean that he is 'dated'. He is no longer with us. Some aspects of his life, work and belief make him 'a man for all seasons' but others make him seem 'a child of his time'. Historians, Methodists, citizens of Oxford or members of the University can all 'claim' their Wesley, can all see that his stature requires some 'memorial', but it would be surprising indeed if they all wanted to do so 'wholesale' or for precisely the same reasons. Henry Rack, at the end of his 1989 biography, concluded that John Wesley 'retains, one supposes, a secure if perplexing place in the history books'.[4] His use of 'one supposes', however, perhaps indicates a little doubt, or perhaps merely reinforces the element of perplexity about what that place is. He emphasises that the paradox of a 'reasonable enthusiast', of a precise clergyman reaching and organising 'the submerged religious frustrations of his time' remains. This bringing together which Wesley accomplished – though not without preserving a certain distance – can be symbolised, he suggests, in the relationship between the simple elegance of the curving rails on the stairs of the Bristol New Room pulpit on the one hand and the sighs, cries and convulsions of the people he addressed from it.[5] Wesley succeeded in harmonising – and the use of a musical term in this connection is rather appropriate – at least some parts of those two otherwise distinct aspects of Georgian England.

If Wesley is dead, the same cannot be said for the movement which he 'founded'. Methodism lives on. It is suggested that the 'world Methodist community' now numbers over seventy-five million people in more than 130 countries. In its manifold manifestations, Wesley remains with us through Methodism. *Si monumentum requiris circumspice*. Yet it would be quite misleading to suppose that the 'Wesleyan heritage' has entailed the straightforward transmission of an unambiguous legacy. The history of nineteenth-century Methodism, to think merely of Britain, makes it plain that Wesley could be interpreted in different ways, with different outcomes. The claim to 'own' the historical Wesley buttressed rival interpretations of his meanings and intentions. And it could be claimed that, just as the opinions and policies of Wesley himself evolved over his long life, so the next generation, and generations, should modify and adapt. If Wesley himself was pragmatic in terms of structures and methods, so should the 'Wesleyan tradition' be. But to make pragmatism a principle might be to go too far. There was such a thing, many supposed, as 'authentic Methodism' and its 'heritage' had to be preserved. This tension, of course, is not unique to Methodism. It applies to all social institutions, religious or secular, which find themselves buffeted by changes which they only imperfectly understand, and frequently resent when they do understand. It may even apply to the University of Oxford. So, as in the case of any ecclesial body which owes it origins to the role of an individual – a Luther or a Calvin – the thought and actions of those individuals still constitute defining markers of a kind, even in circumstances which are radically different from the social, political or intellectual climates in which they emerged.

---

[4] Henry Rack, *Reasonable Enthusiast: John Wesley and the Rise of Methodism* (London: Epworth, 1989), 553.

[5] Ibid., 53–4.

And the world in which we live *is* very different from that of 1738. Hence the need for a consideration of Methodism and 'globalisation'. As we have noted, a quest for holiness in Oxford in the early eighteenth century has led to a world-wide fellowship in a contemporary world structured and organised in a manner which would have been inconceivable to Wesley. Not in his wildest imagination would he have supposed that a body calling itself the World Methodist Council would have been holding one of its five-yearly assemblies in 2006 in Seoul, Korea, bringing together men and women representing Methodists from Slovakia and Sierra Leone, from Italy and Taiwan, from Fiji and Finland – to name only some of the many unlikely pairings to be represented. 'World Methodists', thus assembled, are 'Wesley's children' – but he might not have recognised them and they, in turn, in many cases standing quite outside the cultural milieu of early-eighteenth-century England, may find their 'father' difficult to place.

The World Methodist Council only adopted that title in 1951 at the meeting held in Oxford of the ten-yearly 'Ecumenical Methodist Conference'. That body had been formed in 1881 when a gathering of Methodists of various kinds, drawn largely from the United States and the United Kingdom (and its Dominions) met in London. The word 'ecumenical' in the title was used to emphasise that its purpose was to try to draw together all the divided branches of Methodism across the world. In essence that meant trying to develop a dialogue between British and American Methodism, something which had been largely lacking for a hundred years.[6] It gave some impetus to the stirrings towards Methodist Union in Britain, and indeed, twenty years later, the Ecumenical Conference again meeting in London, formally adopted a resolution suggesting that the British should follow the example which had already been set by the Methodist churches in Australia and Canada. That process, of course, was to take another thirty years. Making something of a reality of 'world Methodism', however, was fundamentally a matter of trying to comprehend the differences of structure and ethos which had emerged, over time, between the Methodist churches of Britain and of the United States – for these in turn were being replicated across the globe by the missionary activity which had been promoted separately by these churches. It was appropriate, therefore, that the 1891 Ecumenical Conference, in the centenary year of Wesley's death, was held in Washington. Hugh Price Hughes was one of the representatives from Britain, having not forgotten to dictate a book of fourteen sermons in one week to his secretary prior to departure. The United States (and its President with whom he shook hands) impressed him enormously but at the same time he felt that 'this light-hearted and prosperous people have never yet taken life quite seriously enough'. Everything was so extremely in favour of the United States that it was difficult 'for this privileged people to avoid the intoxication of success'.[7]

---

[6] These matters are much more thoroughly explored in Kenneth Cracknell and Susan J. White (eds), *An Introduction to World Methodism* (Cambridge: Cambridge University Press, 2005).

[7] Hughes, *Hughes*, 325–7.

The reality, as twentieth-century 'Ecumenical Methodist Conferences' were to show, was that this privileged people provided the finance which makes them possible, but with this has come a particular vision of what 'world Methodism' should be. In the post-Second World War climate, and in the organisational changes which accompanied the 1951 transformation to the World Methodist Council, there was a cleavage between those who wanted to build a 'World Methodist Church' and those whose priorities were less denominational, a gap which substantially, though not exclusively, divided the Americans and their overseas offspring from the British and their overseas offspring. In the ecclesiastical, no less than in the political world, there was also, though rarely acknowledged, resentment at the arrival of 'the American Century'. To take that point one stage further, the fact that President George W. Bush of the United States worshipped with the United Methodist Church did not exempt him from Methodist criticism outside the United States (and from within).

The delegates to the World Methodist Council do indeed represent their respective Methodist Conferences, but these are national and autonomous, though still clearly betraying their 'parentage'. It was only after constitutional changes made at the World Methodist Council in Denver in 1971 that what might be called this rather problematic Anglo-American dominance was modified to make more space for 'Third World' representatives. It is an ecclesial world which is not held together, insofar as it can be said to hold together, by a Holy Father, an Archbishop who is (currently problematically) *primus inter pares*, or a Supreme Governor. It is one in which bishops – of a certain kind – exist and do not exist. When we list Oslo, London, Denver, Hawaii, Singapore, Dublin, Nairobi, Rio de Janeiro and Brighton, described by recent authors as 'centres of global Methodism' – that is to say, places where the World Methodist Council has met over the last half century – what are we saying both about the 'globe' and 'Methodism'?[8]

To deal fully with these questions in more detail than I have sketched would require far more than one chapter. We could pause over each of these cities and ponder in what sense any of them constitutes a 'centre of global Methodism' other than in providing a temporary location for a conference. We may note, however, that these locations are not accidental, neither are they the product of Olympic Games-style lobbying. They reflect where Methodism has 'belonged' or might be thought to have 'settled down'. Two Councils, perhaps predictably, have taken place in Wesley's England and two in the United States (though neither Denver nor Hawaii featured in Wesley's United States); two others in other European countries (Ireland and Norway) and one in Africa, followed by one each in South-East Asia and Brazil. Only in Norway and Brazil in the past has the conference been held in a country which is not in some sense part of the 'English-speaking world'. Norway and Korea apart, none has been held in a country which has not been colonised, in one or other senses of that word, by a European power, that is to say chiefly by Britain itself. Methodism may be global, but it inhabits particular places. It resonates with particular pasts – but it also mutates and interacts. British

---

[8] Cracknell and White, *World Methodism*, 251.

Methodist congregations may not be 'dislocated' by the fact that the World Methodist Conference takes place elsewhere across the globe but nevertheless the venue represents, symbolically at least, a loosening of historical moorings. But is it still true, as the late Rupert Davies wrote, that 'World Methodism, in spite of its potentialities, has never come to count much in British Methodism'?[9] And, when we talk about time, place and space, about unity and diversity, let us not suppose we are only talking of the problem of the contemporary world. We come back to John Wesley himself.

Rack's reference, quoted earlier, to 'the history books',[10] may sound a little antiquated. It seems to assume that there is a prescribed canon which 'the historians' must attend to. The reality seems to be that historians now have very different views on what is and what is not significant or 'worth writing about'. 'Great men', in some quarters, are long past their sell-by date. The miscellaneous contemporary preoccupations of historians are indeed often supposed, implicitly or explicitly, to be by-passing concern with people who have been deemed by their predecessors to have merited a 'place in history/books'. What is now in vogue, if biography is attempted, is a more sophisticated variant of that *Life and Times* genre familiar to Victorians. It is not exactly a new discovery that individuals are 'made' as well as 'born', though any attempt to say where one begins and the other ends is fraught with difficulty. It was over a quarter of a century ago that John Pudney wrote a lavishly illustrated *John Wesley and His World* which provided a popular account with the specific objective of 'placing' him. He did not do so, however, in any sustained fashion.[11] Academic historians since, however, have become much more interested in the significance of 'place'.

Yet it would be too easy to succumb to a secure sense of continuity. To repeat, we know that John Wesley's world is not *our* world. Even to make such an obvious point, however, at once forces us to ask the much more difficult question of whether there is such a thing as *our* world, that is to say, one which an individual or group would be able to identify with and 'own'. That we are all alive in the same era is indisputable. We all receive, on a daily basis, images of 'the world'. We constantly hear of natural disasters, political crises and wars before they pass away from our fleeting attention to be replaced by others equally disturbing, but also equally evanescent. Those of us who are international historians try to piece together the flood of data and information in the hope, possibly vainly, of trying to develop a coherent and comprehensive picture of 'the world'. Even in the act of doing so, however, we know how partial are our perspectives and how random, or perhaps not so random, are the images which flash across the screen and then are gone. 'Our world' is not so much one that 'adds up' in some universally acknowledged and comprehensive manner – 'the international community' – but a set of intersecting, but not interlocking, worlds. We may be in the middle of a 'clash of civilisations',

---

[9] In Rupert Davies, A. Raymond George and Gordon Rupp (eds), *A History of the Methodist Church in Great Britain*: vol.3 (London, 1985), 381.
[10] Rack, *Reasonable Enthusiast*, 553.
[11] John Pudney, *John Wesley and His World* (London: Thames & Hudson, 1978).

or not, and that this matter is itself unclear only illustrates how difficult it is to tie down the contours of any civilisation in the contemporary world. And we also know that the boundaries of a civilisation may not be identified on a map. The 'centres of global Methodism' which we referred to earlier we know are not in fact 'centres' at all. There are Methodists in London and there are Methodists in Singapore but neither population is 'Methodist'. Our neighbour's 'civilisation' may not be ours. The character of 'our world' is that such *coherence* as it possesses stems paradoxically from the juxtaposition and uneasy co-existence of *difference*. There is, therefore, no simple way in which we can contrast 'our world' with that of John Wesley because, beyond certain general beliefs which we may think (or hope) that we all have in common, there is no consensus which we all recognise as constituting the defining characteristics of 'our world'.

There is no single definition of 'globalisation' or agreement about what it entails. 'Realist' theorists do not deny the increased interconnectedness between economies, societies and cultures but contend that the struggle for political power between states continues unabated. 'Liberal' theorists suggest that we are currently witnessing a 'world society', or at least the closest approximation to one which has yet existed, itself the product of a long evolution which has seen, though in no smooth fashion, the erosion of the 'sealed units' of the past. States are ceasing to be the central actors in the way the world works. They are being by-passed by a vast network (and a technological word is significant) of organisations and individuals which make up a connected world. 'World-Systems' analysts see 'globalisation' as fraudulent, identifying it as a Western-led phenomenon, a further phase in the development of international capitalism.[12] Naturally, there are refinements and elaborations of these broad-brush characterisations and we may be inclined to see substance in aspects of all of them, without being persuaded to adopt one of them in its entirety. What we respond to may in turn relate to our own experience of it, our own particular points of contact and interaction. However, as I put it in a book on the world since 1945, 'The genie of globalisation cannot be put back into the bottle. It plays havoc with the political and constitutional concepts inherited from the past: sovereignty, boundaries, frontiers, citizenship, political loyalty being among them.' The individual, or at least the privileged individual, 'communicates' with 'the world' without much regard for particular places; 'it is sufficient for the interlocutor to be familiar with the English language'. I added, however, that there appeared to be a 'loneliness at the heart of this enveloping and developing cybernetic universalism'.[13] Global culture is at once desirable and threatening. Individuals and societies seek reassuring anchorage in established identities or

---

[12] John Baylis and Steve Smith, *The Globalization of World Politics: An Introduction to International Relations* (Oxford: Oxford University Press, 1997), 6; see also Philip Jenkins, *The Next Christendom: The Coming of Global Christianity* (Oxford: Oxford University Press, 2011) and Zvi Ben-Dor Benite, 'Religions and World History', in Jerry H. Bentley (ed.), *The Oxford Handbook of World History* (Oxford: Oxford University Press, 2011), 210–28.

[13] Keith Robbins, *The World since 1945: A Concise History* (Oxford: Oxford University Press, 1998), 252.

invent new ones. These tensions, it need hardly be said, manifest themselves as much in the world of religion as in any other.

It is tempting sometimes to suppose that this ever-present world, and our own inner conflicts in relation to it, is peculiar to our own times. There has indeed been no other in which so many millions have had the ability to 'see the world' at such speed and in such comfort, or to communicate with such facility (normally) with the ends of the earth at the touch of a keyboard. Yet, of course, at different levels and to different degrees, there has always been contact between peoples, and travellers have recorded their impressions, by no means all uniform, of the 'other' they encountered. Langford has indeed written a book in which 'Englishness' – manners and character – is identified through the observations of foreign visitors. I think I am right in saying that none of the visitors he discusses observed John Wesley in action. If they had seen him on Hanham Mount or at Gwennap Pit, they might have modified the overall verdict which the book attributes to them – namely that preachers in the Church of England were 'stiff and unappealing'.[14]

John Wesley has not been used, by any foreign visitor that Paul Langford has drawn upon, as a person embodying 'characteristic' facets of Englishness under the headings of Energy, Candour, Decency, Taciturnity, Reserve or Eccentricity. 'National character' is a perilous construct and foreign visitors during this period were by no means in agreement concerning the ticks in boxes which ought to have been conveniently placed for the benefit of the systematising historian. *The Englishman* may be only an ideal type but certain facets of Wesley's character and, shall we say, his 'life-style', can be matched against the portrait of him which successive biographers have drawn. It is not my objective here, however, to redraw that portrait in detail, to try, as it were, to rebrand 'a brand plucked from out of the burning'. To have attempted another summary 'portrait of Wesley' could necessarily only rehearse a story the salient elements of which are likely to be familiar to many Methodist readers – and there are, as we know, recent lives, building on the admired work of scholars at Oxford and other universities.

If, as Langford does, we take 'Energy' as a starting point, John Wesley may be taken to be the very paradigm of an Englishman. The editor of travellers' tales, Charles White,[15] admittedly only born in the year of Wesley's death, 1791, spoke of a 'craving for locomotion, which is, perhaps, a distinctive characteristic of the English nation'. The marquis de Bombelles, in 1784, thought that 'one does not travel anywhere so much as in England, nowhere has one so many means of departing' – a remark made, of course, well before the era of free coach passes for pensioners. The English, it seemed, suffered from 'la maladie de change de place'.[16] They always seemed to be on the move, but not quite to know why. The equestrian statue of Wesley outside the New Room, situated as that in turn was in the area

---

[14] Paul Langford, *Englishness Identified: Manners and Character, 1650–1850* (Oxford: Oxford University Press, 2000), 183.
[15] Charles White (ed.), *The Courts of Europe at the Close of the Last Century* (London, 1841), I, viii, cited in Langford, *Englishness Identified*, 36.
[16] Langford, *Englishness Identified*, 36–7.

of the Horsefair in central Bristol, makes an immediate point, one not lost on me when I first saw it as a schoolboy. Wesley was perpetually peripatetic. The usual computation is that he travelled altogether some 250,000 miles – an achievement which certainly put him in the eighteenth-century premier league. He needed to have an intimate awareness of the needs and habits of horses, roads and tracks. He knew about the vagaries of the climate of the British Isles. If he had been so inclined he could have anticipated Robert Louis Stevenson and written *Travels with a Donkey*. He walked from the centre of Bristol to the outlying district where I was brought up without thinking about it. I assumed that it was not a journey to be made on foot. He walked from Oxford to London (not because he was conscious of any governmental fiat on the subject of obesity) but because it was a 'natural' thing to do. Of course, he was not unique in his mobility. Although life in his era is sometimes romantically (or not so romantically) thought to be lived intensely locally and horizons thought to be limited to the next village, we should certainly not take too far any notion of self-contained communities living in isolation.

The grumble of the noble French marquess, just cited, was that it was the desire for constant motion, not the necessity of getting anywhere, which seemed to motivate English travellers. Such an observation, however, cannot apply to Wesley. He was a traveller with a purpose. He had particular destinations in mind. If we distinguish between tourists and travellers, he was not a tourist. In his own *Journal* Wesley mentions reading Johnson's *Tour to the Western Isles of Scotland* and Boswell's *Tour to the Hebrides* and *Journal of a Tour to Corsica* but he was only incidentally, rather than deliberately, concerned to record his impressions of his 'environment' (to use a word with which he would not have been familiar). He was not looking deliberately for 'a change of scene' as an aspect of his own 'personal development'. He was not acutely sensitive to the extent to which travel brought with it at least the possibility (or is it threat?) of what might now be described as 'cultural transformation'. He was not a tourist, that is to say, someone for whom the journey is an end in itself bringing with it the excitement and stimulus provided by sights and sounds whose attraction lies in their 'difference'. Wesley was not to be found on the 'Grand Tour'. As Elisabeth Jay noted, even where there are descriptive passages in the *Journal* they are 'almost entirely devoid of the individual response to the environment which lend the best travellers' tales their charm'.[17]

But even if we note that Wesley was a traveller with a message, a message that was not, in principle at least, 'location specific', the intensity of his being 'on the move' stands out. He was a man of 'rooms'[18] not of 'homes'. One might say that the home that Epworth Rectory had been might not have encouraged an enthusiasm for homes. The cultivation of domestic arts and a sense of 'belonging' to a particular place were not for him. His curacy of Wroote, on behalf of his father, between 1727 and 1729, was the only time as a clergyman in which he was anchored in a particular place. That Wesley had no wish to 'settle' there may come as no surprise

---

[17]   Elisabeth Jay (ed.), *The Journal of John Wesley: A Selection* (Oxford: Oxford University Press, 1987), xv.

[18]   Some early Methodist buildings were termed 'rooms' rather than 'preaching houses'.

to those of you who know the Isle of Axholme, and also know Graham Swift's *Waterland*.[19] And of course, not unreasonably, a Fellow of Lincoln College might be expected to come to Lincoln College. A college in Oxford was (and let us hope may still remain) a special kind of place. Boy and man, at Charterhouse, Christ Church and Lincoln, he had lived in enclosed places with their own regulations and conventions, and the intimacies and enmities which arise in 'clubs', even holy ones. This is not the place to embark on a lengthy discussion of Wesley's troubled relationships with women – that desire for commitment and companionship so mixed up with vacillation, clumsiness, distance and detachment – which culminated in his disastrous marriage and the eventual departure of his wife.

To be torn between travel and domesticity, between having 'no particular place to dwell' and recognising that 'there is no place like home' perhaps makes Wesley at least approachable today. In his Isaiah Berlin Lecture before the British Academy in October 2004 Stewart Sutherland began by putting forward a proposition. 'There was a time', he said, 'and perhaps there is still for some, when the metaphor appropriate to the individual in search of moral and spiritual fulfilment was "pilgrim". The goal or *telos* of human life was known and identifiable under some description; the problem was, how to get there.' The problems of the journey were recognised, but the point of arrival was not in dispute. The problem for today, he suggested, is not simply 'how to get there' but rather where 'there' is. He went on to elaborate on two further possible metaphors: 'tourist' or 'nomad' rather than 'pilgrim'. Sutherland identified himself as a 'nomad', someone who does not believe that we can transcend space and time and realise a certain *telos*. He believes that while some elements of integrity can be achieved in life they will always fall short of a full revelation.[20] To be in the company of fellow nomads might be more helpful than to be with guides who claim to possess the full truth. Be that as it may, it comes as no surprise to learn that Bunyan's *Pilgrim's Progress* featured among the practical books of divinity which Wesley recommended for morning or evening meditation.[21] It was a part of his ancestral Dissenting past which had not been blotted out. I have already suggested that Wesley was not a tourist in the sense of someone who starts out from a fixed point and then returns home again, laden down with sights and sounds. A 'traveller' may fall into a slightly different category.

In March 1739 Wesley wrote a strong rejoinder to James Hervey, who had been one of his pupils at Lincoln and one of the Oxford Methodists. The original of that letter has not survived but Wesley's response contains the famous saying, 'I look upon all the world as my parish', reproduced on the Wesley tablet in Westminster Abbey, which might be said to be the text for this chapter. Hervey had obviously put various possibilities for the future before Wesley. One of them was that John should 'settle in college'. There was (and no doubt is) much to be said for such a course. Wesley demurred. He had no business there, having then no office and

---

[19] Graham Swift, *Waterland* (London: Heinemann, 1983).
[20] Lord Sutherland, 'Nomad's Progress', *Proceedings of the British Academy*, 131 (2005), 443–63.
[21] Albert C. Outler (ed.), *John Wesley* (New York: Oxford University Press, 1964), 162.

no pupils. Alternatively, Hervey suggested that he should accept a cure of souls somewhere. Wesley waved that aside by saying that he would think about it – when he was offered one. Hervey wanted him to settle in a particular place, being concerned as to how Wesley could justify assembling Christians to sing psalms and pray and hear the Scriptures expounded when none of them was in his charge. Wesley replied that God in Scripture commanded him to instruct the ignorant, reform the wicked and confirm the virtuous. It was Man who forbade him to do this in another's parish; such a prohibition was to say, in effect, not to do it at all, 'seeing I have no parish of my own, nor probably ever shall'. Should he obey God or man? 'I look upon all the world as my parish', he declared in words which even undergraduates on *University Challenge* might be expected to know.[22] Hervey was shocked and returned to the topic in August. He declared that itinerant preaching was repugnant to the Apostolical as well as the English Constitution – a formidable double-whammy of a rebuke. Timothy was settled at Ephesus. Titus was stationed at Crete. Other of 'our Captain's commanders', he went on, were assigned to their particular posts. These labourers, industrious labourers, did not think it either necessary or expedient 'to travel from this country to that with words of exhortation in their mouth'. They laid out their pastoral vigilance upon the flock assigned to their care. 'Fix in some parish', he earnestly concluded, but Wesley was not to be persuaded.[23]

'All the world is my parish' has become so familiar that we perhaps both fail to grasp what an extraordinary statement it was and neglect to consider what 'all the world' might have seemed to be. He argued that on Hervey's principles there would be nowhere left for him to preach, 'not in any of the Christian parts, at least, of the habitable earth' for he claimed that all of these were, after a sort, divided into parishes. Nor could he go back 'to the heathens' because all those in Georgia now belonged to the parish either of Savannah or Frederica.

The Epworth Rectory of his childhood, one suspects, was not much concerned to 'situate' a Lincolnshire boy in 'the world' as it would have been perceived in the first decade of the eighteenth century. Father was much more concerned with the text of the Book of Job. 'Georgia', scene of Wesley's disappointments, did not exist. Education at Charterhouse and Christ Church took him into the ancient world, its authors and its languages, rather than enabling him to unravel the mysteries of the expanded and expanding 'England'. In addition to Latin, Greek and Hebrew, the Latin-derived languages of his Europe – French, Italian, Spanish – were all mastered to a substantial degree. Yet this did not produce a 'European man'. He was an Englishman to the core and the continent was unknown territory. 'History', conceived as a distinct discipline, did not feature in his studies and although it seems that he read some 'histories' it does not appear that he did so with the conscious intention of learning 'the history of the world' or of trying deliberately to reflect on what it might be to 'think historically'. The 'Holy Experiment' of

---

[22] J. Telford (ed.), *The Letters of the Rev. John Wesley, A.M.*, I (London: Epworth Press, 1931), 285–6.

[23] Ibid., I, 333.

the late 1720s and early 1730s was of course an Oxford affair. Even if his visits to Oxford were few, and much later in life, and his comments on the university equivocal, nevertheless the city and the university had entered his soul. Having an hour to spare – itself a fact worth remarking on – he walked to Christ Church in 1778, a place for which he retained 'a peculiar affection'. There were indeed lovely mansions there, but without experimental knowledge of God nothing could make their inhabitants happy.[24] He was the last person to wallow in 'place' for its own sake. It was 'people' who mattered. Oxford had seen him attempting to practise discipline but perhaps a perfect realisation of the mind and life of Christ could not be attained through the Oxford course which he had set himself.

Georgia was a new beginning. 'Our end in leaving our native country', Wesley wrote, 'was not to avoid want … nor to gain the dung or dross of riches or honour; but singly this – to save our souls; to live wholly to the glory of God.' A journey deserves a *Journal* and it is now that this famous document began. It scarcely needs to be said that it was a record for an apologetic purpose. He had undoubtedly picked up a good deal about what 'Georgia' was to be but, since it was a new venture – its charter had been granted in 1732 – there was no question of the traveller coming guide-book in hand. What beliefs 'Indians' might have could only be a matter for speculation. His fellow-passengers included a party of Germans – of Moravian persuasion. He resolved to learn German in order to converse and to make more meaningful his participation in their services – and was greatly taken with their singing of hymns. The 'new world' which had unexpectedly opened up to him on a ship in the middle of the Atlantic was the Pietism of 'old central Europe'. Sailing westwards, his mind was opened to a continental world to the east of which he knew little. He was asked on the voyage whether he knew that Jesus Christ had died to save him – and felt that the words of his reply had been vain. The 'servile offices', without pay, which Moravians undertook for other passengers contrasted favourably with the behaviour of the English, none of whom would do menial tasks. Their fortitude in the storms that were encountered, however, was not a matter of their national character but of their faith.

The new world was meant to be a new beginning for Wesley himself. Asking himself whether his soul could not as well have been saved in England as in Georgia, he had answered No. He was intending to be an Indian missionary, populating the idealised wilderness with new Christians. On first encountering the small group of Indians who had been brought over to England, Wesley was initially impressed that they did not wish to be made Christians as the Spanish made people Christians. They wanted to be taught before they were baptised. He had a conversation, through an interpreter, in July 1736. Wesley was impressed by their apparent belief that there was One who lived 'in the clear sky' and 'Two' with him. He drew attention to a book which told many things of the beloved ones above. The warriors replied that, should they ever be at peace, they would be glad to know of it. For the moment, however, they only had time for fighting. Wesley concluded that they appeared the most likely of all the Americans to receive the Gospel but he

---

[24] Rack, *Reasonable Enthusiast*, 105.

did not know what would become of them when he was called from among them. He had to admit that the work was too weighty even when he was there. A parish of above two hundred miles in length laughed at the labours of one man. In the event, while the detail need not detain us here, following the varied disputes and personal issues in which he became involved, Wesley departed from among them rather earlier than he had anticipated. On the voyage home, perhaps appropriately, he immersed himself in the Works of Machiavelli. According to George Whitefield, however, the good that Wesley had done in America was inexpressible. His name had become very precious among the people. No doubt that was true for some but there were others, as was reported to him, who could not tell what religion he was of: 'They never heard of such a religion before.' The Indian mission, however, had got nowhere.

The unsettlement in his mind and spirit, however, was not due to his encounter with the 'newness' of the new world. His contacts with Indians, much more limited than he had hoped, had not led him to recoil from the notion of converting them, though it had perhaps led to some erosion of that belief in 'noble savages' with which he had arrived. Encounter with the new – though a new, in all probability one which had already prudently picked up some theological concepts from Spanish Catholics – in its own place had not at all produced the notion that Indians should be left alone and inviolate. He did not sail back as a neophyte cultural anthropologist glorying in the multiplicity of global value-systems. No, he thought the trouble was with himself. As he later put it, no doubt with a particular spin, he had gone to Georgia to teach the Indians the nature of Christianity but had found, what he had least of all suspected, that he was not himself converted to God. He had thrown up his country and wandered into strange lands but did all that give him the claim to the divine character of a Christian? *That* was what he had learned 'in the ends of the earth'.

He took the voyage 'home' in December 1737 but he was both spiritually and physically 'unsettled'. Was he doomed to be a 'Flying Dutchman' endlessly sailing the oceans of the world, 'at home' nowhere? It was, however, to be at a particular place, at the meeting in Aldersgate St. on 24 May that his heart was strangely warmed. The 'conversion experience' had come. It was followed, almost immediately, by the urge to travel again – this time to Germany – he had had the idea in Georgia – to converse with holy men who might help him go on 'from strength to strength' in faith. It was his first time on the continent. What he saw surprised him. He went out with the idea that the Dutch were a 'dirty, slovenly, unpolished people, without good nature, good manners, or common decency'.[25] He found none of that to be true. There was scarce a speck of dirt to be seen and the people were remarkable for the 'mildness and lovingness in their behaviour'.[26] He and his party committed a *faux pas* by removing their hats on entering the Grote Kerk in Gouda. They obviously did things differently here. The destination,

---

[25] http://wesley.nnu.edu/john-wesley/the-letters-of-john-wesley/wesleys-letters-1738/ (accessed 16 September 2012).

[26] Ibid.

of course, was Marienborn, where Count Zinzendorf was installed. Here were Christians who conspicuously loved one another. Further on, at Herrnhut, here was living proof that Christianity was the same yesterday, to-day and for ever. Yet, as events over the next few years were to demonstrate, while Wesley absorbed (and adapted) many Moravian insights there were to prove deep differences between himself and Zinzendorf.

Consonant with our general theme, however, and what is perhaps worth stressing, is the degree to which understanding of doctrinal issues, complex enough in all conscience, was complicated by language. Wesley's famous conversation with Zinzendorf in Lincoln's Inn Fields on 3 September 1741 took place in Latin. Engaging with a foreign world brought inescapable complications. His wanderings, however, had not turned Wesley into a rootless cosmopolitan. While he did not waste time, as he would doubtless have put it, in elaborating comprehensive notions of nationality, we have just noted the extent to which he was aware of 'peculiarities' of peoples. His later travels in the British Isles, both inside and outside England, made him aware of diversities of language and culture. He could not preach in Welsh, and who knows what may have been lost (or gained) in translation when he spoke to Welsh audiences. He did not cease to be an Englishman and thus to possess certain prejudices. Reading Voltaire's *Henriade* in 1756, for example, caused him to remark that 'the French is the poorest, meanest language in Europe, that it is no more comparable to the German or the Spanish, than a bag-pipe is to an organ.'[27]

His experiences in Georgia, despite their difficulties, had naturally left him with a personal interest in 'the English-speaking world'. His mission had left little if any legacy and cannot be taken to constitute the beginning of Methodism in America. That honour belongs rather to the 1760s in Maryland and New York to emigrating Irish families who had become Methodists before they left home. Wesley, of course, travelled widely in Ireland. It has been calculated that in aggregate he spent a total of nine years there. The 'American question' was later to cause him much difficulty – not least with Dr Johnson in the matter of copyright. He sometimes saw the Americans as 'oppressed people' and at other times thought all their talk of 'liberty' windy rhetoric. What about their black slaves, he asked. Wesley contended, of course, that politics was 'quite out of my province' and that all he was doing was applying biblical principles.

Methodism in America was beginning to go its own way. Its first conference was held in 1774; a decade later its membership had increased fourfold to some 13,000 and would go on expanding at a rapid rate. Wesley had considered going to America again after the death of Whitefield there in 1770 but the following year he wrote that he had 'no business there so long as they can do without me'. And so it proved. In 1784, writing to 'Our Brethren in America' Wesley had to admit that 'By a very uncommon train or providences, many of the provinces of North America are totally disjoined from their mother country and erected into independent states. The English government has no authority over them...'.[28]

---

[27] Jay, *Journal of John Wesley*, 135.
[28] Outler, *John Wesley*, 82–3.

In that same month, the Bishop of London declining, Wesley himself set apart Thomas Coke as 'Superintendent of the Societies in America'. Just as the schism in the English world was complete so, in large measure, was that between the Church of England and Methodists. In March 1785 Wesley reflected on 'how strangely the grain of mustard-seed, planted about half a century earlier, had grown up'. It had 'spread through all Great Britain and Ireland; the Isle of Wight ['an island oddly disjoined from Great Britain!'] and the Isle of Man; then to America, from the Leeward Islands, through the whole continent, into Canada and Newfoundland'.[29] He might have added how, in turn, it was brought back to the Channel Islands by their fishermen, French-speaking, who caught Methodism as well as fish off the coast of Newfoundland.

Looking around at the ecclesiastical scene in the British Isles in 1788, Wesley claimed that Methodists were alone in not insisting that adherents held the same opinions or followed the same mode of worship. He did not know of 'any other religious society, either ancient or modern, wherein such liberty of conscience is allowed'. Fifty years earlier he had reproached the Moravian Brethren for resting as mere shadows before Count Zinzendorf, almost implicitly both believing and obeying him. The position which Wesley built for himself, to his critics, seemed very similar. Few would doubt, however, that Methodism's uneasy and precarious balance between liberty and order, between specific dogmatic formulations and an engaging 'enthusiasm', grew out of the way in which a remarkable man fused together, consciously and unconsciously, discordant elements both in his own make-up and in the institutional and social contexts in which he operated. What happened to Methodism in the half century after his death illustrates only too graphically how difficult it was to maintain that fusion. What continued to be insisted upon, however, was the itinerancy principle, with all the difficulties it entailed. Particular places had particular meanings for Wesley. They made him what he became, but he always moved on. Even if, from 'our' perspective, his world was a necessarily limited one, and 'we' might consider, perhaps erroneously, its boundaries, both spatial and metaphysical, ones which 'we' have transcended, for Wesley to see the world as constituting a 'parish' was revolutionary.

His actual 'world' was of that English expansion/consolidation/disruption in the eighteenthcentury. The mustard-seed had sprouted, as we have seen from Wesley's own remarks, in a 'world' conquered, settled and partially, and perhaps fatally, disrupted by his own Englishmen (joined by Scotsmen). That there was another 'world' which was 'out there' Wesley well knew. He had met Sephardic Jews in the new world. He knew of, though did not meet, Moslems. The world, he recognised, also contained, among other races, Negroes who had 'the nicest ear for music' of any people he ever encountered. Reading a volume of Captain Cook's Voyages, however, he was enormously disappointed. It provided an account of a people in the South Pacific apparently without any curiosity and without any sense of shame. Men and women coupled together in the face of the sun and in public

---

[29] Jay, *Journal of John Wesley*, 230.

view.[30] Things 'absolutely impossible' were narrated. The 'real world' world was evidently a very strange place.

And so it remains. In it, however, World Methodism now sits alongside such bodies as the Anglican Communion, the Lutheran World Federation, the Baptist World Alliance, the World Alliance of Reformed Churches, bodies likewise coming together more coherently around the turn of the nineteenth/twentieth centuries, as an ecclesial global network of autonomous churches. The World Council of Churches, roughly half a century later, represents another global layer. The Roman Catholic Church, of course, embodies another global presence. Whether, in consequence, we speak of 'World Christianity', or whether we join with the new volume of the Cambridge *History of Christianity* in speaking of 'World Christianities' in the period 1914–2000, is a matter for debate. Whatever view we take, however, the 'parochial' world mission which John Wesley began in Oxford can be said to have played its part in bringing this complexity to pass.

---

[30]   Jay, *Journal of John Wesley,*, 188.

# PART IV
# Belief and Practice

# 13

ASHGATE
RESEARCH
COMPANION

# Methodism and the Bible

Peter Phillips

## Introduction

Ever since John and Charles Wesley's grouping at Oxford was nicknamed the 'Bible Moths', there has been an essential link between Methodists and the Bible. But how do contemporary Methodists engage with the Bible? Indeed, what do we mean by contemporary Methodists – now a worldwide body of huge variety and richness. In fact, Methodism in the twenty-first century is hugely diverse. In its many hues, it embraces over 75 million people worldwide. There are differences within each branch of Methodism – reflecting many of the theological opinions of the present day, not to mention the many branches of the Wesleyan/Methodist family – the Holiness Movements, the Salvationists, the Nazarenes, the Independent Methodists, British Methodists and the United Methodists of the USA and beyond. Indeed, as Methodist and Wesleyan churches grow in confidence and strength in Africa, Asia and Latin America, so different understandings of 'Methodism' and also the Church's understanding and use of the Bible will naturally develop.[1] So how could one essay embrace such diversity? Is there some general approach to the Bible which could be a common element across the rich diversity of contemporary Methodism?

This common element, this general approach to the Bible, could be found in our shared inheritance from the Wesleys. Is there a family resemblance in our approach to Scripture which is shared across world Methodism? It is true that the Methodist people of today still reflect many of the traits of the Wesleys' own approach to the Bible. The ways in which Methodism today tends to understand the Bible, and the way internationally renowned Wesleyan[2] scholars read the Bible, bear a striking

---

[1] For an introduction to the development and breadth of Methodist/Wesleyan traditions across the globe, see R. L. Maddox and J. E. Vickers (eds), *The Cambridge Companion to John Wesley* (Cambridge: Cambridge University Press, 2010), Part IV, 245–316.

[2] Throughout this essay, 'Wesleyan' is used to refer to scholars who would see themselves in the broader Methodist family, but who would not necessarily want to call themselves 'Methodist' because of that term's denominational specificity. The term is

resemblance to the way John, in particular, read the Scriptures in his own day – not as an inerrant, confining, world-denying weapon, but rather as an authoritative rule of both faith and practice.[3] Two words from that last sentence mark out the difference. On the one hand, despite insistence on the inherent truth of Scripture, Wesley was careful when exploring whether the Bible was without error in content. Indeed, there were times when he would point out minor errors. As such, he avoided, or rather was not interested in, what would later become the doctrine of the inerrancy of Scripture. Wesley was too engaged in the use of Scripture and the application of those Scriptures to real life to be caught up in questions of inerrancy. As Franz Hildebrandt said when exploring Wesley's preface to the *Standard Sermons*:

> Fundamentalism? A cheap label. Like its modernist counterpart it is really concerned with the closed Bible. Both fundamentalist and modernist have arrived at their conclusions before they ever start to open the Book. Wesley cannot afford the luxury of such theories: he is too busy using the contents of Scripture.[4]

However, Wesley also argued strongly for the absolute authority/sufficiency of Scripture, as we will see below: Scripture was to be authoritative without needing to be inerrant, in that it was all that was needed for salvation – authoritative in sufficiency not inerrancy.[5]

Has that core understanding of Scripture held within Wesley's legacy? Amidst all the variety, it would be almost impossible to research all the various forms and distil a hypothetical common approach to Scripture among contemporary Methodists. However, it might be possible to look back to Wesley's own use and then ask whether contemporary Methodists continue with this emphasis; by looking at how Wesley developed a rule for his engagement with Scripture and asking whether contemporary Methodists maintain a link to this rule. Is there

---

not used here to denote 'Wesleyan' in distinction from 'Primitive' traditions in the British Methodist Church.

[3] Robert W. Wall, 'Wesley as Biblical Interpreter', in Maddox and Vickers (eds), *Cambridge Companion*, 113–28; Randy Maddox, 'The Rule of Christian Faith, Practice, and Hope: John Wesley on the Bible', *Methodist Review*, 3 (2011) (published online at https://www.methodistreview.org/index.php/mr/article/view/45/68; accessed December 2011), 1–35.

[4] F. Hildebrandt, *Christianity according to the Wesleys* (reprinted Grand Rapids, MI: Baker Books, 1996, originally London: Epworth Press, 1956), 17. Robert Wall talks of Wesley's interpretation of the Bible 'whose practices actively participate in a people's ongoing struggle to live holy lives before a God who is light and love': 'Wesley as Biblical Interpreter', 115.

[5] W. Stephen Gunter, 'Beyond the Bible Wars: Why Inerrancy is Not the Issue for Evangelical Wesleyans', *Wesleyan Theological Journal*, 46:2 (Fall 2011), 56–69: 'It is *soteriological sufficiency* and not *factual inerrancy* that lies at the heart of Scripture's authority for Wesleyans' (emphasis in original).

still evidence for this rule within the reception and use of the Bible within World Methodist scholarship at the start of the twenty-first century?

This essay begins, then, with John Wesley's own approach to Scripture and his understanding of Scripture *as a rule of faith and practice*, before looking briefly at how this approach was then reified in the texts about Scripture (especially his *Notes on the New Testament*) which he bequeathed to those denominations and churches which his teachings have influenced. In this part of the essay, we will explore whether a Wesleyan approach to Scripture necessarily engages with the Bible not merely through erudite academic objectivity but also through a radical understanding of the Bible as *Scripture for practice* – or rather, in Wesley's terms, as a rule of Christian faith and practice. As the essay then turns to explore the reception of the role of Scripture within key sections of the contemporary Methodist Church and the work of a number of internationally recognised Wesleyan Bible scholars, we will also explore whether contemporary Methodism, as Church and scholarly community, maintains Wesley's understanding of the Scriptures: is there, in fact, a family resemblance in the way we handle the Bible?

## Scripture as rule of faith and practice

> The distinguishing marks of a Methodist are not his opinions of any sort ... We believe, indeed, that 'all Scripture is given by the inspiration of God'... We believe the written word of God to be the only and sufficient rule both of Christian faith and practice...

So said John Wesley in his description of *The Character of a Methodist* (1742),[6] putting positively that which Article VI of the Church of England's Thirty Nine Articles had said in a complex double negative:

> Holy Scripture containeth all things necessary to salvation: so that whatsoever is not read therein, nor may be proved thereby, is not to be required of any man, that it should be believed as an article of the Faith, or be thought requisite or necessary to salvation...[7]

Methodists are not people of opinion but people of the Bible; and in good post-Reformation style, Wesley maintains a focus on the Bible as the exclusive arbiter of faith – 'the only and sufficient rule both of Christian faith and practice'. But it is not quite that simple. John Wesley's approach to the Bible is worthy of a book in

---

[6] John Wesley, 'The Character of a Methodist' (1742), §1, in R. E. Davies (ed.), *The Works of John Wesley*, vol. 9: *The Methodist Societies, I: History, Nature and Design* (Nashville, TN: Abingdon Press, 1989).

[7] *Book of Common Prayer*, Standard Edition (Cambridge: Cambridge University Press, 2004), 613.

itself and several have been written.[8] In a recent article on Wesley's use of the Bible, Randy Maddox says that it has become traditional, 'indeed, almost obligatory', for studies on Wesley's approach to Scripture to cite the following, somewhat strange, passage from the preface to his first volume of *Sermons on Several Occasions*:

> I am a spirit come from God and returning to God; just hovering over the great gulf, till a few moments hence I am no more seen – I drop into an unchangeable eternity! I want to know one thing, the way to heaven – how to land safe on that happy shore. God himself has condescended to teach the way: for this very end he came from heaven. He hath written it down in a book. O give me that book! At any price, give me the Book of God! I have it. Here is knowledge enough for me. Let me be *homo unius libri*.[9]

Despite the eccentric imagery of a spirit come from and going to God, this passage clearly understands the Bible as a means of grace – as a way to learn more about the Christian faith and the saving grace of God. Indeed, Wesley included the searching of the Scriptures among the means of grace: 'outward signs, words, or actions, ordained of God, and appointed for this end, to be the ordinary channels whereby He might convey to men, preventing, justifying or sanctifying grace'.[10] In other words, the Bible for Wesley is not just a collection of words to be dissected and studied. The Bible, and our searching the Scriptures contained therein, is an active process by which we may receive the grace of God. In this way, the Bible provides the 'knowledge' to show a questing individual the way to heaven. The Bible itself is the place to find *saving* knowledge and engagement with the Bible an active part of our sanctification. Because of this, Wesley wants to be 'a man of one book' (*homo unius libri*) in that he needs only the Bible to find this knowledge of salvation – reflecting the Protestant cry of *sola scriptura* – 'Scripture alone'. However, as a means of grace, of course, searching the Scriptures is not just a matter of justification but also a sign of prevenient grace and of sanctification: the Bible provides not only *justifying* knowledge ('how the sinner may receive justification'), but also *preventing* knowledge ('conviction and education about sin and human nature') and *sanctifying* knowledge ('how as Christians we live a life of holiness'). This one book, then, is for Wesley both 'the whole and sole rule of my faith', as well as the 'one, and only one, rule of judgment with which to regard all [his] tempers, words

---

[8] See, for example, Scott Jones, *John Wesley's Conception and Use of Scripture* (Nashville, TN: Kingswood Books, 1995); Donald Bullen, *A Man of One Book? John Wesley's Interpretation and Use of the Bible* (Milton Keynes: Paternoster, 2007); Mark Weeter, *John Wesley's View and Use of Scripture* (Eugene, OR: Wipf & Stock, 2007).

[9] *Sermons on Several Occasions*, vol.1 (1746), preface. See Maddox, 'John Wesley on the Bible', 1.

[10] John Wesley, 'The Means of Grace', §II.1, in Albert C. Outler (ed.), *The Works of John Wesley*, vol.1: *Sermons 1: 1–33* (Nashville, TN: Abingdon Press, 1984), 376–97.

and actions'.[11] The following quotation is from a late sermon, 'On God's Vineyard', written at Witney, Oxfordshire, in 1787, but it refers back to the time of the Holy Club in Oxford over fifty years earlier, and seeks to establish this as a key marker of the Methodist movement throughout:

> First, what could have been done in this his vineyard which God hath not done in it? What could have been done more with regard to *doctrine*? From the very beginning, from the time that four young men united together, each of them was *homo unius libri* – a man of one book. God taught them all to make his 'Word a lantern unto their feet, and a light in all their paths'. They had one, and only one rule of judgment with regard to all their tempers, words, and action, namely, the oracles of God. They were one and all determined to be *Bible-Christians*. They were continually reproached for this very thing; some terming them in derision *Bible-bigots*; others *Bible-moths* – feeding, they said, upon the Bible as moths do upon cloth. And indeed unto this day it is their constant endeavour to think and speak as the oracles of God.[12]

To some extent, you could be forgiven for thinking Wesley had always been and remained to the end an ardent fundamentalist when it came to the Bible – were that term not so anachronistic for an eighteenth century High-Church Arminian – or, as Outler somewhat carelessly comments, an example of '"high-church" evangelicalism – a rare combination then and since.'[13] But, just as Sermon 107 comes from 1787 but points back to the Holy Club in Oxford, so Donald Bullen points to an entry in Wesley's *Journal* from a mid-point in Wesley's travelling (1766) which makes the same point. In this passage, while travelling around Dundee, Wesley gives a summary of his defence against objections to his ministry that he has received while in Scotland. He characterises himself and his ministry in just the terms that will appear in 'On God's Vineyard', twenty years later:

> I love plain dealing. Do you not? I will use it now. Bear with me. I hang out no false colours, but show you all I am, all I intend, all I do. I am a member of the Church of England, but I love good men of every church. My ground is the Bible. Yea, I am a Bible-bigot. I follow it in all those things, both great and small.[14]

---

[11] Maddox, 'John Wesley on the Bible', 31, citing 'On God's Vineyard'.
[12] 'On God's Vineyard', §I.1, in Outler, *Sermons 3: 71–114*, 502–17.
[13] On the development of fundamentalism, see George Marsden, *Understanding Fundamentalism and Evangelicalism* (Grand Rapids, MI: Eerdmans, 1991). On Wesley, inerrancy and fundamentalism, see Gunter, 'Beyond the Bible Wars' and Maddox, 'John Wesley on the Bible', especially 9–13. For Outler's brief comment, see his preface to 'The Means of Grace', §II.1, *Works*, vol.1, 377. Maddox cites James Thomas Clemons, 'John Wesley – Biblical Literalist?', *Religion in Life*, 46 (1977), 332–42.
[14] Bullen, *Man of One Book?*, 178, quoting the *Journal* entry for 5 June 1766 as 'a typical entry'. See W. Reginald Ward and Richard P. Heitzenrater (eds), *The Works of John Wesley*,

In such terms, Wesley sounds to the modern ear like a classic Biblicist. But that term remains anachronistic since it comes out of nineteenth and twentieth century evangelicalism. The context for Wesley's understanding of Scripture and reading of the Bible is in eighteenth century England, in the understanding of biblical interpretation within the Church of England and in the early development of biblical criticisms and the Enlightenment.[15] However, Wesley does not fit neatly into a post-Reformation understanding of *sola scriptura* – or rather he fits into all the Reformation slogans rather than just one – *sola scriptura, sola Christe, sola gratia, sola fide*. But Wesley's understanding of the Bible reflects the more open practical Biblicism of Luther, rather than the more restrictive understanding of Zwingli.[16] Indeed, although many scholars[17] would see Wesley within the general flow of Reformation thinkers, there are those who see Wesleyan Arminianism as a challenge to more radical aspects of the (Calvinist) Reformation, with Wesley's attacks on limited atonement and double predestination being good examples of a more Catholic-leaning emphasis, embracing the dichotomies which were set up in the Reformation between faith/reason, gospel/law, faith/works.[18] So Dayton points to the practical heritage of Wesleyanism – the campaigns against slavery, concern for the poor and the reform of society; or as it says in the *Large Minutes*: 'to reform the Nation, particularly the Church; and to spread scriptural holiness over the land'.[19] In other words, for Wesley the Bible was both the place to explore the life in God and also a guide for how to live out that faith in every part of life – it was a rule for both faith *and practice*.

It is interesting to note that this emphasis reflects Paul's development of *paranesis* in his own letters. Pauline letters are written generally in two halves – first the theology and then the practical outworkings of this theology. Within this second section (the *paranesis*) can be found virtue lists, household codes, and guidance for moral behaviour and for social interaction.[20] In other words, Paul advocates that Scripture is a rule of faith but also a rule of practice – if we believe a certain doctrine then it must have practical outworkings within our daily lives.

---

vol. 22, *Journal and Diaries V (1765–75)* (Nashville, TN: Abingdon Press, 1993), 42–3.

[15] See note 12 above; see also Wall, 'Wesley as Bible Interpreter', 113–16, Bullen, *Man of One Book?*, 177–81 and Jeremy Gregory, 'The Long Eighteenth Century', in Maddox and Vickers (eds), *Cambridge Companion*, 13–42.

[16] Donald W. Dayton, 'The Use of Scripture in the Wesleyan Tradition', in Robert K. Johnston (ed.), *The Use of the Bible in Theology: Evangelical Options* (Atlanta, GA: John Knox Press, 1984).

[17] Dayton suggests William Cannon, Philip Watson and George Croft Cell. See also Hildebrandt, *Christianity according to the Wesleys*, 15; Maddox, 'Wesley on the Bible', 20 and Wall, 'Wesley as Bible Interpreter'.

[18] Dayton, 'Use of Scripture'.

[19] *Minutes of several conversations between The Rev. Mr Wesley, and others. From the year 1744, to the year 1789* (London, 1789). (Facsimile version in Eighteenth Century Collections Online, Gale, image 1, accessed from Durham University, 1 February 2012.)

[20] David B. Capes, Rodney Reeves and E. Randolph Richards, *Rediscovering Paul* (Nottingham: Apollos Books, 1997), 64–5.

Wesley did not relativise the biblical text. But he did argue strongly that the Scriptures could only be understood within the context of study and searching. He set around the Bible a process of interpretation and testing which ensured that Methodism did not descend into the vagaries of enthusiastic interpretation. So, Wesley insisted that he and his helpers made use of contemporary study tools to guide their interpretation, as well as embracing his own passion for the Early Church theologians, while also emphasising the need to interpret Scripture in conference with others. As such, although he calls himself a 'Bible-bigot', Wesley clearly had a very nuanced understanding of this term.[21] Wesley was a gifted Bible scholar – exploring the Scriptures in their original language through the latest editions of the New Testament texts. He read extensively and recommended texts to his helpers. He made use of and recommended commentaries and texts on biblical interpretation. When he says that he is 'a man of one book', Wesley is simply not saying that he reads only this one text.[22] Indeed, in the 1766 *Minutes*, he castigates those who claim to read nothing but the Bible.[23]

The truth is that although Wesley *reads* many texts, he only places supreme *authority* in one text – the Bible. Maddox puts it another way: 'to be *homo unius libri* is to hold no book *comparatively* but the Bible'.[24] Wesley points to the Bible as the exclusive filter for all his other reading. While that reading should be scrutinised through the Bible, the Bible should not be scrutinised in the same way by other texts. The point is to allow those other texts to interpret the Bible more fully, more in keeping with the Church's tradition and the guidance of the Holy Spirit.

The actual origin of the phrase seems to be in doubt. So in a footnote on the use of the phrase in the preface to his edition of the *Sermons*, Albert Outler suggests that the phrase was coined by Bishop Jeremy Taylor (1613–67). However, Outler traces a negative usage, via another collection of sermons, quoting an unsubstantiated line from Aquinas: '*cave ab illo qui unicum legit librum*' (beware the man who only reads one book).[25] But this phrase by (pseudo-) Aquinas can be read in both negative and positive ways. On the one hand, the phrase seems to disparage the exclusivity of the 'person of one book': how can anyone living in our plural and multicultural world simply use one text to guide them? Such a person should surely be seen as shallow and ignorant. However, an alternative reading of the term could suggest that Aquinas fears a 'man of one book' because of his passion and enthusiasm for one idea; such a man focuses on one book, on one set of ideas, such that it allows the reader to know that book through and through and to be deeply influenced and guided by the book's ideas and thoughts. In comparison, the 'man of many books', whose understanding and authority lie in diffuse texts and reading, on a

---

[21] Maddox, 'Rule of Christian Faith', 22; Bullen, *Man of One Book?*, 180.
[22] See Maddox, 'Rule of Christian Faith', 2.
[23] *Minutes of some late conversations, between the Reverend Mr Wesley, and others* (London, 1766). (Eighteenth Century Collections Online, Gale, accessed from Durham University, 24 February 2012.)
[24] Maddox, 'Rule of Christian Faith', 2.
[25] For Outler's footnote, see *Works*, vol. 1, 105, fn. 53.

multiplicity of authority structures, is pushed in all different directions at once and his own authority and guidance are therefore dissipated.

Wesley's self-designation as a man of one book points to the unique role which the Bible was to play within his own understanding. However, his own appreciation of Scripture is sometimes quite quixotic. He refutes those who suggest there are mistakes within the Bible but castigates others who understand the text to be inerrant; he criticises sections of the Psalms as 'unfit for Christian lips' while making frequent use of James, the butt of Luther's ire.[26]

It does not seem to be absolutely clear how Wesley understood Scripture as an authoritative principle. Or rather, it is clear that he used it pragmatically as a rule of faith and practice without getting caught up in extensive arguments about the very nature of Scripture itself. Pragmatic application was the key. The point was not what opinion Methodists had about the Bible, but rather how Methodists made use of the Bible to receive the means of grace in their own life and to spread scriptural holiness through the land. But, it was not a case of Methodists being pragmatic and then finding a proof text in Scripture. Rather, Methodists were urged to read their Bible and act accordingly. It was, if anything, a biblical pragmatism. As such, Dayton suggests that the Methodist tradition is not so much in the '*Evangelisch*' tradition, but within the '*Pietismus*' or 'Awakening' movement – or that Wesley inherited much more of the Lutheran Reformation than of the Calvinistic Reformation.[27] As such, Wesley offers a pragmatic, Lutheran, understanding of the Bible which centres on the believer's own faith and on the Christian community's outworking of that faith rather than the more legalistic and biblically restrictive traditions developed in Switzerland under both Zwingli and Calvin.[28]

## Wesley's *Notes on the New Testament*

A good many of the points made so far are found in Wesley's preface to his *Notes on the New Testament* (1755) – a guide for his preachers and helpers and for Methodists in general to understand how to read the Bible and engage with biblical principles. First, Wesley notes that he is not writing for those of learning (who have their own texts), or those of long and deep experience of the word of God (he would rather sit at their feet), but to 'plain unlettered men, who understand only their mother tongue, and yet reverence and love the Word of God and have a desire to save their souls'.[29] In other words, these notes offer a way of engaging with Scripture as a means of grace for all people, especially those with no other means of engaging with the depths of Scripture – who have neither external learning nor internal

---

[26] Dayton, 'Use of Scripture'.
[27] Ibid.
[28] Maddox, 'Rule of Christian Faith', 21.
[29] John Wesley, *Explanatory Notes upon the New Testament* (1755), preface, §3 (http://www.bible-researcher.com/wesley-nt.html; accessed 24 February 2012).

guidance from extensive tradition and long experience of the Spirit's work (see below on the Wesleyan Quadrilateral which seems to underlie this section).

Secondly, Wesley offers a translation based on the most up-to-date text-critical scholarship and says that in places he will add to that learning himself. In other words, and although Wesley couches this among many caveats, Scripture can be changed through the application of the results of scholarship. The Bible is not a fixed and immutable text but one which needs to be read in the light of scholarship and through the tools of scholarship. However, it is clear that Wesley intends to ensure that such scholarship is put across simply – or rather that the use of scholarly language is limited so that the ordinary reader will not be confused. This is scholarship to make clear the plain meaning of Scripture, not scholarship for scholarship's sake.

Thirdly, Wesley's *Notes* are part of a conversation with his contemporaries. He explicitly mentions a number of sources for his ideas – drawn from both contemporary Bible scholarship such as Johann Bengel, John Heylyn and the more populist writer Philip Doddridge, author of the *Family Expositor*.[30] Robert Wall says of these, and others: 'these … were counted among the leading biblical interpreters of his day and formed with Wesley a diverse community of interpretation'.[31] Wesley's own dependence on the Church Fathers and contemporary Pietist movements is wellknown.[32] The point here is that interpretation for Wesley is itself a social enterprise and not the work of the individual alone. It is part of the outworking of social holiness – a holiness established through conversation within groups both for Bible study and for personal accountability.

Fourthly, Wesley outlines the nature of Scripture as 'the most solid and precious system of Divine truth. Every part thereof is worthy of God; and all together are one entire body, wherein is no defect, no excess.'[33] Here is Wesley as the 'Bible-bigot', enthusing on the truth of the Scriptures, which he also refers to as 'exact' or 'precise' on a number of occasions. So, as a whole he argues for a Scripture which is 'true' but which can be amended by scholarship and which needs to be interpreted by his contemporaries as part of a conversation between tradition, reason and experience.

## The Place of Scripture in Contemporary Methodist Traditions

Interestingly, contemporary doctrinal statements within the British and American Methodist traditions are not so focused on 'Bible-bigotry'! So, the contemporary

---

[30] See Henry D. Rack, *Reasonable Enthusiast: John Wesley and the Rise of Methodism* (London: Epworth, 1989), 347; Bullen, *Man of One Book?*, 183–5.
[31] Wall, 'Wesley as Biblical Interpreter', 125.
[32] Maddox, 'Rule of Christian Faith', 20–21; John Munsey Turner, *John Wesley, The Evangelical Revival and the Rise of Methodism* (London: Epworth, 2002), 3–10; Dayton, 'Use of Scripture'.
[33] Wesley, *Explanatory Notes*, preface, §10.

British Methodist authoritative statement on the use of the Bible is bound up within some rather convoluted material in Clause 4 of the Deed of Union.[34] Before looking at the references to Scripture in this text, it is important to trace the line of heritage which the document draws for Methodism:

> The Methodist Church claims and cherishes its place in the Holy Catholic Church which is the body of Christ. It rejoices in the inheritance of the apostolic faith and loyally accepts the fundamental principles of the historic creeds and of the Protestant Reformation.

We would expect subsequent specific comments, therefore, to align with these general principles – essentially creedal but interpreted through the Protestant Reformation. As such, Scripture would be expected to have high standing within the subsequent doctrinal comments. However, there is some ambiguity about the wording of what follows which suggests that the content of Holy Scripture is a matter of some interpretation:

> The doctrines of the evangelical faith which Methodism has held from the beginning and still holds are based upon the divine revelation recorded in the Holy Scriptures. The Methodist Church acknowledges this revelation as the supreme rule of faith and practice.

This statement is somewhat mixed, perhaps seeking to offer different conciliation points to the different bodies coming together at the time of Union.[35] On the one hand, there is much here of the supremacy of … what? In this reading, doctrine is founded on divine revelation founded on Scripture. Indeed, we can make this even more evangelical in noting the suggestion that the revelation is divine, of God, and is recorded in the Holy Scriptures. As such, the doctrines of the Methodist Church in Great Britain are founded on Holy Scripture which is itself a recorded divine revelation. However, another reading could suggest a differentiation between the divine revelation which is not co-terminous with the Holy Scriptures but rather a subset of those Scriptures – a divine revelation which has to be interpreted and distilled out of the Holy Scriptures. Moreover, the doctrines are themselves only based upon this divine revelation, not dependent upon or founded upon it. Methodist doctrine could therefore be quite different from Holy Scripture by these various processes of distancing: doctrine based on divine revelation recorded (somewhere, somehow) in Holy Scriptures.

---

[34] The Deed of Union is the document drawn up when three main strands of the Methodist Church in Great Britain united in 1932. The text of the Deed can be found in Volume 2 of *The Constitutional Practice and Discipline of the Methodist Church*, published annually.

[35] For a full discussion, see Martin Wellings, '"Throttled by a Dead Hand?": The Wesleyan Standard in Nineteenth and Early Twentieth Century British Methodism', *Methodist History*, 3 (1999), 162–74.

We will return later to a developed argument on those terms. However, it is interesting to note the flexibility which is contained within Clause 4 and the apparent ambiguity. That same ambiguity is found in the current British Methodist catechetical resource teaching on Scripture which says:

> The Bible is the record of God's self-revelation, supremely in Jesus Christ, and is a means through which he still reveals himself, by the Holy Spirit.[36]

The United Methodist Church in the USA took a different path in accepting Wesley's *Articles of Faith* and the Evangelical United Brethren *Confession of Faith* as their foundation documents. Article V follows the normative Protestant stance that the Holy Scriptures contain all things necessary to salvation. However, it is Article IV of the *Confession of Faith* which focuses on the role of those Scriptures:

> We believe the Holy Bible, Old and New Testaments, reveals the Word of God so far as it is necessary for our salvation. It is to be received through the Holy Spirit as the true rule and guide for faith and practice. Whatever is not revealed in or established by the Holy Scriptures is not to be made an article of faith nor is it to be taught as essential to salvation.[37]

To some extent, this article goes further than the British Methodist Deed of Union in that it recognises the Word of God as a canonical text ('a true rule and guide') and argues, in the final sentence, that faith issues require a biblical mandate. However, at the same time the article witnesses to the same ambiguity about the text: the text only reveals the Word of God 'so far as it is necessary for our salvation'. It would seem that the Word of God could be revealed elsewhere, through some other means, for other purposes? Indeed the final sentence seems to open up the possibility of faith statements (not articles) being promulgated which do not have a biblical foundation as long as they do not replace the Bible as being essential to salvation. Both traditions, then, reflect the biblical pragmatism of Wesley as well as his avoidance of authority issues. They also offer the route to develop a broader theology which does not necessarily depend upon the Bible itself for its authority apart from the central tenets of salvation.

Some of the tension in the United Methodist Church's formularies is explored further in the *Book of Discipline* in a section on Scripture (2008, paragraph 104, section 4). This section makes a number of important points. First, the theological task involves attention to the interplay within the so-called 'Wesleyan Quadrilateral' (see below): 'the Christian faith revealed in Scripture, illumined by tradition, vivified in personal experience, and confirmed by reason'. However, Scripture

---

[36] *A Catechism for the People called Methodists* (Peterborough: MPH, 2000), Q. 52.

[37] The foundational documents of the United Methodist Church can be found online at: http://www.umc.org/site/c.lwL4KnN1LtH/b.2299855/ (accessed 24 February 2012).

remains primary ('sacred canon for Christian people') but its interpretation must be within the context of contemporary scholarship, learning and experience ('our attempts to grasp its meaning always involve tradition, experience, and reason'). Thirdly, Scripture remains the central criterion for assessing reason, tradition and experience: 'the norm by which all traditions are judged'.

The theological task for the United Methodist Church is therefore couched heavily in terms of the 'Wesleyan Quadrilateral'. In a classic statement of the concept, Albert Outler goes back to the texts in which Wesley re-addresses the arguments of the Anglican divines such as Richard Hooker, in affirming the 'the judgment bar of Scripture, right reason and Christian antiquity'.[38] Wesley, Outler argues, added to these three the sense of Christian experience – a heart-faith, a vital faith, rather than the nominal faith he had known himself before Aldersgate. As such, the fourfold track of the theological task is asserted.

However, the four elements are not equal – not even in Outler's argument. Throughout, Scripture is supreme. Indeed, when discussing his own coining of the word 'quadrilateral', Outler expresses some regrets. The point remains the same as we have seen throughout this essay – a true understanding of the Bible within the Methodist tradition places Scripture as supreme, as the rule of faith and practice. However, that same Holy Scripture must be interpreted and understood without the context of Christian history, contemporary scholarship and the experience of the faith community within which it is being interpreted. Any attempt to reset the power dynamics of the Quadrilateral away from the supremacy of Scripture represents a move away from an authentically Wesleyan understanding of Scripture. As can be seen within Outler's own discussions, the Quadrilateral has become a subject of much debate in recent decades both within the United Methodist Church and beyond.[39]

It is interesting that when it was coming to terms with its initial conversations about human sexuality, the Methodist Church in Great Britain asked its Faith and Order Committee to explore the authority of Scripture – specifically, 'to consider the nature of biblical authority and how it is implemented within the life of the Methodist Church'.[40] The Committee accepted the basic thrust of the first request, although it slightly adapted the focus to explore the nature of authority more generally within the life of the Church and the place of the Bible within this authority structure. The Conference received the report and commended it for study within the Church, but it did not adopt the report, that is to say that the

---

[38] Hooker, cited in Albert C. Outler, 'The Wesleyan Quadrilateral in Wesley', *Wesleyan Theological Journal*, (1985), 7–19, cited at 10 (found online at http://wesley.nnu.edu/sermons-essays-books/wesleyan-theological-journal-1966-2010/; accessed 24 February 2012).

[39] See, for example, William J. Abraham and Steven J Gunter, 'What should Methodists do with the Wesleyan Quadrilateral?', *Quarterly Review*, 2:1 (2002) (online at http://www.quarterlyreview.org/pdfs/VOL22NO1SPRING2002.pdf; accessed 24 February 2012).

[40] 'A Lamp to my Feet and a Light to my Path: The Nature of Authority and the Place of the Bible in the Methodist Church', *Methodist Church Conference Agenda*, 1998 (archived at http://www.methodist.org.uk/downloads/conf98_alamptomyfeet_0309.pdf; accessed 24 February 2012).

Conference did not give the report the status which would have made it a formal theological statement of the Conference.

The report reflects a theological approach to interpretation, exploring the history of interpretation (early development, Reformers, modern biblical criticism, twentieth century). In this section, Wesley is not mentioned at all. It is in the next section, on the place of the Bible within the Methodist tradition, that the report explores Wesley, having stated already the more open reading of the Deed of Union discussed above:

- It does say that there is such a thing as a *supreme rule of faith and practice* for the Church.
- It says that *the divine revelation*, which is *recorded in the Holy Scriptures* is the supreme authority for the Church. It does not say that *the Bible* is the supreme authority.
- It does not define what it means by *the divine revelation recorded in the Holy Scriptures*. One could interpret this as meaning that it is the actual words of the Bible that form the divine revelation. Alternatively, one could understand it to mean that the self-revelation of God took place in the great events of the Old and New Testaments, in the words of the prophets and biblical writers and supremely in Jesus, and that the Bible is the record of that self-revelation.
- It says that our doctrines are *based upon* God's revelation which is recorded in the Bible. It does not say that our Methodist doctrines are taken straight from the Bible.[41]

We have already seen that this is one way to read the Deed of Union within the British Methodist tradition. However, the report goes on to explore seven different ways in which the Bible might be interpreted within that tradition – and acknowledges that 'most, if not all, of these positions are compatible with possible interpretations of this [sc. the Deed of Union's] ambiguous phrase'. It is worth quoting the seven alternatives directly from the report itself:

> 7.9.1 The Bible is the Word of God and is therefore inerrant (free of all error and entirely trustworthy in everything which it records) and has complete authority in all matters of theology and behaviour …
> 7.9.2 The Bible's teaching about God, salvation and Christian living is entirely trustworthy. It cannot be expected, however, to provide entirely accurate scientific or historical information since this is not its purpose …
> 7.9.3 The Bible is the essential foundation on which Christian faith and life are built. However, its teachings were formed in particular historical and cultural contexts, and must therefore be read in that light …
> 7.9.4 The Bible's teaching, while foundational and authoritative for Christians, needs to be interpreted by the Church. In practice it is the interpretation and guidance offered by Church leaders and

---

[41] Emphasis in original.

preachers which provides authoritative teaching. Church tradition is therefore of high importance as a practical source of authority.
7.9.5 The Bible is one of the main ways in which God speaks to the believer. However, the movement of God's Spirit is free and unpredictable, and it is what the Spirit is doing today that is of the greatest importance. The Bible helps to interpret experience, but much stress is placed on spiritual experience itself, which conveys its own compelling authority.
7.9.6 The Bible witnesses to God's revelation of himself through history and supremely through Jesus Christ. However, the Bible is not itself that revelation, but only the witness to it. Christians must therefore discern where and to what extent they perceive the true gospel witness in the various voices of the Bible. Reason, tradition and experience are as important as the biblical witnesses.
7.9.7 The Bible comprises a diverse and often contradictory collection of documents which represent the experiences of various people in various times and places. The Christian's task is to follow, in some way, the example of Christ. And to the extent that the Bible records evidence of his character and teaching it offers a useful resource.

After a period of reflection, these models came back to the Methodist Conference in 2001 and the recommendations of the Faith and Order Committee specifically citing the seven models were adopted, although it was decided that no one particular model should be advocated above another. It is perhaps somewhat debatable whether the models actually derive from a Wesleyan understanding of the Bible. However, we have already seen that such an understanding contains considerable elasticity. Certainly, the final three models seem to move beyond the supremacy of Scripture recommended in Wesley and in Outler's Quadrilateral for the theological task, in seeing Scripture as a secondary source of inspiration or as an additional source of reflection. This is particularly so in the final example where we are told that 'reason and experience provide much more important tools for faith and practice'. By this point, it could be argued, we have left Mr Wesley well behind.

## Methodist Scholars in the Biblical Studies Guild

Biblical scholars are not primarily known for their denominational loyalties, but Methodism has nonetheless made a significant contribution to North American and British biblical scholarship.[42] Two eponymous texts which quickly established a reputation in and beyond the academy, and which have been revised and reprinted

---

[42] A list of names would be invidious, but for a survey of the Methodist contribution, see Morna D. Hooker-Stacey, 'Methodism's Contribution to New Testament Scholarship', *Epworth Review*, 27:1 (January 2000), 56–62; compare John Munsey Turner, *Modern Methodism in England 1932–1998* (Peterborough: Epworth, 1998), 80–83. Details of individual scholars

for generations, *Strong's Exhaustive Concordance of the Bible* (1890) and *Peake's Commentary on the Bible* (1919) were initiated and edited by Methodist scholars, the American James Strong (1822–94)[43] and the British Primitive Methodist Arthur Samuel Peake.[44] Strong and Peake stood midway in a tradition running from Adam Clarke in the early nineteenth century via J. H. Moulton (1863–1917), W. F. Howard (1880–1952) and Vincent Taylor (1887–1968) in the early and mid-twentieth century to C. Kingsley Barrett (1917–2011), Morna Hooker and James D. G. Dunn at the turn of the millennium.[45] Methodist biblical scholarship has always included the practical theologians and those involved in ministerial training. It is perhaps only recently that some aspects of that training have moved into a more professional mode which has tended to exclude the biblical scholars from theological training.

The question is whether the latent ambiguity within a Wesleyan understanding of the Bible, and the need for radical contextualisation for that text, have had some influence on the work of these Bible scholars. There are probably several research projects' worth of work here. But it is intriguing to note the emphasis of some of the scholars' work, for instance James Dunn's exploration of the Scriptures as *The Living Word* and the openness of the early traditions of the Church in *Unity and Diversity*, as well as his preference for a synthesis between the revolutionary approach of E. P. Sanders and traditional scholarship on Paul.[46] Other examples might be Frances Young's exploration of the crucial role of performance in the interpretation of Scripture[47] or Richard Hays' explorations of the intertextuality of texts and his work with Ellen Davis on *The Art of Reading Scripture*.[48] All of these texts represent the pragmatic element of Wesley's teaching on the Scriptures while at the same time engaging with contemporary and historical scholarship. However, they also explore not just the nature of the biblical text but also move from scholarship into life application. Many of the contributions show a tendency towards an open

---

may be found in John A. Vickers (ed.), *A Dictionary of Methodism in Britain and Ireland* (Peterborough: Epworth, 2000).

[43] For Strong, a lay member of the Methodist Episcopal Church, see *Encyclopaedia Americana* (New York, NY: Americana Corporation, 1970), vol. 25, 739–40, and 'The Translation of Dr James Strong', *Christian Advocate* (Chicago), 16 August 1894, 1–2.

[44] John T. Wilkinson, *Arthur Samuel Peake* (London: Epworth, 1971).

[45] For biographical details, see Vickers, *Dictionary of Methodism*; for Dunn, see Graham N. Stanton, Bruce W. Longenecker and Stephen Barton (eds), *The Holy Spirit and Christian Origins: Essays in Honor of James D. G. Dunn* (Grand Rapids, MI: W. B. Eerdmans, 2004).

[46] James D. G. Dunn, *The Living Word* (2nd edn, Minneapolis, MN: Fortress Press, 2009); *Unity and Diversity in the New Testament: An Inquiry into the Character of Earliest Christianity* (London: SCM Press, 1980); *The Theology of Paul the Apostle* (Grand Rapids, MI: W. B. Eerdmans, 1998).

[47] Frances Young, *The Art of Performance: Towards a Theology of Holy Scripture* (London: Darton, Longman and Todd, 1990).

[48] Richard B. Hays, *The Conversion of the Imagination: Paul as Interpreter of Israel's Scripture* (Grand Rapids, MI: W. B. Eerdmans, 2005); *Echoes of Scripture in the Letters of Paul* (New Haven and London: Yale University Press, 1989); Richard B. Hays and Ellen F. Davis (eds), *The Art of Reading Scripture* (Grand Rapids, MI: W. B. Eerdmans, 2003).

Arminian approach to integrating theology and Scripture – an open tradition of interpretation akin to Wesley's own understanding.

Wesley's passion and zeal for the Scriptures have been taken up within Ben Witherington III's exhaustive studies, leading to the publication of a commentary on every book of the New Testament. He explores each in depth while still being engaged in contemporary thinking and scholarly conversation. Witherington's embrace of, and conversation with, contemporary scholarship mirrors Wesley's own engagement with the world of eighteenthcentury biblical scholarship.

For the postmodern world, too, Methodist scholars have explored the impact of power and non-conformity through the postcolonial and ideological criticism pioneered by Israel Selvanayagam and Itumeleng Mosala, in close association with R. S. Sugirtharajah.[49]

# Conclusion

We have seen that although Wesley proclaimed the Bible as the rule of faith and practice, this understanding has been variously interpreted across the years within the Methodist traditions, with some traditions reflecting the supremacy of Scripture and others focusing on the need to bring other aspects of Wesley's theological repertoire into play in a more concerted way. To some extent, some of Wesley's own statements about the Bible seem somewhat odd to the modern, or postmodern, ear. Certainly, although he prescribed the *Notes on the New Testament* as a core text for preachers, few would now go to that text as a serious contribution to contemporary scholarship – the field has simply moved on too far. Indeed, this may be the issue with Wesley himself. Just as he sought to amend the understanding of Scripture in Calvin or in the Anglican divines, so others within the tradition which he began have sought to move that tradition even further down the same lines – reflecting on contemporary study of the Bible and contemporary reflection on contextual studies of sacred texts.

---

[49] Israel Selvanayagam, *Tamilnadu: Confrontation, Complementarity, Compromise* (Geneva: WCC, 1996); Itumeleng Mosala, 'Wesley Read from the Experience of Social and Political Deprivation in South Africa', *Journal of Theology for Southern Africa*, 68 (September 1989) (available at http://web.uct.ac.za/depts/ricsa/jtsa/; accessed 24 February 2012); Mosala, 'The Meaning of Reconciliation: A Black Perspective', *Journal of Theology for Southern Africa*, 59 (September 1986).

# 14

# Music, Hymnody and the Culture of Methodism in Britain

## J. R. Watson

Methodism was not born in song. It was born in youthful idealism, seriousness and a determination to be different. In 1729, when Charles Wesley and his friends founded the Holy Club in Oxford, they were rebelling against carelessness, self-indulgence and indifference. Song was a part of it, for they sang hymns together. But primarily they were 'serious', using the word in its eighteenth-century sense of being 'serious in matters of religion', but also in the wider sense of seeking a worthwhile purpose and direction in their lives. Unlike many of their contemporaries, who mocked their 'methodical' way of life, they were disciplined, earnest and caring, praying together, studying the Bible and visiting the prisoners in Oxford gaol. They sang hymns in their morning devotions, but such singing was a part of a complex life of worship, study and practical Christianity.

The resonant opening sentence from the preface to the 1933 *Methodist Hymn Book*, 'Methodism was born in song', has been around for so long that it has become what Robin A. Leaver has called 'a familiar truism'.[1] It has sufficient truth to ensure its continued use whenever the origins of Methodism are discussed; but the situation was more complicated and more delayed, affected by the chance encounter with the noble band of Moravian missionaries on board the *Simmonds* in 1735–36. All the evidence suggests that John Wesley became fully aware of the power of hymns to express faith and to unite a community when he joined the Moravians in worship during the voyage to Georgia. They were using their new hymnbook, *Das Gesangbuch der Gemeine in Herrnhut*, printed in the same year, 1735.

To a young English clergyman, accustomed to singing metrical psalms and hymns to traditional tunes, the great riches of German hymnody must have been astonishing. The singing of these hymns must have opened up a new world of spiritual experience, an exploration of the human soul in its joys, its sufferings and its needs. John Wesley, who had used the time of the voyage to learn German,

---

[1] Robin A. Leaver, 'Psalms and Hymns and Hymns and Sacred Poems: Two Strands of Wesleyan Hymn Collections', in Nicholas Temperley and Stephen Banfield (eds), *Music and the Wesleys* (Urbana, Chicago and Springfield, IL: University of Illinois Press, 2010), 41.

translated thirty-three of them during the next few years. He included five of his translations in the hymnbook that he produced during the time in Georgia, *A Collection of Psalms and Hymns*, published in 1737.[2] He used them extensively in Georgia. Carlton R. Young quotes from the diary entry of 10 June 1736: 'Our design was, on Sundays in the afternoon and every evening after public service, to spend some time with the serious of the communicants in singing, reading, and conversation.' Young suggests that the singing would have been of Watts's metrical paraphrases; but for German congregations Wesley wrote (18 October): 'we first sung a German hymn'.[3] One of the charges against Wesley in 1737 was that he had introduced unauthorised hymns and psalms into public worship,[4] and Frank Baker has noted that the phrase 'at the altar' in the charge suggests that the singing was a devotional background while communicants moved to and from the communion rail.[5] Its importance is demonstrated by the way in which Wesley took hymns or poems, particularly those of George Herbert, and forced them into different metre, using only six metres (Young suggests some tunes that Wesley might have used).[6]

Wesley continued to translate hymns from the German; and on his return to England he lost no time in publishing another *Collection of Psalms and Hymns*, with a similar arrangement of texts though with a different selection. But the 'conversion' experiences of May 1738, of Charles on the Sunday and John during the following week (21 and 24 May respectively) marked a new start, as the brothers sought to find their true and authentic Christian selves. And if 1738 is taken as the date of the beginning of Methodism, rather than the date of the formation of the Holy Club, then there is some justification for saying that the denomination was born in song. Charles was, it seems, struggling to express his deepest feelings: what is sometimes called 'the Wesleys' conversion hymn' was evidently written in response to his experience on Sunday 21 May (phrases from it are found in his journal for 23 May), and it was sung by both brothers on 24 May. Its first line, 'Where shall my won'dring soul begin?', is a cry of amazement and awe, the question looking forward to one of the fundamentals of Methodist belief and culture, the insistence on the astonishing and undeserved grace of God in Jesus Christ.

The 'conversion hymn' was succeeded, a few days later, by 'And can it be that I should gain', significantly entitled 'Free Grace'. Both hymns are in the same metre, begin with a question, and are impassioned in idea and expression. 'And

---

[2] See the facsimile with additional material, Frank Baker and George Walton Williams (eds), *John Wesley's First Hymn-Book*, (Charleston, SC: the Dalcho Historical Society; London: The Wesley Historical Society, 1964).

[3] Carlton R. Young, *Music of the Heart: John and Charles Wesley on Music and Musicians* (Carol Stream, IL: Hope Publishing Co., 1995), 48–50.

[4] Luke Tyerman, *The Life and Times of the Rev. John Wesley*, 3rd edn (London, 1876), I, 159, quoted in Leaver, 'Psalms and Hymns', 44.

[5] Frank Baker, *John Wesley and the Church of England* (Nashville, TN: Abingdon Press, 1970), 86; quoted in Young, *Music of the Heart*, 40.

[6] Young, *Music of the Heart*, 47–51. He suggests ST MARY'S TUNE and BURFORD (Common Metre), WIRKWORTH (Short Metre), TALLIS' CANON (Long Metre) and VATER UNSER (Six 8s).

can it be that I should gain' is the better known of the two: indeed it has become a central artefact of Methodist culture, celebrating the glorious liberty of the children of God, freed from the imprisonment of the self and resolved to lead a new life: 'My chains fell off, my heart was free,/ I rose, went forth, and followed thee.' This hymn is more dependent than the 'conversion hymn' on New Testament imagery, especially Acts 12 and Romans 8. I have argued elsewhere that the 'conversion hymn' is in part a response to the contemporary situation in London, with its prostitution, unfair taxes and widespread crime;[7] 'And can it be', on the other hand, is a personal meditation on these great passages from the New Testament, applied to the individual soul.

Part II of the 1739 *Hymns and Sacred Poems*, in which both hymns appear, announces itself as something new. It is one of the great books of Methodism. Part I had contained a miscellaneous selection, including much from George Herbert, altered for the worse, and poems by the Wesleys' friend John Gambold. Part II begins with what seems an entirely new note, a kind of hymnody that is manifestly superior to anything in Part I: 'Where shall my won'dring soul begin?' The excitement of the hymn is felt in the language:

> Should know, should feel my sins forgiven,
> Blest with this antepast of heaven!

The hymn not only begins Part II of the 1739 book; language as spectacular as this signals a new beginning in Charles Wesley's life. It gives the reader or singer the shock of the new, in the individual consciousness and in the attitude to the world. It inaugurates a whole new mode of thinking and feeling. It is impassioned about the assurance of salvation, and also about the need to transform society.

'Where shall my wond'ring soul begin?' is a question that is never answered, because it is in part rhetorical. How shall I find words to express what I feel? But it also looks forward to that element of Methodist culture that turned outward from the self to the world in social concern and Christian service:

> No need of him the righteous have;
> He came the lost to seek and save.

We have in this hymn the first indication of the incomparable greatness of Charles Wesley as a hymn writer. The precision of these lines, their exact statement of what is needed, is found in hymn after hymn, with what Donald Davie called 'the classicism of Charles Wesley'. Davie pointed to the line 'This man receiveth sinners still' as an example of the ability of Charles Wesley to utter the central truths of the Christian faith with what he calls 'a poignant simplicity';[8] although there is also a

---

[7] J. R. Watson, *The English Hymn: A Critical and Historical Study* (Oxford: Clarendon Press, 1997), 226ff.

[8] Donald Davie (ed.), 'The Classicism of Charles Wesley', in *Purity of Diction in English Verse* (London: Routledge and Kegan Paul, 1967), 70–81 (72).

flamboyant splendour of vocabulary and phrase. For Methodists these hymns have been their magnificent heritage, their great glory.

To the prolific splendour of Charles Wesley must be added the translations of John Wesley mentioned above. John picked up from the Germans the same kind of passionate joy in the contemplation of divine grace that is found in the hymns of Charles. Most were written by Pietists or Moravians: some were long, in the tradition of classic German hymnody, and were shortened by Wesley, with verses being omitted, amalgamated with others or transposed.[9] Perhaps the greatest example is the translation of Johann Andreas Rothe's '*Ich habe nun den Grund gefunden*', beginning 'Now I have found the ground wherein'. Every verse of Rothe's hymn ends with the wonderful German word for mercy, a softening of the heart, sometimes repeated; 'Barmhertzigkeit! Barmhertzigkeit!' Wesley thrills to the idea:

> While Jesu's blood through earth and skies
> Mercy, free boundless mercy! cries.

These magnificent translations from the German gave Methodism, long before other British denominations, a small insight into the great riches of post-Reformation devotion. James Martineau even thought that 'after the Scriptures, the Wesley Hymn-book appears to me the grandest instrument of popular religious culture that Christendom has ever produced. But for the German antecedents, however, it would never have come into existence.'[10]

To the passionate declarations of free grace in the hymns of Charles Wesley, and the Reformed spirituality of John Wesley's translations, must be added two other elements. The first was the rejection of Calvinist doctrine, as Arminian Methodism defined its belief in its hymns. *Hymns on God's Everlasting Love* (1741) was a counter to the preaching of George Whitefield, John Cennick and others. The second was a recognition of the structure of the Christian year and the practice of the Church of England. This is found in the 1739 *Hymns and Sacred Poems* in five hymns, for Christmas-Day, the Epiphany, Easter-Day, Ascension-Day and Whitsunday. They are all in the same metre, 77.77, which suggests that Charles Wesley had a tune in mind for them; three of them have remained among the best-loved and best-known hymns in the English language: 'Hark, how all the welkin rings', with its more familiar first line, 'Hark, the herald-angels sing'; '"Christ the Lord is risen to day"', quoting from *Lyra Davidica* (1708); and 'Hail the day that sees him rise'. In due course there was a succession of books: *Hymns on the Nativity of our Lord* (1745), *Hymns for our Lord's Resurrection* (1746), *Hymns for Ascension Day* (1746). The

---

[9] See John L. Nuelsen, *John Wesley und das deutsche Kirchenlied* (Bremen, 1938), trans. Theo Parry, Sydney H. Moore and Arthur Holbrook, *John Wesley and the German Hymn* (Calverley, Yorkshire: Arthur Holbrook, , 1972).

[10] James Drummond and C. B. Upton (eds), *The Life and Letters of James Martineau* (London: James Nisbet & Co. , 1902), II, 99. For a full study of the German influence on Wesley, see Franz Hildebrandt, *From Luther to Wesley* (London: Lutterworth Press, 1951).

most important were *Hymns on the Lord's Supper* (1745), based on the writings of the seventeenth-century Anglican divine Dr Daniel Brevint, which had been abridged by John Wesley; and *Short Hymns on Select Passages of the Holy Scriptures* (1762), a two-volume collection that included 'A charge to keep I have' and 'O thou who camest from above'.

From the beginning John Wesley had encouraged singing in worship, following the example of the Moravians with whom he made common cause in the Fetter Lane Religious Society of 1738. When he left the Society in 1740 to found his own at the old cannon foundry (or 'Foundery'), he continued the practice of singing. This is made explicit in the title of his first tune book, *A Collection of Tunes, Set to Music, As They are commonly sung at the Foundery* (1742). It contained thirty-three tunes, some of which are still sung.[11] The music was often defective, but the book was connected to three words-only early Methodist books, the *Hymns and Sacred Poems* of 1739, 1740 and 1742, marked in the tune book as 1, 2 or 3. The tune book enabled the Methodists to sing with fervour, again following the practice of the Moravians, who had their 'Singstunde' or 'singing hours'. Such hours enabled a tune to become familiar, so that it did not have to be slowly introduced to the congregation in the 'old way of singing' (very slowly, and often with 'lining out'). Once it had become known, the men and the women could sing separately, or antiphonally, or in a simple harmony, and with a quicker tempo. There is evidence that this was very attractive. *A Fine Picture of Enthusiasm, Chiefly Drawn by Dr John Scott, Formerly Rector of St Giles's in the Fields* was published in 1744. The preface, signed 'Eusebius' was dedicated to the Bishop of London. Eusebius was evidently nettled by the growth of the Methodist societies:

> Your Lordship knows that there are Thousands flocking after those Enthusiasts, Whitefield and Westley's [sic.], who appear, upon the most candid and impartial Examination of their public Labours, to be deluding Crowds of People into a passionate, mechanical Religion.[12]

By 'mechanical religion' the author seems to be indicating a religion that is assured of salvation. Scott's 'fine picture' is then printed, 'Wherein The Danger of the Passions Leading in religion is strongly described' (title page). Scott gives an illuminating glimpse into the world of the 1740s and Methodists in it:

> And, as to their Singing, they, perhaps, have got some of the *most melodious* Tunes that ever were composed for *Church Music*; there is *great Harmony* in their Singing, and it is very *inchanting*. I say very *inchanting*; because the Hymns they Sing, *i.e.* all I have seen or heard of, are not *rational* Compositions, nor do they accord with the first Principles of all Religion, but like their Prayers, dwell upon a Word,

---

[11] Young, *Music of the Heart*, 55–6.
[12] *A Fine Picture of Enthusiasm, Chiefly Drawn by Dr John Scott, Formerly Rector of St Giles's in the Fields…*, (London: J. Noon, 1746), Preface, A2.

> or are immediate Addresses to the *Son of God*, as the supreme Object of Worship: And do represent him as much *more* friendly and compassionate to the human World than God the Father ever was – So that their *Singing* is calculated to engage the *Passions* by nothing more than Words, and the Melody of the Sounds, or Voices; but if you would sing with *Understanding*, or have a Reason of Praise, or pray with the Understanding, you must have other Sorts of Compositions both for Psalmody and Prayer, than what the FOUNDERY or the TABERNACLE do afford you.[13]

The accusation here seems to be that the singing prevented thought, what Scott calls 'the Understanding'. His opinion was probably influenced by a general disquiet felt at the progress of the Methodist movement in the early years. It is significant that the publication of his 'fine picture' was dedicated to the Bishop of London, who might well have been disturbed by the unusual happenings in his diocese. But the other principal feature of his portrayal is worth examination, because it tallies with the evidence of the hymns in the early Methodist books. The concentration on the Son of God, and the emphasis on his compassion, was fundamental to the hymnody of these years. Scott's observation that the Son of God was 'much *more* friendly … than God the Father ever was' in these hymns is quite true: 'I know Thee, Saviour, who Thou art,/Jesus, the feeble Sinner's Friend'; 'Jesus, hail! the Sinner's Friend,/ Friend of Publicans – and Me!'

These are two examples from many in which Jesus is the friend of sinners. And a Methodist hymn lover would respond to Scott with a reasoned defence of such a stress on redeeming love. This would have been a hymnody of enthusiastic believers singing in praise of the Name of Jesus, music and words united in allowing the soul to express its deepest needs. And John Wesley, who loved hymn singing, would have cautioned his followers against the charge of singing without understanding. He did so explicitly in his 'directions for singing' in his next tune book, *Select Hymns with Tunes Annext* (1761). After instructing them to learn the tunes, to sing lustily but modestly, to sing in time and not to bawl, he added:

> Above all sing *spiritually*. Have an eye to God in every word you sing. Aim at pleasing Him more than yourself, or any other creature. In order to do this attend strictly to the sense of what you sing, and see that your *Heart* is not carried away with the sound, but offered to God continually; so shall your singing be such as the *Lord* will approve of here, and reward when he cometh in the clouds of heaven.[14]

---

[13] Ibid., 24.
[14] Young, *Music of the Heart*, 72–3.

The instruction might have been designed to counter Scott's suggestion that the Methodists sang without 'Understanding'; although Scott was not the only one who believed that the early Methodists were thoughtless enthusiasts.[15]

Before 1761 there had been a remarkable hymn and tune book, John Frederick Lampe's *Hymns on the Great Festivals and Other Occasions* (1746), setting to music twenty-three hymns by Charles Wesley and one by his brother Samuel. Words and music were printed together, making a rich combination. Lampe's operatic setting of Charles Wesley's 'Lamb of God whose bleeding love' is one example. Martin Clarke has described this, and the tune for 'Rejoice, the Lord is King', as demonstrating 'Lampe's bold musical language, characterized by considerable momentum toward the cadence points, a firm harmonic grasp, melodically interesting bass lines, detailed figuring, and chains of modulations'.[16]

It is arguable, therefore, that by 1780, when John Wesley published *A Collection of Hymns for the Use of the People called Methodists*, his followers had access to a rich and complex verbal and musical culture. The 1780 *Collection*, sometimes known as the 'large hymn-book', was John Wesley's answer to the problem of so many little books available in different places. It contained 535 hymns, arranged in an order that reflected the experience of the individual and the Methodist societies. It was a remarkable book: Bernard Manning described it extravagantly as 'perfect, unapproachable, elemental in its perfection … a work of supreme devotional art by a religious genius'.[17] Manning was no doubt anxious to prevent Methodist undergraduates at Cambridge from taking their hymnbook for granted; but it would be better described as a book with a particular agenda, constructed by John Wesley for his followers at that time. Because it was more interested in the individual experience than in the Christian year, it omitted some of Charles Wesley's hymns that would now be thought essential to any mainstream hymnbook. But the richness of the collection, and its psychological insights, are undeniable. At the same time John Wesley wanted them to continue to sing their faith, and to that end he produced a third tune book, *Sacred Harmony* (1780). The sub-title of this book, 'Set to Music in two or three parts for the Voice, Harpsichord & Organ', indicates that by this time the Methodist societies were using instruments to accompany the singing.[18]

John Wesley was keen to encourage reading among his followers, and sought to educate them: his 'Christian Library' was a treasure-house of devotional literature. At the same time, however, Methodist culture reached out through its field-preaching to the poor and unchurched. To them the gospel of salvation was expressed through sermons and hymns. George Eliot, who admired and loved her Methodist preacher aunt, described one such occasion in *Adam Bede*. Dinah Morris preaches a simple gospel:

---

[15] See Hogarth's engraving, 'Credulity, Superstition and Fanaticism' (1762).
[16] Martin Clarke, 'John Frederick Lampe's *Hymns on the Great Festivals and Other Occasions*', in Temperley and Banfield (eds), *Music and the Wesleys*, 59.
[17] B. Manning, *The Hymns of Wesley and Watts* (London: Epworth Press, 1942), 14.
[18] Young, *Music of the Heart*, 100.

> But now Dinah began to tell of the joys that were in store for the penitent, and to describe in her simple way the divine peace and love with which the soul of the believer is filled – how the sense of God's love turns poverty into riches, and satisfies the soul, so that no uneasy desire vexes it, no fear alarms it: how, at last, the very temptation to sin is extinguished, and heaven is begun upon earth, because no cloud passes between the soul and God, who is its eternal sun.[19]

After the sermon, the little meeting sings one of Charles Wesley's hymns. As the passing traveller goes on his way, 'the voices of the Methodists reached him, rising and falling in that strange blending of exultation and sadness which belongs to the cadence of a hymn'. They sing of the love of God:

> Its streams the whole creation reach,
>   So plenteous is the store;
> Enough for all, enough for each,
>   Enough for evermore.

The novel is set in 1799, though written sixty years later. George Eliot, though a Victorian atheist, recognised the unique value of early Methodist culture, and in a few deft and loving pages she articulates its appeal. From Methodism 'a crowd of rough men and weary-hearted women drank in a faith which was a rudimentary culture, which linked their thoughts with the past, lifted their imagination above the sordid details of their own narrow lives, and suffused their souls with a sense of a pitying, loving, infinite Presence, sweet as summer to the houseless needy'.[20]

The death of John Wesley in 1791 led almost immediately to divisions within Methodism. As early as 1791 itself, Alexander Kilham pressed for a new governance of the Church, which would give equal status to ministers and lay people. His expulsion in 1796 created the Methodist New Connexion of 1797. In 1807 a group led by William Clowes and Hugh Bourne began camp meetings, marking the beginning of Primitive Methodism, and another group led by William O'Bryan and James Thorne took the name 'Bible Christians' in 1816. Each of these groups established its own culture, and published its own hymn book, and the book expressed the hopes and aspirations of its followers. The Wesleyan Methodists continued to rely on the 1780 *Collection of Hymns*, with additions culminating in an established collection with a supplement in 1831. The 'Kilhamites', or Methodist New Connexion, began work almost immediately on a book, *A Collection of Hymns for the Use of the People called Methodists to which is added nearly two hundred Sacramental and Other Hymns*, and published in 1804 *A Collection of Hymns for the Use of the Methodist New Connexion*. This continued in use until 1863, when *Hymns for Divine Worship* was produced, containing no fewer than 1,091 hymns, together with

---

[19] George Eliot, *Adam Bede* (Edinburgh and London: William Blackwood and Sons, 1859), chapter 2, 'The Preaching'.

[20] *Adam Bede*, chapter 3, 'After the Preaching'.

doxologies and canticles. The Primitive Methodists published *A General Collection of Hymns and Spiritual Songs for Camp Meetings* in 1809, which went through several editions before it was superseded by the *Large Hymn Book for the Use of the Primitive Methodists* in 1824. The Bible Christians published their own supplement to the Wesleyan collection in 1820, and *A Collection of Hymns for the Use of the People called Arminian Bible Christians* in 1824.

These early books are important evidence of the importance of hymns to the separated bodies. The Primitive Methodists, for example, required a hymnbook that reflected the ecstatic experience of gospel grace in their camp meetings, and the ranting style was closer to the world of street ballads than to the staid severities of the Wesleyans; James T. Lightwood suggested that it was 'very difficult to identify the music used by the first members' but that it was 'quite likely that many of the hymns were sung to popular tunes of the day'.[21] Similarly, the Bible Christians had their own needs. Wesleyan Methodism, meanwhile, became respectable and ordered, distancing itself from its fissiparous branches. George Eliot, who had admired the Wesleys and their early followers, deplored the transition, contrasting the Wesleys and their preachers with 'that modern type which reads quarterly reviews and attends in chapels with pillared porticoes'.[22]

Throughout the nineteenth century, the various Methodist churches continued to produce their own books. Thirty years after the *Large Hymn Book*, the Primitive Methodists produced the *Primitive Methodist Hymnal* of 1854, edited by John Flesher, described unkindly in Julian's *Dictionary of Hymnology* as 'the worst edited and most severely mutilated collection of hymns ever published'.[23] Whether or not this is true, and an inspection of the book suggests that it is unfair, it certainly suited the denomination, for a sixth edition appeared in 1856. Beside it was another book that stressed the 'revival' element, the *Primitive Methodist Revival Hymn Book* (three editions, 1857, 1861, 1863). Earlier, the Bible Christians had published *A Collection of Hymns for the Use of the People called Bible Christians* in 1838, with a revised edition in 1862. A further group was formed in 1857 from various split-offs: the Protestant Methodists of 1827–28, the Wesleyan Methodist Association of 1834–35 and the Wesleyan Reformers of 1849–50 joined to form the United Methodist Free Churches in 1857. The individual groups had produced their own supplements earlier, but the newly formed church promptly set about providing a new book, commissioned at the Annual Assembly of 1859 and published with a preface dated 1860.

These were words-only books. For tunes, the various branches of the Methodist church would have relied upon the many available tune books, such as *The Copious Tune Book* (1860), *The Bristol Tune Book* (1863), *The Leeds Tune Book* (1868), *The London Tune Book* (1875) or *The Burnley Tune-Book* (1875). There were very many of these: the preface to *The Burnley Tune-Book* noted that 'Tune-Books are counted

---

[21] James T. Lightwood, *The Music of the Methodist Hymn-Book* (London: Epworth Press, 1935), introduction, xxi.
[22] *Adam Bede*, chapter 3, 'After the Preaching'.
[23] J. Julian, *Dictionary of Hymnody* (London: John Murray, 1907), 730.

by hundreds'.[24] Of particular Methodist provenance was *The Wesleyan Psalmist, a collection of psalm & hymn tunes, chiefly selected from the compositions of the old masters, together with the most approved modern tunes now in congregational use, expressly adapted to the various metres in the Wesleyan hymn book* (1843). It was edited by Edward Booth, organist of Brunswick Chapel, Leeds, where fifteen years earlier there had been a fierce controversy over the installation of an organ. The minister and stewards, supported by the hierarchy of the Wesleyan Methodist Church, installed an organ against the wishes of many of the members, who thought that it would undermine the traditional simplicity and purity of worship (it was said that the organ cost a thousand pounds and lost a thousand members). The publication of Booth's book suggests that by 1843 the organ had become accepted in Wesleyan chapels. Similarly, the *Companion to the Wesleyan Hymn-Book* of 1843, with many subsequent editions, contained 'accompaniments for the organ and pianoforte'. It was 'intended for use in Wesleyan congregations, classes, prayer-meetings, schools, and families'. The Wesleyan teachers' training college (Westminster College, founded 1851) had its own book, *The Wesleyan Hymn-Tune Book compiled for the students of the Wesleyan Normal Institution, Westminster* (1857, 1859), edited by E. J. West; other specifically Methodist books included *The Wesley Tune Book* (1871), for which the music adviser was Henry Hiles.[25] The tunes were arranged by metre, with special attention to the '"peculiar metres", of which there are so many in the *Wesleyan Hymn Book*, but whose varied music and sentiment remain in almost entire neglect, from want of suitable tunes'. Prominent among the composers were Hiles himself,[26] Gauntlett, Dykes (HOLLINGSIDE to 'Jesu, Lover of my soul') and William Henry Monk, music editor of *Hymns Ancient and Modern*. Among the curiosities were COBURG, by 'H.R.H. the late Prince Consort'.[27] Other books of this period included John Moxon's *The Methodist Hymn-Tune Book and Psalter* (1877) and Walter Battison Haynes's *Methodist Free Church Tune Book* (1892).

Methodist Sunday Schools had *The Methodist Scholars' Tune Book* (1871), if they were not already using the book for Sunday Schools of all denominations, *The Union Tune Book* of 1837. Sunday Schools were an important element in the religious life of the nineteenth century: this was the age of the 'Big Sings' in places such as Halifax in Yorkshire, where the children from Sunday Schools in Halifax and the surrounding area were trained in singing, gathered together and coached as one

---

[24] *The Burnley Tune-Book* (Burnley: Pitman, 1875), iii.

[25] Hiles was a well-known organist, composer and teacher, a lecturer at Owens College, Manchester (later the Victoria University of Manchester). See J. C. Bridge, 'Hiles, Henry (1826–1904)', rev. Anne Pimlott Baker, *Oxford Dictionary of National Biography* (Oxford University Press, 2004).

[26] Hiles's tunes are still found in some evangelical books, such as *Christian Hymns* (1977). HARSTON and ST LEONARD'S (used three times) survived into the Wesleyan *Methodist Hymn Book* (1904). ST LEONARD'S is found once in *MHB* (1933), set to 'The Galilean fishers toil'. TREVES was used in *Congregational Praise* (1951).

[27] Loyally, this tune was retained in the Wesleyan *Methodist Hymn Book* (1904). It is not the same as the anonymous German tune COBURG that is still in use in *Rejoice and Sing* and *Peculiar Honours*, and in some earlier Free Church books.

huge choir. The effect must have been inspiring: the programmes for these events suggest that they went on for many years, and that they were a high point in the Free Church culture of the cities and towns of the north of England. The centenary of the Sunday School Union in 1880 was marked by a public holiday, and a huge conference to which delegates came from all over the world. It was symptomatic of the importance of religion in society, and was marked by the singing of massed choirs. They sang the great and familiar hymns, often those associated with the blood of the Lamb which washed the sinner clean: 'Rock of Ages, cleft for me'; 'There is a fountain filled with blood/Drawn from Immanuel's veins'.[28]

Music, hymnody and Methodist culture proceeded with this kind of ramshackle enthusiasm, involving word books, tune books and Sunday-School books, big sings and little sings, until the 1870s. But all the denominations of Methodism (and the other Free Churches) were forced to think about revising their hymnbooks by developments in the Church of England. The translations of Latin hymns by John Mason Neale and others helped to pave the way for a gradual acceptance of hymns in worship; and the phenomenal success of *Hymns Ancient and Modern* (1861, *Appendix* 1868, Second Edition 1875) alerted all branches of Methodism to new possibilities. The new acceptance of hymns was confirmed by the SPCK's *Church Hymns* of 1871, with a music edition, *Church Hymns with Tunes* (1874).

The Methodists responded. The Wesleyans, who had relied on the 1780 *Collection of Hymns* with its supplement of 1831, produced a new edition in 1876. It consisted of the revised *Collection*, followed by nine further sections from hymn 540 to hymn 1,008, together with eighteen graces. From the Church of England tradition came hymns that were new to Methodist books by writers such as Thomas Ken, Reginald Heber, Henry Hart Milman, John Keble and Henry Francis Lyte, with translations from Latin and Greek by John Mason Neale. Like the words, the tunes were often new: two distinguished editors, Henry John Gauntlett and George Cooper, died during the compilation, but the music editing was completed by E. J. Hopkins, including many new and recent tunes by the editors themselves and by composers such as John Bacchus Dykes, Joseph Barnby, Samuel Sebastian Wesley and William Henry Monk. It was given the *Collection of Hymns* title of the 1780 book, with the addition of 'With a New Supplement' (to distinguish it from the 1831 supplement). On the cover it was entitled 'Wesley's Hymns', and was often known by that shorter title. It was published first in a words-only edition (1876) and then as 'Wesley's Hymns with Tunes' (1877).

The Primitive Methodists and the United Methodist Free Church followed a decade later. The former published the *Primitive Methodist Hymnal* in 1887 in a words-only edition, with a music edition in 1889. It was a massive collection, ending with the 'Te Deum Laudamus', and containing a remarkably catholic selection, with eleven of the translations of Neale and two hymns by Newman ('Praise to the Holiest in the height' and 'Lead, kindly Light'). 'No church', said the preface, 'has had a monopoly of the gift of sacred song.' At the same time, it had its own

---

[28] For a description of the 1880 celebrations, see Arnold Bennett, *Clayhanger* (London: Egmont, 1910), chapter 10.

denominational character. After sections on the three persons of the Trinity and on the Holy Trinity itself, it went to 'The Holy Scriptures', as source and authority, and then straight to 'Man: His Fallen Condition. His Redemption. Warnings and Invitations'. The final hymn in the 'Redemption' section of the *Primitive Methodist Hymnal* is characteristic of a focus on salvation and the promise of eternal life:

> The voice of free grace cries, 'Escape to the mountain,
> For Adam's lost race He has opened a fountain,
> For sin and uncleanness, and every transgression,
> His blood flows so freely in streams of salvation:'
> Hallelujah to the Lamb Who has bought us a pardon,
> We will praise Him again when we pass over Jordan.

The compilers showed themselves sensitive to the time. They believed a new book to be necessary:

> Considering how new hymn writers continue in the order of Providence to be raised up; the constantly increasing number of hymn books; the progress made in hymnology and church music; and, owing to the spread of education, the altered tastes and preferences of vast numbers who worship with us – it can scarcely be expected that any hymn book, however carefully compiled, will, without addition or alterations, meet the wants of our church for more than thirty years.[29]

This was a respectful nod to Flesher's book, but a firm commitment to produce a book that would incorporate all that had been done since 1854. The astonishing achievement of Victorian hymnody in the decades between 1854 and 1887, the work of Alford, Baker, Caswall, Ellerton, How, Neale, Plumptre and others simply cried out to be recognised. The Primitive Methodists did so with confidence. The reference to the 'vast numbers' reads sadly now, but in 1887 it celebrated a church full of energy (in 1932, at the time of Methodist Union, the Primitive Methodists had just over 222,000 members and claimed over 377,000 Sunday School pupils).[30] There was no defensiveness in this book: the committee found that 'the richness of our age in good hymns' increased their problems, because 'there were not only the accumulated treasures of the past, but also the abundant stores of modern hymnologists, from which to make selections'. The result was a huge and comprehensive book of 1,052 hymns.

Two years later, in 1889, *The United Methodist Free Church Hymnal* appeared in a words-only edition; a music edition followed in 1893. It was described by James T. Lightwood as containing tunes 'of a somewhat sterner kind' than those in

---

[29] *Primitive Methodist Hymnal* (London: R. Bryant, 1887), iii.
[30] Rupert Davies, A. Raymond George and Gordon Rupp ( eds), *A History of the Methodist Church in Great Britain*, vol. IV (London: Epworth Press, 1988), 649.

the Wesleyan and Primitive Methodist books.[31] The hymnbooks of these various denominations were reflections of their culture. That of the Wesleyans was described at the turn of the century by Arnold Bennett in *Anna of the Five Towns*, published in 1902. It portrayed the chapel and its activities: the morning and afternoon Sunday-School classes with their book prizes, the men's Bible class with seventy members on Sunday afternoon, the rich family who 'gave to the society monetary aid and a gracious condescension'. It was this kind of thriving activity that formed the background to the hymnbook of 1904, designed as a book for a new century. It was entitled simply *The Methodist Hymn Book*, a break with the past, but one that signalled the new unity between the Wesleyan Methodists, the Methodist New Connexion and the Wesleyan Reform Union; its title could also be seen as claiming to be the pre-eminent book of the Methodist church as a whole.[32] The compilers claimed that it was 'the lineal descendant, after the lapse of one hundred and twenty-five years, of the volume so long known as "Wesley's Hymns", for which John Wesley wrote a celebrated preface in 1779'. It saw itself as maintaining 'not only the evangelical doctrine, but the earnest spirit, the distinctive devotional tone, and the characteristic phraseology of the book which played so large a part in the Evangelical Revival of the eighteenth century' and also as providing for the needs of Methodist churches at the beginning of the twentieth.

The music editor was Sir Frederick Bridge, King Edward Professor, University of London and Organist of Westminster Abbey. Such grandeur was hard to match. The Primitive Methodists were the only ones to try, by producing quantity rather than quality. *The Primitive Methodist Hymnal Supplement* of 1912 took the 1887 *Primitive Methodist Hymnal*, which already had over one thousand hymns, and added another 295. Among them was a section of Temperance Hymns, not present in 1887; but even this was free of the fanatical denunciation of alcohol in books such as *Hoyle's Temperance Hymns*. Methodism has so long been associated with teetotalism that it should be remembered that, while the church was rightly conscious of the evils of drink and the misery that often went with it, its hymnbooks preached compassion and responsible living.[33]

By now the various strands of Methodism had inherited the hymns of the eighteenth century, and added to them to suit their own needs. With the coming of Methodist union in 1932, the individual insights had to be accommodated into one book. The result was *The Methodist Hymn Book* of 1933. It was intended as a unifying force for the new church: if all parts of the church could be made to sing the same hymns, then Methodist union might become a reality, a true union of the spirit as well as an administrative and financial necessity. The book certainly helped to bring this about, although old loyalties were hard to shift, and some residual

---

[31] Lightwood, *Music of the Methodist Hymn-Book*, preface, xxii–xxiii.
[32] The book was published by the publishing offices of both the Wesleyans and the Methodist New Connexion.
[33] See Maldwyn Edwards, *Methodism and England: A Study of Methodism in its Social and Political Aspects during the Period 1850–1932* (London: Epworth Press, 1943), chapter 6, 'Methodism and the Temperance Problem'.

suspicions remained for many years. It did so by looking back with rose-tinted spectacles: 'Methodism was born in song.' This was a useful fiction. It appealed to a romantic idea of Methodism, a church united against the wickedness of the world ('harlots, and publicans, and thieves') and precious in the sight of God because John and Charles Wesley and their followers had preached the gospel to the poor and needy and sinful at the right time and in the right place. In 1932–33, there was a need to recover their practical Christianity and their vision, and *The Methodist Hymn Book* was a powerful tool in that recovery.

It had two prefaces. The first, by the compilers, emphasised that it was 'issued for the use of *all* British Methodists, and for not a few Methodists "beyond the seas" as well'.[34] This was clearly an appeal to those who had signed up to Methodist Union in 1932 to get behind the book, because it could have the power to unite the new denomination. 'We hope', said the preface, 'that none of our people will consent to be cut off from any part of their heritage of song.'[35] The second was a reprint of John Wesley's 1779 preface to *A Collection of Hymns*. This was a masterstroke: it leaped back across almost two centuries to hear the authentic words of the founder of Methodism. No-one could question that voice. It was there before the divisions, before the rivalries and animosities, before names and sects and parties. The 1904 book had mentioned it: now it was available in all its glory.

The contents of the book, as Andrew Pratt has pointed out, were determined to some degree by a Wesleyan majority of the compilers,[36] although some favourites from elsewhere remained, notably 'Hark! the gospel news is sounding', a benchmark hymn for nineteenth-century Primitive Methodism:

> Hark! the gospel news is sounding:
>   Christ hath suffered on the tree;
> Streams of mercy are abounding;
>   Grace for all is rich and free.
> Now, poor sinner,
>   Look to Him who died for thee.

The verses continue, with the fountain to wash sins away, through the river of grace, until finally, 'we'll bathe in the full ocean/Of the great Redeemer's love'. The progression is splendid, irresistible: the omission of the hymn must have seemed impossible to the committee. However, the bias towards the Wesleyan tradition was justified because the hymns of Charles Wesley contained so much fervour, doctrine and psychological insight, and John's translations carried the wisdom of German theology. To these were added the hymns that had become established in the nineteenth century and the early twentieth as common to all British churches. The result was a great book. It succeeded wonderfully in its aim of uniting the

---

[34] *Methodist Hymn Book* (London: Methodist Conference Office, 1933), preface, iv.
[35] *Ibid.*, iv.
[36] Andrew Pratt, *O for a Thousand Tongues: The 1933 Methodist Hymn Book in Context* (Peterborough: Epworth Press, 2004).

various parts of the denomination, and it carried the Methodist Church through the Second World War and the turbulent times that followed. Its principal weak point was the section 'For Children', hymns 834 to 866, which failed to grasp the example given by *Songs of Praise* of hymns that engaged with children's experience rather than hymns that reflected the adult's view of children. In spite of this, the book became deeply loved by all parts of the new Methodist Church. The supplement, *Hymns & Songs* (1969), added a mixture of traditional hymns and less successful experimental numbers; but it did not shake the firm hold of 'MHB' (as it was affectionately known) on the hearts and minds of the Methodist people. Thus in 1979 the announcement that a new book was planned caused shock and dismay. At the Methodist Conference at Sheffield in 1980 there was a passionate debate, and the commitment to a new book survived only when two conditions were agreed: that there should be two hundred Wesley hymns in it, and that the word 'Methodist' should appear in the title.[37]

The 1933 *MHB* had been a rock of stability in a world of change. But it was also a register of Methodist culture. It had a dignified format, with Gothic lettering for the sub-sections, clear print and an elegant layout, at least in the full music edition (there was a much inferior words-only edition). It began with Adoration and Worship, reflecting the pattern of Free Church liturgy, and followed with sections on God, on the Lord Jesus Christ (including a section on 'His Priesthood and Sympathy', beautifully named and executed) and on the Holy Spirit. This was followed by 'The Holy Scriptures' and 'The Gospel Call': even in the latter section the instant solutions of Frances Jane van Alstyne (Fanny Crosby) and the tinny music of Ira D. Sankey were tempered by the hopeful solemnity and psychological insight contained in Charles Wesley's calls to sinners. The remainder of the book, on 'The Christian Life', 'Death, Judgement, the Future Life' and 'The Church', provided for the experience of the soul on pilgrimage, and for the individual in a Methodist society; and a final series of sections provided for national and social life, and for times and seasons. It was a collection that reflected what went on in Methodist chapels throughout the land: adoration, confession, scriptural reading, intercession and the preaching of the word. It combined the dignity of Free Church worship with a strong sense of personal and social responsibility, and in the full representation of Charles Wesley's hymns and John Wesley's translations it maintained the great traditions of evangelical fervour and Reformation theology.

*Hymns and Psalms*, when it came in 1983, never quite captured the affection of Methodists in the way that the old *MHB* had done. It tried hard: it avoided some of the mistakes of the 1933 book by having no separate children's section, but this required that there should be hymns that were thought to be suitable for children in each section (this was the time of the well intentioned but disastrous 'all-age family worship', which – except in the hands of highly skilled communicators – irritated

---

[37] In the event, the number of Wesley hymns fell short of the target, and 'Methodist' was relegated to a sub-title.

most adults and annoyed most children).[38] It had a substantial second section entitled 'God's World', which contained hymns that were concerned with the natural world, such as Fred Pratt Green's 'God in his love for us lent us this planet', with its prayer to be delivered 'from its [earth's] pollution, misuse and destruction'. But the section, while containing hand-wringing hymns on the human condition, never quite succeeded in capturing the poetic energy that expressed the original Methodist concern for the poor and outcast in the hymns of Charles Wesley.

Nevertheless, Pratt Green's hymns were rightly prized by Methodists. He was certainly the most consistent, skilful and relevant hymn writer that the denomination had produced since the eighteenth century. His hymns were finely crafted and were a deeply spiritual response to the world around him, including its materialism and increasing secularism. Few people would have had the strength, one might almost say the confidence, to write 'When our confidence is shaken/In beliefs we thought secure'. With twenty-seven hymns, he was the most prominent contemporary writer represented in the book. Others included Albert Bayly, Fred Kaan, Caryl Micklem and Brian Wren from the Congregationalist/United Reformed Church tradition, and the supreme Anglican hymn writer, Timothy Dudley-Smith. Their work was valuable, but it had one unforeseen consequence: it left people wanting more. What has been called the 'hymn explosion' of the 1970s was the beginning of a sustained output of new hymnody, some of it good, some not so good, but all fresh and new.

*Hymns and Psalms* was unfortunate in its publication date. It could not have anticipated the great wave of worship songs that have proved so attractive to many people, nor the more traditional hymns that have enriched worship since 1983. Hymns such as Timothy Dudley-Smith's 'Lord, for the years your love has kept and guided' or Michael Saward's 'Christ triumphant, ever reigning', have become essential to any hymnbook. And to those people who admire worship songs, the work of Bayly and Pratt Green must seem like the work of a much older generation. Contemporary culture, driven by television and other media, naturally encourages the new, the temporary and the transient. One result is that more and more Methodist churches have created their own hand-made supplements, easily and cheaply produced in the age of desk-top publishing.

Even more significant is the revolution of the internet. New hymns and worship songs can be downloaded with the click of a mouse and projected on to a screen. This is obviously an opportunity to try out new material, and it is hard to resist the call to do this. For so long congregations have been told that they need to change their ways in the face of the decline in religious attendance, and it would take a brave soul to speak up in a Church Council against anything new or experimental. There has been a huge increase in the writing of hymns and songs during the last twenty years. New books come out; writers post hymns on the internet, or send them round by email. Novelty is easy, and the consequences of failure are negligible: if it doesn't work, a hymn or worship song can be abandoned after a

---

[38] A national survey, ca. 2000, indicated that those most absent from Methodist churches belonged to the 18–40 age group.

first showing on the screen. Hymns and songs are a part of this glorious freedom of opportunity, this perpetual encounter with the new and ephemeral; and in this brave new world the hymns, and even the songs of last year, appear like the fossils of some long-forgotten ancient time.

The problem with this huge increase in the hymns and songs that are available is its failure to relate to the culture of the past. The singing of hymns has been one of the great strengths of Methodism, from the time of John and Charles Wesley, through the problems of the nineteenth century and the turmoil of the twentieth, to the uncertainties of the twenty-first. As I write this, a new hymnbook, *Singing the Faith*, is imminent, and by the time that this essay is published it will be in print. How it will relate to the computer-and-screen provision is hard to predict. How it will relate to its predecessor, *Hymns and Psalms*, is easier to see. According to the list of contents, it will contain many more hymns and songs from modern sources, and fewer from the past. There are seventy-nine hymns by Charles Wesley and three translations by John, against the one hundred and seventy-three in the 1983 book. There are many hymns from the Iona Community, and from the 'Jubilate Group' responsible for *Hymns for Today's Church*, and hymns by many other contemporary writers. This is all to be expected. However, there is no doubt that in the process of responding to the opportunities provided by contemporary hymns and songs, there has been a diminution of traditional Methodist culture.

It is possible that something will remain. But there is also a possibility that the desire to use new music and new words will mean that Methodism will become indistinguishable from any other Protestant denomination. In these ecumenical days this may be no bad thing. But something of a culture that was distinctive and valuable, a noble contribution to national and religious life, will have disappeared. In some places it may be possible to think that this process can be reversed, and that the glorious inheritance of the Wesleys can be preserved. But there are others where the changes are irreversible. There are Methodist institutions which congratulate themselves on having sold the organ and closed the chapel. It is difficult, if not impossible, to sing the great hymns of Charles Wesley under such circumstances. And while some may applaud this, as a necessary break with the past, to others it will seem as if the barbarians are at the gates.

# Episkopé and Connexionalism: Ecclesiology and Church Government in Methodism

### Russell E. Richey

Since 1744 the two constant factors of Methodist polity (1) a superintending and appointing power, and (2) a consulting body, called the Conference, have been continuously operative.

> These two factors are constitutional or elemental in the government of Methodism. The system itself changes as either of these elements changes or is variously combined with the other: the disappearance of either is the destruction of the system. Something better might take its place, but it would be also something different. The peculiar economy of Methodism would cease to exist'.[1]

The world-wide family of Methodist/Wesleyan denominations exhibits an array of patterns of church government and of modes of appointing and consulting, particularly impressive in its variety if the offspring churches across the globe and the extended family of united/uniting churches and Pentecostalism are included. Certainly within Methodism one can find divers forms of congregational, presbyterian and episcopal polities and divers contextualisations or acculturations of these classic forms in the global array of Methodisms. A British or American polity behaves differently when fully indigenised in Africa or Asia. However, two patterns predominate, both framed by John Wesley in 1784. They care in different ways for the two constant factors of Methodist polity. By his provisions for the American movement Wesley created an independent episcopal church, a Church

---

[1] Jno. J. Tigert, *A Constitutional History of American Episcopal Methodism*, 3rd. edn (Nashville, TN: Publishing House of the Methodist Episcopal Church, South, 1908), 15. On the relation and tension between these principles and the overall concerns of this essay, see Thomas Edward Frank, *Polity, Practice, and the Mission of The United Methodist Church*, 2006 edn (Nashville, TN: Abingdon, 2006), 41–114.

of England modified for the new nation, perhaps an Anglicanism-lite, a church that looked and behaved something like colonial Anglicanism. So it named itself, the Methodist Episcopal Church (MEC). By contrast, anticipating British Methodism's need for governance after his death Wesley in 1784 granted supremacy not to superintendents, bishops or key leaders but to Conference, a deliverance that would eventuate in Presbyterian-like structure and later, when ordination was regularised, in leadership by presbyters.[2] The bishop-led church in the newly independent and proudly democratic nation would look royal. The Conference in Georgian and Victorian Britain, once led autocratically by John Wesley, would elect presidents and chairs and look democratic. In both contexts, however, Conference and centralised power (formal and informal) would interact, collaborate and vie in complex fashion.

Both patterns, similar in some respects, radically different in others, might be seen as alternative ways by which Wesley sought to sustain Methodism's mission of leavening the Church of England. Both honoured Wesleyanism's purpose – God's design 'in raising up the Preachers called *Methodists*' – which the 'Large' *Minutes* identified as 'Not to form any new sect; but to reform the nation, particularly the Church; and to spread scriptural holiness over the land'.

By the first, Wesley put the reforming leaven of Methodist discipline, doctrine, mission and structure within an independent, modified Anglicanism at a point in time when it was by no means clear that what had been the colonial Church of England would even survive in the new nation. Or perhaps it would be more accurate to say that Wesley interjected essentials of Anglicanism into the already operative American Methodist system of discipline, doctrine, mission and structure. Revising the 'Large' *Minutes* into a *Discipline*,[3] Wesley ordered American Methodism with a threefold ministry of superintendents, elders and deacons. By ordaining Thomas Coke as superintendent and directing that Francis Asbury be ordained superintendent by Coke, and other Americans be ordained elders and deacons, Wesley made provision for a transmission of orders and of sacramental authority to the new church, albeit a transition that churches claiming the historic episcopate would not recognise. To the *Book of Common Prayer*, dear to the Wesleys, John took scissors, digesting it into the *Sunday Service of the Methodists in North America*. Despite the restrictive title, it provided a full set of rituals – morning prayer, evening prayer, weekday litany, Sunday service, Eucharist, two baptismal rites and marriage, as well as orders for communion of the sick, and burial and ordination

---

[2] John C. Bowmer, *Pastor and People: A Study of Church and Ministry in Wesleyan Methodism from the Death of John Wesley (1791) to the Death of Jabez Bunting (1858)* (London: Epworth, 1975), 62–7.

[3] *Minutes of Several Conversations Between the Rev. Thomas Coke, LL. D., the Rev. Francis Asbury and others, at a Conference, Begun in Baltimore, in the State of Maryland, on Monday, the 27th of December, in the Year 1784* (Philadelphia: Charles Cist, 1785). For the text of the first *Discipline* in parallel columns with the 'Large' *Minutes* see Tigert, *Constitutional History*, 532–602. I use this abbreviation – *Discipline*/church year – for the book of *Discipline* (under the varying names employed by Methodism's several denominations). So this one would be *Discipline*/MEC 1785.

services for deacons, elders and superintendents. It also included a brief lectionary and twenty-four Articles of Religion, excerpted from Anglicanism's Thirty-Nine.[4] With these provisions plus a revised hymnal (*A Collection of Psalms and Hymns for the Lord's Day*), his *Explanatory Notes on the New Testament* and the collected *Sermons* (paralleling the Anglican *Homilies*), Wesley created for the Americans a Methodised Anglicanism.[5]

By the second 1784 action, Wesley sought to sustain Methodism's leaven within the British churches with the *Deed of Declaration*, which settled church government for Great Britain, legally defining the Conference with a specified 'Legal Hundred' preachers.[6] The first leavened Anglicanism by replacing it with a superintendent-led, soon bishop-led, church. The second continued Methodism's leaven within the Church of England and engagement with other churches of the British Isles. In the one year, as Kenneth Cracknell and Susan White observe, Wesley established 'two quite distinct traditions' and released 'two streams' which would 'flow in decidedly different directions'..[7]

## Contrasting Exercises of Episkopé

The distinctive flow of the two 1784 Wesley provisions can be seen in recent American and British statements about episkopé.[8] The United Methodist Church (UMC) in 2008 affirmed the following concerning the superintending and appointing authority:

> Bishops are elected from the elders and set apart for a ministry of servant leadership, general oversight and supervision.... As followers of Jesus Christ, bishops are authorized to guard the faith, order, liturgy, doctrine, and discipline of the Church. The role and calling forth of the bishop is to exercise oversight and support of the Church in its mission of making disciples of Jesus Christ for the transformation of the world. The basis of such discipleship of leadership (episkopé) lies in discipline and a disciplined life.[9]

---

[4] *John Wesley's Sunday Service of the Methodists in North America*, with an introduction by James F. White (Nashville: Quarterly Review, 1984).

[5] Richard P. Heitzenrater, *Wesley and the People Called Methodists* (Nashville, TN: Abingdon, 1995), 288–90.

[6] Ibid., 283–5; Rupert Davies and Gordon Rupp (eds), *A History of the Methodist Church in Great Britain*, 4 vols (London: Epworth, 1965–88), I, 244–6.

[7] Kenneth Cracknell and Susan J. White, *An Introduction to World Methodism* (Cambridge: Cambridge University Press, 2005), vii.

[8] To simplify contrasts I focus on the United Methodist Church and the Methodist Church of the U.K., churches constituted by the uniting of several of the American and British streams.

[9] *Discipline*/UMC 2008, 296, ¶ 403.

The *Discipline* follows this statement with six paragraphs elaborating the disciplines of (episcopal) servant leadership, oversight and supervision. The UMC understands its bishops as 'itinerant general superintendents', terminology protected by the third of the 'Restrictive Rules',[10] each a bishop of the whole church. Reinforcing that catholic aspect and also as a separate expression of episkopé, the UMC looks for oversight and leadership to the Council of Bishops, a body created in the 1939 union (MEC, Methodist Episcopal Church, South (MECS), Methodist Protestant Church) and continued in that of 1968 (Methodist Church and Evangelical United Brethren Church):

> There shall be a Council of Bishops composed of all the bishops of The United Methodist Church. The council shall meet at least once a year and plan for the general oversight and promotion of the temporal and spiritual interests of the entire Church and for carrying into effect the rules, regulations, and responsibilities prescribed and enjoined by the General Conference and in accord with the provisions set forth in this Plan of Union.[11]

In addition, the UMC understands the district superintendency and the cabinet of superintendents (and other Conference officers) 'as an extension of the superintending role of the bishop within the annual conference'. A long discussion, 'Expressions of Superintendency', in the episcopacy section of the *Discipline*, covers these several modalities of episkopé, perhaps because its location does not touch on episkopé as exercised in the general agencies of the UMC, a matter to which we return below.[12]

The Methodist Church of Great Britain, by contrast, defines episkopé in relation to Conference:

> After Wesley's death, the Conference was given legal continuity by the Deed of Declaration, which Wesley had executed in 1784 to bestow upon the Legal Hundred those powers which he himself had held. The Legal Hundred (whose original members were selected by Wesley to provide a cross-section of the itinerant preachers) was the 'official' Conference, though other preachers were eligible to attend and it was the whole Conference which exercised general oversight within the Connexion. From that time onwards, the Conference exercised, as it still exercises, episkopé over the people called Methodists.

Though the character and constitution of the Conference has changed over time, the Conference continues to exercise a corporate rule of episkopé over the connexion.

---

[10] *Discipline*/UMC 2008, 27, ¶ 19.
[11] *Discipline*/UMC 2008, 35, ¶ 47.
[12] *Discipline*/UMC 2008, 297, ¶ 403; 316–318, ¶¶ 426–9.

This 2000 report illustrates Conference's corporate rule of episkopé in four ways. It exercises the teaching office by making 'authoritative statements on matters of faith and order', seeking thereby 'to preserve and transmit the apostolic faith'. Conference 'can and does establish the constitution of Methodism at every level'. It oversees all aspects of the ordaining and stationing of ministry. And Conference authorises those who preside at Holy Communion.[13] This report and others occasioned as well by the prolonged engagement between the Methodist Church and the Church of England (and the Church in Wales and the Scottish Episcopal Church), then proceed to problematise the above formulation by indicating how the entire connexion and its lay and clergy leaders exercise episkopé in its several modes (communal, collegial and personal)[14] by delegation, ad interim, in execution and in mission.[15]

A similar ambiguity exists in United Methodism. Though UMC bishops do exercise episkopé in its several modes, as the language quoted above indicates, the teaching office formally belongs to General Conference. That body, quadrennially convened since 1792 and operating under Restrictive Rules adopted in 1808, has constitutional responsibility for the *Discipline* and other such official resources (hymnals, book of worship, books of resolutions).[16] So the UMC indicates that only General Conference speaks for the church:

> Speaking for the Church –1. No person, no paper, no organization, has the authority to speak officially for The United Methodist Church, this right having been reserved exclusively to the General Conference under the Constitution. Any written public policy statement issued by a general Church agency shall clearly identify either at the beginning or at the end that the statement represents the position of that general agency and not necessarily the position of The United Methodist Church.

---

[13] *Methodist Church Reports*, Special Reports, *Episkope And Episcopacy*, http://www.methodist.org.uk/static/news/papers/episkope_and_episcopacy03.htm, 4 (accessed 2 March 2011). See also *The Nature of Oversight* and *What Sort of Bishops? Models of Episcopacy and British Methodism*, both of which continue to be available on the http://www.methodist.org.uk website as this essay is being drafted.

[14] To these dimensions of the exercise of episkopé, the important ecumenical statement *Baptism, Eucharist and Ministry*, the World Council of Churches' Faith and Order Paper 111, 1982 summons the churches.

[15] See Conference reports *Methodism and Episcopacy* (1978), *Episcopacy in the Methodist Church* (1981), *Episcopacy and Methodist Doctrinal Standards* (1982), *Episcopacy* (1998), *Called to Love and Praise* (1999), *Episkopé and Episcopacy* (2000), *The Nature of Oversight* (2005), *What Sort of Bishops* (2005).

[16] *The Book of Resolutions of the United Methodist Church 2008*; *The United Methodist Book of Worship* (Nashville, TN: Abingdon, 1992) and *The United Methodist Hymnal* (Nashville, TN: Abingdon, 1989). The first, like the *Discipline*, is revised and a new version published after each General Conference, typically quadrennially.

2. Any individual member called to testify before a legislative body to represent The United Methodist Church shall be allowed to do so only by reading, without elaboration, the resolutions and positions adopted by the General Conference of The United Methodist Church.[17]

The British Church operates with a much more nuanced and flexible understanding, outlined in a 2001 report, *Speaking for the Methodist Church.* Various designated leaders and bodies are charged and empowered to speak in so far as they do so 'in harmony with the existing statements and resolutions of the Conference'. A second 'Standing Order' governs activities of the Methodist Council: 'Between the close of any Conference and the opening of the next succeeding Conference the council is authorised to act on behalf of the Conference, provided that such action is not contrary to the Deed of Union or Standing Orders or any subsisting resolution of the Conference.'[18] The *Deed of Union* puts it succinctly: 'The Conference shall be the final authority within the Methodist Church with regard to all questions concerning the interpretation of its doctrines.'[19]

The comparable constitutional UMC statement is: 'The General Conference shall have full legislative power over all matters connectional ....' The *Discipline* then itemises sixteen matters over which General Conference might exercise its authority, following these responsibilities with the current version of the six 'thou shalt nots' which constitute the Restrictive Rules.[20] British and American churches thereby recognise Conference or General Conference as the ultimate authority and the church as connexional in nature.

---

[17] *Discipline*/UMC 2008, 329, ¶ 509.

[18] *Speaking for the Methodist Church.* Methodist Conference 2001 Reports, 5.5. http://www.methodist.org.uk/index.cfm?fuseaction=opentogod.content&cmid=361 (accessed 2 March 2011). The Standing Orders referenced are 301(5) and 211(1).

[19] *The Constitutional Practice and Discipline of the Methodist Church*, published by order of the Methodist Conference, now in two volumes, frequently updated, and at this writing available as free downloads, http://www.methodist.org.uk/index.cfm?fuseaction=churchlife.content&cmid=1644, 2010 edition, II, 214 (accessed 2 March 2011).

[20] *Discipline*/UMC 2008, 24–7. The first two of the Restrictive Rules pertain to doctrine: 'The General Conference shall not revoke, alter, or change our Articles of Religion or establish any new standards or rules of doctrine contrary to our present and existing and established standards of doctrine.' The second recognises the standard contributed from the Evangelical United Brethren side: 'The General Conference shall not revoke, alter, or change our Confession of Faith.'

## Connectionalism/Connexionalism

The term 'connexional'[21] conventionally distinguishes churches with one or another system of centralised authority from those that function with congregational, free church or independent systems. Methodism alone gives connexionalism ecclesiological force. Its understanding of this ecclesial principle is, or ought to be, a central feature of its bi-lateral and multi-lateral encounters with other churches. And British Methodism has done better than its American counterparts in theologising 'connexion' and 'connexionalism', a consequence perhaps of its prolonged engagement in unity explorations with the Church of England and therefore in efforts at self-understanding. Among its richly nuanced expressions is the 1999 Conference Statement, *Called to Love and Praise*. This long, full-orbed, scripturally grounded and 'authoritative account of the official position of the Methodist Church' on ecclesiology begins exposition of the 'connexional principle' affirming:

> Although this principle has not always come to expression in a complete or balanced way in Methodist structures and practice, it enshrines a vital truth about the nature of the Church. It witnesses to a mutuality and interdependence which derive from the participation of all Christians through Christ in the very life of God himself.

The Statement continues, elaborating the 'complementarity of connexionalism and local autonomy':

> First, at all levels of the Church, the structures of fellowship, consultation, government and oversight express the interdependence of all churches, and help to point up, at all levels, necessary priorities in mission and service. Second, alongside this, as the natural corollary of connexionalism, local churches, Circuits and Districts exercise the greatest possible degree of autonomy.

Further paragraphs detail the foundation of connexionalism in scriptural practice, specifically in the understanding of the church as the Body of Christ, in the

---

[21] See the several essays by Brian E. Beck, 'Some Reflections on Connexionalism', *Epworth Review*, 18 (May 1991), 48–59 and (September 1991), 43–50; 'Connexion and Koinonia: Wesley's Legacy and the Ecumenical Ideal', in Randy L. Maddox (ed.), *Rethinking Wesley's Theology for Contemporary Methodism* (Nashville, TN: Kingswood Books, 1998), 129–41; and his chapter along with those by David M. Chapman, Tim Macquiban and David Carter in Richard Sykes (ed.), *Methodism Across the Pond* (Oxford: Applied Theology Press, 2005). I have dealt with connexionalism in American Methodism in several places: *Marks of Methodism: Practices of Ecclesiology*, with Dennis M. Campbell and William B. Lawrence, United Methodism and American Culture, 5 (Nashville, TN: Abingdon, 2005); *Doctrine in Experience: A Methodist Theology of Church and Ministry* (Nashville, TN: Abingdon, 2009) and *Methodist Connectionalism: Historical Perspectives* (Nashville, TN: Abingdon, 2010).

travelling of the apostles and in the *koinonia* that bound early Christian communities in mission. Methodism, the Statement insists, concretises its connexionalism in multiform fashion, a few expressions of which should be illustrative: in the oversight exercised by Conference; in the stationing of ministers by Conference 'an acknowledgement that the ministry as a whole is at the disposal of the entire connexion'; in the grouping of churches into Circuits, an indication that 'no local church is an autonomous unit complete in itself' and that the Circuit is 'the primary church unit'; in the gathering of its people into small groups for fellowship, shared discipline and faithful living (traditionally understood as personal and social holiness); in the holding of Methodist land and buildings under the Model Trusts 'for which the custodian trustees are a connexional body'; in the understanding that structure and order must remain responsive to the Spirit, therefore flexible and pragmatic so as to remain faithful to and oriented to the church's mission; and in its various links with Methodism globally.[22]

The UMC's Committee on Faith and Order, currently at work on ecclesiology, expects to produce a document comparable to *Called to Love and Praise* and hopes that it will gain official status comparable to *By Water and the Spirit: A United Methodist Understanding of Baptism* and *This Holy Mystery: A United Methodist Understanding of Holy Communion*.[23] Currently, the UMC's most formal statement on the principle is in an obscure, short *Disciplinary* paragraph entitled 'The Journey of a Connectional People'.

> Connectionalism in the United Methodist tradition is multi-leveled, global in scope, and local in thrust. Our connectionalism is not merely a linking of one charge conference to another. It is rather a vital web of interactive relationships.

The statement then briefly itemises the connective bonds – 'a common tradition of faith, including our Doctrinal Standards and General Rules', 'a constitutional polity, including a leadership of general superintendency', 'a common mission' executed 'through conferences that reflect the inclusive and missional character of our fellowship' and 'a common ethos that characterizes our distinctive way of doing things'.[24] The paragraph makes no mention of the connective role of boards and agencies, a concern to which we return below.

Regrettably this short paragraph replaced a statement with the same title, which appeared in the *Discipline* in 1988 and 1992, and provided an exposition of connexionalism comparable in prominence, length, nuance and fullness to that in *Called to Love and Praise*. A couple of paragraphs from that no longer authoritative statement deserve citation:

> Ever since John Wesley began to refer to the scattered Methodist classes, bands, and societies throughout eighteenth-century England

---

[22] *Called to Love and Praise*, 1999, Foreword, ¶¶ 4.6.1–5, 4.6.7, 4.7.4, 4.7.1, 4.7.6, 4.7.9, 4.7.8.
[23] *Resolutions*/UMC 2008, 941–61, 961–1009.
[24] *Discipline*/UMC 2008, 90–91, ¶ 131.

as 'the connexion,' Methodists everywhere have embraced the idea that as a people of faith we journey together in connection and in covenant with one another. Expressing the high degree of cohesiveness and centralized organization among Methodists, the connectional principle became the distinguishing mark which set them apart from the normal patterns of Anglican ecclesiastical organization as well as the more loosely organized Protestant bodies of the day.

This acceptance of strong covenantal bonds among the Methodists was no accident. There were deep theological roots, including the concept and experience of covenant and the resulting emphasis on faith journeying in covenant with God and one another. The connectional idea is a style of relationship rather than simply an organizational or structural framework. . . .

There were deep biblical roots as well. Images of the church, especially in the New Testament – the vine and the branches, the wedding feast, the household or commonwealth of God, the new humanity with cosmic and kingdom dimensions, the fellowship of the saints, the Body of Christ, and a host of others – supplemented the covenant concept. The very structure of the Apostolic Church was connectional and covenantal. Paul realized very early the importance of superintending scattered congregations.

In exposition of 'the principle itself' and its covenantal interdependence, this 1988/92 statement emphasised the theological, missional, unitive and identity-providing nature of connexionalism with separate paragraphs on shared vision, memory, community, discipline, leadership, mobilisation and linkage. It concluded noting both stresses on connexionalism and its importance as a uniquely Methodist witness and gift to the larger Christian community.[25]

## Connexionalism as Ecclesiology

This last point deserves emphasis. In recognising, affirming and developing the Biblical, Apostolic, missional, ecumenical and theological nature of connexionalism, Methodism has a distinctive ecclesiology to share with Christians generally and certainly with other churches with connexional polities (including Presbyterians and Lutherans as well as Anglicans, Catholics and Orthodox). Methodists typically do not treat polity and policy as adiaphora as do some churches. Nor do they

---

[25] *Discipline*/UMC 1992, 111–14; *Discipline*/UMC 1988, 116–18. This earlier statement implicitly and explicitly referenced the church's agencies: '*Leadership* – The principle provides a sharing of resources and resource persons for mission and ministry – for pastors and laypeople in local settings or beyond local settings. This is done through superintending pastors, boards, and agencies that serve the denomination in ways it may determine.'

deem our structure, order and organisation as the only one that is true or Biblically warranted. Methodist connexionalism takes a middle path. To the Lutherans and others who treat polity as adiaphora, Methodists say a 'No' because 'connection' has ultimately to do with social holiness, the kingdom, the Christian journey. To the Orthodox, Roman Catholics and sectarians, Methodists say a 'No' presuming that Christians remain pilgrims – struggling under a covenant whose terms and expectations Christ alone satisfies, and functioning with a connexionalism which, though Christ- and his treasure-oriented, remains an earthen vessel. And perhaps this explains why Methodists can be so committed to ecumenism and at the same time reluctant to yield their way(s) of doing and being – an ambivalence well suited to arrangements of full communion which provide for sacramental and ministerial comity without sacrificing the independence and integrity of the churches involved.

Further, it might behove Methodists in conversations with Anglicans and Episcopalians to be as insistent on the theological/missional/soteriological purposes of *actual* polity as they are in having *active* bishops stand in the historic episcopate. The former attests corporate faithfulness. The latter (theirs) its leadership and its faithfulness. Methodist polity emphasises the mission of the church. Theirs its nature. Methodism's signals that the people of God and the structures, policies, systems and processes by which they commit to the *missio dei* do and must orient themselves to the kingdom, to the future, to the promise, to hope. Theirs, the insistence on the historic episcopate, signals that the church and its leadership are and must be oriented to that faith and worship which has been apostolically given.

The British Methodist exposition of episkopé as communal, collegial and personal – in Conference, in the other levels of connexional governance and in connexional leaders from local church to Conference president – provides perhaps the most satisfactorily laid foundations for an ecclesiological nuancing of polity, a connexionalism ecclesiology, a theology of church order.[26] If so, in conversations with Anglicans and Episcopalians Methodists might be as insistent on connexionalism (hope and love) as they are on episcopacy and the historic episcopate (faith). Methodists indeed have something to give as well as to receive.[27]

In its orientation to the future, the American title 'Journey of a Connectional People' gets the theme right. Perhaps Methodism would do best with the American title and British exposition. The two 'streams' or traditions do, in fact, share this connexional ecclesial self-understanding. And at points in the several histories, Methodists have affirmed that, in some fashion or to some degree, Methodists

---

[26] *Methodist Church Reports*, Special Reports, 'Episkope And Episcopacy'.

[27] The preceding paragraphs reflect my participation in the U.S. dialogue between the Episcopal and United Methodist churches and by no means are meant to imply that Episcopalians lack commitment to and efforts towards the *missio dei*. Indeed, Episcopalians have for well over a century led the American churches on social justice concerns. Instead, in our dialogue, Episcopal members, insisting that full communion involves a giving and receiving of gifts, have suggested that Methodists bring a commitment to mission and evangelism as one of our gifts. The foregoing represents, then, an effort to say what that gift might look like.

across the world are one connexion, one people. Such an identity the American movement recognised at its beginning. The first *Discipline* queried:

> Q. 2. What can be done in order to the future Union of the Methodists?
>
> A. During the Life of the Rev. Mr. Wesley, we acknowledge ourselves his Sons in the Gospel, ready in Matters belonging to Church-Government, to obey his Commands. And we do engage after his Death, to do every Thing that we judge consistent with the Cause of Religion in *America* and the political Interests of these States, to preserve and promote our Union with Methodists in *Europe*.[28]

Citing this affirmation, the American constitutional historian Tigert insisted that 'The evidence is conclusive that nothing lay nearer Wesley's heart than the continued union of Methodists throughout the world after his decease. He did not intend the separation of the American and English Methodists into two communions, one under the government of Bishops and the other under that of the Conference.'[29] Tigert went on to argue that Wesley had imagined the new American church to be overseen by and accountable not only to himself, while living, but also and after his death to the English Conference (so implied in the Deed of Declaration).Wesley made no provision for the convening of the Christmas Conference and American ratification of the structures and provisions for a new church, nor for the election of superintendents (both Coke and Asbury), nor for refusal by the MEC of his selection of further superintendents, nor for anything like an American General Conference with plenary authority. The latter, created the year after Wesley died, completed the trajectory towards an independent connexion signalled by the American Conference's 1787 deletion of the above pledge and even earlier by the colonial Conference's relative autonomy.[30] That taking of Wesley off the minutes in 1787 responded to his 'appointment' of Richard Whatcoat and Freeborn Garrettson as superintendents, an exercise of authority that the Americans refused to accept.[31]

So, two connexions, two streams, eventually two churches – one that looked very Anglican, one that would continue as leaven for the Church of England and other churches, though looking ever more church-like after Wesley's death.[32] Each understood itself as connexion, though the Americans chose to replace

---

[28] *Discipline*/MEC 1785, 3; Tigert, *Constitutional History*, 534. Portions of the first *Discipline* are reproduced in Russell E. Richey, Kenneth E. Rowe and Jean Miller Schmidt (eds), *The Methodist Experience in America: A Sourcebook* (Nashville, TN: Abingdon, 2000), 123–33.This volume is identified as vol. 2. Vol. 1 is our *The Methodist Experience in America: A History* (Nashville, TN: Abingdon, 2010). I will identify these as MEA 1 and 2.This quotation is MEA 1 (1785), 82.
[29] Tigert, *Constitutional History*, 187–8.
[30] Richey, *Methodist Conference*, 27–32; MEA 2, 41–8.
[31] Tigert, *Constitutional History*, 188–94.
[32] Bowmer, *Pastor and People*, 34–6, 51–67. Note as well Heitzenrater's repeated emphasis in *Wesley and the People Called Methodists* on the separatist effect of Wesley's own initiatives.

that word with 'church' in 1816. That year Asbury died and General Conference took a number of initiatives towards social and ecclesial self-respectability. From that point on, and especially by the dropping of the word 'connexion' as self-description, American Methodists lost some of the incentive and motivation to reflect on connexionalism theologically and ecclesiologically. And lacking a theological account of connexionalism, American Methodists could readily take polity as merely a pragmatic and instrumental matter. Two centuries later perhaps the two Methodist streams, British and American, might profitably work together on understanding or re-understanding connexionalism and on the relation of the connexion to its leadership.

## Presidency and Connexionalism

In bi-lateral dialogues, Anglicans have pressed Methodists on the world level (through the World Methodist Council) and in both British and American contexts to clarify their understandings of themselves as 'church', their sacramental practices, their patterns of ministry and their exercise of episkopé.[33] After years of on-again, off-again conversations the Church of England and Methodist Church of Great Britain (U.K.) have entered into *An Anglican–Methodist Covenant*, now guiding efforts at various levels towards unity. In the U.S., the UMC and the Episcopal Church will entertain proposals for full communion. These conversations seemingly bring to a close two centuries of apologetics in which Methodists have sought to defend their ministerial orders and explain John Wesley's reasons for raising up preachers and, in the case of the MEC, undertaking to ordain. In a prescriptive and directive letter 'To Dr. Coke, Mr. Asbury and our Brethren in North-America', Wesley addressed himself to the legitimacy of his act of ordaining Coke, arguing that bishops and presbyters were of the same order and that precedents existed in the church for ordination by the latter.[34] Coke made the same case in his ordination sermon for Asbury.[35] These preemptive efforts to defend the MEC orders did not suffice with Episcopalians (and others). And Coke did the MEC no favours by secret exchanges

---

[33] For the exploration on the world level see *Sharing in the Apostolic Communion, a Report of the Anglican–Methodist International Communion to the World Methodist Council and the Lambeth Conference, 1996*.

[34] MEA 2 (1784a), 71–2 and John Telford (ed.), *The Letters of the Rev. John Wesley*, 9 vols (London: Epworth, 1931), 7, 237–8: 'Lord King's Account of the Primitive Church convinced me many years ago, That Bishops and Presbyters are the same Order, and consequently have the same right to ordain. For many years I have been importuned from time to time, to exercise this right, by ordaining part of our travelling Preachers. But I have still refused, not only for Peacesake: but because I was determined, as little as possible to violate the established Order of the national Church to which I belonged.'

[35] 'Substance of a Sermon preached at Baltimore, Maryland before The General Conference of The Methodist Episcopal Church, December 27, 1784 at the Ordination of The Rev. Francis Asbury to the Office of a Superintendent' (New York, 1784).

with Episcopal bishop William White exploring unity between the two churches, letters subsequently published, much to Coke's embarrassment.[36] Thereafter Methodist apologists periodically felt impelled to respond to Episcopal critics of Methodist orders (and Presbyterian critics of Wesleyan doctrine).[37]

Critics from without were a bother. Critics within – obsessed over autocratic bishops, presiding elders, presidents, chairs and superintendents and/or over aristocratic governance and authority exercised by Conferences solely of preachers – greatly troubled American and British connexions, indeed split them. In the case of the MEC, one schism after another focused on bishops, their suffragan-like deputies the presiding elders (now district superintendents) or other undemocratic features of Methodist polity. James O'Kelly, in virulent attacks on Asbury, led the first of a long series of efforts to constrain the seemingly arbitrary appointive power of the bishop. The departure of his Republican Methodists posed such a threat that Coke and Asbury, at the behest of General Conference, undertook an extraordinary effort to annotate the *Discipline* and explain MEC polity and practice (in 1798). Defending the episcopacy, they insisted,

> [N]othing has been introduced into Methodism by the present episcopal form of government, which was not before fully exercised by Mr. Wesley. He presided in the conferences; fixed the appointments of the preachers for their several circuits; changed, received, or suspended preachers, wherever he judged that necessity required it; travelled through the European connection at large; superintended the spiritual and temporal business; and consecrated two bishops, Thomas Coke and Alexander Mather, one before the present episcopal plan took place in America, and the other afterwards, besides ordaining elders and deacons.

Explaining that in other respects their authority was more limited than that of Wesley (particularly in regards to property), Coke and Asbury then made a case for episcopacy (as later for the presiding elder's office) on missional grounds. They insisted on the 'high expediency, if not necessity, of the present plan'.

> How could an itinerant ministry be preserved through this extensive continent, if the yearly conferences were to station the preachers? They would, of course, be taken up with the *sole* consideration of the spiritual and temporal interests of *that part* of the connection, the direction of which was intrusted to them. The necessary consequence of this mode of proceeding would probably, in less than an age, be *the division of the*

---

[36] See John Vickers, *Thomas Coke: Apostle of Methodism* (Nashville, TN: Abingdon, 1969), 176–91.
[37] See Lawrence O. Kline, 'Anti-Methodist Publications (American)', in Nolan B. Harmon (ed.), *The Encyclopedia of World Methodism*, 2 vols (Nashville, TN: Abingdon, 1974), 1, 115–19. See also Frank Baker, 'Anti-Methodist Publications (British)', ibid., 119–22.

*body* and *the independence* of each yearly conference. The conferences would be more and more estranged from each other for want of a mutual exchange of preachers: and *that grand spring, the union of the body at large*, by which, under divine grace, the work is more and more extended through this vast country, would be gradually weakened, till at last it might be entirely destroyed. The connection would no more be enabled to send missionaries to the western states and territories, in proportion to their rapid population. The grand circulation of ministers would be at an end, and a mortal stab given to the itinerant plan. The surplus of preachers in one conference could not be drawn out to supply the deficiencies of others, through declensions, locations, deaths, &c. and the revivals in one part of the continent could not be rendered beneficial to the others. *Our grand plan*, in all its parts, leads to an *itinerant* ministry. Our bishops are *travelling* bishops. All the different orders which compose our conferences are employed in the *travelling line*; and our local preachers are, *in some degree*, travelling preachers. Everything is kept moving as far as possible; and we will be bold to say, that, next to the grace of God, there is nothing *like this* for keeping the whole body alive from the centre to the circumference, and for the continual extension of that circumference on every hand.[38]

Eloquent on connexionalism, instructive on the missional purposes of appointment, insistent on itinerancy as imperative for all ministries, the bishops were clear and forceful, perhaps, but not persuasive to O'Kelly or others who would follow in his democratising train – the several African Methodists, Methodist Protestants, Wesleyan Methodists, Free Methodists, Nazarenes – movements that in one way or another contended with authorities and/or authoritarianism and found it imperative to organise on more egalitarian principles. And the 1844 split, north and south, though preeminently over slavery, entailed differing notions of the relation of bishops to General Conference. The office and its authority would be an issue in dispute after dispute in large part because Asbury successfully exercised his episcopacy and created episcopal government in the style of Wesley.[39] Remaining 'elders', occupying an office not an order, being (eventually) consecrated not ordained, American Methodist bishops in the MEC and MECS nevertheless inherited tremendous authority and exercised great power.[40]

---

[38] Thomas Coke and Francis Asbury, *The Doctrines and Disciplines of the Methodist Episcopal Church, in America* (Philadelphia, 1798), 40–44; MEA 1 (1798), 123, 124–5.

[39] See James E. Kirby, *The Episcopacy in American Methodism* (Nashville, TN: Abingdon, 2000), Gerald F. Moede, *The Office of Bishop in Methodism: Its History and Development* (Zurich: Abingdon, 1964); Richey, *Doctrine in Experience*, chapter 6: 'Itinerant General Superintendency' and Richey and Thomas Edward Frank, *Episcopacy in the Methodist Tradition: Perspectives and Proposals* (Nashville, TN: Abingdon, 2004).

[40] Conversations between American Lutherans and Methodists on episcopacy are instructive here. The dialogue which led to full communion between the ELCA and UMC identified two themes as primary: 'that episcopacy is an *office* of the Church (not of its

Similarly, disquiet over one or another dimension of authority within Wesleyan Methodism led to schisms in the British movement, most notably producing the Methodist New Connexion, the Protestant Methodists and the Wesleyan Association (and to a lesser extent the Bible Christians and Primitive Methodists).[41] And the 1790s protest spearheaded by Alexander Kilham that led to his expulsion from Conference and the formation of the Methodist New Connexion occurred in the same time frame and raised very similar issues to that led by O'Kelly. Indeed, Kilham sought more thoroughly democratic and republican governance than O'Kelly – lay representation at all organisational levels including Conference, elective Conference presidents and District chairs, a say by leaders and stewards in the stationing of preachers – a thorough-going revolt against authoritarianism of bishops, presidents and superintendents (assistants).[42]

Tigert's two factors of Methodist polity – the superintending and appointing power and the consulting conference – constants, to be sure, have frequently, if not constantly, been in tension. And Methodists divide more typically over polity rather than doctrine.

## Connexionalism, Agencies, Superintendency and Congregationalism

Tensions in the connexions – over authority, resources, mission, social issues, money, prerogative – have increased as church membership has declined in the U.S. and the U.K., prompting various reactions, among them provincialisms and localisms (hunkering down by congregations). In *The Nature of Oversight*, the British Conference, acknowledging the Circuit as 'one of the main organisms of British Methodism and of its way of being Church', [43] concedes recently 'there has been a

---

essence) and that it is the *mission* of the Church that determines the shape of that office'. Jack M. Tuell and Roger W. Fjeld (eds), *Episcopacy: Lutheran–United Methodist Dialogue II* (Minneapolis, MN: Fortress, 1991), 12.

[41] Bowmer, *Pastor and People*, 15.

[42] Ibid., 45–50; John Munsey Turner, *Conflict and Reconciliation: Studies in Methodism and Ecumenism in England, 1740–1982* (London: Epworth, 1985), 65–78.

[43] *The Nature of Oversight*, 3.1. The following, a note from *The Nature of Oversight*, references Standing Order 500: '(1) The Circuit is the primary unit in which Local Churches express and experience their interconnexion in the Body of Christ, for purposes of mission, mutual encouragement and help. It is in the Circuit that ministers, deacons and probationers are stationed and local preachers are trained and admitted and exercise their calling. The purposes of the Circuit include the effective deployment of the resources of ministry, which include people, property and finance, as they relate to the Methodist churches in the Circuit, to churches of other denominations and to participation in the life of the communities served by the Circuit, including local schools and colleges, and in ecumenical work in the area including, where appropriate, the support of ecumenical Housing Associations.'

growing tendency in some areas towards local autonomy and congregationalism', but also the 'countervailing tendency to re-establish the circuit as the main entity' when finances stress human and financial resources of the local church. It insists on the importance of the connexional principle – that there be mutuality, interdependence, as well as a measure of autonomy:

> The local churches are not independent, primary entities but interdependent cells of the organism which is the circuit.
>
> The local churches are therefore the interdependent cells of circuits, circuits of districts, and districts of the Connexion, with the greatest weight still being on the structures of the circuit and the wider Connexion (e.g. Conference and Methodist Council).[44]

Localisms of several sorts beset the UMC as well, including a pervasive congregationalism. Indeed, the church now formally circumscribes its mission congregationally:

> The Mission – The mission of the Church is to make disciples of Jesus Christ for the transformation of the world. Local churches provide the most significant arena through which disciple-making occurs.[45]

How such delimitation fits with the pluriformity of the UMC's ministries, the various structures and systems by which it historically undertook missions and evangelism (including camp meetings) and its continuing understanding of the 'annual conference is the basic body of the Church',[46] the *Discipline* does not explain. More strikingly, perhaps, the *Discipline* elaborates that mission statement for several pages – outlines mission in the world and in the community, views it as local and global, and insists that both laity and clergy undertake mission and ministry – without mentioning the corporate structures, the boards and agencies, through which American Methodism carried on mission for nearly a century and a half. Scarcely an oversight, the omission reflects the rather considerable criticism of, even attacks on, the agencies. Some of that, paralleled in American politics, derives from lay and congregational unhappiness over the apportionments (they say 'taxes') that support Conference apparatus as well as that of the general church. But the negativity over these connectional agencies goes beyond money, reflects competition for prerogative and control, and is heard from UMC leaders (bishops, General Conference delegates and Conference principals).

The now thirteen agencies, created by and accountable to General Conference, include huge, powerful entities like the General Board of Global Ministries, successor to the MEC Missionary Society (1819), and small, recently established

---

[44] *The Nature of Oversight*, 3.1 , 3.2.
[45] *Discipline*/UMC 2008, 87, ¶ 120.
[46] *Discipline*/UMC 2008, 31, ¶ 33, a definition within the 'Constitution' section.

bodies like the General Commission on United Methodist Men.Connexional, by composition, constitution, definition and precept, the agencies until the last couple of decades were often seen as what connected Methodism and United Methodism, what held the church together, what did or facilitated its work, what shaped and enabled its mission. To think connexional was to think about the agencies.[47] In 1996, about the point when hostility towards agencies became most open and became focused on the General Council of Ministries, a scapegoat for the system, General Conference lodged in the *Discipline* a statement about agencies as expressions of connexionalism, perhaps ironically an epitaph:

> Connectionalism is an important part of our identity as United Methodists. . . . It provides us with wonderful opportunities to carry out our mission in unity and strength. We experience this connection in many ways, including our systems of episcopacy, itinerancy, property, and mutual cooperation and support. Our connectional system performs at least three essential tasks: embracing God's mission for the church as making disciples for Jesus Christ; organizing our whole Church to enable local congregations, the primary arena for mission, faithfully and fruitfully to make disciples for Jesus Christ; and ensuring that all components in the connection carry out their appropriate responsibilities in ways that enable the whole United Methodist Church to be faithful in its mission. . . . General agencies, in particular, are important to our common vision, mission, and ministry. They provide essential services and ministries beyond the scope of individual local congregations and annual conferences through services and ministries that are highly focused, flexible, and capable of rapid response.[48]

The antagonism towards general agencies, unhappily, is not the only force fraying connexional bonds. Culpability, indeed, belongs everywhere. The agencies compete with one another, duplicate services and vie for resources – despite the newly established Connexional Table. Annual Conferences act as though they were separate churches, behaviour reinforced by legislation permitting idiosyncratic (i.e. missional) rather than connexional template organisation.[49] Bishops, though playing connected roles with agencies and connected globally in the Council, function in their appointive responsibilities as diocesans. Caucuses give expression to distinctive, distinguishing and separating ethnic, gender, theological and social concern identities.

---

[47] *Discipline*/UMC 2008, 473–94, ¶¶ 701– 21. See R. Richey, D. M. Campbell and W. B. Lawrence, *Connectionalism: Ecclesiology, Mission and Identity*, United Methodism and American Culture, 1 (Nashville, TN: Abingdon, 1997); Richey, *Doctrine in Experience*; and Richey, *Methodist Connectionalism*.

[48] *Discipline*/UMC 1996, 397, ¶ 701; *Discipline*/UMC 2008, 473, ¶ 701. The ellipses represent spots in the 1996 text at which other descriptive material has been inserted.

[49] *Discipline*/UMC 2008, 380–82, ¶ 610.

Jurisdictions, the conferences charged with electing bishops, reinforce strong regional orientations. Culture war issues, particularly over homosexuality and abortion, create broad divisions across the church, uniting some Americans with compatriots in Europe, Africa or Asia. On other matters, U.S. members vie with United Methodists from elsewhere. And local churches, especially mega-churches, can operate as independently as Baptists if they have the numbers and money to pay off the system and pay their own way. Congregations, too, can now structure idiosyncratically.[50]

## Concluding Queries

Have Methodists, in the U.K. and in the UMC (U.S. at least) become more articulate about their connexionalism and their exercise of episkopé at points of stress, loss, confusion, conflict and/or desperation? Does the UMC accent the connexionalism of its corporate, centralised, apportionment-funded agency structure as church-wide criticism of and alienation from it increase? Do agencies themselves and correlative Conference boards affirm the importance of connexionalism to counteract the pervasive localism? Have Conference boards of ordained ministry and the General Board of Higher Education and Ministry to which they relate put higher and higher premium on Wesleyan theology, on itinerancy and on polity as commitment to these connective bonds erodes? Does the Council of Bishops ramp up its efforts to lead and enhance the *Discipline*'s understanding of episcopacy to take advantage of the power vacuum as agency influence wanes and United Methodist membership erosion continues?

Similarly, across the pond, what is one to make of the stronger and stronger statements about connexionalism and episkopé that the Conference makes? Do they represent healthy self-reflection as Methodism has entertained unity with the Church of England, claimed the authority of Conference and Circuit, and considered reception of the historic episcopate? Or does the resource investment (leadership and support) focused internally on Methodist self-understanding undercut mission and outreach as Methodism's numbers continue to fall and finances become more problematic?

---

[50] *Discipline*/UMC 2008, 157–8, ¶¶ 243–4.

# 16 Methodist Liturgy and Worship

Karen B. Westerfield Tucker

## Introduction

Because of the relative ease in collecting worship books and hymn books, and on account of the long-standing philological methodology used in liturgical studies, research on Methodist liturgy and worship until the mid-twentieth century tended to focus on printed texts: worship-related books and pamphlets produced by John Wesley and his brother Charles, authorised or official worship resources approved at the highest level by Methodist or Wesleyan denominations, and materials produced by a denomination's publishers but without the denominational imprimatur. Such an approach to research is limited in its ability to capture the actualities of Methodist worship since not only does it assume that worship is done 'by the book' but it also ignores matters such as ethos, performance and setting as well as the participation and response of the congregation (both as individuals and as corporate body) in the liturgical event. The application of social science methodologies and various performance theories to liturgical investigations from the 1980s onward has started to expand the range of research, as has the realisation (and recovery) that worship is an articulation of theological claims. Much work remains to be done in examining published and unpublished theological statements about worship written by Methodists in various locations and time periods, and in uncovering historic eyewitness accounts of Methodist worship recorded in the personal diaries and journals of Methodists and non-Methodists, depicted visually, circulated in denominational and other periodicals, and contained in manuscript documents of various types. Much research on present-day worship practices draws upon multiple methodologies, but given the complexity of such work, the majority of studies produced have focused in general on single congregations; much more synthetic works remains to be done.

By utilising the research already completed, it is possible to identify several trends related to corporate worship that hold true from Methodism's emergence in the eighteenth century as a movement – a 'society' – within the Church of England to its global presence in the twenty-first century as dozens of discrete Methodist/Wesleyan denominations:

1. The traditions of the church catholic inform and shape worship as do new worship styles, current circumstances, theological trends, and local customs and innovations.
2. Corporate worship may follow a structure authorised (usually not mandated) by a denomination's worship books, take up forms drawn from or inspired by other sources (including the liturgical materials or resources of other ecclesiastical traditions), and be derived from a community's or a pastor's preferences.
3. The worship style – and also the worship space – may be formal, informal or something in between. Rarely is corporate worship completely spontaneous from beginning to conclusion.
4. Heart-felt experience within worship is more highly valued than intellectual engagement with worship's purposes and the theological meanings of the words (print or not) that are used.
5. While corporate worship is to edify spiritually, it is also expected to propel worshippers into further and deeper engagement with discipleship and ministry.

These five trends are highlighted in the historical investigation below.

## Eighteenth-Century Foundations

The Methodist movement emerged during a renaissance in the theology and practices of Christian antiquity. While at Oxford John Wesley came to know well the efforts of William Whiston, Non-Jurors such as Thomas Deacon, and others to move Anglican worship more closely to what they perceived to be the 'original' Christian liturgies. The liturgical revisions taken up by Whiston (*The Liturgy of the Church of England, Reduc'd Nearer to the Primitive Standard* [1713]) and Deacon (*A Compleat Collection of Devotions* [1734]) relied on the supposedly 'primitive' components of the 1549 *Book of Common Prayer* and upon the oldest known church order, the *Apostolic Constitutions* and *Canons*. Wesley early in his ministry concurred with Whiston and Deacon that the *Constitutions* and *Canons* were genuinely apostolic, and so turned to those sources and others to promote practices among the fledgling Methodists that were considered 'purer' because of their antiquity, such as the Wednesday and Friday 'stationary' fasts.[1] Wesley's reading of the Non-Juror Robert Nelson's book, *Companion for the Festivals and Fasts of the Church of England* (1704), reinforced fasting as a scriptural and primitive practice, and so he

---

[1] Wesley had read William Cave's *Primitive Christianity*, which noted that fasts in antiquity were held weekly on Wednesdays (the day on which Christ was betrayed by Judas) and Fridays (the day of crucifixion), and that these fasts were called 'stations' because participants were to 'keep guard' until at least 3 p.m. See William Cave, *Primitive Christianity*, 3rd edn (London: Printed by J. G. for R. Chiswell, 1676), 179–80.

kept – and encouraged – the discipline (though not the 'stations') he identified as a means of grace for the remainder of his life.[2]

Wesley soon distanced himself from Whiston and his Unitarianism, and by 1738 he had rejected the apostolic authorship of the *Constitutions* and *Canons* and thus doubted the antiquity of certain practices.[3] But he remained committed to imitating the worship of the early Christians as recorded in scripture and in bona fide ancient texts, a position that accorded him some affinity with the puritan wing of the Church of England, though unlike the puritans he did not expect scripture to provide the blueprint for worship. In consideration of the scriptural and apostolic injunctions to offer God 'hymns, psalms and spiritual songs' (cf. Ephesians 5:18–20; Colossians 3:16–17), Wesley's worship for the Methodists expanded upon the authorised sung repertoire of the Anglican liturgy – the Psalms – with the singing of recently and newly composed hymns on numerous theological themes. Under Wesley's direction, Methodists engaged in love feasts (inspired by the primitive *agape* and Moravian practices; cf. Acts 2:46–7) and watch nights (the ancient vigils, which were allowed by the 1662 *Book of Common Prayer* but infrequently used, and which were also used by the Moravians), and at least annually renewed their covenantal promises to God (based on biblical precedent and borrowed from the puritan Richard Alleine's *Vindiciae Pietatis* [1663]). In addition to hymn singing, each of these special Methodist observances shared in common with other occasions of Methodist corporate worship the core components of prayer, the reading of scripture, preaching and exhortation found in Christian worship from the earliest times (cf. Justin Martyr's *First Apology*, chapter 67). Only for the renewal of the covenant did Wesley provide a printed ritual text;[4] the unscripted Methodist 'preaching services,' love feasts and watch nights developed customary patterns and orders while still allowing for Spirit-inspired flexibility. Prayers could come from print sources (most notably the Prayer Book), but more often were extemporary and even spontaneous.

As did their ancient exemplars, Methodists congregated for worship on days in addition to the Lord's day, and in any space indoors or out that could accommodate their numbers. As the Methodist movement spread, 'plain and decent' preaching houses were constructed according to Wesley's specifications; fourteen of them were in octagonal design, a configuration possibly chosen on account of the early

---

[2] Wesley met with both Whiston and Deacon to discuss the historic stational fasts, and Deacon included in the 'Appendix' of his *Compleat Collection* an excerpt of Wesley's 'Essay upon the Stationary Fasts'. See John Wesley's manuscript diary for February and December 1734 (copy in the possession of Richard P. Heitzenrater); Thomas Deacon, *A Compleat Collection of Devotions* (London: Printed for the Author, 1734), 72–4; and William Whiston, *Memoirs of the Life and Writings of Mr. William Whiston*, 2nd edn, corr. (London: Printed for J. Whiston and B. White, 1753), 121.

[3] See John Wesley's journal entries for 20 September 1736 and 24 January 1738 in W. Reginald Ward and Richard P. Heitzenrater (eds), *The Works of John Wesley*, vol. 18 (Nashville,TN: Abingdon Press, 1988), 171–2; 212 n.95.

[4] *Directions for Renewing Our Covenant with God* (London: Printed by J. Paramore, 1780).

church's association of the number eight with new life or new creation.[5] Worship occurred in small groups – including families and households – and in large assemblies drawn by the prospect of an inspiring preacher or the celebration of the Lord's Supper. Wesley advised the Methodists to attend the sacrament as frequently as possible,[6] using as justification scripture (cf. Matthew 6:11; Acts 2:46) and primitive custom (according to Wesley's interpretation) as well as the Prayer Book's rubric permitting a weekly observance at cathedral and collegiate churches. The Lord's Supper was for Wesley principal among the means of grace instituted by Christ and, though a 'great mystery,' was a true communion with the real presence of the risen Christ and with Christian sisters and brothers on earth and in heaven.[7] Methodists satisfied their spiritual hunger by receiving the sacrament in the parish church and at other places where an Anglican clergyman would be presiding – including the bedside of a person sick or dying as permitted by canon law.

Wesley's designs for corporate worship were not limited to borrowing from the Christian traditions of the first three centuries, for though scripture was the supreme standard and norm, and Christian antiquity carried significant authority, the traditions of the Church of England were to be accorded a special place. Wesley considered the Anglican liturgy to be scripturally sound and the best extant representative of apostolic practice by a national church. His esteem for Prayer Book and Church was evident by his insistence that the Methodists hold their worship at a time other than 'church hours' (frequently 5 a.m.) so that (ideally) they could attend services in the parish church. Even so, Wesley was not without criticism of both the performance of the Church's worship and its liturgical texts. Worship in some parish churches seemed captivated by form and formality, indifference and inattentiveness (and thus 'coldness'); it appeared not to be done 'in spirit and truth' (cf. John 4:23–4), and so lacked the necessary 'power of godliness'. The problem resided not with the liturgical texts themselves, but with this erroneous orientation or focus.[8] By cultivating the 'warm' religion of the heart, the Methodists believed that their worship provided an exemplary remedy for and supplement to the Church's worship. On the matter of the liturgical texts, Wesley took issue with certain rites (e.g., confirmation) and ritual components (e.g., the answers of the

---

[5] Karen B. Westerfield Tucker, '"Plain and Decent": Octagonal Space and Methodist Worship', *Studia Liturgica*, 24 (1994), 129–44.

[6] John Wesley, 'The Duty of Constant Communion', in Albert C. Outler (ed.), *The Works of John Wesley*, vol. 3 (Nashville, TN: Abingdon Press, 1986), 428–39.

[7] From the *Hymns on the Lord's Supper*, see in particular hymns 28, 66, 81 (possibly inspired by *Apostolic Constitutions* VIII.12.35), 116, 165; cf. hymn 166. John Wesley and Charles Wesley, *Hymns on the Lord's Supper* (Bristol: Printed by Felix Farley, 1745; repr. edn Madison, NJ: The Charles Wesley Society, 1995).

[8] Cf. Charles Wesley's Sermon on Romans 3:23–5, in Kenneth G. C. Newport (ed.), *The Sermons of Charles Wesley* (Oxford: Oxford University Press, 2001), 192; and John Wesley's Letter 'To a Friend' (20 September 1757), in John Telford (ed.),*The Letters of the Rev. John Wesley, A.M.*, vol. 3 (London: Epworth Press, 1931), 226–8.

baptismal sponsors).⁹ He was not opposed to altering the performance of the set liturgies and added, for example, extemporary prayer and the singing of hymns.¹⁰ Although disinclined to overhaul the Prayer Book as Whiston, Deacon and numerous other eighteenth-century redactors had done,¹¹ Wesley was nonetheless willing to make adjustments. A diary entry for 5 March 1736 notes cryptically that he 'Revised Prayerbook', an action that foreshadowed the abridgement he made in 1784 of the 1662 Prayer Book under the title *The Sunday Service of the Methodists in North America, with other Occasional Services.*

Despite Wesley's insistence that the Methodists would never separate from the Church of England, the situation in the newly created United States altered Wesley's plan. A liturgical connection to the Church was maintained, however, by the *Sunday Service*, which arrived on American shores shortly before the founding of the Methodist Episcopal Church at the 1784 'Christmas' Conference. Wesley's revision of the Prayer Book was done principally by deletion; only a few items were added (e.g., a rubric for extemporary prayer at the conclusion of the communion liturgy) and some substitutions were made for selected words (e.g., 'priest' became 'minister'). In general, the material omitted was peculiar to a national church; was judged incompatible with the North American setting; assumed a settled congregation with a building and a choir; was intended for private or daily use; appeared to serve no present need (e.g., confirmation, saints' days, and certain days and seasons of the church year); and was considered inappropriate according to the witness of scripture and the early church. Some of the deletions corresponded with historic puritan objections to the Prayer Book, but whether or not Wesley intentionally took a 'puritan' direction is not entirely clear. Regardless, a leaner book – and more a service book than a prayer book – was the result, but it was a book that showed an unmistakable indebtedness to its original source. Thus Wesley passed on to the Methodist people an abbreviated lectionary, a set of collects, the Litany (for use on Wednesdays and Fridays) and an edited psalter ('Select Psalms') that excluded psalms and verses deemed by Wesley to be unsuitable for Christian mouths. Revised services included morning and evening prayer (intended for Sunday corporate use), the baptism of infants and adults (with the language of baptismal regeneration softened or removed), the Lord's Supper (the most conservative revision), the communion of the sick, matrimony (minus the giving of the bride and wedding rings), burial of the dead (lacking the committal), and the ordination of deacons, 'elders' and 'superintendants' (*sic*). *A Collection of Psalms and Hymns for the Lord's Day* (a revision of the 1741 *Collection of Psalms and Hymns*) was

---

⁹ 'Ought we to Separate from the Church of England', in Rupert E. Davies (ed.), *The Works of John Wesley*, vol. 9 (Nashville, TN: Abingdon Press, 1989), (III).8, 571–2. Wesley's attitude towards baptismal sponsors and confirmation was similar to that expressed by puritans dissatisfied with the Prayer Book from the sixteenth century onward.

¹⁰ See, for example, John Wesley, 'The Principles of a Methodist Farther Explained', 3.3–4, ibid., 187–8.

¹¹ See A. Elliott Peaston, *The Prayer Book Reform Movement in the XVIIIth Century* (Oxford: Blackwell, 1940).

sent to be bound in with the *Sunday Service*, so it is surprising that Wesley did not add rubrics into the liturgical texts to indicate the singing of congregational hymns.

New printings of the *Sunday Service* for the Methodists in the United States (no longer 'North America') were sent from England in 1786, 1788 and 1790, each with a few changes. Although Wesley to his death insisted that the British Methodists should not separate from the Established Church, versions of the *Sunday Service* for use in Britain and 'His Majesty's Dominions' were published in 1786, 1788 and 1792, and were largely similar to the editions used in the United States, the one exception being the retention of the royal and national references that had been expunged from the U.S. versions.[12] The history of the *Sunday Service* after Wesley's death in 1791 differs for the United States and for Britain (and its territories) as the result of political, cultural, theological and ecclesiastical factors, but for Methodists in each location the book would play a key role in later liturgical developments.

The trends that can be identified for more than two centuries of Methodist corporate worship are clearly grounded in the practices and theological understandings laid out by Wesley and the earliest Methodists. The liturgical traditions of the church of the first three centuries and the traditions of the Church of England were presented as equally vital and appropriate. In a letter dated 10 September 1784, Wesley informed the North American Methodists that he had 'prepared a liturgy little different from that of the church of England'; yet he also indicated that they were to 'follow the scriptures and the primitive church' and in accordance with that plan advised 'the elders to administer the supper of the Lord on every Lord's day'.[13] Methodist worship thus was to be both formulaic and free, formal and informal, attentive to specific traditions of the church while simultaneously speaking the language of the times and of the particular worshipping community. While Wesley managed to keep together these poles of tension, doing so would prove to be difficult for Methodists of later generations.

# Developments in the Late Eighteenth and Nineteenth Centuries

### Reception of the double inheritance: forms and freedom from forms

In 1810, Methodist leader and clergyman Jesse Lee recalled the reception of Wesley's *Sunday Service* by the Methodists in the United States:

---

[12] Inexplicably, a few royal references crept back into morning and evening prayer and the communion liturgy in the 1790 edition designated for the United States.

[13] Letter to 'Our Brethren in America' (10 September 1784), Telford, *Letters*, vol. 7, 238–9.

> At this time [1784] the prayer book, as revised by Mr Wesley, was introduced among us; and in the large towns, and in some country places, our preachers read prayers on the Lord's day: and in some cases the preachers read part of the morning service on Wednesdays and Fridays. But some of the preachers who had been long accustomed to pray extempore were unwilling to adopt this new plan. Being fully satisfied that they could pray better, and with more devotion, while their eyes were shut than they could with their eyes open. After a few years the prayer book was laid aside, and has never been used since in public worship.
>
> The Superintendents, and some of the Elders, introduced the custom of wearing gowns and bands, but it was opposed by many of the preachers, as well as private members, who looked upon it as needless and *superfluous*. Having made a stand against it, after a few years it was given up, and has never been introduced among us since.[14]

Lee's recollection reveals two unexpected practices: certain 'preachers' (in this case the ordained clergy) read parts of the liturgy for Morning Prayer on weekdays (which had not been Wesley's direction) and wore 'gowns and bands'. More expected is the witness that Wesley's *Sunday Service* – at least as it pertained to Sunday mornings – did not take hold, likely on account of both the general anti-English political climate and the fact that worship for many American Methodists had never included a prayer book or any set forms. By action of the General Conference in 1792, the Lord's day-related materials from the *Sunday Service* were supplanted by a series of instructions in the section 'Of Public Worship' in the *Doctrines and Discipline of the Methodist Episcopal Church* that codified the common and long-standing worship practice: Sunday morning, afternoon and evening services consisting of singing, prayer and preaching, with scripture reading designated for the first two services of the day. The observance of the Lord's Supper each Lord's day that Wesley advised may have been possible for the elder presiding at the table, but it was less likely for others, though conscientious residents of some larger cities may have been able to receive weekly by attending the service at the Methodist community assigned to hold the communion that Sunday of the month.[15] Outside of the urban areas, the quarterly meeting ensured that most Methodists could receive at least four times yearly.[16]

Lee's comment that the prayer book was 'laid aside' was not entirely accurate, for the 1792 General Conference approved revisions of Wesley's rites for baptism,

---

[14] Jesse Lee, *A Short History of the Methodists, in the United States of America; Beginning in 1776, and Continued till 1809* (Baltimore, MD: Magill and Clime, 1810), 107.

[15] Karen B. Westerfield Tucker, *American Methodist Worship* (New York, NY: Oxford University Press, 2001), 148.

[16] Lester Ruth, *A Little Heaven Below: Worship at Early Methodist Quarterly Meetings* (Nashville, TN: Kingswood Books, 2000), 103–55.

Holy Communion, marriage, burial and ordination that were then included within a section of 'Sacramental Services, &c.' in the 1792 *Discipline*. These survivors from the *Sunday Service* would, over the course of the nineteenth century, be subjected officially to further revisions by the Methodist Episcopal Church and also by the other Methodist/Wesleyan denominations that soon emerged and drew initially upon the Methodist Episcopal Church's liturgical texts. Most of the denominations had some type of formulation for these occasional services (ranging from the texts inherited from the Methodist Episcopal Church to little more than expanded rubrics), which were placed in the respective *Discipline* or other-named book of polity.[17] The liturgical heritage of the *Sunday Service* often remained clear in the printed texts, even when a freer style of prayer was adopted or when quotes and paraphrases from scripture and snippets of liturgical texts from other sources were added and interwoven. The second of four paragraphs constituting the Methodist Protestant Church's communion prayer authorised in 1830 exemplifies such textual cobbling in its inclusion of portions of the Prayer of Humble Access, the General Confession from Morning and Evening Prayer (that had been deleted in 1792!), and Psalm 51:12:

> We are not worthy, O Lord, to gather up the crumbs from under thy table, for we have sinned and come short of thy glory; we have erred and strayed from thy ways like lost sheep; we have left undone those things which we ought to have done; and we have done those things which we ought not to have done. Have mercy on us, O God, our heavenly Father, forgive our sins, and restore unto us the joy of thy salvation, through Jesus Christ who hath redeemed us by his own most precious blood.[18]

Methodists in the congregation may never have heard these authorised texts, given the propensity of some clergy to 'neglect' or 'mutilate' them.[19] Debates within the Methodist Episcopal Church in the first decades of the 1800s on the uniform use of the authorised liturgical texts across the denomination led to legislation in 1824 insisting that the 'form of discipline invariably be used' for services of baptism, the Lord's supper and burial.[20] Though the regulation persisted in the Methodist

---

[17] Studies of these revisions include, for example: Charles R. Hohenstein, 'The Revision of the Rites of Baptism in the Methodist Episcopal Church, 1784–1939' (Ph.D. diss., University of Notre Dame, 1990); Gayle Carlton Felton, *This Gift of Water: The Practice and Theology of Baptism among Methodists in America* (Nashville, TN: Abingdon Press, 1992); and Karen B. Westerfield Tucker, '"Till Death Us Do Part": The Rites of Marriage and Burial Prepared by John Wesley and Their Development in the Methodist Episcopal Church, 1784–1939' (Ph.D. diss., University of Notre Dame, 1992).

[18] Methodist Protestant Church, *Constitution and Discipline of the Methodist Protestant Church* (Baltimore, MD: J. J. Harrod, 1830), 77.

[19] *Journals of the General Conference of the Methodist Episcopal Church, 1796–1836* (New York, NY: Carlton and Phillips, 1855), 298.

[20] *The Doctrines and Discipline of the Methodist Episcopal Church* (New York, NY: N. Bangs and J. Emory, 1824), 72.

Episcopal *Discipline* until 1904, the clear evidence is that it was largely ignored.[21] The predominant practice throughout the century and across the different American Methodist denominations seems to have been to intermingle parts of the authorised liturgy with pastoral innovation, though in the case of the Lord's Supper, the Words of Institution tended to be used consistently.

For Methodists in the United States, the double inheritance was clear – the printed texts of Wesley's *Sunday Service* and its liturgical derivatives that stood in contrast with locally designed services of extemporary prayer where the use of printed texts was limited to the Bible and the hymn books that might be available. For Methodists in Britain and 'His Majesty's Dominions' (e.g., Newfoundland, Nova Scotia and the [British] West Indies), the preaching service that took a shape similar to the one practised by their American kindred represented the informal and free approach also appreciated by other evangelical Protestant groups:

> The service commences with singing, in which the greatest part of the congregation joins. The preacher next makes an extempore prayer, and after a few more verses of a hymn have been sung, the sermon follows, which is likewise delivered extempore. The people now join in another hymn, and the whole is concluded with a prayer and blessing from the minister. This, tho' a very plain and simple, is nevertheless a solemn and edifying manner of celebrating Divine Worship.[22]

But regarding texted liturgies, there were two choices to be had, both endorsed by Wesley himself: the *Sunday Service* and the 1662 *Book of Common Prayer*.[23] As in America, the *Sunday Service* appears to have had a limited reception by those inclined to use liturgical texts, though in Britain this was largely because Wesley's publication was judged inferior to the liturgically and culturally familiar Prayer Book.

For some Methodists, Sunday morning worship drew heavily upon the Prayer Book's Morning Prayer and perhaps its ante-communion (the first and non-eucharistic part of the Lord's Supper rite), while gatherings on Sunday afternoons and evenings and on other days engaged the more informal style. Internal disputes regarding liturgical resources and worship times appropriate for Sunday morning in the years after Wesley's death found some resolution in the 'Articles of

---

[21] See, for example, Freeborn Garrettson, *Substance of the Semi-Centennial Sermon, Before the New-York Annual Conference, at Its Session, May, 1826* (New York, NY: N. Bangs and J. Emory, for the Methodist Episcopal Church, 1827), 26.

[22] [Disney Alexander], *Reasons for Methodism; Briefly Stated: In Three Letters to a Friend* (London: Printed for G. Whitfield, 1799), 40 (from the section 'On the mode of performing Divine Service among the Methodists' in the third letter). The text appears to have been first published in 1793.

[23] Cf. *Minutes of the Methodist Conferences, from the First, Held in London, by the Late Rev. John Wesley, A.M. in the Year 1744*, vol. 1 (London: Printed in the Conference Office by Thomas Cordeux, 1812), 191 (*Minutes* for 1786) and 208 (*Minutes* for 1788); and Samuel Bradburn, *The Question, 'Are the Methodists Dissenters?' Fairly Examined: Designed to Remove Prejudice, Prevent Bigotry, and Promote Brotherly Love* ([Liverpool]: n.p., 1792), 13–14.

Agreement for General Pacification' of 1795, which stated that for services held in England during church hours, 'the officiating preacher shall read either the service of the Established Church, our venerable father's abridgement, or at least, the lessons appointed by the calendar'.[24] The 'Articles' also addressed long-standing concerns about Methodist administration of the Lord's Supper, and resolved that the Conference approve places, times and administrators for the sacrament, clearly stipulating that the sacramental occasion was for society members only; the same conditions applied to baptism. Methodist services of Holy Communion were to take place on Sundays when it was not available in the parish church and, at least in England, were to be done according to the Prayer Book's liturgy, with allowances made for the addition of hymns, extemporary prayer and exhortation.[25] Conference *Minutes* after 1795 indicate that reinforcing the rules on the books was as difficult in Britain as it was in the United States.

For legal and ecclesiastical reasons, Wesley's *Sunday Service* rites of matrimony and burial of the dead saw little to no use in England. Lord Hardwicke's Marriage Act (1753) required that all marriages be solemnised within the Church of England; thus only after the law was altered in 1836 could the *Sunday Service* liturgy possibly have been done for a Methodist couple. Interment in the Church of England's consecrated ground was contingent upon the use of the burial office read by a priest, and although the Methodists established their own limited number of burial grounds where the graveside portion of Wesley's abridgement would have been permissible, Methodists were regularly laid to rest in the Church's cemeteries; only in 1880 did the Burial Act permit other Christian rites within the churchyards. Wesley had allowed his (unordained) preachers to lead Methodist funerals and bury the dead, both of which were to be characterised by simplicity and decorum (certainly not the latest cultural fashions for obsequies), and by the singing of hymns, the reading of scripture, the offering of prayer and fervent preaching. Funerals, like other Methodist gatherings, were occasions for evangelism.

Although the *Sunday Service* was little used for Sunday and other occasions, it survived in a series of revisions in the branch of British Methodism known as the Wesleyan Methodist Connexion from 1816 (the next version after 1792) until 1910. Although the title *The Sunday Service of the Methodists* remained the same, the number of rites included in the book and the textual formulations within individual rites could vary from year to year. As with Wesley's original publications, the evidence suggests that the nineteenth-century versions of the *Sunday Service* did not enjoy wide appeal.

In Britain, as in the United States, numerous Methodist/Wesleyan denominations emerged throughout the late-eighteenth and nineteenth century as the result of ruptures over issues such as authority, polity, theology, economics, race and faithfulness to Wesley's original intentions – this latter including practices of worship. Some Methodists on both sides of the Atlantic read Methodist worship history through the lens of the informal and evangelistic preaching service, and

---

[24] William Peirce, *The Ecclesiastical Principles and Polity of the Wesleyan Methodists*, 3rd edn, revised by Frederick J. Jobson (London: Wesleyan Conference Office, 1873), 768.

[25] Ibid., 767–8.

regarded formal ritual expressions not only to be Spirit-quenching and scripturally unfounded, but also to be alien to an authentic Wesleyanism. From their perspective, simple worship for simple people – with preaching as its core – was what Wesley had used to correct – and replace – rigid, formulaic, lifeless and 'liturgical' worship. Holiness and revival-focused Methodist denominations typically took this line, even though they did not entirely abandon print forms (usually retaining at least some text for the sacraments). They saw their separation as an opportunity to create a true Methodism purged of liturgical and worldly accoutrements that they believed stifled the power of godliness and heart-felt emotion. This position was also held by persons within denominations that authorised formal, printed liturgical texts, thereby creating lively intra-denominational discussions and debates on worship-related topics.

## A New Look at Forms

As the nineteenth century progressed, Methodists in Britain and America – and in areas to which Methodism was intentionally (by missionary activity) and unintentionally (by immigration) transplanted – typically worshipped on Sundays and on other occasions in the manner of the previous generation. For the majority of Methodists – no matter the location or denomination – Sunday morning worship continued to consist only of the core ingredients of singing, prayer, scripture reading and preaching. Methodist Episcopal preacher Leonard Smith noted in a diary entry the details of worship for his Sunday congregations in Illinois which seems to corroborate the persistence of these core components alone even into the 1860s:

> I arose about 5 ½ a.m. & paid my morning sacrifice to God. At the ringing of the second bell I repaired to the house of prayer to talk to the people on the Exercise of Godliness. I opened the exercise by singing the 297 Hymn to the tune Umbridge after which I prayed. Then I read the morning lesson in the 4$^{th}$ Ephes. Then sang again the 570 Hymn to Boylston. Took my text from 1 Tim 4:7. Closed by singing & prayer. At 2 ½ p.m. I met a few at our Chapel at Pipers Corners. Talked from the same text as I did in the a.m. Class meeting immediately after.[26]

But increasingly after the century's midpoint, new additions began to fill out the familiar core, eventually even in the practices of those Methodists who had been staunchly resistant to liturgical forms. The fact that several of these 'innovations' could be justified by scripture certainly aided their adoption. For example, the so-called apostolic benediction (2 Corinthians 13:14), freely composed pastoral blessings and

---

[26] Leonard Smith, 12 February 1860, Journal, Typescript, Archives, Illinois Great Rivers Annual Conference, United Methodist Church, Springfield, Illinois.

free-standing, single-stanza doxologies (often placed just prior to the benediction) were among the first to make an appearance; doxologies of different meters could be found in authorised Methodist hymnals by the 1820s, and numbered among them early on was Thomas Ken's text 'Praise God, from whom all blessings flow', written in 1695 as a final stanza for several hymns. Also making an appearance in the Sunday worship of some of the denominations, particularly toward the century's end: the saying of the Lord's Prayer, the Decalogue (which had been part of Wesley's ante-communion)and/ or the Apostles' Creed (from Wesley's Morning Prayer); the collection of monetary offerings; the speaking or chanting of the Psalms or other texts; responsive readings of scripture; and, where permitted by a denomination's rules, anthems from a church choir and voluntaries from the organ. The growing acceptance of these components is indicated by their appearance at different occasions for worship, including camp meetings (an event not endorsed by all Methodist denominations), revivals (indoor and outdoor), and the quarterly meeting's highly organised sequence of preaching services, love feast and Lord's Supper.

Not only did some of these new components appear in local practice, but they also began to be included in formal printed orders of worship found in a denomination's book of polity and/or in the denominational hymnal. In 1900, the African Methodist Episcopal Church supplied directions for practice with their order that had expanded significantly beyond its original, simple core:

> Voluntary by choir
> Scripture Sentences: 'I was glad' etc.
> Singing a hymn from our hymnal, after its announcement by the officiating minister
> Prayer, minister and congregation kneeling
> Voluntary by choir
> Scripture lesson, minister and people reading alternately
> Scripture lesson by minister
> Singing
> Reading of the Decalogue; minister leading, the people responding
> Singing
> Announcements
> Preaching or Exhortation
> The Lord's Prayer or an extempore prayer, the minister and congregation kneeling
> Collecting Offerings
> Doxology and Benediction.[27]

At the same time, Lord's Supper liturgies and the occasional services sometimes underwent substantial revisions that reflected internal theological shifts or external influences from other Christian denominations and from the broader society. For

---

[27] *The Doctrines and Discipline of the African Methodist Episcopal Church* (Philadelphia, PA: A.M.E. Book Concern, 1900), 51–2.

example, the Primitive Methodists' 1860 order for the administration of the Lord's Supper consisted of an extended scriptural warrant citing the Matthean, Lukan and Pauline narratives of institution; extemporary prayer or, alternatively, a long instructive prayer written in the free style (e.g., 'O that the great things represented to us at this ordinance, may deeply affect our hearts'); the distribution of communion with suitable accompanying words; and suggested concluding elements of song, monetary collection, exhortation, prayer and benediction.[28] Forty years later, their order of service had stronger associations not only with the Prayer Book, but also with the communion liturgy in use by the Wesleyan Conference.[29]

Various factors fanned these flames for liturgical revision in the late nineteenth century. With multiple copies of the *Sunday Service* in circulation that contained different contents, it was necessary for the Wesleyan Methodists in Britain to consolidate the materials, which they did in the *Book of Public Prayer and Services* (1882). There were also external pressures that drove this work, namely fears among some that Anglicanism might be moving in a more Roman Catholic direction, which pushed the revisers to produce a book that was recognisably evangelical and Protestant. The prospect of a Methodist union may also have encouraged some of the smaller denominations to move toward the practices and textual forms of the larger. In the United States, Methodism was no longer perceived as the denomination of the poor but rather of the rising middle class, and it had become a major player in national affairs. Many of the denominations, and especially the Methodist Episcopal Church and the Methodist Episcopal Church, South, saw the increasing formalisation of the liturgy as a type of coming of age: just as they had traded 'plain and decent' log preaching houses and brush arbours for houses of worship that embodied architectural and aesthetic elegance, and the clergy had been lifted up from the self-taught to the seminary educated, so too worship practices should signal a movement away from humble beginnings to the more sophisticated. In some cases this meant looking back to the form that Wesley had bequeathed. The Methodist Episcopal Church, South, in 1867, produced *The Sunday Service of the Methodist Episcopal Church, South*, which combined their current ritual material with portions of the Lord's day texts from Wesley's *Sunday Service* of 1786; and in 1880 the African Methodist Episcopal Church approved the optional use of 'Wesley's Prayer Book'.

Not all Methodists were enamoured of the increasing formality in worship. Some asked if it was truly a sign of progress to abandon Spirit-aided prayer in favour of 'dry' read prayers. Some expressed concern that the movement in the direction of more liturgical texts and formality in worship was accelerating the decline in the frequency of love feasts and camp meetings, and stifling worship at the family altar – in other words, cooling the heart-warming worship with which early Methodism had been identified. Essays appeared in the Methodist Episcopal

---

[28] *Forms for the Administration of Baptism . . . for the Use of Such Primitive Methodist Ministers as May Require Them* (London: Richard Davies, 1860), 33–9.

[29] *Order of Administration of Baptism and Other Services for the Use of the Primitive Methodists* (London: Joseph Toulson, n.d.), 35–9.

Church's *Methodist Review* with such titles as 'Ritualistic Tendencies of Our Time', 'More Liturgy or More Life' and, referring to Wesley's *Sunday Service*, 'Is It a Good or a Bad Inheritance'?[30] But the movement toward more liturgical complexity would continue into the next century in a majority of Methodist denominations worldwide even as cautious voices persisted.

While many Methodist denominations were engaging in liturgical reform they were also actively seeking the reform of the nations via missionary activity. Missionaries introduced the practices of worship that they knew and used, and brought with them their conscious and subconscious (and culturally informed) values for Christian worship. Little attention was given to matters of inculturation in the late nineteenth century except for linguistic adjustments, so the worship practices taken up in the new lands were typically translations of imported liturgical texts and hymns or adaptations of the preaching service in the free style. Those who received the missionaries' 'gift' of worship practices and texts sometimes accorded them special status and were hesitant to alter them, thus effectively freezing them in time: when the liturgical texts and practices in the denominations of the missionaries were revised, the recipients of the mission kept their liturgical inheritance intact, though after a delay of time they might begin their own process of revision, sometimes influenced by the changes undertaken within the 'mother' denomination. In some places, inculturated revisions, the production of new materials attentive to local cultural expressions, and the inclusion of local musical instruments previously deemed 'unchristian' – and hence unsuitable for worship – only started to occur in the late twentieth century, as was the case for Methodists in Singapore, Malaysia, Korea, Kenya, Zimbabwe and South Africa. Methodist worship leaders in Zimbabwe, for example, began to dance their opening procession while singing Christian texts to traditional folk tunes; and before the first prayer, the congregation sang a *kuhuhudza* – an invocation or 'call' to God reminiscent of the communicative cry used by the Shona people while herding livestock.[31]

## Liturgical Diversity in the Twentieth Century

As had their spiritual ancestors in the eighteenth and nineteenth centuries, Methodists throughout the world in the twentieth century desired to participate in distinctive – and unscripted – 'Methodist' forms of worship deemed appropriate by

---

[30] 'Ritualistic Tendencies of Our Time', *Methodist Review*, 81 (May 1899), 467–8; Charles M. Giffin, 'More Liturgy or More Life', *Methodist Review*, 84 (January 1902), 71–9; and Daniel A. Goodsell, 'Is It a Good or a Bad Inheritance?', *Methodist Review*, 85 (March 1903), 177–92.

[31] Paul W. Chilcote, with Katheru Gichaara and Patrick Matsikenyiri, 'A Singing and Dancing Church: Methodist Worship in Kenya and Zimbabwe', in Karen B. Westerfield Tucker (ed.), *The Sunday Service of the Methodists: Twentieth-Century Worship in Worldwide Methodism* (Nashville, TN: Kingswood Books, 1996), 239–40. See other essays in this collection for additional accounts of liturgical reception and revision.

their affinities with scriptural and early Christian praxis and by their ability to assist in the conversion of the hardest heart. Yet the dawn of the twentieth century brought with it for some Methodists a greater openness to receiving and appropriating social influences and the worship texts and traditions of other Christian denominations. Several movements during the century – for example, ecumenical, liturgical and charismatic – impacted the theology of worship and the development of liturgical practices in each denomination, but to greater or lesser degrees.

## Ecumenical Interests and Influences

Inter-Methodist conversations both national and international begun in the late nineteenth century only improved as communication technologies advanced in the twentieth. Increased fraternity between denominations frequently led to the borrowing or sharing of liturgical resources, especially hymn and prayer texts. In several instances, rifts were healed between Methodist denominations that then united to form a new denomination. With such mergers came the question of what patterns of worship should be used: the resources of the largest denomination? A conflation of the worship patterns favoured by the participants in the merger? Something new, drawing upon common historic precedents and/or other material? With the creation of worship books for the Methodist Church of Great Britain (1932) and the Methodist Church (1939) in the United States, all three approaches were taken. The *Book of Offices* (1936) of the British church incorporated recognisable versions of older texts for the sacramental and occasional rites (many taken from the Wesleyans' 1882 book), but also provided forms for practices (e.g., the dedication of church school teachers) already improvised in local congregations. Some of the resources incorporated were borrowed from other Christians – the Church of England's 1928 proposed *Book of Common Prayer* to satisfy Methodists inclined toward that style and for others printed prayers from the *Free Church Book of Common Prayer*[32] – which, according to the editors, served to unite their church with the 'universal Church of Christ, dispersed throughout all ages and all lands'.[33]

Ecumenical engagement across denominations meant that Methodists in many parts of the world became more willing to accept the liturgical practices of other Christian groups and even adopt them. For example, thanks to the resources made available by national and international councils of churches, Methodists once wary of the church year – which had been preserved in part by the topical headings in certain hymn books – began to introduce prayers and actions that referenced liturgical days and seasons into their regular worship. Methodists discovered – and used – a lectionary to aid with the design of worship and preaching. With the production of *Baptism, Eucharist and Ministry* (1982) by the Commission on Faith

---

[32] *A Free Church Book of Common Prayer* (London and Toronto: J. M. Dent, 1929).
[33] *The Book of Offices, being the Orders of Service authorized for Use in the Methodist Church, together with The Order for Morning Prayer* (London: Methodist Publishing House, 1936), 7.

and Order of the World Council of Churches, Methodist denominations took the opportunity to assess their practices and theologies in light of that ecumenical convergence document.[34] Worship resources produced by the intentionally ecumenical communities of Taizé (France), Iona (Scotland) and Bose (Italy) found a place in many Methodist congregations outside of Europe.

Inter-Christian cooperation also provoked some Methodist denominations to take to heart Jesus' prayer that his followers might be one (John 17:22), with the result that they joined with other Christian bodies to form a united church. The Church of South India, created in 1947 from a union of Anglicans, Methodists and Reformed, wove together several liturgical threads – including the liturgical traditions of the founding denominations, patristic practices and textures from the Indian context – into a single strand in order to create new liturgies, which were heralded as models for liturgical renewal within Methodism and across the churches.[35]

## The Liturgical Movement

Dovetailing with the ecumenical movement was the liturgical movement, which originated in European monastic communities in the nineteenth century and, as it developed, was characterised by a two-pronged approach: recovery of patristic (and early medieval) theologies and practices (*ressourcement*) in response to the predominating rationalism of the time; and updating in light of the signs of the time (*aggiornamento*). Essays related to worship produced by representative Methodists in Europe, the United States and Australia show that at least by the early twentieth century there was some awareness of the movement which would significantly impact the proceedings of the Second Vatican Council. In response to this renewal, coupled with a growing interest in the recovery of a Wesleyan sacramental piety, certain Methodist communities undertook to encourage informed and frequent sacramental practices. For some denominations, this meant beginning in the 1970s the adoption of Sunday services of 'word and table' or 'word and sacrament' (cf. Luke 24:27–35) that presupposed the normativity of a Lord's day 'eucharist' even when bread and wine were not shared. The table liturgy was frequently structured to correspond with the fourfold 'shape' that the Anglican Benedictine Gregory Dix observed to be present in the New Testament narratives describing Christ's actions

---

[34] See Geoffrey Wainwright, 'Methodism through the Lens of Lima', in Tucker (ed.), *The Sunday Service of the Methodists*, 305–22.

[35] See Eric J. Lott, 'Historic Tradition, Local Culture: Tensions and Fusions in the Liturgy of the Church of South India', in Tucker (ed.), *The Sunday Service of the Methodists*, 53–66; and Samson Prabhakar, 'The Church of South India', in Geoffrey Wainwright and Karen B. Westerfield Tucker (eds), *The Oxford History of Christian Worship* (New York, NY: Oxford University Press, 2006), 534–40.

around the bread and cup;[36] headings in the *United Methodist Book of Worship* (1992) stated them as 'taking the bread and cup', 'the Great Thanksgiving', 'breaking the bread' and 'giving the bread and cup'.[37] Great Thanksgivings or eucharistic prayers often imitated the three-part, trinitarian structure of the ancient West Syrian anaphora that also served as a model for other Christian communities engaged in their own processes of revision and renewal. The language of these prayers sometimes reflected the geographic and cultural locations of the praying communities. Such inculturation is found in a prayer of the Uniting Church in Australia (a union of Methodist, Congregationalist and Presbyterian churches in 1977) which alludes to the aboriginal concept of 'dreamtime' with the words 'In time beyond our dreaming, you brought forth life out of darkness'.[38] Even when prayers were provided in books of worship, the historic Methodist preference for extemporisation was acknowledged by the provision of outlines so that while a common structure might be followed, the specific words used could be highly localised. Thus, as specified for the Uniting Church in Australia: the prayer begins with thankful praise to God; continues with thankful recalling of the acts of salvation in Jesus Christ (including the sacrament of the Lord's Supper); then God is invoked to send the Holy Spirit upon the people and the communion gifts; and the prayer concludes with an ascription of praise to the triune God.[39]

## Charismatic Influences

The wave of charismatic worship practices that swept across independent and mainline denominations from the 1960s onward has its roots in the nineteenth-century Wesleyan Holiness tradition and in Pentecostal stirrings that arose in the early twentieth century. Charismatic emphases on the outpouring of the Holy Spirit's gifts, signs of God's power in the midst of God's people, personal conversion, and enthusiastic and spontaneous praise thus echoed Methodism's own liturgical heritage and was easily recovered in some congregations, especially those in Latin America. Despite its Methodist roots, worship was often modelled upon independent church designs. Congregations with a charismatic orientation developed worship by utilising the simple preaching service – with significant attention given to the 'message' delivered by homiletic monologue or dramatic skit – or by overlaying a charismatic veneer on more formal liturgical structures. These services, often identified as 'contemporary' worship, were typically influenced by the global contemporary Christian music phenomenon which developed out of the

---

[36] Gregory Dix, *The Shape of the Liturgy* (Westminster: Dacre Press, 1945).
[37] *The United Methodist Book of Worship* (Nashville, TN: United Methodist Publishing House, 1992), 36–9.
[38] *Uniting in Worship: Leader's Book* (Melbourne: Uniting Church Press, 1988), 93.
[39] Great Prayers of Thanksgiving #22, *Uniting in Worship 2*, CD-ROM, Uniting Church in Australia, 2005.

'Jesus movement' of the 1960s. Worship tended to be informal but often relied on the latest technological innovation; printed texts, if any were used, were projected on overhead screens. Music in locally popular styles often was delivered by a team of vocalists accompanied by a band usually constituted by guitars, electronic keyboard and percussion.

## Diversity in Practice

At the end of the twentieth century, worship shaped by ecumenical, liturgical and charismatic influences, along with the characteristic Methodist preaching service, could all be found in a single denomination – and even within one local congregation. Such diversity in practice is typical of Korean Methodist Church communities, especially those where the membership numbers in the thousands. Early each morning the congregation gathers for 'dawn prayer' (cf. Mark 1:35), a simple preaching service that bears charismatic as well as Buddhist, Taoist and Confucian influences. A regular component of the service is *'tongsung kido'*: spontaneous and simultaneous prayers offered out loud by each member of the congregation. On Sundays at different hours (and sometimes at the same hour) may be held a 'traditional' preaching service reminiscent of the missionary inheritance, a 'liturgical' service that may use the *Korean Methodist New Book of Worship* (2003) and include the Lord's Supper, and 'contemporary' services of various types highly populated by the young.

## A Look to the Future

In the first decade of the twenty-first century, worship influenced by the ecumenical and liturgical movements continued, but was largely overshadowed by worship forms in charismatic/'contemporary' styles. Approaches combining these three that had emerged in the latter part of the twentieth century – for example, 'ancient/future' worship, 'emerging' worship and 'postmodern' worship – still found a home in Methodist congregations. Persisting into the new century were also styles attentive to issues of liberation and social justice, which strove to produce inclusive, diverse and multicultural worship in keeping with early Methodism's attention to 'social holiness'.

The United Methodist Church in 2008 undertook an experiment to bridge historic and emerging liturgical forms and to resolve the long-standing tension between forms and freedom from forms. The 'Open Source Liturgy Project',[40] which used as its model open source software development, sought to establish

---

[40] See http://www.gbod.org/site/apps/nlnet/content3.aspx?c=nhLRJ2PMKsG&b=5715377&ct=7657815 (accessed 25 September 2011).

core understandings of worship and to determine liturgical essentials that would serve as a skeletal framework for locally developed 'flesh' of different styles and textual formulations. This new approach fully captured the persisting trends of Methodist worship – historic and contemporary, formulaic and free, formal and informal, heart-felt and mindful, edifying and discipling – and extends them into the future.

# Methodist Spirituality

## Ian M. Randall

'John Wesley', writes Phyllis Mack in *Heart Religion in the British Enlightenment*, 'was an exponent of practical piety'.[1] Mack argues that for John Wesley, Methodism was not defined by a set of 'opinions' but by a way of life. Central to his concern was authentic religious experience. Thus to examine Methodist spirituality is to look at the heart of Methodism. In similar vein, Kenneth Cracknell and Susan White argue that 'in many ways the Methodist movement was in its beginnings primarily a *spiritual renewal* movement'.[2] Yet few authors have given sustained, detailed attention to Methodist spirituality. Gordon Wakefield's work has, however, been of great importance.[3] In my analysis I am following to a large extent the thinking of Cracknell and White in looking at what they describe as 'a number of persistent features that tie Methodists around the globe to their origins in John Wesley's devotional insight'; my 'hallmarks of Wesleyan piety' (to use another of their phrases) coincide at most points with what they suggest, albeit with some differences.[4] I am using an analytical framework proposed by Philip Sheldrake, in which spirituality is seen as concerned with the conjunction of theology, communion with God and practical Christianity.[5] This is particularly helpful as a framework within which to examine the inner and outer dimensions of Methodist spirituality.

---

[1] P. Mack, *Heart Religion in the British Enlightenment: Gender and Emotion in Early Methodism* (Cambridge: Cambridge University Press, 2008), 32.

[2] K. Cracknell and S. J. White, 'Methodist Spirituality', in Cracknell and White (eds), *An Introduction to World Methodism* (Cambridge: Cambridge University Press , 2005), 141. Italics original.

[3] G. Wakefield, *Methodist Devotion: The Spiritual Life in the Methodist Tradition* (London: Epworth Press, 1966); *Fire of Love: The Spirituality of John Wesley* (London: Epworth Press, 1976); *Methodist Spirituality* (Peterborough: Epworth Press, 1999).

[4] Cracknell and White, 'Methodist Spirituality', 151.

[5] P. Sheldrake, *Spirituality and History* (London: SPCK, 1991), 52.

## The Formation of Methodist Spirituality

The context in which Methodist spirituality was shaped is generally held to be the Evangelical Revival of the eighteenth century. This involves, however, a contested concept, with John Kent, in *Wesley and the Wesleyans* (2002), speaking about the 'so-called evangelical revival' as one of 'the persistent myths of modern British history' – although even he has to admit that Wesleyanism grew because John Wesley 'responded to the actual religious demands and hopes of his hearers'.[6] The view of Henry Rack, who connects the Evangelical Revival with the rise of Methodism, represents a position which has been one that has been widely accepted.[7] David Bebbington, in his seminal work, *Evangelicalism in Modern Britain*, goes so far as to argue that the decade beginning in 1734 'witnessed in the English-speaking world a more important development than any other, before or after, in the history of Protestant Christianity: the emergence of the movement that became Evangelicalism'.[8] Bebbington has proposed that evangelicalism is a movement comprising all those who stress the Bible, the cross, conversion and activism.[9] This quadrilateral can be set alongside the well-known 'Methodist Quadrilateral' – scripture, tradition, reason and experience. Both illuminate Methodism.

In coming to their understanding of Methodism, John and Charles Wesley were influenced by three differing traditions, largely through their family. One was the English Puritan tradition, which helped to shape English Dissent. The Puritans had spoken of the experience of conversion and of the preaching of the gospel, and although John and Charles Wesley's parents were staunchly Church of England they came from Puritan stock. The second stream of influence on the Wesleys was Catholic and high church devotion, which set out rigorous demands in the spiritual life. While at Oxford, where he was part of the 'Holy Club', John Wesley read Jeremy Taylor's *Holy Living* and *Holy Dying* (1650 and 1651), which made a profound impact on him. In this period he also read the *Imitation of Christ* and other early and medieval classics. He was affected, too, by the writings of the high churchman, William Law, *On Christian Perfection* (1726) and *A Serious Call to a Devout and Holy Life* (1728). All of these works 'provided a treasury of spiritual insight from which Wesley freely drew'.[10] A final element in the mix was the more mystical stream of spirituality, such as that expressed in the book, *The Life of God in the Soul of Man*, by Henry Scougal of Aberdeen, a Scottish Episcopalian.[11] William

---

[6] J. Kent, *Wesley and the Wesleyans: Religion in Eighteenth-Century Britain* (Cambridge: Cambridge University Press, 2002), 1–2.

[7] H. D. Rack, *Reasonable Enthusiast: John Wesley and the Rise of Methodism* (3rd edn, London: Epworth Press, 2002), 158–250.

[8] D. W. Bebbington, *Evangelicalism in Modern Britain: A History from the 1730s to the 1980s* (London: Unwin Hyman, 1989), 20.

[9] Ibid., 2–17. In my *What a Friend we have in Jesus; The Evangelical Tradition* (London: DLT, 2005), I have drawn from Bebbington but have argued for several other strands in evangelical spirituality. In this present study I have incorporated some of that material.

[10] Cracknell and White, 'Methodist Spirituality', 144–6.

[11] Bebbington, *Evangelicalism in Modern Britain*, 38.

Law's work was particularly important.[12] As an example of how the message of the need for spiritual reality was spread, Scougal's book was lent by Charles Wesley to another subsequent leader of the Evangelical Revival, George Whitefield.[13]

A movement of spiritual renewal in central Europe was also highly influential. In 1722 Nicholas Ludwig von Zinzendorf, a Saxon Count who had been educated in a German Pietist environment, opened his estate in south-east Saxony to Protestant refugees from Bohemia and Moravia.[14] This group, which was escaping from persecution by the Roman Catholic Habsburgs, was known as the Unity of the Brethren or the Moravians, but the community created was an ecumenical one. Zinzendorf's estate, Herrnhut (under the Lord's Protection), became the scene in 1727 of a profound spiritual renewal. Four girls came to a powerful spiritual assurance and the intensity of their experiences spread to the whole community. This was to lead to a significant Moravian missionary movement. It was at a Moravian-led meeting in Aldersgate Street in 1738 that John Wesley had an experience of assurance. Charles Wesley was similarly influenced by the Moravians and this contributed to his own evangelical conversion.[15] The way in which Methodism felt the impact of several traditions and movements contributed to what John Wesley described as a 'Catholic Spirit', and he argued for 'the crossing of boundaries on the basis of love' in his sermon on this topic. He looked for those to whom he could say, 'if your heart be right with my heart', hoping for an affirmative reply. It is this spirit which has characterised Methodists in all generations.[16]

## Conversionist Spirituality

A primary 'hallmark' of Methodist spirituality has been its conversionism. John Wesley recorded in his diary for 24 May 1738 the following words, which were to become among the most famous in the story of Christian experience:

> In the evening I went very unwillingly to a society in Aldersgate Street, where one was reading Luther's Preface to the Epistle to the Romans. About a quarter before nine, while he was describing the change which God works in the heart through faith in Christ, I felt my heart strangely warmed. I felt I did trust in Christ, Christ alone, for salvation; and an assurance was given me that He had taken away *my*

---

[12] See D. L. Jeffrey (ed.), *A Burning and a Shining Light* (Grand Rapids, MI: Eerdmans, 1987), 143, 146.
[13] G. Whitefield, *Journals* (Edinburgh: Banner of Truth, reprint 1960), 46–7.
[14] For Zinzendorf see A. J. Lewis, *Zinzendorf: The Ecumenical Pioneer* (London: SCM, 1962).
[15] F.C. Gill, *Charles Wesley: The First Methodist* (London: Lutterworth Press, 1964), 65–71.
[16] Cracknell and White, 'Methodist Spirituality', 150.

sins, even *mine*, and saved *me* from the law of sin and death ... I then testified openly to all there what I now first felt in my heart.[17]

This account, describing as it does how John Wesley came to a point of personal reliance on God's grace and Christ's work on the cross for salvation, later came to be seen as a description of a typical experience of Methodist conversion, although there has been considerable discussion as to whether it should rather be seen as an expression of assurance of salvation.[18] Three days before John Wesley's experience, his brother Charles came to know what he termed 'peace with God', and he wrote a hymn, 'Christ the friend of sinners', followed later by his much more famous conversion hymn, 'Wrestling Jacob':

> Where shall my wond'ring soul begin?
> How shall I all to Heaven aspire?
> A slave redeemed from death and sin,
> A brand plucked from eternal fire.
> How shall I equal triumphs raise,
> Or sing my great Deliverer's praise?[19]

Phyllis Mack notes the words in this hymn speaking of 'mighty faith' which 'cannot ask in vain', and highlights the 'witness of the Spirit', or 'direct perception of God's presence' in these early conversions.[20]

The firm conviction of John Wesley was that this assurance was open to all. Wesley expounded an evangelical Arminian position, believing that grace had opened a path to salvation for everyone, and that in turn it was open to any person to choose Christ as Saviour.[21] John Wesley and the Calvinist George Whitefield, the two most powerful leaders of the Evangelical Revival, despite their common affirmation of conversion, were divided over the doctrines of predestination, divine election to salvation and the possibility of losing salvation.[22] There were huge debates in early Methodism on these issues. For John Wesley the key issues were related to spirituality, which in turn was connected to human agency. In 1757 he wrote to Dorothy Furly stating

---

[17] W. R. Ward and R. P. Heitzenrater (eds), *The Works of John Wesley*, vol. 18 (Nashville, TN: Abingdon Press, 1988), 249–50.

[18] For a full discussion of the meaning of John Wesley's experience see Rack, *Reasonable Enthusiast*, 144–57.

[19] Gareth Lloyd notes the connection between Charles Wesley's evangelical conversion in 1738 and the publication a year later of his *Hymns and Sacred Poems*: G. Lloyd, *Charles Wesley and the Struggle for Methodist Identity* (Oxford: Oxford University Press, 2007), 74–5. See also M. A. Noll, 'Evangelicalism at its Best', in M. A. Noll and R. F. Thiemann (eds), *Where Shall My Wond'ring Soul Begin?* (Grand Rapids, MI: Eerdmans, 2000), 2.

[20] Mack, *Heart Religion in the British Enlightenment*, 39.

[21] For Wesley's understanding of salvation see H. B. McGonigle, *Sufficient Saving Grace: John Wesley's Evangelical Arminianism* (Carlisle: Paternoster Press, 2001).

[22] For George Whitefield see H. S. Stout, *The Divine Dramatist: George Whitefield and the Rise of Modern Evangelicalism* (Grand Rapids, MI: Eerdmans, 1991).

his belief that it was possible to lose a sense of God's love through committing sin or omitting duty or through other wrong actions, but he insisted that none of this was necessary for a believer.[23] Selina, Countess of Huntingdon, a significant supporter of Whitefield, was so incensed by the anti-Calvinism of the Wesleyan Conference that she had the minutes of the 1770 Conference burned.[24] From 1778 the Methodist *Arminian Magazine* began to be published, partly to promote certain Methodist views. But for Wesley the distinguishing marks of a Methodist – the 'character' of a Methodist, as he put it – were not 'opinions' but the work of God in the heart. True religion for the Wesleys was, as Frank Whaling suggested, 'inward and social rather than merely doctrinal'.[25]

As well as the experiences and the theology of these shapers of Methodism, there were many others in the eighteenth century who experienced conversion in a Methodist setting. Mrs Platt, a poor woman in Oxford who was helped by Charles Wesley, wrote about her deep experience of Christ and of 'the Holy Ghost upon me, wherein I have sure pardon of my sins'. She concluded, with reference to her spiritual struggles: 'It is hard work to be born again.'[26] In 1779, William Black, a nineteen-year-old from Yorkshire who had emigrated to Nova Scotia, Canada, and who later became the leading Canadian Methodist of his period, wrote about his conversion in his journal:

> We tarried … singing and praying for about two hours when it pleased the Lord to reveal his free grace; his fullness and his suitableness as a Saviour: his ability and willingness to save *me* …. My burden dropped off: my guilt was removed: condemnation gave place to mercy: and a sweet peace and gladness were diffused through my soul.[27]

A study by Linda Wilson of the obituaries of one hundred women, which includes comparisons with men, from English Nonconformist denominations in the period 1825–75, found that among the Methodists included in the sample 83 per cent of male Wesleyans and 88 per cent of female Wesleyans mentioned conversion explicitly. Among Primitive Methodists the percentages were higher.[28] The spirituality of Methodism has been strongly conversionist.

---

[23] John Wesley to Dorothy Furly, 18 May 1757, in J. Telford (ed.), *The Letters of John Wesley, A.M.*, 8 vols (London: Epworth Press, 1931), vol. III, 215.

[24] M. Noll, *The Rise of Evangelicalism: The Age of Edwards, Whitefield and the Wesleys* (Leicester: IVP, 2004), 8.

[25] F. Whaling (ed.), *John and Charles Wesley* (New York, NY: Paulist Press, 1981), 62 (introduction); cf. Mack, *Heart Religion in the British Enlightenment*, 32–3.

[26] Cited by D. B. Hindmarsh, '"My Chains Fell Off, My Heart was Free": Early Methodist Conversion Narrative in England', *Church History*, 68: 4 (1999), 926.

[27] *Arminian Magazine* (London, 1791), 68–70, cited by G. A. Rawlyk and M. A. Noll (eds), *Amazing Grace: Evangelicalism in Australia, Britain, Canada, and the United States* (Montreal and Kingston: McGill-Queen's University Press, 1994), 16–17.

[28] L. Wilson, *Constrained by Zeal: Female Spirituality amongst Nonconformists, 1825–1875* (Carlisle: Paternoster Press, 2000), 45.

## The Bible: 'O Give Me that Book'

For the early-eighteenth-century Methodists, personal experience of Christ through conversion, which was of paramount importance, was nourished by Bible reading, and so Methodists were constantly encouraged to read and meditate on the Bible.[29] John Wesley often referred to himself as a *'homo unius libri'*, a man of one book. In the preface to his sermons, where he used this phrase, he spoke of the way of salvation as being 'written down in a book', and he continued: 'O give me that book! At any price give me the Book of God! I have it. Here is knowledge enough for me.'[30] Yet this exalted estimation of the Bible was not one that Wesley came to hold only as a result of his evangelical conversion. As early as 1729, a decade before that event, he and others in the Holy Club in Oxford had the desire to be, as it was put, 'downright Bible-Christians'.[31] Later, Rule 26 of Wesley's Rules for Methodist societies spoke of 'searching the scriptures', and many of the hymns written by Charles Wesley were 'paraphrases of or expansions on biblical verses'.[32]

In his thinking about the Bible, John Wesley combined some Enlightenment ways of thinking with a profoundly devotional engaging with the scriptures. The Bible was seen as containing a 'system of divine truth'. John Wesley used this phrase in 1754 when writing about the Bible. He continued in similar vein:

> Every part thereof is worthy of God; and all together are one entire body, wherein there is no defect, no excess. It is the fountain of heavenly wisdom, which they who are able to taste prefer to all writings of men, however wise, or learned or holy. An exact knowledge of the truth was accompanied in the inspired writers, with … precise expression of their meaning.[33]

However, there was another level of biblical reading, as seen in the hymn by Charles Wesley, 'Wrestling Jacob'. The hymn tells the story of Jacob seeking a blessing from God, but at the end the biblical narrative undergoes a transformation. The one with whom Jacob wrestles is Christ. 'Thou diedst for me.' These words reveal a new 'Christian' identity, one that arises from an 'imaginative, Christological reading of the Old Testament text'. The Bible is not read so much for information as for spiritual insight.[34] Scripture is a means of grace.

---

[29] Noll, *The Rise of Evangelicalism*, 141.

[30] A.C. Outler (ed.), *The Works of John Wesley*, vol. 1, Sermons, I (Nashville, TN: Abingdon Press, 1984), 105.

[31] T. Jackson (ed.), *The Works of John Wesley*, vol. 8 (Kansas, MO: Beacon Hill Press, 3rd edn, 1978), 348.

[32] Cracknell and White, 'Methodist Spirituality', 151.

[33] J. Wesley, *Explanatory Notes upon the New Testament* (first published 1754; London: Epworth Press, 1976), preface, paragraph 10.

[34] Cracknell and White, 'Methodist Spirituality', 152–3.

The study of the Bible could take place in small groups. Count Zinzendorf understood the importance of organising his followers into different types of cell groups and this concept was exported to Britain and elsewhere.[35] John Wesley's Methodist societies – which met in class meetings and smaller 'bands' each week – drew from the model of spirituality expressed by the Moravians. Wesley saw his societies as standing firm 'in the good old Bible way' and on one occasion told a group in Derbyshire to 'go straight forward, knowing nothing of various opinions, and minding nothing but to be Bible Christians'.[36] The meaning and application of the Bible has also been communicated in Methodism through preaching. The tradition of preaching, by lay members and by ministers, has continued. In the mid-twentieth century, in England, W. E. Sangster regularly attracted congregations of 3,000 at the Methodist Westminster Central Hall, London. Sangster's advice to preachers regarding the message they brought was: 'Believe in it. Keep to centralities. Work at it. Make it plain. Make it practical ... Steep it in prayer.'[37] Later in the century, Methodism's most famous international preacher was Donald English, who was twice President of the Methodist Conference and was chair of the World Methodist Council. Paul Smith, another Methodist minister, wrote of Donald English that the 'clarity of his exposition left his hearers wondering why they had read that passage so often and never grasped its heart before'.[38] The Bible has been central to Methodist spirituality.

## Ecclesiastical and Spiritual Order

The establishment and maintenance of proper discipline and order have been another crucial feature of Methodist spirituality. An early evangelical example of this process is the way in which John Wesley established his societies. These highlight the importance of communal spirituality: Wakefield speaks of the hymns and the communal discipline as 'rapture and order'.[39] The account of the development of the societies was first published in 1743 as preface to *The Nature, Design, and General Rules of the United Societies, in London, Bristol, Kingswood, and Newcastle-upon-Tyne*:

> In the latter part of the year 1739 eight or ten persons, who appeared to be deeply convinced of sin and earnestly groaning for redemption, came to Mr. Wesley in London. They desired, as did two or three more

---

[35] G. and M. Stead, *The Exotic Plant* (Peterborough: Epworth Press, 2003), chapters 2 and 3.
[36] N. Curnock (ed.), *Journal of John Wesley*, vol. 6 (London: Epworth Press, 1938), 100.
[37] P. Sangster, *Doctor Sangster* (London: Epworth Press, 1962), 277.
[38] P. Smith, 'Donald English – Preacher', in R. W. Abbott (ed.), *Donald English: An Evangelical Celebration* (Ilkeston, Derbys.: Headline Special/Moorley's, 1999), 20.
[39] Wakefield, *Methodist Spirituality*, 10–13.

> the next day, that he would spend some time with them in prayer and advise them how to flee from the wrath to come, which they saw continually hanging over their heads.

Wesley organised a weekly meeting in London, on a Thursday evening, at which he gave the group spiritual advice and at which communal prayer was made.[40] Methodist society or class meetings, with class leaders, then spread. In a sermon on 'Obedience to Pastors', Wesley argued that Methodists did not need to regard the parish priest as their pastor. He envisaged people finding a 'spiritual pastor' or 'spiritual guide'.[41] Local class leaders often functioned in this way.

David Lowes Watson has argued that the class meetings provided a sense of mutual accountability which went along with the cultivation of a catholicity of grace.[42] In his *Christian Library*, which drew from the classics of the Western Church and also some Eastern Church authors, from a number of high Anglicans and supremely from the English Puritans, Wesley intended to draw together material which was 'practical, unmixed with controversy of any kind; and all intelligible to plain men: such as is not superficial, but going down to the depth, and describing the height of Christianity'.[43] The catholic view of the Church, which gives a central place to episcopally ordained ministry and Apostolic tradition, might seem to have been in opposition to Wesley's encouragement of lay ministry, but the societies drew from the Anglican concept of religious societies of lay people.[44] As Frank Baker suggests, Wesley can be found supporting 'a historical institution of bishops and inherited customs', with ministers expounding the Bible and administering the sacraments 'in such a way as to preserve the ancient tradition on behalf of all those who were made members by baptism', while also promoting groups in which believers shared 'the apostolic experience of God's living presence and also a desire to bring others into this same personal experience'.[45]

Ultimately, Wesley's thinking about church order and discipline was evangelistic, activist and pragmatic. He asked: 'What is the end of all ecclesiastical order? Is it not to bring souls from the power of Satan to God, and to build them up in His fear and love?' Given the priority for him of conversion and spiritual growth, Wesley

---

[40] See *John Wesley the Methodist: A Plain Account of his Life and Work* by a Methodist Preacher (New York, NY: Methodist Book Concern, 1903), chapter 9.

[41] A. C. Outler (ed.), *The Works of John Wesley*, vol. 3, Sermon on 'On Obedience to Pastors', Sermons, III (Nashville, TN: Abingdon Press, 1986), 380.

[42] D. L. Watson, 'Methodist Spirituality', in F. Senn (ed.), *Protestant Spiritual Traditions* (New York, NY: Paulist Press, 1986), 217–73.

[43] For the Christian Library see G. Rupp, 'Introductory Essay', in R. Davies and G. Rupp (eds), *A History of the Methodist Church in Great Britain*, vol. 1 (London: Epworth Press, 1965); for the 'Catholic spirit' of Methodism, see J. L. Schwenk, *Catholic Spirit* (Lanham, MD: Scarecrow Press, 2008).

[44] P. W. Chilcote (ed.), *Early Methodist Spirituality: Selected Women's Writings* (Nashville, TN: Kingswood Books, 2007), 23.

[45] F. Baker, *John Wesley and the Church of England* (New York, NY: Abingdon Press, 1970), 137.

concluded: 'Order, then, is so far valuable as it answers these ends; and if it answers them not, it is worth nothing.'[46] Preaching on 'The Church', and in particular on 'One Lord, one faith, one baptism', Wesley typically emphasised the internal rather than the external. Believers had 'one Lord', the one 'who has now dominion over them, who has set up his kingdom in their hearts'.[47] The 'order' which Wesley commended above all was the kind of attitude and behaviour which promoted the spiritual life. Helpful religious acts were 'ordinances'. In this category could be found prayer, fasting, the Love Feast, conferences, diary-keeping, use of money and modest dressing. In many of these areas women took the lead, for example in organising the first Love Feast, which was a symbolic meal with testimony, prayer and singing.[48] Cracknell and White note that in every period of Methodism there has been persistent diary-keeping. The journal of Mary Lyth of York ran to twenty volumes. Many Methodist materials are being produced to reclaim a range of classical spiritual disciplines.[49]

## Constant Communion

John Wesley preached that the redemption of Christ on the cross was for all humankind. In a sermon preached in 1740 in Bristol, on the theme of 'Free Grace', he referred to the text in Romans (10:12) concerning the Lord being 'rich in mercy to all that call upon him'. Wesley addressed the objection: 'But you say, "No; he is such only to those for whom Christ died. And those are not all, but only a few, whom God hath chosen out of the world; for he died not for all".' In response, Wesley quoted a number of biblical texts speaking of Christ taking away the sins of the world and being the Saviour of all.[50] Because Christ was saviour of all, but not all were necessarily saved, the implication was that there had to be human cooperation. David Trickett argued that the theme of divine–human cooperation 'lies at the heart of John Wesley's theological perspective', and that it was this understanding that led Wesley to see 'the Eucharist as paradigmatic of all the means of grace'.[51] It also seems to have been the case that many early Methodist women

---

[46] F. Baker (ed.), *The Works of John Wesley*, vol. 26 (Nashville, TN: Abingdon Press, 1984), 206.
[47] A. C. Outler (ed.), *The Works of John Wesley*, vol. 3, Sermon on 'Of the Church', Sermons, III (Nashville, TN: Abingdon Press, 1986), 49.
[48] Mack, *Heart Religion in the British Enlightenment*, 150–51.
[49] Cracknell and White, 'Methodist Spirituality', 161–2.
[50] A. C. Outler (ed.), *The Works of John Wesley*, vol. 3, on 'Free Grace' (1739), Sermons, III (Nashville, TN: Abingdon Press, 1984), 558–9.
[51] D. Trickett, 'The Sense of God's Presence: Spiritual Vision and Witness in the Early Wesleyan Witness', in B. C. Hanson (ed.), *Modern Christian Spirituality* (Atlanta, GA: Scholars Press, 1990), 172–3.

in particular were able to identify, in their sometimes unremitting hardships, with the sufferings of the crucified Christ.[52]

The death of Christ on the cross is also the focus of several much-sung Methodist hymns. An example is Charles Wesley's hymn 'O for a thousand tongues to sing', which was the first hymn in the later Wesley hymnbooks and was intended 'for the anniversary day of one's conversion'. After the initial verses expressing general praise and prayer, there is a focus on Christ's redemption, through his blood being shed:[53]

> He breaks the power of cancelled sin,
> He sets the prisoner free;
> His blood can make the foulest clean;
> His blood availed for me.

In another of Charles Wesley's hymns there is an invitation to look at the suffering of Christ through the imagination, in the words 'See there! His temples crown'd with thorns.' The hymn also describes his 'bleeding hands'. Phyllis Mack cites this hymn in the context of arguing that there are similarities between the Wesleyan approach and that of the Ignatian tradition – for instance in training, discipline and mutual confession. In this case the similarities have to do with the focus on Christ suffering and the call to 'visually follow him to the cross'.[54] The Moravians were also distinctive for the stress they placed on the cross of Christ, and an emphasis on the wounds of Christ produced intense devotion among Moravian believers.[55] This became the famous 'Blood and Wounds Theology' of the Moravians. One of John Wesley's leading associates, John Cennick, became a Moravian. Cennick was attracted by the power of the 'Blood and Wounds Theology', and when he read a 'Litany of the Wounds' composed by Zinzendorf, Cennick shed tears of joy. By 1743 Zinzendorf was stating: 'We will look for nothing else in the Bible but the Lamb and His Wounds.' This intense form of spirituality did not, however, impress John Wesley.[56]

Rather, Wesley made a strong experiential connection between the cross and Holy Communion. Wesley's views about the benefits of Holy Communion were formulated when he was a young Church of England priest, before his later evangelical experiences, but his approach to Communion remained substantially the same throughout his life. In a sermon preached in 1788, 'The Duty of Constant Communion', Wesley urged the observance of the Lord's Supper on the grounds

---

[52] D. Hempton, *Methodism: Empire of the Spirit* (New Haven, CT and London: Yale University Press, 2005), 142; cf. Mack, *Heart Religion in the British Enlightenment*, chapter 5, 'Mary Fletcher on the cross'.

[53] F. C. Gill, *Charles Wesley: The First Methodist* (London: Lutterworth Press, 1964), 72.

[54] Mack, *Heart Religion in the British Enlightenment*, 49–52, especially 51.

[55] Bebbington, *Evangelicalism in Modern Britain*, 39.

[56] J. E. Hutton, *A History of the Moravian Church* (London: Moravian Publication Office, 1909), 265, 275–6, 322.

that it was 'a plain command of Christ'. In addition to that, there were 'great benefits' in Communion, notably 'the forgiveness of our past sins and the present strengthening and refreshing of our souls'. The Lord's Supper also, said Wesley, 'gives strength to perform our duty, and leads us on to perfection'. Clearly for him this was a meal with considerable spiritual significance. Wesley encouraged proper preparation for the Lord's Supper through meditation on scripture and self-examination. For Wesley, frequent celebration was the ideal. He wrote:

> Let every one therefore who has either any desire to please God, or any love of his own soul, obey God and consult the good of his own soul by communicating every time he can; like the first Christians, with whom the Christian sacrifice was a constant part of the Lord's day service. And for several centuries they received it almost every day: Four times a week always, and every saint's day beside. Accordingly those that joined in the prayers of the faithful never failed to partake of the blessed sacrament.[57]

He added by way of explanation in the printed version of this sermon that it had been written over five-and-fifty years before, for the use of his pupils at Oxford. 'I have added very little', said Wesley, 'but retrenched much; as I then used more words than I do now. But I thank God I have not yet seen cause to alter my sentiments in any point which is therein delivered.'[58] In 1745 the Wesleys published *Hymns on the Lord's Supper*, which contained 166 items, among them lines like these:

> From house to house they broke the bread,
> Impregnated with life divine,
> And drank the Spirit of the head
> Transmitted in the sacred wine.

As F. C. Gill notes, these are Communion hymns which convey the depths and mystery of the Eucharist and which are intended to nourish spiritual experience.[59] This emphasis has continued within Methodism.

## Prayer and Praise

Methodism can also be described as a prayerful spirituality. 'There is no single entry in Wesley's diary where he does not mention having prayed, usually several

---

[57] A. C. Outler (ed.), *The Works of John Wesley*, vol. 3, Sermon on 'The Duty of Constant Communion', Sermons, III (Nashville, TN: Abingdon Press, 1986), 430.
[58] Ibid., 428.
[59] Gill, *Charles Wesley: The First Methodist*, 123.

times in the day.'[60] The journals of early Methodists have the same emphasis. Jane Treffry, in her *Memoirs*, described how in daily prayer she tried to give thanks and offer intercession 'in a very extensive and minute manner'.[61] John Wesley also inculcated through his teaching the biblical idea of 'praying without ceasing'. He explained that the Methodist believer was not always in the house of prayer

> ... though he neglects no opportunity of being there. Neither is he always on his knees, although he often is, or on his face, before the Lord his God. Nor yet is he always crying aloud to God, or calling upon him in words: For many times 'the Spirit maketh intercession for him with groans that cannot be uttered'.[62]

Wesley continued to speak in typical fashion in this passage about prayer and the language of the heart. Prayer, for Wesley, was not only to be expressed in words, but also through silence, groans, adoration and a constant sense of God's presence.[63] Wesley set out a scheme for prayer in 1730 and he reprinted this in 1781, showing that his thinking about the approach to prayer and the importance of this aspect of devotion had not changed significantly over these decades. His scheme encouraged both spontaneous prayer and also the use of the Anglican Collect.[64]

Despite his strong Anglican commitment, Wesley was somewhat ambivalent about the use of set prayers. In giving instructions (probably in 1786) about visiting the sick, he advised that every visit should conclude with prayer. He continued: 'If you cannot yet pray without a form you may use some of those composed by Mr. Spinckes, or any other pious writer. But the sooner you break through this backwardness the better. Ask of God, and he will soon open your mouth.'[65] Nathaniel Spinckes' *A Complete Manual of Private Devotions*, which drew on prayers going back to the early church, was the volume that was being commended by Wesley, but only as a second best. Wesley believed that in praying for someone it was important to pray in a personal way. Yet in a letter about public worship written in 1778 to Mary Bishop, Wesley commented: 'I myself find more life in the Church prayers than in the formal extemporary prayers of Dissenters.'[66] Methodist spirituality has incorporated free prayer and set prayers. It is 'life' that has been seen as crucial.

As well as prayer made in solitude, there has been a strong belief in Methodism that prayer made in company with others is a source of blessing. John Wesley's *Journal* for 1 January 1739 records that he was with about sixty friends, including his

---

[60] Cracknell and White, 'Methodist Spirituality', 153.
[61] Ibid., 154.
[62] J. Wesley, 'The Character of a Methodist', in Jackson (ed.), *The Works of the Rev. John Wesley*, vol. 8, 404.
[63] G. Mursell, *English Spirituality: From 1700 to the Present Day* (London: SPCK, 2001), 96.
[64] Jeffrey, *A Burning and a Shining Light*, 229–30.
[65] A.C. Outler (ed.), *The Works of John Wesley*, vol. 3, Sermon on 'On Visiting the Sick', Sermons, III (Nashville, TN: Abingdon Press, 1984), 392.
[66] Telford, *The Letters of the Rev. John Wesley, A.M.*, vol. VI, 326.

brother Charles, George Whitefield and other prominent leaders in the Methodist Awakening, for a 'love feast' in Fetter Lane, London, and that they experienced God's power and also great joy in their communal prayer. He wrote:

> About three in the morning, as we were continuing instant in prayer, the Power of God came mightily upon us, insomuch that many cried out for exceeding joy, and many fell to the ground. As soon as we were recovered a little from that awe and amazement at the presence of his Majesty, we broke out with one voice, 'We praise thee, O God; we acknowledge thee to be the Lord.'[67]

Closely linked to communal prayer has been communal praise, expressed in hymns. Many hymns of praise could be used to illustrate this aspect of Methodist spirituality. Charles Wesley's 'And can it be?' is notable for its expression of heart-felt praise and wonder at what Christ has done:

> 'Tis mystery all! Th' Immortal dies:
> Who can explore His strange design?
> In vain the first-born seraph tries,
> To sound the depths of love divine.
> 'Tis mercy all! Let earth adore!
> Let angel minds inquire no more.

This is followed by a typical Methodist expression of assurance:

> No condemnation now I dread;
> Jesus, and all in Him, is mine!
> Alive in Him, my living Head,
> And clothed in righteousness divine,
> Bold I approach the eternal throne,
> And claim the crown, through Christ my own.

Charles Wesley is estimated to have written over 8,000 hymns – on average more than one each week. In introducing the *Collection of Hymns for the Use of the People of God Called Methodists* (1780), John Wesley spoke of the book as expressing 'experimental and practical divinity'. John Wesley, who liked bold songs of assurance, encouraged his brother in his work (although he once described some of his brother's hymns as 'namby-pambical'), and in fact it was through the hymns written by Charles, marked as they were by vibrant theology and splendid poetry, as much as through preaching, that the Methodist message spread.

---

[67] W. R. Ward and R. P. Heitzenrater (eds), *The Works of John Wesley*, vol. 19: Journals and Diaries, II (Nashville, TN: Abingdon Press, 1990), 29.

## Perfect Love

Some have regarded John Wesley's conception of Christian perfection or of 'perfect love' as the most original of his doctrinal contributions. Wesley regarded the doctrine of 'full sanctification' or Christian perfection as the 'grand *depositum* which God has lodged with the people called Methodists'.[68] In this area, however, he was out of line with much common Protestant thinking of his time. Sanctification was understood by Wesley as the developing work of God in the human soul from the time of conversion. There was also, for him, a definite stage and consequent condition that he called full or entire sanctification. This blessing was attainable, but once attained could be lost. At the heart of Wesley's thinking about the fully sanctified life were the concepts of an undivided desire to please and serve God and a 'perfect love' for God which excluded sin. In his famous 'Brief Thoughts on Christian Perfection', Wesley said that by perfection he meant 'the humble, gentle, patient love of God, and our neighbour, ruling our tempers, words and actions'. This was 'always wrought in the soul by a simple act of faith' and therefore happened 'in an instant'. Where this experience of sanctification did take place it was usually 'many years after justification'.[69]

This was not a doctrine of 'sinlessness'. There was, according to Wesley, no absolute perfection before heaven, and indeed Wesley maintained that the term 'perfection' had been thrust on him. The way in which Wesley described his position is carefully nuanced, although he is perhaps not always consistent. Crucially, human failures that were not intentional were not seen by him as sins. What Wesley was looking for, above all, was growth in grace. It was not the case, as Wesley saw it, that the whole of salvation was given at once. He wrote:

> Neither dare we affirm, as some have done, that all this salvation is given at once. There is indeed an instantaneous, as well as a gradual, work of God in His children; and there wants not, we know, a cloud of witnesses who have received, in one moment, either a clear sense of the forgiveness of their sins, or the abiding witness of the Holy Spirit. But we do not know a single instance, in any place, of a person's receiving, in one remission of sins, the abiding witness of the Spirit, and a new, a clean heart.[70]

Although (as noted) Wesley had been influenced by writers in the field of spirituality such as William Law and Jeremy Taylor, he had not found in them the spiritual assurance he was seeking. It was the discovery of this assurance that led him to look for a life of perfect love, of purity of heart. The themes of assurance

---

[68] Telford (ed.), *The Letters of the Rev John Wesley, A.M.*, vol. 8, 238.
[69] J. Wesley, 'Brief Thoughts on Christian Perfection', in T. Jackson (ed.), *The Works of the Rev John Wesley*, Vol. XI (Kansas, MO: Beacon Hill Press, 3rd edn, 1978), 446; A. S. Wood, *Love Excluding Sin*, Occasional Paper No. 1 of the Wesley Fellowship (1986), 5, 8–9.
[70] Wesley, 'Brief Thoughts', 443.

and purity of heart were summed up by Charles Wesley in one of his finest hymns, 'Love divine, all loves excelling' with its words:

> Jesu, Thou art all compassion,
> Pure, unbounded Love Thou art ...
> Finish then Thy new creation,
> Pure and spotless let us be ...[71]

This experience meant being changed 'from glory into glory' and as a consequence the Christian had greater enjoyment of God, with a resultant increase in happiness. For Wesley the Methodist was 'happy in God, yes, always happy'. In a study of 'Sanctification as Lived by Early Methodist Women', Paul Chilcote highlights a number of features related to 'inward' and 'outward' holiness: the all-sufficiency of God's grace; the goal of happiness in Christ; the necessity of growth into deeper love; the witness of service to others; and the proclamation of God's love.[72]

What part did the Holy Spirit play in this experience of perfect love? John Wesley was wary of those, as he put it, who had 'imagined themselves to be endued with a power of working miracles, of healing the sick by a word or a touch, of restoring sight to the blind; yea, even of raising the dead', and he referred to a recent 'notorious instance' that he and others knew of false claims being made.[73] Wesley was, nonetheless, committed to the crucial role of the Holy Spirit. Unlike John Fletcher of Madeley, and his wife Mary, however, Wesley did not see the experience of entire sanctification in terms of a baptism of the Spirit similar to that experienced by the disciples on the day of Pentecost. Wesley wrote many pastoral letters, and in 1749 he said this to a Roman Catholic:

> I believe the infinite and eternal Spirit of God, equal with the Father and the Son, to be not only perfectly holy in Himself, but the immediate cause of all holiness in us; enlightening our understandings, rectifying our wills and affections, renewing our natures, uniting our persons to Christ, assuring us of the adoption of sons, leading us in our actions, purifying and sanctifying our souls and bodies, to a full and eternal enjoyment of God.[74]

Inward renewal through the Holy Spirit produced a full-orbed holiness which had outward effects.

---

[71] Gill, *Charles Wesley: The First Methodist*, 66–7.
[72] P. W. Chilcote, 'Sanctification as Lived by Early Methodist Women', *Methodist History*, 32:2 (January 1996), 90–103.
[73] A. C. Outler (ed.), *The Works of John Wesley*, vol. 2, Sermon 37, 'The Nature of Enthusiasm', Sermons II (34–70) (Nashville, TN: Abingdon Press, 1985), 52.
[74] John Wesley to a Roman Catholic, 18 July 1749, in Telford (ed.), *The Letters of the Rev John Wesley, A.M.*, vol. III, 9.

In the mid-nineteenth century, holiness teaching in North America and then in Britain was revitalised, arguably in a way that diverged somewhat from Wesley's thinking.[75] James Caughey, an American revivalist who also preached in England, emphasised the possibility of instant sanctification. Methodist 'camp meetings' (so called because families camped during these gatherings), at which the messages of salvation and sanctification were proclaimed, became highly popular. In New York, popular 'Tuesday' meetings, as they came to be known, were addressed by a Methodist, Phoebe Palmer. The holiness theology expounded by Palmer was taken up by William and Catherine Booth and the Salvation Army. Phoebe Palmer's introduction of 'altar terminology' – a 'shorter way' to holiness through laying one's all on the altar, often signified by kneeling at the communion rail – affected British and American revivalism.[76] In the later nineteenth and early twentieth century, 'full salvation' (as the experience of perfect love was by then often termed) was widely claimed by people within the Wesleyan movements. Compared with John Wesley himself, these holiness teachers made more of instantaneous experience and less of love perfected.[77] Nonetheless, holiness advocates of this period often appealed to Wesley and Fletcher. Modern Methodism has been concerned to recover the early Wesleyan vision of holiness involving a life-long journey.

## The Main Preoccupation: Salvation

Lester Ruth speaks about shared traits in Methodism, such as experiential religion, an immediate experience of God, discipline, expressive spirituality and, finally, 'Methodists' main preoccupation', which was 'salvation'. Ruth argues that all other concerns orbited around this centre of gravity.[78] Charles Wesley made a point of speaking about Christ to fellow-passengers when travelling by coach. On one occasion a lady was so offended she threatened to beat him, but on another occasion Charles so impressed another passenger that the coach stopped for a time of prayer. Charles recorded: 'We sang and shouted all the way to Oxford.'[79] Wesley followed both George Whitefield's example and that of Howell Harris in Wales in preaching in the open air in Bristol in April 1739. In Wesley's famous words, 'At four in the afternoon I submitted to be more vile, and proclaimed in the highways the glad tidings of salvation … to about three thousand people.'[80] Wesley never

---

[75] For streams of holiness teaching, see D. W. Bebbington, *Holiness in Nineteenth-Century England* (Carlisle: Paternoster, 2000).

[76] M. McFadden, 'The Ironies of Pentecost: Phoebe Palmer, World Evangelism, and Female Networks', *Methodist History*, 31:2 (1993), 428.

[77] For more see J. L. Peters, *Christian Perfection in American Methodism* (New York, NY: Abingdon, 1956).

[78] Lester Ruth, *Early Methodist Life and Spirituality* (Nashville TN:Abingdon, 2005), 19.

[79] Gill, *Charles Wesley: The First Methodist*, 75.

[80] Ward and Heitzenrater (eds), *The Works of John Wesley*, vol. 19, 46.

felt at ease with field preaching, but he believed that this was an important way to reach the people. Up to that point preaching outside one's parish had been a Dissenting activity, but Wesley insisted that the world was his mission field – 'I look upon all the world', he stated, 'as my parish.'[81]

The evangelistic work of the Methodists drew together all the strands of spirituality that have been outlined. The outlook was conversionist. There was a desire that everyone should have assurance and a testimony to pass on to others. This was not something original to Methodism: Hindmarsh shows how many Moravian testimonies of conversion contained vivid descriptions of an apprehension of the atonement.[82] However, the preaching within Methodism was more reasoned, as the Bible was explained. Wesley, although indebted to the Moravian vision, never embraced Moravian intensity.[83] Nonetheless, Methodist preachers, like the Moravians, did share with others the message of the power of the cross. As Ruth notes, their goal was 'to orchestrate experiences of justification – the initial experience of salvation including forgiveness of sins and justification – and sanctification'.[84] John Wesley repeatedly noted in his *Journal*, 'I offered them Christ'.

Wesley was not content to see individuals experiencing conversion. He wanted to establish communities of accountability. Many Methodist societies flourished. In Norwich, for example, in late 1751, Methodist preaching led to a huge revival. Over 2,000 people joined the Methodist Society, despite considerable violence against the Methodists.[85] By the time of his death John Wesley had travelled about 300,000 miles and preached about 45,000 sermons. He established a Methodist Connexion which grew during his life-time until it had about 1,500 lay preachers. Part of his achievement was to encourage women to take leadership.[86] The example of John Wesley also had a profound impact on William and Catherine Booth and the Salvation Army. In 1882 George Scott Railton, the son of a Methodist minister and one of William Booth's earliest helpers, wrote *The Saved Clergyman or the Story of John Wesley*, a book which consisted of descriptions of early Methodist evangelism. We Railton concluded: 'Whoever wishes well to the Church or the nation, let him follow John Wesley's example.'[87] In the same period, in 1885, the Methodist Southport Convention was started as a contribution to the renewal of Methodism, and Hugh Price Hughes, who combined progressive evangelistic and social concern with revivalist spirituality, hoped that Southport would be 'the Pentecost

---

[81] Telford (ed.), *The Letters of the Rev John Wesley, A.M.*, vol. I, 286.

[82] D. B. Hindmarsh, *The Evangelical Conversion Narrative: Spiritual Autobiography in Early Modern England* (Oxford: Oxford University Press, 2005), 177–80.

[83] J. Walsh, 'Religious Societies, Methodist and Evangelical, 1738–1800', *Studies in Church History*, 23 (1986), 279–302 and H. D. Rack, 'Religious Societies and the Origins of Methodism', *Journal of Ecclesiastical History*, 38 (1987), 582–95.

[84] Ruth, *Early Methodist Life and Spirituality*, 19.

[85] Rack, *Reasonable Enthusiast*, 300–302.

[86] P. W. Chilcote, *John Wesley and the Women Preachers of Early Methodism* (Metuchen, NJ: Rowman and Littlefield, 1991).

[87] D. Guy, 'The Influence of John Wesley on William and Catherine Booth', in P. Taylor (ed.), *Wesley Pieces* (Ilkeston, Derbys: The Wesley Fellowship, 1996), 17.

of modern Methodism'.[88] This desire for a renewal which involved effective mission – evangelistic and social – has continued.

## Conclusion

In this study I have concentrated on the early period in Methodism when Methodist spirituality first took shape. The ways in which the Methodist tradition has developed have meant that there has been great variety over time and across the world. In my study of evangelical spirituality in England between the First and Second World Wars, I found that the Wesleyan tradition, like other traditions, was divided because some wanted to go back to an earlier period while others wanted to explore new spiritual possibilities.[89] This tension remains. While there has been adaptation, as Cracknell and White argue, 'at its core [Methodism] has been a remarkably stable spiritual tradition'. The original vision of Wesley, drawing explicitly from the teaching of Jesus, has remained, that a Methodist is one who loves the Lord his God with all his heart, soul, mind and strength and his neighbour as himself.[90] This love is seen in the response of conversion, in serious engagement with the Bible, in a disciplined commitment, in use of the means of grace offered in Holy Communion, in a life of prayer and praise, in a desire for love to be perfected, and in active service in mission. In exhorting Hannah Ball to give advice to a male Methodist preacher, Wesley offered this general counsel: 'Go on in the Lord and in the power of his might. Warn every one ... and exhort every one, that you may present every one perfect in Christ.'[91] This is the Methodist spiritual vision.

---

[88] See R. C. Standing, 'The Relationship between Evangelicalism and the Social Gospel with Special Reference to Wesleyan Methodism', University of Manchester M. Phil. thesis (1992), 110.

[89] I. M. Randall, *Evangelical Experiences: A Study in the Spirituality of English Evangelicalism, 1918–1939* (Carlisle: Paternoster, 1999).

[90] Cracknell and White, 'Methodist Spirituality', 162, 168.

[91] John Wesley to Hannah Ball, 12 April 1774, in Telford (ed.), *The Letters of the Rev John Wesley, A.M.*, vol. VI, 79.

# 18

# Methodism and the Evangelical Tradition

## Martin Wellings

One of the most striking phenomena in the story of late-twentieth-century Christianity has been the resurgence of evangelicalism in the transatlantic West and its expansion across the Global South. The fundamentalist controversies of the 1910s and 1920s left Anglo-American evangelicalism divided, discredited and demoralised, but in the years after 1945 a remarkable renaissance took place.[1] The 'new evangelicalism' in the United States, associated particularly with Carl Henry and Billy Graham, saw evangelicals eschew the shibboleths of 'fighting fundamentalism' and regain a position of influence in the ecclesiastical and cultural mainstream, to the extent that *Newsweek* magazine could respond to the inauguration of President Jimmy Carter by labelling 1976 'the year of the evangelical'.[2] A comparable transformation took place in Great Britain, with the revival and strengthening of conservative evangelical strands in the historic denominations from the 1950s and then from the late 1960s the growth of new churches, some charismatic in worship style and theology, and some appealing to a particular national or ethnic constituency. The historians of the Evangelical Alliance characterised its history in the late twentieth century in terms of 'renewal' and 'resurgence', while the Alliance's sesquicentenary in 1996 prompted serious reflection on the opportunities and challenges of greater numbers and growing influence.[3] Church leaders, scholars and secular commentators, moreover,

---

[1] This topic has generated an extensive and increasing literature. See, for example, D. W. Bebbington, *Evangelicalism in Modern Britain: A History from the 1730s to the 1980s* (London: Unwin Hyman, 1989); Oliver Barclay, *Evangelicalism in Britain 1935–1995: A Personal Sketch* (Leicester: IVP, 1997); Joel A. Carpenter, *Revive Us Again: The Reawakening of American Fundamentalism* (New York: Oxford University Press, 1997); and George M. Marsden, *Fundamentalism and American Culture* (Oxford: Oxford University Press, 1980; 2nd edn, with additional material, 2006).

[2] Alister McGrath, *Evangelicalism and the Future of Christianity* (London: Hodder and Stoughton, 1993), 32.

[3] Ian Randall and David Hilborn, *One Body in Christ: The History and Significance of the Evangelical Alliance* (Carlisle: Paternoster, 2001), vi; Steve Brady and Harold Rowdon (eds),

recognised that evangelicalism was a significant force in the non-Western world. As the numerical balance within Christianity shifted to the Global South, so the strength of burgeoning evangelical churches in Africa, Asia and Latin America became increasingly important.[4]

The resurgence in evangelical numbers and influence has been matched by a revival of debate about evangelical identity. This has been contentious in the church and in the academy. 'New evangelicals' have been anxious to distance themselves from fundamentalism, while liberal critics have questioned the distinction.[5] Many evangelical leaders have emphasised unity in diversity, trying to hold together a coalition of disparate groups, while hard-liners have worried about doctrinal indifference and cultural accommodation. Manifestoes with telling titles have appeared: *Together We Stand*; *Lord, Make Us One – But Not All The Same!*; *Evangelicalism Divided*; *The Futures of Evangelicalism*.[6] In 1992 the ultra-conservative Banner of Truth Trust published *What is an Evangelical?*, three addresses given in 1971 by Martyn Lloyd-Jones, urging the need for clarity of definition and earnest contending for the faith.[7] Two years later Harper Collins published Derek Tidball's *Who are the Evangelicals?*, mapping the varieties of evangelicalism in an endeavour to avoid 'narrowness of vision and rigidity of judgement'.[8] The controversy has raged in the academy as well as in the church, and all parties have appealed to history for examples, warnings and insights. This has both stimulated historical research into evangelicalism and made such research highly contentious. The outcome overall has been a flourishing of historical scholarship and a lively debate about lines of interpretation.

Where does Methodism stand in this world of evangelical resurgence and disputed identities?

---

*For Such a Time as This: Perspectives on Evangelicalism, Past, Present and Future* (Milton Keynes: Scripture Union, 1996).

[4] Jeremy Morris, *The Church in the Modern Age* (London: I. B. Tauris, 2007), chs 9, 10, 14, 15; Diarmaid MacCulloch, *A History of Christianity* (London: Allen Lane, 2009), 958–1016; Philip Jenkins, *The New Faces of Christianity: Believing the Bible in the Global South* (New York: Oxford University Press, 2006).

[5] See John Stott, 'The Authority of the Scriptures – Response', in David L. Edwards and John Stott, *Essentials: A Liberal–Evangelical Dialogue* (London: Hodder and Stoughton, 1988), 89–95; compare Harriet A. Harris, *Fundamentalism and Evangelicals* (Oxford: Oxford University Press, 1998) and George M. Marsden, *Understanding Fundamentalism and Evangelicalism* (Grand Rapids, MI: Eerdmans, 1991), with the celebrated opening sentence 'A fundamentalist is an evangelical who is angry about something.'

[6] Authored or edited respectively by Clive Calver and Rob Warner (1996), Joel Edwards (1999), Iain Murray (2000) and Craig Bartholomew, Robin Parry and Andrew West (2003).

[7] Lloyd-Jones deprecated division over 'non-essentials', but gave a list of 'essentials' which included the historicity of Genesis, the sole authority of the Bible, and the consequent rejection of evolution, tradition, sacerdotalism and ecumenism.

[8] Derek J. Tidball, *Who are the Evangelicals?* (London: Marshall Pickering, 1994), cover. The change from Lloyd-Jones' 'what is' to Tidball's 'who are' says much about the difference in tone and approach.

In the Winter 2010 issue of *metconnexion*, the magazine of Methodist Evangelicals Together, the retiring General Secretary of MET reflected on the position of evangelicals in British Methodism a decade into the twenty-first century. Listing 'the things MET stands for' as 'upholding the authority of Scripture ... seeking spiritual renewal ... praying for revival ... spreading Scriptural holiness ... [and] emphasising the centrality of the cross', Richard Iball celebrated 'the way the church has moved over the last decade', but justified the continuing need for a definite evangelical organisation within the Methodist Church. British Methodism, he wrote, 'is ... certainly not an evangelical church ... yet!'[9] It is interesting to juxtapose this cautious assessment with the official doctrinal standards of the Church, enshrined in the 1932 Deed of Union, which affirm that the Connexion 'ever remembers that in the providence of God Methodism was raised up to spread scriptural holiness through the land by the proclamation of the evangelical faith and declares its unfaltering resolve to be true to its divinely appointed mission'. Furthermore, according to the Deed, Methodism 'has held [these evangelical doctrines] from the beginning', and still holds them.[10] This confident claim would certainly not be accepted by all within the wider evangelical movement; indeed, a leading historian of evangelicalism, when asked whether late- twentieth-century Methodism was an evangelical denomination, replied: 'It used to be.'[11]

From these three conflicting perspectives it may be seen both that there is a relationship between Methodism and evangelicalism, but also that the nature of the relationship requires some investigation and elucidation. This chapter seeks to map the relationship, both historically and theologically, and to indicate the state of current research. Much of the material used will be drawn from British and North American sources, although it is recognised that Methodism and evangelicalism are worldwide phenomena, with increasing representation in the Global South. In what follows it should be noted that 'Methodism' will be used to refer to the movement tracing its origins to the work of the Wesley brothers and those who operated 'in connexion with' them, while the definition of 'evangelicalism' will be considered below, because it is a significant part of the historiography of recent years.

## The Evangelical Revival and Methodism

Although Rupert Davies claimed that 'Methodism is ... a recurrent form of Christianity' with manifestations in many ages of the Church,[12] the historical phenomenon of the Methodist movement came to birth in conjunction with the

---

[9] 'From the General Secretaries', *metconnexion* (Ilkeston), Winter 2010, 12–13.
[10] *The Constitutional Practice and Discipline of the Methodist Church* (Peterborough: Methodist Publishing, 2010), ii, 213.
[11] Martin Wellings, *Evangelicals in Methodism: Mainstream, Marginalised or Misunderstood?* (Ilkeston: Moorley's, 2005), 5.
[12] Rupert E. Davies, *Methodism* (London: Epworth Press, 1963), 1.

Evangelical Revival of the eighteenth century. Indeed, for generations popular Methodist history and Wesley hagiography were inclined to collapse the revival into John Wesley's autobiography, as if it began in Aldersgate Street in May 1738 and continued as Wesley 'leapt on his horse and rode off in all directions'.[13] At the other end of the historical spectrum, John Kent has described the revival as itself 'one of the persistent myths of modern British history', a provocative judgement which has not won widespread support among historians, although many recognise the abundant mythology associated with the movement.[14] Encouraged by the surge in evangelical numbers in the last third of the twentieth century, the revival has attracted considerable scholarly attention in recent years, and three important areas of research may be identified.

First, careful work has been done on the roots of the revival in Britain, North America and Continental Europe. Thus movements of reform and renewal have been detected in the Church of England from the late 1670s to the 1730s, including religious societies, societies for the reformation of manners, missionary enterprises like the SPG and SPCK, and agencies fostering contact with European Protestants.[15] In *The Great Awakening: The Roots of Evangelical Christianity in Colonial America* (2007) Thomas Kidd has discerned 'clear antecedents' of the revival in the covenant renewals in New England in the 1670s and 1680s, and in the 'harvests' reaped by Solomon Stoddard in Northampton, Massachusetts.[16] The wider European background has been illuminated by W. R. Ward in *The Protestant Evangelical Awakening* (1992) and *Early Evangelicalism: A Global Intellectual History, 1670–1789* (2006). Significantly, Ward devotes five chapters to revival in the Hapsburg lands and the Holy Roman Empire, reaching his discussion of America and Britain only towards the end of the book.

Secondly, the geographical spread and diversity of the revival have been increasingly recognised and explored. The essays in the symposium *Evangelicalism: Comparative Studies of Popular Protestantism in North America, the British Isles, and Beyond, 1700–1990* (1994) reflect on transatlantic publishing networks, communication through journals and letters, and the itineraries of leaders like George Whitefield, whose travels disseminated news of revival widely. In 2004 the evangelical publishing house Inter-Varsity Press launched a five-volume history of evangelicalism, promising 'a connected history of evangelical movements throughout the English-speaking world, from the 1730s to the 1990s'. The first book in the series, Mark Noll's *The Rise of Evangelicalism*, offered a multi-national

---

[13] John A. Vickers, *Myths of Methodism* (Oxford: Wesley Historical Society, 2008), 30.

[14] John Kent, *Wesley and the Wesleyans* (Cambridge: Cambridge University Press, 2002), 1. On Methodist mythology, see Vickers, *Myths of Methodism*; for the mythology of evangelicalism in relation to the American Revolution, see Thomas S. Kidd, *The Great Awakening: The Roots of Evangelical Christianity in Colonial America* (New Haven, CT: Yale University Press, 2007), 288–90.

[15] Jeremy Gregory, 'The Long Eighteenth Century', in Randy L. Maddox and Jason E. Vickers (eds), *The Cambridge Companion to John Wesley* (Cambridge: Cambridge University Press, 2010), 32.

[16] Kidd, *The Great Awakening*, 3–9.

narrative of evangelical movements in the age of Jonathan Edwards, George Whitefield and the Wesleys, synthesising a large body of research.

Thirdly, as noted above, the definition and identity of evangelicalism have come under scrutiny. No study of evangelicalism can escape the work of David Bebbington, whose *Evangelicalism in Modern Britain: A History from the 1730s to the 1980s* (1989) made two seminal proposals. First, Bebbington offered a definition of evangelicalism, suggesting four 'special marks of evangelical religion': 'conversionism, the belief that lives need to be changed; activism, the expression of the gospel in effort; Biblicism, a particular regard for the Bible; and ... crucicentrism, a stress on the sacrifice of Christ on the cross'.[17] Secondly, Bebbington traced the interplay between these 'four qualities' or 'main characteristics' and a series of social and cultural movements, arguing that evangelicalism retained its essence while expressing itself in a variety of forms, influenced by the Enlightenment, Romanticism and modernism.[18]

As Tim Larsen has demonstrated, the 'Bebbington quadrilateral' has become an accepted truth in much of the literature on evangelicalism, although debate continues about the relationship between evangelicalism and culture.[19] The four characteristics usefully indicate areas of resemblance among evangelicals, but the peculiarities of different groups also remain significant, as the case of Methodism illustrates. More precisely, Methodism shared a 'family resemblance' with all evangelicals, it held certain aspects in common with particular evangelical groups, and it possessed several distinctive features which gave Methodist evangelicalism a unique flavour.

Early Methodism in Britain and America comfortably fits within the Bebbington criteria and qualifies as a strand of the wider eighteenth-century evangelical movement. Methodism's founding narrative focussed on the conversion of the Wesley brothers in May 1738, and although the contemporary importance of the Aldersgate Street events remains contentious, conversion was certainly central to the experience of the first Methodists and to the priorities of the movement's mission. Accounts of conversion featured prominently in the exemplary biographies which John Wesley solicited, collected and edited for publication in his *Arminian Magazine*, while conversion underpinned the deep personal piety and strenuous labours of the early preachers.[20] The whole machinery of Methodism

---

[17] Bebbington, *Evangelicalism in Modern Britain*, 2–3.
[18] Ibid., 275.
[19] Timothy Larsen, 'The Reception Given *Evangelicalism in Modern Britain* since its Publication in 1989', in Michael A. G. Haykin and Kenneth J. Stewart (eds), *The Emergence of Evangelicalism: Exploring Historical Continuities* (Nottingham: Apollos, 2008), 21–36, esp. 27–9. The entire volume is an engagement with 'the Bebbington thesis'. Larsen has offered his own definition, modifying the Bebbington 'quadrilateral', in 'Defining and Locating Evangelicalism', in Timothy Larsen and Daniel J. Treier (eds), *The Cambridge Companion to Evangelical Theology* (Cambridge: Cambridge University Press, 2007), 1.
[20] John H. Wigger, *Taking Heaven by Storm: Methodism and the Rise of Popular Christianity in America* (Urbana, IL: University of Illinois Press, 1998), 53–4; John Lenton, *John Wesley's Preachers* (Milton Keynes: Paternoster, 2009), 50–52; D. Bruce Hindmarsh, *The Evangelical*

functioned as a structure for effective evangelism. Turning to the Bible, John Wesley was famously 'a man of one book';[21] Methodism's doctrinal standards were not creeds or confessions, but expository sermons and 'explanatory notes' on Scripture; and Charles Wesley's hymns were soaked in biblical references, imagery and vocabulary.[22] Methodist crucicentrism was experiential rather than doctrinal: for the Wesleys, the grace and love of God were seen supremely in the cross, and this was reflected in Charles Wesley's lyrical hymns on the Passion.[23] As Lester Ruth observes, early American Methodists placed their emphasis less on the dogmatic interpretation of the atonement than on an affective encounter with an atoning Christ.[24] As for activism, the first of the 'Twelve Rules of a Helper', formulated at the first Methodist Conference in June 1744, began 'Be diligent. Never be unemployed a moment.'[25] This rule was bequeathed to the British Connexion, where it came to be read annually in the May Synods,[26] and it was reinforced for American Methodists in Coke and Asbury's annotated *Discipline* of 1798.[27] John Wesley matched precept by example, as did the Methodist preachers on both sides of the Atlantic. Thus John Walsh can describe Wesley's ideal Christian life as 'one of ceaseless, cheerful activism',[28] while Francis Asbury criss-crossed North America, travelling thousands of miles on horseback even in his final years, becoming so wellknown in the process that mail from Europe could be addressed simply to 'Francis Asbury, America'.[29]

Having placed the Wesleys' Methodism within the broadest understanding of the evangelical movement, some finer distinctions may now be drawn, beginning with four aspects characteristic of, though not unique to, Methodism.

First, Methodism represented a popular and populist strand within eighteenth-century evangelicalism. In John Wesley himself an authoritarian temperament and instinctive High Churchmanship coexisted with an apostolic concern for the poor and a readiness to discard ecclesiastical tradition and social proprieties for the sake

---

*Conversion Narrative: Spiritual Autobiography in Early Modern England* (Oxford: Oxford University Press, 2005), 226–60.

[21] 'Preface', in Albert C. Outler (ed.), *The Works of John Wesley: Sermons I* (Nashville, TN: Abingdon, 1984), 105.

[22] John Lawson, *A Thousand Tongues: The Wesley Hymns as a Guide to Scriptural Teaching* (Exeter: Paternoster, 1987) gives numerous examples.

[23] Ibid., 59–65, 167.

[24] Lester Ruth, *Early Methodist Life and Spirituality*. (Nashville, TN: Kingswood, 2005), 35.

[25] *Minutes of the Methodist Conference* (London: Thomas Cordeux, 1812), 1744, 15.

[26] *The Constitutional Practice and Discipline of the Methodist Church* (Peterborough: Methodist Publishing House, 1988), i, 77. The wording was slightly amended in 1753.

[27] Wigger, *Taking Heaven by Storm*, 8.

[28] John Walsh, *John Wesley 1703–1791: A Bicentennial Tribute* (London: Dr Williams's Trust, 1993), 7.

[29] John Wigger, *American Saint: Francis Asbury and the Methodists* (New York, NY: Oxford University Press, 2009), 302, 375.

of the gospel.[30] The Methodist movement was predominantly lay-led, giving status, recognition and authority to lay men and women as preachers, exhorters and class leaders. These characteristics, apparent and inevitable in Britain from the 1740s, were even stronger in America after the Revolution, and they cemented a powerful bond with the democratic impulses of the new republic which helped Methodism achieve astonishing growth in the period between 1780 and 1820.[31] Methodists were not the only populist evangelicals: similar features may be discerned among American Baptists and Disciples of Christ, for example, but populism marked a distinction between Methodists and more respectable evangelicals in the Church of England and the established denominations in North America.[32]

Linked to populism, secondly, was a thorough-going enthusiasm and supernaturalism. To their critics, all evangelicals were enthusiasts, and evangelical apologists, including John Wesley, tried variously to refute or to nuance the accusation. The Methodist worldview, however, remained one in which dreams, visions and providential happenings bulked large, and the movement was known for the exuberance of its spirituality and worship.[33] On New Year's Day 1739 the Wesley brothers attended a love feast in Fetter Lane at which '[A]bout three in the morning, as we were continuing instant in prayer, the power of God came mightily upon us, insomuch that many cried out for exceeding joy, and many fell to the ground.'[34] Such dramatic experiences were commonplace in British and American Methodism. While Wesley valued reason and rationality, justifying Henry Rack's description of him as a 'reasonable enthusiast', what John Wigger denominates 'militant supernaturalism'[35] was prevalent among the preachers, lay leaders and converts of the Methodist movement, forging a connection with existing traditions of popular religion. Again, Methodism was not unique in this; again, genteel evangelicals like the Episcopalian Devereux Jarratt and the Congregationalists Timothy Dwight and Lyman Beecher found such antics deeply uncongenial.[36]

---

[30] Walsh, *Wesley*, 8, 13–17; J. D. Walsh, 'John Wesley and the Community of Goods', in Keith Robbins (ed.), *Protestant Evangelicalism: Britain, Ireland, Germany and America c. 1750–c. 1950* (Oxford: Blackwell, 1990).

[31] Nathan O. Hatch, *The Democratization of American Christianity* (New Haven, CT: Yale University Press, 1989), 9–11. Mark A. Noll, *The Rise of Evangelicalism: The Age of Edwards, Whitefield and the Wesleys* (Leicester: IVP, 2004), 205, has a graph of American Methodist membership 1773–91; Wigger, *Taking Heaven by Storm*, 197–200, gives figures for 1773, 1780, 1790, 1800 and 1810.

[32] Bebbington, *Evangelicalism in Modern Britain*, 30–31, maps attitudes to church order among English evangelicals.

[33] Wigger, *Taking Heaven by Storm*, ch. 5; Phyllis Mack, *Heart Religion in the British Enlightenment* (Cambridge: Cambridge University Press, 2008), 219–260. Compare Russell E. Richey, 'Methodism and Providence: A Study in Secularization', in Robbins (ed.), *Protestant Evangelicalism*.

[34] W. Reginald Ward and Richard P. Heitzenrater (eds), *WJW 19 Journal and Diaries II (1738–1743)* (Nashville, TN: Abingdon, 1990), 29 (entry for 1 January 1739).

[35] Wigger, *Taking Heaven by Storm*, 115.

[36] Hatch, *Democratization of American Christianity*, 17–18, 21.

Given the populist and enthusiastic nature of early Methodism, it is not surprising, thirdly, that Methodists placed a saving experience of Christ above concern for the minutiae of doctrine. John Wesley included in his Connexion's doctrinal standards a sermon on 'Catholic Spirit' in which he urged Christians to be of one heart, even if they could not be of one opinion. Wesley was no advocate of easy-going toleration, a tendency he stigmatised as 'speculative latitudinarianism', but he held that Christians could all too easily elevate minor disagreements into causes of schism.[37] Mark Noll, in discussing 'theological differentiation' within the evangelical movement, places the Wesleys with those who emphasised preaching Christ and urging holiness of life, rather than focussing on doctrinal precision.[38] Although John Wesley expected his preachers to take reading seriously, it may be seen that evangelical activism and an emphasis on experience could easily produce an anti-intellectualism scornful or suspicious of 'lettered learning'. In the American context, this placed Methodists with the Baptists, in opposition to the college-educated clergy and appealing to anti-elitist sentiment in the new nation.

Fourthly, the Wesleys' Methodism, although not uniquely so, was undoubtedly the most aggressively Arminian element in the Evangelical Revival. Many of the leaders of the revival leant towards moderate Calvinism, because they found that the Reformed understanding of divine sovereignty made sense of their experience of grace.[39] The Wesleys, nurtured in Arminianism at Epworth and Oxford, abhorred Calvinism, holding it to be the antithesis of Methodism.[40] If salvation was about unconditional election and irresistible grace, there was no point in preaching or evangelism, and there was no truly good news in the gospel, because only the chosen, the foreordained, would be able to respond. Predestination and perseverance, John Wesley argued, destroyed moral responsibility, undermined holiness and encouraged antinomianism. The whole system, said Wesley, was a blasphemy which made Scripture untrue, Jesus a hypocrite and God a monster. 'What are all the absurd opinions of all the Romanists in the world', asked Wesley, preaching in Cork in 1775, 'compared to that one, that the God of love, the wise, just, merciful Father of the spirits of all flesh, has from all eternity fixed an absolute, unchangeable, irresistible decree that part of mankind shall be saved, do what they will, and the rest damned, do what they can!'[41] The consequence of this robust Arminianism was conflict with Whitefield in 1740 and with another generation of Calvinist evangelicals in the 1770s. In America, where Calvinist denominations were established in pre-Revolutionary New England, theological controversy was exacerbated by tensions between elite

---

[37] 'Catholic Spirit', in Outler (ed.), *Works of John Wesley: Sermons II*, 81–95, esp. 82 and 92.
[38] Noll, *Rise of Evangelicalism*, 111.
[39] D. Bruce Hindmarsh, *John Newton and the English Evangelical Tradition* (Grand Rapids, MI: Eerdmans, 1996), 50–51, citing examples of Newton, Berridge, Venn and Scott.
[40] Herbert B. McGonigle, *John Wesley's Arminian Theology: An Introduction* (Lutterworth: Wesley Fellowship, 2005), 37.
[41] 'On the Trinity', in Outler (ed.), *Works of John Wesley: Sermons II*, 376.

and popular religion, as Methodism claimed to champion an accessible religion for all the people against an erudite creed for the few.[42]

Turning finally to features unique to the Wesleys' Methodism, two may be identified. The first was the structure of the movement: the machinery of bands, classes and societies to husband, organise and nurture converts; the pattern of meetings in society and circuit; the preachers and the itinerancy to serve and supervise the societies; the connecting threads of hymns and publications; the oversight exercised by Wesley and his 'assistants' through travel and correspondence; the authority embodied in the annual Conference, and codified in the *Large Minutes* and the *Discipline*.[43] These were the physical components of connexionalism, both expressing and reinforcing a distinctive ecclesiology – 'our discipline'. Many of the parts of Wesley's system were borrowed or adapted from elsewhere, and elements of his organisation were used by other leaders – Whitefield, Lady Huntingdon and Benjamin Ingham, for instance, had 'connexions' of their own. Wesley, however, created a system without parallel in Britain, and Asbury used the same structure to build the Methodist Episcopal Church in America.[44]

Wesley saw the Connexion as a tool serving the mission of Methodism, and his understanding of that mission incorporated a doctrine of holiness which was his movement's second distinctive feature. For John Wesley, the goal of the Christian life was perfect love: the renewing of the image of God in the believer and the eradication of sin. Wesley taught that the experience of entire sanctification, or freedom from sin, was possible in this life, and he claimed that this doctrine was the 'grand depositum' lodged with the people called Methodists, and the reason why the movement had been raised up. For evangelicals in the Reformed tradition, such teaching was at best naïve and at worst a long step towards Roman Catholicism or Pelagianism.[45]

Eighteenth-century Methodism shared much common ground with all evangelicals. Taken together, however, the particular structures and emphases of Methodism gave the movement an unusual degree of success, especially in America, and a distinctive identity. Unusually Arminian in its soteriology, uniquely promoting entire sanctification as a present experience and organised in a tight-knit connexion, Methodism emerged from the Evangelical Revival as a strong sub-

---

[42] Wigger, *Taking Heaven by Storm*, 17; Hatch, *Democratization of American Christianity*, 170–79.

[43] The cumulative Minutes of the annual Conference were produced as the *Large Minutes* in Britain from 1753; the equivalent for the Methodist Episcopal Church was the *Discipline*, first published in 1785.

[44] John Lawson, 'The People called Methodists – 2. "Our Discipline"' and Frank Baker, 'The People called Methodists – 3. Polity', in Rupert Davies and Gordon Rupp (eds), *A History of the Methodist Church in Great Britain*, i (London: Epworth Press, 1965); Wigger, *Taking Heaven by Storm*, ch. 2.

[45] Herbert Boyd McGonigle, *Sufficient Saving Grace: John Wesley's Evangelical Arminianism* (Carlisle: Paternoster, 2001), 258–62. Mack, *Heart Religion*, 296, identifies the tension between self-transcendence and personal agency, made most acute in Wesleyan perfectionism, as the torque which drove the movement forward.

culture, aware of its relationships with other evangelicals, but also conscious of its differences. These elements were all carried forward into the next century.

## Nineteenth-Century Methodists and Evangelicalism

In entitling his history of the mid-nineteenth century *The Dominance of Evangelicalism*, David Bebbington summed up the strength of the evangelical movement in the century after Wesley's death. In North America and Great Britain evangelical denominations flourished, evangelical organisations multiplied, and evangelical values and shibboleths entered into the Christian cultural mainstream. Evangelicals from different denominational and theological traditions banded together in a whole range of devotional, philanthropic and missionary agencies, such that James Stephen could write in 1844: 'Ours is the age of societies. For the redress of every oppression that is done under the sun, there is a public meeting. For the cure of every sorrow by which our land or our race can be visited, there are patrons, vice-presidents and secretaries. For the diffusion of every blessing of which mankind can partake in common, there is a committee.'[46] At the symbolic centre of this structure was the Evangelical Alliance, established in London by an Anglo-American initiative in August 1846.

Historians of the Alliance have not always recognised the extent of the Methodist involvement in the founding conference. Almost a quarter of the nine hundred delegates were Methodists. Two of the four major donors to the fledgling organisation were Methodists. Methodists were well represented on the Alliance's committees and in its secretariat. It is not surprising, therefore, that the speaker chosen to open the conference, and to conclude it a fortnight later, was also a Methodist, the Wesleyan elder statesman Jabez Bunting.[47]

Although the Evangelical Alliance failed to fulfil the high hopes of its progenitors, its inauguration accurately placed Methodism at the heart of the wider evangelical movement. For the whole of the nineteenth century, Methodism continued to share the defining characteristics of evangelical religion, as well as sustaining its own specific emphases. As will be seen, however, for Methodists in particular, as for evangelicals in general, the interpretation and expression of the emphases evolved in the course of the century.

Beginning with the 'Bebbington quadrilateral', Methodists maintained their adherence to the core characteristics of Bible, cross, conversion and action.

---

[46] James Stephen, 'The Clapham Sect', *Edinburgh Review*, clxi (London:Longman, Brown, Green and Longmans and Edinburgh:Adam and Charles Black, 1844 [vol. lxxx]), 306.

[47] *Report of the Proceedings of the Conference held at Freemasons' Hall, London, from August 19 to September 2 inclusive, 1846* (London: Partridge & Oakley, 1847). The delegates are listed in appendix C, lxxvii–xcvii, with denomination. There were 162 Wesleyan Methodist delegates, sixteen from the Methodist Episcopal Church and one from the African Methodist Episcopal Church .

Methodist preaching and piety were Bible-based; Methodists supported the efforts of Bible societies to circulate the Scriptures and of Sunday schools to equip people to read the Bible; and Methodist theology emphasised the authority of Scripture. In the words of the *Free Methodist* newspaper in January 1881: 'There is but one final standard of Christian living, or Christian doctrine. That standard is the Word of God, revealed to man in the Holy Scriptures.'[48] The cross of Christ stood at the heart of Methodist dogmatics, seen, for example, in the massive *Compendium of Christian Theology* published by the British Wesleyan William Burt Pope in 1875. The pivot of Pope's system was 'the mediatorial ministry', the plan of salvation focussed on the death of Christ. The cross, wrote John Miley in the New York *Christian Advocate* five years later, was 'the symbol of all that is most vital in Christianity'.[49] The Australasian Conference, meeting in Hobart Town in February 1858, assured its British parent that 'With you, we will steadfastly and fully preach the good old Methodist doctrine. We are "determined to know nothing among men, save Jesus Christ, and Him crucified."'[50] Conversion, too, remained central to the Methodist understanding of Christianity and of the Church's mission. Memoirs and biographies dwelt on this theme; preachers were clear that conversion was essential to real Christianity; and when an Anglican bishop cast aspersions on Methodist meetings as over-heated exercises in emotional manipulation, the Wesleyan veteran Thomas Jackson penned a magisterial reply, concluding: 'Take away conversion, in doctrine and experience, from Wesleyan Methodism, and you have nothing left but what is as unsubstantial as the shadow that follows a man in a moonlight night.'[51] Activism, too, remained a hallmark of Methodism, expressed in the ethos of the movement and demonstrated by the statistics meticulously assembled, testifying to the growth of the denomination in members, societies, buildings, institutions and agencies.

In crafting his quadrilateral, David Bebbington deliberately identified characteristics capable of re-interpretation in changing times. It is not surprising, therefore, that Methodists, in common with other nineteenth-century evangelicals, articulated their evangelicalism in new ways as the century wore on. While Methodists continued to uphold the authority of Scripture, from the 1890s the 'higher criticism' of the Bible began to make inroads into Methodist colleges, publications and pulpits. George C. Workman and George Jackson in Toronto, Borden Parker Bowne and Hinkley G. Mitchell in Boston, Charles Garland in New Zealand and A. S. Peake in Great Britain were among those who championed

---

[48] Cited in David W. Bebbington, *The Dominance of Evangelicalism* (Nottingham: IVP, 2005), 23.
[49] John Miley, 'The Cross', *Christian Advocate* (New York), 29 January 1880, 65.
[50] 'Address of the Conference of the Australasian Wesleyan-Methodist Church to the British Conference', *Minutes of Conference 1858* (London: John Mason, 1862), 148.
[51] T. J[ackson], 'The Wesleyan Doctrine of Conversion', *Wesleyan Methodist Magazine* (London), 1868, 414–26, quote at 426.

'believing criticism' around the turn of the century.[52] Bowne's personalist teaching, moreover, represented a striking move away from the traditional Methodist view of the atonement; less influential in the long term, but also provocative in its context, was the British Wesleyan John Scott Lidgett's Fernley Lecture of 1897, *The Spiritual Principle of the Atonement*. Bowne drew on idealist and neo-Kantian philosophy, while Lidgett echoed in a Free Church setting the shift in theology's centre of gravity from the atonement to the incarnation, principally associated with the Anglican *Lux Mundi* school. Conversion, although still important, lost some of its immediacy. Kenneth Brown has claimed that the *Methodist Recorder* reported in August 1903 that less than half of the candidates accepted for the ministry at the recent Wesleyan Conference had testified to a definite conversion experience: most had spoken instead of processes of gradual enlightenment or conviction.[53] Although Methodists remained busy, the scope of their activism changed. Church programmes expanded and diversified; traditional Methodist activities, particularly class meetings, love feasts and camp meetings, waned; and leisure pursuits, formerly shunned as worldly, began to feature in chapel programmes.[54]

These developments were not unique to Methodism, for they may be discerned across the spectrum of evangelical churches in Great Britain and North America in the course of the nineteenth century.[55] It is worth considering, however, how the changing expression of Methodist evangelicalism interacted with Methodism's more distinctive features.

It has already been seen that early Methodism was populist and enthusiastic, appealing to anti-elitist sentiment and finding common ground with folk superstition. Just over twenty years after Asbury's death, Nathan Bangs nuanced a celebration of his leadership with an identification of two oversights: lack of concern for a learned ministry and educational institutions, and lack of provision

---

[52] David B. Marshall, *Secularizing the Faith: Canadian Protestant Clergy and the Crisis of Belief, 1850–1940* (Toronto: University of Toronto Press, 1992), 76–9, 289; Russell E. Richey, Kenneth E. Rowe and Jean Miller Schmidt, *The Methodist Experience in America: A History* (Nashville, TN: Abingdon, 2010), i, 301; Susan J. Thompson, *Knowledge and Vital Piety: Education for Methodist Ministry in New Zealand from the 1840s* (Manukau: WHS New Zealand, 2010), 31; John T. Wilkinson, *Arthur Samuel Peake* (London: Epworth Press, 1971), 115–17.

[53] Kenneth D. Brown, *A Social History of the Nonconformist Ministry in England and Wales 1800–1930* (Oxford: Clarendon Press, 1988), 53. The article 'Candidates for Ordination', *Methodist Recorder*, (London), 6 August 1903, 25, does not wholly support Brown's argument, since twenty-one of the thirty-four ordinands refer to a definite experience, albeit using a variety of terms.

[54] Dominic Erdozain, *The Problem of Pleasure: Sport, Recreation and the Crisis of Victorian Religion* (Woodbridge: Boydell, 2010) claims that this shift eviscerated Victorian Nonconformity.

[55] It may be noted that the availability of publications and the exchange of personnel across the Atlantic and across the British Empire sustained a common English-speaking evangelical world in this period.

for ministers and their families.⁵⁶ Like his close contemporary Jabez Bunting in Great Britain, Bangs was anxious to garner the fruits of Methodism's success, to retain the loyalty of the upwardly mobile and respectable members of society, to give the Church an infrastructure commensurate with its numerical strength and missionary opportunities and, where necessary, to curb the extravagances of revivalism. In their recent account of *The Methodist Experience in America*, Russell Richey, Ken Rowe and Jean Miller Schmidt discern a dialectic between appeals to the 'churchly' Wesley and the 'revivalistic' Wesley in this period.⁵⁷ As American Methodism acquired parsonages and opted for 'stationed' preachers instead of Circuit riders, as British and American Methodists began to build imposing Gothic churches and to train their preachers in seminaries, and as denominational bureaucracies developed to manage the burgeoning connexions, Methodism did not wholly cease to be populist and enthusiastic; rather, it added a new strand of educated respectability which contributed to its success with a rising urban middle class. This strand, however, came into conflict with the older tradition, giving real concerns and rhetorical space to 'Primitive' Methodists in Britain, 'croakers' in America and 'reformers' on both sides of the Atlantic. Different visions of Methodism emerged, and the resulting tension spawned new denominations, in some of which the same issues of cultural accommodation were played out a couple of generations later.⁵⁸

There was no slackening in Methodism's commitment to Arminian theology in this period. Indeed, Nathan Bangs' reputation as a Methodist spokesman was made with apologetic works attacking Calvinism, while Bunting broke with the promoters of the pan-evangelical *Eclectic Review* when it 'impugned the principles of Evangelical Arminianism'. For Bunting, this was a salutary experience, cementing his preference for 'denominational methods'.⁵⁹ Particularly in the British context, Arminianism marked Methodists off from most other evangelicals and encouraged a degree of theological insularity.

Experience also remained important to Methodists, to such an extent that the Tractarian E. B. Pusey could accuse the Wesleyans of advocating justification by feelings: an accusation indignantly rebutted by Thomas Jackson.⁶⁰ It may be suggested that the nineteenth century saw a change in the Methodist use of the language of experience, from Wesley's emphasis that saving faith must be

---

⁵⁶ Richey, Rowe and Schmidt, *Methodist Experience in America*, 103–4; Nathan Bangs, *A History of the Methodist Episcopal Church*, ii, citing the third edition (New York: Lane and Tippett, 1845), 413–17.

⁵⁷ Richey, Rowe and Schmidt, *Methodist Experience in America*, 104.

⁵⁸ This was the experience of the Primitive Methodists in Great Britain: Geoffrey Milburn, *Primitive Methodism* (Peterborough: Epworth Press, 2002), 43–53.

⁵⁹ Abel Stevens, *Life and Times of Nathan Bangs, DD* (New York, NY: Carlton and Porter, 1863), 208–10, 223–4; Richey, Rowe and Schmidt, *Methodist Experience in America*, 107; T. P. Bunting and G. Stringer Rowe, *The Life of Jabez Bunting, DD* (London: T. Woolmer, 1887), 211–13.

⁶⁰ Mats Selén, *The Oxford Movement and Wesleyan Methodism in England 1833–1882* (Lund: Lund University Press, 1992), 179–83.

'a disposition of the heart', rather than merely 'a cold, lifeless assent' or 'a train of ideas in the head' to a prioritising of experience over all doctrinal tests and considerations. This was not unique to Methodists, and not all Methodists moved away from doctrinal standards, but it was a discernible trend which opened the movement to theological change.[61]

If nineteenth-century Methodists re-interpreted experience, they also recast their understanding of Christian perfection. Entire sanctification as a decisive stage in the Christian life, obtained by faith after ardent seeking and evidenced in a transformed lifestyle clearly separate from the 'world', was variously diluted by rising respectability, challenged by the teaching of 'holiness by faith' and supplanted by the social gospel.[62] Methodist belief and practice became less distinctive and more diverse, and this generated significant secessions to new holiness denominations in the United States in the years after the Civil War.[63] Meanwhile, some British Wesleyans sought to return to their roots with the establishment of the Southport Holiness Convention in 1885.

Nineteenth-century evangelicalism rested on a knife-edge between optimism and anxiety. Even as they celebrated their successes at home and abroad, evangelicals were aware of the rival attractions of Roman and Anglo-Catholicism, concerned about the challenge of Darwinian biology, biblical criticism and liberal theology, and conscious of the incursion of worldliness into the Church. Largely untouched by pre-millennial gloom, Methodists remained confident, buoyed up by numerical strength, impressive resources, growing foreign missions and significant domestic influence. As the twentieth century dawned, however, tensions within the evangelical world exploded into conflict, and Methodism was inevitably affected by this development.

## The Twentieth Century

The story of twentieth-century evangelicalism has often been told in terms of polarisation.[64] As evangelicals responded to the developments already outlined – biblical, theological and cultural – it is often suggested that a gulf of separation

---

[61] 'Salvation by Faith', in Outler (ed.), *Works of John Wesley: Sermons*, i, 120; Wilfred R. Wilkinson, *Religious Experience: The Methodist Fundamental* (London: Holborn Publishing House, 1928), 7. Wilkinson mentions James Denney as an example of a similar outlook: ibid., 11.

[62] David Bebbington, *Holiness in Nineteenth-Century England* (Carlisle: Paternoster, 2000), 62–7; Kathryn T. Long, 'Consecrated Respectability: Phoebe Palmer and the Refinement of American Methodism', in Nathan O. Hatch and John H. Wigger (eds), *Methodism and the Shaping of American Culture* (Nashville, TN: Kingswood, 2001), 281–307.

[63] Melvin E. Dieter, *The Holiness Revival of the Nineteenth Century* (Lanham, MD: Scarecrow Press, 1996 [2nd ed.]), ch. 3.

[64] Seen particularly in accounts of the divisions in the student movement, for example Douglas Johnson, *Contending for the Faith* (Leicester: IVP, 1979).

opened up in the movement between those who embraced 'modern thought' and those who adhered steadfastly to the 'old paths' in what they saw as increasingly perilous times. Such a reading enables the protagonists in late-twentieth-century debates to label their opponents 'modernists' or 'fundamentalists'. The historical reality, however, was more complicated. Evangelicalism, already a broad coalition, showed an ability to accommodate many aspects of 'modern thought' while remaining true to the core principles of Bible, cross, conversion and action. Biblical authority could be upheld while welcoming responsible critical scholarship. The cross could remain central to preaching and systematic theology without necessarily endorsing penal substitution. Conversion could be sought while also emphasising growth in spirituality. Activism could continue but with changes in priorities and prohibitions. It is true that the most conservative or paranoid members of the evangelical family saw and denounced any nuance of doctrine or change of practice as apostasy, but many evangelicals were able to adopt a 'central' or 'liberal' position in the first third of the twentieth century.[65]

Methodism, too, moved with the times. In Great Britain the theological centre of gravity shifted to a liberal evangelical position. The assumptions and methodology of biblical criticism were adopted in the training of ministers and Local Preachers, and in A. S. Peake the Primitive Methodists produced a biblical scholar of international renown. Lidgett and Russell Maltby wrote creatively on the atonement. The Fellowship of the Kingdom, founded in 1919, offered ministers a forum for study, discussion and spiritual exploration free of the stale shibboleths of the past and seeking 'a reborn Methodism' in the post-war world.[66] Late-Victorian Methodists took up the Christian Endeavour movement with enthusiasm, and the Wesleyans formed their own organisation, the Wesley Guild, in 1896 to give a structure to the cultural as well as spiritual nurture of young people. The first third of the twentieth century was the Guild's heyday, and its ethos was a moderate evangelicalism.[67]

A similar trajectory may be discerned in North America. Canadian Methodists tackled their newlyprosperous society with a positive approach to leisure and with an increasing advocacy of the social gospel, associated with the leadership of Samuel Dwight Chown.[68] The controversy generated by George Jackson's advocacy of biblical criticism in Toronto in the early 1910s showed that there was keen debate over the acceptability of 'modern thought', but that a broadly liberal evangelical position was tenable. In the United States, Robert Chiles characterises the decades around the turn of the century as years of transition from 'liberal evangelicalism' to 'evangelical liberalism', as the generation of John Miley (1813–95) gave way to that

---

[65] Bebbington, *Evangelicalism in Modern Britain*, ch. 6.
[66] Ian M. Randall, *Evangelical Experiences: A Study in the Spirituality of English Evangelicalism 1918–1939* (Carlisle: Paternoster, 1999), 110–34, at 114; K. Harley Boyns, *The Fellowship of the Kingdom* (London: Epworth Press, n.d. [1922]), 17.
[67] William Leary, *Wesley Guild: The First Hundred Years* (Liverpool: Wesley Guild, 1995), 20, 43.
[68] Marshall, *Secularizing the Faith*, 131, 145–50.

of Borden Parker Bowne (1847–1910) and then that of Albert C. Knudson (1873–1953). Chiles suggests that American Methodism moved further and faster from its evangelical roots than its British cousins, so that 'Methodism was dominated by liberalism in the first third of the twentieth century'.[69] Dominance in seminaries and denominational publications, however, should not obscure the existence of much more conservative attitudes in local congregations: not all conservative evangelicals in American Methodism had left for the holiness movement.[70]

'Central' or 'constructive conservative' evangelicals remained wellrepresented in Methodism. In Britain this outlook was epitomised by Samuel Chadwick (1860–1932), Principal of Cliff College and president of the Southport Convention, by the evangelist Charles Hulbert (1878–1957), the connexional statesman Colin Roberts (1886–1975) and the pre-eminent preacher W. E. Sangster (1900–1960).[71] In the United States, bishops like Warren Candler and Horace DuBose expounded a conservative understanding of Methodist evangelicalism.[72]

Writing in 1934, DuBose made it very clear that 'I am not a fundamentalist, as the term is strictly defined.'[73] The historiography notes, and seeks to account for, the weakness of organised fundamentalism in Methodism, on both sides of the Atlantic.[74] Two points of interpretation are important. First, Methodists of conservative inclinations tended not to endorse such key fundamentalist tenets as biblical inerrancy and premillennialism. Secondly, Methodists generally eschewed the militancy and divisiveness of 'fighting fundamentalism'. Methodism had its staunch conservatives, some of whom were even prepared to adopt the fundamentalist label, like Dinsdale Young, Harold P. Sloan and Robert P. 'Fighting Bob' Shuler. It had a fringe of militants, like the Wesley Bible Union and the Methodist League for Faith and Life.[75] Methodism's experientialist emphasis and connexional ethos, however, acted against the formation of fundamentalist groups within the denomination. This did not mean, though, that liberal or liberal evangelical assumptions were accepted and adopted across the Church, for conservative networks and publications continued to nurture 'folk fundamentalism' in local congregations and Circuits.[76]

---

[69] Robert E. Chiles, *Theological Transition in American Methodism 1790–1935* (Lanham, MD: University Press of America, 1983 [reprint of 1965 Abingdon Press original]), 61–75, at 65 and 71.

[70] On the 'stay-inners', see Howard Glenn Spann, 'Evangelicalism in Modern American Methodism: Theological Conservatives in the "Great Deep" of the Church, 1900–1980', Ph.D. diss., The Johns Hopkins University, 1994, 79–86.

[71] Martin Wellings, 'Evangelicalism in Twentieth-Century Methodism', in Mark Smith (ed.), *British Evangelical Identities Past and Present* (Milton Keynes: Paternoster, 2008), i, 53–5.

[72] Spann, 'Evangelicalism', 39, 217–20 [Candler], 51 [DuBose].

[73] Ibid., 51.

[74] Ibid., 43–50.

[75] Wellings, 'Evangelicalism in Twentieth-Century Methodism', 53–4; Spann, 'Evangelicalism', 52, 189–211, 256–337.

[76] Wellings, 'Evangelicalism in Twentieth-Century Methodism'', 55–7. The phrase 'folk fundamentalism' was coined by Stephen Dawes.

Four important developments took place in the evangelical world after the Second World War.[77] First, the liberal evangelical position suffered serious erosion, and then almost complete collapse. Secondly, there was a renewal of conservative evangelicalism, pioneered in the United States by a loose coalition of radio preachers, evangelists and para-church organisations of which Youth for Christ was the most significant. Militant fundamentalism, eclipsed since the 1920s, metamorphosed into the new 'evangelicalism'.[78] In Great Britain, the student work of the Inter-Varsity Fellowship created new leadership for the evangelical movement, fostering scholarship and confidence. Reformed theology experienced a renaissance, and the Billy Graham 'crusades' of 1954–55 put conservative evangelicalism centre stage. Thirdly, charismatic renewal touched traditional denominations from the 1960s, and created new churches, agencies and alliances, as well as a more far-reaching change in styles of music and worship. Fourthly, evangelical forms of Christianity spread rapidly in the Global South, both in new denominations and in existing churches, enjoying autonomy from the control of Western mission boards. The result was the confident, growing and diverse phenomenon of evangelicalism in the worldwide Church at the start of the twenty-first century.

In British Methodism, where liberal evangelicalism had been strong between the World Wars and thereafter, the collapse of this influential outlook in the 1960s produced a Connexion struggling to come to terms with an acknowledged pluralism, including radicals, charismatics and newlyconfident conservative evangelicals. To the Southport and Cliff College networks were added the Revival Fellowship, formed in 1952, Conservative Evangelicals in Methodism, set up in 1971, and the readership of the charismatic magazine *Dunamis*, launched in 1972. Mergers in 1987 and 1995 brought these groups together as Headway, 'a movement of Methodists committed to prayer for revival and witness to the evangelical faith'.[79] Methodist evangelicals were connected to the wider evangelical movement through festivals and para-church organisations, burgeoning worship resources and all the paraphernalia of the new evangelical sub-culture. How far they remained connected to their roots in the Wesleyan tradition was a moot point.[80]

In the United States the institutional expression of conservative evangelicalism within the Methodist Church (formed in 1939 by the merger of the Methodist Episcopal Church, Methodist Episcopal Church South and Methodist Protestant Church) and in the United Methodist Church (resulting from the union of the Methodist Church and the Evangelical United Brethren in 1968) was the 'Good News' movement, based around a magazine of that name which first appeared in spring 1967.[81] Good News sought to give a voice to the denomination's hitherto 'silent minority', taking up such issues as Sunday school literature, theological

---

[77] Bebbington, *Evangelicalism in Modern Britain*, chs 7 and 8.
[78] Carpenter, *Revive Us Again*.
[79] Headway was re-named Methodist Evangelicals Together (MET) in 2007.
[80] Wellings, 'Evangelicalism in Twentieth-Century Methodism', 57–60.
[81] Riley B. Case, *Evangelical and Methodist: A Popular History* (Nashville, TN: Abingdon, 2004), 25–33; Spann, 'Evangelicalism', 343–7, 361–86.

education, mission policy and acceptance of homosexual practice by the Church.[82] Like Headway in Great Britain, Charles Keysor, the founder of Good News, sought to ensure that conservative evangelicals were heard in a pluralist denomination.[83] Particularly over issues of human sexuality, that conversation became increasingly acrimonious as the century drew to a close.[84] Meanwhile the rediscovery of Wesleyan theology and spirituality gave Methodist evangelicals opportunities to re-appropriate long-lost traditions and claim to represent authentic Methodism.[85]

Mission policy was one of the areas of concern among conservative evangelicals, fearful lest intentional evangelism be lost in a welter of inter-faith dialogue. Growing churches in the Global South, however, have included strong evangelical elements, so that Methodist or Methodist-related denominations in Korea and the Philippines, in Nigeria and elsewhere have displayed a more conservative theology than the former 'sending' churches in the West.

The Wesleys' Methodism formed one strand of the broader evangelical movement of the eighteenth century. In its British and North American manifestations Methodism marched with developments in evangelical faith and practice for the next two centuries, while maintaining its own identity as an Arminian holiness movement with a connexional polity. In its nineteenth-century heyday Methodism lost evangelically minded adherents to revival and holiness movements; in the twentieth century cultural and theological changes transformed Methodist denominations into broad churches where conservative evangelicals might find a place among a spectrum of opinions. To be Methodist was no longer synonymous with being evangelical, and it remains to be seen whether Methodist evangelicalism will renew itself from its Wesleyan roots or draw its inspiration from other streams of the global evangelical movement.

---

[82] Ibid., chs 6–9; Case, *Evangelical and Methodist*, passim.

[83] Spann, 'Evangelicalism', 346.

[84] Richey, Rowe and Schmidt, *Methodist Experience in America*, 467–85; Case, *Evangelical and Methodist*, 236–7; Spann, 'Evangelicalism', 449–83.

[85] For example, Case, *Evangelical and Methodist*, 73–6. Good News did not respond well to the section 'Our Theological Task' added to the *Discipline* in 1972 through the work of a Study Commission chaired by the pre-eminent Wesley scholar Albert Outler: Richey, Rowe and Schmidt, *Methodist Experience in America*, 459–62. Outler's legacy, and the interpretation of 'Wesleyan' identity, remain contested territory.

# A Historical Survey of Methodist Preaching

John Munsey Turner

Recently the transatlantic Evangelical Revival has come into the centre of research. It was well under way before John and Charles Wesley began their 'second journey' in May 1738.[1] The Revival in Europe and America had a fascinating 'network' of styles.[2] Professor David Bebbington[3] sets out a 'quadrilateral' which can be applied across the rift between the 'Arminians of the heart' – the Wesleys and John Fletcher – and the 'Calvinists of the heart', like George Whitefield and, later, the Countess of Huntingdon. New birth or conversion was an ever-present focal point. This was the 'religion of the heart'. Activism was a second characteristic leading to evangelism, missionary endeavour and social action, not least the campaign against slavery. The third feature was a fervent preaching of the cross as the heart of devotion with, fourthly, a stress on the Bible as the final authority. John Wesley said that he was 'a man of one book' but that did not imply that the Bible alone mattered. In his advice to preachers the Bible was the source of authority and teaching, endorsed by tradition, not contradicted by reason and confirmed by experience in the fullest sense.[4]

What of Wesley's preaching? We have the Forty Four Sermons, certainly preached – yet they are in the style often of the Oxford don. Wesley's style in the open air and, later, in Methodist societies was what may be called 'illustrious vulgar', everyday speech which, nevertheless, conveys an air of distinction and

---

[1] G. O'Collins, *The Second Journey* (London: Paulist Press, 1987), 21ff.
[2] W. R. Ward, *The Protestant Evangelical Awakening* (Cambridge: Cambridge University Press, 1992).
[3] D. W. Bebbington, *Evangelicalism in Modern Britain: A History from the 1730s to the 1980s* (London: Unwin Hyman, 1989), 15–17; John Walsh, 'Methodism and the Origins of English-Speaking Evangelicalism', in Mark Noll, David Bebbington and George Rawlyk (eds), *Evangelicalism 1700–1900* (Oxford: Oxford University Press, 1994).
[4] Scott J. Jones, *John Wesley's Conception and Use of Scripture* (Nashville, TN: Abingdon, 1995); Richard Heitzenrater, 'John Wesley's Principles and Practice of Preaching', in R. Sykes (ed.), *Beyond the Boundaries: Preaching in the Wesleyan Tradition* (Oxford: Applied Theology Press, 1998).

authority. 'I now write, as I generally speak, *ad populum*, to the bulk of mankind, *plain truth for plain people.*'⁵

One of Wesley's definitions of preaching was: 'To invite, to convince, to offer Christ, to preach him in all his offices, to set forth Christ as evidently crucified before their eyes, justifying us by his blood and sanctifying us by his Spirit.' He also said: 'I think the right method of preaching is this – at our first beginning to preach at any place. After a personal declaration of the love of God to sinners and his willingness that they should be saved ... to preach the law in the strongest, the clearest, the most searching manner possible, only intermixing the gospel here and there and showing it, as it were, afar off.'⁶

Wesley preached extempore, using the same material countless times – a feature of Methodist preaching to this day, as preachers, ministerial and lay, preach in many different places. Wesley insisted on frequent pulpit change: 'This preacher has one talent ... No-one whom I ever yet knew has all the talents, which are needed for beginning, continuing and perfecting the work of grace in any one congregation.' The preachers' 'plan' from 1787 became a document quite unique to Methodism.⁷ Wesley's preaching, said Sir Walter Scott, included 'many excellent stories' making people feel he was preaching to them personally. As John Nelson describes hearing Wesley preach at Moorfields in 1739: 'I thought his whole discourse was aimed at me.'⁸ To summarise: as early as 1746 Wesley wrote: 'Our main doctrines which include all the rest are three – that of repentance, of faith and of holiness. The first of these we account, as it were, the porch of religion, the next the door, the third religion itself.'⁹ In 1790 he wrote to Robert Carr Brackenbury: 'I am glad brother D. has more light with regard to full sanctification. This doctrine is the grand depositum which God has lodged with the people called Methodists and for the sake of propagating this chiefly he appeared to have raised us up.'¹⁰

Who were the early preachers of the Methodist 'societies' which became the Methodist Connexion and eventually split from the Church of England? If John Wesley's creation of 'societies', circuits (7 in 1746, 50 in 1770, 114 by 1791) and the Conference from 1743 is an example of evangelistic pragmatism, it is a fact that without the itinerant preachers there could have been no Methodist Connexion. They were a diverse group – many from what came to be called the 'labour

---

⁵ 'Preface' to *Sermons* (1746), in Albert Outler (ed.), *The Works of John Wesley* [hereafter *WJW*], *Sermons*, vol. i (Nashville, TN: Abingdon, 1984), 104.

⁶ Albert Outler (ed.), *John Wesley* (Oxford: Oxford University Press, 1964), 232; R. E. Davies, A. R. George and G. Rupp (eds), *A History of the Methodist Church in Great Britain*, vol. iv (London: Epworth, 1988), 109; *WJW* (*Letters*, vol. ii), 482–9; Richard Heitzenrater, *Wesley and the People Called Methodists* (Nashville, TN: Abingdon, 1995), 164, 175, 235.

⁷ Alan Rose, 'The Evolution of the Circuit Plan', *Proceedings of the Wesley Historical Society*, 37 (1969–70), 50–54; Alan Rose, 'Local Preachers and the Circuit Plan', in Geoffrey Milburn and Margaret Batty (eds), *Workaday Preachers* (Peterborough: MPH, 1995).

⁸ W. L. Doughty, *John Wesley – Preacher* (London: Epworth, 1955), 96.

⁹ *WJW*, vol. ix, 227; J. Telford (ed.), *Letters of John Wesley* (London: Epworth, 1960), vol. ii, 268.

¹⁰ Telford, *Letters*, vol. v, 316; vol. viii, 237–8; cf. *Large Minutes*, 1763.

aristocracy': skilled labourers, builders, bakers, ex-soldiers, stonemasons like John Nelson, teacher Christopher Hopper, a squire Robert Carr Brackenbury (1752–1818), an alumnus of St Catharine's College, Cambridge. With the brilliant young Irishman Adam Clarke (1760–1832), Brackenbury evangelised the Channel Isles. John Lenton,[11] in a massive piece of research, shows that 23 per cent came from the West Riding of Yorkshire and 21 per cent from Ireland. They were men who showed 'gifts, graces and fruits' with the task: 'to reform the nation, particularly the Church and to spread Scriptural holiness over the land'.[12]

Lenton describes the lifestyle of these men and their wives dependent on the Methodist people – ladies like Frances Pawson, whose journal, some in French, describes grim houses in Scotland and Halifax.[13] There was Mrs John Furze, whose husband, an itinerant, rode seventy miles to find her naked in bed, her clothes sold for food.[14] Wesley set up Kingswood School for the sons of the preachers, allowed them £12 per year but could be insensitive: 'You'll have time to preach', he told Christopher Hopper (1722–1802) when his wife died.[15]

What happened to the 800 who were itinerants even for a short time? In 1781 there were 178 itinerants at work. A total of 53 per cent left the itinerancy, many becoming Local Preachers. Fifty- seven became Dissenting ministers, like John Bennet (1714–59), who had married Grace Murray, Wesley's 'lost love' and had rumpuses in Bolton with both Wesley and his wife Mary over doctrine. Forty-seven became Church of England priests, like Melvill Horne, John Fletcher's successor at Madeley. Fifty-two were expelled, fifteen more for immorality, eleven over drink. John Wesley was more lax over some of the eccentrics like George Bell than his brother Charles, who was much less taken in by some of the more emotional attitudes and claims of perfection.[16]

The preachers certainly met the needs of the people for a 'religion of the heart', like Nelson, who stood on 'The Rocks' at King's Cross, Halifax, beginning the

---

[11] *History of the Methodist Church in Great Britain*, iv, 70, 84, 109, 116–19; John Lenton, *John Wesley's Preachers* (Milton Keynes: Paternoster, 2009); John Lenton, *My Sons in the Gospel* (Loughborough: WHS, 2000); D. Bruce Hindmarsh, *The Evangelical Conversion Narrative* (Oxford: Oxford University Press, 2005); A. Kingsley Lloyd, *The Labourer's Hire: The Payment and Deployment of the Early Methodist Preachers 1744–1813* (Chester: WHS, 1988); James Hogg, 'John Nelson (1707–1774): Stonemason and Itinerant Preacher', *Proceedings of the Wesley Historical Society*, 56 (2007), 146–62.

[12] 'Large Minutes', in Thomas Jackson (ed.), *The Works of the Revd John Wesley* (London: Mason, 1856), vol. viii, 288; Adrian Burdon, *Authority and Order: John Wesley and His Lay Preachers* (Aldershot: Ashgate, 2005).

[13] Copy in the Methodist archives, John Rylands University Library of Manchester.

[14] Thomas Jackson (ed.), *Lives of the Early Methodist Preachers* (London: W. M. Bookroom, 1865 [4thh edn]), vol. v, 152.

[15] *WJW*, vol. xxvi, 587ff.

[16] John Lenton, 'Charles Wesley and the Preachers', in Kenneth Newport and Ted A. Campbell (eds), *Charles Wesley: Life, Literature and Legacy* (Peterborough: Epworth, 2007); Kenneth Newport (ed.), *The Sermons of Charles Wesley* (Oxford: Oxford University Press , 2005).

work there, when the parish church could not cope with increased population,[17] a common factor. Phyllis Mack[18] has recently given a vivid picture of what the life of the early Methodist people – especially the women, a majority, – was like. There was order and discipline as well as ardour and ecstasy, concern for personal evangelism and care for the poor. Mary Bosanquet (1739–1815), who became John Fletcher's wife, felt 'a special call' and continued to preach well after the Wesleyan Conference in 1803 forbad women to preach except to female audiences. She still preached five times a week at the age of seventy-five. Sarah Crosby (1729–1804) took 220 services in one year and Mary Barrit (Mrs Taft) (1772–1851) also continued to preach after the Conference decision. Her preaching led to the conversion of Thomas Jackson (1783–1873), who became a leading expert on Wesley's writings. Methodists realised that Conference is not infallible. Phyllis Mack shows also great changes in styles of preaching between John Pawson[19] (1737–1806), critical of other itinerants and especially Alexander Kilham (1762–98), whose expulsion in 1796 led to the Methodist New Connexion in 1797, and Adam Clarke who was President in 1806, 1814 and 1822.[20] Clarke's vast eight volume *Commentary on the Bible* (1825) was clearly significant even if his Christology was suspect. He preached extempore expository sermons and advised preachers to 'exhort those who are justified to look for all deliverance from sin now'. Recent research by John Lenton[21] has revealed many women preachers in Wesleyanism in the nineteenth century. Some were on 'full plan' before the creation of the various diaconal orders and Sisters of the People, and long before the 1803 rule was repealed in 1910. In 1918 the Wesleyan Conference declared that women could become Local Preachers under the same rules as men.[22]

---

[17] J. M. Turner, *John Wesley, the Evangelical Revival and the Rise of Methodism* (Peterborough: Epworth, 2002), 89.

[18] Phyllis Mack, *Heart Religion in the English Enlightenment: Gender and Emotion in Early Methodism* (Cambridge: Cambridge University Press, 2008).

[19] John C. Bowmer and John A. Vickers (eds), *The Letters of John Pawson, Methodist Itinerant, 1762–1806* (Emsworth: WMHS, 1994–95); M. L. Edwards, *Adam Clarke* (London: Epworth, 1942), 25–8; S. B. Dawes, *Adam Clarke: Methodism's First Old Testament Scholar* (Truro: Cornish Methodist Historical Association, 1994).

[20] D. W. Bebbington with K. Dix and A. Ruston (eds), *Protestant Nonconformist Texts*, vol. iii, *The Nineteenth Century* (Aldershot: Ashgate, 2006), 16 and 129; J. A. Vickers (ed.), *A Dictionary of Methodism in Great Britain and Ireland* (Peterborough: Epworth, 2000) and T. Larsen (ed.), *Biographical Dictionary of Evangelicals* (Leicester: IVP, 2003).

[21] John Lenton, 'Labouring for the Lord: Women Preachers in Wesleyan Methodism', in Sykes (ed.), *Beyond the Boundaries*; Janet Burge, 'Impudent Women: The Women Preachers of Early Methodism', *Epworth Review*, July 1994.

[22] Paul W. Chilcote, *John Wesley and the Women Preachers of Early Methodism* (Metuchen, NJ: Scarecrow, 1991); Dorothy Graham, 'Women Local Preachers', in Milburn and Batty (eds), *Workaday Preachers*; E. Dorothy Graham, 'The Early Deaconess Evangelists', in Sykes (ed.), *Beyond the Boundaries*; David East, *My Dear Sally* (Emsworth: WMHS, 2003); David East, *Women Preachers in Early Methodism* (Norwich: WHS East Anglia, 2005); Gareth Lloyd, 'Repression and Resistance: Wesleyan Female Public Ministry in the Generation after 1791', *PWHS*, 55 (2005), 101–14.

What of the position of Local Preachers? They were trained in a manner similar to that of apprenticeship at the time. A preacher was given a 'note' to preach with an established preacher, then put 'on trial', permitted to preach alone, and then admitted as a 'fully accredited' preacher (on 'full plan') after an oral examination. This is still the case, with the eighteenth-century language still used, although with much more written study requirements. It was only in 1796 that Local Preachers were given a proper place in the Wesleyan Methodist constitution. By then changes had come through 'preaching houses' being built – 40 in 1760, 120 in 1770, 470 at Wesley's death in 1791. The Local Preachers' Meeting was constituted then. The Local Preachers were a mixed group – shopkeepers, farmers, schoolteachers, skilled artisans, doctors like James Hamilton (1740–1827) and Dr John Whitehead (1740–1804). Clive Field has shown that the preachers became more middle class in Victorian days with, later, a large number of teachers in their ranks.[23] Occasionally some Local Preachers felt downgraded by the itinerants, not preaching often in the large chapels or missions.

Local Preachers were found on all sides of the many divisions in Methodism from the Methodist New Connexion onwards. In 1811 the 'Sidmouth Bill' would have been disastrous for lay preaching. It was a Local Preacher, Thomas Allan (1774–1845), backed up by Thomas Thompson MP (1754–1828) who was able to assure the government that 'we are not a political people, we simply wish to worship God and promote Christianity by all means and have been the steady friend of government'.[24] Before we explore the nineteenth century we need to realise that there were 'many Methodisms' and that the system was able to be adopted around the world, not least in America, but also in new 'mission fields' through the flexibility of the stationing of ministers.[25]

Following the American war of independence, when Methodism was unpopular due to Wesley's opposition, great changes took place. First, Wesley 'set apart' Dr Thomas Coke (1737–1814) as 'Superintendent' of work in America. He, in America in 1784, ordained the Black Countryman Francis Asbury[26] (1745–1816), who became the bishop of the American Methodist Church. Charles Wesley wrote scurrilous verses:

---

[23] Clive Field, 'The Methodist Local Preacher: An Occupational Analysis', in Milburn and Batty (eds), *Workaday Preachers*.

[24] D. Hempton, *Methodism and Politics in British Society, 1750–1850* (London: Hutchinson, 1984), 102.

[25] D. Hempton, *Methodism: Empire of the Spirit* (New Haven, CT and London: Yale University Press, 2005).

[26] John H. Wigger, *American Saint: Francis Asbury and the Methodists* (Oxford: Oxford University Press, 2009); John. H. Wigger, *Taking Heaven by Storm: Methodism and the Rise of Popular Christianity in America* (Oxford: Oxford University Press, 1998); Frank Baker, *From Wesley to Asbury* (Durham, NC: Duke University Press, 1976); Lester Ruth, *Early Methodist Life and Spirituality* (Nashville, TN: Abingdon, 2005).

> A Roman Emperor, 'tis said
> His favourite horse a consul made
> But Coke brings greater things to pass
> He makes a bishop of an ass.

Clearly Wesley could not dominate American Methodism. Asbury realised the significance of independence. He was an 'apostolic bishop' who believed in itinerancy and practised it. This enabled him to have a strong rapport with ordinary people. He had to relate to able preachers like John Dickins, Thomas Rankin and Richard Whatcoat, and while not a charismatic preacher, he combined support of revivalist styles with strong discipline – the vital 'both . and' nature of Methodism, rugged individualism and communal accountability. He stressed the class meeting, the love feast, the two-day-long Quarterly Meeting and, after 1800, the Camp Meeting, which was Pentecostal in style – 'fishing with a large net', he called it. Small schisms occurred, but very different was the resolution in 1816 by Richard Allan (1760–1831) to form the African Methodist Episcopal Church – a pointer to the great division over slavery which was to lead later to the Civil War – and the continuity of the charismatic styles of preaching – holiness and 'happiness' side by side as Lester Ruth depicts it.[27] By 1816 there were 214,000 Methodist members in the USA. White Methodism was to become more middle class – 'nobodies' became 'somebodies'. The unmarried itinerants on their horses like Asbury were outmoded. The intense charismatic style was, for a time, diminishing. Nathan Bangs (1778–1862) was the leading preacher in the new style, disliking enthusiastic revivalism.

The Camp Meeting came to England through the eccentric Lorenzo Dow, whom Dr Coke thought was a spy – and led to Primitive Methodism as an independent denomination.[28] It was part of the Second Evangelical Revival, as it is often called, led by Hugh Bourne (1772–1852) and William Clowes (1789–1851), a carpenter and a potter. In Primitive Methodism the distinction in the early days between 'local' and 'travelling' preachers was one of payment and administrative functions. The Local Preacher could preside at the Lord's Supper at the Superintendent's behest. A circuit plan from Brandon in Suffolk in 1854 says:

---

[27] Ruth, *Early Methodist Life And Spirituality*.

[28] Geoffrey Milburn, *Primitive Methodism* (Peterborough: Epworth, 2002); Julia S. Werner, *The Primitive Methodist Connexion* (Madison, WI: University of Wisconsin Press, 1994); John E. Minor, 'The Mantle of Elijah – Nineteenth Century Primitive Methodism and Twentieth Century Pentecostalism', *PWHS*, 23 (1982); Robert Moore, *Pitmen, Preachers and Politics* (Cambridge: Cambridge University Press, 1994); Robert Colls, *The Pitmen of the Northern Coalfield* (Manchester: Manchester University Press, 1987); E. Dorothy Graham, *Chosen by God: A List of the Female Travelling Preachers of Early Primitive Methodism* (Banbury: Bankhead Press, 1989); *From Mow Cop to Peake, 1807–1932: Essays to Commemorate the 175th Anniversary of Primitive Methodism* (Leeds: WHS Yorkshire Branch, 1982); David Stacy, 'Women May Preach, but Men Must Govern', in R. N. Swanson (ed.), *Studies in Church History*, 34 (Woodbridge: Boydell, 1998).

> Beloved brethren never disappoint a congregation if you can possibly attend. Go to your important work in the spirit of prayer. Choose the plainest text you can. In your discourse aim at the glory of God and the conversion of sinners. Do not allow bodily imposition, a long journey, a dark night and inclement weather deter you from your important duties – proclaim redemption and pull sinners out of the fire![29]

Primitive Methodism produced Chartists like Joseph Capper and William Thornton of Amber Thorn who prayed at the great Chartist rally at Peep Green on Whit Monday 1839. After the meeting Feargus O'Connor, the Chartist leader, clapped his hand on Thornton's shoulder. 'Well done Thornton. When we get the People's Charter I will see you are made archbishop of York!' Thornton emigrated to America. Later Primitive Methodists took part in 'the revolt of the field' in Norfolk and Suffolk in the 1870s. Typical was Sir George Edwards (1850–1933), who learned to read so that he could become a Local Preacher in 1872: 'With my study of theology I soon began to realize that the social conditions of the people were not as God intended them to be. The gross injustice meted out to my parents and the terrible suffering I had undergone in my boyhood burned themselves into my soul like a hot iron. Many a time did I vow I would do something to better the condition of my class.'[30] A report of a service in the North East describes the worship and the sermon:

> It was a sermon to be heard not reported. What a mixture of humour, passionate appeal, thrilling exhortation and apposite illustration it was – laughter and tears the preacher commanded at will and when he closed with heartsearching appeals to the unconverted to fly to the Cross for pardon, one almost wondered that men and women did not spring to their feet and rush somewhere, anywhere, exclaiming with Bunyan's Pilgrim: 'Life, life, eternal life.' Here was a rugged Elijah of the coalpit, a hewer of coal for six days in the deep, dark mine, and a very flame of fire on the seventh.[31]

The town of Peterlee was named after a Methodist preacher – the trade unionist Peter Lee (1864–1935). Primitive Methodism, like the Bible Christians in the South West, had women preachers – the last Primitive Methodist itinerant woman Elizabeth Bultitude died in 1890. Here was a mixture of a Quaker and charismatic style not unlike the Black churches of America. We should mention the Tent Methodists, led by G. Pocock and John Pyer, who sought a means of reaching people outside the

---

[29] Printed in Bebbington (ed.), *Protestant Nonconformist Texts*, iii, 205.

[30] George Edwards, *From Crow-scaring to Westminster* (London: Labour Publishing Co., 1922).

[31] John Briggs and Ian Sellers (eds), *Victorian Nonconformity* (London: Edward Arnold, 1973), 35–6, from *Primitive Methodist Magazine*, 1896, 830–31; John K. Lander, *Itinerant Temples: Tent Methodism 1814–1832* (Carlisle: Paternoster, 2003).

churches. This petered out, with Pyer becoming a Congregationalist minister and Pocock returning to Wesleyanism.

What of Wesleyanism in the nineteenth century? We cannot analyse here the divisions of Methodism, save to note the effect on preaching of divergence over the whole concept of sanctification. Theologians like Richard Watson (1781–1833) and W. B. Pope (1822–1903) saw sanctification as a gradual process, a matter agreed to by Jabez Bunting (1779–1858) whose sermons were very much in that tradition. He was convinced that the progress of Methodism in the West Riding after the short-lived revival of 1792 onwards was 'more swift than solid'.[32] Dr James Dixon[33] (1788–1871) can represent the still difficult problems of rural circuits. He was stationed at one time in Hereford, where 'the labour and fatigue of visiting the thin and scattered population was immense' – Dixon started on long preaching rounds of a month's duration. He walked on foot twenty miles or more every day, preached nearly every day and on Sundays walked twenty miles and preached four times. In some places neither food nor bed were offered him. The circuit was too poor to pay his nominal stipend and his own little savings were consumed by the necessities of life. He became in the end President of Conference in 1841.

Later the railways saw the arrival of the itinerant preacher of a very different style, typified by Robert Newton (1781–1854), four times President of Conference, who was well known on the railway system. Newton would repeat himself countless times. It meant professional skill and sometimes artificiality, but Newton had the knack of immediately grabbing a congregation's attention and holding it. A later popular figure was William Morley Punshon[34] (1824–1881). He preached, raising money for 'The Watering Places Fund' and the Metropolitan Chapel Fund:

> He spoke with immense energy … feeling among the audience grew, enthusiasm was awakened and gathered force as he went on. At last in one of the magnificent climaxes, the congregation sprang simultaneously to their feet. Hats and handkerchiefs were waved, sticks and umbrellas were used in frantic pounding of the floor … such a tornado of applause swept through Exeter Hall and swelled from floor to ceiling as has never been witnessed before.'[35]

This was a style of charismatic romantic preaching very different from Clarke or Bunting.

---

[32] David Hempton, *The Religion of the People: Methodism and Popular Religion c. 1750–1900* (London: Routledge, 1996), 100.

[33] R. W. Dixon, *The Life of James Dixon* (London: Wesleyan Conference Office, 1874), 27–8.

[34] Gordon Rupp, 'The Influence of Victorian Nonconformity', *The Listener*, 17 March 1955; T. S. A. Macquiban, 'A Prince among Preachers – a Short Biography of William Morley Punshon', *West Yorkshire WHS Bulletin*, 39 (1981).

[35] F. W. MacDonald, *The Life of William Morley Punshon* (London: Hodder & Stoughton, 1888), 97.

This style had been foreshadowed by those who saw conversion and sanctification as an immediate experience with a great deal of charismatic fervour. Typical was William Bramwell[36] (1759–1818). At a love feast at West Moor colliery in May 1817 he asked penitents to express their feelings, '... instantly there were fifteen or sixteen persons on their feet, all in tears ... In a little while he again requested the remaining penitents to stand up ... and this he repeated until there was no-one left in unbelief.'[37] Later James Caughey came to England from America in 1841. He was forbidden to preach in Wesleyanism in 1847, but at Rochdale he claimed to have 'sanctified' hundreds of people. Adam Clarke, and later William Arthur (1819–1901) picked up thinking from the USA. Arthur's *Tongue of Fire* (1856) was formative, though he did not like 'speaking in tongues', a reflection of mid-Victorian sensibilities. In the USA the rather different style of Phoebe Palmer (1807–74) propounded a view of 'total consecration', laying one's whole life on the altar. For Phoebe Palmer the act of consecration and reception of the blessing of entire sanctification were linked as cause and effect. The influence here was great on the Church of the Nazarene and the Pilgrim Holiness Church, and greatly influenced Catherine Booth and the Salvation Army.

In Wesleyanism this style emerged in Bolton with Thomas Champness[38] (1832–1905) whose work was the ancestor of Cliff College. In *Joyful News* in 1883 he writes of kindling the 'holy flame' of revival. He asks: 'What we want – news of recent revival, stories of remarkable conversions, answers to prayer, illustrations of Providence. What we do not want – politics, controversy, Connexional finance!' The first Principal of Cliff College, Thomas Cook[39] (1854–1912) clearly saw sanctification as 'the removal of all the roots of bitterness ... we are cleansed from all sin now'. Samuel Chadwick (1860–1932) was much richer in his preaching. He was able to preach through the Nicene Creed and W. B. Pope's *Compendium* to the congregation at Oxford Place, Leeds, and to introduce the innovation of Passiontide services.[40]

This was the period of the Forward Movement, which featured new Methodist city missions. Hugh Price Hughes[41] (1847–1902) was concerned to save people's

---

[36] John Kent, *Holding the Fort* (London: Epworth, 1978), 25–7, 77–90; H. McGonigle, 'William Bramwell: A Reappraisal', *PWHS*, 54 (2004); D. W. Bebbington, 'The Holiness Movement in British and Canadian Methodism in the Late Nineteenth Century', *PWHS*, 50 (1996); Richard Carwardine, *Transatlantic Revivalism: Popular Evangelicalism in Britain and America, 1760–1865* (London: Greenwood, 1978); Charles E. White, *The Beauty of Holiness: Phoebe Palmer as Theologian, Feminist and Humanitarian* (Grand Rapids, MI: Zondervan, 1986).

[37] Colls, *Pitmen of the Northern Coalfield*, 175.

[38] *Joyful News*, 23 February 1883.

[39] Thomas Cook, *New Testament Holiness* (London: Epworth, 1948), 25ff, 39; A. Skevington Wood, *On Fire for God: The Story of Thomas Cook* (Calver: Cliff College, 1983).

[40] J. M. Turner in *HMGB*, vol. iii; D. H. Howarth, *How Great a Flame: The Story of Samuel Chadwick* (Calver: Cliff College, 1983); T. D. Meadley, *The Story of Thomas Champness* (Calver: Cliff College, 1983); Howard Mellor, *Cliff – More than a College* (Calver: Cliff College, 2005).

[41] C. Oldstone-Moore, *Hugh Price Hughes* (Cardiff: University of Wales, 1998).

souls, but also 'to sanctify their circumstances'.[42] He rejected the three year itinerancy as irrelevant to city life. There were now long ministries like that of Samuel Collier (1855–1931) in Manchester and the Central Hall, Birmingham, under Luke Wiseman (1858–1944). There was evangelistic preaching of a simple but powerful style. All centred on the preacher. The pulpit was his throne and this was still the age of platform oratory. Charles Hulbert recalls how he would carefully record all the verdicts for Christ in his notebook and would deem a service a failure if there were none.[43] Hughes used a different style – in the morning Mark Guy Pearse (1842–1930) would preach to 'the saints', building up faith. In the afternoon political matters were featured, in the evening evangelism. J. E. Rattenbury (1870–1963) later recalled his observation on the style of 1900: 'The great difference between congregations then and now is the difference between a sense of guilt and a sense of doubt. Guilt is the tinder which blazes when the spark of emotion is applied to it. Doubt is like a rust which can only be removed by careful polishing.'[44] John Scott Lidgett[45] (1854–1953) rejected the individualistic style of social witness at the Bermondsey Settlement, where he ministered in many ways for decades, still preaching in 1952. He took Frederic Denison Maurice's view of Christ as the Head of the human race rather than John Wesley as his starting point. In a more conservative evangelical style was Dinsdale Young (1861–1938) at Central Hall Westminster – very different from the moderates like J. A. Beet (1840–1924) and George Jackson (1864–1945) who were violently attacked by some, although Samuel Chadwick acknowledged Jackson as a genuine evangelist.[46] We end this section with Thomas Bowman Stephenson (1829–1912) whose work has endured remarkably well. In 1865 he was in Bolton among the poor, appointing a Miss Entwistle as a 'Deaconess' – the first in Methodism. He pioneered the National Children's Home (now Action for Children) with its Order of Sisters of the Children. A logical development was the Wesley Deaconess Institute. Its concept was an 'order' with vocation but no vow, discipline without servility, association not excluding freedom. By the time of his death there were 229 Deaconesses, paralleled by Sisters of the People in Manchester and, in London, by Katherine Price Hughes, who brought some very able women into her 'order'. The other Methodist churches also had Deaconesses who were preachers also.[47]

Moving into the twentieth century we begin with Liberal Protestantism. It was Friedrich Schleiermacher who stressed religious consciousness. Besides knowing and doing – that is, science and morality – there was the activity of

---

[42] Kenneth Cracknell and Susan J. White, *An Introduction to World Methodism* (Cambridge: Cambridge University Press, 2005), 238.
[43] Kenneth Hulbert, *Passion for Souls* (London: Epworth, 1959), 30ff, 95.
[44] Donald Soper, *The Advocacy of the Gospel* (London: Hodder and Stoughton, 1961), 18; J. E. Rattenbury, *Evangelism and Pagan England* (London: Epworth, 1954), 25ff.
[45] Alan Turberfeld, *John Scott Lidgett* (Peterborough: Epworth, 2003).
[46] D. W. Bebbington, 'The Persecution of George Jackson', in W. J. Sheils (ed.), *Persecution and Toleration* (SCH) (Oxford: Blackwell, 1984), 421–31; M. Wellings, 'The Wesley Bible Union', *PWHS*, 53 (2002).
[47] E. Dorothy Graham, *Saved to Serve: The Story of the Wesley Deaconess Order* (Peterborough: MPH, 2002).

feeling, immediate self-consciousness. This was the source of religion. Methodist preaching, as we have seen, stressed experience as well as Bible, tradition and reason. Certainly Methodist historians like Henry Bett (1876–1953) and Herbert Workman (1862–1951) used Schleiermacher and Adolf Harnack, who said that the essence of it all was the Fatherhood of God and the infinite value of the human soul.[48] It can be shown that there was a shift from atonement to incarnation in the late nineteenth century. Nevertheless Lidgett and W. F. Lofthouse (1871–1965) wrote outstanding books on the atonement.[49] At the time of Methodist Union, preachers – not only in Primitive Methodism – were much influenced by Professor A. S. Peake (1865–1929) who combined Biblical criticism – progressive revelation, the record of revelation – with a liberal evangelism which he offered as a Local Preacher. Religious experience in the widest sense was stressed. Maldwyn Hughes (1875–1940), E. S. Waterhouse (1879–1964) and Ryder Smith (1875–1956) stressed this and, like Peake, deeply influenced many ministers whom they taught. There was a book in this genre from the lay educationalist and Primitive Methodist Local Preacher Victor Murray (1890–1967),:*Personal Experience and the Christian Faith*.[50] In it Murray showed how feeling, knowing and believing were essentials of full Christian experience, a matter agreed by J. T. Wilkinson (1893–1980), another scholar from that tradition which was taught to student ministers in colleges at this time. Alongside and following the theology of experience was some renaissance of Methodist spirituality associated especially with W. R. Maltby (1886–1951), said by William Temple to be the finest preacher at the time to students, and the New Testament scholar J. A. Findlay (1880–1962). Bodies like the School of Fellowship and the Fellowship of the Kingdom (now Spectrum) exemplify this, with the more 'catholic' wing associated with T. S. Gregory (1897–1975), A. E. Whitham (1878–1938) and J. E. Rattenbury, who created the Methodist Sacramental Fellowship. Rattenbury combined this with a passion for evangelism which in various styles

---

[48] Karl Barth, *The Theology of Schleiermacher* (Edinburgh: T and T Clark, 1983); Henry Bett, *The Spirit of Methodism* (London: Epworth, 1937); H. B. Workman, 'The Place of Methodism in the Catholic Church', in W. J. Townsend, H. B. Workman and George Eayrs (eds), *A New History of Methodism* (London: Hodder & Stoughton, 1909); A. Harnack, *What is Christianity?* (London: E. T. Benn, 1958); J. M. Turner, 'Preaching, Theology and Spirituality in Twentieth Century Methodism', *Expository Times*, January 2000.

[49] J. S. Lidgett, *The Spiritual Principle of the Atonement* (London: Kelly, 1897); W. F. Lofthouse, *Ethics and Atonement* (London: Methuen, 1906); W. F. Lofthouse , *Altar, Cross and Community* (London: Epworth, 1921).

[50] C. Ryder Smith, *The Christian Experience* (London: Epworth, 1926); H. Maldwyn Hughes, *The Theology of Experience* (London: Kelly, 1915); A. Victor Murray, *Personal Experience and Christian Faith* (London: Epworth, 1939); F. B. James (ed.), *William Russell Maltby: Obiter Scripta* (London: Epworth, 1952), 15; John T. Wilkinson (ed.), *Arthur Samuel Peake, 1865–1929* (London: Epworth, 1958); John T. Wilkinson , *Arthur Samuel Peake: A Biography* (London: Epworth, 1971); A. S. Peake Memorial Lectures by Ian Sellers (*Epworth Review* 1997), Graham Slater (2002) and Henry Rack (2004).

was never far below the surface of any of the Methodist groups, including those surrounding Samuel Chadwick at Cliff College.[51]

No church illustrates the power of preaching better than Brunswick Church, Leeds. Successively Alfred Whitham,[52] Leslie Weatherhead (1893–1976) and William Sangster (1900–1960) filled that church from 1920 to 1939. Whitham had a delightful mixture of genuine folksiness with a deep sacramentalism and a rich conception of the Incarnation. Weatherhead, whose *Discipleship* was still a classic in the 1940s, exploited the discoveries of psychology, not only to counsel people but in his preaching. He used every service to make Jesus real to people. His theology was liberal protestant with a deep sense of the historical Jesus, not yet dimmed by the scepticism of the 'form critics'. After 1936 he was able to exercise his skill at the City Temple in London – an outstanding ministry of twenty-four years. He said that the aim of preaching was making the gospel real and changing lives. William Strawson sums him up:

> Christianity is the acceptance of the gift of friendship in Jesus. The reality of this is known through imagination, not rational argument. Despite its dangers, the experience is shown to be real in its effect – good impulses, victory over faults, a sense of beauty, deeper self-understanding and integration of personality.'[53]

Weatherhead was no mean theologian, though his later speculations made him suspect to evangelicals. Little books like *The Will of God* helped many to come to terms with suffering in the Second World War.

Sangster was a more conventional evangelical, though never fundamentalist. He had an immense knowledge of the saints and of ordinary human nature, with enormous skill in sermon construction and illustration. To some in Leeds he seemed more in touch with ordinary people in the area of the church than Weatherhead.[54] Sangster's last service at Brunswick attracted 2,000 people in August 1939 before

---

[51] Rattenbury, *Evangelism and Pagan England*; J. E. Rattenbury, *Evangelism, Its Shame and Glory* (London: Epworth, 1932); W. Chilcote, 'The Legacy of J. E. Rattenbury', *Doxology*, 3 (1986).

[52] A. E. Whitham, *The Discipline and Culture of the Spiritual Life* (London: Hodder and Stoughton, 1938), *The Pasture of His Presence* (London: Hodder and Stoughton, 1939) and *The Catholic Church* (London: Hodder and Stoughton, 1940).

[53] J. Travell, *Doctor of Souls – Leslie Weatherhead 1893–1976* (Cambridge: Lutterworth, 1999), with bibliography 308ff citing seventy books by Weatherhead; W. Strawson, 'The Significance of L. D. Weatherhead as a Preacher', *Methodist Recorder*, 9 June 1977; Horton Davies, *Worship and Theology in England: The Ecumenical Century, 1900–the Present* (Grand Rapids, MI: Eerdmans, 1996), chs 4 and 6.

[54] W. E. Sangster, *Westminster Sermons* (2 vols) (London: Epworth, 1960, 1961), *The Craft of Sermon Illustration* (London: Epworth, 1956), *The Craft of Sermon Construction* (London: Epworth, 1949), *The Approach to Preaching* (London: Epworth, 1951) and *Power in Preaching* (London: Epworth, 1958); cf. Susan White, *The Craft of Sermon Illustration Revisited* (York: College of Preachers, 1995).

he went to his great ministry at Westminster Central Hall. His successor, Garfield Lickes, a fine preacher, had 200 at his first service. The war had begun and its effect on preaching was grim. It became easy to denigrate Liberal Protestantism but it was always evangelism. Maldwyn Hughes, the Principal of Wesley House, Cambridge, whose book on theology helped thousands of Local Preachers, could end a sermon asking if his congregation had 'seen the light'. All this impinged on me as a teenager at Beckminster Methodist Church, Wolverhampton. The minister, H. M. Sinfield, a pupil of J. A. Findlay and deeply influenced by Sangster, made Jesus real – human, Master, example, Lord and Saviour. Sinfield would preach on themes like 'Why do people suffer?' or 'How do we know what God is like?' and then, quite frequently, make an appeal for discipleship – and many of us young people responded.[55]

Donald Soper[56] (1903–98) was also an important figure in Methodist preaching. 'The true preparation for the preaching of the gospel is the possession of the golden secret of the love of God, a personal experience of forgiveness of sins and an overwhelming desire to communicate that experience to others that they may come to the saving grace of their Lord and ours.'[57] Soper was the most well-known Methodist preacher for decades. He inherited the radical tradition of the Forward Movement, Liberal Protestantism, philosophical theology from F. R. Tennant at Cambridge, and socialism, pacifism and sacramentalism of the Whitham style. Soper caught the imagination of many by his logical and debonair method and his superb skill at communication including radio, television and the House of Lords. He saw the need for two pulpits, one in church, the other outside, but he was as much at home in his college chapel, St Catharine's Cambridge, where he was Honorary Fellow, as in Hyde Park. Adrian Hastings was right to state: 'Remove a few idiosyncrasies and Soper's Methodism in its wide social and sacramental character fits very much within the mainstream of modern English religion just as the evangelism of Billy Graham does not!'[58]

Were there other styles besides Liberal Protestantism? The revival of Protestantism through Karl Barth, the 'biblical theology' of C. H. Dodd, T. W. Manson and the Methodists Vincent Taylor (1887–1968) and Norman Snaith (1898–1982) was very important, and not least the writings of Joachim Jeremias, especially on the parables of Jesus. The popular writings of William Barclay were pillaged by Local Preachers and ministers alike. There was in the 1930s a rediscovery of the great Reformers, led in England by a group of Methodist scholars who had studied in Germany or Sweden, led by Gordon Rupp (1910–86), Philip Watson (1909–83), Percy Scott (1910–91) and Stanley Frost (1913–), who later taught in

---

[55] H. M. Sinfield, *Methodism's Message in Modern Terms* (London: Epworth, 1945).
[56] Donald Soper, *All His Grace* (London: Epworth, 1951); *The Advocacy of the Gospel* (London: Hodder and Stoughton, 1961), 39, 115; and 'Preaching in the Open Air', *Epworth Review*, 1985; B. Frost, *Goodwill on Fire: Donald Soper, Life and Mission* (London: Hodder and Stoughton, 1996).
[57] Soper, *Advocacy of the Gospel*, 39.
[58] A. Hastings, *A History of English Christianity 1920–1985* (London: Collins, 1986), 462–4.

Canada, Raymond George (1912–98) and Rupert Davies (1909–94). They had the 'optimism of grace' combined with a wider application of classic Protestantism.[59] Gordon Rupp was the guru of the more theologically minded Methodists after the Second World War. As a preacher (or speaker) he was remarkably able to be *en rapport* with any congregation, with a range of illustrations and metaphors from art and church history, the latest television programmes and detective stories old and new. He said that his one constant vocation was that of a Methodist preacher. These were the days of the rise and fall of Hitler, the German church struggle and the division and reconstruction of Germany after the war. Most of Rupp's sermons were never committed to paper. He caught his vision of ministry, not in church but on hearing Donald Soper on Tower Hill in the 1920s. The Local Preachers' Department report on Doctrinal Preaching in 1951 was written by Rupp and it is interesting to compare it with the writings of W. E. Sangster at that time.

By 1960 preaching was in a crisis. Neville Ward[60] twisted the knife in the wound in 1967: 'Among Methodists this is particularly true in the contemporary decline of preaching, a decline so devastating that many Methodists now are reaching the exasperation long since reached by Anglicans and Roman Catholics in which one expects little from the sermon and often finds the expectation justified.' But in the 1970s students began to learn how to preach.[61] The Local Preachers' Department in Methodism eventually began to be much more positive about preaching and, indeed, theology.[62] The factors here were clearly a decline of authority; oratory was at a discount. In an electronic age 'eye-gate' is as important as 'ear-gate'. Educationalists said that sermons were an outmoded style of teaching.

In Methodism radicalism did not suggest much scope for the preacher, but radicals cannot exist without the institutions they want to revolutionise. John

---

[59] R. N. Flew and R. E. Davies (eds), *The Catholicity of Protestantism* (London: Lutterworth, 1950); E. Gordon Rupp, *The Righteousness of God* (London: Hodder and Stoughton, 1953); E. Gordon Rupp, *The Sixty Plus and Other Sermons* (London: Collins, 1978).

[60] Neville Ward, *The Use of Praying* (London: Epworth, 1967), 15.

[61] Trevor Rowe (ed.), *Queen's Sermons* (London: Epworth, 1973); *The Preachers' Handbooks*, 11 vols (London: Epworth Press, 1949–69); John Stacey (ed.), *Doing Theology: An Introduction for Preachers* (London: Epworth, 1972); J. M. Turner, *Introducing Theology: A Companion to Doing Theology* (London: LP Dept, 1972); John Stacey, *Groundwork of Theology* (London: Epworth, 1977); Richard G. Jones, *Groundwork of Worship and Preaching* (London: Epworth, 1980); John Stacey, 'Local Preachers and Theological Change in the 1960s and 1970s', in Milburn and Batty (eds), *Workaday Preachers*; M. Wellings, 'The Methodist Revival Fellowship', *PWHS*, 57 (2009); J. S. Lampard, '*Faith and Worship*: The Local Preachers' Training Course', *Worship and Preaching*, (1990).

[62] M. Willshaw, 'The Decline and Rise of Preaching', in R. E. Davies (ed.), *The Testing of the Churches 1932–1982* (London: Epworth, 1982); Valerie Edden, 'The Changing Role of the Sermon', *Epworth Review*, 5 (1978); H. McLeod, *The Religious Crisis of the 1960s* (Oxford: Oxford University Press, 2007); M. Townsend, 'Preaching – 25 Years of Ups and Downs', *Expository Times*, 95 (1983–84); John Stacey (ed.), *About Preaching* (London: LP Dept, 1970); John Stacey, *About Faith* (London: LP Dept, 1972).

Vincent moved from rejection of Wesley to an attempt to rehabilitate essential Methodism. Here is a typical Vincent homiletic:

1. Christ is where his deeds are done and the disciple is called to service.
2. Christ is where his ministry of healing and redemption is continued and the disciple is called to healing.
3. Christ is being dealt with, ministered unto or rejected in the person of others, hidden within the secular, and the disciple is called to recognition.
4. Christ is on the cross, and the disciple is called to suffering.
5. Christ is ruling the universe both openly and secretly, and the disciple is called to indication.[63]

At this time Colin Morris was a missionary in what is now Zambia.[64] For some in the 1960s he was a new hero – the reverse of the pacifism of Soper, because he supported violent means to bring down racist regimes. He affirmed his sources were Reinhold Niebuhr and Karl Barth, and he often quoted P. T. Forsyth – very different from the liberation theologians in America like the Argentinian José Miguez Bonino.[65] Morris stated that the central function of preaching was to make Christians by confronting people with the claims of Jesus – at its heart must be the articulation of God's imperious demands, the offer of his forgiveness and the gift of his grace.

The 1960s also saw the radical theologies eclipse the biblical theology of the 1930s–1950s, but it also marked the beginning in Britain of the charismatic movement and the renewal of Evangelicalism across the churches. If in the 1950s and 1960s no great ecumenical assembly was without a rousement by Rupp, after 1970 his place was taken by Donald English (1930–98).[66]

The British story is one of a Methodist thread of apostolic optimism and the centrality of Christ in devotional evangelism. But most Methodist sermons are still preached by Local Preachers. The philosopher T. E. Jessop (1896–1980),[67] for instance, or the long and persuasive preaching of Dr Pauline Webb[68] are worth

---

[63] John Vincent, *Secular Christ* (London: Lutterworth, 1968), 218.
[64] Colin Morris, *Unyoung, Uncoloured, Unpoor* (London: Epworth, 1965); *Mankind My Church* (London: Hodder and Stoughton, 1971); *The Word and the Words* (London: Epworth, 1975), 38, 145; and *Raising the Dead – The Art of the Preacher and Public Performance* (London: Fount, 1996).
[65] José Miguez Bonino, *Doing Theology in a Revolutionary Situation* (Philadelphia, PA: Fortress, 1975); Graham Slater, 'Liberation Theology', *Epworth Review*, 2 (1975).
[66] Donald English, *The Meaning of the Warmed Heart* (London: Methodist Home Mission Division, 1984); 'John Wesley as Preacher for Today', in Sykes (ed.), *Beyond the Boundaries*; and 'Local Preachers and the Church's Mission', in Milburn and Batty (eds), *Workaday Preachers*.
[67] T. E. Jessop, *Effective Religion* (London: Epworth, 1944); *Law and Love* (London: SCM, 1940); *Social Ethics, Christian and Natural* (London: Epworth, 1952); and *The Enduring Passion* (London: Epworth, 1961).
[68] Pauline Webb, *Salvation Today* (London: SCM, 1974); and *World Wide Webb* (London: SCM, 2006).

analysis. There was Charles Coulson (1910–74),[69] who did so much to enable scientists and Christians to cease viewing one another with suspicion – before the new atheism of Richard Dawkins. One might select educationalists like Marjorie Lonsdale or Ernest Taylor of Wolverhampton Grammar School, whom the writer remembers preaching a fine sermon called 'A historian looks at the Resurrection', still needed when the media can get excited over an ossuary. As important were Dr Dorothy Farrar (1899–1987)[70] and the Regius Professor of History at Cambridge, Sir Herbert Butterfield (1900–1979), one of whose lectures ended:

> I have nothing to say at the finish except if one wants a permanent rock in life and goes deep enough for it, it is difficult to meet the future with sufficient elasticity of mind especially if we are locked in contemporary systems of thought. We can do worse than remember a principle which both gives a firm rock and leaves us the maximum elasticity for our minds – the principle hold to Christ and for the rest be totally uncommitted.[71]

Even if Clive Marsh asserts that 'preaching may have had its day as an art form in our present culture',[72] Methodists still seek to preach the gospel in many diverse forms – the twenty minute expository sermon – 'reason, doctrine and use', as the Puritans put it; all-age dialogues, now more difficult as the age of children in church declines; the short, sharp sermon at Holy Communion, and many 'fresh expressions'. An interesting selection of sermons and work on preaching has appeared in the early twenty-first century.[73] The Epworth *Companions to the Revised Common Lectionary* are very positive about preaching.

---

[69] C. A. Coulson, *Science and Christian Belief* (London: Fontana, 1951); and *Science, Technology and the Christian* (London: Epworth, 1960); D. and E. Hawkin, *The Religious and Social Thought of C.A. Coulson* (London: Epworth, 1965).

[70] D. H. Farrar, 'A Preacher's Life of Prayer', in G. P. Lewis (ed.), *The Preachers' Handbook*, vol. 1 (London: LP Dept, 1949), 1–6.

[71] H. Butterfield, *Christianity and History* (London: Bell, 1949), 146; C. T. McIntire (ed.), *Writings on Christianity and History* (Oxford: Oxford University Press, 1979); and, *Herbert Butterfield* (New Haven, CT: Yale University Press, 2004).

[72] Clive Marsh, *Christianity in a Post-atheist Age* (London: SCM, 2002), 54; cf. Neil Richardson, *Preaching from Scripture* (London: Epworth, 1983); and 'Preaching in the Twenty First Century', *Ichthus*, Spring 2001; John A. Newton, 'True and Living Word: Preaching with Integrity in the Third Millennium', *Worship and Preaching*, 1999.

[73] Brian Galliers, *Variety in Preaching* (Peterborough: Epworth, 2000); Martyn Atkins, *Preaching in a Cultural Context* (Peterborough: Epworth, 2001); Jane Craske, *A Woman's Perspective on Preaching* (Peterborough: Epworth, 2001); John B. Taylor, *Preaching as Doctrine* (Peterborough: Epworth, 2001); Cyril Rodd, *Preaching with Imagination* (Peterborough: Epworth, 2001); J. M. Turner, 'Preaching and Theology', in Cyril Rodd (ed.), *Church and Theology: Reflections on Ministry* (Buxton: Church in the Market Place, 2004); A. Shier-Jones (ed.), *Forty Four Sermons to Serve the Present Age* (Peterborough: Epworth, 2007); Michael Townsend, *Thinking About Preaching* (Peterborough: Epworth, 2009); volumes of sermons by John B. Taylor (1996), Gordon Wakefield (1999), Geoffrey Eddy (2003), John Farley (2006)

In America mention should be made of three matters. First, a recent stress in American Methodism on what they call the 'Wesleyan heritage'. Secondly, the whole area of 'Liberation Theology', as it developed after the collapse of the Soviet Union, and, thirdly, the area of Black theology and Black preaching, culminating historically in the election of the first Black President, Barack Obama. In this Theodore Runyon, Thomas Langford, José Miguez Bonino and James Cone are significant. There is also the relationship with Pentecostalism, which David Hempton sees as a development of Methodism on which one has to point out the 'both ... and' combination of elation and discipline in Methodist preaching, which is somewhat lacking in some Pentecostal styles.[74]

Theodore Runyon's work on Wesley is splendid,[75] especially the section on experience – 'orthopathy', he calls it. It must transcend subjectivism, transform life, have social effect, be rational, sacramental and teleological, but he tends to relate Wesley to contemporary matters like the environment, feminism and relationships with other faiths – ignoring Wesley's hostile attitude to 'the Turks', that is, Islam. This tends to make Wesley an 'icon' rather than the 'folk theologian' of the Albert Outler era. Langford takes us from Wesley to Wainwright – descriptive rather than critical and featuring few lay voices or preachers. 'Contemporary voices' feature James Cone, José Miguez Bonino, Rupert Davies, Frances Young, Geoffrey Wainwright, Stanley Hauerwas and Rebecca Chopp.

Liberation Theology is not an easy era to summarise. Pope John Paul II was very critical from his Polish perspective, seeing too much uncritical Marxism. This is clearly true of Bonino,[76] the Argentinian theologian and preacher. In his early work he certainly eulogised Marx and saw the Soviet Union and Cuba as model states.

---

and J. M. Turner (2006) published by Church in the Market Place, Buxton; Gordon Wakefield, *Methodist Spirituality* (London: Epworth, 1999).

[74] Essential are the Oxford Institute of Methodist Theological Studies' 11 handbooks (Abingdon); cf. Brian Beck, *Exploring Methodism's Heritage:. The Story of the Oxford Institute of Methodist Theological Studies* (Nashville, TN: General Board of Higher Education and Ministry of the United Methodist Church , 2004).

[75] Theodore Runyon, *The New Creation: John Wesley's Theology for Today* (Nashville, TN: Abingdon, 1998), esp. 160ff; and 'Introduction', in *Sanctification and Liberation* (OIMTS handbook 1977 [Abingdon, 1981]); Thomas Langford, *Practical Divinity; Theology in the Wesleyan Tradition* (Nashville, TN: Abingdon, 1983, 1998); *Readings in Wesleyan Theology* (Nashville, TN: Abingdon, 1984, 1999); and *Methodist Theology* (London: Epworth, 1998); Richard B. Steele (ed.), 'Honest Religion', in *The Methodist Tradition and Related Movements* (Metuchen, NJ: Scarecrow, 2001); Lovett H. Weems, Jr., *Leadership in the Wesleyan Spirit* (Nashville, TN: Abingdon, 1999); John B. Cobb, Jr., *Grace and Responsibility: A Wesleyan Theology for Today* (Nashville, TN: Abingdon, 1995); Kenneth J. Collins, *A Faithful Witness: John Wesley. Homiletical Theology* (Nashville, TN: Abingdon, 1993); Randy Maddox, *Responsible Grace: John Wesley's Practical Theology* (Nashville, TN: Abingdon, 1994); and *Rethinking Wesley's Theology for Contemporary Methodism* (Nashville, TN: Abingdon, 1998).

[76] José Miguez Bonino, *Christians and Marxists: The Mutual Challenge to Revolution* (London: Hodder and Stoughton, 1976); *Doing Theology in a Revolutionary Situation*; 'Wesley's Doctrine of Sanctification from a Liberation Perspective', in Runyon (ed.), *Sanctification and Liberation*; and 'The Poor are Always with Us – Can Wesley Help us to Discover how to Serve

He later supported Argentina against Britain in the war over the Falklands. Then he appears to have left Marxism behind and fastened on Wesley and the 'Wesley for Today' school.

Black theology is very much in an American context. James Cone is a fine example.[77] Preaching to Cone must be exuberant. It must appeal to the heart, the emotions and the will. This style could be exemplified in Black preaching in Great Britain,[78] which is now studied at the Queen's Foundation in Birmingham.

There are now an outstanding number of American books on preaching, especially from the Black traditions, Baptist and Methodist especially. They mark a renewal of interest in the nature of preaching in contexts very different from the 'post-modernism' and secularism of Europe.[79] Perhaps we finally say with Richard Jones that 'preaching is good story-telling controlled by good Christian theology' and with Archbishop John Habgood that 'the aim of preaching is to arouse, strengthen and deepen faith'.[80]

---

our Poor Today?', in Richard Heitzenrater (ed.), *The Poor and the People Called Methodists, 1729–1999* (Nashville, TN: Abingdon, 2002).

[77] James H. Cone, *A Black Theology of Liberation* (New York: Orbis, 1986); *Black Theology and Black Power* (New York: Orbis, 1987); 'Sanctification and Liberation in the Black Religious Tradition', in Runyon (ed.), *Sanctification and Liberation*; and *The Gospel of the Oppressed* (San Francisco: Harper, 1975).

[78] Robinson Milwood, *Liberation and Mission* (London: ACER, 1997); Robert Beckford, *Jesus is Dread: Black Theology and Black Culture in Britain* (London: DLT, 1999).

[79] Martha J. Simmons (ed.), *Preaching on the Brink: The Future of Homiletic* (Nashville, TN: Abingdon, 1996); Karen B. Westerfield Tucker, *American Methodist Worship* (Oxford: Oxford University Press, 2001); Henry H. Mitchell, *Black Preaching: The Recovery of a Powerful Art* (Nashville, TN: Abingdon, 1990); Henry H. Mitchell , *The Recovery of Preaching* (London: Hodder and Stoughton, 1979); James H. Harris, *Preaching Liberation* (Philadelphia, PA: Fortress, 1995); David Buttrick, *Homiletic* (London: SCM, 1987); David Buttrick, *Preaching – the New and the Now* (Louisville, KY: John Knox Press, 1998); Samuel Proctor, *The Creative Sound of the Trumpet* (Valley Forge, PA: Judson Press, 1994); William J. Abraham, *The Art of Evangelism* (Calver: Cliff College, 1993); William J. Abraham , *The Logic of Renewal* (London: SPCK, 2001); Anthony G. Reddie, *Nobodies into Somebodies: A Practical Theology for Education Liberation* (Peterborough: Epworth, 2003); Anthony G. Reddie , *Is God Colour Blind?* (London: SPCK, 2009), esp. chs 5 and 6.

[80] Jones, *Groundwork of Worship and Preaching*, 139; Rowe, *Queen's Sermons*, 13. Cf. John Sawkins and Margaret Batty, 'Methodist Local Preachers in Great Britain: A Millennial Profile', *Epworth Review*, 29 (2002); Clive Field, 'The Social Structure of English Methodism, Eighteenth–Twentieth Centuries', *British Journal of Sociology*, 28 (1977); Jonathan Hustler, *Making the Words Acceptable: The Shape of the Sermon in Christian History* (Peterborough: Epworth, 2009).

# PART V
# Culture and Society

# Methodism and Politics: Mapping the Political on the Methodist Genome

Stephen J. Plant

> How far is it the duty of a Christian minister to preach politics? … this is rarely to be done, and only when fit occasion offers; it being our main business to preach 'repentance towards God, and faith in our Lord Jesus Christ'
>
> John Wesley, 9 January 1782[1]

## Introduction

Many Methodists take political engagement to be an important and distinctive part of their ecclesial tradition. It is widely assumed that though the Methodist Church may be said to be disestablished in relation to the state in almost all countries,[2] it has often 'punched above its weight' politically. In their politics Methodists understand themselves to tread in John Wesley's footsteps. His aim to 'reform the nation and, in particular, the Church; to spread scriptural holiness through the land' was expressed in preaching but also in determined campaigning on political issues such as slavery, economics, religious liberty and civil obedience.[3]

---

[1] Thomas Jackson (ed.), *The Works of the Rev. John Wesley, A.M.* (London: John Mason, 1872), vol. ix, 154–5.

[2] The term 'disestablished' is best used cautiously with respect to Methodist Churches. Even where it is not the state church, a Methodist Church may have a legal relationship with the state (see, e.g., the Methodist Church Acts of the British Parliament passed in 1939 and 1976 that constitute the Methodist Church in Britain as a legal entity); and, where Christianity has been afforded special status in a national constitution and the Methodist Church is in the majority, it may nonetheless find itself in conflict with the state, as is the case in Fiji at the time this essay is being written.

[3] Minutes of Conference 1763.

Such assumptions are not false; but in this essay I will argue that there are significant tensions within the Methodist tradition shaping Methodists' engagement with politics. These tensions create impulses in Methodist political theology that have repeatedly pushed Methodists in competing directions, each claiming to be authentically Methodist. A growing body of recent historical literature on Methodism and politics on both sides of the Atlantic provides evidence of such tensions. But, with a few exceptions, Methodist theology has been slow to respond constructively with strategies able to resolve the tensions. In this essay I highlight how recent historical research has challenged the polemically driven interpretive proposals of preceding generations. Moving through the sparser theological literature I argue that Methodists must look *outside* their tradition for the resources with which to sort out their internal conflicts. I propose one example of how this might be done.

Methodist thinking about politics typically took place as a by-product of engagement with 'concrete' issues such as slavery, war and peace, the birth of a welfare state and state education policy.[4] These issues are dealt with in other essays in this volume and this essay should be read alongside them.[5]

## John Wesley and the Evolution of a Methodist Genome

Most of the patterns in subsequent Methodist political thinking were established by John Wesley. The source material for Wesley's political thought is varied and little of it is intentionally ordered into a coherent theory. Wesley involved himself in political issues by means of letters, pamphlets, sermons and actions, some of which are recorded in his journal. He often wrote in response to contemporary events and, absent that context, their content is difficult to interpret.

Among the key controversies affecting Wesley's political thinking three stand out:[6]

---

[4] The extent to which Methodists were active in relation to political issues is described by D. W. Bebbington in *The Nonconformist Conscience: Chapel and Politics, 1870–1914* (London: George Allen and Unwin, 1982). Bebbington identifies several neuralgic points, to only some of which this essay can refer, including religious equality, social problems (e.g., prostitution and drink), the Irish Question and education. Bebbington iterates that Methodists were at once constituents of a broader grouping of nonconformists and distinct from the generality of nonconformists in important respects. For another account of the relation of Methodists to other forms of religious dissent see Michael R. Watts, *The Dissenters: Volume II* (Oxford: Oxford University Press, 1995).

[5] One important tradition of interpretation of Methodist political thought is absent from this essay because it is covered elsewhere in this volume. This is the liberation theological interpretation of Wesleyan politics and economics; see e.g., Theodore W. Jennings Jr.; *Good News to the Poor: John Wesley's Evangelical Economics* (Nashville, TN: Abingdon, 1990).

[6] For an example of a study that identifies these issues as central see Theodore R. Weber, *Politics in the Order of Salvation: Transforming Wesleyan Political Ethics* (Nashville, TN: Kingswood, 2001), 41–154.

1. The first had its origins in the Glorious Revolution of 1688 that replaced James II on the English and Irish thrones (James VII on the Scottish) with William and Mary as joint sovereigns. A division of opinion was created in the British Isles between those willing to transfer their loyalty to the new monarchs and those unwilling to abjure their oath of loyalty to King James (becoming 'non-jurors' or 'Jacobites').The division was felt nowhere more keenly than in the Wesley family, in which William of Orange was acknowledged as sovereign by Samuel but regarded as a usurper by Susanna. When Samuel registered his wife's reluctance to pray for King William and Queen Mary in 1702, he insisted they separate: John owed his conception to their reunion.[7] By the time John went to Oxford University the political situation was *de facto* resolved, but the return of Charles Stuart in 1745 brought it to the surface again. On 21 September 1745, the day Stuart's clansmen routed the British army at the battle of Prestonpans, Wesley was in Newcastle writing to the City's mayor that '[a]ll I can do for his Majesty, whom I honour and love – I think not less than I did my own father – is this: I cry unto God day by day, in public and private, to put all his enemies to confusion. And I exhort all that hear me to do the same, and in their several stations exert themselves as loyal subjects, who so long as they fear God cannot but honour the king.'[8] Differences of opinion endure about the extent to which Wesley ever held Jacobite sympathies, but by 1745 Wesley exhibited unflinching loyalty to the House of Hanover.
2. A second key series of events was the Radical political agitation associated with British constitutional crises of the 1760s. A central figure in this agitation was John Wilkes, who became a Member of Parliament (MP) in 1757, but was arrested for libelling the King and his minister in 1763. While an outlaw he was elected MP for the county of Middlesex in 1768, a result hotly contested by the Government against the run of popular opinion. Wilkes took his seat in 1774, by which time his populism had taken a patriotic turn.[9] Wesley was never slow to express views about the impropriety of popular political agitation directed against the King and his representatives. But his advocacy for order and obedience became increasingly bound up with his anxiety about widespread conservative suspicions that Methodism was associated with political disorder.
3. A third key event was the American Revolution leading to the Declaration of Independence in 1776. Whereas, with respect to the Glorious Revolution, Wesley had accommodated the principle that leading establishment figures could stage-manage the replacement of one monarch by others (he was careful not to attribute this change either to the people or to Parliament),

---

[7] For an account of this incident see Henry D. Rack, *Reasonable Enthusiast: John Wesley and the Rise of Methodism* (London: Epworth, 1992), 48.

[8] W. Reginald Ward and Richard P. Heitzenrater (eds), *The Works of John Wesley Volume 20: Journals and Diaries III (1743–1754)* (Nashville, TN: Abingdon, 1991), 78.

[9] It was with Wilkes in mind that John Wesley's friend, Dr Johnson, wrote in his dictionary that patriotism was the last resort of the scoundrel.

he could see no good reason for the American colonies to withdraw their allegiance to King George III.[10] By 1784, however, Wesley had little choice but to accept that over the newly independent American States the 'English Government has no authority... either civil or ecclesiastical, any more than over the States of Holland'.[11]

In exploring Wesley's responses to these contextual challenges I want to employ an analogy through which I interpret Wesley and the political theological traditions that originate with him. The analogy is that of a Methodist genome in which hereditary information is recorded in a DNA sequence of two complementary strands connected in a number of base-pairs. The human genome has around three billion base-pairs, but thankfully for my purposes the sequence on the Methodist genome in which I am interested has only two.[12]

The first base-pair is *liberty* and *order*. Wesley believed that religious liberty and social order were both basic to political life. These dual commitments were, however, held together in a state of tension. Wesley's 1772 essay 'Thoughts on Liberty'[13] contains both halves of the first base-pair, though his emphasis here is liberty. He begins by asserting that a desire for liberty is universal, natural and – since only human beings desire it – is 'the glory of rational beings'.[14] Laying irony on with a trowel, Wesley asks if contemporary fascination with liberty is 'because of the inseparable connexion between Wilkes and liberty...?'[15] Turning from libertarian rhetoric, Wesley advances an understanding of that liberty which the good and wise desire: 'It is either religious or civil. Religious liberty is a liberty to choose our own religion, to worship God according to our own conscience, according to the best light we have.'[16] Religious liberty, according to Wesley, has not been unfailingly defended by the English crown, a fact that makes George III's undertaking to defend it the more commendable. A second kind of liberty is civil liberty, which is '[a] liberty to enjoy our lives and fortunes in our own way; to use our property, whatever is legally our own according to our own choice.'[17] Wesley insists that '[w]e enjoy at this day throughout these kingdoms [i.e., Britain and

---

[10] See especially his 'Calm address to our American Colonies'(London: Hawes, 1775).

[11] See Wesley's letter to American Methodists dated 10 September 1784, in John Telford (ed.), *The Letters of John Wesley, AM.* (London: Epworth, 1931), 238.

[12] The idea of a Methodist genome is indebted to Hempton's organisation of the chapters in *Empire* 'around parallel or competing concepts' and to his thesis that '[t]he contents of Methodist archives throughout the world display the trace elements of Methodism's origins in enthusiasm and enlightenment as children carry the genetic code of their parents': D. Hempton, *Methodism: Empire of the Spirit* (New Haven, CT and London: Yale University Press, 2005), 7.

[13] John Wesley, 'Thoughts on Liberty', in Jackson (ed,), *Works*, 34–46.

[14] Ibid., 34.

[15] Ibid., 35.

[16] Ibid., 37.

[17] Ibid., 41.

Ireland] such liberty, civil and religious, as no other kingdom or commonwealth in Europe, or in the world, enjoys'[18]

The other half of this first base-pair is *order*. For Wesley, liberty was made possible by laws binding subject and sovereign to each other. On his part, the King was bound by law to honour the civil and religious liberties of his citizens, while the citizens were also bound by the law to honour the King. For Weber, this reciprocal pattern of liberties defended by the crown on the one hand, and of political duty and order binding sovereign and subject on the other, makes for an 'organic constitutionalism' that is 'Wesley's primary political tradition'.[19] An important issue at stake is the extent to which Wesley subscribed to a theory of the divine right of kings to rule. The question is moot; but at the least we may note in passing the similarity between a poem of Wesley's 'For His Majesty King George' and the National Anthem, 'God save our Gracious King', written about the same time. Wesley too invokes God's help in saving his sovereign from his enemies:

> Confound whoe'er oppose,
> Or force them to retire;
> Be thou a tower against his foes,
> Be thou a wall of fire.[20]

On the face of it, the Royalist sentiment expressed here suggests that it is accurate to describe Wesley as a Tory; certainly this is what may be called the 'standard portrait'.[21] Wesley thought kings ruled by a divine authority and that, consequently, their power derived from God and not the people. He believed further that such authority ought to command obedience. Yet, as we shall see when we turn to trends in recent theological research, this rather bald description of Wesley's political position has been challenged by those arguing in several ways that it does Wesley an injustice. Certainly the term 'Tory' is not infrequently applied to Wesley as a term of abuse, for which reason alone it should be treated with caution.

The political base-pair of liberty and order resembled closely other base-pairs on the Methodist genome, perhaps especially one base-pair governing Methodist ecclesiology and polity: connexional discipline and charismatic energy.[22] Just as that base built into the Methodist genome a tension between a centralising connexion and charismatic individuals pushing at the boundaries, the political base-pair of liberty and order proved unstable even in Wesley's lifetime. Where liberty was emphasised at the expense of order, Methodists were liable to find their Christian radicalism subsumed by political radicalism; where order was emphasised at the

---

[18] Ibid., 45.
[19] Weber, *Politics in the Order of Salvation*, 32.
[20] Jackson (ed.), *Works*, 187.
[21] For this term and the position it is intended to describe see Jason E. Vickers, *Wesley: A Guide for the Perplexed* (London: Continuum, 2009), 62–82.
[22] See Hempton, *Empire of the Spirit*.

expense of liberty Methodists were liable to give unthinking obedience to the authority of the state.

The second base-pair is *evangelism* and *social holiness*. Both liberty and order were, for Wesley, never more than secondary goods from the perspective of the Gospel: '[f]or it is our main and constant business "to preach Jesus Christ, and him crucified".'[23] Religious liberty was to be defended by magistrates because ministers must be free to preach the Gospel, and order was to be defended because it provided the condition wherein that liberty could be exercised. On Wesley's account, therefore, politics was to be left to politicians, for '[i]t is always difficult and frequently impossible for private men to judge of the measures taken by men in public offices'.[24] In a similar vein Wesley remarked that 'I am no politician; politics lie quite out of my province.'[25] But that remark prefaced a treatise on public affairs. To which Wesley are we to give credence: to the Wesley who eschewed politics for the Gospel, or the Wesley for whom salvation could not be separated from politics? The answer lies in the tension between evangelism and social holiness. Basic to Wesley's thinking was that once an individual has accepted Jesus as saviour, the Holy Spirit sanctifies her life in a process leading towards Christian perfection in love. That process of sanctification has social consequences: it transforms whole persons embedded in social relationships. This means that proclamation of the Gospel of salvation is inextricably intertwined with a *social* holiness. On the one hand, therefore, Wesley enjoined upon Methodists the importance of keeping out of politics, and, on the other, gave to them a Gospel with profound social – and therefore political – consequences.

How have these two base-pairs, together with the irresolvable tensions between them, genetically determined the history of Methodism? To begin to answer that question we may turn first to the history of Methodism in Britain and Ireland.

## Recent Trends in Historical Research: Britain and Ireland

The shadow cast on historical research on Methodism and politics in the British Isles by the French historian Elie Halévy has been a long one. *In nuce,* Halévy asked why revolution against the state had occurred in 1789 in France, again in 1830, and then on a Europe-wide scale in 1848, while in the country where the Industrial Revolution began and in which it went furthest, no popular revolution occurred. Halévy's answer was that in England social and political revolutionary impulses had been moderated and redirected into a Protestant evangelical revival in which Methodism played the leading role.[26] Halévy's thesis still excites interest a century after its first

---

[23] Jackson (ed.), *Works*, 155.
[24] Ibid., 155.
[25] Ibid., 14.
[26] E. Halévy, 'La Naissance du Méthodisme en Angleterre', *Revue de Paris*, 1 and 15 August 1906, 519–39 and 841–67; trans. B. Semmel, *The Birth of Methodism* (Chicago, IL:

publication,[27] but its importance for recent research is the reaction to it of several Marxist historians beginning in the 1960s. Eric Hobsbawm is a good example: he accepted uncritically the view that '[t]he new Methodist type of sectarianism was anti-revolutionary' but thought that attributing 'the immunity of Britain to revolution in our period' (i.e., 1789–1848) was nonetheless mistaken.[28] Hobsbawm maintained that 'the new sects and trends were initially a-political or even (like the Wesleyans) strongly conservative for they turned away from the evil outside world to personal salvation or to the life of the self-contained group, which often meant that they rejected the possibility of any collective alteration of its secular arrangements'.[29] Still more polemically driven, E. P. Thompson also critiqued the malign influence of Methodism on working people. Thompson maintained that Methodism served simultaneously 'as the religion of the industrial bourgeoisie ... and of wide sections of the proletariat'.[30] While older traditions of Dissent promoted laudable traditions of intellectual independence and democratic practice, the general tenor of the new Wesleyan traditions was of submission to authority: '[i]n his theology, Wesley appears to have dispensed with the best and selected unhesitatingly the worse elements of Puritanism: if in class terms Methodism was hermaphroditic, in doctrinal terms it was a mule'.[31] Thompson's rhetorical skill alone, particularly in his chapter on 'The Transforming Power of the Cross', makes him essential reading for any serious student of Methodism and politics, and it was the liveliness of E. P. Thompson's polemic that drove the succeeding generation of historians back to the historical sources for evidence with which to construct their rebuttals.

Foremost among contemporary historians who have worked on Methodism and politics is David Hempton. His *Methodism and Politics in British Society 1750–1850*[32] and *Religion and Political Culture in Britain and Ireland*[33] are significant contributions, and in Methodism: *Empire of the Spirit* he extends his reach into North America. Hempton credits the generation of Marxist and Socialist historians for prompting an increase in research in Methodism and politics. Though Methodism has long exercised a strange power over generations of researchers, the subject matter catching researchers' interests has altered: '[m]ost obviously, there has been a marked decline in the number of words devoted to Methodist theology, spirituality and biography, and a corresponding increase in studies of the personal, social and

---

University of Chicago Press, 1971).

[27] See e.g., G. W. Olsen (ed.), *Religion and Revolution in Early Industrial England* (Lanham, MD: University Press of America, 1990).

[28] Eric Hobsbawn, *The Age of Revolution: 1789–1848* (London: Weidenfeld and Nicolson, 1962), 277.

[29] Ibid., 277.

[30] E. P. Thompson, *The Making of the English Working Class* (London: Victor Gollancz, 1963), 391.

[31] Ibid., 398.

[32] David Hempton, *Methodism and Politics in British Society 1750–1850* (London: Hutchinson, 1984).

[33] David Hempton, *Religion and Political Culture in Britain and Ireland* (Cambridge: Cambridge University Press, 1996).

political impact of Methodism on English localities'.[34] The last phrase is important: while Halévy and the Marxist historians who followed him were concerned with political theories at the macro level, much recent historical research has been concerned with mapping the impact of Methodism at the micro level. As quickly as recent historians of Methodism in the British Isles achieved a sense of the scale, complexity and local variation of the historical record, they became increasingly reticent about proposing grand theories to interpret it.

From 1791 Methodism underwent what Hempton describes as a 'decade of crisis'. External factors played a role as Methodism found itself under the pressure of an Industrial Revolution at home, and of a political revolution in France leading to war. But the 1790s also saw the tensions on the Methodist genome leading to internal conflicts resulting in splits within the Methodist movement that, deploying my analogy, ran between the halves of the two binary pairs I have identified. Take the dispute between Alexander Kilham and the Wesleyan connexion, leading to his expulsion in 1796 and the formation of the Methodist New Connexion. Kilham, as Hempton reminds us, 'in his opposition to Catholicism, absolutism, corruption and legal manipulation, was firmly within the old-fashioned tradition of the freeborn Englishman'.[35] Kilham's Methodism emphasised liberty over order. Those in the Wesleyan establishment, however, which saw in the Kilhamites a 'Methodist Jacobinism' that must be extirpated, emphasised order over liberty. Thus, already by the 1790s, the Wesleyans had become, on the one hand, 'the most centralised, most clerically dominated and most conservative of all the Nonconformist denominations' while, on the other, 'in its chapels it fostered lay participation, free debate, and frequently radicalism'.[36] Wesleyan conservatives could claim to be authentically Methodist because of their emphasis on order for the sake of evangelism, and the radicals could claim to be authentically Methodist because of their emphasis on religious liberty to the same end: neither party was wrong but the failure to hold the base-pair of order and liberty together made conflict between them inevitable. By the end of the next phase in Methodist development '[a] generalized Wesleyan conservatism was now well rooted, at least among the men of influence, but it could not be converted into a politically active Toryism until religion emerged as a major political issue in the late 1820s'.[37]

That activism was prompted by two overlapping issues that were of major political importance. The first issue was Catholic emancipation[38] and the second, the politics of education.[39] A heavy political investment in the anti-Catholic campaign set Wesleyans against the liberal cause of religious liberty for which they had formerly been vocal advocates. The reasons may be interpreted in light of the idea of flaws on the Methodist genome. Wesleyans had two anxieties with respect to

---

[34] Ibid., 25.
[35] Ibid., 68.
[36] Watts, *The Dissenters*, 358.
[37] Ibid., 110.
[38] See Hempton, *Methodism and Politics*, 116–48.
[39] Ibid., 149–78; see also Bebbington, *Nonconformist Conscience*, 127–52.

Catholic emancipation. The first was that Roman Catholics owed ultimate allegiance to a Church that was oppressive of liberty of religious conscience; the second that Catholic emancipation would remove a social and political dam that held back Catholic evangelisation among sections of the population where it might compete with Methodist evangelism. The first may be seen as an imbalance on the first base-pair in emphasising order above liberty; the second an imbalance on the second base-pair in allowing evangelism to override commitments to social equality.

With respect to education, the issues were certainly challenging. The 1902 Education Act raised hackles because it taxed people who were not members of the Church of England to pay for schools where only Anglicans could teach and in which children baptised as Anglicans were given priority. Methodists feared that the Church of England was being granted a franchise to educate the nation as Anglicans. In a catchy slogan eliding disestablishment and anti-Catholic sentiments, the 1902 Act was described as 'Rome on the Rates'. As part of the campaign between 1902 and 1906 over 170 men were jailed for refusing to pay that proportion of their Rates that funded Church of England schools: many more were issued with summonses. In very strong language the Wesleyan Conference of 1902 vented its view that a right of conscience and of public justice demanded that the new local education authorities be largely publicly elected, in order to moderate the proposed control of state education by Anglicans.[40] The campaign was very successful and the Liberal party electoral landslide of 1906 rode this wave of nonconformist conscience and represents its high-water mark. At its best, Methodist engagement with educational policy in the late nineteenth and early twentieth centuries represents a canny and courageous campaign in defence of civil rights and religious liberty. But even here, perhaps, signs of genetic flaws are discernible in a debasement of the laudable goal of religious liberty into an assertion of nonconformist rights against the established Church.

## Recent Trends in Historical Research: North America

One of the most important trends in recent historical research has been a shift from histories written about, by and for particular Methodist denominations towards histories that explore the embeddedness of Methodism in the development of American nationhood and culture. This approach is peculiarly apt for Methodism because, as Russell Richey notes, 'in 1784 [Methodists] became the first denomination to organise themselves nationally [and], from that date were the most national American church'.[41] A good exemplar of this approach is the recent two-volume history written and edited by Russell E. Richey, Kenneth E. Rowe and

---

[40] See Rupert E. Davies, Raymond George and Gordon Rupp (eds), *A History of the Methodist Church in Great Britain*, vol.4 (London: Epworth Press, 1988), 616.

[41] Russell E. Richey, *Early American Methodism* (Bloomington and Indianapolis, IN: Indiana University Press, 1991), 34.

Jean Miller Schmidt.[42] These volumes identify 'three distinct Methodist phases ...: a Pietist, a nurturing, and an advocating. Methodism features/featured all three – piety, nurture, and advocacy – in every period but, we think, has tended to accent one.'[43] The narration of this history is further focussed by taking three snapshots, each at an important transitional moment between phases: 1816, 1884 and 1968. This structure is a convenient one for the purposes of this chapter: how did the binary pairs on the Methodist genome I have mapped affect political behaviour during these three phases?

The founding myth of North American nationhood is that the Puritan Fathers of the nation fled to America in search of religious liberty because of persecution of religious minorities by European states in which the principle *'cuius regio, eius religio'*[44] pertained. In that context Wesley's allegiance to the crown and to the establishment of the Church of England proved inconvenient. Following the Declaration of Independence in 1776, Methodists found themselves divided by competing political allegiances to the British crown on the one hand and to the nascent American States on the other. In this heated context Wesley's 1775 *Calm Address to Our American Colonies* proved a political liability, and this was exacerbated by internal struggles about leadership of the new Methodist movement facing the questions: '[w]as Methodism part of the feared Anglican plot to impose an episcopate on the colonies? Was it a friend or foe to the colonial cause and American liberties?'[45] As with British Methodists, American Methodists found themselves wrestling with irresolvable tensions between order and liberty. When American Methodism emerged from its earliest period it was as a movement deeply suspicious of politics, keen to get on with its core business of spreading scriptural holiness.[46] This was clearly expressed by Francis Asbury, who wrote in 1813:

> As to temporal power, what have we to do with that in this country? We are not senators, congressmen or chaplains; neither do we hold any civil offices. We neither have, nor wish to have, anything to do with the government of the States, nor, as I conceive, do the States fear us. Our kingdom is not of this world.[47]

The paradox was this: on the one hand, patriotism, and on the other a rule of 'no-politics'. 'Why,' asks Richey, 'the aversion to politics and the passion for

---

[42] Russell E. Richey, Kenneth E. Rowe and Jean Miller Schmidt, *The Methodist Experience in America: A History* vol. 1 (Nashville, TN: Abingdon, 2010) and *The Methodist Experience in America: A Sourcebook*, vol. 2 (Nashville, TN: Abingdon, 2000).

[43] Ibid., 1, xv.

[44] I.e., the principle that the religious confession adopted by a state's Prince should be the confession of his people.

[45] Richey, *Methodist Experience*, 1, 26.

[46] Ibid., 73–89.

[47] Cited in Richey, *Early American Methodism*, 33.

patriotism?'⁴⁸ In this instance, the answer lies in a tension between evangelism and social holiness. Just as Wesley was not telling the whole truth when he claimed to eschew politics, Asbury too was not wholly truthful in claiming that Methodists wanted nothing to do with the States: 'The Methodists did not simply want to be left alone by the nation. They wanted to convert it.'⁴⁹

From around 1816 the pattern shifted discernibly towards building for ministry and nurture.⁵⁰ In this period the now denominationally fragmented Methodist movement in America lay down deep roots into national life. Its faith became more scripted, more ordered; conversion, while remaining an important emphasis, was supplemented and structured by Sunday Schools and by the foundation of educational establishments and Seminaries for clergy training. The base-pair of order and liberty pivoted towards order.

Thus established in the life of the nation, in the third phase, Methodists began flexing their political muscles from around 1884. Politically central to this was a decided shift from evangelism towards advocacy for a social gospel, a development from the social holiness of the preceding generations:⁵¹ '[w]hen they (northern Methodists particularly and quite early) grasped its import, they embraced, institutionalised, and internalised it much as they had the camp meeting a century earlier'.⁵² To an extent the rise of a social gospel represented an assertion of the importance and social value of Christianity in the wake of a crisis of confidence provoked by the acceptance, particularly in educated circles, of the insights of biblical criticism and of a concomitant liberal theology. At its best, the social gospel was an energetic expression of 'concern for workers, immigrants, slum dwellers, and poor persons'⁵³ in obedience to the biblical prophets and the teachings of Jesus. At its worst it drew close to substituting the Gospel of Christ with the gospel of human progress in the attempt to build God's kingdom on earth by human hands. In addition to a theological critique of the social gospel going back at least to 1919,⁵⁴ from the late 1960s there has been a conservative evangelical

---

⁴⁸ Ibid., 34.
⁴⁹ Ibid., 34.
⁵⁰ Richey, *Methodist Experience*, 1, 103–40.
⁵¹ Ibid., 299–309.
⁵² Ibid., 299.
⁵³ Ibid., 299.
⁵⁴ Karl Barth's rebuttal of the social gospel, to which he had himself once subscribed, in his Tambach Lecture in September 1919 marks the beginning of the dialectic/neo-orthodox theological 'revolution' that reshaped contemporary Protestant political theology: , Karl Barth, *The Word of God and the Word of Man* (New York, NY: Harper & Row, 1957; English tr. 'The Christian's Place in Society'), 272–327. Barth writes: 'For it is one thing to entertain critical doubts regarding the god of this world, and another thing to perceive the δύναμις, the meaning and the might of the living God who is building a new world. And yet without that perception the idea of "social Christianity" is sheer nonsense'; ibid., 280. The Barthian critique of the social gospel has influenced recent Methodist political theology in the US, not least through the work of Stanley Hauerwas, e.g., in his Barthian critique of Reinhold Niebuhr in *With the Grain of the Universe* (London: SCM, 2001).

reaction, led by 'Good News' as a campaigning caucus, against the dominance of a social gospel perspective in the political and moral outlook of the United Methodist Church.[55] In terms of my analogy, the tendency towards the social gospel and the subsequent conservative reaction to it, suggest an imbalance on the 'base' pairs of the Methodist political genome. Most obviously it evidences an enduring inability in American Methodism to achieve a balanced and theologically convincing account of the relationship between evangelism and social holiness. But the assertion of the Church's moral agenda in Federal and in State politics, for example on prohibition (from 1920–1933)[56] and on abortion legislation, may also repeat a tendency, stemming from John Wesley, too readily to see the divine hand in the politics of the earthly city.

## Recent Trends in Theological Research

While historical research has flourished in recent years, there have been lamentably few contributions of significance to *theological* thinking about politics by Methodists. But two books stand out. In *The Methodist Revolution*[57] Bernard Semmel responds theologically to the Marxist historical critique of Methodism's historical role in British history. Where I have seen tension in base-pairs on the Methodist genome with respect to politics, Semmel sees balance and strength. Semmel argues that the 'Methodist Revolution' can be interpreted as the English counterpart to the democratic revolution of the eighteenth century. In this way, Semmel proposes, Methodism may 'have had a decisive impact in the shaping of what foreign observers consider the unique qualities of nineteenth-century England, with its blending of liberty and order, and its special sense of national mission'.[58] Theology comes into play because, for Semmel, Methodism's political engagement followed, sometimes intentionally and sometimes less intentionally, from its doctrines. The theological doctrine with the most obvious political consequences in this very English revolution was Arminianism, which had the potential to underwrite a political commitment to liberty of conscience. Semmel sees in Kilham an interesting case, in whom an egalitarian Arminian theology translated into political ideas.[59] Similarly, the doctrine of assurance had 'levelling tendencies'.[60] Tensions there were, to be sure, but '[t]he "revolutionary" implications of Methodist doctrine …

---

[55] See Richey, *Methodist Experience*, 1, 502 ff.

[56] For an account of the influence of 'Pietist' religion on the temperance campaigns leading up to Prohibition, in which Methodists played a key role, see James. A. Morone, *Hellfire Nation: The Politics of Sin in American History* (New Haven, CT and London: Yale University Press, 2003), 281–344; see too 'Social Gospel at High Tide (1932–1973)', in Richey, *Methodist Experience*, 1, 350–445.

[57] Bernard Semmel, *The Methodist Revolution* (London: Heinemann, 1974).

[58] Ibid., vii.

[59] Ibid., 120.

[60] Ibid., 96.

led to the contradictory effect of the Connection [sic.] leadership to counter the political translation: the consequence of this clash was what I call the Methodist synthesis'[61] in which a resolution occurred between the contradictory forces making for order and liberty, revolution and counter- revolution. That resolution came about, for Semmel, because of the political journey Wesley made in transitioning from a divine right thinker to a more libertarian approach.

For Theodore R. Weber, Wesley is not best understood of as having developed in his political outlook from a hard-line Tory position to one with more libertarian notes, but as holding these elements together throughout his lifetime. Weber's *Politics in the Order of Salvation* (2001) is an outstanding book; thorough and insightful, it is the most important contribution to a Wesleyan political theology in this generation. Weber agrees with Semmel that Wesley was not, as the Marxists would have us believe, an unreconstructed divine-right Tory, but promoted both liberty and order. But Weber sets out to trace the political traditions that might afford a better account of what Wesley's political views actually were. His conclusion is that 'Wesley was an *organic constitutionalist*',[62] whose sources were England's reciprocating political institutions of King, Lords and commons, with the rights and traditions that undergirded them; first and especially the settlement following the Glorious Revolution that bound the king to the law of the land. Weber is a skilled and thorough exegete of Wesley's writings, but of greater interest here is what Weber himself does theologically with the historical texts he interprets, on which methodological aim Weber writes:

> The focus on Wesley's political thought is essential, because John Wesley is the only specifically Wesleyan resource common to all branches of the Methodist family ... One must offer an invitation to reconnect directly with the founder of the movement not as an act of filial piety or an exercise in antiquarianism, but as a necessity imposed by a history of abandonment and fragmentation in Methodist political thinking.[63]

To do this, Weber proposes to work out a Methodist political theology that proceeds on the basis of the comparatively well-developed Wesleyan theological language of 'the *ordo salutis*, the order or way of salvation – God's prevenient, justifying, sanctifying grace ... Any specifically *Wesleyan* theological reformulation, not excepting efforts to develop a Wesleyan *political* language, must either proceed from this language or at least be integrated with it.'[64] In short, Weber's proposal is to repair the Methodist political genome *from within*, using Wesleyan theological resources as the only appropriate treatment. But even if Methodist theology were able to heal itself – and in this chapter I am suggesting this may not be the case – why should repairing the Methodist genome (or, in Weber's parallel analogy,

---

[61] Ibid., 171.
[62] Weber, *Politics*, 30.
[63] Ibid., 27–8.
[64] Ibid., 33.

'why should the formulation of a Wesleyan political language') be done using only *Wesleyan* resources? While it may be true that Wesley's writings are a common resource for Methodists, so too are the Fathers, so too the teachings of the Reformers, and above all the Scriptures.

Weber makes a second methodological move that is equally puzzling. He assumes that the reason Wesley must be reinterpreted is (though he doesn't put it quite this way) because Wesley failed to integrate his egalitarian theology with his political thought. Exegetically, Weber successfully establishes that Wesley maintained that *'authority is from God through the people'*;[65] but for Weber, this axiom still falls short of the ideal. On just this point D. Stephen Long points out, in my view quite rightly, that Weber's assumption should not pass unchallenged:

> Wesley's political ethics is not the solution but the problem to be overcome. It is a problem because Wesley did not ground political authority in the people, rather he grounded it solely in God. But Weber never tells us exactly why this is a problem. He seems to assume that a theocratic politics is so obviously wrong that it does not need to be argued against.[66]

Weber has simply assumed that a modern western democratic tradition, in which political authority is understood to arise from the people, is the only acceptable norm and has, as Long puts it, reformulated 'Wesley's theology to fit it'.[67]

There remains enormous scope for theological research into Methodist political thinking, both by historical theologians and by those seeking to contribute to contemporary Methodist political theology.

## Global Perspectives

The greater part of both historical and theological literature deals with the United States and the British Isles. That is understandable, but it is not satisfactory. Political engagement by Methodists outside America and the British Isles is no less interesting, and indeed other contexts cast cross lights that bring the contours into relief. Two examples must suffice to represent the whole.

By the twentieth century Methodists in Germany had become a constituent part of the Methodist Episcopal Church.[68] This international connection placed German Methodists in a delicate position in a period of growing nationalism.

---

[65] Ibid., 203, author's italics.
[66] D. Stephen Long, *John Wesley's Moral Theology: The Quest for God and Goodness* (Nashville, TN: Kingswood, 2005), 235.
[67] Ibid., 236.
[68] It is now a Conference of United Methodist Church called the Evangelisch-methodistischen Kirche (EmK).

According to its Episcopal Methodist theological foundations German Methodists were committed, on the one hand, to obedience to the state in all things according to conscience, and, on the other, to the independence of the Church from the state.[69] The theological principles affirmed by this position here are:

- that Christian faith is voluntary, and is not appropriately a matter of belonging to a national Church (*Volkskirche*); the Church is not of the people but for the people: this principle was based upon the Methodist imperative to evangelise;
- that the Church owes ultimate obedience to God and penultimate obedience to the state: this principle was based on the Methodist imperative to promote political and social order.

In most circumstances, these principles might have worked out well enough. But the pressures of life in a Nazi state between 1933 and 1945 exposed the difficulties in holding these principles together. As a minority Church, Methodists in Germany were above all keen to remain distinct from the formation of a national Protestant *Reichskirche* that, following 1933, became an objective of Nazi policy towards Protestant Churches in Germany. Nazism had its attractions for Methodists in any case, on account of a shared moral emphasis on healthy living and pulling together for the common good. German Methodism in the main accommodated itself to the authority of Nazism politically in exchange for freedom to evangelise Germans as a Church with a distinct identity. Methodists took this course in order to abide by the two principles identified above, but an unintentional consequence was that their freedom to evangelise as Methodists and of political obedience tended to outweigh the Church's other political obligations, for example defence of the weak against state persecution. In sum, the response of German Methodism to Nazism provides an instructive example of the failure of political theology in action.[70]

In different circumstances the recent history of the Methodist Church in Fiji and Rotuma exhibits similar patterns.[71] A key feature of the Pacific context is a close interweaving of land, (ethnic) identity and religious faith. A majority of ethnic Fijian islanders are Methodist and, though some 42 per cent of the 920,000 people living in the islands are of Indian origin, the national constitution – until it was abrogated following the 2006 military *coup* – defended Christianity in Fiji based on the conviction, widely held by Fijian Christians, that God entered into a

---

[69] For a fuller account of the theological position of the EmK with respect to politics see: Walter Klaiber and Manfred Marquardt, *Gelebte Gnade: Grundriß einer Theologie der Evangelisch-methodistischen Kirche* (Stuttgart, Christliches Verlagshaus, 1993), 380–92.

[70] For a fine essay on German Methodism during the Nazi period see Herbert Strahm, 'Die Bischöfliche Methodistenkirche im Dritten Reich (1933–1945)', in Michel Weyer (ed.), *Der kontinentaleuropäische Methodismus zwischen den beiden Weltkriegen* (Stuttgart: Christliches Verlagshaus, 1990), 93–132.

[71] For background see Jacqueline Ryle's ethnographical study, *My God, My Land: Interwoven Paths of Christianity and Tradition in Fiji* (Farnham: Ashgate, 2010).

sacred covenant with Fijians to be a Christian nation when the Islands became a British colony in 1874. In recent years, however, Methodism's desire to maintain Christianity as a fundament of Fijian national identity arguably led some to defend a political assertion of ethnic Fijian interests at the expense of Indo-Fijian interests. In 2009 the head of the interim military administration, Commodore Frank Bainimarama, abrogated the constitution of Fiji and Rotuma, bringing the interim administration into conflict with the Methodist Church. Ironically, the intervention by Methodists in several of Fiji's periodic *coups d'état* may have been a factor in Commodore Bainimarama's decision to arrest several leaders of the Methodist Church and to prohibit the annual Conference in 2011. What may be happening once more is that flaws in the Methodist DNA governing political behaviour adversely affect the Church's political actions. In this case we may be seeing Methodists act to defend their freedom to evangelise the nation, for example by maintaining a constitutional commitment to Christianity, while falling short in their determination to defend the equality for *all* citizens and the freedom of religion for *all*.

Beyond North America and the British Isles there are real opportunities for research into Methodism and politics for historians and theologians. Jacqueline Ryle's detailed study of Fiji illustrates the potential for ethnographical research to shed light on Methodism in its concrete political engagement.[72] Compared with the well-tilled soil of historical research on Methodist political engagement in the English-speaking world, Methodism in Africa and the Pacific offers virgin territory crying out for research.

## From Diagnosis to Treatment: Augustine

In the concluding phase of this chapter I move from diagnosis to treatment of the flaws on the Methodist political genome in dialogue with Augustine's mature theology in book XIX of *City of God*.[73] My thesis has been that there are worrying faults on the Methodist genome at two points: at the base-pair of liberty and order, and at the base-pair of evangelism and social holiness. In varied historical and geographical contexts in which Methodists have lacked a robust political theology able to keep in balance the halves of both base-pairs, Methodist political engagement has often become unstable. I suggest that the Methodist tradition needs resources from outside in order to repair its political genome. For a tradition 'that claims and cherishes its place in the Holy Catholic Church which is the Body of Christ' and 'rejoices in the inheritance of the apostolic faith and loyally accepts the fundamental

---

[72] Ibid.

[73] Augustine, *Concerning the City of God against the Pagans*, tr. Henry Bettenson (Harmondsworth: Penguin, 1972). For a Latin text see Augustine, *City of God Books XVIII.36–XX*, ed. Jeffrey Henderson, Loeb Classical Library, (Cambridge, MA: Loeb, 1960), 96–245.

principles of the historic creeds and of the Protestant Reformation',[74] thinking in dialogue with sources without the Methodist tradition ought to be essential. The point is neatly made by Long: '[w]ithout the context of these kinds of arguments, the Wesleyan tradition quickly becomes unintelligible. It needs a richer intellectual tradition than Wesley's work alone to bring out the best of his work.'[75]

Augustine began work on *City of God* following the sack of Rome by Alaric's (Arian) Goths in 410, which some in the empire blamed on the replacement of Rome's ancient religious allegiances with the Christian God. Already in his fifties, Augustine could look back over a life in which the Church had passed through several political contexts: it had experienced persecution; it had been effectively the 'official' religion of the empire; now it was threatened by the disintegration of the empire. Earlier, when Christianity had cohabited symbiotically with the state, Augustine had flirted with the idea that the state was God's providential instrument for the advancement of the Christian Gospel. But by 410 he had long since abandoned that view as theologically mistaken. This was not a question of disillusionment with politics: it was a realisation that the destinies of the earthly city and the heavenly city are simply different. For one thing, the earthly city's hopes – even its political hopes – will always in the end prove empty, for true happiness lies only in the salvation of God. And then there is the obvious point that all earthly empires pass away sooner or later: little wonder, since they spend their time 'generally divided ... by litigation, by wars, by battles, by the pursuit of victories that bring death with them'.[76] Conflict is endemic, part of the human condition even in loving families.

Yet Augustine recognised, especially now that the empire was collapsing, that the earthly peace maintained by civil magistrates benefited citizens of both the earthly city *and* the heavenly city who sojourned among them like Jewish captives in Babylon. The authorities played an important – and God-given role – in keeping the peace and guarding life. The earthly city affords not only protection from violence and the provision of material needs such as food and shelter but also provides the conditions for social intercourse that is essential to human life. In such ways it may even be said to foster 'a kind of compromise between human wills about the things relevant to mortal life'.[77]

The upshot of all this for Augustine was that non-Christians and Christians alike will make use of peace and other temporal goods afforded by the earthly city, but they will make use of them in quite different ways: 'the Heavenly City ... must make use of this peace also, until this mortal state, for which this kind of peace is essential, passes away'.[78] It is a question of what one loves, since '[w]e see then that the two cities were created by two kinds of love: the earthly city was created by

---

[74] Citation from the doctrinal statement of the Deed of Union of the Methodist Church in Britain.
[75] Long, *John Wesley's Moral Theology*, 171.
[76] Augustine, *City*, 15:4, 599.
[77] Ibid., 877, XIX:17.
[78] Ibid., 877, XIX:17.

self-love reaching the point of contempt for God, the heavenly city by the love of God carried as far as contempt of self. In fact, the earthly city glories in itself, the Heavenly City glories in the Lord.'[79] The cities are allegiances, not territories, in which Christians are intermingled with others, like wheat and tares sown together, their ultimate allegiances known only to God in time's fullness. Nonetheless the Church is a *sign* of the heavenly city.[80]

Augustine can help Methodists *orient* themselves to politics in authentically Christian ways. This will mean, on the one hand, resisting the temptation to invest too *much* in politics. With the advent of the social gospel, for Methodists this became perhaps the greater temptation. There is a point – perhaps the point where the pursuit of social holiness transforms into a social gospel – at which a Methodist political practice loses sight of the distinction between hope in human progress and hope in God. Augustine teaches that though God can make providential use of 'prince' and of magistrate, the earthly city will always have purposes distinct from those of the heavenly city. Augustine believed *both* that humankind is fallen physically, spiritually and intellectually *and* that God's image in humankind was not erased and that it was redeemable by God's grace. Unlike his opponents the Pelagians, Augustine did not, therefore, think that Christians simply need to try harder in order to transform this world into the kingdom of God. What is needed in politics from an Augustinian point of view is not more moral effort, but more God. Methodists are political optimists; Augustine was neither optimist nor pessimist: when it came to politics he was simply melancholic because he saw in the earthly city a politics motivated by self-love rather than the love of God.

An Augustinian approach would mean, on the other hand, that Methodists may not invest too *little* in politics. Christians may make *use* of politics, but they may not *enjoy* politics as if politics were God, or as if they could transform the earthly into a heavenly city. As John Wesley puts it, in a decidedly Augustinian moment, in the quotation with which this essay began: 'politics…when fit occasion offers; it being our main business to preach "repentance towards God, and faith in our Lord Jesus Christ"'. In the earthly city politics promotes, even at its very best, penultimate

---

[79] Ibid., 593, XIV:28.

[80] Opinion divides between those who think Augustine means that in spite of their different allegiances citizens of the earthly and the heavenly cities *cooperate* in a limited sense; or whether all Augustine's talk of intermingling is merely a qualification of the fundamental point, which is that the two cities are in *competition* with each other. For the first approach, Augustine's key image is taken to be that of Christian *pilgrims* passing through the earthly city; for the second the key image is taken to be the *Babylonian captivity* of the citizens of the heavenly city in the earthly. For a representative of the 'liberal' approach that sympathises with intermingling and cooperation see R. A. Markus, *Saeculum: History and Society in the Theology of Augustine* (Cambridge: Cambridge University Press, 1970). For an advocate of the second, more 'combative' approach see Gregory W. Lee, 'Republics and their Loves: Rereading *City of God* 19', *Modern Theology*, 27:4 (2011), 553–81. See also the debate on Augustine's political thought between Christopher J. Insole's (323–35) more 'cooperative' model and William T. Cavanaugh's (299–321) assertion that the two cities are in competition: *Political Theology*, 7:3 (2006).

goods of peace, justice and prosperity. These are genuine goods, but they are not to be mistaken for ultimate goods. Liberty and order are also both goods and, where they are both promoted and defended by politicians of the earthly city, Christians may make penultimate use of them. But what Christians pursue as an ultimate end is contemplation of the liberty and order perfectly revealed in the trinitarian life of God. Likewise, an Augustinian approach promotes the view that since all human life is life in society, there can be no opposition between evangelism and social holiness as both have the same proper aim: to draw humankind into the knowledge and love of God.

# The Methodist Conscience: Slavery, Temperance and Pacifism

Jennifer L. Woodruff Tait

Is there a Methodist conscience? And if so, what does it look like? Methodists have been prophetic activists on a number of social issues, including those named in this essay's title. But Methodists also have a long history of preserving the status quo as part of their process of moving from countercultural religious movement to culturally influential church. This essay focuses on British and American Methodism, but recognises that what it means to be a socially involved Methodist is a contested concept across the globe. It also recognises that the official pronouncements of any religious group do not always parallel the thoughts of people in the pews, and that this tension runs strongly through Methodist stance(s) on race, alcohol and war.[1]

## The Nonconformist Conscience

Whether or not there is a Methodist conscience, there was, historically, a 'Nonconformist Conscience'. Many Nonconformist denominations were involved

---

[1] See Steven Tipton, *Public Pulpits: Methodists and Mainline Churches in the Moral Argument of Public Life* (Chicago, IL: University of Chicago Press, 2007), for opposition to the political involvement of the General Board of Church and Society of the United Methodist Church (UMC); Donald Collins, *When the Church Bell Rang Racist: The Methodist Church and the Civil Rights Movement in Alabama* (Macon, GA: Mercer University Press, 1998), for resistance to Methodism's movement towards racial equality; Bill Kellerman's 'A Methodist Pastor', in Jim Wallis (ed.), *Peacemakers: Christian Voices From the New Abolitionist Movement* (San Francisco, CA: Harper and Row, 1983), for his congregation's dislike of his peace activism; and Heather Walton's *A Tree God Planted: Black People in British Methodism* (London: Ethnic Minorities in Methodism Working Group, 1985), for Methodist troubles with racial pluralism in Britain. A good survey of Methodist social thought, including on these three issues, is the chapter 'Methodist Social Ethics' in Kenneth Cracknell and Susan White's *An Introduction to World Methodism* (Cambridge: Cambridge University Press, 2005), 209–42 (bibliography, 274).

in agitation against social evils throughout the nineteenth century, but the phrase itself arose in 1890 when Nonconformist leaders ceased to support Irish Nationalist leader Charles Parnell when his extramarital affair was discovered. Like the term 'Methodist', it was originally derogatory, indicating legalistic moralism, but was soon proudly adopted by Nonconformists themselves.[2] It has been defined as 'a conviction that there is no strict boundary between religion and politics; an insistence that politicians should be men of the highest character; and a belief that the state should promote the moral welfare of its citizens'.[3] Prominent Wesleyan Methodist Hugh Price Hughes became a leader in Nonconformist social agitation through his 1870s campaign against the Contagious Disease Acts and remained one of its most well-known spokesmen. Indeed all branches of British Methodism were central to the expression of the 'Conscience'.[4] Hughes repeatedly enumerated the 'great evils' that Christians needed to work against as 'slavery, drunkenness, the social evil, ignorance, pauperism, and war' (he later added gambling and 'mammonism').[5] The 'Nonconformist Conscience' became part of campaigns for disestablishment, sexual purity, alcoholic prohibition and Irish Home Rule – and part of protests against gambling, imperialism and the favoured position of the Church of England in public education.[6]

America, in contrast, contained no state church against which Nonconformists could claim moral superiority. Early American Methodists stood in a marginal relation to social and cultural centres of power, but the nineteenth century saw them grow in numbers and influence until they were one of America's largest and most powerful denominations. They were no strangers to controversy over social issues. But as America's de facto 'established church', their areas of crusade versus compromise varied from their British compatriots.[7] Their 1968 merger with

---

[2] D. W. Bebbington, *The Nonconformist Conscience: Chapel and Politics, 1870–1914* (London: George Allen and Unwin, 1982), ix–x, 11–12, 100–101; Christopher Oldstone-Moore, *Hugh Price Hughes: Founder of a New Methodism, Conscience of a New Nonconformity* (Cardiff: University of Wales Press, 1999), 209–19.

[3] Bebbington, *Nonconformist Conscience*, 11.

[4] Ibid., 3–4, 38, 40–43, 59–60. See Oldstone-Moore, *Hugh Price Hughes*, 145–53 for Hughes' entry into 'Christian politics'. Robert Wearmouth, (*Methodism and the Common People of the Eighteenth Century* (London: Epworth, 1945); *Methodism and the Working Class Movements of England, 1800–1850* (London: Epworth, 1937); *Methodism and the Struggle of the Working Classes, 1850–1900* (Leicester: Edgar Backus, 1954); and *Social and Political Influence of Methodism in the Twentieth Century* (London: Epworth, 1957) gives detailed statistics on the growth of Methodism and its involvement, by connexion and region, in social causes and political activity. Wearmouth was a Primitive Methodist and lamented a perceived decrease in Methodist social concern after the 1932 union (*Social and Political Influence*, 77–9).

[5] Oldstone-Moore, *Hugh Price Hughes*, 132, 181.

[6] Bebbington, *Nonconformist Conscience*, and Oldstone-Moore, *Hugh Price Hughes*, passim; Lilian Shiman, *Crusade Against Drink in Victorian England* (New York, NY: St Martin's Press, 1988),1–2.

[7] See Tipton, 82–3; Herman Will, *A Will for Peace* (Washington, DC: GBCS, 1984), 277–79 (the latter charts the dates of founding of Methodist/EUB social agencies).

the Evangelical United Brethren (EUB) connected them with a tradition which on the whole bore a stronger tradition of countercultural witness; some recent United Methodist attempts to speak on social issues have drawn from this perspective.[8]

## 'O, He is Preaching Politics!'

Despite his avowal that Christians ought to preach repentance often and politics rarely – except when necessary to defend the King – John Wesley was not shy about expressing his political and economic opinions.[9] While they remained throughout his life the political opinions of an educated upper-middle-class Tory, Wesley was genuinely concerned for problems in English society, including poverty, lack of education and health care, drunkenness and the liquor trade, slavery and war.[10]

While Wesley made little early public protest against slavery before the 1774 publication of *Thoughts Upon Slavery*, Methodists on the whole accepted 'white and black, free and slaves' as long as they submitted to Methodist discipline.[11] *Thoughts Upon Slavery*, adapted from the writings of abolitionist Anthony Benezet, argued:

> I deny that villainy is ever necessary. It cannot be, that either war, or contract, can give any man such a property in another as he has in his sheep and oxen. Much less is it possible, that any child of man should ever be born a slave. Liberty is the right of every human creature, as soon as he breathes the vital air; and no human law can deprive him of that right which he derives from the law of nature[12]

---

[8] D. Stephen Long, *Living the Discipline: United Methodist Theological Reflections on War, Civilisation and Holiness* (Grand Rapids, MI: Eerdmans, 1992), 40. An excellent introduction to the EUB's tradition of social witness is J. Steven O'Malley and Jason Vickers, *Methodist and Pietist: Retrieving the Evangelical United Brethren Tradition* (Nashville, TN: Kingswood, 2011).

[9] John Wesley, 'How Far is it the Duty of a Christian Minister to Preach Politics?' (1782), in Thomas Jackson (ed.), *The Works of the Rev. John Wesley, A.M.* (London, 1872)) 9, 154–5.

[10] Wearmouth, *Social and Political Influence*, 185–9; Jeffrey Williams, *Religion and Violence in Early American Methodism: Taking the Kingdom by Force* (Bloomington, IN: Indiana University Press, 2010), 15–26; Manfred Marquardt, *John Wesley's Social Ethics: Praxis and Principles* (Nashville, TN: Abingdon, 1992), 17–86; Ronald Stone, *John Wesley's Life and Ethics* (Nashville, TN: Abingdon, 2001), 70–76, 137–41, 172–98.

[11] Marquardt, *John Wesley's Social Ethics*, 71–2; Stone, *John Wesley's Life and Ethics*, 187–97; Wellman Warner, *The Wesleyan Movement in the Industrial Revolution* (New York, NY: Russell and Russell, 1930), 239–45; William McClain, *Black People in the Methodist Church* (Nashville, TN: Abingdon, 1984), 7–14. Two excellent books on the life of free and enslaved blacks in Great Britain are Gretchen Gerzina's *Black London* (New Brunswick, NJ: Rutgers University Press, 1995) and Julie Flavell's *When London Was Capital of America* (New Haven, CT: Yale University Press, 2010), 1–61, 242–4.

[12] John Wesley, 'Thoughts Upon Slavery' (1774), *Works* (Jackson ed.), 11, 59–79 (quote from 72).

After he published this tract Wesley's support became more vocal and was backed up by petitions from the Methodist Conference. Methodists also cooperated with abolitionist groups such as the Society for the Suppression of the Slave Trade.[13] Famously, Wesley's last known letter, to William Wilberforce, argued that Wilberforce should 'go on, in the name of God and in the power of his might, till even American slavery (the vilest that ever saw the sun) shall vanish away before it'.[14]

Nineteenth-century claims that Wesley was a teetotaller were false – he drank both wine and beer in a moderate and disciplined fashion – but he was no friend of drunkenness nor of trade in distilled spirits.[15] The Methodist General Rules forbade 'drunkenness, buying or selling spirituous liquors, or drinking them, unless in cases of extreme necessity'.[16] His *A Word to A Drunkard* minced no words in its description of the drunkard's desire to 'stir up all the devilish temptations that are in you, and gain others' while at the same time grieving the Spirit of God and running 'the hazard of committing all manner of villainies; and this only for the poor pleasure of a few moments, while the poison is running down your throat'.[17] *Thoughts on the Present Scarcity of Provisions* rooted that scarcity in three related causes: 'distilling, taxes, and luxury', and argued in favour of 'prohibiting forever' and 'making a full end of that bane of health, that destroyer of strength, of life, and of virtue – distilling'.[18]

Wesley spoke less directly to the issue of war, though his descriptions of it were generally negative, as seen in the *Seasonable Address to the More Serious Part of the Inhabitants of Great Britain*. While asking his hearers to 'survey the desolation' caused by the American Revolution, he refused to attribute to either side a just cause for it.[19] In *The Doctrine of Original Sin* and *The Dignity of Human Nature* he famously asked, 'Who can reconcile war, I will not say to religion, but to any degree of reason

---

[13] Stone, *John Wesley's Life and Ethics*, 197; Marquardt, *John Wesley's Social Ethics*, 74–5; Warner, *Wesleyan Movement*, 242–3; Williams, *Religion and Violence*, 44–5.

[14] John Wesley to William Wilberforce (24 February 1791) in *Works* (Jackson ed.), 13, 153; Donald Mathews, *Slavery and Methodism: A Chapter in American Morality 1780–1945* (Princeton, NJ: Princeton University Press, 1965), 5–6. Wilberforce sent anti-slavery literature to Methodist preachers for distribution (Warner, *Wesleyan Movement*, 243).

[15] Jennifer Woodruff Tait, *The Poisoned Chalice: Common-sense Realism and Eucharistic Grape Juice in Victorian Methodism* (Tuscaloosa, AL: University of Alabama Press, 2011), 11–12; Daniel Swinson, 'American Methodism and Temperance in the Antebellum Period', PhD thesis, University of Chicago Divinity School, 1992, 37–68.

[16] 'Nature, Design, and General Rules of the United Societies' (1743), *Works* (Bicentennial ed. [Baker]), 9, 69–73; 'Directions Given to the Band Societies' (1744), *Works* (Bicentennial ed.), 9, 79.

[17] John Wesley, 'A Word to A Drunkard', *Works* (Jackson ed.), 11, 169–71. Also see George Brake, *Drink: Ups and Downs of Methodist Attitudes to Temperance* (London: Oliphants, 1974), 1–3.

[18] John Wesley, 'Thoughts on the Present Scarcity of Provisions' (1773), *Works* (Jackson ed.), 11, 57–8.

[19] John Wesley, 'Seasonable Address' (1776), *Works* (Jackson ed.), 11, 120–21.

or common sense?'[20] Yet Wesley did consider war just in certain circumstances.[21] His *Advice to a Soldier* was advice not on conscientious objection, but on how best to live as a Christian in a profession beset with horrors and temptations.[22] Despite a clear understanding of war's financial cost, human sacrifice and sinful causes, Wesley several times reiterated his support of the Thirty-Nine Articles' decree that it was lawful for Christians to bear arms, although he did not include this article in the abridgement of twenty-four Articles he sent to the newly formed American Methodist church in 1784.[23]

## 'Madam, There Were No Black People in Britain Before 1945'

After Wesley's death, British Methodists continued advocacy against the slave trade. Many Methodist preachers wrote abolitionist pamphlets or signed petitions, and Methodist missionaries to the West Indies were criticised for being anti-slavery activists.[24] In no small part through Methodist influence the slave trade was abolished in Britain in 1807 and slavery in British colonies in 1833, and later advocates of the 'Nonconformist Conscience' often looked back fondly on this as one of Nonconformity's finest moments of social witness.[25]

During the nineteenth century, the Black population of Britain never entirely died out, although to some degree it was absorbed through intermarriage. But the racial attitudes spread through imperialistic conquests laid the groundwork for future problems.[26] These problems became more acute after World War II when immigrants from former colonies, now members of the Commonwealth, began to come to Britain in large numbers for employment opportunities.[27] This immigration

---

[20] John Wesley, 'Doctrine of Original Sin' (1757), *Works* (Jackson ed), 9, 194–464 (quote from 221).

[21] Michael Hughes, *Conscience and Conflict: Methodism, Peace and War in the Twentieth Century* (Peterborough: Epworth, 2008), 5; also see Williams, *Religion and Violence*, 42–55, for Wesley's conflicting attitudes on war as both an example of human sin and a 'responsibility of obedient citizens submitting to the just actions of a divinely instituted sovereign'. (49).

[22] John Wesley, 'Advice to a Soldier', *Works* (Jackson ed.), 11, 198–202.

[23] Long, *Living the Discipline*, 37–40; Williams, *Religion and Violence*, 47.

[24] Warner, *Wesleyan Movement*, 244–5.

[25] Roger Anstey, *The Atlantic Slave Trade and British Abolition 1760–1810* (Atlantic Highlands, NJ: Humanities Press, 1975), 157–99, 233–5; also Stone, *John Wesley's Life and Ethics*, 197; Bebbington, *Nonconformist Conscience*, 14–16, 110–13; Oldstone-Moore, *Hugh Price Hughes*, 132, 178, 181.

[26] Gerzina, *Black London*, 202–4. Kenneth Leech's *Struggle in Babylon: Racism in the Cities and Churches of Britain* (London: Sheldon Press, 1988) and G. I. T. Machin's *Churches and Social Issues in Twentieth-Century Britain* (Oxford: Clarendon Press, 1998) both deal with immigration's social context and the church's response.

[27] Tony Holden, *People, Churches, and Multi-racial Projects* (London: DSR, n.d.), 9, 53; Walton, *A Tree God Planted*, ii, 1–2; Leech, *Struggle in Babylon*, 7–117; Brian Frost and Stuart

became controversial on both social and legal fronts, with repeated acts passed to restrict the flow of immigrants and sharp social debate on whether Britain ought to be a multiracial and multicultural society.[28] (When Gretchen Gerzina asked during her research for a copy of a particular book on black history in Britain, she 'received a stern look from the saleswoman. "Madam, there *were* no black people in England before 1945," she said.'[29]) Methodists, like all British churches, began to struggle with how to integrate White, Black and Asian Methodists into a common connexional life.[30] The arm of the Wesleyan Missionary Society had been long, and many of these Black immigrants had been Methodist in their countries of origin, but found the growing number of Black Pentecostal churches more congenial than facing the racism in White Methodist churches. This led Methodists to seek out new ways to partner with these denominations.[31] While meeting no small amount of resistance, many Methodist leaders argued – in terms that would have been familiar to their nineteenth-century Nonconformist counterparts – that 'when individuals or groups find themselves poor, disadvantaged, the victims of prejudice, discrimination, or racism – they should find the followers of Christ on their side'.[32] In 1987 the church issued the report *Faithful and Equal*, which continues to be the official policy on issues of immigration and racism, and has subsequently published statements and resources dealing with racist political parties.[33]

## 'The Church Must Preach to the Slave Even if it Could Not Emancipate Him'

Slavery died a slow and painful death in the United States, only abolished in 1863 in the middle of America's bitter and destructive Civil War. Here the Methodist witness was mixed. Early American Methodists brought anti-slavery principles with them from Britain; the 1780 Conference required all ministers to free their

---

Jordan, *Pioneers of Social Passion: London's Cosmopolitan Methodism* (Peterborough: Epworth, 2006), 138–9, 202–23.

[28] Machin, *Churches and Social Issues*, 206–9.

[29] Gerzina, *Black London*, 3.

[30] Holden, *People, Churches and Multi-racial Projects*, passim and Walton, *A Tree God Planted*, passim; Leech, *Struggle in Babylon*, 119–19; Frost and Jordan, *Pioneers of Social Passion*, 202–14; Machin, *Churches and Social Issues*, 205–9.

[31] Holden, *People, Churches and Multi-racial Projects*, 51–9. See Anthony Reddie's *Faith, Stories, and the Experience of Black Elders* (London: Jessica Kingsley, 2001); a good introduction to the place of Black Pentecostal denominations in British society is Joe Aldred and Keno Ogbo( eds), *The Black Church in the 21st Century* (London: DLT, 2010).

[32] Holden, *People, Churches and Multi-racial Projects*, 13, 129.

[33] See http://www.methodist.org.uk/index.cfm?fuseaction=opentogod.content&cmid=1551; http://www.methodist.org.uk/index.cfm?fuseaction=opentoworld.content&cmid=105 (accessed 27 September 2012).

slaves, and the Christmas Conference in 1784 gave all members a year to free their slaves or risk expulsion. However, this policy faced immediate opposition and was suspended.[34] Methodists who bought slaves were still supposed to report this to the Quarterly Conference, which would determine how long the slave had to serve before being freed.[35] But there was a growing concern that this emphasis would antagonise slaveholders, who would then prevent missionary preaching to slaves.[36] Furthermore, repeated discrimination in worship and polity led to groups of African-Americans leaving the MEC in the 1780s and establishing African Methodist denominations.[37]

While the General Conference continued an anti-slavery message, many Annual Conferences in the South refused to comply, and leadership became less strident: 'The ideological justification for this retreat was … that the Church must preach to the slave even if it could not emancipate him.'[38] The 1804 General Conference voted to suspend enforcement of the entire section on slavery in the *Discipline* south of Virginia. This official compromise produced a wave of abolitionist sentiment in the Northeast. One leading abolitionist, Orange Scott, left in the 1840s to form the Wesleyan Methodist Church, which wrote opposition to slavery into its founding documents.[39] On the other hand, Annual Conferences in the South developed evangelistic missions to the slaves, which acknowledged the slaves' need for redemption while not advocating any change in their status.[40] In 1844 a split between North and South occurred when a clergyman who had inherited slaves, James Andrew, was elected to the episcopacy.[41]

After the Civil War neither Northern or Southern White Methodists wanted bureaucratic equality with newly freed slaves. Free Blacks in the North had been part of White Annual Conferences, but their leaders were rarely ordained, and when they were it was for local ministry (non-itinerating) or for missionary service in Africa.[42] In 1864, the MEC established segregated Annual Conferences

---

[34] Mathews, *Slavery and Methodism*, 7–8, 10–12. Mathews lists all the *Disciplinary* statements on slavery from 1784–1844 (293–303).

[35] Warner, *Wesleyan Movement*, 245; Lester Ruth, *Early Methodist Life and Spirituality* (Nashville, TN: Abingdon, 2005), 228–30, 245–56; McClain, *Black People*, 55–9; Mathews, *Slavery and Methodism*, 8–10.

[36] Ibid., 13–19. See Mark Noll, *America's God: From Jonathan Edwards to Abraham Lincoln* (Oxford: Oxford University Press, 2002), for how pro- and anti-slavery advocates justified their positions exegetically (386–438).

[37] G. Shockley (ed.), *Heritage and Hope: The African American Presence in United Methodism* (Nashville, TN: Abingdon, 1991), 30–36.

[38] Mathews, *Slavery and Methodism*, 20–21.

[39] Ibid., 26, 113–76, 231–3. The Free Methodists, who left the MEC in 1860, also did so in part because of its failure to oppose slavery.

[40] Ibid., 62–87.

[41] Ibid., 246–82; also see William Gravely's *Gilbert Haven: Methodist Abolitionist* (Nashville, TN: Abingdon, 1973), the life story of a MEC bishop and abolitionist.

[42] Ordinations for Africa occurred in part because African missions were seen as the 'white man's graveyard' due to disease (John D'Amico, 'Spiritual and Secular Activities of

for African-American members; this did allow African-Americans to have fully itinerating deacons, elders, presiding elders and bishops, as well as a voice in General Conference.[43] The MECS separated their formerly enslaved African-American members into the Colored Methodist Episcopal Church in 1870.[44]

Discussions about reunification began in the 1870s but repeatedly foundered on racial issues. (Southern Methodists also distrusted the 'modernism' of the MEC.)[45] The MECS proposed plans that would give African-Americans their own General Conference or separate them into a new denomination.[46] The eventual price of the 1939 union was the segregation of African-American Methodists into the racial Central Jurisdiction while White Methodists were divided into the five geographical jurisdictions that still exist in the modern UMC.[47]

Almost from the beginning of the Central Jurisdiction, its leaders began to work for its dissolution.[48] At first a few individual churches managed the cumbersome constitutional procedure of transferring into regional jurisdictions. In 1956 the General Conference proposed a constitutional amendment that allowed a more streamlined procedure for transfers out of the Central Jurisdiction, which would then be dissolved. However, it did not set a date for this dissolution, relying on the voluntary good will of White Methodists. Not until the 1968 merger with the EUB

---

the Methodist Episcopal Church in Liberia,1833–1933', PhD thesis, St John's University, 1977, 263–7).

[43] Shockley, *Heritage and Hope*, 48–56; McClain, *Black People*, 65–7. Richard Allen, founder and first bishop of the African Methodist Episcopal Church, was originally ordained as a local deacon by Francis Asbury. See Oldstone-Moore, *Hugh Price Hughes*, 223, for Hugh Price Hughes' reaction to American Methodist anti-slavery activism.

[44] Shockley, *Heritage and Hope*, 17–18, 44; Peter Murray, *Methodists and the Crucible of Race, 1930–1975* (Columbia, MO: University of Missouri Press, 2004), 19–22, 32.

[45] Ibid., 42–3. See Robert Sledge, *Hands on the Ark: The Struggle for Change in the Methodist Episcopal Church, South, 1914–1939* (Lake Junaluska, NC: GCAH, 1975), for a narrative of the struggle between conservatives and progressives in the MECS.

[46] Ibid., 45–9; McClain, *Black People*, 75–9; Murray, *Methodists and the Crucible of Race*, 29–44. Morris Davis' *The Methodist Unification* (New York, NY: New York University Press, 2008) interprets the entire struggle towards merger through a racial lens.

[47] Murray, *Methodists and the Crucible of Race*, 38–47; McClain, *Black People*, 75–82; Shockley, *Heritage and Hope*, 99–115.

[48] See especially Murray, *Methodists and the Crucible of Race*, 53–199 (which sets the Central Jurisdiction in the context of American civil desegregation); James Thomas, *Methodism's Racial Dilemma* (Nashville, TN: Abingdon, 1992); Shockley, *Heritage and Hope*, 117–207; McClain, *Black People*, 83–92. Alice Knotts' *Fellowship of Love* (Nashville, TN: Abingdon, 1996) describes the fight of Methodist women against racism in church and society, and David Cooney's 'A Consistent Witness of Conscience: Methodist Nonviolent Activists, 1940–1970', PhD thesis, Iliff School of Theology/University of Denver, 2000, 195–280, discusses the influence of Methodist nonviolent activists, including those trained in India, on the American civil rights movement.

was a commitment made to abolish the Central Jurisdiction. The EUB had very few African-American members, but it also had a history of opposing racism.[49]

While the number of African-Americans in leadership positions has increased in the UMC, de facto segregation remains. Cross-racial appointments are a matter of course, but few local churches are integrated.[50] Organisations such as Black Methodists for Church Renewal and denominational agencies such as the General Commission on Religion and Race continue to work for integration and inclusiveness, and there is cooperative discussion with members of African Methodist denominations through the Pan-Methodist Commission.[51]

## 'No, They Have Joined Me'

British Methodists after the death of Wesley supported temperance – defined as moderation – and opposed drunkenness, but alcohol was still part of church functions.[52] Wesleyan Methodists were the least supportive of the total abstinence movement. The 1841 Conference passed resolutions which forbade the use of 'unfermented wine' in the Eucharist and the use of Wesleyan Methodist chapels for meetings of the Temperance Society, a teetotal organisation.[53] Many Wesleyans saw teetotal groups as entirely secular organisations and total abstinence as unscriptural, and while teetotal organisations repeatedly advocated the use of unfermented wine in Communion, Wesleyans continued to oppose it.[54] Temperance advocacy grew in Wesleyan Methodism in the 1860s, when the publication of the *Methodist Temperance Advocate* began.[55] The Conference also began to express support for the United Kingdom Alliance, an organisation which campaigned for prohibitionary legislation. In 1874 a permanent Temperance Committee was formed and reports made regarding the work of Bands of Hope and temperance societies; membership in these grew widely. The Temperance Committee in time took up advocacy of

---

[49] Murray, *Methodists and the Crucible of Race*, 82, 115, 186–231; Shockley, *Heritage and Hope*, 223, 287, 318; O'Malley and Vickers, *Methodist and Pietist*, 186.
[50] Shockley, *Heritage and Hope*, 209–84.
[51] Ibid., 285–305; McClain, *Black People*, 93–9; see Black Methodists for Church Renewal, http://www.bmcrumc.org/ (accessed 27 September 2012).
[52] Good summaries of the campaigns against alcohol in Nonconformity and Anglicanism are Shiman's *Crusade Against Drink* and Brian Harrison's *Drink and the Victorians* (Pittsburgh, PA: University of Pittsburgh Press, 1971); Brake's *Drink* focuses on Methodist involvement. Irish Methodists until nearly the end of the 1800s 'broach[ed] a keg of ale for the refreshment of the members after a quarterly meeting' (Dudley Cooney, *The Methodists in Ireland* (Blackrock: Columba Press, 2001), 220). See Machin, *Churches and Social Issues*, 8–9.
[53] Brake, *Drink*, 3–4; Bebbington, *Nonconformist Conscience*, 46–7. Shiman, *Crusade Against Drink*, 63–73, addresses the general hostility to the idea of unfermented Eucharistic wine.
[54] Ibid., 69–73.
[55] Brake, *Drink*, 11–15; Oldstone-Moore, *Hugh Price Hughes*, 30–35. See Shiman, *Crusade Against Drink*, 99–133, 240–41, for the history of Gospel Temperance.

other issues, including gambling and social purity.[56] Wesleyans began to pressure Parliament to pass laws regulating or suppressing the liquor traffic, and established a Temperance Sunday.[57] In 1912, under the leadership of Henry Carter, a Wesleyan Temperance Movement was officially established.[58]

By and large, total abstinence was more firmly preached in the other Methodist connexions (Hugh Bourne, one of the founders of the Primitive Methodists, commented when asked if he had joined a total abstinence society, 'No, they have joined me.')[59] Primitive Methodist preachers were not explicitly forbidden to drink alcohol (though they were forbidden to smoke or hold tea parties), but few did. The Primitive Methodist Conference explicitly encouraged formation of temperance societies, support of the United Kingdom Alliance and work for legal prohibition. Primitives established a Connexional Temperance Movement in 1883, a Temperance Sunday and Temperance Week in the late 1890s, and passed a resolution encouraging the use of non-alcoholic wine in Communion in 1912.[60] For Primitives, this advocacy – and that of other issues related to the Nonconformist Conscience such as gambling and social purity – was strongly rooted in a desire to improve the condition of the working classes.[61] The Bible Christians also expressed a commitment to the temperance movement beginning as early as the 1830s, although they were in general less inclined to political advocacy. They founded a denominational Total Abstinence Society in 1892.[62] The United Methodist Free Churches formed a Temperance League in 1880; while at first they did not support non-alcoholic wine in Communion, this had changed by the late 1880s. Interestingly, while the Methodist New Connexion expressed support for the temperance cause and contained many total abstainers, it never founded an official temperance society.[63]

Union in 1932 brought together the existing Temperance Committees of the Methodist connexions into a Temperance and Social Welfare department. Among the other causes this new department advocated was peace, as Henry Carter was also a well-known pacifist. However, the department also continued to work for abstinence, temperance instruction and governmental regulation.[64] The Standing Orders of the Methodist Church forbade gambling and dancing, although it was not until 1942 that liquor was actually forbidden on Methodist church premises. The Standing Orders also allowed for the use of non-alcoholic wine in the Eucharist, and Methodist candidates for the ministry were also asked if they were

---

[56] Brake, *Drink*, 17–18, 19–23, 44, 58; Oldstone-Moore, *Hugh Price Hughes*, 63–4, 75–6, 176.
[57] Brake, *Drink*, 24–5; Oldstone-Moore, *Hugh Price Hughes*, 46–51, 59–60, 248–50.
[58] Brake, *Drink*, 32–41; Machin, *Churches and Social Issues*, 17–18, 59–60.
[59] Brake, *Drink*, 63.
[60] Ibid.; Shiman, *Crusade Against Drink*, 56–7.
[61] Brake, *Drink*, 71–2; Shiman, *Crusade Against Drink*, 19, 256.
[62] Brake, *Drink*, 84–94; Shiman, *Crusade Against Drink*, 57.
[63] Brake, *Drink*, 95–107, 75–82.
[64] Ibid., 109, 125, 111–12; Machin, *Churches and Social Issues*, 63–7.

total abstainers.⁶⁵ Generally, though, the presence of non-abstainers in Methodism grew among both laity and clergy.⁶⁶ In the 1970s, the requirement that ministers be total abstainers was changed to one respecting the 'sincerity and integrity of those who take differing views on whether they should drink or abstain', and an official report, *Through a Glass Darkly*, commending both abstinence and responsible drinking, was issued in 1987.⁶⁷

## 'Unfermented Wine is Fermented Nonsense'

Early American Methodists spoke repeatedly about the dangers of drinking distilled spirits at all, and drinking alcohol to excess or as part of frivolous social occasions (such as 'treating' at elections).⁶⁸ As with language on slavery, Wesley's General Rule against drunkenness and the liquor trade was toned down through the early 1800s in an attempt to minister to liquor-sellers. Opposition to the rule was focused in the South, where Southern clergy hesitated to tie themselves too closely to a cause identified with abolitionism. Northerners, on the other hand, re-adopted the original rule after the 1844 split.⁶⁹

From the 1830s on, Americans began to define temperance as total abstinence from all intoxicating drinks, and Methodists were in the forefront of this total abstinence activity.⁷⁰ The MEC formed committees on temperance, constitutional prohibition and the liquor traffic in the 1880s. In 1912 they established a general church Board of Temperance; the name was soon changed to the Board of Temperance, Prohibition, and Public Morals, one of the ancestors of the General Board of Church and Society.⁷¹ The MEC also supported the work of the Women's Christian Temperance Union (WCTU), founded in 1874, and the movement for Scientific Temperance Instruction in public schools.⁷² The most famous president of the WCTU, Frances Willard, was an active Methodist as well as an advocate of women's suffrage.⁷³

---

⁶⁵ Brake, *Drink*, 113–14, 118. These regulations are now more lenient; see *Statements on Social Responsibility: 1946–1995*, 40–51.

⁶⁶ Brake, *Drink*, 119–21.

⁶⁷ See http://www.methodist.org.uk/index.cfm?fuseaction=opentogod.content&cmid=142 (accessed 27 September 2012) for current policies.

⁶⁸ Ruth, *Early Methodist Life*, 243–5, 280; Swinson, 'American Methodism and Temperance', 37–68.

⁶⁹ Woodruff Tait, *Poisoned Chalice*, 11–13. Swinson gives a detailed account of the debates over the General Rule on alcohol.

⁷⁰ Woodruff Tait, *Poisoned Chalice*, 8–10, 21–2.

⁷¹ Will, *Will for Peace*, 277; Tipton, *Public Pulpits*, 69–70, 84–5.

⁷² Woodruff Tait, *Poisoned Chalice*, 12, 24.

⁷³ Ruth Clifford Engs, *Clean Living Movements: American Cycles of Health Reform* (Westport, CT: Praeger, 2000), 123–4, 130. See Carol Mattingly, *Well-Tempered Women: Nineteenth Century Temperance Rhetoric* (Carbondale, IL: Southern Illinois University, 1998) for the

The MEC was one of the earliest American Protestant denominations to introduce grape juice into the celebration of the Eucharist. The first known recommendation against intoxicating Communion wine, an article by Congregationalist Moses Stuart, appeared in the *Methodist Review* in 1835, and his 'two-wine' theory of Biblical exegesis was adopted and enlarged upon by a number of MEC authors. The MEC General Conference began to recommend unfermented wine in the early 1860s; notes to this effect were added to the Communion liturgy in 1876, and in 1916 the words 'whenever practicable' were deleted from these requirements, making the use of grape juice mandatory.[74] It remained mandatory until the 1992 *United Methodist Book of Worship* replaced this language with, 'Although the historic and ecumenical Christian practice has been to use wine, the use of unfermented grape juice by The United Methodist Church and its predecessors since the late nineteenth century expresses pastoral concern for recovering alcoholics, enables the participation of children and youth, and supports the church's witness of abstinence.'[75]

Southern Methodists finally returned prohibition of the liquor traffic to their *Discipline* with the re-adoption of Wesley's original rule in 1886. MECS Annual Conferences formed Temperance Committees throughout the post-Civil War era and the denomination formed a Board of Temperance in 1926.[76] While the General Conference began recommending grape juice in 1887 its use was never made mandatory (until the 1939 merger) and many prominent church leaders opposed it – including the editor of the *Methodist Review*, who remarked, 'Unfermented wine is fermented nonsense.'[77]

Methodists strongly supported the move towards national Prohibition (which was in legal effect from 1919–33).[78] Several Prohibitionists were prominent Methodists: Bishop James Cannon Jr. of the MECS, who was president of the Anti-Saloon League, and Clarence True Wilson, head of the Board of Temperance, Prohibition, and Public Morals in the MEC and author or editor of a number

---

arguments of Willard and others; Jack Blocker's *Give to the Winds Thy Fears* for the Women's Crusade and the founding of the WCTU; and Jonathan Zimmerman's *Distilling Democracy* (Lawrence, KS: University Press of Kansas, 1999), for the history of Scientific Temperance Instruction .

[74] Woodruff Tait, *Poisoned Chalice*, 15–16, 12–13.

[75] Ibid., 123. *This Holy Mystery*, adopted by the 2004 General Conference as the official denominational Eucharistic theology, recommended the use of wine but did not require it.

[76] Will, *Will for Peace*, 277.

[77] Woodruff Tait, *Poisoned Chalice*, 13–14. See also Joe Coker, *Liquor in the Land of the Lost Cause* (Lexington, KY: University Press of Kentucky, 2007).

[78] Woodruff Tait, *Poisoned Chalice*, 122; Engs, *Clean Living Movements*, 126–9. One of the best introductions to Prohibition is Norman Clark's *Deliver Us From Evil* (New York, NY: Norton, 1976). Also helpful, and fair to religious motivation, are Ian R. Tyrell, *Sobering Up* (Westport, CT: Greenwood, 1979); Jack Blocker, *American Temperance Movements* (Boston, MA: Twayne, 1989); and James Timberlake, *Prohibition and the Progressive Movement* (Cambridge, MA: Harvard University Press, 1963).

of temperance books.⁷⁹ In 1924 the MEC dedicated the Methodist Building in Washington D.C. to serve as a staging ground for temperance activism. (Today, in addition to hosting the General Board of Church and Society (GBCS) it also contains the offices of a number of mainline Protestant denominations and religious nonprofits.) The Methodist Church prohibited drinking by its clergy and laypeople until the late 1960s, and the GBCS has continued to maintain an 'abiding concern' for the 'family and personal problems of addiction (gambling, pornography, drugs, and alcohol)'.⁸⁰

## 'I Would Welcome the Russians With Cups of Tea'

Some individual British Methodists were pacifists during Wesley's lifetime, and prominent nineteenth-century leaders – including Percy Bunting and Hugh Price Hughes – were active in branches of the interdenominational Peace Society, founded in London in 1816.⁸¹ Hughes spoke regularly of his dislike of war, and resisted attempts to introduce a draft.⁸² However, Methodist leaders generally subscribed to the idea that Britain's advancing empire was destined to play a civilising and converting role in the world and that Methodism was crucial to that advance.⁸³ While not all Methodists supported the Boer War as the logical next step in that advance, many did, Hughes chief among them.⁸⁴ The years following the Boer War showed a growth in imperialist sentiments, supported by nationalism grounded in the perceived superiority of the Anglo-Saxon race – although there was some consensus that Britain should seek to be part of international treaties and arbitration organisations.⁸⁵

---

[79] Robert A. Hohner's *Prohibition and Politics* (Columbia, SC: University of South Carolina Press, 1999) is a detailed, if laborious, account (and has superseded Virginius Dabney's vitriolic *Dry Messiah* (New York, NY: A. A. Knopf, 1949)). Clarence Wilson was responsible in part for both *Temperance Sermons* and *Cyclopedia of Temperance, Prohibition, and Public Morals* produced by the MEC. The only current biographies of him are Robert Dean McNeill's hagiographic *Valiant for Truth* (Portland, OR: Oregonians Concerned about Addiction Problems, 1992) and *Clarence Darrow's Unlikely Friend* (Portland, OR: Spirit Press, 2007).

[80] Tipton, *Public Pulpits*, 85–6. The 1964 *Discipline* enjoined total abstinence for clergy and church leaders (100, 142, 149); the 1968 *Discipline* continued to commend it in the Social Principles (57) but not require it (112–13); and the 1972 *Discipline* listed it as one possible avenue of witness (89, 147).

[81] Hughes, *Conscience and Conflict*, 9; Oldstone-Moore, *Hugh Price Hughes*, 79; Bebbington, *Nonconformist Conscience*, 107–8, 119.

[82] Hughes, *Conscience and Conflict*, 6–9, 18; Oldstone-Moore, *Hugh Price Hughes*, 132–3; Wearmouth, *Methodism and the Struggle of the Working Classes*, 210–12.

[83] Hughes, *Conscience and Conflict*, 22–5; Oldstone-Moore, *Hugh Price Hughes*, 311–16; Bebbington, *Nonconformist Conscience*, 107, 113–24.

[84] Hughes, *Conscience and Conflict*, 25–34; Oldstone-Moore, *Hugh Price Hughes*, 313–16.

[85] Hughes, *Conscience and Conflict*, 34–44; Bebbington, *Nonconformist Conscience*, 120, 124–5.

World War I was a turning point in building support for the pacifist cause. Although all the connexions officially supported Britain's entry into the war, a growing minority of members maintained that war was contrary to the teachings of Christ.[86] After the draft was introduced in 1916, the Methodist press supported the rights of conscientious objectors, and Methodists were wellrepresented among COs.[87]

British Methodists in the 1930s after their own unification expressed more formal interest in ecumenical and international cooperation, backing the League of Nations and participating in consultations on issues of peace and war. In 1933 a Methodist Peace Fellowship was set up with the support of leading Methodist pacifists such as Donald Soper, Henry Carter, Charles Coulson and Leslie Weatherhead. Weatherhead later moved away from the pacifist position under consideration of the evils of Nazism; the others remained committed to an unconditional pacifism.[88] While Methodists generally stood behind statements against war in the abstract, the buildup to World War II saw tensions between Soper and Carter and those who felt the Nazi menace deserved a military response. The Methodist Conference continued to express strong support for conscientious objectors, but also went on record in 1941 as being committed to the war as a 'sacred cause'.[89]

Postwar Methodist leaders generally supported Britain's retreat from imperialism, opposed Communism (though they did not favour American capitalism as an alternative) and spoke out against the stockpiling of nuclear weapons. The Methodist Peace Fellowship remained active, but the church as a whole did not adopt a pacifist position. Soper became President of Conference in the 1950s, but this did not lead to Methodism espousing his positions wholesale. (When interviewed by former pacifist John Middleton Murry in 1950 Soper announced that 'if the Russians invade "I would welcome them with cups of tea … you may think this is crazy but it is no more crazy than blowing the whole universe to pieces with hydrogen bombs."')[90]

During and after the Cold War, many prominent Methodists took radical anti-institutional views (one, Colin Morris, quipped in 1968, 'I am the son of a prophetic movement which became an institution by mistake.') They were critical of the various 'hot' wars of the later twentieth century, although the people in the pews did not always follow suit. Opposition to Britain's nuclear arsenal continued and in some cases led to civil disobedience, although controversy remained over whether the Methodist Church should endorse such disobedience. Britain's decision to join the U.S. in the war in Iraq came in for much criticism; combined with a desire to attend to issues of global poverty and injustice, this led to a 2006 joint report with

---

[86] Ibid., 125–6; Hughes, *Conscience and Conflict*, 76–8.
[87] Ibid., 58–70, 95. Methodists were about as likely to be found among COs as other Nonconformists, who were much better represented than Anglicans and Roman Catholics (ibid., 68).
[88] Ibid., 80–81, 90, 95–100, 115.
[89] Ibid., 113–14, 123, 138–9.
[90] Ibid., 161–72 (quote from 162).

the United Reformed Church titled *Peacemaking: A Christian Vocation*. The report allowed the use of force only in rare circumstances where clearly indicated by human rights violations and approved by the United Nations. It was only received, not adopted, by Conference.[91]

## 'The Bishops Want to be a Little Bit Pacifist'

While early American Methodists were frequently accused of loyalist sympathies, many were in fact neutral or supportive of the Revolution. But there was a strong streak of pacifism as well. John Littlejohn told of hearing another preacher maintain that 'no Man can be a Christian who goes to War', and seeing preachers put in jail as conscientious objectors or forced to hire substitutes. Littlejohn himself was among the Maryland preachers who refused to take an oath of allegiance against the British (Francis Asbury moved to Delaware to escape it).[92] Jesse Lee decided when drafted as a young farmer that 'as a Christian and a preacher of the Gospel I could not fight. I could not reconcile it to myself to bear arms, or to kill one of my fellow creatures.' Lee ended up serving for some months as a noncombatant and spent much of the time preaching to his fellow soldiers.[93]

Methodist support for war as an instrument of national policy grew in the nineteenth century, a fact seen most clearly in the support of all of United Methodism's predecessor denominations for the Civil War – including the Evangelical Association and United Brethren in Christ, earlier known for strong peace statements. The EA had adopted a statement in its Confession of Faith in 1839 stating, 'We believe that wars and bloodshed are not agreeable to the Gospel of Christ', but replaced this for the duration of the Civil War by: 'It is the imperative duty of our Government to use the sword intrusted to it of God.'[94] Some conferences passed loyalty resolutions, and preachers and laypeople served in the armed forces of both the Union and the Confederacy. While in many cases preachers served as chaplains, they were also active in recruiting, which sometimes occurred in church. Methodists and EA/UBs were also largely in support of the Spanish-American War.[95]

While World War I drew broad support among American churches, peace action intensified after the war was over. Many Methodists supported the League of Nations and attempts at world disarmament, and issued statements asking

---

[91] Ibid., 181, 200–202, 247–9.
[92] Will, *Will for Peace*, 7–8, 168–9; Murray, *Methodists and the Crucible of Race*, 12–13; Williams, *Religion and Violence*, 55–67. Williams argues that many Methodist preachers 'refused to intersect the political struggle with the cosmic struggle for redemption' (65).
[93] Peter Brock (ed.), *Liberty and Conscience* (Oxford: Oxford University Press, 2002), 57–61.
[94] Long, *Living the Discipline*, 36. The statement against war returned and became part of the Confession of Faith of the Evangelical United Brethren Church (1946) and the UMC (1968).
[95] Will, *Will for Peace*, 13–14, 169–71, 16–18.

that Methodist conscientious objectors be granted the same rights as those from historic peace churches. The 1924 MEC General Conference created a World Peace Commission, stating: 'We recommend that a prayer for peace be prepared and used at every communion service ... Our church must do its full share to mold the present youth of all races into a peace-loving generation ...The glorification of war must end.'[96] Leadership in this area was undertaken by a dedicated core group of young activists, many of whom had been influenced by the Methodist Student Movement and learned nonviolent tactics abroad from Gandhi and his followers. Some of them also played roles overseas in campaigns for Indian independence and against South African racism.[97]

Early in World War II the 1940 General Conference of the Methodist Church stated that the denomination would not 'officially endorse, support, or participate in war'. However, a report asserting 'the necessity of the use of military forces to resist aggression which would overthrow every right which is held sacred by civilized men' was narrowly adopted in place of this statement in 1944.[98] The Methodist Youth Fellowship and the Women's Division of the Board of Missions continued to protest the 1944 statement and proclaim support for ending war, ending the draft and protecting the rights of conscientious objectors. The church also objected to the forced internment of Japanese-Americans.[99]

Methodists supported the establishment of the U.N. as part of their Crusade for a New World Order and spearheaded the building of the Church Center for the United Nations.[100] During the war in Vietnam Methodist leaders spoke out strongly and consistently against the war and in support of ending the draft; the 1972 General Conference issued a statement 'call[ing] upon the leadership of the United States to confess that what we have done in Indochina has been a crime against humanity'.[101] That same General Conference adopted a set of Social Principles for the newly merged UMC, including a statement (still in force) that war was 'incompatible with the teachings and example of Christ'.[102] Methodists were active in work for world disarmament and concerned over the growing development of nuclear weapons. In 1960 the Methodist Boards of Temperance, Social and Economic Relations, and World Peace merged (and moved to the Board of Temperance headquarters) as the Board of Christian Social Concerns/GBCS.[103] This inaugurated a sharper focus

---

[96] Ibid., 36–43, 173–84. See also Paul Ramsey and Stanley Hauerwas, *Speak Up for Just War or Pacifism* (University Park, PA: Pennsylvania State University Press, 1988), 68.

[97] See David Cooney, 'A Consistent Witness', esp. 8–12 and 133–94.

[98] Will, *Will for Peace*, 70–72; Long, *Living the Discipline*, 36–7, 42–62. Long sees Methodist willingness to change on this issue as being a sign that the ultimate goal was to civilise, not discipline Methodist followers (62).

[99] Will, *Will for Peace*, 66–70; David Cooney, 'A Consistent Witness', 77–132.

[100] Will, *Will for Peace*, 81–4, 97–101. Will was head of the Board of World Peace and its later subdivisions within the GBCS for over fifty years (Tipton, *Public Pulpits*, 85–6).

[101] Will, *Will for Peace*, 157–8.

[102] Long, *Living the Discipline*, 63–7.

[103] Will, *Will for Peace*, 186–221; Tipton, *Public Pulpits*, 69–103. Amy Laura Hall argues in *Conceiving Parenthood* (Grand Rapids, MI: Eerdmans, 2008) that the growth of atomic power

on peace, as well as growing grass-roots opposition to what was seen as excessive involvement by the GBCS in left-of-centre political activity.[104]

In 1986 the Council of Bishops stated that United Methodists should respond to the growing nuclear crisis as pacifists, and the American government should seek a nuclear freeze and disarmament even if the USSR did not do likewise.[105] Among responses was *Speak Up for Just War and Pacifism*, by respected Methodist just war theorist Paul Ramsey and a young pacifist ethicist named Stanley Hauerwas. They accused the bishops of being ultimately willing to trust national politics: 'The Bishops', Hauerwas argued, 'want to be a little bit pacifist. But it is no easier to be a little bit pacifist than it is to be a little bit pregnant. The peace that is sought is not the peace that has been given by Christ. Instead it is a peace that encourages us to put our faith in the threat of nuclear war'.[106] Among other theologians calling for Methodism to acknowledge itself as a peace church was D. Stephen Long: 'Is the United Methodist Church pacifist? Constitutionally we are, practically we are not.'[107]

## 'The World is Not Consisting Only of Black and White'

The Methodist conscience moved with Methodist missions, although imperialistic and colonial attitudes meant that it sometimes moved in contradictory and counter-productive ways. This was especially acute in Africa, where the spread of Christianity was inexplicably interwoven with the slave trade and where even acts seen as 'enlightened' in their day – such as the establishment of the Liberian colony

---

actually served as a powerful organising metaphor for the American Methodist vision of the good life (291–361).

[104] Tipton, *Public Pulpits*, 104–228. The GBGS has recently emerged victorious in a lawsuit alleging that since the building and endowment were given specifically for temperance work, any other social activism constitutes a misappropriation of funds (http://www.umc-gbcs.org/site/apps/nlnet/content2.aspx?c=frLJK2PKLqF&b=3631941&ct=8756451; accessed 27 September 2012).

[105] The United Methodist Council of Bishops, *In Defense of Creation: The Nuclear Crisis and a Just Peace* (Nashville, TN: Graded Press, 1986), 62–90. The accompanying *Guide for Study and Action* (Gary Ball-Kilbourne and Jack Keller, *In Defense of Creation: The Nuclear Crisis and a Just Peace: Guide for Study and Action*, (Nashville, TN: Graded Press, 1986)) includes an extensive bibliography on war and peacemaking.

[106] Ramsey and Hauerwas, *Speak Up for Just War*, 125–82; Hughes, *Conscience and Conflict*, 15; Cracknell and White, *Introduction to World Methodism*, 210. See Long, *Living the Discipline*, 120–28, for a concise description of just war criteria, and Tipton, *Public Pulpits*, 430–32, for Hauerwas, who became one of the most prominent Methodist theologians of the twentieth century (http://www.time.com/time/magazine/article/0,9171,1000859,00.html; accessed 27 September 2012).

[107] Long, *Living the Discipline*, 1–2. Many of the peace activists David Cooney studied felt they were rejected by a church which practised both racism and militarism ('A Consistent Witness', 314–15).

– were heavily fraught with White racism.In the postcolonial era, many indigenous Methodist churches in Africa, Asia and Europe have been involved in witnessing against racism, intertribal conflict and government corruption.[108] The witness of Methodists such as Nelson Mandela and Peter Storey in South Africa may be the most notable, but is far from the only example.[109]

A late 1980s study under the auspices of the World Methodist Council named the primary theological and ethical issues facing world Methodism as: lack of belief in God; lack of striving for holiness; poverty, war and arms races; misuse of the environment; and racial, gender, economic and religious oppression. The surveyors found Methodists worldwide to be concerned on all these fronts, though with considerable geographical variance.[110] Methodists in the developing world were more concerned for issues of personal holiness than those Methodists in the 'mother' churches in Britain and the U.S. But social concern was certainly important to the 'daughter' churches, with Asian and Pacific Methodists showing particular interest in issues of war and peace, and African and Central and South American Methodists being extremely concerned about issues of race, class and gender oppression.[111] One can question the actual amount of power over its constituencies wielded by the World Methodist Council – and the actual amount of power within the World Methodist Council given to representatives of the global South – but the WMC has certainly continued to keep these issues at the forefront of its advocacy, especially those of racial and economic oppression and environmentalism.[112]

---

[108] See Casely Essamuah, *Genuinely Ghanaian* (Trenton: Africa World Press, 2010) (Ghana); James Campbell, *Songs of Zion* (Chapel Hill, NC: University of North Carolina Press, 1998) (South Africa); D'Amico,'Spiritual and Secular Activities' (Liberia); Charles Cole (ed.), *Christian Mission in the Third Millennium* (New York, NY: GBGM, 2004), 77–119 (Europe). Ruben Trinidad's *A Monument to Religious Nationalism* (Quezon City: Evangelical Methodist Church, 1999) explores how the racism of White missionaries led to a breakaway indigenous Filipino Methodism; Earnest Lau's *From Mission to Church* (Kent Ridge, Singapore: Genesis, 2008) explores how the same issue led to autonomous Methodist churches in Southeast Asia; and Cole, *Christian Mission in the Third Millennium* considers how ethnic churches around the world are developing issues with Anglo-American ways of 'doing church'. Uta Theilen's *Gender, Race, Power, and Religion* (Frankfurt: Peter Lang, 2005) outlines both Methodist women's witness against racism and gender oppression in South Africa and the lengths still to go, including the difficulty of integrating Black, White and 'coloured' women's organisations (see esp. 235–51). Many South African theologians clearly see a connection between witness against racism and witness against heterosexism (see Dion Forster and Wessel Bentley (eds), *What Are We Thinking?* (Cape Town: MPH, 2008), 71–95, 107–16).

[109] Cracknell and White, *Introduction to World Methodism*, 209–10.

[110] Earl Brewer and Scott Thumma, *World Methodism and World Issues* (Atlanta, GA: Center for Religious Research, 1990), 4–5. The accompanying study book, *Wesleyan Transformations*, focuses largely on pacifism and environmentalism.

[111] Ibid., 11–23. Though the data are now some decades old, they are considerably detailed, separating opinions by age, gender, urban–rural location and clergy–laity status.

[112] This is clearly seen in the proceedings of the last two WMC meetings, *Jesus Christ: God's Way of Salvation* (2001) and *God in Christ Reconciling* (2006).

Surprisingly, perhaps, to some Anglo-American Methodists, temperance remains extremely central to the Methodist witness in many of Methodism's 'daughter' churches. Early Methodist missionaries naturally established temperance organisations as a crucial part of their outreach.[113] The message was particularly attractive in Eastern Europe and Russia, where the emphasis – even when defined as abstinence – drew many converts.[114] Methodism actually came to Lithuania in 1900 as a result of an independent house church of German-speaking former Lutherans discovering, 'quite coincidentally, that [their] evangelical emphases of prayer, Bible study, proclamation, witness, and abstinence from alcohol were akin to Methodist emphases'.[115] Abstinence was also central to the formation of Methodist women's organisations in South Africa and remains the official policy of the Methodist Church of South Africa.[116] It is true, though, that while Methodists around the world continue to make ministry to those struggling with alcohol and drug addiction as a priority, some see the total abstinence message as an American import.[117]

While the conflict between pacifist and militarist approaches has been largely a matter of wars abroad for Anglo-American Methodists (with the exception of the American Civil War, where militarism won out), Methodists in 'daughter' churches have wrestled at length with the degree to which they will cooperate with military conflict or occupation. In India, American Methodist missionaries assisted the Indian independence movement and helped organise nonviolent protests against British rule, even in the face of opposition from the U.S. Board of Missions.[118] Methodists in Ghana were a force in the drive towards Ghanaian independence and have continued to see themselves as having a 'calling to remind temporal authorities of the limits of their political power'.[119] The Philippines, Singapore and Malaysia were all occupied by the Japanese during World War II (as well as being bombed). Both segments of Filipino Methodism resisted pressure to join the union of Protestant

---

[113] Wesley Parker, *In the Midst of the City* (Auckland: Methodist Central Mission, 1971), 22; Cooney, *Methodists in Ireland*, 88–9, 218–22; Cracknell and White, *Introduction to World Methodism*, 229–30; Lau, *From Mission to Church*, 29 (among the items supplied by the early Methodist Publishing House in Malaysia was grape juice for the Eucharist). D'Amico, 'Spiritual and Secular Activities', maintains that while American Methodists established temperance societies in Liberia (218, 253), enforcing temperance precepts was another matter (242–3).

[114] ST Kimbrough (ed.), *Methodism in Russia and the Baltic States* (Nashville, TN: Abingdon, 1995), 61, 66, 94, 102, 131, 171.

[115] Ibid., 171.

[116] Theilen, *Gender, Race, Power and Religion*, 86–7, 97.

[117] See Cooney, *Methodists in Ireland*, 88–9, 178, 218–22, for resistance to the total abstinence message in Ireland; also Parker, *In the Midst of the City*, 10, 22, 58.

[118] Cooney, 'A Consistent Witness', 133–50. Many of the same missionaries later attempted to work nonviolently for Puerto Rican and Algerian independence and against apartheid in South Africa (151–94).

[119] Essamuah, *Genuinely Ghanaian*, 69–95. He does identify cases where prominent Ghanaian Methodists have collaborated with corrupt governments (81–2, 94).

churches which the Japanese imposed.[120] In Singapore and Malaysia, the White missionaries who remained during the occupation were interred in prison camps; Asian leadership took over and functioned for the large part congregationally. Many churches were destroyed, pastors arrested and preaching activities restricted, but the church at the end of the war reported itself to be stronger and more fully indigenised.[121] Irish Methodists have remained united in the Methodist Church in Ireland across Ulster and the Republic, and many helped work for a peaceful solution to the Troubles, continually asserting that 'communities live rather by debate than by confrontation'.[122] There have been times, though, when Methodists have compromised – perhaps most notably in the case of Bishop Otto Melle in Germany, who collaborated with the Nazis in the service of German nationalism and received official legal favour as a result.[123] Methodists under Communism also faced difficult choices: Heigo Ritsbek, discussing the ways in which he and other Methodist leaders tried to make a space for the Gospel in Estonia, said, 'Being myself a minister under Communism over ten years, I know that the world is not consisting only of black and white. Sometimes there are shades, but we do not see them.'[124]

This narrative certainly does not exhaust the areas of Methodist concern – or the areas in which that concern has been misguided or culturally conditioned. In Britain, opposition to gambling was always a strong component of the Nonconformist Conscience, and the Methodist Church there continues to oppose it while avoiding 'the heavy-footed pursuit of the trivial'.[125] American Methodists likewise disapproved of gambling and its stimulating associations with saloons and prostitution; in the twentieth century, opposition to casinos, lotteries and other forms of legalised gambling has continued to be one of the signature social issues of the UMC.[126] Methodists in both 'mother' and 'daughter' churches worldwide have also spoken out, firmly and repeatedly, on our need to care

---

[120] Trinidad, *A Monument to Religious Nationalism*, 203–6. As a result, the Japanese army occupied and later destroyed the Evangelical Methodist Church in the Philippine Islands Cathedral in Tondo.

[121] Lau, *From Mission to Church*, 155–78.

[122] Cooney, *Methodists in Ireland*, 108–16.

[123] Will, *Will for Peace*, 74–6; see also Roland Blaich, 'A Tale of Two Leaders', *Church History*, 70:2 (2001).

[124] See 'Methodism in Estonia Under Communism', in Tim Macquiban (ed.), *Methodism in its Cultural Milieu* (Oxford: Applied Theology Press, 1994), 72; Kimbrough, *Methodism in Russia and the Baltic States*, 145–50.

[125] *Statements on Social Responsibility*, 40–51; Machin, *Churches and Social Issues*, 146–9; Bebbington, *Nonconformist Conscience*, 51–3; Oldstone-Moore, *Hugh Price Hughes*, 2, 177–81; Brake, *Drink*, 44, 132 (where he comments that the Methodist Church's Gambling Commission has had better recent success than its temperance work because 'it was created to do a job in this century and not the last').

[126] Woodruff Tait, *Poisoned Chalice*, 44, 64, 69; http://archives.umc.org/interior.asp?ptid=1&mid=1743 (accessed 27 September 2012).

for the environment.[127] Of all the issues originally formative to the Methodist conscience, temperance is perhaps the least affirmed in the 'mother' churches as an expression of fundamentalist legalism despite the fact that it still serves as a defining characterisation of Methodism to outsiders and continues to draw attention abroad.[128]

Some have recently argued that modern Methodism focuses on social and corporate sins to the exception of personal ones. But the evidence above favours the contention that Methodists, from Wesley onward and worldwide, have always been concerned that society, and not just individuals within it, be changed.[129] What remains unanswered is the question with which this essay began. Is the way in which Methodists have lived out their conscience any different, any more successful, than the works of mercy and justice in which other parts of the Body of Christ have engaged? Jim Winkler, former head of the GBGS in the UMC, once commented that United Methodists would best live out their prophetic witness by understanding 'how important our denomination is in the life of this nation, indeed in the world … People depend on the United Methodist Church. Praise God. We have much work to do.'[130] In his words could be heard the echo of Hugh Price Hughes. Yet the question remains whether or not Winkler and Hughes were right. Is not the Methodist witness on these issues only, in the end, the witness that any Christians should make? And is it not best understood not as making Methodists distinctive, but as making them obedient to the Gospel of Christ and part of the Body of Christ?

---

[127] http://www.umc.org/site/apps/nl/newsletter.asp?c=lwL4KnN1LtH&b=5065913#e6794177 (UMC) (accessed 27 September 2012).See also Forster and Bentley, *What Are We Thinking?*, 117–36; Brewer and Jackson, *Wesleyan Transformations*, 53–64; Brewer and Thumma, *World Methodism and World Issues*, 14–23 (the last notes how different regions of Methodists ranked issues of environmental justice in comparison to other social issues).

[128] Tipton, *Public Pulpits*, 82–3, 236–7; Woodruff Tait, *Poisoned Chalice*, 7–8, 121–6; Machin, *Churches and Social Issues*, 67–8.

[129] Tipton, *Public Pulpits*, 106–45.

[130] Ibid., 144.

# Material and Cultural Aspects of Methodism: Architecture, Artefacts and Art[1]

## Peter Forsaith

Until recent decades, any sense of a cultural history of Methodism might have been thought a misnomer approaching a contradiction in terms. Accurately or otherwise, Methodists could be perceived as 'thin-lipped laughterless spoil-sports'[2] who shunned the cultural sphere – or at best engaged only in terms of a narrow world of those senses they inhabited, such as church music.[3] Their functional architecture could be considered as plain or parody, the artefacts of their religion mere frippery and their art generally nondescript.

Such views, if they were ever tenable, should no longer be sustained,[4] as this essay endeavours to demonstrate. At its genesis, the Methodist movement arose at a time of particular transition in the cultural life of Britain, and indeed of western Europe, and needs to be read alongside that process. During the first half of the eighteenth century the expressive 'baroque' style was struggling for supremacy with a stricter and more severe classicism; chiefly evident in art, architecture and music. Nor was this simply and solely a question of fashion and appearance; it was allied to political philosophies, indeed to the whole 'enlightenment' movement, which in turn were linked to churchmanship. So any examination of the cultural contexts of Methodism has to be wider than a narrative of changing styles. It needs to place such trends within wider cultural landscapes and those currents of thought which underpinned them.

---

[1] I am grateful to a number of people for their assistance and advice, some of whom I have quoted, others whose work has been usefully informative. They include Debby Gaitskell, Mike Leigh, Ken Rowe, Ian Serjeant, Terry Wall and Andrew Worth.

[2] Leslie Weatherhead, quoted in F. H. Everson, *This is Methodism* (London: Epworth Press, 1957), 11.

[3] For a discussion, see D. Rosman, *Evangelicals and Culture* (Eugene, OR: Pickwick, 2011, 2nd edn).

[4] Ibid, 1–13.

The subsequent trajectory of the movement is closely linked to the cultural histories of the host communities in which Methodism has taken root. Predominantly this has been allied to the rise and decline of the British, then American, imperial projects; latterly to the exponential growth of Christendom in the global south which, as David Hempton has observed, 'would not look the same if Methodism had never existed'.[5]

Nevertheless, the writing of such a chapter is seriously impeded by a dearth of research and literature around the subject. Specialist or summative works are few: recent compendium volumes on the Wesleys and Methodism are generally negligent on cultural aspects of the movement.[6] It has to be a key purpose of this chapter, therefore, both to understand Methodism within relevant cultural contexts and to view it as a source and setting for material and cultural research.

The following section of this chapter will outline the overall cultural context within which the subject is to be set, after which come themed sections on architecture (focusing upon churches, although Methodist building types include schools, universities, hospitals and homes); artefacts (the material evidence of the movement); then aspects of visual art, before a brief conclusion. To reiterate, works on Methodist art, architecture or artefacts are not plentiful – something which may also be said of other nonconformist traditions. There seems to be a tacit assumption that not much is written because there is not much to write about. As Dolbey, writing of architecture, put it a half-century ago: 'There is an attitude of mind outside the Methodist Church, and not unknown within it, that asks "Can anything good come out of Methodism?"'[7]

This essay seeks to demonstrate that there is indeed something to discuss.

## Mapping the Landscape

On the afternoon of 24 May 1738 John Wesley 'was asked to go to St. Paul's. The anthem was, "Out of the deep have I called unto Thee"'[8] by Henry Purcell.[9] Thus

---

[5] D. Hempton, *Methodism: Empire of the Spirit* (New Haven, CT and London: Yale University Press, 2005), 209.

[6] See P. Forsaith, 'Methodism and its Images', in C. Yrigoyen, Jr. (ed.), *T&T Clark Companion to Methodism* (London and New York: T&T Clark, 2010); otherwise there is negligible material besides treatments of literature or music as they relate narrowly to the Wesleys or Methodism in either W. J. Abraham and J. E. Kirby (eds), *The Oxford Handbook of Methodist Studies* (Oxford: Oxford University Press, 2009) or R. L. Maddox and J. E. Vickers (eds), *The Cambridge Companion to John Wesley* (Cambridge: Cambridge University Press, 2010).

[7] G. Dolbey, *The Architectural Expression of Methodism: The First Hundred Years* (London: The Epworth Press, 1964), v.

[8] John Wesley, *Journal*, 24 May 1738, in W. R. Ward and R. P. Heitzenrater (eds), 'Journals and Diaries' I–VII, in *The Works of John Wesley* [hereafter *WJW*] (Nashville, TN: Abingdon Press, 1988–2003,vols 18–24).

[9] Identified as Purcell by Sir Frederick Bridge in N. Curnock (ed.), *The Journal of the Rev. John Wesley* (London: Epworth, 1909), i, 472.

the prelude to Wesley's evangelical Aldersgate experience was hearing the music of England's leading baroque composer, in its most vaunted baroque ecclesiastical edifice. This represents an ideological struggle, for Wesley was wedded to the quest for the 'primitive',[10] a mantra of Whig classicism, rather than the progressive and elaborate baroque, with its association with Catholic Europe, more usually linked to the Tory stance to which he would in other ways incline.

The 'baroque' – a term, like 'renaissance' or 'enlightenment', which was applied retrospectively and can best be defined loosely – describes a dominant stylistic European cultural current of the seventeenth century. Rooted in the resurgence of papal Rome, it was typified by a grand appeal to the senses. In England it was exemplified by such architects as Wren, Vanbrugh and Hawksmoor; painters like Vandyke, Lely and Kneller and musicians including Purcell and Handel.

Increasingly opposed to baroque style through the first half of the eighteenth century, was a neo-classicism. In Renaissance Italy, Andrea Palladio promoted a recovery of the mathematical relationships of Greek architecture: his *I Quattro Libri dell'Architettura*[11] became profoundly influential. In England the 'architect-Earl' Lord Burlington from around 1720 became the nation's apostle of Palladianism, adhering to its strict classical 'orders', although his classicism was perhaps already anticipated by Dean Aldrich's 'Peckwater Quad' at Christ Church, Oxford, which the Wesleys would have known in its newness.

A parallel trend was happening in the field of art. In 1715 Jonathan Richardson (1666–1745) published *An Essay on the Theory of Painting*, followed in 1722 by *An Account of Some of the Statues, Bas-Reliefs, Drawings, and Pictures in Italy* (with his son Jonathan, 1694–1771). Arguably the earliest art-theory writing in Britain, the principles enunciated by Richardson influenced such prominent artists as Thomas Hudson, Richardson's son-in-law, and Joshua Reynolds. The emphasis on modelling upon the 'Old Masters', later heavily insisted upon in Reynolds' *Discourses*, was again a throwback to the past, and guided wealthy young men on their 'grand tour' in Italy to study and acquire classical antiquities.

These movements were more than stylistic; they represented different approaches to a search for a purity of church and state through a recovery of the 'primitive', primarily associated with the Whigs, who were the dominant political force under the first two Hanoverian monarchs. Hence 'this had a politico-cultural dimension, as the Baroque could be presented in terms of a papalism, Italianism and even Frenchification of these [originally classical] forms, with Palladianism a return to them comparable to that of the Primitive Church and of virtuous, public, non-authoritarian, politics'.[12]

So the roots of Methodism are not found in some arbitrary cultural setting, but in identifiable styles and modes of thought with a wider currency and material existence. John Wesley's endeavours to replicate aspects of the 'primitive' church,

---

[10] See G. Hammond, *Restoring Primitive Christianity: John Wesley and Georgia, 1735–1737* (unpubl. Ph.D. thesis, University of Manchester, 2008).
[11] Andrea Palladio, *The Four Books of Architecture* (Venice, 1570).
[12] J. Black, *A Subject for Taste* (London and New York: Hambledon, 2005), 175.

first at Oxford and then in Georgia,[13] which so shaped the mores of the 'connexion' he established, were endemic to the politics, society and churchmanship of his formative years. So, for instance, his adoption of octagonal chapel designs (to which we shall return) reflected a Palladian embrace of this form.

In mid-century, just as the neo-classical had superseded the baroque, a range of other styles, less easily defined, began to be pursued and practised. These included the 'rococo', with its decorative ebullience mainly applied to interiors and objects; and the rise of 'sensibility', which related more to Methodism in the areas of literature and morality. The growing interest in the 'sublime', seen particularly in 'picturesque' landscape painting (but also in the landscape itself) reflected the rise of 'natural philosophy', a theological approach which viewed the universe as fundamentally the handiwork of God. Scientific enquiry was not, therefore, antithetical to Christianity.

But what was to become the most influential architecture for (Anglo-American) churches was the 'Gothic', usually identified as originating with Horace Walpole's eccentric 'Strawberry Hill' from 1747. By the 1760s the style was catching on, and was used by Lady Huntingdon for her Bath chapel and College at Trevecca, Wales. But it was not until the 1840s, following the success of Barry and Pugin's use of Gothic decoration for the new British Houses of Parliament, and the related Tractarian insistence on the style as representing true Christian building, in its authentic medieval form, that it became the unquestioned face of nineteenth-century church-building.

At the same time, the age of political democracy was spawning numbers of public institutions and universal education, and with them a new genre of scene-painting, depicting and heroicising triumphant episodes from the past. The 'pre-Raphaelites' and then the 'Arts and Crafts movement' can both be seen as examples of looking back to move forward. The wars of the twentieth century largely put paid to such romantic retrospection and resulted in abstraction in art, brutalism in buildings and functionalism in furniture.

It may seem strange, from the present time, how the architecture of a building can be so directly linked to religious beliefs, cultural assumptions or political values, though this might be more obviously apparent in decoration. After a century of styles such as modernity or expressionism it is more usual to see the design of a building as purely related to its functional use and purpose, or a picture to its sensory impact. However, the embodiment of such values was indeed the case, and it is equally possible to argue that fashions in twentieth-century Western architecture, art and design are similarly allied to atheistic or totalitarian perspectives.

Lest it be thought that Methodism is oblivious to messages and values embodied in design, it has recognised and used the presentation of publications (hymnbooks, newspapers, magazines, websites), church furniture and other aspects of its activities to reflect cultural mores. They do not exist in a valueless void. In the 1970s the U.S.A.-based United Methodist Church adopted the 'cross and flame' logo to embody missiological and symbolic meaning, which has become its global

---

[13] Hammond, *Restoring Primitive Christianity*.

trademark.[14] Similarly the British Methodist Church adopted the 'orb and cross' logo, again to convey a specific message.[15]

## Architecture

John Wesley's 'New Room' at Bristol, originally built in 1739 but significantly enlarged and remodelled in 1748, remains in many ways the archetypical Methodist religious and social space. The term 'chapel' is technically inaccurate as Wesley called such places 'preaching-houses' or just 'rooms' to differentiate them from either parish churches or Dissenting 'meeting-houses' (it also avoided the requirement to license them as the latter). 'Church' is similarly anachronistic since members were expected to attend parish church services, and particularly the sacraments. In at least the initial decades of the movement, the function of a building was as a space for Methodist 'society' meetings which chiefly consisted of preaching and hymn-singing. Methodist buildings were designed as auditory spaces for preacher and people, although they needed to be adaptable for smaller meetings and other purposes.

In the 'New Room', the communion area and pews were later additions: in its early form it comprised a high pulpit, gallery and (un-pewed) 'pit' and incorporated architectural features such as fenestration which makes considerable use of indirect lighting. The open ground floor was multi-functional, being used as a school, dispensary, bookroom and general social area, while above was living accommodation for travelling preachers. Its style is loosely neo-classical; it is not a building type with a solely religious pedigree, for although its antecedents can be detected in Greek and Roman temples, or Saxon churches, it is not unrelated

---

[14] '... some expression of warmth would be conveyed – a warmth such as John Wesley had experienced on a long-ago spring evening in Aldersgate Street. Following some two dozen conceptualisations, a traditional symbol – the cross – was linked with a single but dual flame. The insignia thereby relates our church to God by way of the second and third persons of the Trinity: the Christ (cross) and the Holy Spirit (flame). Apart from Wesleyan Trinitarian theology and warmth, the flame has two other connotations. The flame suggests Pentecost when witnesses saw "tongues as of fire." And the duality of the flame was meant to represent the merger in 1968 of two denominations: The Methodist Church and the Evangelical United Brethren Church.' http://www.bmk.ee/jonah/history.htm (accessed 8 February 2011).

[15] 'The cross being in radiant form to symbolise the Glory of the risen Lord. The orb to symbolise the world. The colours red and white are used: Red for the orb to symbolise the (Arminian) doctrine of the possibility of a universal salvation for all humanity through the power of the Holy Spirit – represented by the Whitsun colour. White for the risen Saviour of Eastertide. The whole logo in symbolic form summarises the Mission and Message of Methodism first set out by John Wesley: "I look upon the whole world as my parish".' http://www.methodist.org.uk/index.cfm?fuseaction=churchlife.content&cmid=782 (accessed 8 February 2011).

to Assembly Rooms (the fashionable social spaces of the time) nor to the theatre.[16] Indeed, it still functions well as performance space.

The two other earliest buildings associated with Wesley's Methodism, the 'Foundery' in London and the 'Orphan House', Newcastle-on-Tyne,[17] which delineated the triangle of Wesley's annual itinerancy, have both long since disappeared. While the 'Orphan House' was purpose-built, the 'Foundery' was constructed from a ruined military arsenal which had exploded in 1716 – quite possibly Wesley had heard the explosion while at school a half-mile or so away.

Wesley held clear views on the design and building of 'preaching-houses', iterated in several editions of the 'Minutes of Conference', which served as the Connexion's code of law and polity. In the 'Large Minutes' of 1770–72, which were a consolidated disciplinary document, in response to the question 'Is anything further advisable with regard to building?', it was recorded:

> A. 1. Build all preaching-houses, if the ground will admit, in the octagon form. It is best for the voice, and on many accounts more commodious than any other. 2. Let the roof *rise* only one-third of the breadth: this is the true proportion. 3. Have enow windows and doors; and let all the windows be sashed, opening downward. 4. Let there be no tub-pulpit; but a square projection with a long seat behind. 5. Let there be no backs to the seats, which should have aisles on each side, and be parted in the middle by a rail running all along, to divide the men from the women.[18]

Two decades later the proscription was twice as long, adding clauses about the building of square houses 'after the model of Bath or Scarborough'; 'Let there be no Chinese paling' (a reflection on the fashion for 'chinoiserie'); that 'all preaching-houses be built plain and decent; but not more expensive than is absolutely unavoidable'; and, lastly, 'wherever a preaching-house is built, see that lodgings for the Preachers be built also'.[19]

Of all Methodist building styles, the early octagons have attracted most attention. Their inception is generally attributed to Wesley viewing the 1756 'eight-square' meeting-house in Norwich,[20] although the octagonal plan had a long history in ecclesiastical and other buildings. It was favoured by Wren and found a vogue

---

[16] See T. Friedman, *The Eighteenth-Century Church in Britain* (New Haven, CT and London, Yale University Press, 2011).

[17] T. Hurst (ed.), *The Orphan House of John Wesley* (Wesley Historical Society North East Branch, 2007).

[18] H. D. Rack (ed.), 'The Methodist Societies, The Minutes of Conference', in *WJW* (Nashville, TN: Abingdon Press, 2011), vol. 10, 896–7.

[19] Ibid., 930–31.

[20] J. Wesley, *Journal*, 23 November 1757, *WJW*, 21 (Journals and Diaries IV), 131. 'I was shown Dr. Taylor's new meeting-house, perhaps the most elegant one in Europe. It is eight-square, built of the finest brick, with sixteen sash-windows below, as many above, and eight skylights in the dome.'

in the eighteenth century, notably in the Radcliffe Observatory at Oxford (from 1772), modelled on the 'Tower of the Winds' at Athens. Theologically, octagons are symbolically linked with rebirth, and so the traditional shape for baptismal fonts.[21]

However, Wesley's stated reasons were entirely functional, that it was best for preaching, communality and economy. Its disadvantage lay chiefly in roof construction, which restricted size. As the movement, and society memberships, grew it became less practicable; and increasing sacramental use of Methodist buildings demanded a less auditory layout. Most of the fifteen octagons built between 1761 and 1776 were demolished or sold: the largest, at Bradford, became structurally unsound and was abandoned.[22]

For his flagship London 'chapel' of 1778, to replace the Foundery, Wesley reverted to a rectangular form closely related to Anglican preaching-house design, such as at St. James, Piccadilly. Nonetheless, Thomas Telford used an octagonal plan for the large and methodistical St. Michael's, Madeley (1793), with its wide unsupported ceiling, and the octagon has been intermittently revived in Methodism.

Two hundred years after John Wesley's evangelical experience at Aldersgate, Frank Lloyd Wright – consciously or otherwise – used an essentially octagonal floor plan for his Annie Pfeiffer Chapel (1938) for the Methodist Florida Southern College. The building was largely constructed by the students, redolent of early Methodist self-sufficiency. Wright, drawing on Eastern philosophy, saw spiritual integrity as fundamental to an organic unity through which the appearance, function and life of any building is set.[23]

Wright also believed in the transformative power of interior space, which offers a useful analytical approach to Methodism's relations with its buildings. If, as has been argued, the design of a building reflects and represents the underlying substructure of the society in which it was created; its usage over the years, and peoples' interaction with and within it, form another, and perhaps more pertinent, dimension – a subject which has been explored in the proliferation of Cornish Methodist chapels in Britain's isolated southwestern peninsula.[24]

This principle is closely echoed at the heart of a book which, despite its shortcomings,[25] remains the chief single-volume treatment of Methodist architecture, George Dolbey's *The Architectural Expression of Methodism*. In its opening paragraphs he stated:

---

[21] Dolbey, *The Architectural Expression of Methodism*, 99ff.
[22] Ibid., 113.
[23] R. L. Sommer, *Frank Lloyd Wright: American Architect for the Twentieth Century* (Greenwich, CT: Brompton, 1993), 135–6.
[24] J. Lake, J. Cox and E. Berry, *Diversity and Vitality: The Methodist and Non-conformist Chapels of Cornwall* (Truro: Cornwall Archaeological Unit, 2001).
[25] See H. T. Fowler, *Methodist History*, 3 (1964–5), 56–7: 'This book … is disappointing in what it does not say … what Methodism is, or what about Methodism is expressed in the scores of edifices it discusses.'

> There is a relation between the theology, worship and organization of a church and the building in which these things are practiced ... it is accepted there is a relation between the way men worship and the way men build. Doctrines and liturgies and architectural styles are both the crystallized formal expressions of the fluid, life-giving Spirit of God in man.[26]

To adopt David Hempton's term, a symbiosis subsists between a building and its usage; to apply his methodology, to what extent in Methodism is there a disjuncture between the designs of its buildings and the purposes and practices of its peoples? Is the dialectical tension which Hempton and others observe in Methodism a feature of its architectural environment?

By covering the first hundred years, to 1840, and only in Britain, Dolbey avoided addressing the multifarious mutations of Methodism as it spread globally and rapidly through the nineteenth century, building schools, hospitals and housing as well as churches. In some places settler congregations were established quickly, aspiring to the kind of permanent structures they had known back home. Elsewhere, mission movements demanded flexibility and portability; there was enormous variety, with little coherent pattern. In Burma 'expensive buildings, once built, seemed immediately to be consumed by fire, washed away in floods, blown down by winds or destroyed in war and had to be built all over again'.[27] It was dictated by pragmatism, and what was written of an Australian Congregational church might equally apply to Methodist buildings as

> characterised by confusion. Seeking to avoid any suggestion of altar-worship, the original designers had made the focus of worship a huge organ and in front of it the choir stalls ... The pews were built to last a thousand years and keep you awake through any sermon ...
>
> The adjoining School Hall was also too big. To a child it was a huge, draughty, exciting place, with passages behind the stage and even a route to the roof of the stage.[28]

Thus some of the critical parameters for its buildings were established in the dawn of Methodism: plain, decent and multi-functional, with building types extending beyond the recognisably religious to domestic housing for preachers as well as educational and medical. Yet the argument that they were merely a functional shell within which the transactions of an inner life were conducted is demonstrably

---

[26] Dolbey, *The Architectural Expression of Methodism*, 1–2.
[27] M. Leigh, 'The Upper Burma Wesleyan Mission 1887–1966: A Note on Buildings' (email to the author, February 2011).
[28] S. Firth, 'Strathfield-Homebush Church, 1950–1965: A Recollection', *Church Heritage* (Journal of the Church Record and Historical Society, Uniting Church in Australia), 1:4 (September 1990), 350.

fallacious. The elevated pulpit, to cite one example, both symbolises and actualises the prioritisation of the (biblical) 'word', read and preached. The interior space, as Wright averred, was at least formative and could become transformational.

Wright's English near-contemporary, C. F. A. Voysey was related to the Wesleys (the 'A' stood for Annesley). His architectural principles might be thought close to Methodist ideals: 'his clarity of vision; his refined sense of simplicity; the insistence on harmony and balance in his work and an uncompromising scrutiny of every detail, could all be described as consciously developed family traits'.[29] Ever scrupulous about the absolute integrity of building and design, his iconic style influenced a generation of housing design although late in life he returned to the by then unfashionable Gothic.

A major exponent of the Gothic was Sir George Gilbert Scott, a scion of the Gilbert family of Antigua, stalwarts of early Methodism. The 'Gothic' style cut across the precepts of early Methodist buildings to create a tension which has arguably never entirely been resolved. Following the Reformation 'Gothic' could be regarded as outmoded, eccentric and faintly dissolute, and hardly Christian or Protestant. It was, after all, Goths who had sacked Rome, and Greco-Roman renaissance and reformation had supplanted medieval Gothicism (originally derived from Islamic Spain).[30] Its transformation in the 1830s into *the* Christian style arose with the High Church Oxford Movement and its leading architect was the prodigiously productive A. W. N. Pugin (1812–52),[31] who designed or decorated a swathe of (mostly church, and many Catholic) buildings, and published several influential works including *The True Principles of Pointed or Christian Architecture* (1841).

The impact of the Gothic was sweeping, even among non-conformist bodies generally suspicious of Catholic tendencies. The Wesleyan minister F. J. Jobson originally trained as an architect under Edward Willson,[32] perhaps the father of the movement. His 1850 *Chapel and School Architecture*,[33] followed by Gothic designs for two important Methodist institutions, Westminster College (London) and Kingswood School (Bath), led to this becoming the dominant Methodist style for the remainder of the century, not only in Britain but around the world. Some idea of the rapidity and ubiquity of the international gothicisation of church architecture is evident from a small and simple 1856 Primitive Methodist chapel at Penfield (Adelaide, S. Australia), with its pointed window heads and door.[34]

Two churches which might epitomise Methodist Gothic carry Wesley dedications. Wesley Memorial Methodist Church (1877, Oxford, U.K.) was built

---

[29] W. Hitchmough, *C. F. A. Voysey* (London: Phaidon, 1995), 7.

[30] See Friedman, *The Eighteenth-Century Church in Britain*, 185ff.

[31] R. Hill, *God's Architect: Pugin and the Building of Romantic Britain* (London: Allen Lane, 2007).

[32] 'Jobson, Frederick James, D. D.', in J. A. Vickers (ed.), *A Dictionary of Methodism in Britain and Ireland* (Peterborough: Epworth, 2001).

[33] F. J. Jobson, *Chapel and School Architecture* (London: Hamilton, Adams, 1850).

[34] B. Andrews, *Australian Gothic: The Gothic Revival in Australian Architecture from the 1840s to the 1950s* (Victoria: Melbourne University Press (The Miegunyah Press), 2001), 3.

close by the first (1783) Methodist meeting-house in Oxford, where John Wesley had preached. In Savannah, Wesley Monumental Methodist Church (1875–90, Georgia, U.S.A.) was built on one of the squares the Wesleys would have known. Though similar and contemporary, the styles embody key differences.

The architect of the Oxford church was Charles Bell (1846–99), designer of many Methodist churches, as well as schools such as Kent College, Canterbury[35] and other church and civic buildings. Despite the 'Wesley' dedication there is no Wesleyan reference in design or decoration. Its floor-to-ceiling columns give the interior a verticality which enhanced the original layout of pulpit, choir, organ and pews. The floral features in the windows and on the capitals of the columns link the architecture to the natural world.

The Savannah church, with its steel-reinforced hammerbeam roof retains its original, unpillared interior, while windows and other decoration commemorate not only the Wesleys but historic American Methodist figures. It was possibly styled after the (late medieval) Nieuwe Kerk in, Amsterdam.[36] Yet its interior space is openly rectangular: the Gothic is mostly decorative.

And this represents the tension created by Methodist Gothic, for with few exceptions it is an exuberant (and expensive) decorative style applied to what are fundamentally auditory boxes. Methodism catholicised neither its liturgy nor its ecclesiology. The pulpit remained the focal feature of the building, backed by the choir: table and font occupy subsidiary places. The preached Word and congregational and choral singing outranked the sacrament. Yet its critical significance is that function followed form: the style represented not merely the Catholic or High Church but a moral and cultural formality which was just as true of nonconformity.

The ubiquity of the Gothic is such that a considerable book could be written on the range and variety of its Methodist usage worldwide, as well as what it may have represented in terms of doctrinal understandings and practices – Methodism's and the Oxford Movement's shared territories. From the stylistically precise Metropolitan Church (Capetown, S. Africa, 1878) by Charles Freeman, who was responsible for many of Cape Town's municipal buildings, to free Gothic forms as at Manners Street, Wellington (New Zealand, 1868),[37] it continued through permutations of style into the twentieth century. Highland Park Methodist Church (Dallas, U.S.A., 1926) was 'inspired by [the minister's] dream of a campus cathedral … rich in gothic detail', carried onwards into a twenty-first-century extension.[38] (By contrast, the nearby 1950s Perkins Chapel of Southern Methodist University is in unashamedly eighteenth-century Gibbseian style.)

---

[35] Originally known as the Wesleyan College.
[36] www.wesleymonumental.org (accessed 15 February 2011), which states 'Queen's Kirk in Amsterdam'. The Nieuwe Kerk (New Church, c.1400) is the traditional setting for Dutch coronations.
[37] Anon., 'Methodist Churches in New Zealand: Legacy from Britain', *Proceedings of the New Zealand Wesley Historical Society*, 62 (1995), 23–5.
[38] www.hpumc.org (accessed 1 June 2011).

One single aspect for such a study might be spires or towers,[39] which externally characterise a Gothic composition. Yet for Methodist buildings this – almost unexceptionally – serves only as a skyline presence, a symbolic pointing to the heavens. With no rings of bells, and few clocks, such an aspirational structure is otherwise functionless. So the Methodist use of 'Dissenting Gothic'[40] poses a further issue, for this was an exhibitionist style. As with other Protestant traditions, Methodist buildings had not only been economically modest but closely related to domestic architecture. Persecution, but also a theology which understood the temple of God to be the household of ordinary believers, resulted in unobtrusive buildings. In Wesley's 'New Room', Bristol, the high fenestration was partly protection against the mob – a feature which was not unique. Some early British Primitive Methodist chapels appear to have been designed to be converted to or from houses. Of this, the Gothic was the antithesis.

Late in the nineteenth century the 'arts and crafts' movement reintroduced a preference for the vernacular, styles related to the environment, which did not stand out. In New Zealand, Edmund Anscombe was one who exemplified this transition, a move which was part of a tendency to make religious space more familiar.[41] On a larger front, the 'central halls' movement similarly sought, on a much larger scale, to mimic the music halls (and, later, cinemas) rapidly becoming popular and drawing crowds away from the churches.

In Britain, the Wesleyan connexion marked the new century with a building to signify the church's considerable social presence, opposite Westminster Abbey and the Houses of Parliament. Massive and impressive, Westminster Central Hall (architects Lanchester & Rickards, 1912) in 'French chateau' style provided connexional offices as well as meeting rooms and a hall with a capacity of over 2,000, topped by a vast ferro-concrete dome.

This monumental edifice became the flagship of a string of 'central halls' in cities and large towns in Britain and worldwide – one of the first, and most notable, is that in Sydney, Australia.[42] This 'Forward Movement' sought to recover an original Methodist emphasis on social outreach to the marginalised as integral to the church's mission, in the changed circumstances of urban life. Moreover, its religious spaces were re-shaped for audiences more used to secular entertainment.

Such buildings were therefore multi-functional, generally with a large central auditorium – the 1946 inaugural assembly of the United Nations was held at Westminster Central Hall. The multifarious needs of the central missions, extending to hostels or hospitals, had no identifiable unifying architectural style.

---

[39] Proscribed for dissenting buildings under the Toleration Act 1689; Friedman, *The Eighteenth-Century Church in Britain*, 28.

[40] Cf. C. Binfield, *So Down To Prayers: Studies in English Nonconformity 1780–1920* (London: J. M. Dent, 1977), 145–6.

[41] See C. McCarthy, 'Against 'Churchianity': Edmund Anscombe's Suburban Church Designs', (New Zealand) *Architectural History*, 51 (2009), 170–200.

[42] Originally founded 1885, www.wesleymission.org.au (accessed 17 February 2011).

This movement had a parallel in the U.S.A. in the late twentieth century in the rise of the 'mega-church', although the objective was to offer a neutral environment to the unchurched rather than outreach to the socially marginalised. Willow Creek Community Church (Illinois, 1982), with its strikingly secular appearance, is identified as its first main model.[43] In this movement the Methodists have not been prominent: it is not the purpose of this chapter to discuss this, but to note that it is an architectural development which has not found significant currency in U.S. Methodism, although the world's largest Methodist Church (Kumran, Seoul, S. Korea) may be cited as an example.

Methodist churches in the U.S.A. are numerous and architecturally multifarious. Rowe notes that the 1890s rebuilding of 'Methodism's flagship Christchurch, Pittsburgh' with a Romanesque frontage for an auditory space utilised a plan which integrated the children's activities with the main preaching service, first used at Akron, Ohio:

> Methodists were one of the first to accept the auditorium plan for worship use and the Akron plan was created for a Methodist sunday school in Akron, Ohio. Methodists were deeply involved in the spread of both plans by their newly formed denominational departments of architecture. The two plans shaped the interiors of Methodist churches (and other mainline Protestant churches) for fifty years. Much maligned and misunderstood, auditorium plan churches with Akron style sunday schools represent what may be the most common type of Methodist church building still in use today.[44]

Although much of American Methodism then reverted to the Gothic, in the latter part of the twentieth century a number of experimental church designs have been noted, including hexagonal and semi-circular, even boat-shaped, and utilising modern materials and technology.[45] These trends may also be noted in the United Methodist Church global diaspora.

The very size and spread of Methodism, currently estimated at some 75 million members and 'adherents',[46] demonstrates that even generalisations about its built heritage are ill-advised. Much of its growth has been through the twentieth century, and in the global south where stylistic coherence is less amenable to mapping. The political and social pressures of the century produced a cultural shift in which form

---

[43] A. C. Loveland and O. B. Wheler, *From Meetinghouse to Megachurch: A Material and Cultural History* (Columbia, MO and London: University of Missouri Press, 2003), 120–35.

[44] K. Rowe, *Main Street Monuments: Architectural Form Follows Spiritual Function in Methodist Church Building in late Victorian America* (Madison, NJ: Drew University Press, 1997).

[45] K. Rowe, *The Liturgical Movement and Modern American Church Architecture* (Drew University seminar notes, 2006).

[46] www.worldmethodistcouncil.org (accessed 3 June 2011).

became shaped, or even dictated, by function, as well as the dominance of new materials, steel, concrete and plastics.

Of these the Bauhaus was precursor, which style the architect Wells Coates (1895–1958) brought to his (mostly domestic) projects. Brought up in Japan, son of Canadian Methodist missionaries, his mother apparently studied architecture under the doyen of Chicago skyscraper designer Louis Sullivan. The minimalist principles Coates embraced might relate to his religious background as well as to Japanese or other influences. As his daughter was to write: 'The Methodist missionary message of Wells' youth had been transformed into a deeply felt radical ethos.'[47]

Coates' career, rejecting the stultifying weight of nineteenth-century traditionalism and turning to clean, streamlined design, was axiomatic of the ambiguity to which the denomination – and indeed churches generally – found itself exposed with stark twentieth-century modernity. As individuals and communities faced rapid change in virtually every sector of life, architecture became a language through which to side with the past or meet new challenges, evidence for which can be seen in many Methodist buildings.

## Artefacts: Material Objects

A visit to the Methodist Museum in London will readily indicate the numbers and variety of material objects relating to Methodism, ranging from the large and obvious – pulpits and pews – to the small and ephemeral, such as the 'class ticket'. As with all religious movements, Methodism has constructed a material environment which is at once the familiar furniture for its inhabitants, yet may be a barrier to the outsider.[48] Indeed, probably for most Methodists their religious life was focused, not on great movements, theological nuances or liturgical niceties, but on the people and place of the week-by-week life of their local chapel.

Artefacts, like Methodist buildings, covers a multitude of things. These might, from the viewpoint of research, be classified straightforwardly into those for which there is existing literature and those for which there is not. The latter are in the preponderance: it is intriguing that to some key areas so little scholarly or other consideration appears to have been given. While, for instance, the words and music of hymnody have received extensive attention, negligible interest has been directed to the mechanics of the production, sale and use of Methodist hymnals. Preaching is prominent in Methodist worship but where are the studies of pulpits (or – hitherto – pews[49]) and their usage?

---

[47] L. Cohn, *The Door to a Secret Room: A Portrait of Wells Coates* (Aldershot: Scolar, 1999), 39.
[48] See P. Collins and P. Dandelion, 'Wrapped Attention: Revelation and Concealment in Nonconformism', in E. Arweck and W. Keenan (eds), *Materializing Religion: Expression, Performance and Ritual* (Aldershot: Ashgate, 2006), 45–61.
[49] T. Cooper and S. Brown (eds), *Pews, Benches and Chairs: Church Sseating in England from the Fourteenth Century to the Present* (Donington: Tyas (for The Ecclesiological Society), 2011).

Two influential factors may be discerned in the level of attention paid in this area. The first is collectability; the second, relevance to mainstream research interests. So, with reference to the first, one area to have received attention is that of ceramics.[50] These range from commemorative pottery and china, including busts and statuettes of Wesley, to tableware produced for chapels, which was generally marked with the chapel name. There are arguably three reasons for this. The first is its ubiquity, the 'ware' found its way into the experience of Methodists throughout the nineteenth and twentieth centuries, as shared meals were focal to chapel life. The second is that, in Britain, the centre of production was in the Potteries area of the English Midlands, around Stoke-on-Trent, heavily industrialised and a stronghold of Methodism.[51] Further, the distribution networks, often through itinerant peddlers or fairs, also may have served an evangelistic role. Thirdly, the variety of the genre, with greater and lesser differences in style, inscription and condition, makes it eminently appealing to collectors.

The phenomenon of 'Wesleyana' marks Methodism aside from most other Christian traditions. Neither Lutherans, Calvinists, Jesuits nor Franciscans make such play of the image of their founding father. Yet busts, plaques, plates, statuettes and pulpit figures of Wesley were extensively produced, circulated and displayed through Methodism in the nineteenth century. These, together with visual images, reinforced the denominational creation myth of providential causality that Wesley himself had arguably originated as he described himself as 'a brand plucked as from the burning'. By comparison, the incidence of other ceramics is limited. Yet the implications of the totemic place of Wesleyana is a subject which has received little or no critical attention.

While decorated tableware for shared meals or artefacts for display are widespread, not only in Methodism, something peculiar to the British Methodist system is the circuit plan. The evolving system of itinerant and local (later ministerial and lay) preachers, operating in growing numbers of places of worship, grouped in 'circuits', led by the 1770s to the production of a simple matrix for the quarterly scheme of appointments. This developed into a kind of directory, to include preachers' addresses, details of the chapels and other information. For an active Methodist this was an indispensable guide (and diary) to their social, and often working, networks – some were printed on fabric to ensure durability as they might be carried in working clothing and in all weathers.

These are more closely relevant to mainstream research interests, the second area noted above, for historically their usefulness as a source can be considerable. Hundreds of circuits, each issuing four plans annually, over nearly a quarter-millennium indicates the scope of the research field, as well as archival issues. The circuit plan has generated its own specialist research society of Cirplanologists,

---

[50] See R. Lee, *Wesleyana and Methodist Pottery* (Lee: Wembley, 1988); J. Roberson, *Treasures of the World Methodist Museum* (Lake Junaluska: World Methodist Council, c. 1983); also Donald Ryan has compiled catalogues of Wesleyana at several Methodist Heritage sites in Britain.

[51] J. M. Turner, *John Wesley: The Evangelical Revival and the Rise of Methodism in England* (Peterborough: Epworth, 2002), 170ff.

whose publications are hugely useful in understanding and interpreting these documents.[52] But as artefacts they were embellished by printers and sometimes framed for display while special plans – a preacher's first services, for instance – were carefully preserved.

In similar vein are class tickets. The 'class meeting' was the cell group of which membership was vital. This was the Methodist's closest family in the church: to lapse in attendance was to risk being struck off membership of the 'society', the larger unit. Without a valid class ticket one was not admitted to the sacrament of Communion (although Communion tokens were also issued but are much rarer).[53] Class tickets were plentiful objects; they varied in decoration and style; were kept, collected and valued. Yet they are little studied.

'Methodism's infatuation with education and the cultivation of the mind'[54] was mirrored in its publishing, which was far from restricted to religious books. Yet a book is also a material object: a hymnal must be portable and durable while a pulpit Bible may be large, symbolically visible and finely bound. It may be wise not to judge a book by its cover, yet outward appearance plays a part in the appeal to a potential purchaser. It would seem that some Wesleyan Book Stewards paid closer attention to the physical presentation of their products than others, so the design and manufacture of books are again an overlooked sector of Methodism's material culture, as are the media of a technological age.

While Methodism's artefacts were often domestic, church furnishings might be cited (as already hinted) as a significantly under-researched area. There seems little literature or research on pulpits, pews, stained glass, commemorative plaques or other facets which typify the worshipping environment of Methodism. Dolbey, cited above, has nothing, nor does the *Dictionary of Methodism* have an entry on either. The study of 'material culture', using 'things' as sources for historical research, is still an emerging field, particularly around religion, which in part explains the paucity of research and writing in this area. The discourse of material culture seeks to interrogate not simply the object but its usage and wider social significance. However, it is a field with its own journal,[55] and one which is likely to grow in significance. As a research area this is promising territory.

# Art

Against the sheer numbers of Methodist buildings which have dictated the predominance of architecture in this chapter, the area of art cannot command

---

[52] *Cirplan*, from 1955.
[53] J. C. Bowmer, *The Sacrament of the Lord's Supper in Early Methodism* (London: A & C Black (Dacre Press), 1951), 115ff.
[54] Hempton, *Empire of the Spirit* , 54.
[55] S. B. Plate, D. Goa, D. Morgan and C. Paine (eds), *material religion: the journal of objects, art and belief* (Oxford: Berg).

comparable attention, although sources are more plentiful than those relating to artefacts.[56] There have been Methodist artists, although generally few and far between, who have achieved public recognition. Although artistic depictions of Methodist scenes are not manifold, portraits of key individuals are. While Methodism has not developed a tradition of patronage, yet there is art in Methodist settings. This section will attempt to delineate those three areas.

If in architecture consideration has been given to the transformative nature of structures and space, the creation, perception and impact of works of art are predicated upon a triangulation between artist, subject and audience. On this John Wesley himself, of whom there is a bewildering multiplicity of representations, two- and three-dimensional, as a subject offers an intriguing example. He was a man clearly careful to promote and guard a particular image of himself, yet he seemed to have been unconcerned about visual depictions. 'I yielded to the importunity of a painter'[57] is a typical comment, as if he had no part in the process. Wesley seems to have lacked visual astuteness, and images of him have a semblance of caricature about them. But late in life he had the sculptor Enoch Wood adjust the 'melancholy expression'[58] on his bust while he proudly presented to Adam Clarke's wife a 'fine large print of himself', although she thought 'it is by no means a striking likeness'.[59]

This print had been engraved by the evangelical Jonathan Spilsbury[60] from the portrait by George Romney, a libertarian freethinker who supported the French revolution that year and probably had little empathy with Wesley, whose sittings took place early on four consecutive winter Monday mornings.[61] Indeed, it has been proposed that Romney actually depicted Wesley as a bulky Falstaff, which Spilsbury overpainted.[62] So the triangulation between sitter or subject, artist and audience is far from straightforward.

The extensive and complex matter of the iconography of the 'founder of Methodism' could exemplify and illustrate many aspects of Methodism's engagement with art. Images of the 'founder of Methodism' have an iconic, and sometimes ambivalent, place within the tradition and, as a director of the National Portrait Gallery has noted, 'a detailed critical survey of the portraiture is overdue'.[63] Nevertheless, it will be more appropriate to consider Methodism and art in a wider perspective.

---

[56] For an overview in this area see P. Forsaith 'Methodism and its Images', in Yrigoyen, *T&T Clark Companion to Methodism*, 350–68.

[57] J. Wesley, *Journal*, 22 December 1787, *WJW* 24 (Journals and Diaries VII), 68.

[58] Enoch Wood to Adam Clarke, 6 October 1830, ms. in United Library, Garrett Theological Seminary, IL, U.S.A.

[59] Mrs Mary Clarke to Miss Cottie, 11 August 1789, in M. A. Clarke Smith, *Mrs. Adam Clarke, Her Character and Correspondence* (London: Partridge & Oakey, 1851), 76.

[60] See C. Yeldham, *Maria Spilsbury (1776–1820): Artist and Evangelical* (Farnham: Ashgate, 2010).

[61] D. A. Cross, *A Striking Likeness: The Life of George Romney* (Aldershot: Ashgate, 2000), 167–9.

[62] See P. Forsaith, 'The Romney Portrait of John Wesley', *Methodist History*, XLVII:4 (July 2004), 251–5.

[63] J. Kerslake, *Early Georgian Portraits* (London: HMSO, 1977), 301.

The affiliation of particular artists with Methodism is not always straightforward. John Russell, sometimes cited as the first Methodist Royal Academician,[64] while a friend to Charles Wesley's family, was more inclined to the Calvinistic Methodists. The successful American artist John Wesley Jarvis (1781–1839), named after his great-uncle,[65] had little other connection with the movement. However, James Barton Longacre (1794–1869), engraver to the U.S. Mint, was a lifelong member.[66] In Britain John Jackson R.A.(1778–1831) was a successful society portraitist and Wesleyan Methodist.

Antje Matthews has pointed out that the transition between eighteenth and nineteenth centuries marked the onset of a cultural segregation: John Russell (and his friend, sculptor John Bacon) saw little tension between their art and their religion; for both their sons there was an inherent contradiction and William Russell 'swore an oath not to touch brush and palette again'.[67] Such hostility between church and art is particularly evident in the life of the pre-Raphaelite associate James Smetham (1821–89), whose mental illness was arguably exacerbated by his divided loyalties (as well as his failure to sell successfully),[68] although his contemporary, successful seascape painter James Clarke Hook (1819–1907) sat more comfortably in both spheres.

In an article of 1895 W. G. Beardmore in the (British) *Wesleyan Methodist Magazine* reviewed artists of that closing century it numbered within its church ('who have carried off academic renown').[69] But he also offered insights into that dominant Methodist denomination's attitudes to art. Having expiated on the virtues of pious art in Christian history he continued: 'In these ancient and hoary and almost classic glories, our Church has no part – except that of inheritance.'[70]

Those listed had demonstrated both success and denominational loyalty: Smetham's difficulties were omitted as were G. P. Everett-Green's links with the dissident minister James Everett. All are male: the article closes with a demure anonymous mention of 'two young lady students … whose gifts will one day revive contemporary honours'.[71]

Two British Methodist contributors to art in Australia were Marshall Claxton and Herbert Beecroft. Claxton (1813–81) exhibited many works at the Royal Academy, including 'Holy Triumph' (Wesley's deathbed scene), although he was unsuccessful in competitions for the murals in the new Houses of Parliament. In

---

[64] W. B. Brash, 'John Russell R.A.', *Proceedings of the Wesley Historical Society*, xxv, 52–56.

[65] John Wesley's sister Anne was his grandmother (L. D. Case, 'Jarvis, John Wesley', in N. B. Harman (ed.), *Encyclopaedia of World Methodism* (Nashville, TN, United Methodist Publishing House, 1974), 1262–3.

[66] N. B. H., 'Longacre, James Barton', in Harman (ed.), *Encyclopaedia of World Methodism*, 1449–50.

[67] A. Matthews, 'John Russell (1745–1806) and the Impact of Evangelicalism and Natural Theology on Artistic Practice' (unpubl. PhD thesis, University of Leicester, 2005), 163.

[68] S. Casteras, *James Smetham: Artist, Author, Pre-Raphaelite Associate* (Aldershot: Scolar, 1995).

[69] W. G. Beardmore, 'Wesleyan Artists, Past and Present', *Wesleyan Methodist Magazine*, vol. CXVIII, 1895, 583–90, 649–57.

[70] Ibid., 569.

[71] Ibid., 657.

1850 he went to Australia, introducing history-painting to the continent, but his pictures largely went unsold and his projected art academy was not realised.[72]

By contrast, Beecroft (1864–1951) set up as a portrait painter and caricaturist entertainer in his home town of Reading, then in London, before emigrating to Australia in 1905 where he again established himself successfully. He produced religious pictures and also tracts, with more masculine depictions of Christ than those familiar from pre-Raphaelite imagery in Britain. His most famous picture, which became widely reproduced for evangelistic purposes, was 'And Jesus Looked at Peter…'.[73]

The twentieth century brought two successful society painters who were Methodists, also the illustrator Henry Tidmarsh.[74] Arthur Trevivian Nowell (1862–1940)[75] and Frank Salisbury (1874–1962)[76] were contemporaries although seem not to have had personal or professional links. But the century also brought modern art to which all three were resistant (and Salisbury in particular reviled) which, with its secularity and challenge to the establishment of which Methodism was now part, set itself against many tenets of religious belief. Methodist practitioners of art have largely been absent in modernist and following schools.

One artist who was not reticent to depict Methodism was W. H. Y. Titcomb, whose oeuvre includes religious scenes in the Methodist stronghold of West Cornwall such as 'Primitive Methodists at Prayer'.[77] An exception to the general paucity of images of Methodist scenes might be noted among missionaries who used graphic representation as well as the camera to record their work and surroundings.

Depictions of Methodist scenes may be unusual, and three images often understood to represent early Wesleyan Methodist preaching are demonstrably not so.[78] However, a cult of personality, a feature of Protestantism, has been evident in Methodism from John Wesley himself. Images of Methodist personalities are manifold and were significant features of denominational life. The *Arminian Magazine*,[79] carried totemic frontispiece portrait prints from the outset which soon became artistically competent. Examples were collected and displayed in

---

[72] 'Claxton, Marshall', *Oxford Dictionary of National Biography* (online http://www.oxforddnb.com/) (henceforth *ODNB*).

[73] E. M. Waugh, *Lawrence Herbert Beecroft: An Entertaining Artist* (Sydney: Randwick and District Historical Society, 1997).

[74] R. Hyde, *The Streets of London: Evocative Watercolours by H. E. Tidmarsh* (Colchester: Red Scorpion, 1993).

[75] 'A. T. Nowell', *ODNB*.

[76] N. McMurray, *Frank O. Salisbury, Painter Laureate* (1st Books Library, 2003).

[77] D. Tovey, *W. H. Y. Titcomb* (2 vols) (Tewkesbury: Wilson, 2003), i, 46–9, pl.6.

[78] [Attrib.] Francis Hayman, 'John Wesley Preaching at Old Cripplegate Church' (Dr Johnson's house, London); Phillip de Loutherbourg, 'A Midsummer Afternoon with a Methodist Preacher' (National Gallery of Canada, Ottawa, NGC4057); Print: 'John Wesley and Preachers in the City Road Chapel, 1779'.

[79] First published in 1778, becoming the *Methodist Magazine* in 1798 and the *Wesleyan Methodist Magazine* in 1822.

Grangerised formats.[80] The extent to which such a personalisation told against Methodist spiritual or democratic principles is an interesting question.

Methodism's engagement with art may have been rarely official or consistent but possibly one of the most surprising has been the establishment and use of the British Methodist Church's outstanding Collection of Modern Art. Comprising works which represent aspects of the Christian narrative, including several abstracts, it includes pieces by such significant artists as Edward Burra, Elisabeth Frink, Eric Gill, William Roberts and Graham Sutherland – none of whom was Methodist. Largely the achievement of Dr. John M. Gibbs in the 1960s, it is exhibited regularly as a medium of the church's mission, and represents a leading example of patronage of art in a Methodist context.

The Collection has flourished as interest in the visual and creative arts has grown and continues to grow. No longer are prohibitions or discouragement the normative response to art and culture across Methodism. Beardmore's 1895 article, with its faint patronising of art and artists, could hardly have been written a century later.

# Conclusion

A critical theme which has emerged in this chapter has been to note certain tensions which have subsisted in Methodism relating to both its own cultural and material expressions as well as those of the environments in which it has subsisted. A further tension is created by the differentiation of Methodism's cultural expressions into built, material and visual heritage, distinctions which may at times be arbitrary and artificial. Nevertheless this offers a route into intersecting disciplines and dialogues which can both inform studies of Methodism's heritage as well as bringing this often neglected aspect of cultural history into the mainstream.

Yet in order for this transition to be enabled, those who engage with Methodism's cultural past have a two-fold task. There is both a need to establish a solid body of competent research accessible to wider scholarship, as well as an imperative of serious engagement with the discourses of cultural study. Without these, Methodism may well continue to fail to be taken seriously beyond its own borders. It could continue to be thought, as has been suggested of other areas of Protestantism, that Methodism has suffered from 'severe visual anorexia';[81] that any appetite towards aspirational, artistic or material culture has been delusional, and responded to by an emetic urge triggered by the philistinism with which Methodism has tended to be popularly associated.

---

[80] See M. Pointon, *Hanging the Head: Portraiture and Social Formation in Eighteenth-Century England* (New Haven, CT and London: Yale University Press, 1993), 53ff.

[81] See P. Collinson, *The Birthpangs of Protestant England* (Basingstoke: Palgrave-Macmillan, 1988), 119. I am indebted to Prof. John Coffey for this reference.

Eighteenth-century English religion, the seedbed of Methodism, is one area which has latterly been treated more seriously by cultural historians.[82] Recent decades have generally seen more readiness to relate religion to the broader cultural life of society; and among students of the churches, including Methodism, the denominational interface with the worlds of art, design and material culture is significant. A conference today entitled 'Methodism in its Cultural Milieu' would likely have a very different complexion than the so-titled Wesley Historical Society's centenary conference in 1993, of which only one paper might be considered 'material'.[83] A decade ago a book such as this might not even have considered including an essay on Methodism's material or cultural aspects, yet they inform not only internal denominational narratives but wider studies of religion and culture.

The extent of Methodism's enculturation into the environments in which it has taken root; or whether, indeed, it has been counter-cultural, are questions which follow from the discussions in this chapter. But in the compass which has been its scope it should have become evident that while Methodism can hardly lay claim to prominence in cultural fields, nevertheless it has not been absent and there are significant aspects of its life which remain under-researched. Can a tacit assumption remain that not much is written because there is not much to write about? I hope not.

---

[82] See Black, *A Subject for Taste*, 83ff.
[83] R. Glen, 'The Fate of John Wesley in English Satiric Prints', in T. S. A. Macquiban (ed.), *Methodism in its Cultural Milieu* (Oxford: Applied Theology Press, 1994), 35–43.

# Methodism and Education

## John T. Smith

John Wesley once claimed that if the Methodists were not a reading people the work of grace would die out in a generation. Thirty years ago Frank Pritchard described Wesley's pragmatism, seeing the need for the teaching of reading to enable Bible study for both preachers and congregations.[1] He established both the Orphan House in Newcastle, and Kingswood school, supported the Grey Coat Charity School in Oxford in the 1720s and a school in Georgia. His sermons 'On Obedience to Parents' and 'On the Education of Children', and his 'Thoughts on the Manner of Educating Children' of 1783 stressed the centrality of religion in education.

Rupert Davies describes John Wesley as 'a great collector of other people's ideas',[2] and J. Estep describes him as a 'synthesizer' of educational theories, picking and choosing what fitted a situation.[3] There is general agreement on the influence of his mother, Susanna, whose long letter on education from the 1730s was preserved in his journal.[4] She was herself influenced by the ideas of John Locke, most famously stressing the need for 'breaking the will' to ensure conformity of the child's behaviour to that of the parents until it could make informed decisions. Martha Bowden argues that this originated from Susanna's very practical concerns of regulating a household of nine children, and that it did not imply the extinction of personality, but rather the elimination of selfishness.[5] Davies similarly claims

---

[1] F. C. Pritchard, 'Education', in R. Davies (ed.), *The History of the Methodist Church in Great Britain* (London: Epworth Press, 1983), iii, 279.

[2] R. Davies, 'John Wesley, Kingswood and Kingswood School', *Wesleyan Historical Society Bristol Branch Bulletin*, 51 (1988), 11.

[3] J. R. Estep, 'John Wesley's Philosophy of Formal Childhood Education', *Christian Education Journal*, (1997), 44.

[4] E. L. Towns, 'John Wesley and Religious Education', *Religious Education*, 65:4 (1970), 318–28; H. Rack, 'John Wesley', in J. A. Palmer (ed.), *Fifty Major Thinkers on Education* (London: Routledge, 2001), 50–58; D. Tranter, 'John Wesley and the Education of Children', in T.Macquiban (ed.), *Issues in Education: Some Methodist Perspectives* (Oxford: Applied Theology Press, 1996), 17–40.

[5] M. F. Bowden, 'Susanna Wesley's Educational Method', *Journal of the Canadian Historical Society*, 44 (2002), 60.

that the target was to undermine the 'self-will' in children.[6] Wesley himself advised close supervision, believing that children would be ruined by free play, a reaction, according to Elmer Towns, to his own experiences as a victim of bullying at school. Alfred Body discerned the influence of Moravian schools visited by Wesley, and the German belief that 'those who play when they are young, will play when they are old'.[7] Whatever the motivation, Towns has shown the ensuing 'marked resemblance in expression' in the works of Locke and Wesley.[8]

Richard Heitzenrater places Wesley within the contemporary theological debate on the innate innocence or depravity of children.[9] Wesley rejected Rousseau's philosophy of childhood innocence, claiming 'a more consummate coxcomb never saw the sun!'[10] Donald Tranter and Henry Rack use his instructions to Kingswood to explain his view that the child inherited Adam's sinful nature, that salvation could not come from education *per se*, and 'all our wisdom will not even make them [children] *understand* much less *feel*, the things of God.'[11] Gary Best quotes Wesley's own words:

> The bias of nature is set the wrong way. Education is designed to set it right. This, by the grace of God, is to turn the bias from self-will, pride, anger, revenge and the love of the world, to resignation, lowliness, meekness, and the love of God. And from the moment we perceive any of those evil roots springing up, it is our business immediately to check their growth, if we cannot root them out.[12]

However, while baptism might infuse grace, children had to be protected from 'contamination during their helpless years' to 'build character'.[13] Religious instruction should thus begin with 'the dawn of reason'.[14]

The influence of other philosophers has featured in recent writings. Tranter and Towns outline the significant differences with the views of Comenius, the Dutch educationalist, who believed that all good things existed in children and education was thus 'to cultivate and not to transform'. He recognised that children had different aptitudes and learned at different speeds. While some could 'progress in abstract science', others had 'as little aptitude for practical subjects as an ass playing

---

[6] Davies, 'John Wesley, Kingswood and Kingswood School', 10.

[7] Towns, 'John Wesley and Religious Education', 327.

[8] Ibid., 320. A. N. Body, *John Wesley and Education* (London: Epworth Press, 1936) showed the similarities in Wesley's and Locke's *Some Thoughts concerning Education*.

[9] R. P. Heitzenrater, 'Wesley and Education', in S. J. Hels (ed.), *Methodism and Education: From Roots to Fulfilment* (Nashville, TN: General Board of Higher Education and Ministry, United Methodist Church, 2000), 1–13; R. P. Heitzenrater, 'John Wesley and Education', in M. J. Bunge (ed.), *The Child in Christian Thought* (Grand Rapids, MI: W. B. Eerdmans, 2001), 279–99.

[10] Heitzenrater, 'Wesley and Education', 8.

[11] Rack, 'John Wesley', 51.

[12] G. M. Best, 'Wesley and Kingswood', in Hels (ed.), *Methodism and Education*, 37.

[13] Towns, 'John Wesley and Religious Education', 322.

[14] Ibid., 324.

the lyre'. Wesley, however, had little time for such individuality in children. While Comenius advocated games and nature study, Wesley discouraged learning by investigation, maintaining that talk of nature could lead children into atheism.[15] Both accepted the need for repetition in teaching, Wesley advising that 'you had to tell a child the same thing ten times over or you do nothing'.[16] However, he deplored the 'common but accursed way' of children learning parrot-fashion, and wanted children to understand 'every single sentence which they read'.[17]

Wesley nonetheless valued education, accepting that the thirst for knowledge was natural in man, but rejecting any intellectual endeavour that failed to reinforce theological understanding. Methodist reading was confined to works which he considered useful, to be read in the order he advised, with 'no room for diversions inspired by curiosity'.[18] Although he placed Newton's *Principia* on the reading list for his academic course, he warned that a deep study of mathematics, arithmetic or algebra might lead to a questioning of faith. Reason alone was incapable of producing faith and education was regarded as reason 'learned at second hand, which is, as far as it can, to supply the loss of original perfection'.[19] Heitzenrater concludes that, for Wesley, knowledge was not 'a purely intellectual attribute but rather a channel of self-understanding', which was itself crucial for salvation.[20]

## Kingswood

Wesley's first foundation, Kingswood, which opened in 1749, has been featured in many recent studies. Its origins are shown by Michael Bishop to lie in George Whitefield's plan to educate the godless coalminers of Kingswood in Bristol. He argues that Wesley himself intended a complex of four schools rather than a single institution, initially a boys' school and a girls' school, boarding and day.[21] With other writers, John Barrett points to Wesley's desire that Kingswood 'shield children from the corrupting influence of much of their environment' and showed his revulsion against the 'idleness and laxity of contemporary public schools … nurseries of all manner of wickedness'.[22] The breadth of its curriculum was exceptionally wide, supposedly 'every branch of useful learning', and, according to Barrett, rested on Wesley's insistence that 'education is a search for truth' and an 'exploration into

---

[15] Tranter, 'John Wesley', 28.
[16] Towns, 'John Wesley and Religious Education', 325.
[17] Ibid., 325.
[18] Tranter, 'John Wesley', 28.
[19] Rack, 'John Wesley', 51.
[20] Heitzenrater, 'Wesley and Education', 10.
[21] M. Bishop, 'Wesley and his Kingswood Schools', in J. H. Lenton (ed.), *Vital Piety and Learning: Methodism and Education –Papers Given at the 2002 Conference of the Wesley Historical Society* (Oxford: Applied Theology Press, 2005), 16–24.
[22] J. Barrett, 'The Methodist Church and Education in Britain', in Hels (ed.), *Methodism and Education*, 24.

God'.[23] However, Gary Best cautions that the pursuit of knowledge for its own sake was seen to encourage boys to 'probe God's mysteries irreverently'.[24]

Best has described Kingswood's progress through the generations in *Continuity and Change*[25] and in 'Wesley and Kingswood'.[26] In order to shield the school from the world, no child over the age of twelve was accepted, as Wesley judged that by then he or she would have been already corrupted by the world.[27] Best describes the rigidity of the routine. One of Wesley's objections to the schools of his day was the tendency to let children do as they wished outside the classroom, exposing them to 'idleness and all manner of vice'.[28] Industriousness was a 'sign of moral character'. Kingswood pupils came for two years without holidays. Best contrasts this rigidity with Wesley's own good humour with children and with the tempering of his views after 1788, in 'A Thought on the Manner of Educating Children', advocating 'softness and gentleness' in teaching and that religious education needed to be prescribed in terms of 'humility, gentleness, patience, long-suffering, contentedness'.[29]

In America, Wesley's Methodist 'bishops' both believed in the expansion of schools. They together established Cokebury on similar lines to Kingswood. Their General Conference of 1828 encouraged the growth of classical schools for 'literature, morality, industry and a practical knowledge of the arts'. However, some preachers here fiercely resisted this, one calling students 'the greatest drones in the Gospel ministry, idlers in the vineyard, useless cucumbers of the ground who ever afflicted and cursed the Church'. As this Mr Reece claimed, 'larnin isn't religion, and eddication don't give a man the power of the spirit. It is grace and gifts that furnish the real live coals from off the altar.'[30]

## Sunday Schools

John Wesley's work in teaching children in Savannah in Georgia in 1737 is frequently cited as the first American Sunday school.[31] In England, he felt such activity was 'one of the noblest specimens of charity' since the Norman Conquest and the great means of reviving religion throughout the nation. Wesleyans were particularly

---

[23] Ibid., 26.
[24] Best, 'Wesley and Kingswood', 48.
[25] G. M. Best, *Continuity and Change: A History of Kingswood School, 1748–1998* (Bath: Kingswood School, 1998).
[26] Best, 'Wesley and Kingswood', 37–55.
[27] Ibid., 44.
[28] Ibid., 45.
[29] Ibid., 46, 51.
[30] T. Macquiban, 'Body, Mind and Spirit: Westminster College's Contribution to Higher Education', in C. E. Joynes (ed.), *The Quest for Wisdom: Essays in Honour of Philip Budd* (Cambridge: Orchard Academic Press, 2002), 92.
[31] Towns, 'John Wesley and Religious Education', 327.

active in the early stages of the movement – with 30 per cent of all Sunday scholars by 1851, in comparison to the Anglicans' 42 per cent.[32] Their profusion in America gave rise to the 'Akron Plan' design of churches, with folding wooden partitions which could separate the Sunday school space from the main church.[33] Neil Semple describes the growth of Canadian Methodist Sunday schools after the mid nineteenth century as 'truly remarkable'.[34] In Central Canada, Wesleyan Sunday schools had taught 175,000 students by 1883 and in Atlantic Canada they had 25,518 scholars by the time of the union of the Methodist Episcopal Church, the Bible Christian Church and the Primitive Methodist Church in 1884. The United Methodist Church boasted over 2,600 Sunday schools and over 191,000 scholars by 1886 and over 3,800 schools and over 420,000 scholars by 1915. Hempton sees these schools reflecting 'many of the tensions of the early nineteenth century, including class conflict, anticlericalism, anti-centralisation and sectarianism'.[35] He also points to the wide diversity of the Sunday schools themselves.[36] These themes are featured in recent scholarship.

Such establishments were traditionally viewed in Britain as a means of class control, often provided by industrialists to pacify their workers. Patrick Joyce, for example, claims through his study of records in the towns of northern England that they were managed by the middle classes.[37] Malcolm Dick claims that they were conservative and evangelical institutions 'promoted and staffed by individuals from social classes which were higher than those of the scholars who attended them, and espousing an ideology which attacked the allegedly depraved behaviour and radical inclinations of the poor'.[38] In 1985 however, Walter Laqueur challenged these views. Utilising the minutes of teachers' meetings in the north of England, he propounded the thesis that they were predominantly working-class institutions 'taught primarily by working-class teachers in schools largely financed and sometimes also run, by working-class men and women'.[39] Their teachers determined internal school policies and a broadening of their financial support made them less dependent on benefactors. Within two decades of their foundation, they had become 'one strand of a uniquely working class constellation'.[40] Ronald

---

[32] D. Hempton, *Methodism and Politics in British Society, 1750–1850* (London: Hutchinson, 1984), 90.

[33] K. Cracknell and S. J. White, *An Introduction to World Methodism* (Cambridge: Cambridge University Press, 2005), 134.

[34] N. Semple, *The Lord's Dominion: The History of Canadian Methodism* (Montreal: McGill-Queen's University Press, 1996), 371.

[35] D. Hempton, *The Religion of the People: Methodism and Popular Religion c.1750–1900* (London: Routledge, 1996), 95.

[36] Hempton, *Methodism and Politics*, 88.

[37] P. Joyce, *Work, Society and Politics: The Culture of the FactoryiIn Late Victorian England* (London: Methuen, 1982).

[38] Dick quoted in Hempton, *Methodism and Politics*, 88.

[39] T. W. Laqueur, *Religion and Respectability: Sunday Schools and Working Class Culture, 1780–1950* (London: Yale University Press, 1976).

[40] Ibid.

Coxford has investigated the occupations of the teachers of Sun Lane Methodist Sunday School in New Catton in the period 1841 to 1856 and finds them to be predominantly working class.[41] The teachers subscribed one penny per month to the school's Benevolent Fund (for sick scholars) and small sums were given to sick teachers, showing something of their own parlous financial position. Extensions to schoolrooms were aided by J. Colman (the mustard manufacturer), although fundraising from teachers and scholars allowed Colman to deny any control over the school.[42] Keith Snell has addressed the class issue in his recent quantitative analysis of the statistics from the 1851 Religious Census (which gave attendances on Census Sunday).[43] He finds schools 'crucial venues for the public activities of lower and middle-class women', who were often their founders, managing finances, holding offices and acting as teachers.[44] Anglican schools dominated the field, with parishes connected to landed estates having the highest indexes of attendance, while Primitive Methodism 'perhaps the most proletarian denomination' is shown to be negligible as a provider of Sunday School education.[45] Snell thus concludes that paternalistic parishes, of all denominations, established effective Sunday Schools, although examples of 'humble people' helping to organise schools could be found, particularly in Lancashire.[46]

Hempton, in his investigation of Jabez Bunting's papers, describes the struggle to impose central control.[47] The 'General Principles and Rules' of 1827 required all Sunday schools to be connected to a chapel.[48] Bunting faced a formidable task in trying to impose Methodist discipline over such schools, characterised by the issue of the teaching of writing. Reading was accepted as essential for Bible study, but writing was seen by some as too utilitarian for the Sabbath. Bunting persuaded the 1809 Conference to accept that all new schools should limit writing tuition to weekdays, although this ban was only partly successful and was repeated in 1814 and 1827. Hempton points out that every northern circuit in the period 1810–30

---

[41] R. Coxford, 'A Working Class Sunday School?', *Proceedings of Wesley Historical Society*, 54 (2003–4), 11–16.

[42] Ibid., 15.

[43] K. D. M. Snell, 'The Sunday School Movement in England and Wales: Child Labour, Denominational Control and Working-Class Culture', *Past and Present*, 164 (August 1999), 122–68.

[44] Ibid., 131.

[45] Ibid., 148. Of 2,323 Anglican parishes, 1,679 (72.3 per cent) had Sunday schools. Welsh Calvinistic Methodists dominated Anglesey and Caernarvonshire with 60 per cent of total attendances.

[46] Ibid., 164. Welsh Sunday-schools appear independent of landowning structures.

[47] Hempton, *The Religion of the People*, 96.

[48] Hempton, *Methodism and Politics*, 90. Bunting advocated 'denominational drill' to control children, as six of the seventeen Luddites hanged at York in 1813 were sons of Methodists. Cf. J. A. Hargreaves, 'Methodist Attitudes to Education and Youth, 1800–2000', in D. Bebbington and T. Larsen (eds), *Modern Christianity and Cultural Aspirations* (Sheffield: Sheffield Academic Press, 2004), 202–3.

was riddled with angry clashes over the issue.[49] By the 1840s the local circuits had capitulated. Chris Hughes Smith's recent analysis of the 1827 Rules drawn up by the Grimsby circuit, which barred Sabbath writing lessons, shows the strong recommendation 'that writing, and the elements of arithmetic, shall be taught to the elder scholars, both male and female, on one or more week-day evenings, as a reward for their regular attendance and good conduct on the Sabbath'.[50] He shows from Selly Oak that, although secular education was subordinate to the religious instruction, it was nevertheless important in this school.

David Harvey et al. have explored the relationship between the Sunday school parades, which began in the eighteenth century, in the formation of religious identity in Cornwall.[51] These promoted Methodism as respectable, emphasising 'order, continence, propriety, sobriety, seemliness and rectitude, which ensured, if not the patronage of the ruling elite, then at least their acquiescence'.[52] The orderly use of public space contrasted with 'the perceived chaotic use of public space evidenced by carnivals'.[53] The Sunday school (and Methodism itself) was thus portrayed as disciplined, temperate and respecting religious and secular authority. Moreover, as the tea treats were open to outsiders, they attracted non-attending children into membership. Using extant records of Sunday schools, as well as public reports, Harvey reconstructs several such parades. That at Morvah in 1836 passed through all the important areas of the parish, terminating on the most conspicuous hill, which was highly visible throughout the whole area.[54] That at Camborne in 1880 had 6,000 Methodists from five different denominations, with a rigid hierarchy in the march, led by the Wesleyans, followed by other Methodist denominations in numerical order. In Penzance in 1890 scholars gathered from outlying areas, some walking over six miles in mini-parades.

John Hargreaves' research on Halifax finds that Sunday schools remained the most popular vehicle for Methodist work there throughout the nineteenth century.[55] However, numerical decline began before the First World War, with attendances halving between 1900 and 1950, and by 1995 the collapse was described as 'catastrophic'. The same collapse is noted in Canada and led to the development of new partnerships with non-Methodist organisations, including the student Christian movement.[56] In Britain, uniformed organisations offered some remedy

---

[49] Hempton, *The Religion of the People*, 96. Cf. Hargeaves, 'Methodist Attitudes', 205. Joseph Barker, of the Methodist New Connection, also argued in 1829 that teaching children, who lacked other educational opportunities, to write on the Sabbath was an act of mercy.

[50] C. Hughes Smith, 'The Sunday School Movement and Education', in Lenton (ed.), *Vital Piety and Learning*, 42.

[51] D. C. Harvey, C. Brace and A. R. Bailey, 'Parading the Cornish Subject: Methodist Sunday Schools in West Cornwall, c.1830–1930', *Journal of Historical Geography*, 33 (2007), 24–44.

[52] Ibid., 30.
[53] Ibid., 31.
[54] Ibid., 38.
[55] Hargreaves, 'Methodist Attitudes', 208.
[56] Semple, *The Lord's Dominion*, 387.

for the decline.⁵⁷ Nevertheless, Hargreaves portrays the growing pragmatism in Halifax in the second half of the twentieth century, in a desperate attempt to attract youth.⁵⁸ Methodist youth clubs were a successful approach, with seven in Halifax (more than any other denomination).⁵⁹ Methodists still struggled to maintain a continuing influence on even their own children in an age of cultural postmodernity, characterised as witnessing 'the haemorrhage of British Christianity'.⁶⁰

## Day Schools

Several themes appear in recent research into Methodist day schools. Hempton showed thirty years ago that the Methodists entered elementary education 'surprisingly late', having concentrated on their Sunday school provision.⁶¹ He describes the context of this entry, with growing suspicion of the Anglican Church, formerly seen as 'a great breakwater against the swelling tide of Popery' but which, under the influence of Pusey, was 'full of popish holes'.⁶² *Methodism and Education* reiterates the importance of anti-Catholicism and the fear of the 'romanised' Church of England as motivation for building day schools.⁶³ *A Victorian Class Conflict* argues that the motivation was threefold – a desire to educate the young in Christianity, to equip them with secular skills, and to counter the perceived aggression of other religious bodies.⁶⁴ Wesleyan ministers resented Wesleyan children being forced to attend Anglican schools, Anglican services (particularly Tractarian ones) and Anglican Sunday schools. However, they became divided over support for their own schools after the creation of school boards in the 1870s. Some ministers saw the advantage of a universal board system to take over all denominational schools, thereby ending Anglican influence. Others argued that village school boards remained dominated by local Anglican clergy and called for the maintenance of rural Wesleyan schools for protection. The 1888 Conference showed particular division, with a majority no longer supporting their continuation. As a Wesleyan witness to the Royal Commission commented, Wesleyan schools were becoming 'a dead weight in the circuits', injuring 'all the Connexional funds'.⁶⁵

---

⁵⁷ Hargreaves, 'Methodist Attitudes', 212–13.
⁵⁸ Ibid., 217.
⁵⁹ Ibid., 219.
⁶⁰ Ibid., 222.
⁶¹ Hempton, *Methodism and Politics*, 150.
⁶² Ibid., 166.
⁶³ J. T. Smith, *Methodism and Education: Rigg, Romanism and Wesleyan Schools* (Oxford: Clarendon Press, 1998).
⁶⁴ J. T. Smith, *A Victorian Class Conflict: Schoolteaching and the Parson, Priest and Minister, 1837–1902* (Brighton: Sussex Academic Press, 2009).
⁶⁵ M. Cruickshank, *Shifting Alliances: Church and State in English Education* (London: Continuum, 1963), 60.

However, and in spite of the polemics of the Wesleyan factions, recent research into the period 1860 to 1910 has shown that less than 20 per cent of Wesleyan schools were situated in villages.[66] In 1860, 45 per cent were situated in the six northern industrial districts of Liverpool, Halifax–Bradford, Manchester–Bolton, Leeds, Sheffield and Hull. These proportions remained throughout the Victorian period, with 44 per cent of all Wesleyan schools in 1885 within the 'Bolton ring' and only eighty-five village schools in total. They did little to prevent their rural children being, in Wesleyan words, 'badly cooked' educationally by their denominational enemies.

Several local studies have been made of day schools. Mary Hulton shows, in her analysis of the surviving Minutes of Smethwick Methodist School, how proposals to create a 'Romanist' school triggered the Wesleyans 'in self-defence, and to prevent the aggression of error' to establish a school in their former chapel building.[67] She discovers the generally 'non-interventionist' approach of the governing body, composed of local iron masters and other businessmen, who are seen to have an 'amateurish and limited approach' to educational management.[68] Julia Carter's analysis of the failed plans to establish a Wesleyan day school in Wimborne Minster gives an indication of Wesleyan attitudes to schools in the later 1880s.[69] The proposal was instituted after the closure of the BFSS (British & Foreign School Society) school, and when Baptists and Congregationalists refused to join them, the Wesleyans proceeded alone. However, the school was never completed. Carter concludes that the financial demands were too great for the circuit, which was always short of funds.[70] Moreover, as similarly noted by Kay Laister with regard to East Yorkshire schools,[71] the impetus for the proposal came from the minister and after he left the circuit subsequent ministers did not have the same enthusiasm. *A Victorian Class Conflict* reiterates these limitations on the influence of circuit ministers caused by the three year itinerancy.[72] From the 1870s the teachers themselves assumed a role of leadership as lay preachers and stewards and the Wesleyan minister did not demand a similar deference from his schoolteacher as the Anglican clergyman. The minister often came from a background similar to that of the teacher, with equivalent intellectual accomplishments and a manse equal in size to the schoolteacher's house, although with poorer salaries throughout the

---

[66] J. T. Smith, 'The Geographical Distribution of Wesleyan Schools, 1860–1910', *History of Education Researcher*, 86 (2010), 49–60.

[67] M. Hulton, 'The Trials of School Management: Smethwick 1860–1932', in Lenton (ed.), *Vital Piety and Learning*, 106–21.

[68] Ibid., 119.

[69] J. Carter, 'What Went Wrong? The Attempt to Establish a Wesleyan Day School in Wimborne Minster in the 1880s', *Family and Community History*, 10:1 (2007), 35–46.

[70] Ibid., 43.

[71] K. Laister, *Methodist Day Schools in East Yorkshire* (Hull: Humberside Christian Press, 2001), 10–11.

[72] Smith, *Victorian Class Conflict*, 46. The itinerant nature of the ministry also prevented ministers from sitting on school boards, although Wesleyan laymen were elected for long periods of time.

Victorian period.[73] The headteachers often dominated their schools and the low number of disagreements between ministers and teachers recorded in minute books is a testimony to largely harmonious relationships, in stark contrast to the experiences of Anglican schoolteachers.[74]

The educational contributions of several important leaders of the church have been the subject of recent researchers. Hempton analyses Bunting's attitude to the Brougham Education Bill of 1820, showing the developing Wesleyan opposition to the privileged position of the Established Church.[75] Bunting similarly led the Wesleyan opposition to the 1839 Russell Bill, which would have allowed grants to schools outside the two major national societies, the National Society and the BFSS. His stance was intensified in the era of the pamphlet wars of 1842, with him concluding that no person could 'reconcile Methodism and High Churchism'.[76] The Graham factory education proposals of 1843 were again opposed because of the 'exclusiveness of the measure which virtually ensured that the boards of trustees, masters and schools would be established on terms favourable to the Church of England'.[77] This was particularly alarming because of the growing influence of those Anglicans who adopted 'popish doctrines, superstitious practices, and unfairly proselytising operations'.[78] Denominational rivalries scuppered attempts to aid schools, although by 1847 chronic shortage of funds led Wesleyans to accept grants, alongside other churches. Hempton concludes that Bunting's 'intensely sectarian position' after 1832 hindered the development of a national system of schools, although it also ensured that English education in the nineteenth century 'would neither be under the control of a secular bureaucracy, nor tied too closely to the Church of England'.[79]

John Scott was personally determined to establish a network of schools, as well as the new Westminster Training College, nicknamed 'Scott's Folly'.[80] Scott is shown to have encouraged the increase of the Wesleyan contingent to 700 schools by the time of his death. He was personally convinced of the value of schooling, believing it would improve the material comfort of the poor and that 'the foundation of all improvement' was to 'make children generally intelligent … to teach them to think'.[81] He was also determined to maintain the connection of education to religion, vigorously opposing the Milner Gibson Education Bill of 1855 and Pakington's Bill of 1857, which would have proscribed all religious instruction in schools receiving

---

[73] Ibid., 100.
[74] Ibid., 155.
[75] D. Hempton, 'Wesleyan Methodism and Educational Politics in Early Nineteenth Century England', *History of Education*, 8:3 (1979), 209.
[76] Ibid., 213.
[77] Ibid., 215.
[78] Ibid., 215–16.
[79] Hempton, *Methodism and Politics*, 174.
[80] J. T. Smith, '"Scott's Folly": John Scott and the Development of the Wesleyan Educational System', in S. Gilley (ed.), *Victorian Churchmen* (Woodbridge: Boydell and Brewer, 2005), 292–307.
[81] Ibid., 300.

state grants. He told his students, 'Why limit education at any of its stages to the lower views of man, and not adapt to the higher? Why confine it to what is ephemeral, and exclude from it what is enduring?'[82] He displayed a similar energy against the Government's Revised Code of 1862, which allowed payment of grants only in the three Rs and deplored that pupils were seen as machines, to be taught in mechanical ways. His Wesleyan inspector, Armstrong, typified Wesleyan reactions, that 'reading, writing and arithmetic cannot be accepted as the complete curriculum of education even for the most neglected and ignorant of our population'.[83]

In both *Methodism and Education*, and in David Carter's article, '*Against the Tide*', Scott's successor, J. H. Rigg, is seen as one of the forgotten giants of Methodism, who swam against the tide of contemporary opinion on educational matters.[84] He clashed with both William Arthur and Hugh Price Hughes, who no longer saw the usefulness of their own denominational schools after the establishment of school boards. Rigg saw their continuing value in championing religious education in the face of secularism and as a bulwark against the encroaching influence of the High Anglican Church. Nevertheless, he accepted the need for a growing rapprochement with other denominations as long as their schools respected the conscience clauses of the 1870 Act. His personal influence on educational policy is seen as most significant, as a member of the Cross Commission of 1886 and a member of the first London School Board.

Alan Turberfield describes the still under-researched influence of John Scott Lidgett on education. He shows his work at Bermondsey Settlement and as a member of the London School Board and the London County Council. Lidgett believed passionately in the fundamental importance of education, 'the opening of the mind to desire to seek after and to enjoy knowledge for its own sake'. Education had a divine sanction and was needed to 'develop personality, to help people rise above depressing, monotonous, squalid, even brutal and immoral surroundings, enjoy all God's creation and practise creativity'.[85] He campaigned against both sectarian Religious Instruction and a secular curriculum in schools.[86] John Gibbs describes Lidgett securing the withdrawal of the 1890 bill to give additional financial help to denominational schools. He was 'a constant visitor to the educational corridors of power and his friendship with individual government leaders… ensured that the Methodist voice was heard, albeit unofficially before legislation was introduced'.[87] Communications from Whitehall were received by the Methodist Church at the same time as those to the Anglican and Roman Catholic Churches, 'a result of the

---

[82] Ibid., 302.

[83] Ibid., 305.

[84] D. Carter, 'Against the Tide? James Harrison Rigg and Education', in Macquiban (ed.), *Issues*, 79–95.

[85] A. Turberfield, *John Scott Lidgett: Archbishop of Methodism?* (London: Epworth Press, 2003), 42.

[86] Ibid., 378.

[87] J. Gibbs, 'Methodist Influence on National Education Policy', in Macquiban (ed.), *Issues*, 69.

historic Wesleyan stake in national education through their provision of schools and training colleges'. Although the Methodist contribution to education remained small, Gibbs does show, from his personal experience as Treasurer of the Methodist Education Committee, that the Church's influence remained 'out of all proportion to its size', with access to the Department of Education that other Free Churches did not have.[88]

The decline of the Wesleyan system had begun by the 1890s, with the rigorous application of government rules by Her Majesty's Inspectorate of Schools (particularly the call for 10 square feet of floor space per pupil) bringing many schools into what was described as 'a position of peril'.[89] Over 100 schools were closed between 1892 and 1902 for financial reasons, with Wesleyans relying on the security of school boards to protect their children from Anglican and Catholic influence. Wesleyan policy by then was to secure a universal system of such non-denominational elementary schools. The 1902 Education Act hardly satisfied this and it also led to deep divisions within the Connexion. The Act replaced the school board system with Local Education Authority (LEA) schools, but gave Church schools rate aid, instead of tax grants. Single school areas continued to exist, 5,600 of these being Anglican, and Wesleyans complained that 700,000 Methodist children were compelled to attend such schools, making themselves conspicuous by withdrawal from religious instruction or suffering petty proselytism. Some Wesleyans welcomed the financial support for their own denominational schools, 738 of which still survived, while others, led by Hugh Price Hughes, were disgusted that there would be a permanent minority of only two LEA appointees on the managing body of five in voluntary schools. Some Wesleyans joined the Passive Resistance Movement, refusing to pay local rates intended to support denominational schools, although the Conference would not support this institutionally and John Scott Lidgett spoke out against such extremism. Rigg wrote to Balfour, the author of the Act, criticising the 'intensely sectarian, anti-sectarian blind-eyed zealots who would land us in a blind, atheistic chaos'.[90]

Closures accelerated throughout the twentieth century, and this decline has been analysed in the context of growing ecumenism.[91] As the churches drew together in the face of a growing secularisation of society, Methodist schools were no longer deemed necessary to protect Wesleyan children from High Church Anglican schools. Secularism became the chief enemy, as shown by J. Osborn in 1903:

---

[88] Ibid., 72.

[89] The arguments are discussed in Smith, *Methodism and Education*, 204.

[90] Ibid., 229. Cf. D. R. Pugh, 'English Nonconformity, Education and Passive Resistance, 1903–6', *History of Education*, 19:4 (1990), 355–73; D. R. Pugh, 'Wesleyan Methodism and the Education Crisis of 1902', *British Journal of Educational Studies*, 36:3 (1988), 232–49.

[91] J. T. Smith, 'Ecumenism, Economic Necessity and the Disappearance of Methodist Elementary Schools in England in the Twentieth Century', *History of Education*, 39:5 (2010), 631–57.

> Methodism has always opposed Sacerdotalism ... in our fury against this evil, are we to let secularism severely alone? There is a great danger of religious education to go by default when the demand waxes louder and louder, that we must at all costs compete with America and Germany in secular education.[92]

However, financial difficulties largely precipitated school closures, with rigorous HMI inspections leading to unaffordable demands for renovations. A survey in 1928, for example, reported that the majority of the remaining 135 schools were over 60 years old, 44 being built before 1860, 26 in the decade 1860–70, 22 between 1871 and 1881 and a further 6 in the following decade.[93] Such old premises were often beyond improvement. The issue of single school areas was largely resolved by the 1936 Education Act which obliged denominational schools to provide Religious Instruction according with the LEA 'provided school syllabus', if children were unable to reach an LEA school.[94] From 1937 to 1941, Scott Lidgett held unofficial conferences on religious education with members of the Anglican Church and Evangelical Free Churches, in order to secure corporate worship in all schools and an Agreed Syllabus in 'provided' (LEA) schools. Society was seen as increasingly irreligious, with large numbers of evacuated children showing no religious knowledge at all.[95] By 1942 deficiencies in religious education were seen as so grave that 'a united Christian front' was considered essential. Such arguments convinced Butler, the Minister of Education, who felt it imperative to make 'the old faiths ... vivid to the next generation'.[96] The 1944 Act therefore legislated for compulsory acts of worship in all schools, and a locally agreed syllabus of religious education in all provided schools, and voluntary schools which opted for 'controlled' status.[97] The developing closeness of the Anglican and Methodist Churches finally led to the amalgamation of some of their primary schools, with eight such amalgamations by 1969. A heated debate in the 1970 Methodist Conference called for such Methodist–Anglican schools to replace existing schools, and a working party of 1996 declared openly that if there were a clean sheet Methodism would not set up a handful of primary schools 'eccentrically distributed across the country', although it would not abandon its schools.[98]

The secularism of society pushed the churches into further common approaches to education. The National Curriculum of 1988 was seen as indicative of the 'utilitarian and materialistic approach to education in which market economies

---

[92] *Weslyan Education Report*, 1904–1905, p. 21.
[93] Smith, 'Ecumenism, Economic Necessity and the Disappearance of Methodist Elementary Schools',, 644.
[94] Ibid., 645.
[95] Ibid., 649.
[96] S. J. D. Green, 'The 1944 Education Act: A Church–State Perspective', *Parliamentary History*, 19 (2000), 155.
[97] Controlled schools were financed from public funds with four LEA nominees in the six person managing committee.
[98] Ibid., 655.

would be the overriding ethos of schools'.[99] The new statement of Methodist policy, the *Essence of Education*, in 2000 reaffirmed the belief that education was about the whole person and condemned 'all rhetoric which threatens to reduce human beings to units of employment or pawns on a political chess board'.[100] Such views are reflected in the Anglican *Way Ahead* Report of 2001 and the statements of the Roman Catholic Cardinal Hume from 1988 until his death.

## The Mission Schools

Methodist missionary enterprise invariably went hand in hand with the establishment of schools. David Hempton sees them as 'the chief device of Christianizing native populations'.[101] However, the value of this educational work has been questioned in recent scholarship. David Bebbington claims that Methodists, 'hoping to rescue those whom they evangelised from barbarism', often 'lacked the sensitivity ideally required in cross-cultural mission'.[102] They showed a blindness to cultural relativism and could display insensitivity to local traditions, although they also brought enduring benefits.[103] Simeon Ilesanmi argues more forcefully that the relationship was typified by the postulate that one culture was superior to the other.[104] The missionary would not enter into dialogue with the culture he found. He cites the African scholar, V. Y. Mudimbe, that the missionary programme was more complex than the simple transmission of the Christian faith, and that it is difficult not to identify it with 'cultural propaganda, patriotic motivations and commercial interests', with the missionary becoming 'the best symbol of the colonial enterprise'.[105] K. Cracknell and S. J. White cite an Asian theologian who saw the missionaries arriving with 'attendant parochialism, dogmatism, cultural jingoism, secularism and materialism, demanding rejection of Korean indigenous values, customs, culture and faith'.[106]

However, Cracknell and White also quote Nelson Mandela, himself educated in Methodist schools, who felt that 'the benefits outweighed their disadvantages'. The missionaries ran schools when the government was unwilling or unable to do so. The learning environment of the missionary schools, 'while often morally rigid

---

[99] Ibid., 654.

[100] Ibid., 655.

[101] D. Hempton, *Methodism: Empire of the Spirit* (New Haven, CT and London: Yale University Press, 2005), 157.

[102] D.W. Bebbington, 'Methodism and Culture', in W. J. Abraham and J. E. Kirby (eds), *Oxford Handbook of Methodist Studies* (Oxford: Oxford University Press, 2009), 717.

[103] Ibid., 726.

[104] S. Ilesanmi, 'Methodism and Politics in Africa', in Abraham and Kirby (eds), *Oxford Handbook of Methodist Studies*, 706.

[105] Ibid., 707.

[106] Cracknell and White, *An Introduction to World Methodism*, 90.

was far more open than the racist principles underlying government schools'.[107] Ilesanmi also shows how education was seen to provide temporal blessing, with the creation of a middle class to facilitate progress.[108] He relates James Coleman's conclusions not simply to Nigeria but to other African nations:

> Western education did not merely facilitate the emergence of a separate class; it endowed the individuals in that class with the knowledge and skills, the ambitions and aspirations, that enabled them to challenge the Nigerian colonial government and ultimately to wrest control over the central political power from it.[109]

Luther Oconer similarly sees Methodist medical and educational work in Asia as planting seeds for social transformation in their communities. William Scranton of the MEC Korean mission claimed in 1893 that education was 'our harrow to smooth and dress the ground'.[110] Methodist colleges of repute emerged in Ceylon and in India, where Methodists focused their attentions on the lower caste Hindu population rather than catering for the higher caste Brahmins. Oconer concludes that it presented Methodism as a social religion that concerned itself not only to benefit the underprivileged, but also to empower the helpless.[111] It also effected changes in Chinese society. He points to the Wesleyan missionary, Anna Spears, principal of the girls' boarding school in Peking, refusing to admit girls with bound feet, which encouraged even parents from rural areas to abandon the practice.[112]

David Scott has recently analysed the experience in Malaysia from 1884 in the context of Hempton's hypothesis that Methodism's growth depended on the 'symbiotic fit' between the movement and its environment.[113] The Chinese there acknowledged the value of Western education and this did much, according to Scott, to 'legitimate missionary schools in the eyes of the Chinese People'.[114] The desire for economic advance by learning English was 'a significant influence' which disposed them towards Methodist missionary education.[115] Methodist expansion often followed a call for a school, as in Java in 1905, where the demand was made to B. F. West after an exploratory visit. Methodist establishments thus came to dominate the scene, and by 1914 three quarters of the boys receiving education in

---

[107] Ibid., 90.
[108] Ilesanmi, 'Methodism and Politics in Africa', 708.
[109] J. S. Coleman, *Nigeria: Background to Nationalism* (Berkeley, CA: University of California Press, 1965), quoted in Ilesanmi, 'Methodism and Politics in Africa', 706.
[110] L. C. Oconer, 'Methodism in Asia and the Pacific', in C. Yrigoyen( ed.), *T&T Clark Companion to Methodism* (London: T&T Clark, 2010), 158.
[111] Ibid., 164.
[112] Ibid., 160.
[113] D. W. Scott, 'Missionary Education and the Chinese in Malaysia: A Case Study for the Symbiotic Growth of the Methodist Movement', *Methodist History*, 48:3 (April 2010), 179.
[114] Ibid., 184.
[115] Ibid., 185.

the English language were at these schools.[116] However, there was not a universal agreement that this had been the best way to achieve new Methodist converts. Some visiting missionaries to Malaysia claimed that 'the messengers of the gospel would be better engaged in preaching the New Testament rather than in thumbing schoolbooks'.[117] The efficacy was also questioned in 1914 by the Board of Education for the Malaysia Conference, which concluded: ' It is a matter of deep regret that after 29 years of school work there are not in all our churches in Malaya 50 men and women over 25 years of age who have ever attended our schools.'[118]

Whiteside described over a century ago how, from about 1875, the African chiefs themselves began to see the value of secular instruction. At Clarkebury in South Africa the minister believed that Christian instruction and manual training were both necessary to the 'permanent uplifting of the native races' and established an industrial school to teach handicrafts such as shoemaking, masonry and agriculture.[119] In 1882 the Ayliff Industrial Institution for Girls was established offering household training to lift them, as one ex-missionary phrased it, from their 'mean surroundings', the brightest girls being trained as pupil-teachers. In the following year a Boys' Industrial School was established at Butterworth, and the Lamplough Training Institution for Girls was created there in 1890, instructing the girls in cooking, baking, sewing, ironing and tailoring, in addition to usual school lessons.[120] Bartels' narrative study, fifty years ago, of Ghanaian Methodism showed how the chiefs there recognised the material advantages that could come from mission schools.[121] One of the first missionaries, Thomas Freeman, was concerned that the Ghana schools should include manual training, claiming, 'We take the plough with us. Let it be remembered that in Africa the Bible and the plough go together.'[122] His school at Beulah had its own plantation, which was used for training. Many native Ghanaians were trained to be the teachers in mission schools and Bartels felt that this accounted for the widespread influence of Methodism and its place in Ghana nationalism.[123] Twenty-four per cent of the education of the country was under the management of the Methodist Church in the mid 1940s.[124] However, there remained concerns at overeducating boys in academic subjects, which led them to refuse to work with their hands.[125] These themes might be explored more fully to show the general aims and effectiveness

---

[116] Ibid., 188.
[117] Ibid., 190, quoting the first missionary, W. F. Oldham.
[118] Quoted in Scott, 'Missionary Education and the Chinese in Malaysia', 190.
[119] J. Whiteside, *History of the Wesleyan Methodist Church of South Africa* (London: Methodist Publishing House, 1906), 292.
[120] Ibid.
[121] F. L. Bartels, *Roots of Ghana Methodism* (Cambridge: Cambridge University Press, 1965), 54.
[122] Ibid., 66.
[123] Ibid., 75.
[124] Ibid., 243.
[125] Ibid., 238. The complaint was made by the Asantehene to the Synod in 1942.

of Methodist mission schools. Indeed, the topic is ripe generally for up-to-date scholarship at local and national levels.

## The Education of Girls

Several works have addressed female education, although this important issue also warrants further research. Bowden shows how Susanna Wesley deplored that girls were put to learn sewing before they could read perfectly, which was the 'very reason why so few women can read fit to be heard, and never to be well understood'.[126] William Graham describes the attempt to introduce a girls' school at Kingswood, following Wesley's criticism of existing girls' boarding schools, where girls taught each other 'pride, vanity, affection, intrigue, artifice and in short everything that a Christian woman ought not to learn ... one might as well send a young maid to be bred in Drury Lane.'[127] He preferred private tuition by a mistress who 'truly fears God'. His 1781 letter of advice to one stressed, 'make Christians! Let this be your leading view ... let everything else which you teach be subordinate to this.'[128] Graham has unearthed Wesley's 1748 Rules for girls at Kingswood and compares these with the often quoted Rules for boys, concluding that they were restricted to a curriculum designed to meet 'a somewhat vague feminine vocational need'.[129] Rather than training 'in every branch of useful learning', the girls were taught 'in all such things as are needful for them'.[130] Boys studied reading, writing, arithmetic, English, French, Latin, Greek, Hebrew, history, geography, chronology, rhetoric, logic, ethics, geometry, algebra, physics and music. Girls had a reduced curriculum of reading, writing, sewing 'and if desired, English, Grammar, Arithmetic and other sorts of Needlework'.[131] They did not study music and were not to be employed in 'philosophical experiments' as were the boys.[132] They had the same diet, although girls were allowed cheese for supper.[133]

*Scott's Folly* describes John Scott's enlightened view of female education in the mid nineteenth century, calling for girls to be trained in 'general intelligence and activity'.[134] In 1858 he condemned the long-held conception that it was wrong to educate lower-class girls destined to 'do the drudgery of life', supposing that it would make them 'dissatisfied and unfit for their proper station'.[135] The Wesleyan inspector, Armstrong, predicted in 1858 that the time had not yet come when 'all that

---

[126] Bowden, 'Susanna Wesley's Educational Method', 61.
[127] W. T. Graham, *Wesley's Early Experiments in Education* (Ilkeston: Moorley, 1990), 4.
[128] Ibid., 15.
[129] Ibid., 12.
[130] Ibid., 11.
[131] Ibid., 11.
[132] Ibid., 13.
[133] Ibid., 14. (Fees were 25 per cent cheaper for the girls.)
[134] Smith, 'Scott's Folly', 300–301.
[135] Ibid., 300–301.

belongs to womanly education will be valued and sought', but Wesleyan schools nonetheless offered girls, 'whether among the humble or the well-conditioned' a first-class education. The 1865 specimen timetable for Wesleyan girls' schools was identical to that of boys' schools with only the addition of needlework. Girls were expected to study reading and arithmetic for five hours each per week, with one hour a week spent on history, geography and singing.[136]

Neil Semple shows the high priority given to female secondary education by Canadian Methodists. They still assumed that the purpose of education was to expand the effectiveness of women in their particular roles, or as Alma College announced, to supply 'proper training and culture of the future Queens of the Home Circle'.[137] However, they hoped to supply 'a good, substantial education in which the moral powers have been cultivated in harmony with the intellect'. Even as early as the 1830s at Upper Canada Academy, female students took natural history, natural philosophy, botany, chemistry, algebra, geometry, astronomy, physiology, natural theology, Christian evidences, rhetoric and composition, with senior students reading at university level. In 1840, the school had ninety-six male and seventy-six female students.[138] At Alexandra College, the mistress of liberal arts diploma involved university-level work, with courses and examinations similar to those taken by men. Wesley College in Winnipeg admitted women on the same basis as men from its inception. Some Methodist churchmen still argued that since women had a different destiny, they should be educated separately, and only in this way could 'the true ideal of womanhood' be developed. However, more enlightened educators argued that woman was intellectually man's equal, if not superior, and that coeducation at all levels would promote a broader equality. In fact the Methodist Colleges across Canada took a leading role in promoting higher education for women. Mount Allison enrolled women in 1872, and Grace Lockhart became the first woman to receive a Canadian university degree in 1875.[139]

Clyde Binfield shows something of the Methodist attitude to female education by the 1880s in his analysis of three addresses made by the Rev. John Simon at his sister's school, Wintersdorf at Southport.[140] Contemporary arguments held that girls were to be educated to know their place, which for Methodists was for them to be Christian women, with their faith deepening their duty as daughters, wives and helpmates. However, Simon appears to be more ambitious in his estimate of girls' potential. He recognised their passion for accuracy, inquisitiveness and clear reflection, which were as important to eight-year-old drapers' daughters as to grown men. He welcomed the new conceptions of female education, but claimed that this had been won 'in the face of a pitiless storm of ridicule'. The teaching of

---

[136] Ibid., 301.
[137] Semple, *The Lord's Dominion*, 246.
[138] Ibid.
[139] Ibid.
[140] C. Binfield, '"Having Proved the Past We Need not Fear the Future": Some Sidelights on Wesleyan Girls' Education', in Lenton (ed.), *Vital Piety and Learning*, 122–42.

mathematics, Latin and science had been opposed with 'extraordinary vehemence' which Simon castigates as a folly:

> There is a girl whose mind has been fitted by God for the study of mathematics! She is what is called a 'born mathematician'. Was it not strange that there were many people not long since who thought that they were doing heaven service when they conspired together to defeat the design of God in her creation? Why? Because we had set up an ideal man, and an ideal woman, and in as much as mathematics did not enter into our conception of an ideal woman we determined that she should be delivered up to the working of samplers and the making of wax flowers. Or, perhaps, we said that if we educated her in accordance with her genius, there would be no sphere for her. No sphere! Who was to blame for that? An unenlightened opinion, a bitter prejudice were to blame.[141]

The issue is ripe for more detailed research.

## Non-Wesleyan Methodist Work in Education

Lois Louden has recently researched the influence of non-Wesleyan Methodist congregations in educational provision, a group largely ignored in standard histories.[142] She admits the paucity of evidence, but has described the work of the Primitive Methodists, the Methodist New Connexion, Bible Christians and the United Methodist Free Churches (UMFC). All are shown to support Sunday schools, but several were also interested in the formation of day schools. The New Connexion set up a committee to facilitate this in 1840, hoping schools would provide 'a sound, practical, and religious education'.[143] The Primitive Methodists reflected the general aims of all Methodists for their schools to be 'doors of entrance into the Church of God', but they also wanted to 'protect the child against the carelessness, cupidity, or poverty of the parents'.[144] The Non-Wesleyan Conferences were more wary about accepting government grants than the Wesleyans, the Primitive Methodist Conference of 1868 leaving this decision to local churches. Indeed, these churches were 'bottom up' systems giving much decision making to the local circuits.[145] The Methodist New Connexion similarly left it to local circuits in 1852. Four UMFC and two Primitive schools accepted grants. All the non-

---

[141] Ibid., 129.
[142] L. M. R. Louden, 'Non-Wesleyan Methodist Schools: A Neglected Group of Elementary Day Schools', *Journal of Educational Administration and History*, 36:1 (2004), 78–82.
[143] Ibid., 72.
[144] Ibid., 72.
[145] Ibid., 80.

Wesleyan churches welcomed the school boards, supporting a universal system and the abolition of all voluntary schools. In doing so they aligned themselves more closely with general Nonconformist opinion than the Wesleyan Conference. They also called for teaching in day schools to be confined to secular education, with religious education left to the churches in their own time and on their own premises. They thus all opposed additional government grants to voluntary schools in 1897 and expressed antagonism to Anglican single school areas. This led to extreme hostility towards the 1902 Education Act, which was seen by Primitives as 'a disgraceful, sectarian plot' which supported 'sectarian' teaching from local rates and without adequate control.[146] The passive resistance movement was fully supported by the non-Wesleyan Methodists and thirty Primitive Methodists went to prison for their non-payment.[147] As far as actual schools were concerned, Louden shows that these groups established some 141 schools at some time within the period, with the greatest number open at any one time being 92 in 1890. The vast majority of these schools were in Lancashire, which had 14 UMFC, 11 Primitive and 8 New Connexion schools by 1876.[148] While the actual provision is seen as puny in comparison with the Wesleyans, it exceeded that of any other Nonconformist denomination.

Dorothy Graham has researched several of the non-Wesleyan secondary schools, finding the origins of Primitive Methodism's ventures into education to be initiated by its travelling preachers, who felt their children suffered because of the itinerant system, and that 'their salaries were too low to pay even for "common schooling"'.[149] As a result a Jubilee Fund was initiated in 1860 to found Elmfield College in York. Edward Royle's brief study of the college shows that the original intention had been to create a school for ministers' sons.[150] Graham gives some detail of the boys' experiences at the school, with prayer meetings twice a week and daily worship. Financial problems obliged the college to be scheduled for closure in 1906, although it was saved by a consortium of old students, who turned it into a 'high class boarding school'.[151] It finally closed with the rationalisation demanded by the Methodist Union of 1931. In a comparison with the Wesley College at Eccleshall near Sheffield (opened in 1838), Royle reports that Elmfield had a lower social appeal. It catered for small-businessmen, had a much larger number of boys studying book keeping, with only 13 per cent studying Greek, and did not teach science until 1872. The religious observance was similar to the Wesleyan schools; although prayers were *extempore*, there was no Liturgy or chanting. Royle

---

[146] Ibid., 74.
[147] Ibid., 75.
[148] Ibid., 78. There were 912 Wesleyan schools in existence in 1873.
[149] E. D. Graham, 'Non-Wesleyan Methodist Secondary Education Ventures' in Lenton (ed.), *Vital Piety and Learning*, 81.
[150] E. Royle, 'Methodism and Education – a Question of Denominational Image and Identity?' in Lenton (ed.), *Vital Piety and Learning*, 12.
[151] Graham, 'Non-Wesleyan Methodist Secondary Education Ventures', 83.

concludes that the college showed, 'if the Wesleyans were half-way to Anglicanism, the Primitives were half-way to Dissent'.[152]

A similar Primitive Methodist institution, the Cedars, was established for girls in 1877, although this survived for less than a decade. The girls were given a broad education, and Graham concludes that such a venture indicated 'the growing prosperity and respectability of Primitive Methodism and its movement towards middle-class status'.[153] Although female education was not considered particularly necessary, Primitive Methodism felt concerned enough to make the experiment.[154] In 1875 a second school, Bourne College in Birmingham, was established as a limited liability company to educate the sons of ministers and laymen.[155] Graham shows the comprehensiveness of the curriculum, with church minutes of 1882 reporting the teaching of 'all commercial and classical subjects (including mathematical and languages) for professions, University Examination and matriculation; taking care also to promote their spiritual interests and their instruction in the principles of our Christian faith'.[156] The College continued in some strength until the 1920s, when the advent of State secondary education, the prevailing depression and the prospect of Methodist Union precipitated its closure in 1928.[157] Other colleges were established by the Bible Christians and the United Methodist Free Churches. Graham concludes that both the Primitive Methodists and the Bible Christians felt the need 'to provide education for their denomination's members and friends'.[158] The education was intended for both girls and boys and both used their institutions initially to give some form of ministerial training. However, the location of schools, economic depressions and varying support from influential members determined their failure or survival.

## Higher Education

*A Victorian Class Conflict*, in its comparative analysis of preachers and teachers, shows the consistent mistrust of 'over-educating' both professions.[159] Royle explains how early Methodism remained suspicious that college educated preachers would become a spiritual elite, discerning an 'antinomianism of the intellect – that those who are "in the Spirit" are exempt from the need for formal education'.[160] John Lenton similarly describes the contemporary view that those who 'took their

---

[152] Royle, 'Methodism and Education', 13.
[153] Graham, 'Non-Wesleyan Methodist Secondary Education Ventures', 86.
[154] Ibid., 87.
[155] In 1876 a quarter of its twenty-five boys were the sons of travelling preachers.
[156] Ibid., 88.
[157] Ibid., 93.
[158] Ibid., 103.
[159] Smith, *Victorian Class Conflict*, 115–23.
[160] Royle, 'Methodism and Education', 1.

knowledge from a shelf' would be less concerned about evangelism.[161] Semple shows how the issue similarly unsettled Methodist councils in Canada, which feared that too great an education might lessen the spontaneity of preaching and spoil the preacher's ability to convey Christianity's simple message by introducing complex vocabulary. 'Trivial niceties' would confuse the general membership and create unnatural boundaries between the congregation and the preacher. Charles Stewart, later theological teacher at Mount Allison College, was also concerned that training the intellect often involved introducing students to dangerous, secular rationalism.[162] While seventeen of Wesley's original fifty preachers in 1749 were sent to Kingswood for training, this was only for a one-day course on theology, logic and preaching.[163] Some were poorly educated, with at least one, John Smith, unable to write, though he could read, and one Bristol steward of 1752 blamed Wesley himself for 'taking so many raw, young fellows from their trades to a work they are as utterly unqualified for, as for Minister of State!'[164] Of the 1740s cohort (bolstered by Wesley's own university friends who joined as preachers) 70 per cent did have the best education available, with a classical tutor or at a grammar school, although later cohorts had lower standards, the 1760s cohort having 47 per cent of its number with a 'minimal education'.[165] Bunting accepted the need of training for young preachers as early as 1805 to make them 'more accurately and thoroughly acquainted with Divinity as a science, and qualify them for more extensive and permanent usefulness'.[166] In Canada, the Methodist Episcopal Church expressed concerns in 1825 that they needed 'intellectual improvement among our young preachers ... in order to meet the wants of society now improving in literary acquirements'.[167] Samuel Nelles claimed:

> we live in an intellectual age and men who are behind the age in cultivation are not the men to lead the age in religion ... It is therefore always binding on the Christian ministry to be ready to preach in the Portico as well as in the Market Place, to meet the polished scepticism of the learned as well as the courser iniquity of the ignorant.[168]

However, it was not until 1834 that a theological institution began in Britain, Conference finally recognising the need for preachers to be 'in no way inferior in intellectual standard' to those of other denominations, and even their own congregations. Lenton claims that its focus remained on circuit work and only

---

[161] J. Lenton, 'The Education of John Wesley's Preachers', in Lenton (ed.), *Vital Piety and Learning*, 25–37.
[162] Semple, *The Lord's Dominion*, 254.
[163] Lenton, 'The Education of John Wesley's Preachers', 29.
[164] Ibid., 26.
[165] Ibid., 27.
[166] Pritchard, 'Education', 282.
[167] Semple, *The Lord's Dominion*, 254.
[168] Ibid., 254.

after the First World War, with men like A. S. Peake and W. F. Moulton, was there a 'determined effort to make a worthy Methodist contribution to biblical and theological scholarship'.[169] In Canada, candidates for the ministry by 1884 were at least required to have the equivalent of admission standards of the Methodist university colleges – Mount Allison and Victoria.[170]

Tim Macquiban and Jennifer Bone give general surveys of Westminster Training College, showing its commitment to a religious rather than a secular education for teachers from its beginning.[171] John Scott, its first principal, told student-teachers that it was a 'nursery for religion, that chapel and Bible Study were as important as classroom teaching and that they needed to guard against the temptation to neglect Bible study for geography, history and literature books;.[172] When it moved in 1959 to Oxford, because of its outdated premises, there were concerns that the 'more secular and less Methodist environment' would threaten the religious observance.[173] Such concerns persevered as other changes were made in teacher training. The 1993 Methodist Conference predicted, 'The world of education has entered the market place with a vengeance. Never has it been more important to maintain and develop the Christian community and values which have made Westminster College what it is.'[174] Mary Ludlow has made a similar study of Southlands, opened for female teachers in 1871.[175] In its early days it was a requirement that students be Methodist, although by 1988, after many changes and amalgamations, less than 20 per cent of Southlands students were so. Ludlow concludes that the current institution is no longer a Women's Teacher Training College, most of its students are not Methodists and it no longer produces overseas missionaries, ministers or Methodist leaders as it once did, but its Methodist members and the Christians at the centre make 'a distinctive contribution to the life of the University'.[176]

## Themes and Conclusions

The theme that persists within Methodist policy on education is of being at odds with the ethos of the day. Hempton sees Methodism at its heart to be always a countercultural movement, drawing energy from 'the dialectics arising from its challenge to accepted norms in religion and society'.[177] This can be seen in John

---

[169] Pritchard, 'Education', , 304.
[170] Ibid., 255.
[171] Macquiban, 'Body, Mind and Spirit', 93; J. Bone, *Our Calling to Fulfil: Westminster College and the Changing Face of Teacher Education, 1951–2001* (Bristol: Tockington Press, 2003).
[172] Ibid., 94.
[173] Ibid., 98.
[174] Ibid., 102.
[175] M. Ludlow, 'Southlands: A Moving Story', in Lenton (ed.), *Vital Piety and Learning*, 155–77.
[176] Ibid., 175.
[177] Hempton, *Methodism: Empire of the Spirit*, 201.

Wesley's disgust with the schools of the eighteenth century, which motivated him to build Kingswood. It is seen in Methodist reactions to the Revised Code of 1861, in reactions to the 1988 Education Act and more recently in the condemnation, made by John Barratt, headteacher of The Leys School, Cambridge, of the swing towards a shortsighted, functionalist concept which values education only in terms of producing technical skills.[178] This 'less-than-Christian view of men and women' is seen to detract from the 'hunger for explanation' and 'intellectual curiosity' within the purpose of God that a Christian school should encourage. Methodism challenges the current values of society, which 'is so deeply affected by a humanistic, sophisticated, largely materialistic, and often cynical approach to life'.[179] A final word might be given to Donald Tranter, who, shortly before his death, criticised the attempts to reform the educational system solely to improve economic competitiveness. For him, the creation of wealth was not a sufficiently worthy motive to determine education and he was saddened by a loss of the idealism which valued education for its own sake and recognised man's insatiable appetite to understand. Education, 'like all things joyous, beautiful and good', needed no secondary justification.[180] As Jabez Bunting asserted two hundred years before:

> an education which looks only at the secular interests of an individual, which looks only at his condition as a member of civil society, and does not look on him as a man having an immortal soul ... is not education.[181]

---

[178] Barrett, 'The Methodist Church and Education in Britain', 31.
[179] Ibid., 34.
[180] D. Tranter, 'The Dimming of the Light', in Lenton (ed.), *Vital Piety and Learning*, 180.
[181] G. M. Best, *Shared Aims: A Celebration of Methodism's Involvement in Education* (London: Board of Management for Methodist Residential Schools, 2003), 5.

# Methodists and Business, 1860–1960

## David J. Jeremy

Historians' attention to the role of religion in industry and business has centred on the early Industrial Revolution decades, before 1850. E. P. Thompson's interpretation of Methodism as a malign capitalist influence on the British working classes has inspired similar studies in the USA, and in both countries research has produced opposing views.[1] However, relatively little work has been done on post-1850 developments in either country and for the most part the portrayal of pious entrepreneurs, often struggling with persisting ethical dilemmas, has been unsympathetic. This essay aims to open up the topic. Most attention is paid to the British experience and to those figures who have been most successful, distinguished or otherwise, because they have left most evidence of their activities. Surprisingly, in view of the fact that the vast majority of Methodists have lived in the United States, no systematic collective biographies of Methodists in business in North America have been written although, as will be seen, the religious affiliations of United States business leaders have been identified. Hopefully this essay may stir historians elsewhere to pursue that sort of an approach for an understanding of the interactions between business and faith.

Assuming that the essential task of the historian is to understand and explain change, the challenge posed by Methodist interactions between faith and business resolves into three basic themes. One is related to origins. From what family and social circumstances did these individuals come? What education or training did they receive? How did they advance their careers? What made them stand out against their fellows? How did all these elements change over time?

A second theme pertains to mindsets. What formative influences shaped their Christian faith – parents, wives, teachers, preachers, friends in church, friends in business situations, the Bible, another book, a significant event, something else? Did their understanding of the Christian faith alter as they moved through their lives? How did they reconcile their beliefs with changes in the intellectual climate,

---

[1] Mark A. Noll (ed.), *God and Mammon: Protestants, Money, and the Market, 1790–1860* (Oxford: OxfordUniversity Press, 2002) has very helpful survey articles.

like new findings in modern science? What beliefs about the purpose of life guided their behaviour? How did business attitudes translate into church life and religious practice?

The third theme is about behaviour. In their conduct of business did they aim to follow any set of ethical standards? What happened when standards conflicted with widely accepted business practices? Could ethical behaviour be detected in their treatment of business stakeholders (employees, suppliers, customers, government, local community), or in their accumulation of wealth, or in their dispersal of wealth? Or did they keep belief and behaviour quite separate, holding them simultaneously in separate mental compartments, in neo-Lutheran 'two kingdoms' fashion?[2] How readily did their accommodations between belief and practice adjust to changing temporal environments? And in their local and national churches, what impact did they have?

Since businesspeople before the 1960s (and some since) were often reticent, inarticulate or secretive, the task of penetrating mental horizons is often precluded. However, local church records, denominational archives and publications, the occasional survival of business papers, and, above all (for figures in public life), local newspapers, mean that there are possibilities for learning something more about people in business. What follows focuses upon how Methodist Christians in business in the past might be identified and, secondly, on what may be known about their origins and influence.

# Identities

Leading Methodists in business were not necessarily business leaders; nor were leading businessmen and women affiliated to Methodism necessarily Methodist leaders. This section separates the two groups but acknowledges that there were many examples of individuals simultaneously exhibiting leadership both in business and in Methodism.

## Some Sources

Popularly, Methodists in business are recalled as just a few giant figures. The impression derives from a clutch of full-length biographies or autobiographies. For the British scene, the main older biographies are of William P. Hartley,[3] John

---

[2] William J. Wright, *Martin Luther's Understanding of God's Two Kingdoms* (Grand Rapids, MI: Baker Academic, 2010), chapter 1.

[3] Arthur S. Peake, *The Life of Sir William Hartley* (London: Hodder & Stoughton, 1926).

Mackintosh,[4] William McArthur,[5] Robert Perks,[6] Joseph Rank[7] and Josiah Stamp.[8] More recently two biographies of J. Arthur Rank[9] have appeared and Isaac Holden is well served.[10] The older works badly need revision and a full-length biography of Robert Perks is necessary, not least because of Owen Covick's work on his business activities.[11] The problem with most of these biographies and the shorter biographical treatments found in the national pantheons, the *DBB* and the *ONDB* (see bibliography),[12] lies with their authors' approaches. The older biographies were too close to their subjects. Many suffer from monocular vision. Either their subjects appear as business magnates with little mention of Christian and Methodist activities, or else they are treated as Methodist heroes. For the USA, Kathryn W. Kemp's biography of Asa Candler is good for his Methodist, political and personal involvements, but less strong on the corporate business record of Coca-Cola.[13]

Autobiographies of business figures with Methodist involvements are few. Inevitably they suffer from their authors' subjectivity. Walter Runciman's is mostly filled with tales of life at sea and is disappointing on his business career.[14] Robert Perks's posthumous autobiography is full of intriguing information and is as essential for his career as Denis Crane's biography written well before Perks's life

---

[4] George W. Crutchley, *John Mackintosh: A Biography* (London: The National Sunday School Union, n.d. but 1921).

[5] Thomas McCullagh, *Sir William McArthur KCMG: A Biography, Religious, Parliamentary, Municipal, Commercial* (London: Hodder and Stoughton, 1891).

[6] Denis Crane, *The Life Story of Sir Robert W. Perks* (London: Robert Culley, 1909).

[7] R. G. Burnett, *Through the Mill: The Life of Joseph Rank* (London: Epworth Press, 1945).

[8] J. Harry Jones, *Josiah Stamp, Public Servant: The Life of the First Baron Stamp of Shortlands* (London: Pitman, 1964).

[9] Besides Alan Wood, *Mr Rank: A Study of J. Arthur Rank and British Films* (London: Hodder and Stoughton, 1952), there are Geoffrey Macnab, *J. Arthur Rank and the British Film Industry* (London: Routledge, 1993) and Michael Wakelin, *J. Arthur Rank: The Man behind the Gong* (Oxford: Lion, 1996).

[10] Elizabeth Jennings, 'Sir Isaac Holden, Bart (1807–97): His Place in the Wesleyan Connexion', *Proceedings of the Wesley Historical Society[PWHS]*, 43 (1982), 117–26, 150–58; Katrina Honeyman and Jordan Goodman, *Technology and Enterprise: Isaac Holden and the Mechanisation of Wool Combing in France, 1848–1914* (Aldershot: Scolar, 1986); entries on Holden in the *DBB* by John A. Iredale and J. Malcolm Trickett and in the *ODNB* by Katrina Honeyman.

[11] Owen Covick (Flinders University, Adelaide, Australia), 'Mapping the Career of a Businessman Who Was an "Independent Operator" and Who Left No Substantial Papers: The Case of Sir R. W. Perks, 1849–1934' (paper presented to Conference of the Association of Business Historians Glasgow, 2005) and other papers.

[12] David J. Jeremy (ed.), *Dictionary of Business Biography* (London: Butterworths, 5 vols, 1984–86); Oxford *DNB* as cited elsewhere.

[13] Kathryn W. Kemp, *God's Capitalist: Asa Candler of Coca-Cola* (Macon, GA: Mercer University Press, 2002).

[14] Sir Walter Runciman, *Before the Mast – and After: The Autobiography of a Sailor and Shipowner* (London: Fisher Unwin, 1924).

was over.[15] Harold Bellman's records chapel life and has valuable glimpses of his friend Josiah Stamp.[16] Lord Mackintosh's autobiography is much more balanced but needs to be read against the wider company background found in the business history of Rowntree.[17]

However, these giants are by no means representative of the Methodist lay people who reached business prominence in the localities and industries of the 1860–1960 period, an age when the Christian religion still had some ascendancy.

## Who Were Leading Methodists in Britain and the USA with Business Backgrounds?

In Britain, prior to the merger of the Wesleyans, Primitives and United Methodists, and the formation of the Methodist Church in 1932, leading Methodist laypeople can be identified and their occupational characteristics established in several ways. Late Victorian Methodists met in decennial ecumenical Conferences that brought together hundreds of delegates from both the 'eastern' (mostly British and European) branches of Methodism and the 'western' (mostly United States) branches.[18] The first, in London in 1881, saw 200 delegates from the eastern branches meeting 200 delegates from the western branches. Numbers were equally split between ministers and the laity. Of the hundred laypersons (all men) from the eastern section, 90 were laymen representing eight British Methodist branches. In conjunction with Census, rite of passage records, and denominational and town directories, the occupations for most have been found.

A second technique for tracking leading Methodist laypersons and then discovering their occupational backgrounds is to find those individuals who were the most active on national church committees at particular dates in time. This has been attempted for 1906–07, prior to the merger of the United Methodist Free Churches, the Methodist New Connexion and the Bible Christians. Using the arbitrary criterion for leadership of a minimum presence on five national denominational committees, a laborious computing exercise with spreadsheets discovered the identities of 76 Wesleyan lay leaders and 13 Primitive Methodist lay leaders. For the smaller Methodist branches the criterion had to be relaxed:

---

[15] Perks, Sir Robert William, *Sir Robert Perks, Baronet* (London: Epworth Press, 1936).

[16] Sir Harold Bellman, *Cornish Cockney: Reminiscences and Reflections* (London: Hutchinson, 1948).

[17] *By Faith and Work: The Autobiography of The Rt Hon the First Viscount Mackintosh Halifax*, ed. A. A. Thomson (London: Hutchinson, 1966); Robert Fitzgerald, *Rowntree and the Marketing Revolution* (Cambridge: Cambridge University Press, 1995).

[18] *Proceedings of the Oecumenical Methodist Conference, Held in City Road Chapel, London, September 1881* (London, 1882); *Proceedings of the Second Ecumenical Methodist Conference, Held in the Metropolitan Methodist Episcopal Church, Washington, October 1891* (London, 1892); *Proceedings of the Third Ecumenical Methodist Conference, Held in City Road Chapel, London, September 1901* (London, 1902); *Proceedings of the Fourth Ecumenical Methodist Conference, Held in Metropolitan Methodist Church, Toronto, Canada, October 4–17, 1911* (London, 1912).

to members of four national committees for the Methodist New Connexion, and members of three national committees for the United Methodist Free Churches and the Bible Christians. This spreadsheet exercise provided another 20 laymen. Occupations were then traced in the same way as before.[19]

A third means of identifying leading Methodist laypersons, and then proceeding to discover their occupations, is to limit the definition to those who held the highest office open to laypersons in any branch of Methodism. This has been done for the Vice-Presidents of the Primitive Methodist Connexion (the only Methodist branch before union to have this office) and, after 1932, the Methodist Church.[20]

Depending on the incidence of past donations, or anniversary fundraising projects, it is sometimes possible to detect generous benefactors to Methodist churches, and in some instances to relate them to business. Obviously this hinges on publication of the names of benefactors.

Table 24.1 summarises findings using these techniques for identifying lay leaders and, with them, members of the business community, for Britain. The far left column of percentages is an occupational analysis of the Wesleyan delegates to the 1881 ecumenical Methodist Conference. The next column, moving to the right, is a similar analysis of the 76 individuals identified as members of five or more national committees of the Wesleyan Methodist Church. Then there are occupational profiles of holders of the office of Vice-President of the Primitive Methodist Church, 1872–1913 and 1914–32. The last two columns on the right show the occupational composition of Vice-Presidents of the Methodist Church 1932–59 and 1960–2000.

Two striking conclusions emerge from these analyses. One is that between 1880 and the Second World War, people in business, almost exclusively men, monopolised the lay leaderships of Methodism. The other, equally plain, is that after 1960 business voices were displaced by those of non-business backgrounds, particularly with people from the professions and current or former church administrators.

Bald statistical analyses are insufficient of themselves. A great deal remains to be done in discovering the roles of these lay leaders. The Wesleyan 'workhorses' are analysed in this author's 1990 volume and the Primitive Methodist and Methodist Church lay leaders, in his two articles already cited.[21]

---

[19] David J. Jeremy, *Capitalists and Christians: Business Leaders and the Churches in Britain, 1900–1960* (Oxford: Clarendon Press, 1990), 295–306.

[20] David J. Jeremy, 'Laity in Denominational Leadership: Vice-Presidents of the Primitive Methodist Church, 1872–1932', *PWHS*, 57 (2010), 246–72; David J. Jeremy, 'Laity in Denominational Leadership: Methodist Vice-Presidents, 1932–2000', *PWHS*, 58 (2011), 12–33.

[21] Jeremy, *Capitalists and Christians*, 295–335; 'Laity' (2010); 'Laity' (2011).

Table 24.1  Occupational composition of UK Methodist lay leaders, 1872-2000 (percentages)

|  | Wesleyan Lay delegates, Oecumencial Methodist Conference | Wesleyan 5+ committee memberships | Primitive Methodist Vice-Presidents | | Methodist Church Vice-Presidents | |
| --- | --- | --- | --- | --- | --- | --- |
|  | 1881 | 1907 | 1872–1913 | 1914–1932 | 1932–1959 | 1960-2000 |
|  | 42 men | 76 men | 30 men | 19 men | 26 men<br>2 women | 25 men<br>16 women |
| **Business** |  |  |  |  |  |  |
| **Primary** | 2 | 3 | 3 | 16 | 4 | 2 |
| **Manufacturing** | 33 | 39 | 33 | 32 | 14 | 10 |
| **Services** |  |  |  |  |  |  |
| Utilities |  |  |  |  |  |  |
| Transport & communications | 5 | 7 |  |  | 7 |  |
| Distributive trades | 33 | 17 | 40 | 21 | 11 | 2 |
| Financial services | 5 | 8 | 7 | 16 | 11 | 10 |
| Legal services | 10 | 8 | 3 |  | 18 | 10 |
| Accountancy services | 2 |  |  | 11 |  |  |
| Other business services | 2 | 7 | 3 |  |  |  |
| Miscellaneous services |  |  | 10 |  |  |  |
| **Non-Business** |  |  |  |  |  |  |

| | | | | | | |
|---|---|---|---|---|---|---|
| Education | 2 | 5 | | | 7 | 20 |
| Academia | | | | 5 | 14 | 5 |
| Medicine | 2 | 1 | | | 7 | 10 |
| Church | | | | | 4 | 2 |
| Church admin. | | | | | | 12 |
| Government | | 3 | | | | 7 |
| Social work | | | | | | 2 |
| Media | | | | | | 5 |
| Housewives | | | | | | 2 |
| Private means | 2 | 1 | | | | |
| Other | | 1 | | | | |
| Totals, percentages* | 98 | 100 | 99 | 101 | 97 | 99 |
| Business share, % | 93 | 88 | 100 | 95 | 64 | 34 |

Note: *Where totals do not add up to a hundred, this is due to the removal of decimal places.

One way of identifying American Methodists in business would be to analyse the ca. 100 lay delegates from North America attending each of the six international ecumenical Methodist Conferences between 1881 and 1931, linking their names to Census occupational data. A rapid examination of the American delegates to the 1911 Conference gathered in Toronto finds that among the Methodist Episcopal delegates was Charles W. Fairbanks, originally a railway lawyer but more recently former Vice-President of the USA under President Theodore Roosevelt. Among the Methodist Episcopal Church, South delegates was Asa Candler, the founder of Coca Cola. Another collective profile could be assembled from the names of the laypersons gathered in Kansas City in 1939 to negotiate and organise the formation of the Methodist Episcopal Church.[22]

---

[22] *Journal of the Uniting Conference of the Methodist Episcopal Church; Methodist Episcopal Church, South; and the Methodist Protestant Church*, ed. Lud H. Estes with Edgar Rohrer Heckman and Cuthbert Warner Bates (New York and Cincinnati: Methodist Publishing House, 1939).

## Who in the British and American Business Elites Had Methodist Linkages?

As noted, businesspeople among the lay leaderships of Methodism may not have been major figures in the world of business. To confirm or contradict hagiographical profiles, evaluations from the business community and from business historians are needed. The former might appear in ranked lists of large firms either in an industry or in a particular region or locality.[23] The latter was attempted in two major historical projects at the London School of Economics and at Glasgow University in the 1980s and resulted in two dictionaries of business leaders in Britain between the 1860s and the 1960s.[24] Since the editors were advised by industry specialists, the volumes offer a relatively objective identification and evaluation of careers with major significance. These sources thus serve as universes against which to compare denominational business figures. As seen in Table 24.2, those with adult Methodist commitment in the British business elite comprised only 3 per cent of the 1,500 in the set. Comparing, unfairly perhaps, this share to the presence of Methodists in the UK's churchgoing population in 1907, a highpoint, suggests that other denominations contributed more to the elite.

Table 24.2  Methodist adult affiliations among business leaders in Britain in the *DBB* and the *DSBB* (1,561 individuals) compared with members in 1907

| DBB/DSBB | Nos | Per cent | Church members | | Per cent |
| --- | --- | --- | --- | --- | --- |
| Methodists | | | Wesleyans in England | 447,474 | |
| | | | Wesleyans in Wales | 41,472 | |
| | | | Wesleyans in Scotland | 9,518 | |
| Wesleyans | 34 | 2.2 | TOTAL WESLEYANS | 498,464 | 4.2 |
| Primitive Methodists | 4 | 0.3 | Primitive Methodists | 205,182 | 1.7 |
| United Methodist Free Church | 3 | 0.2 | United Methodist Free Church | 80,323 | 0.7 |

---

[23] An approach exemplified in Simon J. D. Green, *Religion and the Age of Decline: Organisation and Experience in Industrial Yorkshire, 1870–1920* (Cambridge: Cambridge University Press, 1996).

[24] *DBB*; Anthony Slaven and Sydney Checkland (eds), *Dictionary of Scottish Business Biography: 1860–1960* (Aberdeen: Aberdeen University Press, 2 vols, 1986, 1990).

| | | | | | |
|---|---|---|---|---|---|
| Methodist New Connexion | 4 | 0.3 | Methodist New Connexion | 37,017 | 0.3 |
| Bible Christians | | | Bible Christians | 32,317 | 0.3 |
| Others | 4 | 0.3 | Others | | |
| Total | 49 | 3.1 | Total Methodists | 853,303 | 7 |
| | | | TOTAL CHURCH-GOERS | 11,807,644 | 100 |

*Sources*
DBB = 1,181.
DSBB = 380.
Robert Currie, Alan Gilbert and, Lee Horsley, *Churches and Churchgoers* (Oxford: Oxford University Press, 1977).

A list of the Methodists appearing in these two dictionaries (though none were in the Scottish dictionary) is given in Appendix 1.

The figure of 3.1 per cent as the Methodist share of the British business elite 1860–1960 may be compared with the 10.6 per cent found in early Victorian England for the textile masters, the business elite of the country's dominant industry at that time.[25]

In the United States there are plenty of clues about outstanding individuals but, apparently, no systematic work has been done on collective biographies of Methodist business leaders. Over 60 years ago members of the Research Center in Entrepreneurial History at Harvard Business School analysed the collective characteristics of the United States industrial elite in the 1870s and again in the first decade of the twentieth century. In each study and in Mabel Newcomer's study of America's 1950s business elite, aggregated religious affiliations were presented. So percentages could be quoted but the individuals behind them could not be identified.[26] Analysis was further facilitated after John Ingham published his extremely valuable *Biographical Dictionary of American Business Leaders*, which usefully, though not always comprehensively, provides a religious affiliation for most of its subjects and an index to these affiliations.[27]

American Methodists collectively may or may not have been more strongly represented in the United States business elite than their British counterparts were

---

[25] Anthony C. Howe, *The Cotton Masters, 1830–1860* (Oxford: Clarendon Press, 1984), 62.

[26] Frances W. Gregory and Irene D. Neu, 'The American Industrial Elite in the 1870s: Their Social Origins' and William Miller, 'American Historians and the Business Elite' both in William Miller (ed.), *Men in Business: Essays on the Historical Role of the Entrepreneur* (New York, NY: Harper Torch Books, 1962); Mabel Newcomer, *The Big Business Executive and the Factors that Made Him, 1900–1950* (New York, NY: Columbia University Press, 1955).

[27] John N. Ingham, *Biographical Dictionary of American Business Leaders* (4 vols, Westport, CT: Greenwood Press, 1983).

in their business elite. In the 1870s 6 per cent of the United States industrial leaders (of 144 cases) had Methodist backgrounds; in the 1900s, 9 per cent of United States business leaders (of 174 cases) had Methodist backgrounds; and in 1950, 10 per cent (of 390 cases) chose 'Methodist' when asked for their religious preference.[28] Background and preference in the USA might capture much weaker levels of commitment than the strength of the affiliation counted in the British cases in Table 24.2.

Of 971 individuals in John Ingham's *Dictionary*, 53 or 5.5 per cent had Methodist connections (see Appendix 2). However, his list does not distinguish between Methodist upbringing and adult affiliation. It includes, besides Asa Candler, such household names as Harper Bros, publishers; H. J. Heinz, food processor; John Wanamaker, Philadelphia department store chain magnate; and F. W. Woolworth, chain store merchant. Alfred P. Sloan had a devout Methodist father but little adult contact with the church himself. Three other names were synonymous with the American automobile industry: Walter Chrysler, Henry Ford II and Clement Studebaker. Short bibliographical notes append the entries in Ingham. A similar source is the more recent *American National Biography*.

# What Formative Influences Have Methodists in Business Received and How Have they Exercised Their Wealth and Position?

## Formative Influences

A majority of Methodist lay leaders in business in Britain were neither single traders of the corner-shop variety, nor directors of the giant firms of the kind that developed in the first merger wave between the 1890s and the 1900s. A random sample of 5 per cent of the 21,100 local preachers listed in *The Methodist Local Preachers Who's Who, 1934* revealed that the largest occupational group were those in intermediate, non-manual (lower-middle) class occupations (38.7 per cent) and of these 12 per cent with dealers or retailers.[29] So far this is the best national picture of the business backgrounds of Methodist laypersons. Methodists in business frequently seem to have headed small and medium sized firms, between five or ten and 500 employees, often in retailing. Prime Minister Margaret Thatcher's father, Alfred Roberts, owner of two grocery shops in Grantham, Lincolnshire, town councillor and a Methodist lay preacher in the 1940s, epitomised the Methodist businessman: his firm was small in scale, face-to-face in organisation and conservative in its

---

[28] Miller, *Men in Business*, 200, 324; Newcomer, *Big Business Executive*, 47–8.

[29] Clive D. Field, 'The Methodist Local Preacher: An Occupational Analysis', in Geoffrey Milburn and Margaret Batty (eds), *Workaday Preachers: The Story of Methodist Local Preaching* (London: Methodist Publishing House, 1995), 240–41.

values.[30] However, as made clear at the beginning of this essay, the focus here is on members of business elites.

While formal education was important, business abilities rested upon leadership competences. These included interpersonal skills, numeracy abilities and creative opportunism. Sons of businessmen could learn these from their fathers, apprentices from their masters, but without these advantages one route to social advance was the chapel. Examples from the 'pantheon' lives of Methodists in business illustrate the point.

Harold Bellman, prominent Wesleyan and mastermind of the vast expansion of the Abbey Road & St Johns Wood Building Society in the 1920s and 1930s, vividly remembered his chapel upbringing. His father, a coachbuilder, migrated from Cornwall to London in the mid 1880s and joined the Wesleyan Methodist Church in Fernhead Road, Paddington, following a path tracked by other Cornish Methodists.[31]

At the 'old chapel' Harold Bellman had a social education as much as an induction into a life of faith. Distinguished Methodist ministers and local civic dignitaries visited his parents' home and he watched and learned the courtesies of hosting family guests. In the Bible class and the Wesley Guild he honed public speaking skills. From his elders he received encouragement and advice. His father, the chapel choirmaster, ensured that he heard a good diet of evangelical hymns and the choral works of Handel, Haydn and Stainer beloved by Victorians. In the chapel Sunday School he met his future wife. Here too he learned and gained faith, faith mediated through the stories and language of the Bible and the words and tunes of the Wesleyan hymnbook. For Harold Bellman, if age did not lend a roseate tinge to his memories, chapel was an essentially joyful community in which to grow up. Equally significantly, he made friendships with other like-minded youngsters, creating lifetime contacts.[32] No matter that the Wesleyans represented only 2 per cent of the population of inner London in the 1880s and early 1900s, this kind of networking, it is now recognised, was a crucial social mechanism in developing business careers.[33]

Bellman's experience was metropolitan, middle class and socially accommodating. It is likely to have been more typical of Wesleyan than of the smaller, more democratic and less clerically dominated Methodist branches, also drawing on the working and lower-middle classes. Such was the chapel world of John Mackintosh, the Halifax toffee manufacturer. While the textile mill, where he started as a 10-year-old half-timer in 1878, and the Methodist New Connexion chapel in Queens Road, Halifax, were of a similar size – 200 workers compared to 200 members – it was the democratic structures of this chapel that gave him his life opportunities. First, through Sunday School and the young men's Bible class, he learned his Bible stories and came into an evangelical faith. This equipped him

---

[30] Margaret Thatcher, *The Path to Power* (London: HarperCollins, 1995), 4.
[31] Hugh McLeod, *Class and Religion in the Late-Victorian City* (London: Croom Helm, 1974), 61.
[32] Bellman, *Cornish Cockney*, 33–45.
[33] McLeod, *Class and Religion*, 314, Table 20; and Mark Casson, *Information and Organisation: A New Perspective on the Theory of the Firm* (Oxford: Clarendon Press, 1997).

with a vision of life as a Christian moral and spiritual battle. Secondly, from the age of 15 he progressed up the chapel-based hierarchies of the Band of Hope and the Sunday School, serving as librarian and secretary. Eventually he was elected superintendent of the 600-strong Sunday School. In these posts he learned skills vital in both the voluntary and commercial domains: composing minutes; letter writing; teaching; communicating informally; counselling individuals; conducting meetings; public speaking; and accounting. Thirdly, in the chapel he met his wife, the lady whose recipe for toffee laid the foundation for his remarkable business success. Lastly, the chapel supplied John Mackintosh with elements directly transferable for his leap from the factory to entrepreneurial independence. In the chapel's Penny Bank he and his wife saved most of the £100 they used to set up their own shop in 1890. From the publicity drives of the Band of Hope he drew ideas for his own aggressive toffee marketing campaigns. And in the chapel he found his closest network of trustworthy friends, among them, one of two who became directors of his toffee manufacturing company. Clearly the Mackintosh family chapel offered a radical emancipation from the wage dependence and social deference inherent in a late-nineteenth-century paternalistic factory culture.[34]

From the imperfect evidence of the early careers of Primitive Methodist Vice-Presidents, 'a conversion experience, instant or gradual, was the vital portal' to Primitive Methodist membership and leadership.[35] While a life changing conversion experience was not mentioned by Bellman, for other Wesleyans it was typical. Joseph Rank the miller, whose wife took him back to church in 1880, came under the dynamic ministry of the Rev. Simpson Johnson (much later, President of Conference).[36] At an evangelistic mission in 1883 Rank came to personal faith in Christ, expressing that as he sang the hymn, 'I believe on the Son, I'm saved by the blood of the Crucified One'.[37] In contrast, J. Arthur Rank, Joseph's son, like John Mackintosh, apparently gained a personal faith in Christ more gradually. Because a personal faith imparted spiritual energy, meaning and purpose to life, a vision of the future, some understanding of the past, a sense of stewardship and standards of right behaviour for Christian believers, much more needs to be learned about the manner in which business leaders in Methodism came to faith and how they understood that faith.

Good schooling was the other well-travelled route into the late-nineteenth-century business world. Educationally, Wesleyans were the most privileged of the Methodist sects. Kingswood School, Bath was confined to the sons of their ministers. Other Wesleyan schools, with fees of about £30 a year, like Woodhouse Grove near

---

[34] David J. Jeremy, 'Chapel in a Business Career: The Case of John Mackintosh (1868–1920)', in David J. Jeremy (ed.), *Business and Religion in Britain* (Aldershot: Gower, 1988), 95–117; Patrick Joyce, *Work, Society and Politics: The Culture of the Factory in Later Victorian England* (Brighton: Harvester, 1980), 90–157.

[35] Jeremy, 'Laity' (2010), 254.

[36] 'Johnson, Simpson', in John Vickers (ed.), *Dictionary of Methodism in Great Britain and Ireland* [Peterborough: Epworth, 2000].

[37] Burnett, *Through the Mill*, 43.

Bradford, or Truro College (later, School), or The Leys School, Cambridge (set up in 1875 for the sons of Methodist businessmen) catered for the denomination's middle-class members. From school they might be articled to a professional partnership, the law being a favoured one; or else they might gain a place at an Oxford or Cambridge college, once these were freed from religious tests in the early1870s. Or else they might proceed to one of the new civic universities for a technical, scientific higher education. School and college offered some of the early-career networks often important to an individual's social and economic advance. School also supplied training in leadership, but it was leadership exercised in a coercive hierarchy. However trained, the fortunate beneficiaries of these forms of education could return to a family firm or enter one of the professions. Either way, and especially if they were responsible for a workforce of dozens or hundreds, they needed the skills of man-management for which, arguably, the chapel was better at providing than the school.

## Wealth Accumulation

In his sermon on 'The Use of Money', John Wesley advised, 'gain all you can; save all you can; give all you can'. The sermon came to have the force of a papal edict. It was included in the published collection of Wesley's *Sermons* which from 1763 to the present constituted part of the standard doctrine of Methodism.[38] Cited in the trust deeds of every British Methodist chapel, studied by ministers, office holders and lay preachers, the *Sermons*, and this one or its dictum, lurked somewhere in the commercial mentality of many a Methodist.[39] How then did Victorian and later Methodist laymen and women accumulate their wealth?

Judging by the Census evidence behind Table 24.1 and biographical data on Primitive Methodist Vice-Presidents, Methodist businessmen found at least three ways of pursuing successful careers. Some entered manufacturing industries where they met rising economic demand in expanding urban populations, particularly in the cities, and in foreign markets (though increasingly protected from competition), until the First World War. Demand for staples, like coal, food, textiles and clothing, and housing, offered opportunities that men like Alexander Ritson (coalmine owner), Joseph Rank (flour miller), Joseph Hepworth (clothing) and the Walmsley brothers (builders) seized. Another avenue for manufacturers came with a rising standard of living. Luxuries turned into necessities. Toffee made John Mackintosh a fortune of over £250,000 and jam made Sir William Hartley a millionaire.

A second route to wealth came for those who moved from manufacturing into services. Among leading Wesleyan laymen the oft-occurring description of merchant signified distribution activities. Here overheads could be lower and workforces smaller per unit of capital than in manufacturing; consequently profits could be greater. Those in distribution comprised 33 and 17 per cent of the samples

---

[38] No. 44 in the published collection of Wesley's *Sermons*.
[39] See comments in Milburn and Batty (eds), *Workaday Preachers*, 49, 112.

in 1881 and 1907, respectively. Among the Primitive Methodist Vice-Presidents, 1872–1913, this category reached 40 per cent. If other kinds of services are included, then over 60 per cent of the 167 leading Wesleyan and Primitive Methodist laymen gravitated to these intermediary commercial activities.

This might require removal to London, the traditional path to fortune. In the late nineteenth century London harboured the largest concentration of markets in the world and, as Rubinstein found, here the wealthiest found their fortunes – in financial, shipping, commodity and property markets, or in supplying the daily wants of the urban population.[40] An interim analysis of the Wesleyan lay leaders shows that in 1881 some 24 per cent of them lived in London, a proportion that rose to 30 per cent in 1907.[41]

These routes primarily were economic choices. Equally, maybe more, important were networks, particularly Methodist and family networks by which individuals found new opportunities, associates and kin. This has been demonstrated in the case of Sheffield where Methodism was a powerful social influence.[42]

As a result of following these and other business paths, were the Methodists a wealthy group? The evidence suggests that indeed they were. At the conclusion of the Wesleyan Thanksgiving Fund in 1884, out of thousands of names, maybe 47,500 (assuming a rough count of a hundred names per page), 347 were wealthy enough to give over £100, while 34 gave £1,000 or more.[43] These were vast sums when an agricultural labourer was earning about £50 a year. At 2010 prices £100 would be at least £10,000 and £1,000, £100,000.

The *Dictionary of Business Biography* includes 50 British business leaders with adult Methodist connections. Of these, 38 died between 1880 and 1946, when death duties on estates of over £500,000 climbed from 7 per cent to 65 per cent.[44] Despite sharpened motives for tax avoidance, 28 of the 38 left estates of over £100,000. Seven of them left estates of over £500,000, including four millionaires, Lord Furness, Sir Prince Smith and Sir William Hartley and Lord Runciman. Yet these were not true measures of wealth for they missed lifetime accumulations. Joseph Rank left £70,000 but well before he died gave £1 million to each of his seven children and several million to Methodist causes.[45]

---

[40] William D. Rubinstein, *Men of Property: The Very Wealthy in Britain since the Industrial Revolution* (London: Croom Helm, 1981), 102–10.

[41] I have arbitrarily taken London to stretch from Highgate in the North to Beckenham in the South and from Woolwich in the East to Hammersmith in the West. This is an area which by 1900 covered Victorian suburbia and was served by a commuter railway network. See Donald J. Olson, *The Growth of Victorian London* (London: Batsford, 1970).

[42] Clyde Binfield, 'Victorian Values and Industrious Connexions', *PWHS*, 55 (2006), 141–68.

[43] *Report of the Wesleyan-Methodist Thanksgiving Fund, 1878–1883* (London: Wesleyan-Methodist Book-Room, 1884).

[44] See table in David J. Jeremy, *A Business History of Britain, 1900–1990s* (Oxford: Oxford University Press, 1998), 118.

[45] Wakelin, *Man behind the Gong*, 31.

Only two of these four millionaires were Wesleyans. Did the more democratic structures of the Methodist New Connexion and Primitive chapels engender sharper ambitions for the life of an independent tradesman? So many other dimensions come into the equation that it would be hard to demonstrate the point. All that can be said is that the Wesleyans produced 34 members of the *DBB* elite and the Primitives, four. As a ratio of their members in 1932, the Wesleyans produced one for every 15,000 members while the Primitives could manage only one per 50,000 members, making the Wesleyans 3.4 times more efficient. But was this an accident of *DBB* selection? Were Wesleyans more London-based? Were they more educated? Were they more middle class and theologically accommodating? Did their clerically dominated governance free the laity from more of the responsibilities of chapel and circuit, thereby allowing them to dedicate more of their time to business?

## Stakeholder Relations

Business ownership might lead an employer into exercising a suffocating paternalism. Did Methodists resist the temptation to be all-controlling employers? One, albeit disputed, evidence of good intentions as an employer was the introduction of profit sharing schemes. Two of the Primitive Methodist Vice-Presidents, Sir William Hartley and William Ewart Morse, introduced them. Hartley had well over a thousand seasonal fruit pickers plus 600 permanent employees in his jam works at Aintree and London. Morse employed 200 people in his drapery shop chain based in Swindon. On the other hand, the attempts of Christopher Furness, a New Connexion Methodist in the North East, in 1908 to introduce profit sharing to his shipyards and coalmines were choked by trade union opposition.[46] In Northampton during the First World War, Charles Lewis, a boot and shoe manufacturer, provided welfare schemes for his 1,400 employees.[47]

Surprisingly perhaps, North East Primitive Methodist capitalists were involved in trade unions. John Coward, a Durham import and export merchant, was treasurer of the Durham Miners' Federation. James Bell, northern representative (manager) of the Leeds clothing firm of Joseph Hepworth (a United Methodist) was trustee of the Durham Miners' Association (which merged with the Federation in 1897). At Crewe William McNeill, a Primitive Methodist and local Liberal Party leader and a travelling draper, led in defeating the London & North Western Railway Co.'s tyrannical policy of politically intimidating its 6,000 employees, 1885–90.[48]

Were other Methodist lay leaders mindful of the interests of employees, suppliers, customers, local communities? The Wesleyan Joseph Rank was a hard, driven employer, whose upbringing was moulded by a severe stepmother and father. Often harsh and inconsiderate of others, he reportedly always gave a good

---

[46] Gordon Boyce, 'Christopher Furness', *DBB*.
[47] Jeremy, 'Laity' (2010), 255–6.
[48] Diane K. Drummond, *Crewe: Railway Town, Company and People, 1840–1914* (Aldershot: Scolar Press, 1995), 133–85.

price when buying out a rival miller.[49] The Primitive Methodist William Hartley would unexpectedly compensate his suppliers of soft fruits when their crops were damaged by weather. When a trade depression left some Oldham cotton mills unfinished and equipment contractors unpaid, Hartley and fellow Primitive Methodist John Bunting bought several mills, profiting from their sale when trade recovered. Hartley, feeling guilty about his good fortune, surprised one contractor with a compensating cheque for £1,000.[50] What is certain is that motives are usually mixed and almost impossible to disentangle. Self-interest intertwined with altruism. Rank and Hartley would have known that Biblical morality and commercial sense coincided. But all these cases are anecdotal, insufficient for reaching a general verdict on the stakeholder relations of Methodist lay leaders in business.

It should not, however, be assumed that Christians in business, Methodist or otherwise, had an unblemished record in dealing with their stakeholders: employees, suppliers, customers, community, government or the environment. Among Methodists the most deplorable example was that of the Turner family, cotton and asbestos manufacturers at Rochdale, Lancashire from the 1880s. Their failure to protect their employees and foreign mine workers from diseases caused by asbestos exposure might be excused before 1924 when medical science had not cautioned about the material's toxic effects. After that date, Turner & Newall directors' determination to put corporate profits and shareholder interests above those of all other stakeholders was inexcusable and particularly so when perpetrated by pious and otherwise good Methodists.[51]

Ironically, two Methodist businessmen in the House of Lords found themselves promoting forms of gambling, one because he headed a semi-government agency, the other because he chaired a large corporation in the leisure industry. For Lord Rank, the latter, see below. The former, Lord Mackintosh (son of John Mackintosh), Chairman of the post-war National Savings Movement, introduced Premium Bonds in 1956. The backdrop was the rising popularity of football pools and the Treasury's need to increase income. The British Council of Churches, including the Methodist Church, protested that Premium Bonds were a form of gambling. Mackintosh recalled that he 'could not see any harm in the scheme, as the point was that the money was not at stake, only the interest'. At a small dinner party he told the Archbishop of Canterbury, Dr Fisher, 'I know it is the business of the Churches to save sinners, but I didn't know it was their duty to stop sinners saving.'[52] As a member of the Churches Committee on Gambling he seems either to have been inconsistent or else seduced by a benevolent definition of gambling. Contrary to expectations, Premium

---

[49] Burnett, *Through the Mill*, 198–9.
[50] Peake, *Hartley*, 61–4.
[51] See Geoffrey Tweedale, *Magic Mineral to Killer Dust: Turner & Newall and the Asbestos Hazard* (Oxford: Oxford University Press, 2000), the definitive study. For some linkages to Methodism see David J. Jeremy, 'Corporate Responses to the Emergent Recognition of a Health Hazard in the UK Asbestos Industry: The Case of Turner & Newall, 1920–1960', *Business and Economic History: The Journal of the Business History Conference*, (1995), 254–65.
[52] Mackintosh, *By Faith and Work*, 132–3.

Bonds did not divert the public from other forms of gambling. By 1981 35 per cent of the adult population entered football pools every week.[53]

In the USA, late-nineteenth-century business magnates, portrayed as robber barons by the muck-rakers of the Progressive era, having accumulated stupendous fortunes, gave large sums to the churches.[54] As ever their motives were mixed and their methods evinced a transfer of business techniques, especially marketing, into the religious realm. For example, Laurence Moore found parallels between Dwight Moody's evangelistic techniques and the marketing methods of the business barons of the post-Civil War decades; and singled out John Wanamaker, Philadelphia department store chain magnate, pillar of the Methodist Church and promoter of Moody's preaching campaigns.[55] Wanamaker's precise Methodist affiliation is missed. Later Methodists included exploiters and reformers in entangling and yet polarising business–religion relationships in the 1920s. Harry Collins Spillman, author of books on personal development, typewriting and speechmaking, admitted: 'I am a Methodist because it runs in the family like snoring and obesity' and found in the Bible 'the background of the language of all the great advertising experts of the world'.[56] On the other hand, Rev. Harry F. Ward led the most radical liberal Methodists from Social Christianity towards Christian Marxism in the 1920s and 1930s.[57] The British parallel could be found in the career of the Reverend Samuel Keeble, Wesleyan minister and early Christian Socialist. The shift to the left, headed by the clergy, was more successful in Britain than in the USA – though in British Methodism it was strongly resisted in the early 1930s by the ageing Sir Robert Perks and then by Sir Josiah Stamp.[58]

## Wealth Distribution

John Wesley was in no doubt that the resources God gave were to be used in a ranked order. First, the individual should 'provide things needful for himself' (food, clothing, necessities for 'preserving the body in health and strength'). Secondly, 'provide these for your wife, children, your servants, or any others who pertain to

---

[53] George Thompson Brake, *Policy and Politics in British Methodism, 1932–1982* (London: Edsall, 1984), 533–44.

[54] For example, Matthew Josephson, *The Robber Barons: The Great American Capitalists, 1861–1901* (1934; reprint New York: Harcourt Brace Jovanovich, 1962): work now well superseded by a stream of scholarly biographies, studies from those associated with the Harvard Research Center in Entrepreneurial History, and John Ingham, already cited.

[55] R. Laurence Moore, *Selling God: American Religion in the Marketplace of Culture* (New York: Oxford University Press, 1994), 184–8.

[56] Rolf Lunden, *Business and Religion in the American 1920s* (New York: Greenwood Press, 1988), 111.

[57] Harry F. Ward, *The Social Creed of the Churches* (New York, NY: Abingdon Press, 1914); Paul T. Phillips, *A Kingdom on Earth: Anglo-American Social Christianity, 1880–1940* (Pennsylvania, PA: Pennsylvania State University Press, 1996), 257–60.

[58] Jeremy, *Capitalists and Christians*, 176–83.

your household'. If anything remains, 'do good to them that are of the household of faith'. And if there were still resources left (Wesley again quoted Paul), 'as you have opportunity, do good unto all men'.[59]

With the first generations of industrialists came much soulsearching about the age-long problem of covetousness. From the 1850s onwards the concept of systematic beneficence developed among evangelicals.[60] One popular statement of systematisation, William Arthur's *The Duty of Giving Away a Stated Proportion of Income* (1855), had a reported print run of 100,000 copies. Since Arthur was a Wesleyan minister and biographer of Samuel Budgett of Bristol, the model of a Wesleyan retail merchant and philanthropist, this tract strongly influenced Methodist businessmen. Certainly systematic giving determined the amount of William P. Hartley's wealth distribution. On 1 January 1877 (three years after he opened his first jam factory at Bootle and was still paying three-quarters of his profits to creditors) he recorded in a small notebook the following resolution:

> I have for some months back been very seriously impressed that it is my duty to give one-tenth of my income towards religious and charitable objects and, after careful consideration, my wife and myself have agreed to give one-tenth of our total income. This we consider to be our duty and pray for grace to always continue in the same path.[61]

The notebook shows that in 1877 he gave away a tenth of his salary, amounting to £62-18s, and a tenth of his share of the firm's profits, totalling £38-0-6 for eight months to June. Thereafter, each January, as a spiritual discipline, Hartley set aside part of his income for philanthropic purposes. His giving was proportionate as well as systematic. The greater the income, he believed, the greater the proportion that should be given away, and during his career he increased his own donations from a tenth to a third of his gross income.[62]

Hartley's friend and biographer, the Biblical scholar Arthur Samuel Peake, observed that wealth distribution was more costly in time and anxiety than its accumulation. Applications inundated Hartley. Distressing causes, like sickness, bereavement, poverty or disaster, appealed to his human sympathies. Others were religious or ecclesiastical – for church building, church debt reduction, needy societies and circuits, bazaars, forward movements, church institutes, many from the Primitive Methodists, his own denomination. And there were scoundrels.

How could the deserving be sifted and ranked? Hartley amplified Wesley's advice by following a number of principles. Places with which he was specially associated, like his birthplace (Colne in Lancashire), or the places where he had

---

[59] John Wesley, *On the Use of Money*, III/3 in *WJW* (*Sermons*), 624–6.
[60] Jane Garnett, '"Gold and the Gospel": Systematic Beneficence in Mid-19th-Century England' in W. J. Sheils and Diana Wood (eds), *The Church and Wealth* (Oxford: Basil Blackwell, 1987), 355.
[61] Notebook, 1877–84, photocopy in possession of Peter Fearon, Leicester University.
[62] The rest of the information on Hartley comes from Peake, *Hartley*, 78–90.

lived, had his sympathy. Places with which his family was associated also benefited from his generosity. His own denomination ranked highly. Usually he announced a challenge offer, promising a specific amount – 10 per cent on all sums raised, or the last £10 if the sum was raised by a given date. At other times he bore the whole cost.

Eventually the distribution of his charity was too much even for Hartley. In 1908 he appointed a Primitive Methodist minister, Dr Thomas Mitchell, to live in Southport and take over the duties of investigating applications for Hartley's help, recommend policies and undertake the necessary correspondence. After Mitchell's death in 1915 another minister 'of long experience and high character with a wide knowledge of the denomination' was appointed, though he too predeceased Hartley.

Peake recorded that Hartley gave away nearly £300,000, of which £230,000 went to charities serving the whole community, like the Aintree Institute, the Colne Cottage Hospital, Colne Hospital, the Liverpool Maternity Hospital, homes for the aged at Colne, and departments of the Universities of Liverpool and Manchester. It could be argued, however, that Hartley ought to have directed more charity towards relieving the pauper masses of Liverpool and less towards his home town.

## Business People in the Methodist Churches

Since businesspeople had such a heavy presence within British Methodism, it could be expected that they would assume important roles within the life of the Methodist branches before 1932, and the Methodist Church thereafter. Chiefly they provided funds for church expansion at home and missionary work abroad. This frequently included chapel building;[63] outstanding in this respect, for he was active in France as well as Britain, was Isaac Holden.[64] Both nationally and locally they filtered business practices into church organisation and administration. Yet they were not prepared to be passive, uncritical sources of money and business know-how. Habituated to monitoring and controlling, deciding and directing, they occasionally collided with the clergy. Consequently the theological and political tendencies of church professionals, shifting to the left since the 1890s, clashed with the more conservative preferences of laypeople with economic power.

Methodist fundraising before the First World War was spearheaded by men in business. They acted as treasurers, lent their business reputations to fundraising projects ranging from a local church bazaar to a national denominational scheme, and they ensured that due process was followed. As astonishing as their generosity was their willingness to proclaim their good works. In view of the

---

[63] Peter Forsaith suggests that a future researcher might interrogate the register of Methodist Church Listed Buildings to track gifts of business benefactors. It should be added that before 1914 the more substantial ones were acknowledged at the annual Conference (or its equivalent) of the main Methodist branches, acknowledgements that were noted in denominational newspapers and also in the published *Minutes of Conference.*

[64] Jennings, 'Sir Isaac Holden'.

teaching of Jesus that alms should be given in secret (Matthew 6: 3), this seems perverse. Joseph Rank claimed that he was stirred by the text about 'provoking one another to love and good works' (Hebrews 10: 24). The technique of making a challenge offer necessarily required the challenger to go public. Sometimes it was regarded as a challenge if, over a period of two or three years, the names and sums of those who did contribute were published. Perhaps the most remarkable example of this was the large volume produced at the conclusion of the Wesleyan Thanksgiving Fund in 1884 (already mentioned).

A challenge offer was sprung on the Wesleyan Methodist Conference in 1900.[65] Robert Perks, railway lawyer and contractor and treasurer of the Wesleyan Twentieth Century Fund, and one of the most eminent Wesleyan laymen of his day, told the 300 ministers and 300 laypeople gathered at Burslem that July that the million-guineas Fund, launched in 1898, still had £270,000 to raise. Could it be done before the end of December 1900?[66] Conference was not sufficiently moved until the Rev. Hugh Price Hughes, passionate leader of the Forward Movement and prophet of 'Social Christianity' (seeking to save society as well as individuals), rose to his feet and pleaded with 'the men of means in the Conference' to give 'not out of income, but out of capital'. In an atmosphere of high emotion sober commercial men tossed thrift and caution to the winds as, one after another, they stood up to announce new or increased donations. Joseph Rank added 10,000 guineas to the 7,000 he had already promised in his own circuit and district. Between them, in the space of minutes, seven Wesleyan businessmen gave over £65,000, or 26 per cent, of the 250,000 guineas (£262,500) needed. The Twentieth Century Fund target was met on the last day of 1901, when £1,073,682 had been received by the Fund's five treasurers.[67]

Among the Primitive Methodists, William Hartley was not only a judicious benefactor but also an organiser of denominational structures. He established a Chapel Aid Association in 1886–89 to mobilise loans for church building. For three decades, starting in 1890, he served as general treasurer of the Primitive Methodist Missionary Society, and sharply criticised mission station farming from a commercial point of view. He endowed a ministerial training college at Manchester and was responsible for recruiting to it, from Oxford, Arthur Samuel Peake, later to become an internationally regarded Biblical scholar. On his own initiative, Hartley purchased Holborn Town Hall, London, enlarged and refurbished it, and then sold it back at two-thirds of the cost price to the Primitive Methodist Church for its national headquarters and publishing house. His services were recognised in his election as Vice-President of the Primitive

---

[65] *Methodist Recorder*, 2 August 1900. What follows is derived from my essay, 'Late Victorian and Edwardian Methodist Businessmen and Wealth', in David J. Jeremy (ed.), *Religion, Business and Wealth in Modern Britain* (London: Routledge, 1998), 71–85.

[66] For Perks see *DBB, ODNB* and an unpublished paper by Owen Covick, 'R. W. Perks, C. T. Yerkes and Private Financing of Urban Transport Infrastructure in London, 1900–1907' (presented to the ABH Conference, Portsmouth, 2001).

[67] Crane, *Life of Sir Robert W. Perks*, 152.

Methodist Connexion Conference in 1892 and then as President in 1909. In later life he promoted Methodist reunion.

Without being such a controlling figure, Sir Josiah Stamp performed an important organisational role after the Methodist Church in Britain was formed in 1932 by the merger of the Wesleyans, the Primitive Methodists and the United Methodists. Facing the task of unifying the legal, property and financial components of the three connexions, he brought to bear the managerial skills he learned in the Civil Service, the merger experience he gained on the board of Imperial Chemical Industries, and the strategic vision he possessed as President of the London, Midland & Scottish Railway Company.[68] His unrivalled business experience and competence combined with the abilities of William Arthur Sturdy C.B.E. (b. 1877), a senior Civil Servant (in charge of the India Audit Office), and Leslie William Farrow (b. 1888), an LSE-trained accountant, served the newly formed church well.[69] Stamp was one of the new breed of professional corporate executives. In contrast to Hartley, a classic example of a Victorian paternalist, he did not own and control his business, so he could not distribute a fortune and thereby exercise the beneficence and interference that might be troublesome in the life of the church.

Exactly that happened, some would argue, with Joseph Rank and his son J. Arthur Rank, flour miller and film magnate. Enormously rich and generous, they personally through their trusts gave millions to various departments of the Methodist Church, the Methodist Missionary Society and many local churches. Fixing upon the late-nineteenth-century evangelistic panacea of urban Central Halls, they donated large sums in this direction. Arthur Rank latterly spent more than £1 million on renovations at Westminster Central Hall. The preferences of the Ranks in their Methodist benefactions, coupled with their evangelical faith, prompted serious misgivings in the minds of some Methodist clergy. Rev. Donald Soper, Lord Soper, thought that J. Arthur Rank's simple faith and focus upon personal conversion and individual responsibility did not properly reflect the teaching of Jesus about the Kingdom of God and social transformation. Rank thought Soper was too unworldly and too unrealistic. Politically, Soper was a Socialist, Rank a Tory. Another Methodist cleric, Rev. Dr Colin Morris, one-time President of the Methodist Conference, believed that the Central Halls policy was mistaken: 'far from showing the flexibility of the Holy Spirit, it lumbers people down with structures'.[70]

But these were not the only tensions between the Ranks and the Methodist leadership. When J. Arthur Rank, facing a collapse in film-going due to television, authorised bingo sessions in his Odeon cinemas, Methodists deeply opposed to gambling regarded him as delinquent. Conference in 1962 debated

---

[68] See biographical entries by Michael Bywater in the *DBB* and by Jose Harris in the *ODNB*.

[69] W. A. Sturdy, *Methodist Finance: Past, Present and Future* (London: Epworth Press, 1932).

[70] Wakelin, *Man behind the Gong*, 203–5.

whether he should be allowed to remain a member of the Methodist Church. Eventually, convinced of his deep personal faith, Conference declined to expel him.[71] Most disconcertingly, Rank claimed knowledge of the direction of the Holy Spirit which dangerously injected infallibility into his large-scale financial decisionmaking.

The impact of both the Ranks on Methodism is difficult to assess. J. Arthur's biographer Michael Wakelin reaches the extraordinary conclusion that 'there probably wouldn't have been much of a Methodist Church without the Rank connection'.[72] Until access is given to the Methodist Church departmental accounts and the minutes of the various Rank trusts before J. Arthur Rank's death in 1972, these criticisms and evaluations cannot be properly tested.

Much earlier, theology rather than economics was the scene of a clash between powerful laypeople in business and professional clergy. Given the Primitive Methodists' anticlericalism and emphasis on the priesthood of all believers, it was not surprising that controversy broke out at one of their Conferences. In 1907 the Rev. John Day Thompson, a senior Primitive Methodist minister much influenced by the rationalist theologies coming out of Germany, gave a very controversial Hartley Lecture. His Chairman was Councillor George (later Sir George) Green J.P. of Glasgow, Inspector for Scotland of the Prudential Assurance Company (a very senior executive in a company employing 20,000 people). He was also a Primitive Methodist local preacher and former Vice-President. When Thompson expressed doubt about the Second Coming of Christ, the Day of Judgement and the physical resurrection, Green strongly dissented and the Conference refused to let the lecture be published with its usual congratulatory resolution.[73]

## Conclusion

In focusing upon identities, origins and behaviour of Methodist lay leaders in business, mostly in Britain, this essay is no more than a slender introduction to a topic of continuing importance. Little has been said about the mindsets that drove people in business and allowed them to reconcile their faith with sometimes contradictory business behaviour. Very little has illuminated the American scene. Most serious of all is our ignorance of the roles of lay leaders and especially those in business in the countries that in the second half of the twentieth century have seen an explosion of Methodist Christianity: South Africa, Ghana, Chile and South Korea. Are some of the old patterns being

---

[71] Ibid., 223–4.
[72] Ibid., 9.
[73] David J. Jeremy, 'Business Men as Preachers among Methodists in the Early Twentieth Century', in Anthony R. Cross (ed.), *Ecumenism and History: Studies in Honour of John H. Y. Briggs* (Carlisle: Paternoster Press, 2002), 309–15.

repeated? Are there lessons in the British experience? The main one must be that the values of the Kingdom of God inevitably challenge those of the rich and powerful.

# Appendix 1

Table A.1  Methodists among British business leaders, nineteenth and twentieth centuries

|  | U | A |  |  | type | location |
|---|---|---|---|---|---|---|
| W | U | A | Airey, Edwin | Building | i | Leeds |
| W | U | A | Bain, Albert Wellesley | Insurance broking | e | Leeds |
| W | U | A | Bainbridge, Emerson Muschamp | Retailing | e | Newcastle |
| W | U | A | Baldwin, Alfred | Iron and steel | i | Stourport |
| W |  | A | Beale, John Elmes* | Retailing | e | Bournemouth |
| unpl |  | A | Bedford, John | Retailing | m | Plymouth and London |
| W | U | A | Bellman, Charles Harold | Building societies | m | London |
| W | U | A | Boot, Jesse | Pharmaceuticals | e | Nottingham |
| P |  | A | Bunting, John A. | Company promoter | e | Oldham |
| W |  | A | Fenwick, John James | Retailing | e | Newcastle |
| W |  | A | Ferens, Thomas Robinson | Detergent manufacturer | m | Hull |
| NC |  | A | Firth, Mark | Steel manufacturer | e | Sheffield |
| UMF | U | A | Furness, Christopher | Shipowner | i, e | West Hartlepool |
| W | U | A | Gee, Henry Simpson** | Shoe retailing | i | Leicester |
| unpl |  | A | Gomme, Ebenezer | Furniture manufacturer | e | High Wycombe |
| W | U | A | Hartley, James** | Glass manufacturer | e | Sunderland |
| P | U | A | Hartley, William Pickles | Jam manufacturer | e | Liverpool |
| W |  | A | Hattersley, Richard L. | Textile machinery making | i | Keighley |
| NC |  | A | Hepworth, Joseph | Clothing manufacturer | e | Leeds |
| W | U | A | Holden, Isaac | Wool combing | e | Bradford |
| W | U | A | Holland, William Henry*** | Cotton manufacturer | i | Manchester |

| | | Name | Occupation | | Location |
|---|---|---|---|---|---|
| W | A | Jolly, James Hornby | Steel manufacturer | m | Cardiff |
| unpl | A | Kenning, George | Motorcar distribution | i | Derbyshire |
| NC | U | Mackintosh, Harold Vincent | Toffee manufacturer | i | Halifax |
| NC | U | Mackintosh, John | Toffee manufacturer | e | Halifax |
| W | U | Mallinson, Stuart Sidney | Timber merchant | i | London |
| W | U | Mallinson, William J. | Timber merchant | i | London |
| W | A | Mitchell, Henry | Worsted merchant | m | Bradford |
| W | U | Musgrave, John | Steam engine manufacturer | i | Bolton |
| W | U | Owen, Owen**** | Retailing | e | Liverpool |
| W | U | Perks, Robert William | Railways | m | London |
| W | U | Posnett, Robert Harold | Leather | i | Runcorn |
| W | U | Rank, Joseph | Flour miller | e | Hull |
| W | U | Rank, Joseph Arthur | Flour miller & film maker | i & e | Hull, London |
| W | A | Reed, Albert Edwin | Paper manufacturer | e | Kent |
| W | A | Ritson, Utrick Alexander | Coalmine owner | e | Newcastle |
| W | U | Runciman, Walter | Shipowner | e | South Shields |
| W | U | Rushbrook, Frederick William | Cycle retailer | e | Leicester |
| W | A | Sankey, John William | Iron manufacturer | i | Bilston |
| W | A | Sankey, Joseph | Iron manufacturer | e | Bilston |
| W | U | Smith, Prince | Worsted machinery maker | i | Keighley |
| W | A | Stamp, Josiah Charles | Railways | m | London |
| W | U | Stephenson, William Haswell | Coalmine owner | e | Newcastle |
| W | A | Sutherland, Arthur M. | Shipowner | e | Newcastle |
| UMF | A | Thompson, Robert | Shipbuilding | i | Durham |
| UMF | A | Thompson, Robert Junior | Shipbuilding | i | Durham |
| W | A | Turner, John | Coalmine owner | e | Leicester |
| P | A | Walmsley, Benjamin | Building | e | Leeds |
| P | A | Walmsley, William | Building | e | Leeds |

| | | Wood, Edward | Building societies | m | London |
|---|---|---|---|---|---|
| W | U | Ball, Charles James Prior | Magnesium manufacturer | | |
| unpl | U | Bibby, Joseph | Animal food manufacturer | | |
| unpl | U | Edwards, Ronald | Professional manager and academic | | |
| W | U | Farley, Reuben | Iron founder | | |
| unpl | U | Foden, Edwin Richard | Motor vehicle manufacturer | | |
| unpl | U | Foden, William | Motor vehicle manufacturer | | |
| W | U | Gartside, Thomas Edmund | Cotton spinner | | |
| W | U | Holden, Edward Hopkinson | Banker | | |
| unpl | U | Hornby, Frank | Toy manufacturer | | |
| unpl | U | Irving, Henry | Actor manager | | |
| NC | U | Mason, Hugh | Cotton manufacturer | | |
| W | U | Rank, James Voase | Flour miller | | |
| W | U | Reed, Albert Ralph | Paper manufacturer | | |
| W | U | Ruston, Joseph | Agricultural machinery maker | | |
| W | U | Streat, Edward Raymond | Cotton textile trade executive | | |
| unpl | U | Stroudley, William | Locomotive builder | | |
| P | U | Taylor, Frank | Building contractor | | |
| W | U | Weston, Willard Garfield | Food manufacturer and retailer | | |
| P | U | Wycherley, Robert Bruce | Building society manager | — | |

| | A | Adult Methodist commitment | | | |
|---|---|---|---|---|---|
| | U | Methodist upbringing | | | |

*Moved to Congregationalists..
**Became Church of England
***Became Roman Catholic.
****Became Unitarian.

NC  New Connexion.
P   Primitive.
UMF United Methodist Free Church (and predecessors).
W   Wesleyan'
unpl Unplaced.

e   Entrepreneur.
i   Inheritor.
m   Manager.

# Appendix 2

Table A.2  Methodists among American business leaders, nineteenth and twentieth centuries

| Name | State main | Industry | Company |
|---|---|---|---|
| Archbold, John Dustin | Pennsylvania | Oil | Standard Oil |
| Beaty, Amos Leonidas | Texas, New York City | Oil | Phillips Petroleum |

| | | | |
|---|---|---|---|
| Bechtel, Stephen Davison | Indiana | Engineering, construction | Bechtel Corporation |
| Beech, Olive Ann Mellor | Kansas | Aircraft manufacture | Beech Aircraft Corporation |
| Browne, William Washington | Virginia | Banking | Reformers Mercantile & Industrial Association |
| Budd, Edward Gowen | Delaware | Vehicles | E G Budd Co |
| Candler, Asa Grigg | Georgia | Soft drinks | Coca-Cola Company |
| Carr, Julian Shakespere | North Carolina | Tobacco and cotton | Durham Tobacco Co |
| Chrysler, Walter Percy | Illinois | Motor vehicles | Chrysler Corporation |
| Couch, Harvey Crowley | Arkansas | Utilities | Arkansas Light & Power Co |
| Cowles, Gardner | Iowa | Media | Cowles Publications |
| Cowles, Gardner Jr (Mike) | Iowa | Media | Cowles Broadcasting |
| Cowles, John | Minnesota | Media | Minneapolis Star and Tribune |
| DeBardeleben, Henry Fairchild | Alabama | Iron | Alabama Fuel & Iron |
| Duke, James Buchanan | North Carolina | Tobacco | American Tobacco Company |
| Dymond, John | Louisiana | Sugar planter | *Louisiana Planter and Sugar Manufacturer* |
| Ford, Henry II | Michigan | Automobile manufacturer | Ford Motor Company |
| Ford, John Batiste | Indiana; Pennsylvania | Glass manufacturer | Pittsburgh Plate Glass Company |
| Gage, Lyman Judson | Illinois | Banker | First National Bank, Chicago |
| Gary, Albert Henry | New York City | Lawyer & steel co executive | United States Steel Company |
| Gossett, Benjamin Brown | South Carolina | Textile manufacturer | Gossett Mills |
| Gray, Bowman | North Carolina | Cigarette manufacturer | R. J. Reynolds Tobacco Company |

| | | | |
|---|---|---|---|
| Gray, Bowman Junior | North Carolina | Cigarette manufacturer | R. J. Reynolds Tobacco Company |
| Gray, George Alexander | North Carolina | Textile manufacturer | Many textile firms |
| Gray, James Alexander Junior | North Carolina | Cigarette manufacturer | R. J. Reynolds Tobacco Company |
| Harper, Fletcher | New York City | Publisher | Harper Brothers |
| Harper, James | New York City | Publisher | Harper Brothers |
| Heinz, Henry John | Pennsylvania | Food processor | H. J. Heinz Company |
| Hill, George Washington | New York City | Cigarette manufacturer | American Tobacco Company |
| Hill, James Jerome | Minnesota | Railroad entrepreneur | Great Northern Railroad |
| Hillman, Thomas Tennessee | Alabama | Iron | Tennessee Iron, Coal & Railroad Company |
| Hopson, Howard Colwell | New York City | Public utilities entrepreneur | Associated Gas & Electric Company |
| Hudson, Joseph Lowthian | Michigan | Department store founder | J. L. Hudson Company |
| Iliff, John Wesley | Colorado | Cattleman | |
| Johnson, George Francis | Massachusetts | Shoe manufacturer | Endicott-Johnson Company |
| Knapp, Joseph Frederick | New York City | Printers, publishers, insurance co | Knapp & Company; Crowell-Collier Pubg Co, Metropolitan Life Insurance |
| Knapp, Joseph Palmer | New York City | Printers, publishers, insurance co | Knapp & Company |
| Kresge, Sebastian Spering | New York City | Chain store merchant | S. S. Kresge Company |
| Lamont, Thomas William | New York City | Investment banker | JP Morgan |
| Lee, Ivy Ledbetter | New York City | Public relations pioneer | Parker & Lee |
| Lilly, Josiah Kirby | Indiana | Drug manufacturer | Eli Lilly & Company |
| Moody, William Lewis Junior | Texas | Banker &c | W. L. Moody & Company, Bank |

| | | | |
|---|---|---|---|
| Phillips, Frank | Oklahoma | Oil producer and refiner | Phillips Petroleum |
| Rand, James Henry | New York | Office equipment manufacturer | Rand Ledger Company |
| Rand, James Henry Junior | New York | Office equipment manufacturer | Sperry Rand Corporation |
| Saunders, Clarence | Tennessee | Chain store executive | Piggly Wiggly Stores Inc |
| Sloan, Alfred Pritchard Junior | New York City | Automobile manufacturer | General Motors Corporation |
| Studebaker, Clement | Indiana | Wagon & automobile manufacturer | Studebaker Brothers Manufacturing Company |
| Walker, Sarah Breedlove | Indiana | Manufacturer of hair products | Madame C. J. Walker Manufacturing Company |
| Wanamaker, John | Pennsylvania | Department store retailer | John Wanamaker & Company |
| Wilson, Kemmons | Tennessee | Motel and hotel chain owner | Holliday Inns of America |
| Woolworth, Frank Winfield | New York | Chain store merchant | F. W. Woolworth & Company |
| Woolworth, Charles Sumner | New York | Chain store merchant | F. W. Woolworth & Company |

*Note*: Upbringing and adult affiliations conflated

*Source*: John Ingham, *Biographical Dictionary of American Business Leaders*.

# Methodism in Literature

## Laura Davies

Even if we set aside the breadth, instability and opacity of the terms 'Methodism' and 'Literature' the phrase created by the insertion between them of the preposition 'in' opens up a whole series of questions. In order properly to address the matter of how Methodism has been represented in Literature, it is also necessary to consider: the relationship between Methodism and Literature, and indeed between Methodists and Literature; the ways in which the study of Methodism from a literary perspective can be productive; and the bearing that research into Methodism has had, or could in the future have, upon the study of Literature as an academic discipline. This chapter will proceed from the belief that it is important and worthwhile as much for our understanding of the origins and continuing development of Methodism as for the ongoing evolution of Literature studies, to ask and to attempt to answer these questions. Addressing first the issue of Methodist attitudes towards, and practices of, reading, before shifting its focus to writing and publishing by Methodists, and then the representation of Methodism and Methodists in literary works by authors outside the movement, the discussion will move chronologically from the early Methodist period to the present day.

## John Wesley: Reading and Recommendations

It is possible to reconstruct a detailed picture of John Wesley's reading practice and his attitude towards the reading of his followers from a range of sources. These include his diaries and published *Journal*, the inventory of his book collection compiled after his death, the recommendations he made to his preachers, the plan of study he instigated at Kingswood School, and the works which he chose to excerpt, abridge and publish.[1] It is on this account that he has formed the focus of much of

---

[1] The Catalogue of the Methodist Book Concern was published in the *Arminian Magazine*, XIII (1789) and is reproduced in Samuel J. Rogal, *John Wesley's Book Stock and the Arminian Magazine Catalogue of 1789* (Lewiston, NY and Lampeter: Edwin Mellen Press, 2006). The Book Inventory is reproduced as an appendix in Vicki Tolar Burton, *Spiritual*

the existing scholarship on eighteenth-century Methodist reading. Research on this subject has paid particular attention to his belief in the necessity for all believers to improve their knowledge, understanding and conduct by 'reading authors of various kinds'.[2] Therefore, while he acknowledged the inestimable value of the Bible – which he placed alongside tradition, reason and experience as an essential source of divine authority, wisdom and sustenance – he himself read a great deal and recommended that all his followers, to the degree that they were able, should do the same. This is not to say that either his consumption or his recommendations were unreserved. The texts noted in his *Journal*, the book inventory and the works which he chose to publish fall broadly into four categories: practical divinity, both historical and contemporary and from a wide range of Christian sources; autobiography and biography, including a large number of Methodist narratives; collections of sermons and hymns; and 'literary' texts including poetry, and both fictional and non-fictional prose. It has been demonstrated that this taste was influenced by the intellectual environment of Wesley's childhood and by the reading of his mother, Susannah, which concentrated on practical divinity, but also included the poetry of John Milton and George Herbert, the essays of John Locke and a few works of classical literature.[3]

Although he took account of divergences in the abilities and circumstances of his followers, Wesley nevertheless valued some works above others, both on account of their enduring influence upon his own life and because he believed they could prove equally instructive to others. These were Thomas à Kempis' *Christian's Pattern*, Jeremy Taylor's *Holy Living and Holy Dying*, and William Law's *Christian Perfection* and *Serious Call to a Devout and Holy Life*.[4] The works which he made available to the poor through the 'Society for the Distribution of Religious Tracts Among the Poor (established with Thomas Coke in 1782) also indicate those he believed to be most essential. Again, Law's *A Serious Call* appears, but so too do Wesley's own *Instructions for Children* and a selection of sermons, hymns and advices. Within the pages of the *Arminian Magazine* we find the same commitment to practical divinity expressed through a more diverse selection of texts, including letters, essays, poetry, and both historical and contemporary biography and autobiography. With respect to the itinerant lay preachers, the fifty volumes of edited and abridged texts which he produced between 1749 and 1755 as *The*

---

*Literacy in John Wesley's Methodism: Reading, Writing, and Speaking to Believe* (Waco, TX: Baylor University Press, 2008).

[2] *The Letters of the Rev. John Wesley*, ed. John Telford, 8 vols (London: Epworth, 1931), VI.129. Two early works on this topic remain useful: Thomas Walter Herbert, *John Wesley as Editor and Author* (Princeton, NJ: Princeton University Press, 1940) and T. B. Shepherd, *Methodism and the Literature of the Eighteenth Century* (London: Epworth, 1947). More recently Isabel Rivers' extensive scholarship and Tolar Burton's *Spiritual Literacy* are indispensable.

[3] See 'John Wesley's Literary Genealogy', in Tolar Burton, *Spiritual Literacy* and Charles Wallace Jr., '"Some Stated Employment of Your Mind": Reading, Writing, and Religion in the Life of Susannah Wesley', *Church History*, 58:3 (September 1989), 354–66.

[4] Isabel Rivers, 'John Wesley and the Language of Scripture, Reason and Experience', *Prose Studies*, 4:3 (1981), 252–86.

*Christian Library* provide an insight into Wesley's hopes for their more rigorous programme of education through reading. Here too the focus was practical divinity and exemplary 'lives' but also comprised some theology and ecclesiastical history. The Kingswood School curriculum followed a similar pattern with the addition of Latin translations from authors such as Augustine.[5]

These reading lists indicate Wesley's characterisation of valuable literature – be it didactic, exemplary or imaginative – as a source of knowledge and spiritual guidance. They also reveal his understanding of reading as an activity of work, part of a process of self-improvement and thus in essence devotional. It is from this perspective that he urged all his followers to read and encouraged and assisted them to do so through the publishing activities of the Book Room and Foundry Press. Once in hand, he advised that texts were to be approached with a 'purity of intention'. They were to be read slowly and with concentration, 'remarkable sayings or advice' were to be memorised, and their teachings were to be taken from the page and implemented in the heart, mind and life of the reader.[6] In his strict control of the reading of his preachers, his heavy-handed editing and abridging, and his publication choices, Wesley facilitated this kind of reading by making available texts that did not require the reader to separate the salient from the irrelevant or to compare and contrast different interpretations. By the insertion of comments and explanations before, after or even within texts – a practice to which he resorts frequently in the *Arminian Magazine* – Wesley directed the responses of his readers still further.[7]

Isabel Rivers has discussed the distinctiveness of this attitude, observing how Wesley's views differed from those of the Independent minister and educator, Philip Doddridge, to whom he writes in 1746 for advice on the subject. She concludes that where the programme at Doddridge's Academy was grounded on a 'basic principle of free enquiry in education' Wesley 'by no means shared' this principle.[8] His view, by contrast, was that reading should provide access to moral and spiritual exemplars. This motivated his commitment to the publication of spiritual 'lives' but its origins can be found much deeper, in his 'conception of experimental religion':

---

[5] All these publications are discussed in detail by Isabel Rivers in her chapter on 'Religious Publishing' in Michael F. Suarez, S.J. and Michael Turner (eds), *The Cambridge History of the Book in Britain 1695–1830* (Cambridge: Cambridge University Press, 2009), 579–600. See also Randy L. Maddox, 'John Wesley's Reading: Evidence in the Kingswood School Archives', *Methodist History*, 41:2 (2003), 49–67.

[6] *An Extract of the Christian's Pattern*, in *The Works of John Wesley*, ed. Thomas Jackson, 14 vols (London: John Mason, 1872), VII. 308.

[7] Wesley's biblical commentaries provide further evidence of this impulse. See his *Explanatory notes upon the New Testament*, 3 vols (Bristol, 1760–62) and *Explanatory Notes upon the Old Testament*, 3 vols (Bristol, 1765).

[8] Isabel Rivers, 'Dissenting and Methodist Books of Practical Divinity', in Isabel Rivers (ed.), *Books and Their Readers in Eighteenth-Century England* (Leicester: Leicester University Press, 1982), 127–64, at 151, and 'John Wesley and the Language of Scripture, Reason and Experience', 260.

The individual knows God through Scripture and through experience. He can readily compare the two, but he also needs the testimony of others, partly in order to test whether his own experience coheres with common experience, and is not peculiar to himself and hence invalid, and partly to encourage him to persevere. Hence Wesley's experimental method, by which he systematically collected accounts of the experiences of others and published them in a variety of forms – biographies, autobiographies, conversion narratives, deathbed accounts, letters – had a two-fold purpose: to test the validity of his own doctrines, and to give support to his readers.[9]

It is also important to note, however, that the success of this propagation of 'useful' literature equally was determined by an opposite mode of regulation. Believing that only those works which would encourage good conduct and spiritual growth were worthy of reading, Wesley, like many in the eighteenth century, was suspicious of the novel, which was held to promote idleness, inflamed passions and delusions of foolish romance.[10] Thus although he published an edition of Henry Brookes' *The Fool of Quality*, this was an exception to his general rule: 'I should recommend very few novels to young persons'.[11] Not all imaginative literature was rejected though. His essay on taste demonstrates that he was interested in contemporary debates about the process of aesthetic appreciation and he argued that the power of literature (particularly poetry) to illuminate the human condition and to touch the soul, meant that it could function as the 'handmaid of piety'.[12] This belief lies behind his publications of poems on religious themes or topics, including pieces by William Cowper and Hannah More in the *Arminian Magazine* and a number of stand-alone collections and extracts.[13]

---

[9] Ibid., 261. On the novelty of publishing contemporary biography see Rivers 'John Wesley and the Language of Scripture', , 229–33. Additionally Rivers conducts a comparison between Methodist and other interdenominational collections of 'lives' in 'John Wesley and Religious Biography', *Bulletin of the John Rylands Library*, 85 (2003), 209–25.

[10] *Works*, VIII, 270. On the wider eighteenth-century attitude see William B. Warner, *Licensing Entertainment: The Elevation of Novel Reading in Britain, 1684–1750* (Berkeley, CA: University of California Press, 1998).

[11] *The History of Henry, Earl of Morland, abridged by John Wesley*, 2 vols (London, 1780); *Letters*, VI.228.

[12] 'Thoughts Upon Taste' (1780), *Works*, XIII, 465–9. *A Collection of Hymns for the Use of the People called Methodists* (London, 1780), Preface.

[13] For instance, *A collection of moral and sacred poems from the most celebrated English authors* (1744), *An Extract from Milton's Paradise Lost* (1763), *An extract from Dr. Young's Night-thoughts on life, death, and immortality* (1770), and *Select Parts of Mr Herbert's Sacred Poems* (1773).

## The Reading Practices of Ordinary Believers

Of course, making recommendations is never a guarantee that they will be followed. Wesley's charismatic leadership and the practical regulatory steps he took made him much more successful than many in this respect, but it remains instructive to ask, as Tolar Burton does: 'What were the literacy practices of ordinary Methodists? What did they read and write and in what circumstances?'[14] Her answers attend carefully to issues of gender, education and socio-economic status, and consider a comprehensive range of reading practices, from communal reading to private study, annotation to memorisation, and from purchasing books to borrowing them. Through her attention to 'ordinary' Methodists, to the ongoing debates regarding the teaching of writing as well as reading in Sunday Schools, to the activities of preachers such as Samuel Bradburn and Samuel Bardsley, and also to the experiences of women such as Mary Bosquanet Fletcher and Sarah Crosby, she is able to assess the extent to which his intentions were realised and the ways in which practices diverged among different groups and individuals.

Although the eighteenth century is Tolar Burton's focus, her methodology is equally applicable to later periods in the development of Methodism as well as to other geographical areas. It could usefully be extended, for example, to trace changes in Methodist reading practice in England during the nineteenth century, when not only the total number of all publications rose dramatically, and general levels of literacy within the population increased, but when the profile of Methodist membership underwent a process of evolution.[15] Equally, a comparison between these developments and those which took place as Methodism spread and branched in America would be productive.[16] There is a wealth of material relating to this line of enquiry, including the records of book concerns such as those in Philadelphia and New York, various Methodist periodicals, evidence relating to literacy teaching within the Sunday School movement, and published works such as F. A. Archibald's *Methodism and Literature*, which tackles such issues as 'What we read and what we should read' directly.[17] The activities of Methodist missionaries in America and beyond, and the relationship between the literature they disseminated and the texts and practices that were already embedded in the

---

[14] Tolar Burton, *Spiritual Literacy*, 3.

[15] William St Clair's comprehensive study, *The Reading Nation in the Romantic Period* (Cambridge: Cambridge University Press, 2004), discusses these general developments, although unfortunately without reference to Methodism.

[16] Existing studies which focus solely on America include Carl F. Kaestle and Janice A. Radway (eds), *Print in Motion: The Expansion of Publishing and Reading in the United States 1880–1940* (Chapel Hill, NC: University of North Carolina Press, 2009); and David Paul Nord's *Faith in Reading: Religious Publishing and the Birth of Mass Media in America* (New York, NY: Oxford University Press, 2004).

[17] F. A. Archibald (ed.), *Methodism and Literature: A Series of Articles From Several Writers on the Literary Enterprise and Achievements of the Methodist Episcopal Church* (Cincinnati, OH: Walden and Stowe, 1883), 6. Also Addie Grace Wardle, *History of the Sunday School Movement in the Methodist Episcopal Church* (New York, NY: Methodist Book Concern, 1918).

## Methodism and the Reading Revolution

Beyond the benefits for our understanding of the movement itself, studying Methodist reading practices within these contexts is important for another reason. It marks a further stage in a growing move towards the situating of Methodism within wider cultural contexts.[19] Specifically, work such as Tolar Burton's provides strong evidence for the usefulness of Methodism as a case-study relevant to the ongoing debate among historians of reading about the validity of the 'Reading Revolution' hypothesis. It has been posited that this revolution took place during the eighteenth century and was

> a process by which the intensive reading of a small collective canon of texts, mostly of a religious kind and primarily the Bible, that were familiar, normative and repeatedly recited, was replaced with an extensive form of reading. In a modern, secularized and individual way, extensive reading was characterized by an eagerness to consume new and varied reading materials for information, and for private entertainment in particular.[20]

But while the general idea of a shift in reading practice over the course of the century has been largely accepted, elements of the theory remain contentious; not least of which the notions that one form of reading was replaced by another and that the rise of extensive reading was inextricably linked with a process of

---

[18] The potential of this approach is discussed in Kenneth Cracknell and Susan J. White (eds), *An Introduction to World Methodism* (Cambridge: Cambridge University Press, 2005), 90–91. It also appears in the first volume of Amory and Hall's *A History of the Book in America* (Cambridge: Cambridge University Press, 2000) and in Hilary M. Carey, *God's Empire: Religion and Colonialism in the British World, c.1801–1908* (Cambridge: Cambridge University Press, 2011).

[19] For example, Tim Macquiban (ed.), *Methodism in its Cultural Milieu: Proceedings of the Centenary Conference of the Wesley Historical Society 26–30 July 1993* (Oxford: Applied Theology Press, 1994). Jeremy Gregory, 'Wesley's Context: The Long Eighteenth Century', in Randy L. Maddox and Jason E. Vickers (eds), *The Cambridge Companion to John Wesley* (Cambridge: Cambridge University Press, 2010), 13–39 and 'Religion in the Age of Enlightenment: Putting John Wesley in Context', *Religion in the Age of Enlightenment*, 2 (2010), 19–53. Also Brett McInelly, '"I Had Rather be Obscure but I Dare Not": Women and Methodism', in Diane E. Boyd and Marta Kvande (eds), *Everyday Revolutions: Eighteenth-Century Women Transforming Public and Private* (Newark, DE: University of Delaware Press, 2008), 135–58.

[20] Guglielmo Cavallo and Roger Chartier (eds), *A History of Reading in the West*, trans. Lydia G. Cochrane (Amherst, MA: University of Massachusetts Press, 1999), 285.

secularisation. On a number of counts Methodist reading practices are a valuable resource here. In terms of the transition from intensive to extensive reading, they provide evidence of a movement within which both flourished – close Bible reading and memorisation existing side by side with the consumption of a variety of literary forms, including those within the burgeoning sphere of newspapers, periodicals and self-help texts – and, moreover, where both also functioned in close conjunction with an equally vigorous culture of oral performance. The growth of this variety of reading material and practices within a context of intense religiosity has in addition a bearing on the association of extensive reading with a process of secularisation, while the organised structures of Methodist life, within which reading would have been both an individual and a group activity, adds a further dimension to the arguments that have been made about the development of a sense of reading 'community' during this period.[21]

Since it is equally possible to describe changes in reading practice brought about by the growth of the internet, and its concurrent online publishing companies, digitisation projects and blogosphere, as well as the immense popularity of ereaders, as a 'reading revolution', it is today even more important that the history of Methodist reading should be understood, that its connections with wider technological and cultural shifts are explored, and that these findings are made relevant and accessible to scholars working outside the field of Methodist studies.[22]

# Methodist Writing

### John Wesley as Author, Editor and Publisher

The scale of John Wesley's writing, editing and publishing activities was prodigious and has been the subject of a number of studies.[23] In overview, they comprised: i) large and ongoing projects such as his *Journal*, *Sermons*, *The Christian Library*,

---

[21] For instance, Jon Klancher, *The Making of English Reading Audiences 1790–1832* (Madison, WI: University of Wisconsin Press, 1987).
[22] This is briefly mentioned in Tolar Burton, *Spiritual Literacy*, 305. A list of popular Methodist blogs can be found at http://blogs.botw.org/Society/Religion/Christianity/Methodist (accessed 1 October 2012).
[23] In addition to the texts listed in the previous section, see also: Henry D. Rack, *Reasonable Enthusiast: John Wesley and the Rise of Methodism*, 3rd edn (Peterborough: Epworth Press, 2002) and Randy L. Maddox and Jason E. Vickers (eds), *The Cambridge Companion to John Wesley* (Cambridge: Cambridge University Press, 2010). Samuel J. Rogal's *John Wesley's Book Stock* (Lewison, NY: Edwin Mellen Press, 2006) provides useful bibliographical information, while Richard Green's *The Works of John and Charles Wesley: A Bibliography* (London: Charles Kelly, 1906) remains authoritative.

the *Arminian Magazine* and, with his brother Charles, a series of Psalm and Hymn collections; ii) texts relating to practical divinity and to Methodist theology and spirituality; iii) essays and tracts on wider miscellaneous themes; iv) editions of literary works, or extracts thereof; v) a single biography, *A Short Account of the Life and Death of the Reverend John Fletcher* (1786); and vi) instructional works on a range of subjects from logic to medicine.

From the perspective of literary scholarship, the *Journal* has received the most attention.[24] Looking beyond the *Journal*, however, much is relatively unexplored. One such area is Wesley's understanding of, and participation within, the developing periodical culture of the eighteenth century and his legacy of periodical writing and publication which was then developed in different ways by later generations of Methodists around the world, including America, Australia, Asia, Mexico and Russia.[25] Much also remains to be investigated with regard to the tension between his intense commitment to spreading the word and what Rack describes in relation to the *Arminian Magazine* as his aspiration 'to be a semi-popular educator catering for the growing reading public of Georgian England'. And, lastly, there is more to be said about Wesley's understanding of authorship and editorship at a conceptual level, as well as their interconnection in his own practice and in the writing of other Methodists.[26]

A further distinctive feature of Wesley's attitude towards literature was his desire that his followers should write about their spiritual experiences. The lay preachers were required to write an account of God's dealings with them and were also urged to keep journals. However, the value of self-awareness through autobiography and of accounting for one's time through a written record was pressed home to all by the publication of his own *Journal* and in the works of practical divinity that he recommended that they read.

---

[24] It is discussed by Elisabeth Jay in *The Journal of John Wesley: A Selection* (Oxford and New York, NY: Oxford University Press, 1987) and by Felicity Nussbaum in *The Autobiographical Subject: Gender and Ideology in Eighteenth-Century England* (Baltimore, MD and London: Johns Hopkins University Press, 1989).

[25] Useful reference texts here are Samuel J. Rogal, 'A Survey of Methodist Periodicals Published in England, 1778–1900', *Victorian Periodicals Review*, 14:2 (Summer 1981), 66–9; and Josef L. Altholz, *The Religious Press in Britain 1760–1900* (New York, NY and Westport, CT: Greenwood Press, 1989). See also John N. Hollister, *The Centenary of the Methodist Church in Southern Asia* (Lucknow, India: Lucknow Publishing House, 1956); and Don Wright and Eric G. Clancy (eds), *The Methodists: A History of Methodism in NSW* (St Leonards, NSW: Allen and Unwin, 1993). Relevant entries in Charles Yrigoyen, Jr. (ed.), *T&T Clark Companion to Methodism* (London and New York: T&T Clark, 2010) can be found on Gonzalo Baez-Camargo, Henry G. Appenzeller and George Albert Simons.

[26] Rack, *Reasonable Enthusiast*, 349.

## 'The inner life in their own writing'[27]

Many of the resulting texts, written by women as well as men, were published. Some, like the journal of the Methodist Episcopal bishop Francis Asbury – a work easily as interesting as Wesley's own – or the more amateur but immensely popular *Short Account of the Experience of Mrs. Hester Ann Rogers*, were issued as single texts, but most appeared in the *Arminian Magazine* alongside accounts of providences, illness, biographies and narratives recounting 'happy deaths'.[28] Over the course of the eighteenth and nineteenth centuries, furthermore, collected biographies of notable Methodists began to appear, functioning both as celebratory histories and as spiritual exempla.[29] The autobiographies have been subject to more investigation than these biographies, however. By their very nature, of course, it is likely that a good number of the personal narratives, diaries and journals that were not published are no longer extant. Nevertheless, a very active field of research has been built around the material that is available.[30] Studies of Methodist texts from this perspective, however, tend to regard them as a sub-category, different in kind from secular life-writing. There are clearly solid grounds for doing so, especially in the case of conversion narratives, but it is nevertheless an approach which has its limitations. A methodology which instead sought to pursue research questions across what is in many respects a linguistic boundary – between the so-called 'secular' and the 'spiritual' – could, by contrast, facilitate comparisons between texts on the grounds of gender, education, class, race, circumstance or geographical location, and, in this way, could generate new perspectives upon the interplay between faith influences and other factors within the life of the author. To do so would further extend the productive work which has already begun to situate

---

[27] 'In every generation, Methodists have echoed this deep concern for the inner life in their own writing', Cracknell and White (eds), *Introduction to World Methodism*, 141.

[28] F. Hollingsworth (ed.), *Journal of the Rev. Francis Asbury*, 3 vols (New York, NY: Lane & Scott, 1852); Rogers' *Account* was first published in 1793 but went though fifty subsequent editions, including various additions.

[29] For example, *The Methodist Memorial; being an impartial sketch of the lives and characters of the preachers, who have departed this life* (1801) by Charles Atmore; *Biographical sketches of early Methodist women* (1825) by Zachariah Taft; and Thomas Jackson's *The lives of the early Methodist preachers: chiefly written by themselves* (1865).

[30] Nussbaum's *The Autobiographical Subject* was a pioneering study and remains well-regarded. It shares common ground with Phyllis Mack's more recent book, *Heart Religion in the British Enlightenment: Gender and Emotion in Early Methodism* (Cambridge: Cambridge University Press, 2008), and Bruce Hindmarsh, *The Evangelical Conversion Narrative: Spiritual Autobiography in Early Modern England* (Cambridge: Cambridge University Press, 2005). David Hempton, meanwhile, explores the private papers of the Irish preacher Gideon Ousely in *The Religion of the People: Methodism and Popular Religion c. 1750–1900* (London: Routledge,1996). Susie Cunningham Stanley's *Holy Boldness: Women Preachers' Autobiographies and the Sanctified Self* (Knoxville, TN: University of Tennessee, 2002) focuses on the United States, as does Jeffrey Williams' *Religion and Violence in Early American Methodism: Taking the Kingdom by Force* (Bloomington, IN: Indiana University Press, 2010).

Methodism within wider cultural contexts, and, furthermore, would bring much needed literary-critical attention to the large but under-examined body of fictional literature by Methodists.

## Professional Methodist Authors

A small but significant number of early Methodists wrote literary works in forms other than the autobiographical. James Hervey's essay collection, *Meditations and Contemplations*, for instance, went through twenty-five editions from 1748 to 1800.[31] None of these texts, however, have been seriously discussed or analysed as 'literature'. Indeed, the tenor of Donald Davie's remark made in 1978 that 'One looks for a long time before finding any attempt to place Charles Wesley, or Isaac Watts either, in relation to the more secular poetry of their times – in relation to Pope, or Thompson, or Gray or Goldsmith', remains true today, and is, in fact, even more apt with regard to these more minor figures who have largely fallen into obscurity.[32] Given the relatively minimal impact of many of these texts, this lack of consideration is not altogether surprising. Unfortunately, however, it is also the case with regard to the work of much more prolific and influential Methodist authors from the nineteenth and twentieth centuries. Notable figures in this group are primarily novelists and include the Hocking siblings (Silas, Joseph and Salome), Ellen Thorneycroft Fowler and her sister Edith Henrietta Hamilton, and Mark Guy Pearse. Despite the vast number of novels which they produced between them (particularly the Hocking brothers, who wrote over fifty each, and Pearse, who published almost as many as well as numerous shorter works) and the significant sales and popularity which they enjoyed during their lifetimes, they have not been adequately studied.[33] This paucity of scholarship should not, however, be taken as a sign that these works are not worthy of investigation. They are in fact valuable on a number of counts.

Most straightforwardly, they can provide information about Methodism and Methodists. As works of fiction they obviously cannot be regarded as sources of verifiable historical evidence about individuals or events, but they can reveal the ways in which their authors chose to perceive and to represent the beliefs and practices of their faith. Pearse's *Daniel Quorm and his Religious Notions* (1875) achieves this through detailed depictions of the rhythms of the Methodist life, while

---

[31] A useful survey and bibliography of miscellaneous literary publications of this kind by Methodists up to 1914 can be found in Watson Boone Duncan, *Studies in Methodist Literature* Methodist Episcopal Church, South, Smith & Lamar, 1914).

[32] Donald Davie, *A Gathered Church: The Literature of the English Dissenting Interest 1700–1930* (London: Routledge and Kegan Paul, 1978), 48.

[33] At present the only useful studies are: Alan Kent's literary biography, *Pulp Methodism: The Lives and Literature of Silas, Joseph and Salome Hocking, Three Cornish Novelists* (St Austell: Cornish Hillside Publications, 2002), Anthony Perry's *The Fowler Legacy: The Story of a Forgotten Family* (Studley: Brewin, 1997), and Derek R. William's *Cornubia's Son* (London: Francis Boutle, 2008).

the ordered and modest lifestyle of the family of a Methodist minister is contrasted with the London high-society existence of the eponymous heroine in Ellen Fowler's novel, *Concerning Isabel Carnaby* (1899). In Silas Hocking's *The Birthright* (1897) and *The Strange Adventures of Israel Pendray* (1899), written like the work of his siblings from the perspective of his membership of the United Methodist Free Churches, his reflections on Methodism emerge in the character of John Wesley himself, while his brother's *Jabez Easterbrook* (1890) explores the testing of a young minister's faith, placed under pressure by various exponents of industrialisation, capitalism, evolutionary theory and atheism. Depictions of Methodist spirituality also appear in these novels, and many of these glimpses into the inner life reveal threads of continuity between nineteenth-century Methodism and its Wesleyan origins, not only in the type of experiences that are described, but also in terms of their description. A particularly illuminating example can be found in Edith Fowler's novel, *The Farringdons*, when the female protagonist Elizabeth, who has up until this point turned away from her faith under the influence of rational atheistic arguments, attends a sermon and feels a divine presence all around her and an intense burning in her heart. As in the accounts of early Wesleyan Methodists, she is through this feeling instantaneously assured of God's Grace.[34]

Exploring the aims of authors such as these can also provide useful insights into changing Methodist attitudes towards the reading and writing of literature. Kent reports, for instance, that the Hockings' father maintained an old-fashioned suspicion of novels but his children firmly believed that they should embrace them as a new means to spread the word and to educate the faithful.[35] As is evident from the titles of works such as *Where Duty Lies* (1892) Silas' response was to write strongly theological, symbolic and didactic novels. Initially this was also true of his brother, and Mark Guy Pearse's novels fall into the same category. Joseph, however, soon began to think differently. In a talk he was known to give frequently on the subject of 'Novels and Novelists' he asserted that the novel was not a dangerous distraction but rather one of the 'most pleasant and healthful forms of recreation', as well as a powerful 'reforming force'. The authorial task, in his view, therefore, was to amuse, teach and arouse the 'sympathies and emotions' of his readers.[36]

These engagements with authorship as an idea are just one way in which it is apparent that at least some Methodist novels are actively in dialogue with the wider literary culture of their time. The immense but fleeting success of novels such as Silas Hocking's *Her Benny* (1879), which sold over a million copies, provides further evidence of this. These sold so well not because of their exceptional quality but because they appealed to a particular public mood. Acknowledging and exploring this transient popularity, therefore, can offer a glimpse into the reading preferences and habits of the late-nineteenth and early-twentieth-century reading publics.

---

[34] Ellen Thorneycroft Fowler, *The Farringdons* (London: Hutchinson and Co., 1900), 151–2.
[35] *Pulp Methodism*, 68.
[36] Reproduced in ibid.,116–19.

Furthermore, the marked tendency of Methodist literature to be located in specific geographical locations and to depict distinctive local communities provides a strong point of connection with literary scholarship on the relationship between literature and landscape. From the Yorkshire and Lincolnshire countryside celebrated by H. L. Gee in such works as *The Romance of the Yorkshire Coast* (1928) and *Easter at Epworth: The Story of a Pilgrimage* (1944), we can travel to the factory towns of Liverpool and Manchester which feature in *Her Benny*. From here we can proceed to the Staffordshire potteries depicted in Arnold Bennett's 'Five Towns' novels, before arriving in the tin mines and coastal villages of the Cornwall so beloved by Pearse and all three of the Hockings, but captured most famously perhaps in Salome's *Some Old Cornish Folk* (1903).[37] Looking further afield we might choose to follow Edward Egglestone's *Circuit Rider* (1874) through the vast American plains, or to breathe the sea air of nineteenth-century maritime Canada as it is realised in the poetry of Thomas Daniel Cowdell and John Sparrow Thompson.[38] Alternatively, we can journey through India with Edward J. Thompson, by reading novels such as his *An Indian Day* (1927) which draw on his years as a teacher at the Bankura Wesleyan College, or instead experience life in Antigua and the intensity of the debate surrounding the abolitionist movement through the histories, polemical tracts, poems, letters and biographies of Anne Hart Gilbert (1773–1833) and her sister Elizabeth Hart Thwaites (1772–1833).[39]

Given this wealth of material there is no reason at all why an examination of this aspect of Methodist literature could not prove equally as valuable as the existing publications which tackle the relationship between literature, landscape and religion.[40] It is difficult, however, to speculate about the full extent of the dialogue that might be possible between Methodist and literary studies without also examining the ways in which Methodist communities, characters and themes have been represented in works of literature written by non-Methodist authors. This, therefore, will be the focus of the next section.

---

[37] Although born into a Methodist family, Bennett quickly and vehemently rejected the faith. This is discussed in Margaret Drabble, *Arnold Bennett: A Biography* (London: Weidenfeld and Nicolson, 1974).

[38] These poets are discussed in Thomas B. Vincent, 'Methodism and Methodist Poets in the Early Literature of Maritime Canada', in Charles H. Scobie and John Webster Grant (eds), *The Contribution of Methodism to Atlantic Canada* (Montreal and Kingston, London, Buffalo: McGill-Queen's University Press, , 1992), 189–204. The following chapters by Gwendolyn Davies and David G. Pitt are also illuminating.

[39] These works are reproduced in part and discussed at length in Moira Ferguson, *The Hart Sisters: Early African Caribbean Writers, Evangelicals, and Radicals* (Lincoln, NE and London: University of Nebraska Press, 1993).

[40] See, for instance, Robert J. Mayhew's *Landscape, Literature, and English Religious Culture, 1660–1800: Samuel Johnson and the Languages of Natural Description* (Basingstoke: Palgrave Macmillan, 2004) and the essays on 'ecotheology' in Peter Clarke and Tony Claydon's *God's Bounty: The Churches and the Natural World* (Woodbridge: Boydell & Brewer for the Ecclesiastical History Society, 2010).

# Methodist Representations

## Anti-Methodist Literature

During the lifetime of John Wesley the primary representation of Methodists and Methodism in literature was satirical. Appearing in a wide range of poetic, dramatic, novelistic and essay forms, this satire ridiculed every distinctive aspect of Methodist belief and practice, mounting charges of enthusiasm and hypocrisy and mocking the lowly backgrounds and extemporary preaching of the itinerants.[41] With the exception of Richard Graves' gently comic novel *The Spiritual Quixote* (1773), it was not until the nineteenth century that more balanced representations began to appear. These took different forms. In George Eliot's *Adam Bede* (1859) Dinah Morris, the female 'Methody' preacher, is a main character, as are the Methodist ministers at the centre of Mary Braddon's popular novels, *Joshua Haggard's Daughter* (1876) and *The Infidel: A Story of the Great Revival* (1900). By contrast, in the novels of Elizabeth Gaskell and Anthony Trollope, an impression of Methodism is generated through a series of smaller references: the hymns sung by Nicholas Boucher in *North and South* (1854–55), the controversial chapel in *The Vicar of Bullhampton* (1870) or the comparison between Mr Slope and Wesleyan Methodists in *Barchester Towers* (1857). These references do not dominate, but rather sit alongside other perspectives, be they Eliot's secular humanism, Gaskell's Unitarianism or the multiple faces of the Anglican establishment which appear in Trollope's novels.

Arguments have also been made for Methodism as a literary structure or theme. Valentine Cunningham, for instance, claims that *Adam Bede* is the 'first Methodist novel' because in its twin sources – Eliot's reading of Southey's *The Life of Wesley; and the rise and progress of Methodism* (1820) and the personal testimony of her Methodist aunt – it draws on and parallels a distinctive feature of what he terms the Methodist 'memoir'.[42] In a later chapter Cunningham also argues that for Emily and Charlotte Brontë Methodism serves as a 'referent for' and provides a 'rhetoric of' passion.[43] Other scholars too have linked the Methodist doctrine of feeling with wider literary culture. Frederick C. Gill's *The Romantic Movement and Methodism* (1937) provides a notable early example but has been largely superseded by G. J. Barker Benfield's *The Culture of Sensibility: Sex and Society in Eighteenth-Century Britain* (1992), which

---

[41] Bibliographies of these works can be found in Richard Green, *Anti-Methodist Publications Issued during the Eighteenth Century* (London: Kelly, 1902) and Albert M. Lyles, *Methodism Mocked: The Satiric Reaction to Methodism in the Eighteenth Century* (London: Epworth, 1960).

[42] Valentine Cunningham, *Everywhere Spoken Against: Dissent in the Victorian Novel* (Oxford: Clarendon, 1975),164.

[43] Ibid., 124. This assertion draws on the claim of Elsie Harrison that Methodism was 'the clue' to the Brontës but has itself been subject to further interrogation by Emma Mason. See G. Elsie Harrison, *The Clue to the Brontës* (London: Methuen, 1948) and Emma Mason, 'The Clue to the Brontës? Methodism and Wuthering Heights', in Mark Knight and Thomas Woodman (eds), *Biblical Religion and the Novel* (Aldershot: Ashgate, 2006), 69–78.

makes a compelling case for the feminine dimension of this doctrine and for its expression in the discourses of sentiment, sensibility and sympathy that rose to prominence during the mid-eighteenth century, and which are manifest in Eliot's Dinah Morris and Gaskell's Margaret Hale.

Presumably as a consequence of the wide dissemination of such arguments regarding 'feeling', the significant representations of other aspects of Methodist spirituality and practice have been rather overlooked. As a gesture towards a more balanced approach, let us briefly consider what can be gained from just one possible alternative focus. It is not a coincidence, I would argue, that very often when Methodism or Methodists appear in literary texts – whether they are written by Methodists or not – they do so alongside recurrent motifs of reading and writing. To list just a few examples: the multiple prefaces of *The Spiritual Quixote* set up this association from the off, drawing attention to the missing author, the discovered manuscript, and the activities of writers, critics, readers, and booksellers. In *North and South* Gaskell's attention returns repeatedly to libraries, the value of classical literature, to letters, and to the contrasting tone of the New Testament passages Margaret wants to read to Bessy and the verses from Revelation which the dying girl finds thrilling. *Adam Bede* is punctuated by poetical excerpts from Wordsworth's *Lyrical Ballads*, by references to periodicals and newspapers, and by conflicting opinions about the value of the Bible in relation to secular books. And while Dinah opens her Bible for direction, the unfortunate Hetty, like Nelly in *Her Benny*, remains uninterested in learning to read. Meanwhile Braddon's *The Infidel* has as its protagonist an authoress daughter born of a hack-writer father and the plot of *Concerning Isabel Carnaby* revolves around the publication of two books: 'Shams and Shadows' and 'Some Better Thing'. What this suggests is that Methodism, and within it the Wesleyan quadrilateral of scripture, reason, tradition and experience, also functions within these works as a referent for a series of broader cultural anxieties associated with reading and writing. These include, at the very least: uncertainty arising from competing models of textual authority, truth and accuracy, as a consequence not only of developments in Biblical criticism and the impact of geological and evolutionary science, but also from the rapid growth of news and of vehicles for public opinion; differing and often conflicting perceptions of the author's role and responsibilities and the desirable characteristics of the ideal reader; and apprehension about the prospect of universal literacy and its potential political, social and cultural consequences.

## Methodism in Literature Today

It is certainly not the case that these anxieties are an artefact of the early Methodist period. In fact, I would argue that debates about truth, authority and agency have intensified over the intervening centuries, becoming a widespread feature of a whole range of cultural discourses. Within the Methodist movement itself this has perhaps had its clearest expression in the ongoing discussion regarding the legacy of John Wesley and the way in which his writings can or should be 'read'.[44] But it is also the case that Methodists around the world have continued to be authors, editors and publishers, and that their work makes no less of a contribution to this dialogue than that which has preceded it. To name just a few examples from the last hundred years: the Australian poet Alfred Midgley (1849–1930); the Rev. Gaddiel Robert Acquaah, who translated the Bible into Fante and published numerous tracts, poems and songs; the Canadian poet E. J. Pratt (1882–1964); the prolific writings of the St Lucian poet and playwright Derek Walcott; and the ongoing activities of the Methodist minister and storyteller Linda Bandelier, who composes songs and stories which draw on the history of the American frontier and of her adopted Scottish homeland. What I hope to have demonstrated here is that genuine points of connection exist between the questions raised by Methodist Literature, the representation of Methodists and Methodism in literature, and wider cultural concerns. The study of these intersections therefore has a resonance and a relevance beyond the faith, but it is equally an endeavour which can only extend and deepen our understanding of its history and its future.

---

[44] Sarah H. Lancaster, 'Current Debates over Wesley's Legacy among his Progeny', in Maddox and Vickers (eds), *The Cambridge Companion to John Wesley*, 298–315.

# Methodism and Social Justice

## Jonathan Rodell

An active concern for social justice forms a key element in the self-understanding of many contemporary Methodist churches. The mission imperatives of the Methodist Church in Southern Africa, for example, include: 'Justice and service in church and society … Empowerment and development which give dignity and new purpose to those who have been deprived.'[1] The vision statement of the Methodist Church in Aotearoa/New Zealand talks of working: 'For justice for any who are oppressed in Aotearoa/New Zealand.'[2]

Indeed, there is clearly a widespread perception that such concerns form a core element of the Methodist tradition. The official website of the Methodist Church in Great Britain explains that: 'Methodists believe in what John Wesley called "social holiness" … Holiness is not just about personal spirituality and prayer. It will also be expressed through a commitment to social justice.'[3]

The *Book of Resolutions* of the United Methodist Church likewise presents a range of current preoccupations as the latest expressions of a long Methodist heritage of social concern:

> Taking an active stance in society is nothing new for followers of John Wesley. He set the example for us to combine personal and social piety. Ever since predecessor churches to United Methodism flourished in the United States, we have been known as a denomination involved with people's lives, with political and social struggles … The United Methodist Church believes God's love for the world is an active and engaged love, a love seeking justice and liberty. We cannot just be observers.[4]

---

[1] http://www.methodist.org.za/heritage/mission-charter (accessed March 2012).
[2] http://www.methodist.org.nz/about_us/our_vision (accessed March 2012).
[3] http://www.methodist.org.uk/index.cfm?fuseaction=opentogod.content&cmid=1497 (accessed March 2012).
[4] *The Book of Resolutions of the United Methodist Church* (Nashville, TN: Abingdon, 2008), 28.

This essay reviews the history of this particular vision of Methodism's past, looks at the claims that have been made about Methodism's historic commitment to social justice, and highlights some of the more ambiguous legacy that needs to be addressed in any objective assessment of the movement's social impact over the last three centuries.

## An Historiographical Review

In 1834 six farm labourers from the English village of Tolpuddle, in Dorset were arrested, convicted and transported to prison colonies in Australia for being part of a trade union. The petition protesting against their treatment was signed by 800,000 people and 100,000 joined in a protest march through the streets of London, perhaps the first of its kind. Five of the six men were Wesleyan Methodists and as many as three may have been local preachers. Today, the Methodist chapel in Tolpuddle, which was built long after the men had left the village and no longer has any regular congregation, is preserved as a national Methodist heritage site.

The first history of Methodism in Dorset, however, published in 1870 and written by John Simon who would later become President of the Wesleyan Conference and produce a five-volume study of John Wesley's career, saw no connection with the incident:

> Dorset has one claim to notoriety, unfortunately of an unenviable kind. Who has not shuddered over the 'labour' problem? We calm the fears of our readers by assuring them at once that it is not our intention to attempt its solution. There are more pleasant topics upon which we may dwell for a short time, – those arising out of the connexion of Methodism with this supposedly most uninteresting county.[5]

There is no mention of the case in George Smith's three-volume *A History of Wesleyan Methodism* (1858–61) or in Townsend, Workman and Eayrs's two-volume *A New History of Methodism* (1909). In fact, it was not until Robert Wearmouth, a Methodist minister and committed Socialist, published *Methodism and the Working-Class Movements of England 1800–1850* in 1937 that the 'Tolpuddle martyrs' were celebrated as a Methodist contribution to trade unionism.[6]

The evolution of the way in which British Methodists have viewed the activities of the Tolpuddle trade unionists is, perhaps, a salutary warning that works of history often tell us as much about the preoccupations of the time at which they were written as they do about the time of which they write. Wearmouth's

---

[5] J. S. Simon, *Methodism in Dorset – a Sketch* (Weymouth: Sherran, 1870), 1. Simon's work on eighteenth-century Methodism began with *John Wesley and the Religious Societies* (1927).

[6] R. F. Wearmouth, *Methodism and the Working-Class Movements of England 1800–1850* (London: Epworth, 1937), 265–70.

historical work justified the Methodist tradition, of which he was a product, to the new Socialist value system which was rapidly gaining ground in Britain during the 1920s and 30s and in which he shared. To achieve this he re-cast the chapels, which increasingly seemed to personify the prudery of the previous century, as the historic vanguard of mass democracy: 'When no other example of collective endeavour presented itself to the working classes, Methodism became a pattern and parent for their democratic exercises and idealism.'[7]

What is true of Tolpuddle is true also of many other aspects of Methodist history. It is clear that Methodist writers in the twentieth century, and the present day, have found in the movement's past material that underpinned their own commitment to concerns about social justice with an apostolic succession of similar commitments stretching back to the great John Wesley himself. Sometimes such work has had an apologetic quality, selling the Methodist tradition to a new generation; sometimes it has been shaped by internal political debates and the desire to prove that a particular vision of Methodism's future is the true heir to its legacy.

What is also clear is that this is not how Methodists before the beginning of the twentieth century saw or wrote about their past. For Jonathan Crowther, a future president of the British Wesleyan Conference, writing one of the first denominational histories *A portraiture of Methodism: or, the history of the Wesleyan Methodists* in 1814, Methodism's past showed it to be a divine agent for hastening the millennium:

> That Methodism so called, is eminently a work emanating from the counsel and wisdom of God; and that it is the harbinger, and will very powerfully contribute to usher in the glory of the latter day, I do most firmly believe. May the Lord hasten it in time.[8]

He recognised that among Mr Wesley's many virtues, and those indeed of his followers, was an uncommon benevolence, but it was not born of a sense of social justice:

> To relieve and help the poor, was with him a luxury of life. He considered them as if they existed that the followers of Christ might have an opportunity of shewing what benevolence they would shew to their Divine Master had he been now upon earth.[9]

For Abel Stevens, an anti-abolitionist New Englander, trying on the eve of the American civil war to chronicle the growth of Methodism on both sides of the Atlantic, the historic significance of the movement lay in its success in raising moral standards. If Methodism had contributed to social and political reform, he wrote in

---

[7] Ibid., 273.

[8] J. Crowther, *A portraiture of Methodism: or, the history of the Wesleyan Methodists* (2nd edition, London: Richard Edwards, 1815), vii.

[9] Ibid., 124.

*A History of the Religious Movement of the Eighteenth Century called Methodism*, it had been by making the public responsive to moral arguments:

> The Methodist Englishman may, with proper modesty, refrain from claiming the great reforms of English politics, and of even the British constitution, which have occurred since the days of his religious fathers, as due to their Christian labors; the unevangelical Churchman would smile at the claim; but the future impartial and philosophic historian will record that those splendid ameliorations could not have taken place without the popular improvements introduced by Methodism; that the Methodistic influence, as experienced by 'the good men of Clapham,' gave them their effective power; that the reformed moral sense of the nation, responding to the Christian appeals of these good and great men, secured the triumph and permanence of their political reforms, and that when the Church [i.e. the Church of England] itself was impotent, Methodism effectively acted through it, and through Dissent, to reclaim, if not to save the nation.[10]

Not until Townsend, Workman and Eayrs's *A New History of Methodism*, at the turn of the twentieth century, would it be claimed that:

> Wesley anticipated almost all the forms of social work now carried on … If he was not a theoretical socialist, he was a self-denying, practical philanthropist, who gave a new and abiding impulse to social reform.[11]

What is not at all clear, is whether the facts of Methodist history would persuade Stevens's 'impartial and philanthropic historian' (if such a fabled creature were ever to exist) that the much cherished interpretation placed upon them over the last hundred years can be substantiated. Do the claims for Wesley and Methodism as agents of social justice bear scrutiny?

## John Wesley and Early Methodism

Over recent decades, it has sometimes seemed that John Wesley was the harbinger of almost every development in progressive social values. In 1983, in *Women of Mr. Wesley's Methodism*, Earl Kent Brown wrote of Wesley's Methodism as a proto-feminist movement:

---

[10] A. Stevens, *The History of the Religious Movement of the Eighteenth Century called Methodism, Considered in its Different Denominational Forms and its Relations to British and American Protestantism* (3 vols, London: William Nichols, n. d.), II, 111–12.

[11] W. J. Townsend, H. B. Workman and G. Eayrs (eds), *A New History of Methodism* (2 vols, London: Hodder & Stoughton, 1909), I, 225.

It is clear that women in Mr. Wesley's Methodism often did not conform to the stereotypical patterns which have often been seen as limitations on female leadership in religious affairs. Detailed examination reveals that the ministries exercised by women in early Methodism were remarkable both in kind and quality.[12]

In 1990, Theodore Jennings wrote of an eighteenth-century English Lenin:

> If we take seriously the primitive communist, or communalist, ideal as one way of characterizing the aim of the spread of scriptural holiness, then we can also see that Wesley had a rather sophisticated strategy to accomplish that end. He realized that the rich were not promising candidates for such a message. They felt they had too much to lose, were too caught in the snare of riches. Therefore, the message must be directed to the poor, the dispossessed, the marginalized. And these would be organized as disciplined cadres, steeped in the point of view (ideology) that entailed these values and held together by strict discipline. The privileged classes, meanwhile, would be confronted with a relentless call to repentance of their complicity in the snares of wealth and the practice of injustice, in the hope that some at least would respond. In this way would be launched an international movement whose aim would be the realization within a relatively short period of time of a transformed social, economic, and world order.[13]

Two years later, Manfred Marquardt had found the father of European social democracy – free healthcare, mass education, social enterprise and human rights. In *John Wesley's Social Ethics: Praxis and Principle* he concluded that:

> With appropriate scholarly hesitancy, it may be asserted that Wesley was the greatest social reformer of his time because he succeeded in bringing socio-ethical theory and praxis into a close connection that served to advance both ... Wesley was not satisfied with publicly denouncing abuses in his sermons and writings; instead, he also strove, where possible, to initiate practical solutions.[14]

On the eve of the bicentenary of the abolition of the trade in slaves within the British empire, it is perhaps only to be expected that Wesley was ushered centre

---

[12] E. K. Brown, *Women of Mr. Wesley's Methodism* (New York, NY: Edwin Mellen, 1983), 15.

[13] T. Jennings, *Good News to the Poor: John Wesley's Evangelical Economics* (Nashville, TN: Abingdon, 1990), 116.

[14] M. Marquardt, *John Wesley's Social Ethics: Praxis and Principles* (Nashville, TN: Abingdon, 1992), 137.

stage in 2006 to be lauded as the man who 'must be credited with having a unique influence' on the abolitionist campaign.[15]

Two objections can be made against many of these attempts to paint Wesley and early Methodism as champions of social justice. The first is that they are often highly anachronistic, attributing to men and women who lived in the thought-world of eighteenth-century England ideas, ideals and ways of thinking that they quite simply could not have conceived. John Wesley was not an advocate of social justice, he could not have been, for both the term and the concept – of a right to equal treatment, regardless of ethnicity, gender, race, religion, possessions and so on – are the products of subsequent centuries. If he opposed slavery, had a concern for the poor or encouraged women to play a larger role in his societies than we imagine was commonplace at the time, he did so from a standpoint rooted in his own time and context. The second objection against so much that has been written about this facet of early Methodism is that it is often highly selective in its focus, relying on a narrow evidential base and with little reference to what else was being said and done in eighteenth-century England. Given the prolific volume of John Wesley's writings, a collection of quotations can be put together implying his support for all manner of often contradictory opinions, and shorn of their setting, those opinions can take on a wholly misleading significance.

Let us consider for a moment Wesley's 'preference for the life and company of the poor'.[16] There are a number of passages, particularly in Wesley's published *Journals*, that are very quotable and which vividly express his criticism of extravagant consumption, his disdain for the wealthy and his affection for the poor. Perhaps the most often cited is:

> 'Tis well that a few of the rich and noble are called. O that God would increase their number! But I should rejoice (were it the will of God) if it were done by the ministry of others. If I might choose, I should still (as I have done hitherto) 'preach the gospel to the poor'.[17]

Any understanding of Wesley's attitude to both the rich and the poor must, however, take into account the full range of the opinions he expressed on the subject. It must explain how he could describe congregations of poor country people to whom he preached as 'void both of common sense and common decency' (Henley, Oxfordshire) and 'very stupid' (Sundon, Bedfordshire).[18] It must also square with comments such as those made following his meeting with the Baroness van Wassenaer, 'one of the first quality in The Hague', in 1783 when he wrote:

---

[15] I. Brendlinger, *Social Justice through the Eyes of Wesley: John Wesley's Theological Challenge to Slavery* (Ontario: Joshua, 2006), 169.

[16] J. Vincent 'The Poor', in J. Vickers (ed.), *A Dictionary of Methodism in Britain and Ireland* (Peterborough: Epworth, 2000), 276.

[17] W. R. Ward and R. P. Heitzenrater (eds), 'Journals and Diaries IV', vol. 21 in *The Works of John Wesley* [*WJW*] (Nashville, TN: Abingdon, 1992), 233.

[18] Ibid., 442.

'She received us with that easy openness and affability, which is almost peculiar to Christians and persons of quality.'[19] Likewise, it must be able to comprehend both Wesley's denunciation of the 'ambitiosa paupertas' of the children at Lady Maxwell's charity school – 'Be they ever so poor, they must have a scrap of finery. Many of them have not a shoe to their foot but the girl in rags is not without her ruffles'[20] – and his sneering at the failure of the Earl of Salisbury to display properly his wealth and standing in the furnishings of Hatfield House:

> The hall, the assembly-room, and the gallery are grand and beautiful. The chapel is extremely pretty. But the furniture in general (excepting the pictures, many of which are originals) is just such as I should expect in a gentleman's house of five hundred a year.[21]

The ruffle and the furnishings, with their echoes of sumptuary laws and the whole notion that people's consumption should reflect their place in society, are perhaps the starkest reminder that Wesley's world view was essentially conservative. As John Walsh has shown, his political and social thinking was hugely indebted to the Tory, High Church tradition within the Church of England which 'extolled the religious character of magistracy; divine right, passive obedience'.[22] It was, by the mid eighteenth century, an essentially nostalgic vision of the traditional rural community in which the poor were deferential to their social superiors and the rich were obliged to relieve the most pressing needs of the poor. The idea that his societies could become just such a community was certainly one that Wesley returned to several times during his life; but we should be clear that the aim was for Methodists to look after the Methodist poor not to address poverty in society generally:

> is it possible to supply all the poor in our society with the necessaries of life? ... Is it not so among the people called Quakers? Yes, and among the Moravians so called. And why should it not be so with us?[23]

For the most part, however, Wesley's chief concern appears to have been in encouraging the ascetic self-denial of giving rather than any vision of the good that such gifts might bring to the recipients. As John Hampson, one of his preachers and his first biographer, observed however: 'His charities rather seem to have been the result of a sense of duty, than of any peculiar tenderness of heart.'[24] It is a view which has echoes with Jonathan Crowther's, not intentionally critical, claim that

---

[19] *WJW*, vol. 23, 274.
[20] Ibid., 241.
[21] Ibid., 422.
[22] J. Walsh, 'John Wesley and the Community of Goods', in K. Robbins (ed.), *Protestant Evangelicalism: Studies in Church History*, 'Subsidia' series, 7 (Oxford: Blackwell, 1990), 32.
[23] Ibid., 46.
[24] J. Hampson, *Memoirs of the late Rev. John Wesley* (Sunderland: John Hampson, 1791), III, 199.

Wesley believed the poor existed to give the faithful opportunity to show their benevolence.

If Wesley preferred the company of the poor it was not because he felt great empathy or human solidarity with them – compare Whitefield's description of the Kingswood colliers, 'poor lambs needing a shepherd', with his 'Gross, open sinners, common swearers, drunkards, unmerciful wolves and bears in the shape of men' – but because within the hierarchical structure of social relationships in eighteenth-century England, he was far happier assuming the role of the superior than the inferior.[25] As John Pawson, another of his preachers, observed: he was a man who was 'extremely fond of power' and 'never would suffer it [i.e. his authority] to be called into question'.[26] He had a congenital dislike of having to defer to anyone but, if that expectation were removed and his ego was suitably massaged, he had no intrinsic objection to wealth or privilege. Indeed, it is clear that he found great pleasure in the company of wealthy admirers and in the comfort of their homes. A study of Wesley's preaching tours shows that by the latter part of his career, if not before, they had become an annual progress around the homes of wealthy sympathisers.[27]

Even if Wesley did not have the kind of personal solidarity with the poor that some have claimed, the argument that his Arminian theology paved the way for others to experience a new sense of common humanity might still hold. If everyone can be saved, everyone must have value. Except that the charitable record of Calvinistic Methodism fully stands comparison with Wesleyan Methodism. It was Whitefield who initiated the founding of the first school at Kingswood for the children of the local colliers, a project which, under Wesley's management, was terminally overshadowed by a fee-paying boarding school. Whitefield's Tottenham Court Road chapel provided twelve almshouses and his orphan-house in Georgia, unlike Wesley's in Newcastle, did actually provide shelter for orphans. Martin Madan, one of the Countess of Huntingdon's chaplains, was closely involved in London's Lock Hospital for the victims of venereal diseases; and Hywel Harris established a supposedly self-sufficient community at Trefeca.

It is misleading, however, to present charitable initiatives as having played any central role in the life of any branch of early Methodism. Wesley's *Plain account of the Methodists*, first published in 1748, gave prominence to four projects undertaken by the London Wesleyans. Three of these, however (the dispensary, the poorhouse and the charity school), appear to have had a very short life and there is very

---

[25] M. Bishop, 'Wesley and his Kingswood Schools', in J. Lenton (ed.), *Vital Piety and Learning: Methodism and Education* (Oxford: Applied Theology Press, 2005), 18.

[26] H. D. Rack, 'Wesley Observed: An Unpublished Character Sketch by John Pawson', *Proceedings of the Wesley Historical Society* [*PWHS*], 49 (1993), 17. Pawson also observed that Wesley's 'ear certainly was too attentive to hear his own praise'.

[27] Cf. J. Rodell, '"The Best House by Far in the Town": John Wesley's Personal Circuit', in J. Gregory (ed.), *Bulletin of the John Rylands University Library of Manchester*, 85 (2003), 111–22.

little evidence that they were imitated elsewhere.[28] Telling evidence against the importance of charitable acts in early Methodism comes from the obituary columns of the *Arminian Magazine*. In these idealised lives of the saints, charitable works are not among the virtues routinely celebrated. Visiting the sick, particularly the terminally ill, and condemned prisoners was certainly a Methodist preoccupation; but we should be clear that the purpose of such ministrations was not to ease the temporal circumstances of the afflicted but to save their souls from imminent damnation. So, when Richard Crosby and Samuel Rhodes were condemned to death for robbery, while other people in the town vainly attempted to secure a reprieve for them, the Wesleyan preacher, John Hickling, was a regular visitor to the condemned cell and was well satisfied that he had achieved his goal when, standing with the noose around his neck, one of the men said: 'This is the happiest hour I ever knew in my life, I hope in a few minutes we shall be in paradise.'[29]

If Wesley's personality played an important part in shaping his interaction with the rich and the poor, it played an even more central role in shaping his relationships with women. As Pawson, again, observed: 'his greatest weakness was his extreme fondness of the company of agreeable young women.'[30]

In the second half of the twentieth century, as women began to enter the ministries of the main British and American Methodist denominations, interest focused on examples of women acting in leadership roles, and particularly as preachers, during Wesley's lifetime. Paul Wesley Chilcote, author of several works on the leading role played by women in early Methodism, made clear his motivation:

> The voice of women needs to be heard. The stories of the women who shaped the early Methodist movement need to be known. We are poorer for lack of this memory, and, I firmly believe, nothing less than the future of the church is at stake.[31]

He found forty-one women who preached or exhorted to eighteenth-century Wesleyan societies, and concluded that 'the Methodist societies provided an

---

[28] The dispensary was launched in November 1746 but already historic by 1754. The poorhouse was opened in 1749 and may not have lasted a year; it was certainly given up by 1755. The commencement of the charity school is obscure but it was before 1744, when Silas Told was appointed preacher, but it was described in 1772 as having been 'dropped for some time'. The fourth project, the lending stock, which was started in July 1746, was still a going concern in January 1767. (John Wesley, *A Plain account of the people called Methodists in a letter to the Rev. Mr. Perronet, Vicar of Shoreham in Kent* (1749). Rupert Davies (ed.), *WJW*, vol. 9, 252–80.)

[29] *Arminian Magazine*, 1795, 394.

[30] Rack, 'Wesley Observed', 17.

[31] P. Chilcote, *Her Own Story: Autobiographical Portraits of Early Methodist Women* (Nashville, TN: Abingdon, 2001), 10.

environment which was conducive to the empowerment of women'.[32] Indeed, the nurturing nature of class and band meetings was peculiarly feminine.

It is very easy, however, to overstate this case. Wesley allowed a degree of licence to a small number of women with whom he had a personal relationship; he did not write any kind of role for women into the structure of his connexion. Indeed, given the established precedent of women preaching among the Quakers, and the leading role which women played in various eighteenth-century movements, including the Shakers, the Southcottians, the Moravians and, most obviously, the Calvinistic Methodists, the surprise is how few women had leadership roles among the Wesleyans. Even the roles which were formally open to women, such as class leader, were predominantly performed by men. In the Bedfordshire circuit in 1781, for instance, twenty-three of the twenty-six classes were led by men. In fact, although surviving membership lists do suggest that women generally outnumbered men in Methodist societies, what is noticeable is that during the second half of the eighteenth century men made up an increasing proportion of religious communities.[33] The real gender issue of eighteenth-century Methodism appears to be, why was it so attractive to men?

Before moving on to look at the situation after Wesley's death, a word must be said, in passing, on John Wesley's contribution to abolitionism. As Henry Rack has pointed out, Wesley's interest in social issues was peripheral and his views were almost always unoriginal.[34] Much has been made of his opposition to slavery, which is often described as 'lifelong' but, despite having personal experience of slavery during his time in Georgia in 1736/37, there is no record of his having expressed any opinion on the subject before the publication of Anthony Benezet's enormously influential book *Some historical account of Guinea* in 1772 made it a fashionable talking point. Indeed, Wesley's own pamphlet on the subject, *Thoughts on Slavery* (1774), is little more than a popular précis of Benezet's work. In the 1780s he associated himself publicly with the campaign for the abolition of the slave trade on several occasions but he was neither an instigator nor a driving force in the movement.

---

[32] P. Chilcote, *John Wesley and the Women Preachers of Early Methodism* (Metuchen, NJ and London: Scarecrow, 1991), 239.

[33] Among dissenting churches, men grew from 36 per cent of the membership in the period 1726–50 to 45 per cent in 1776–1800. (C. Field, 'Adam and Eve: Gender in the English Free Church Constituency', *Journal of Ecclesiastical History*, 44:1 (1993), 67.) Gail Malmgreen, apparently using figures from the Manchester circuit in 1759 and the Macclesfield circuit in 1794, found that men also formed 45 per cent of Wesleyan membership (G. Malmgreen, 'Domestic Discords: Women and the Family in East Cheshire Methodism, 1750–1830', in J. Obelkevich, L. Roper and R. Samuel (eds), *Disciplines of Faith: Studies in Religion, Politics and Patriarchy* (London: Routledge & Kegan Paul, 1987), 60).

[34] H. D. Rack, *Reasonable Enthusiast: John Wesley and the Rise of Methodism* (London: Epworth, 2nd edition, 1992), 362.

## British Methodism in the Age of Bunting

The half-century between John Wesley's death and the accession of Queen Victoria in 1837 saw British Methodism evolve into a genuinely popular religious movement. Against a background of unprecedented population growth, profound economic changes, prolonged warfare and political tension, Wesleyan Methodism was transformed. Fuelled by an orgy of chapel building, the expansion of the itinerant ministry and the formal organisation of an army of local lay preachers, Methodism gathered around its formal membership an extensive community of 'hearers' who, at any one time, may have represented some 15 per cent of the population. Indeed, given that there was a high turnover of both members and hearers, the influence of the movement may have reached to as many as twice that number.

This was the period in which Methodism was best placed to have significant influence on British society and, not surprisingly, it is the period of British Methodist history that has attracted the greatest interest from social historians. The debate has been lively and, sometimes, fierce. Alan Gilbert is one of those who have argued that Methodism, and evangelical Dissent more generally, were a benign influence, creating new, voluntary communities to fill the gap left by the traditional village community:

> perhaps the most important of the latent functions of Methodism and New Dissent involved the capacity for satisfying the profound associational and communal needs of people experiencing anomie and social insecurity in a period of rapid social change and dislocation.[35]

He has also accepted the argument that these new communities involved some degree of self-assertion, a deliberate stepping aside from deference to social superiors:

> The labourers, artisans and trades people, the school teachers and other minor professionals, and even (albeit to a much lesser extent) the merchant and manufacturing groups that became Methodists in early industrial England, were the kinds of people, who, in matters of politics, industrial relations or social status, often found themselves at odds, in one way or another, with the norms, values and institutions of the ruling classes.[36]

---

[35] A. D. Gilbert, *Religion and Society in Industrial England: Church, Chapel, and Social Change, 1740–1914* (London and New York: Longman, 1976), 89. 'Anomie' is defined as 'social disorganisation' (n. 85).

[36] A. D. Gilbert, 'Religion and Political Stability in Early Industrial England', in P. K. O'Brien and R. Quinault (eds), *The Industrial Revolution and British Society* (Cambridge: Cambridge University Press, 1993), 89.

Nigel Scotland has put it more baldly: 'The building and establishment of a chapel was often an act of open rebellion against parson, squire, and farmers.'[37] It is easy to see how this line of thought breathes new life into Wearmouth's thesis: the protest begins with a chapel, which fosters the skills for a trade union, and paves the way for the Labour party.

Not everyone, of course, has been convinced. E. P. Thompson, the Marxist son of a Methodist minister, stands out as the most outspoken advocate of an entirely contrary interpretation. For Thompson Methodism was 'a component of the psychic processes of counter-revolution'.[38] It fed off the hunger, hardship and anomie of the migrants to the expanding industrial towns, drained them of energy and spirit and taught them to submit to the work-discipline of the factory: 'The box-like, blackening chapels stood in the industrial districts like great traps for the human psyche.'[39] The advance of Methodism represented a retreat from the struggle for social and political progress:

> What we have ... is a revivalist pulsation, or an oscillation between periods of hope and periods of despair ... whenever hope revived, religious revivalism was set aside ... In this sense, the great Methodist recruitment between 1790 and 1830 may be seen as the chiliasm of despair.[40]

It is clear that Thompson has a point, and that the Wesleyan leadership, both the preachers and the wealthy laymen who bankrolled the movement, worked strenuously to maintain Wesley's tradition of political and social conservatism. Maldwyn Edwards, a Methodist historian and President of the British Methodist Conference, wrote before Thompson:

> One cannot easily exaggerate the help Methodism gave to the Government in the early nineteenth century by this attitude of uncritical admiration and unswerving loyalty. Its ultimate effect was to strengthen in a dangerous fashion the forces of reaction and conservatism.[41]

In the writings of W. R. Ward, and more recently of David Hempton, there has been an attempt to synthesise both these arguments based on the observation of Raphael Samuel, that there were 'many Methodisms in many places at many times'.[42] A reactionary leadership does not necessarily mean that what was happening in

---

[37] N. Scotland, *Methodism and the Revolt of the Field* (Gloucester: Sutton, 1981), 22.

[38] E. P. Thompson, *The Making of the English Working Class* (Harmondsworth: Pelican, 2nd edition, 1980), 419.

[39] Ibid., 404.

[40] Ibid., 427.

[41] M. Edwards, *After Wesley: A Study of the Social and Political Influence of Methodism in the Middle Period (1791–1849)* (London: Epworth, 1935), 152.

[42] D. Hempton, *Methodism and Politics in British Society 1750–1850* (London: Hutchinson, 1984), 11.

the smaller chapels, served by the local lay preachers, did not take on a completely different hue. So it was quite possible that even in a village chapel, built with the money of conservative farmers, governed by conservative ministers sent to the circuit by the national leadership, a far more radical version of Methodism might occasionally be glimpsed, as in this prayer meeting from the 1830s:

> The landlords and some of the farmers were prayed for by name 'cursed is he who removeth his neighbour's landmark, and oppresseth the poor and needy, and joineth land to land,' and stoppeth footpaths; these sentences always met with hearty amens.[43]

Official Methodism did its best, however, to stamp out such displays. Back in Dorset, we do not know how the Dorchester circuit responded to the arrest of several of its local preachers as no records from this period have survived, but the minutes of the adjacent Sherborne circuit show that steps were immediately taken to discipline other preachers involved in the union:

> Resolved 2nd That if the said brethren John Smith and Samuel Denman or any other brother or brethren on the plan of the Sherborne circuit enter into any combination against their masters or take any oath of secrecy or make any engagement whatsoever that tends to disturb the public peace – that violates the precepts of the word of God, or the rules of the Wesleyan Methodist Society – the Superintendent Preacher shall be at perfect liberty (without calling any Special Meeting of the Local Preachers) to suspend him or them from preaching.[44]

It was this assertion of traditional Wesleyan control, to the exclusion of those who sought to use the movement as a vehicle for social protest, that in the late 1830s brought Methodist growth (as a proportion of the population) to an end. As Hempton puts it:

> Telling men on rock bottom wages that poverty was a Christian blessing was simply encouraging them to separate their economic from their religious life. Those who did not abandon religion altogether were forced either to join a more radical denomination or else to squeeze religion into a smaller compartment of their lives … [It was] the end of Wesleyan Methodism as a force in working class culture and politics.[45]

Although Methodism resolutely refused to support any movement for political or economic reform in early-nineteenth-century Britain, Methodists were united

---

[43] J. Buckmaster, *A Village Politician* (Horsham: Caliban, 1982), 40.
[44] Sherborne Wesleyan circuit, minutes of local preachers' meeting. Dorset Records Office, NM6 C1/LP1/1.
[45] Hempton, *Methodism and Politics in British Society*, 110.

and vocal in campaigning on one of the key social issues of the period. Throughout the 1820s, despite experiencing continuing disabilities themselves, 'the friends of all and enemies of none' actively and vociferously opposed all attempts to lessen legal discrimination against Roman Catholics. Although held back from campaigning against emancipation as a body, by the single-handed intervention of Jabez Bunting, up and down the country Wesleyan preachers were zealously active in their opposition to reform. The ultra-Protestant Lord Eldon reported to the House of Lords that, having read the

> Reports of the debates which had taken place at numerous meetings across the country, for the purpose of petitioning parliament against further concessions to the Catholics, he had been astonished to observe the ability and knowledge manifested by the ministers of the Wesleyan Methodists who had taken part in those debates.[46]

It was a position which put Methodists at odds with other kinds of Protestant dissenters who generally accepted that, in seeking equality for themselves, they could not justify denying it to others. In Manchester, in 1825, although copies of an anti-Catholic petition were sent to all Dissenting ministers, only the Methodists displayed them in their chapels to be signed.

A deep loathing of Catholicism was also evident in the response of British Methodists to one of the other great social movements of the period, the campaign for mass literacy. Methodists have often claimed, and been accorded, considerable credit for their pioneering work in the spread of Sunday schools. H. F. Mathews went so far as to claim that such schools originated in Wesleyan Methodism:

> Without in any way diminishing the rightful honour paid to Raikes as initiator of the Sunday-school movement, it is right to point out that a Methodist, Hannah Ball, had as early as 1769 (eleven years before Raikes' experiment) opened a Sunday-school at High Wycombe which came under Wesley's patronage.[47]

In fact, the Methodist contribution to the Sunday school movement has probably been overstated. As late as 1837, more than a third of Wesleyan congregations had no Sunday school and among the non-Wesleyans the proportion appears to have been even higher.[48] Even where there were Wesleyan schools, strict sabbatarianism ensured that the curriculum was restricted to reading, with even the teaching of writing being prohibited. Despite the obvious shortcomings of Sunday schools as a vehicle of elementary education, the Wesleyans opposed all Government

---

[46] Ibid., 137.

[47] H. F. Mathews, *Methodism and the Education of the People, 1791–1851* (London: Epworth Press, 1949), 36.

[48] R. Davies, A. R. George and G. Rupp (eds), *A History of the Methodist Church in Great Britain*[ *HMCGB*] (4 vols, London: Epworth, 1965–88), IV, 435.

initiatives to fund day schools until 1847. Their opposition appears to have had several roots: a concern that education would make the poor dissatisfied with their lot; a fear of any scheme that gave advantage to the Church of England; but above all, a determination that no government money should go to support Catholicism. Rather than see any public money facilitate the 'propagation of the corrupt and tyrannical system of Popery', Methodists were willing both to forego State aid for their own schools and to deprive the general population of education.[49] Methodist self-interest and prejudice were certainly not the only reasons that England had to wait until 1870 for a comprehensive system of publicly funded elementary education, but they played their part.

A brief review of recent works on nineteenth-century British social history suggests that the majority of social historians have yet to be convinced that Methodism had any significant impact, for good or ill, on British society.[50]

## Ante-bellum Methodism in America

Crossing the Atlantic, we enter a new world. Whatever other contributions Methodism may have made to philanthropy and social reform in America in the period before the civil war, the test of any claim that it stood for what we might today call social justice must surely rest on its response to the single issue of slavery. The modern historiography of this question can probably be said to begin with Donald Mathews' *Slavery and Methodism: A Chapter in American Morality 1780–1845* (1965). Mathews argued that the anti-slavery sentiment of early Methodism was quickly crumpled in the face of opposition. He traced the retreat in Asbury's position, through 'opposition to slavery ... then caution, then compromise', recording that he told the General Conference of 1804 'I am called upon to suffer for Christ's sake not for slavery' and stood by as:

> the Conference produced an ordinance which further softened the rules on trading in slaves, rescinded the call to petition state legislatures ... [and suspended] the whole Section on Slavery [in the *Discipline*] south of Virginia.[51]

---

[49] J. T. Smith, *Methodism and Education, 1849–1902: J. H. Rigg, Romanism, and Wesleyan schools* (Oxford: Clarendon, 1998), 8.

[50] D. MacRaild's *Labour in British Society 1830–1914* (Basingstoke: Palgrave Macmillan, 2000) contains only one reference to Methodism, as does A. August's *The British Working Class 1832–1940* (Harlow: Longman, 2007). J. Host's *Victorian Labour History: Experience, Identity and the Politics of Representation* (London: Routledge, 1998) contains no references to Methodism; and the only article relating to Methodism that has appeared in the *History Workshop Journal* since 2000 describes its influence on the childhood of radical historian Christopher Hill rather than British society.

[51] D. Mathews, *Slavery and Methodism: A Chapter in American Morality 1780–1845* (Princeton, NJ: Princeton University Press, 1965), 28.

What conscience Methodists had, Mathews maintained, was salved either in missions to slaves or in support for the American Colonization Society's scheme to send freedmen back to Africa. Indeed, such was the complete acceptance of the unassailability of slavery that when abolitionism emerged as a cause within Methodism in the 1830s, it sprang from roots outside the movement rather than from any legacy of earlier opposition to slavery.

Perhaps not surprisingly, there has been greatest interest in the earliest, innocent phase of American Methodism, when interracial congregations and class-meetings were possible and the first *Discipline* of the Methodist Episcopal Church prohibited members from owning slaves. Cynthia Lyerly, in *Methodism and the Southern Mind 1770–1810* (1998), has argued that, even in the South, Methodism offered a radically egalitarian counter-culture well into the first decade of the nineteenth century:

> Methodism challenged ... southern values and practices on a number of levels ... For a few decades, Methodists challenged slavery as well. Their attack ebbed and flowed, they alternately advanced and retreated, and they frequently changed their strategy, but nonetheless they were the most persistent and vocal critics of slavery among the evangelical sects. Among all religious groups, they were second only to Quakers in their opposition to human bondage.[52]

For Lyerly, the exponential growth of Methodism (membership rose from 20,681 in 1786 to 174,060 in 1810) was rooted in its ability to create:

> a public sphere in which southerners at the margins of power [white women, slaves, free blacks and plain folk men] could advance to leadership and earn the esteem of their fellow believers, a public sphere in which southerners from all walks of life were welcomed and valued.[53]

Christopher Owen, whose book, *The Sacred Flame of Love: Methodism and Society in Nineteenth-Century Georgia*, came out in the same year as Lyerley's, has taken the argument a stage further and attempted to rehabilitate Southern Methodists more generally. He argues that the great majority of Georgia Methodists:

> promulgated a position of official neutrality toward the institution [of slavery] and advocated withdrawal, as a church, from politics. They repeatedly maintained that slavery was a civil institution outside the purview of the church. Genuine Christianity, they argued, could exist (and had existed) either with slavery or without it. Religious

---

[52] C. L. Lyerly, *Methodism and the Southern Mind, 1770–1810* (New York, NY: Oxford University Press, 1998), 7–8.

[53] Ibid., vii.

bodies, whose goal should be saving souls, therefore had no business 'intermeddling' with a secular institution.[54]

Owen also argues that what persuaded the non-slave-owning majority of Southern Methodists to part company with the Methodist Episcopal Church was the fact that abolitionism moved the debate about ethical standards away from a purely Biblical basis:

> Georgia Wesleyans continually harangued against the 'higher-law conscience' of northern Methodists. Abolitionists, they argued, derived antislavery principles from certain passages (like the Golden Rule) that did not deal specifically with slavery, but rejected the literal meaning of more pertinent verses. This repudiation of scriptural literalism allowed southern churchmen to launch telling attacks on antislavery forces … In 1850 the Southern Christian Advocate maintained that Methodist reunion was impossible because of the extrabiblical notions of the MEC.[55]

Finally, he argues that while Southern Methodists did nothing to end slavery they did go to substantial lengths to save the souls of slaves:

> Slave missions developed into an extraordinary enterprise. By 1861 membership of MECS slave missions numbered 66,559, a growth of more than 300 percent since 1844 … Methodists no longer needed to beg slave owners to allow evangelization of their charges. Rather, they could expect financial subsidies from slave owners, many of whom welcomed preaching places on the plantation.[56]

There are surprising points of congruence in all of this with British Wesleyanism, which, while firmly abolitionist, also maintained a 'no politics' rule and was seen by some factory owners, including Robert Peel's father, as a steadying influence on workers.

There are, however, some fairly unhelpful facts that sit oddly with these last two interpretations of American Methodist history. Lyerley's vision of a long summer of love before Southern Methodism conformed to Southern culture is hard to reconcile with the suspension of the much quoted prohibition on Methodists owning slaves just six months after it had been promulgated in 1784. Just eight years later, even in Philadelphia, then perhaps the most liberal city in the United States, a special gallery was erected in the Methodist church so that Africans could be seated separately. Here and in other cities, relations between the races were so

---

[54] C. H. Owen, *The Sacred Flame of Love: Methodism and Society in Nineteenth Century Georgia* (Athens, GA and London: University of Georgia Press, 1998), 63.
[55] Ibid., 66.
[56] Ibid., 80.

fraught, in this Methodist golden age, that African Methodists began to take the first steps towards establishing their own denominations.[57] Likewise, Owen's vision of Southern Methodism as slightly detached from the full-blown advocacy of slavery does not square comfortably with rapid growth of the Methodist Episcopal Church South in the run-up to the civil war.

A different voice can be heard in Peter Murray's *Methodists and the Crucible of Race 1930–1975* (2004), which while it primarily deals with history of the reunited Methodist Church's segregated central jurisdiction, contains a brief but useful summary of the experience of black Methodists before that point. Murray notes that at the beginning of the nineteenth century:

> Despite misgivings about the institution of slavery, the Methodist Church decided it was better to grow in the slaveholding South than to rigidly uphold its antislavery position. This alone did not cause a break between African American and white Methodists, but it indicated how white interests dominated the church.[58]

He also draws attention to the fact that very few Methodists seceded with Orange Scott and La Roy Sunderland in 1843 to form a church specifically committed to abolition, and that even after the Southerners had withdrawn, the General Conference of the Methodist Episcopal Church threw out abolitionist revisions to the *Discipline*. African Americans within the Methodist Episcopal Church were segregated in separate congregations and African American preachers were not accorded full ordination until 1864.

There seems very little reason to single Methodists out from their Baptist, Presbyterian or non-churchgoing neighbours in terms of their attitudes to slavery and race. They reflected and followed the outlook and prejudices of their day, and continued to do so after slavery was abolished. After the war, the Southern church sponsored the creation of the Colored Methodist Episcopal Church to divest itself of its remaining African members and the Northern church separated its black congregations into segregated Conferences. When the two reunited, in 1939, those black Conferences were then doubly segregated into a black jurisdiction. Not until the late 1960s, at the height of the civil rights movement, were steps taken to dismantle these structures. The only aspect of this story in which Methodism can be seen leading the development of attitudes and events is in the institutional separation of North and South which prefigured the political division of the country by eighteen years, and some historians argue was an important psychological precursor to war.

---

[57] J. G. Melton, *A Will to Choose: The Origins of African American Methodism* (Latham, MD: Rowman & Littlefield, 2007), 93.

[58] P. Murray, *Methodists and the Crucible of Race 1930–1975* (Columbia, MO: University of Missouri Press, 2004), 13–14.

## The Social Gospel and After

Much less ink has been spilt on the history of Methodism in the late nineteenth and early twentieth centuries, and yet this is a period in which Methodist interest in social reform becomes unquestionably evident. In Britain, Wesleyan Methodism launched a Forward Movement – a large-scale investment programme in missions to the urban poor that combined a new style of worship, organised charitable works and engagement with progressive politics – driven along by the dominating personality of Hugh Price Hughes. In the introduction to his *Social Christianity*, Hughes had written:

> In our reaction from medieval ecclesiasticism we have gone too far. We have practically neglected the fact that Christ came to save the Nation as well as the Individual, and that it is an essential feature of His mission to reconstruct human society on a basis of Justice and Love. It has been well said that 'the power of love as the basis of a State has not yet been tried.' But Christ rose from the dead to try it, and to do it.[59]

The campaign was both a reaction to a number of high-profile reports on working-class living conditions in the cities and a response to the dramatic decline in attendance in some city centre churches. It borrowed shamelessly from the Salvation Army, down to the use of brass bands, and struck a confident, even militant note. Christopher Oldstone-Moore's biography of Hughes bills him as the 'founder of a new Methodism, conscience of a new Nonconformity' and there is certainly much to suggest that twentieth- century Methodism owed more to Hughes than to Wesley.[60]

Most of the developments in Methodism were mirrored in other Evangelical Free churches, and although Methodists formed the largest community they often appeared to be the junior partners in the Free churches' efforts to exert public pressure for social reform. At the election of 1906, the high-water mark of Free church political influence, thirty-five Wesleyans were elected to Parliament, compared with seventy-three men from the much smaller Congregationalists and seventeen from the tiny Unitarians.[61] Central to this Nonconformist Conscience was a concern for social purity. The Wesleyan Society for Securing Repeal of the Contagious Diseases Act (which was seen as condoning prostitution), was the first organisation in British Methodist history to prompt overt political action by Wesleyan ministers against existing legislation.[62] Efforts to legislate against

---

[59] H. P. Hughes, *Social Christianity* (London: Hodder & Stoughton, 1889), viii.
[60] C. Oldstone-Moore, *Hugh Price Hughes: Founder of a New Methodism, Conscience of New Nonconformity* (Cardiff: University of Wales Press, 1999).
[61] S. Koss, *Nonconformity in Modern British Politics* (Hamden: Archon, 1975), 228.
[62] D. Bebbington, *The Nonconformist Conscience: Chapel and Politics, 1870–1914* (London: Allen & Unwin, 1982), 39–40.

gambling followed, but most important of all, of course, was the campaign against alcohol. Temperance secretaries were appointed by all the main British Methodist connexions, abstainers' rolls maintained in all churches and children's temperance meetings, the Band of Hope, widely supported. Despite forming a core element of Methodist identity, politics and social impact in this period, almost nothing has been written about this aspect of British Methodist thought and life.

There were, of course, alternative voices. Samuel Keeble offered the Wesleyans an agenda that was focused much more clearly on the pressing issue of labour relations, and many lay Methodists became involved in the growing trade union and labour movements, but they were in the minority. Most Methodists continued to believe that moral renewal was the key to social reform and, as it became clear that the Free churches did not have the political clout to impose moral legislation, they retreated into forming cricket and football clubs, building temperance hotels in seaside resorts and creating a social enclave in which members and their children could be kept safely away from worldly amusements.[63]

In America, Temperance was, if anything, even more central to Methodist identity than in Britain and became emblematic, not only of a traditional quest for personal holiness but of an Anglo-Saxon, nativist way of life that appeared to be threatened by an extraordinary wave of new immigration from southern and eastern Europe. Prohibition was writing into law the American Protestant way of life and it is no coincidence that the Methodist Episcopal Church petitioned Congress 'to deport aliens upon the second conviction for violation of our prohibition and narcotic laws'.[64] The passage of the eighteenth amendment in 1919 was a triumph for Methodism and prompted dreams of a more extensive programme:

> The prize fight will be outlawed, the stage cleaned up, the moving picture films regulated … A wave of Americanism which has receded will come back enthroning the Bible in the public schools and the American Sabbath on its American foundations.[65]

The Methodist churches, whose strength lay in rural and small-town America, and whose urban membership was drawn from skilled and clerical workers, managers and professionals, were slow to appreciate the appalling living and working conditions of the largely immigrant manual labourers in the rapidly expanding industrial centres. The progressivist, optimistic element in prohibitionism, however, prepared the ground for Methodists to believe, once alerted to the issue, that other social evils could also be addressed through legislation. At the General Conference of 1908 the Methodist Episcopal Church adopted a Social Creed which expressed its support for, among other things:

---

[63] H. D. Rack, 'Wesleyan Methodism 1849–1902', in *HMCGB*, III, 145.
[64] R. M. Miller, 'Methodism and American Society 1900–1939', in E. S. Bucke (ed.), *The History of American Methodism* (3 vols, New York, NY: Abingdon, 1964), III, 340.
[65] Ibid., III, 340.

> ... equal rights and complete justice for all men in all stations of life.
> ... the principles of conciliation and arbitration in industrial dissensions.
> ... the protection of the worker from dangerous machinery, occupational diseases, injuries and mortality.[66]

The MEC was the first denomination to adopt such a statement, but much of its thinking was based on the Social Gospel teachings developed by Washington Gladden (a Congregationalist), Richard Ely (an Episcopalian) and Walter Rauschenbusch (a Baptist); and within a few months a very similar declaration was made by the Federal Council of the Churches of Christ in America, to be followed by others from most of the main Protestant denominations.

The impact of the Social Gospel, and the Social Creed, remains questionable. In the cities the Methodist churches launched 'institutional churches', on lines not dissimilar to the British 'central halls' and beautifully captured in Sinclair Lewis's irreverent odyssey through American religious life, *Elmer Gantry*:

> Dr. Otto Hickenlooper, of Central Church, was an even more distressing rival. His was the most active institutional church of the whole state. His had not only manual training and gymnastics but sacred pageants, classes in painting (never from the nude), classes in French and batik-making and sex hygiene and book-keeping and short-story writing. He had clubs for railroad men, for stenographers, for bell-boys; and after the church suppers the young people were encouraged to sit about in booths to which the newspapers referred flippantly as 'courting corners.'[67]

However, campaigning for legislative reform before 1919 was entirely overshadowed by the priority of prohibition and by the 1920s was undermined by the prevalent assumption that rising prosperity would resolve most of the problems. Certainly Harry Ward, the original author of the Social Creed, was thoroughly disillusioned by the late 1920s and felt that his words had failed to produce any actions. By the 1930s opposition to the creed had gathered and it disappeared from the *Discipline* of the Northern church in 1936. It was brought into the *Discipline* of the reunited Methodist church in 1939 by the Southerners, just as African Methodists were corralled into the Central Jurisdiction. As one historian has noted:

> It is one of the supreme ironies of American history that ... many progressive reformers, including leaders of the Social Gospel, were either indifferent to the Negro's plight or actually hostile to his aspirations.[68]

---

[66] D. K. Gorrell, 'The Social Creed and Methodism through Eighty Years', in R. E. Richey, K. E. Rowe and J. M. Schmidt (eds), *Perspectives on American Methodism: Interpretive Essays* (Nashville, TN: Abingdon, 1993), 388.
[67] Sinclair Lewis, *Elmer Gantry* (New York, NY: Signet Classic, 1980), 313.
[68] Miller, 'Methodism and American Society 1900–1939', 360.

In another irony, in 1951 at the height of the McCarthy witch-hunt, a self-appointed 'Committee for the Preservation of Methodism' denounced the Methodist Federation for Social Action (the original sponsors of the Social Creed) as 'unAmerican' and published a list of MFSA members who, it claimed, were Communists attempting to subvert the Methodist Church.[69]

## Methodism and Nationalism

'The Committee for the Preservation of Methodism' is a useful reminder that the history of both British and American Methodism has had a nationalistic dimension. British Methodists were, from the beginning, vocal in their loyalty to the crown and British Methodist missionaries contributed to Britain's imperial project. In the United States, Methodism has been seen by many as the quintessential American religion, with Theodore Roosevelt describing it as 'peculiarly congenial' to the American character. Although very little of the history of Korean Methodism is available yet in English, it is clear that Methodism's initial success in the country owed much to its adoption by Korean nationalists as a means of protesting against Japanese imperialism.

It is interesting to note, however, and is surely worthy of further research, that nationalism of an exclusive and sometimes chauvinistic kind has been a feature of several other Methodist communities. In Ireland, where religious and national identities were historically closely bound, to be a Methodist was to be a Protestant and to be a Protestant was to be British. Until almost the end of the twentieth century, Methodists were party to a blend of anti-Catholicism and anti-Irish sentiment that supported a political system in the Protestant-dominated enclave of Northern Ireland which discriminated against Irish Catholics. In Germany, in the 1930s, Methodists flowed with the tide of National Socialism and demanded a German Methodist Church:

> The Methodist Episcopal Church in Germany is from now on exclusively under German leadership. German Methodists can now look their racial comrades in the eye and say, 'Methodism is German'.[70]

They found 'congenial association in the moral reform wing of the National Socialist Party', as the Austrian Methodists did with 'a government at war with the Roman Catholic Church and favoring the Free Church movement'.[71] The Nazis, for their part, found a willing apologist in Bishop Melle who, as late as July 1944, was

---

[69] *Is there a Pink Fringe in the Methodist Church?* (Houston, TX: Committee for the Preservation of Methodism, 1951).

[70] P. F. Douglass, *The Story of German Methodism: Biography of an Immigrant Soul* (New York, NY and: Cincinnati, OH: Methodist Book Concern, 1939), 249–50.

[71] Ibid., 252.

submitting proposals to Hitler for propaganda initiatives that would undermine American support for the war on Germany.[72] More recently in Fiji, where Methodists form a higher proportion of the population than any other country, the Methodist Church was closely involved in a military coup to overthrow a democratically elected government supported by non-indigenous ethnic groups. Of course many Christian communities have proved susceptible to nationalist feeling and there is nothing unique to Methodism in this, but it is an aspect of Methodist history which has yet to be explored.

## Myths and Realities

Although the concept of social justice is clearly of central importance to many twenty-first century Methodists, enough has been said, hopefully, to dispel the idea that Methodism has any coherent history as a socially progressive movement, much less a movement for social justice. Indeed, its history tends to suggest that it has generally been a moderately conservative community, following social trends rather than leading them. It is worth recalling, for instance, that there were women doctors in both America and Britain for more than a hundred years before the main Methodist denominations in either country ordained women.

As a final word, it is perhaps worth returning to the work of Robert Wearmouth. Writing in the 1930s, Wearmouth recognised that Wesley's theological legacy was both politically and socially essentially conservative. He argued, however, that at the grassroots, the numerous opportunities to hold some kind of office created by the various Methodist connexions taught ordinary men, and to some extent women, the skills to make themselves heard. Methodism was not in itself a movement for social justice but an unintentional consequence of its bureaucratic structures was to equip people, who went on to become interested in social justice, with organisational skills. Over the last seventy years Wearmouth's thesis has been supported by a number of local studies of trade unionism in Britain, which show that the labour movement benefited from a Methodist legacy of personnel, language and structures if not its active support.[73] A similar case has been made in relation to Canada and to figures like James Shaver Woodsworth, first leader of the Co-operative Commonwealth Federation.[74] It was never an ideological legacy, however, and it could equally be said to have launched the career of some who had no time for the notion of social justice, including a Methodist lay preacher's daughter called Margaret Thatcher.

---

[72] Roland Blaich, 'A Tale of Two Leaders: German Methodists and the Nazi State', *Church History*, 70 (2001).

[73] R. Moore, *Pitmen, Preachers and Politics* (London: Cambridge University Press, 1979).

[74] N. Semple, *The Lord's Dominion: The History of Canadian Methodism* (Montreal and London: McGill-Queen's University Press, 1996), 350.

# Select Bibliography and Further Reading

Abbott, R. W. (ed.), *Donald English: An Evangelical Celebration* (Ilkeston, Derbys.: Headline Special/Moorley's, 1999).
Abelove, H., *Evangelist of Desire: John Wesley and the Methodists* (Stanford, CA: Stanford University Press, 1990).
Abraham, W. J. 'The End of Wesleyan Theology', *Wesleyan Theological Journal*, 40:1 (2005).
Abraham, W. J. and J. E. Kirby (eds), *The Oxford Handbook of Methodist Studies* (Oxford: Oxford University Press, 2009).
Aldred, J. and K. Ogbo (eds), *The Black Church in the 21st Century* (London: Dartman, Longman, and Todd, 2010).
Anderson, A., *Spreading Fires: The Missionary Nature of Early Pentecostalism* (Maryknoll, NY: Orbis Books, 2007).
Anderson, A. and E. Tang (eds), *Asian and Pentecostal: The Charismatic Face of Christianity in Asia* (Oxford: Regnum Books International, 2005).
Andrews, D., *The Methodists and Revolutionary America: The Shaping of an Evangelical Culture* (Princeton, NJ: Princeton University Press, 2000).
Baker, F., *John Wesley and the Church of England* (Nashville, TN: Abingdon Press, 1970).
Barclay, O., *Evangelicalism in Britain 1935–1995: A Personal Sketch* (Leicester: IVP, 1997).
Bartels, F. L., *Roots of Ghana Methodism* (Cambridge: Cambridge University Press, 1965).
Baylis, J. and S. Smith, *The Globalization of World Politics: An Introduction to International Relations* (Oxford: Oxford University Press, 1997).
Bebbington, D. W., *Evangelicalism in Modern Britain: A History from the 1730s to the 1980s* (London: Unwin Hyman, 1989).
Bebbington, D. W., *Holiness in Nineteenth-Century England* (Carlisle: Paternoster Press, 2000).
Bebbington, D. W., *The Dominance of Evangelicalism* (Nottingham: IVP, 2005).
Bebbington, D. W. and T. Larsen (eds), *Modern Christianity and Cultural Aspirations* (Sheffield: Continuum, 2004).

Beck, B. E., *Exploring Methodism's Heritage: The Story of the Oxford Institute of Methodist Theological Studies* (Nashville, TN: General Board of Higher Education and Ministry of the United Methodist Church, 2004).

Binfield, C., 'Victorian Values and Industrious Connexions', *Proceedings of the Wesley Historical Society*, 55 (2006).

Blaich, R., 'A Tale of Two Leaders: German Methodists and the Nazi State', *Church History*, 70:2 (2001).

Bock, K. Y. (ed.), *Minjung Theology: People as the Subjects of History* (Singapore: The Commission on Theological Concerns, The Christian Conference of Asia, 1981).

Bonino, J. M., *Doing Theology in a Revolutionary Situation* (Philadelphia, PA: Fortress Press, 1975).

Bonino, J. M., *Christians and Marxists: The Mutual Challenge to Revolution* (London: Hodder and Stoughton, 1976).

Bowden, M. F., 'Susanna Wesley's Educational Method', *Journal of the Canadian Historical Society*, 44 (2002).

Brady, S. and H. Rowdon (eds), *For Such a Time as This: Perspectives on Evangelicalism, Past, Present and Future* (Milton Keynes: Scripture Union, 1996).

Brake, G. T., *Policy and Politics in British Methodism, 1932-1982* (London: Edsall, 1984).

Brewer, E. and M. Jackson, *Wesleyan Transformations: A Study in World Methodism and World Issues* (Atlanta, GA: ITC Press, 1988).

Brewer, E. and T. Scott, *World Methodism and World Issues: A Research Report* (Atlanta, GA: Center for Religious Research, 1990).

British Methodist Conference, *An Anglican–Methodist Covenant: Common Statement of the Formal Conversations between the Methodist Church of Great Britain and the Church of England* (London: Church House Publishing and Methodist Publishing House, 2001).

Brown, E., *Women of Mr Wesley's Methodism* (New York, NY: Mellen, 1983).

Bruce, S. (ed.), *Religion and Modernization: Sociologists and Historians Debate the Secularization Thesis* (Oxford: Clarendon Press, 1992).

Bundy, D., 'The Holiness Movements in World Christianity: Historiographical Questions', *Wesleyan Theological Journal*, 38 (Spring 2003).

Bundy, D., *Visions of Apostolic Mission: Scandinavian Pentecostal Mission to 1935* (Uppsala: Uppsala Universitet, 2009).

Burton, V.T., *Spiritual Literacy in John Wesley's Methodism: Reading, Writing, and Speaking to Believe* (Waco, TX: Baylor University Press, 2008).

Campbell, T. A., *John Wesley and Christian Antiquity: Religious Vision and Cultural Change* (Nashville, TN: Kingswood Books, 1991).

Campbell, T. A., *The Religion of the Heart: A Study of European Religious Life in the Seventeenth and Eighteenth Centuries* (Columbia, SC: University of South Carolina Press, 1991).

Campbell, T. A., *Wesleyan Beliefs: Formal and Popular Expressions of the Core Beliefs of Wesleyan Communities* (Nashville, TN: Kingswood Books, 2010).

Carey, H. M., *God's Empire: Religion and Colonialism in the British World, c.1801-1908* (Cambridge: Cambridge University Press, 2011).

Carpenter, J. A., *Revive Us Again: The Reawakening of American Fundamentalism* (New York, NY: Oxford University Press, 1997).
Chapman, D. M., *In Search of the Catholic Spirit: Methodists and Roman Catholics in Dialogue* (Peterborough: Epworth Press, 2004).
Chilcote, P., *John Wesley and the Women Preachers of Early Methodism* (Metuchen, NJ: Scarecrow Press, 1991).
Chilcote, P., *She Offered Them Christ: The Legacy of Women Preachers in Early Methodism* (Nashville, TN: Abingdon Press, 1993).
Chilcote, P. (ed.), *Her Own Story: Autobiographical Portraits of Early Methodist Women* (Nashville, TN: Kingswood Books, 2001).
Chiles, R. E., *Theological Transition in American Methodism 1790–1935* (Lanham, MD: University Press of America, 1983).
Clapper, G. S., *John Wesley on Religious Affections: His views on Experience and Emotion and Their Role in the Christian Life and Theology* (Metuchen, NJ: Scarecrow Press, 1989).
Clark, J. C. D., *English Society, 1688–1832* (Cambridge: Cambridge University Press, 1985).
Collins, D., *When the Church Bell Rang Racist: The Methodist Church and the Civil Rights Movement in Alabama* (Macon, GA: Mercer University Press, 1998).
Collins, K. J., *The Theology of John Wesley: Holy Love and the Shape of Grace* (Nashville, TN: Abingdon Press, 2007).
Cone, J., *A Black Theology of Liberation*, 2nd edition (Maryknoll, NY: Orbis Books, 1986).
Cooney, D. L., *The Methodists in Ireland: A Short History* (Blackrock, Dublin: Columba Press, 2001).
Cox, J., 'Master Narratives of Imperial Missions', Introduction to J. S. Scott and G. Griffiths (eds), *Mixed Messages: Materiality, Textuality, Missions* (New York, NY: Palgrave Macmillan, 2005).
Coxford, R., 'A Working Class Sunday School?', *Proceedings of the Wesley Historical Society*, 54 (2003–04).
Cracknell, K., *Towards a New Relationship: Christians and People of Other Faith* (London: Epworth Press, 1986).
Cracknell, K., *In Good and Generous Faith: Christian Responses to Religious Pluralism* (Peterborough: Epworth Press, 2005).
Cracknell, K. and S. J. White (eds), *An Introduction to World Methodism* (Cambridge: Cambridge University Press, 2005).
Daugherty, R. A., *The Missionary Spirit: The History of Mission of the Methodist Protestant Church, 1830–1939* (New York, NY: General Board of Global Ministries of the UMC, 2004).
Davie, D., *A Gathered Church: The Literature of the English Dissenting Interest 1700–1930* (London: Routledge and Kegan Paul, 1978).
Davies, R., A. R. George and G. Rupp (eds), *A History of the Methodist Church in Great Britain* (4 vols, London: Epworth Press, 1965–88).
Davis, M. L., *The Methodist Unification: Christianity and the Politics of Race in the Jim Crow Era* (New York: New York University Press, 2008).

Davis, M. L., 'Early Twentieth-Century Methodist Missions Photography: The Problems of "Home"', *Methodist Review*, 2 (2010).

Dayton, D., *Theological Roots of Pentecostalism* (Peabody, MA: Hendrickson, 1987).

Dickerson, D. C., 'Liberation, Wesleyan Theology and Early African Methodism, 1766–1840', *Wesley and Methodist Studies*, 3 (2011).

Dieter, M., *The Holiness Revival of the Nineteenth Century*, 2nd edition (Lanham, MD: Scarecrow Press, 1996).

Essamuah, C., *Genuinely Ghanian: A History of the Methodist Church Ghana, 1961–2000* (Trenton, NJ: Africa World Press, 2010).

Estep, J. R., 'John Wesley's Philosophy of Formal Childhood Education', *Christian Education Journal*, 1 (1997).

Felton, G. C., *This Gift of Water: The Practice and Theology of Baptism among Methodists in America* (Nashville, TN: Abingdon Press, 1992).

Ferguson, M., The Hart Sisters: Early African Caribbean Writers, Evangelicals, and Radicals (Lincoln, NE: University of Nebraska Press, 1993).

Forsaith, P. S., *John Wesley – Religious Hero?: 'A Brand Plucked as from the Burning'* (Oxford: Applied Theology Press, 2004).

Forster, D. and W. Bentley, *What Are We Thinking? Reflections on Church and Society From Southern African Methodists* (Cape Town: Methodist Publishing House, 2008).

Forward, M., S. Plant and S. White (eds), *A Great Commission: Christian Hope and Religious Diversity* (Frankfurt: Peter Lang, 2000).

Frank, T. E., *Polity, Practice, and the Mission of the United Methodist Church* (Nashville, TN: Abingdon Press, 2006).

Frost, B. and S. Jordan, *Pioneers of Social Passion: London's Cosmopolitan Methodism* (Peterborough: Epworth Press, 2006).

Gesling, L., *Mirror and Beacon: The History of Mission of the Methodist Church, 1939–1968* (New York, NY: General Board of Global Ministries of the UMC, 2005).

Gibson, W., *Church, State and Society 1760–1850* (London: Macmillan, 1994).

Gibson, W., *The Church of England, 1688–1832: Unity and Accord* (London: Routledge, 2001).

González, J., *Mañana: Christian Theology from a Hispanic Perspective* (Nashville, TN: Abingdon Press, 1990).

Graham, D. E., *Chosen by God: A List of the Female Travelling Preachers of Early Primitive Methodism* (Banbury: Bankhead Press, 1989).

Graham, D. E., 'Two Primitive Methodist Women Preachers', *Proceedings of the Wesley Historical Society*, 56:2 (2007).

Gregorson, L. and S. Juster (eds), *Empires of God: Religious Encounters in the Early Modern Atlantic* (Philadelphia, PA: University of Pennsylvania Press, 2010).

Gregory, J., *Restoration, Reformation, and Reform, 1660–1828: The Archbishops of Canterbury and Their Diocese* (Oxford: Oxford University Press, 2000).

Gregory, J., 'Religion in the Age of Enlightenment: Putting John Wesley in Context', *Religion in the Age of Enlightenment*, 2 (2010).

Gutiérrez, G. (trans. Sr C. Inda and J. Eagleson), *A Theology of Liberation: History, Politics, and Salvation*, 15th edition (Maryknoll, NY: Orbis Books, 1988).

# Select Bibliography and Further Reading

Hammond, G. and P. S. Forsaith (eds), *Religion, Gender and Industry: Exploring Methodism in a Local Setting* (Eugene, OR: Pickwick, 2011).

Harman, R. J., *From Missions to Mission: The History of Mission of the United Methodist Church, 1968–2000* (New York, NY: General Board of Global Ministries of the UMC, 2005).

Harmon, N. B. (ed.), *The Encyclopedia of World Methodism* (2 vols, Nashville, TN: United Methodist Publishing, 1974).

Hatch, N. O., *The Democratization of American Christianity* (New Haven, CT: Yale University Press, 1989).

Hatch, N. O. and J. Wigger (eds), *Methodism and the Shaping of American Culture* (Nashville, TN: Kingswood Books, 2001).

Haykin, M. A. G. and K. J. Stewart (eds), *The Emergence of Evangelicalism: Exploring Historical Continuities* (Nottingham: Apollos, 2008).

Heitzenrater, R. P., *The Elusive Mr. Wesley* (Nashville, TN: Abingdon Press, 1984).

Heitzenrater, R. P., 'John Wesley and Education', in M. J. Bunge (ed.), *The Child in Christian Thought* (Grand Rapids, MI: W. B. Eerdman, 2001).

Heitzenrater, R. P. (ed.), *The Poor and the People Called Methodists, 1729–1999* (Nashville, TN: Abingdon Press, 2002).

Hempton, D., 'Wesleyan Methodism and Educational Politics in Early Nineteenth-Century England', *History of Education*, 8:3 (1979).

Hempton, D., *The Religion of the People: Methodism and Popular Religion c. 1750–1900* (London: Routledge, 1996).

Hempton, D., *Methodism: Empire of the Spirit* (New Haven, CT and London: Yale University Press, 2005).

Hindmarsh, B., '"My Chains Fell Off, My Heart was Free": Early Methodist Conversion Narrative in England', *Church History*, 68:4 (1999).

Hindmarsh, B., *The Evangelical Conversion Narrative: Spiritual Autobiography in Early Modern England* (Oxford: OxfordUniversity Press, 2005).

Hollister, J. N., *The Centenary of the Methodist Church in Southern Asia* (Lucknow, India: Lucknow Publishing House, 1956).

Hughes, M., *Conscience and Conflict: Methodism, Peace, and War in the Twentieth Century* (Peterborough: Epworth Press, 2008).

Jeffrey, D. L. (ed.), *A Burning and a Shining Light* (Grand Rapids, MI: Eerdmans, 1987).

Jenkins, P., *The New Faces of Christianity: Believing the Bible in the Global South* (New York, NY: Oxford University Press, 2006).

Jennings, E., 'Sir Isaac Holden, Bart (1807–97): His Place in the Wesleyan Connexion', *Proceedings of the Wesley Historical Society*, 43 (1982).

Jennings Jr., T. W., *Good News to the Poor: John Wesley's Evangelical Economics* (Nashville, TN: Abingdon Press, 1990).

Jeremy, D., 'Chapel in a Business Career: The Case of John Mackintosh (1868–1920)', in D. Jeremy (ed.), *Business and Religion in Britain* (Aldershot: Gower, 1988).

Jeremy, D., *Capitalists and Christians: Business Leaders and the Churches in Britain, 1900–1960* (Oxford: Clarendon Press, 1990).

Jeremy, D., *A Business History of Britain, 1900–1990s* (Oxford: Oxford University Press, 1998).
Jeremy, D., 'Late Victorian and Edwardian Methodist Businessmen and Wealth', in D. Jeremy (ed.), *Religion, Business and Wealth in Modern Britain* (London: Routledge, 1998).
Jeremy, D., 'Business Men as Preachers among Methodists in the Early Twentieth Century', in A. R. Cross (ed.), *Ecumenism and History: Studies in Honour of John H. Y. Briggs* (Carlisle: Paternoster Press, 2002).
Jeremy, D. ,'Laity in Denominational Leadership: Vice-Presidents of the Primitive Methodist Church, 1872–1932', *Proceedings of the Wesley Historical Society*, 57 (2010).
Jeremy, D., 'Laity in Denominational Leadership: Methodist Vice-Presidents, 1932–2000,' *Proceedings of the Wesley Historical Society*, 58 (2011).
Jones, M. P., '"Her Claim to Public Notice": Reflections on the Historiography of Women in British Methodism', in R. Sykes (ed.), *God's Own Story? Some Trends in Methodist Historiography* (Oxford: Applied Theology Press, 2003).
Jones, S. J., *John Wesley's Conception and Use of Scripture* (Nashville, TN: Kingswood Books, 1995).
Kemp, K. W., *God's Capitalist: Asa Candler of Coca-Cola* (Macon, GA: Mercer University Press, 2002).
Kent, A., *Pulp Methodism: The Lives and Literature of Silas, Joseph and Salome Hocking, Three Cornish Novelists* (Truro: Cornish Hillside Publications, 2002).
Kent, J., *Wesley and the Wesleyans: Religion in Eighteenth-Century Britain* (Cambridge: Cambridge University Press, 2002).
Kidd, T. S., *The Great Awakening: The Roots of Evangelical Christianity in Colonial America* (New Haven, CT: Yale University Press, 2007).
Kimbrough, ST (ed.), *Methodism in Russia and the Baltic States* (Nashville, TN: Abingdon Press, 1995).
Kimbrough, ST (ed.), *Orthodox and Wesleyan Spirituality* (Crestwood, NY: St Vladimir Seminary Press, 2002).
Kimbrough, ST (ed.), *Orthodox and Wesleyan Ecclesiology* (Crestwood, NY: St Vladimir Seminary Press, 2007).
Kimbrough, ST and K. G. C. Newport (eds), *The Manuscript Journal of the Reverend Charles Wesley, M.A.* (Nashville, TN: Kingswood Books, 2007–08).
Kinghorn, K. C., *The Story of Asbury Seminary* (Lexington, KY: Emeth Press, 2010).
Kirkpatrick, D. (ed. trans. L. McCoy), *Faith Born in the Struggle for Life: A Rereading of Protestant Faith in Latin America Today* (Grand Rapids, MI: W. B. Eerdmans, 1988).
Kisker, S.T., *Foundation for Revival: Anthony Horneck, the Religious Societies, and the Construction of an Anglican Pietism* (Lanham, MD: Scarecrow Press, 2008).
Knight, H. H. (ed.), *From Aldersgate to Azusa Street: Wesleyan, Holiness, and Pentecostal Visions of the New Creation* (Eugene, OR: Pickwick, 2010).
Knotts, A., *Fellowship of Love: Methodist Women Changing American Racial Attitudes* (Nashville, TN: Abingdon Press, 1996).

Langford, T. A. (ed.), *Doctrine and Theology in the United Methodist Church* (Nashville, TN: Abingdon Press, 1991).
Langford, T., *Methodist Theology* (Peterborough: Epworth Press, 1998).
Larsen, T. and D. J. Treier (eds), *The Cambridge Companion to Evangelical Theology* (Cambridge: Cambridge University Press, 2007).
Lau, E., *From Mission to Church: The Evolution of the Methodist Church in Singapore and Malaysia: 1885–1976* (Kent Ridge, Singapore: Genesis, 2008).
Lawson, J., *A Thousand Tongues: The Wesley Hymns as a Guide to Scriptural Teaching* (Exeter: Paternoster Press, 1987).
Lenton, J. H. (ed.), *Vital Piety and Learning: Methodism and Education – Papers Given at the 2002 Conference of the Wesley Historical Society* (Oxford: Applied Theology Press, 2005).
Lenton, J. H., *John Wesley's Preachers: A Social and Statistical Analysis of the British and Irish Preachers who Entered the Methodist Itinerancy before 1791* (Milton Keynes: Paternoster Press, 2009).
Lloyd, G., *Charles Wesley and the Struggle for Methodist Identity* (Oxford: Oxford University Press, 2007).
Long, D. S., *John Wesley's Moral Theology: The Quest for God and Goodness* (Nashville, TN: Kingswood Books, 2005).
Mack, P., *Heart Religion in the British Enlightenment: Gender and Emotion in Early Methodism* (Cambridge: Cambridge University Press, 2008).
Macquiban, T. (ed.), *Methodism in its Cultural Milieu: Proceedings of the Centenary Conference of the Wesley Historical Society* (Oxford: Applied Theology Press, 1994).
Macquiban, T. (ed.), *Issues in Education: Some Methodist Perspectives* (Oxford: Applied Theology Press, 1996).
Macquiban, T., 'Proto-Methodists of Anglican Piety in Post-Revolution England', in M. Davies (ed.), *A Thankful Heart and a Discerning Mind: Essays in Honour of John Newton* (Dursley: Lonely Scribe, 2010).
Maddox, R. L., 'Celebrating Wesley – When?', *Methodist History*, 29 (1991).
Maddox, R. L., *Responsible Grace: John Wesley's Practical Theology* (Nashville, TN: Kingswood Books, 1994).
Maddox, R. L. (ed.), *Rethinking Wesley's Theology for Contemporary Methodism* (Nashville, TN: Kingswood Books, 1998).
Maddox, R. L., 'Wesley's Understanding of Christian Perfection: In What Sense Pentecostal?', *Wesleyan Theological Journal*, 34:2 (1999).
Maddox, R. L., 'A Change of Affections: The Development, Dynamics and Dethronement of John Wesley's Heart Religion', in R. B. Steele (ed.), *'Heart Religion' in the Methodist Tradition and Related Movements* (Lanham, MD: Scarecrow Press, 2001).
Maddox, R. L., 'John Wesley's Reading: Evidence in the Kingswood School Archives', *Methodist History*, 41:2 (2003).
Maddox, R. L. and J. E. Vickers (eds), *The Cambridge Companion to John Wesley* (Cambridge: Cambridge University Press, 2010).
Marsden, G. M., *Understanding Fundamentalism and Evangelicalism* (Grand Rapids, MI: Eerdmans, 1991).

Marsden, G. M., *Fundamentalism and American Culture* (Oxford: Oxford University Press, 1980; 2nd edition, 2006).
Marsh, C., B. Beck, A. Shier-Jones and H. Wareing (eds), *Unmasking Methodist Theology* (London: Continuum, 2004).
Mason, E., 'The Clue to the Brontës? Methodism and *Wuthering Heights*', in M. Knight and T. Woodman (eds), *Biblical Religion and the Novel* (Aldershot: Ashgate, 2006).
McClain, W., *Black People in the Methodist Church: Whither Thou Goest* (Nashville, TN: Abingdon Press, 1984).
McGonigle, H. B., *Sufficient Saving Grace: John Wesley's Evangelical Arminianism* (Carlisle: Paternoster Press, 2001).
McGonigle, H. B., *John Wesley's Arminian Theology: An Introduction* (Lutterworth: Wesley Fellowship, 2005).
McInelly, B., '"I Had Rather Be Obscure But I Dare Not": Women and Methodism', in D. Boyd and M. Kvande (eds), *Everyday Revolutions: Eighteenth-Century Women Transforming Public and Private* (Newark, DE: University of Delaware Press, 2008).
Meadows, P. R. (ed.), *Windows on Wesley: Wesleyan Theology in Today's World* (Oxford: Applied Theology Press, 1997).
Meeks, M. D. (ed.), *The Future of the Methodist Theological Traditions* (Nashville, TN: Abingdon Press, 1985).
Meeks, M. D., *God the Economist: The Doctrine of God and Political Economy* (Minneapolis, MN: Fortress Press, 1989).
Meeks, M. D. (ed.), *What Should Methodists Teach?* (Nashville, TN: Abingdon Press, 1990).
Meeks, M. D. (ed.), *The Portion of the Poor: Good News to the Poor in the Wesleyan Tradition* (Nashville, TN: Kingswood Books, 1995).
Meeks, M. D. (ed.), *Trinity, Community and Power* (Nashville, TN: Abingdon Press, 2000).
Meeks, M. D. (ed.), *Wesleyan Perspectives on the New Creation* (Nashville, TN: Kingswood Books, 2003).
Míguez, N., J. Rieger and J. Mo Sung, *Beyond the Spirit of Empire: Theology and Politics in a New Key* (London: SCM Press, 2009).
Milburn, G., *Primitive Methodism* (Peterborough: Epworth Press, 2002).
Milburn, G. and M. Batty (eds), *Workaday Preachers: The Story of Methodist Local Preaching* (London: Methodist Publishing House, 1995).
Monk, R. C., *John Wesley: His Puritan Heritage* (Nashville and New York: Abingdon Press, 1966).
Morris, J., *The Church in the Modern Age* (London: I. B. Tauris, 2007).
Morrow, T. M., *Early Methodist Women* (Altrincham: Epworth Press, 1967).
Murray, P., *Methodists and the Crucible of Race, 1930–1975* (Columbia, MO: University of Missouri Press, 2004).
Newport, K. (ed.), *The Sermons of Charles Wesley* (Oxford: Oxford University Press, 2001).

Newport, K. and T. A. Campbell (eds), *Charles Wesley: Life, Literature and Legacy* (Peterborough: Epworth Press, 2007).

Noll, M., *America's God: From Jonathan Edwards to Abraham Lincoln* (Oxford: Oxford University Press, 2002).

Noll, M. (ed.), *God and Mammon: Protestants, Money, and the Market, 1790–1860* (Oxford: Oxford University Press, 2002).

Noll, M., *The Rise of Evangelicalism The Age of Edwards, Whitefield and the Wesleys* (Leicester: IVP, 2004).

Noll, M. and R. F. Thiemann (eds), *Where Shall My Wond'ring Soul Begin?* (Grand Rapids, MI: Eerdmans, 2000).

O'Malley, J. S., *On the Journey Home: The History of Mission of the Evangelical United Brethren Church 1946–1968* (New York, NY: General Board of Global Ministries of the UMC, 2003).

O'Malley, J. S. and J. Vickers, *Methodist and Pietist: Retrieving the Evangelical United Brethren Tradition* (Nashville, TN: Kingswood Books, 2011).

Park, A. S., 'Holiness and Healing: An Asian American Voice Shaping the Methodist Tradition', in J. Rieger and J. Vincent (eds), *Methodist and Radical* (Nashville, TN: Kingswood Books, 2004).

Park, J. C., 'Interliving Theology as a Wesleyan Minjung Theology', in J. Rieger and J. Vincent (eds), *Methodist and Radical* (Nashville, TN: Kingswood Books, 2004).

Parker, W., *In the Midst of the City: The Rise and Growth of the Auckland Methodist Central Mission* (Auckland: Methodist Central Mission, 1971).

Pestana, C., *Protestant Empire: Religion and the Making of the British Atlantic World* (Philadelphia, PA: University of Pennsylvania Press, 2010).

Price, L., *Interfaith Encounter and Dialogue: A Methodist Pilgrimage* (Frankfurt: Peter Lang, 1991).

Pui-lan, K., D. Compier and J. Rieger (eds), *Empire and the Christian Tradition* (Minneapolis, MO: Fortress Press, 2007).

Rack, H. D., 'Religious Societies and the Origins of Methodism', *Journal of Ecclesiastical History*, 38 (1987).

Rack, H. D., *Reasonable Enthusiast: John Wesley and the Rise of Methodism* (London: Epworth Press, 1989).

Rack, H. D., 'Some Recent Trends in Wesley Scholarship', *Wesleyan Theological Journal*, 41:2 (2006).

Randall, I. M., *Evangelical Experiences: A Study in the Spirituality of English Evangelicalism 1918–1939* (Carlisle: Paternoster Press, 1999).

Randall, I. and D. Hilborn, *One Body in Christ: The History and Significance of the Evangelical Alliance* (Carlisle: Paternoster Press, 2001).

Richey, R. E., *Doctrine in Experience: A Methodist Theology of Church and Ministry* (Nashville, TN: Abingdon Press, 2009).

Richey, R. E., *Methodist Connectionalism: Historical Perspectives* (Nashville, TN: Abingdon Press, 2010).

Richey, R. E. and K. E. Rowe (eds), *Rethinking Methodism* (Nashville, TN: Kingswood Books, 1985).

Richey, R. E., K: E. Rowe and J. Miller-Schmidt (eds), *Perspectives on American Methodism: Interpretive Essays* (Nashville, TN: Kingswood Books, 1993).

Richey, R. E., K. E. Rowe and J. Miller Schmidt, *The Methodist Experience in America* (Nashville, TN: Abingdon Press, vol. 1 *A History* 2010, vol. 2 *A Sourcebook*, 2000).

Richey, R. E. with Dennis M. Campbell and William B. Lawrence, *Marks of Methodism: Practices of Ecclesiology*, United Methodism and American Culture, 5 (Nashville, TN: Abingdon Press, 2005).

Rieger, J. (ed.), *Liberating the Future: God, Mammon, and Theology* (Minneapolis, MO: Fortress Press, 1998).

Rieger, J., *God and the Excluded: Vision and Blindspots in Contemporary Theology* (Minneapolis, MO: Fortress Press, 2001).

Rieger, J., *Christ and Empire: From Paul to Postcolonial Times* (Minneapolis, MO: Fortress Press, 2007).

Rieger, J., *No Rising Tide: Theology, Economics, and the Future* (Minneapolis, MO: Fortress Press, 2009).

Rieger, J., *Grace under Pressure: Renegotiating the Heart of the Methodist Traditions* (Nashville, TN: The General Board of Higher Education and Ministry, 2011).

Rieger, J. and J. Vincent (eds), *Methodist and Radical: Rejuvenating a Tradition* (Nashville, TN, Kingswood Books, 2003).

Rivers, I., 'John Wesley and the Language of Scripture, Reason and Experience', *Prose Studies*, 4:3 (1981).

Rivers, I., 'Dissenting and Methodist Books of Practical Divinity', in I. Rivers (ed.), *Books and Their Readers in Eighteenth-Century England* (London: Leicester University Press, 1982).

Rivers, I., 'John Wesley and the Language of Scripture, Reason and Experience', in I. Rivers (ed.), *John Wesley and Religious Biography: Bulletin of the John Rylands Library*, 85 (2003).

Rivers, I., 'Religious Publishing', in M. F. Suarez and M. Turner (eds), *The Cambridge History of the Book in Britain 1695–1830* (Cambridge: Cambridge University Press, 2009).

Robbins, K. (ed.), *Protestant Evangelicalism: Britain, Ireland, Germany and America c. 1750–c. 1950* (Oxford: Blackwell, 1990).

Robbins, K., *England, Ireland, Scotland, Wales: The Christian Church 1900–2000* (Oxford: Oxford University Press, 2008).

Robbins, K. (ed.), *The Dynamics of Religious Reform in Northern Europe 1780–1920: Political and Legal Perspectives* (Leuven: Leuven University Press, 2010).

Robert, D. L., *Converting Colonialism: Visions and Realities in Mission History 1706–1914* (Grand Rapids, MI: Eerdmans, 2008).

Rogal, S. J., 'A Survey of Methodist Periodicals Published in England, 1778–1900', *Victorian Periodicals Review*, 14:2 (Summer, 1981).

Rogal, S. J., *John Wesley's Book Stock and the Arminian Magazine Catalogue of 1789* (Lampeter: Edwin Mellen Press, 2006).

Rowe, K. E., 'Temples of Healing: The Founding Era of Methodist Hospitals, 1880–1900', *Methodist History*, 46:1 (October 2007).

Runyon, T. (ed.), *Sanctification and Liberation* (Nashville, TN: Abingdon Press, 1981).

Runyon, T. (ed.), *Wesleyan Theology Today: A Bicentennial Theological Consultation* (Nashville, TN: Kingswood Books, 1985).
Runyon, T., *The New Creation: John Wesley's Theology Today* (Nashville, TN: Abingdon Press, 1998).
Ruth, L., *A Little Heaven Below: Worship at Early Methodist Quarterly Meetings* (Nashville, TN: Kingswood Books, 2000).
Ruth, L., *Early Methodist Life and Spirituality* (Nashville, TN: Abingdon Press, 2005).
Santa Ana, J. de (trans. Helen Whittle), *Good News to the Poor: The Challenge of the Poor in the History of the Church* (Maryknoll, NY: Orbis Books, 1979).
Schmidt, M., *John Wesley: A Theological Biography* (trans. N. Goldhawk and D. Inman; 2 vols, Nashville: Abingdon Press, 1973).
Scobie, C. H. and J. Webster Grant, *The Contribution of Methodism to Atlantic Canada* (Montreal: McGill-Queen's University Press, 1992).
Scott, D. W., 'Missionary Education and the Chinese in Malaysia: A Case Study for the Symbiotic Growth of the Methodist Movement', *Methodist History*, 48:3 (2010).
Selén, M., *The Oxford Movement and Wesleyan Methodism in England 1833–1882* (Lund: Lund University Press, 1992).
Shockley, G. (ed.), *Heritage and Hope: The African American Presence in United Methodism* (Nashville, TN: Abingdon Press, 1991).
Sledge, R. W., *Five Dollars and Myself: The History of Mission of the Methodist Episcopal Church, South, 1845–1939* (New York, NY: General Board of Global Ministries of the UMC, 2005).
Smith, J. T., 'Ecumenism, Economic Necessity and the Disappearance of Methodist Elementary Schools in England in the Twentieth Century', *History of Education*, 39:5 (2010).
Stanley, B., *The World Missionary Conference, 1910* (Grand Rapids, MI: Eerdmans, 2009).
Stanley, B. and A. Low (eds), *Missions, Nationalism, and the End of Empire* (Grand Rapids, MI: Eerdmans, 2003).
Stanley, S., *Holy Boldness: Women Preachers' Autobiographies and the Sanctified Self* (Knoxville, TN: University of Tennessee, 2004).
Stephens, R., *The Fire Spreads: Holiness and Pentecostalism in the American South* (Cambridge, MA: Harvard University Press, 2010).
Stout, H. S., *The Divine Dramatist: George Whitefield and the Rise of Modern Evangelicalism* (Grand Rapids, MI: Eerdmans, 1991).
Tait, J. W., *The Poisoned Chalice: Common-Sense Realism and Eucharistic Grape Juice in Victorian Methodism* (Tuscaloosa, AL: University of Alabama Press, 2011).
Temperley, N. and S. Banfield (eds), *Music and the Wesleys* (Urbana, Chicago and Springfield, IL: University of Illinois Press, 2010).
Thomas, H., R. Keller and L. Queen (eds), *Women in New Worlds: Historical Perspectives on the Wesleyan Tradition* (Nashville, TN: Abingdon Press, 1982).
Tipton, S., *Public Pulpits: Methodists and Mainline Churches in the Moral Argument of Public Life* (Chicago, IL: University of Chicago Press, 2007).

Trickett, D., 'The Sense of God's Presence: Spiritual Vision and Witness in the Early Wesleyan Witness', in B. C. Hanson (ed.), *Modern Christian Spirituality* (Atlanta, GA: Scholars Press, 1990).

Trinidad, R., *A Monument to Religious Nationalism: History and Polity of the IEMELIF Church* (Quezon City, Phillippines: Evangelical Methodist Church, 1999).

Trueblood, R. W., 'Union Negotiations between Black Methodists in America', *Methodist History*, 8:4 (July 1970).

Tucker, K. B. Westerfield, '"Plain and Decent": Octagonal Space and Methodist Worship', *Studia Liturgica*, 24 (1994).

Tucker, K. B. Westerfield, (ed.), *The Sunday Service of the Methodists: Twentieth-Century Worship in Worldwide Methodism* (Nashville, TN: Kingswood Books, 1996).

Tucker, K. B. Westerfield, *American Methodist Worship* (New York, NY: Oxford University Press, 2001).

Turner, J M., *Modern Methodism in England 1932–1998* (Peterborough: Epworth Press, 1998).

Turner, J. M., *John Wesley, the Evangelical Revival and the Rise of Methodism* (Peterborough: Epworth Press, 2002).

Tyson, J. R., *Charles Wesley on Sanctification: A Biographical and Theological Study* (Grand Rapids, MI: Francis Asbury Press, 1986).

Vickers, J. A., *Myths of Methodism* (Oxford: Wesley Historical Society, 2008).

Wainwright, G., *Methodists in Dialog* (Nashville, TN: Kingswood Books, 1995).

Wallace Jr., C., '"Some Stated Employment of Your Mind": Reading, Writing, and Religion in the Life of Susannah Wesley', *Church History*, 58:3 (1989).

Walsh, J. D., 'Religious Societies, Methodist and Evangelical, 1738–1800', in W. J. Sheils & D. Woods (eds), *Studies in Church History*, 23 (Oxford: Blackwell, 1986).

Walsh, J. D., 'John Wesley and the Community of Goods', in K. Robbins (ed.), *Protestant Evangelicalism: Britain, Ireland, Germany and America c 1750–c 1950: Essays in Honour of W. R. Ward* (Oxford: Blackwell, 1990).

Walsh, J. D., 'Methodism and the Origins of English-Speaking Evangelicalism', in M. Noll, D. Bebbington & G. Rawlyk (eds), *Evangelicalism 1700–1900* (Oxford: Oxford University Press, 1994).

Walton, H., *A Tree God Planted: Black People in British Methodism* (London: Ethnic Minorities in Methodism Working Group, 1985).

Ward, W. R., *The Protestant Evangelical Awakening* (Cambridge: Cambridge University Press, 1992).

Ward, W. R., *Early Evangelicalism: A Global Intellectual History, 1670–1789* (Cambridge: Cambridge University Press, 2006).

Watson, D. L., *The Early Methodist Class Meeting* (Nashville, TN: Discipleship Resources, 1985).

Watson, D. L., 'Methodist Spirituality', in F. Senn (ed.), *Protestant Spiritual Traditions* (New York, NY: Paulist Press, 1986).

Watson, J. R., *The English Hymn: A Critical and Historical Study* (Oxford: Clarendon Press, 1997).

Weber, T. R., *Politics in the Order of Salvation: Transforming Wesleyan Political Ethics* (Nashville, TN: Kingswood Books, 2001).

Weems, Jr., L. H., *Leadership in the Wesleyan Spirit* (Nashville, TN: Abingdon Press, 1999).

Wellings, M., *Evangelicals in Methodism: Mainstream, Marginalised or Misunderstood?* (Ilkeston, Derbys.: Moorley's, 2005).

Wellings, M., 'Evangelicalism in Twentieth-Century Methodism', in M. Smith (ed.), *British Evangelical Identities Past and Present* (Milton Keynes: Paternoster Press, 2008).

Wigger, J. H., *Taking Heaven by Storm: Methodism and the Rise of Popular Christianity in America* (Oxford: Oxford University Press, 1998).

Wigger, J. H., *American Saint: Francis Asbury and the Methodists* (Oxford: Oxford University Press, 2009).

Williams, J., *Religion and Violence in Early American Methodism: Taking the Kingdom by Force* (Bloomington, IN: Indiana University Press, 2010).

Wilson, L., *Constrained by Zeal: Female Spirituality amongst Nonconformists, 1825–1875* (Carlisle: Paternoster Press, 2000).

Wood, L. W., *The Meaning of Pentecost in Early Methodism: Rediscovering John Fletcher as John Wesley's Vindicator and Designated Successor* (Nashville, TN: Abingdon Press, 2002).

Wright, D. and E. G. Clancy (eds), *The Methodists: A History of Methodism in NSW* (St Leonards, NSW: Allen and Unwin, 1993).

Young, C. R., *Music of the Heart: John and Charles Wesley on Music and Musicians* (Carol Stream, IL: Hope Publishing, 1995).

Yrigoyen, Jr. C. (ed.), *The Global Impact of the Wesleyan Traditions and Their Related Movements* (Lanham, MD: Scarecrow Press, 2002).

Yrigoyen, Jr. C. (ed.), *T&T Clark Companion to Methodism* (London and New York: T&T Clark, 2010).

# Index

Abelove, Henry 163
abortion 82, 268
Abraham, William J. 25
Abrams, Minnie 141, 147, 152–153
abstinence 368, 373–377, 383, 496
Acquaah, Gaddiel Robert 475
Act of Toleration (1689) 15
activism 311, 312, 317, 318, 325
*Adam Bede* 239–240, 473
'adherents' 93–94, 96
'Advice to a Soldier' 369
Africa 57, 58, 69–73, 75, 77, 95, 107, 125, 134, 136, 137, 146, 147, 194–195, 202, 282, 324, 339, 421, 422, 477
   see also Ghana; Sierra Leone
African American Pentecostal community 153
African Methodist Episcopal (AME) 58, 59, 67–68, 70, 76
African Methodist Episcopal Zion (AMEZ) 58, 59, 67–68, 70, 76
African Methodist Episcopalians 39, 264, 280, 281, 330
*Against the Tide* 417
Airey, Edwin 454
'Akron Plan' 411
alcohol 368, 373–377, 383, 496
Aldersgate conferences 6, 118–119
All-African Conference of Churches 75
Allan, Richard 330
Allan, Thomas 329
Alleine, Richard 271
Allen, J. Timothy 41–42
altruism 446
Ambler, R.W. 48
'American Methodist Ladies' Centenary Committee' 159

Andrew, Bishop James O. 45, 46, 371
Anglican Collect 300
Anglican Communion 76
Anglican-Methodist Covenant 125–126, 262
Anglican-Methodist International Commission for Unity in Mission (AMI-CUM) 130
*Anna of the Five Towns* 245
Annie Pfeiffer Chapel 393
Anscombe, Edmund 397
apartheid 79, 189–190
Apostle's Creed 280
*Apostolic Constitutions* 270, 271
Apostolic Faith Mission 152
apostolicism 279, 330, 339
Aquinas, Thomas 223
Araya-Guillén, Victorio 181, 182
Archbold, John 457
Archibald, F.A. 465
*The Architectural Expression of Methodism* 393–394
architecture 390, 391–399, 411
   see also preaching houses
Argentina 76
Ariarajah, Wesley 137
Arias, Mortimer 195
*Arminian Magazine* 293, 311, 404, 462, 463, 464, 468, 469, 485
Arminianism 4, 9, 28, 121–122, 131, 138, 222, 232, 236, 292, 314, 319, 325, 356, 484
art 35, 401–405
artefacts, of Methodism 399–401
Arthur, William 93, 333, 417, 448
*Articles of Faith* 227
Arts and Crafts movement 390, 397

Asbury, Francis 37, 41–42, 57, 252, 262–264, 312, 315, 329–330, 354–355, 379, 469, 491
Asia 70, 75, 134, 202, 282
Asuza Street revival 150, 152
Atlanta Institute 74, 77
atonement 318, 321, 335
Augustine 179, 360–363, 463
Australasian Conference 317
Australia 75, 94, 96, 107, 125, 129, 135, 147, 171–172, 285, 394, 397, 403–404
Austria 76, 126
authority
    of Bible 223, 224
    within Methodism 39–42, 265
Ayliff Industrial Institution for Girls 422

Bacon, John 403
Bain, Albert Wellesley 454
Bainbridge, Emerson 454
Bainimarama, Frank 360
Baker, Frank 24, 110, 234, 244, 296
Baldwin, Alfred 454
Ball, Charles James Prior 456
Ball, Hannah 306
Balthasar, Hans Urs von 139
band meetings 19, 25
Bandelier, Linda 475
Bangs, Nathan 318–319, 330
Banner of Truth Trust 308
baptism 78, 126, 273, 275, 408
*Baptism, Eucharist and Ministry* (1982) 284
Baptists 126, 313, 314
*Barchester Towers* 473
Barclay, William 337
Bardsley, Samuel 465
Barker-Benfield, G.J. 164
Barnby, Joseph 243
baroque style 387, 389
Barratt, Thomas Ball 141, 146, 147, 152
Barrett, C. Kingsley 231
Barrett, John 409, 430
Barrit, Mary 328
Bartels, F.L. 422
Barth, Karl 80, 182, 337, 339
Batty, Margaret 167
Bauhaus 399
Bayly, Albert 248
Beale, John Elmes 454
Beardmore, W.G. 403, 405

Beaty, Amos Leonidas 457
Bebbington, David 34, 290, 311, 316–317, 325, 420
'Bebbington quadrilateral' 3, 21, 227–228, 230, 290, 311, 316–317, 325, 474
Bechtel, Stephen 458
Bedford, John 454
Beech, Olive Ann 458
Beecher, Lyman 313
Beecroft, Herbert 403–404
Beet, J.A. 334
Bell, Charles 396
Bell, George 327
Bell, James 445
Bellman, Harold 434, 441, 454
Benezet, Anthony 486
Benfield, G.J. Barker 473
Bengel, Johann 225
Bennet, John 327
Bennett, Arnold 245, 472
Bermondsey Settlement 334, 417
Best, Gary 408, 410
Bethel Bible School 150, 151
Bett, Henry 335
Bibby, Joseph 456
Bible
    authority of 223, 224
    in contemporary methodism 225–230
    John Wesley's reading of 217–225, 271, 294
    Methodism's interpretation of 27, 79–80
    primacy of 21, 196–197, 227–228, 230, 290, 311, 316–317, 325, 462
    as rule of faith and practice 219–224
    study groups 294–295
    Wesley's notes on the New Testament 224–225, 232, 253
Bible Christians 8, 39, 92, 95, 167, 240, 241, 265, 374, 411, 425, 427, 435–437
'Bible Moths' 217
Bible Protestant Church 66
Biblical Studies Guild 230–232
'The Bicentennial Edition of the Works of John Wesley' 17–18
Billington, Louis 41
Binfield, Clyde 424
*Biographical Dictionary of American Business Leaders* 439–440
*Biographical Sketches of the Lives and Public Ministry of Various Holy Women* 158

*The Birth of Methodism in England* 28
*The Birthright* 471
Bishop, Mary 300
Bishop, Michael 409
bishops
    controversy over position of 41, 42, 72, 263, 264–265
    Council of Bishops 254–255
    John Wesley on ordination of 262
    in United States 41, 42, 252, 264–265
    women 69
'Bishops' Initiative on Children and Poverty' 194
Black Methodists for Church Renewal 373
Black theology 183, 187, 196, 341, 342
'blood and wounds theology' 298
Boardman, W.E. 148
Body, Alfred 408
Bolivia 195
Bone, Jennifer 429
Bonhoeffer, Dietrich 79
*Book of Common Prayer* 78, 252, 277
*Book of Public Prayer and Services* (1882) 281
Book Stewards 401
books used in worship 78
Boot, Jesse 454
Booth, Catherine 146, 304, 305
Booth, Charles 89
Booth, Edward 242
Booth, Evangeline 146
Booth, William 146, 304, 305
Bosanquet, Mary 328
Bose Community 284
Bosworth, F.F. 151
Bourne College, Birmingham 427
Bourne, Hugh 38, 240, 330, 374
Bowden, Martha 407, 423
Bowne, Borden Parker 317, 322
Boys' Industrial School 422
Brackenbury, Robert Carr 326, 327
Bradburn, Samuel 465
Braddon, Mary 473, 474
Bramwell, William 333
Brantley, Richard 26
brass bands 495
Brazil 5, 118, 202
Brekus, Catherine 48
Brevint, Dr Daniel 237
Bridge, Sir Frederick 245

British Methodist Relief and Development Fund 73
Brönte, Charlotte 473
Brönte, Emily 473
Brookes, Henry 464
Brown, Earl Kent 163
Brown, Kenneth 318
Browne, William 458
Brunswick College, Leeds 336
Budd, Edward 458
Budgett, Samuel 448
Bullen, Donald 221
Bultitude, Elizabeth 331
Bultmann, Rudolf 80
Bundy, David 155
Bunting, Jabez 40, 316, 319, 332, 412, 416, 428, 430, 490
Bunting, John 446, 454
Bunting, Percy 377
Burbank, J. Maze 35
burial 276
Burlington, Lord 389
Burma 394
Burnet, Elizabeth 164
Burra, Edward 405
Burton, Tolar 465
Bush, George W. 202
business, Methodists and 431–460
Butterfield, Sir Herbert 340

Cagle, Mary Lee 145
*Called to Love and Praise* 257
Calvinism 8, 9, 28, 179, 222, 224, 236, 314–315, 319, 325, 484
    see also Reformed Church
Calvinistic Methodism 4, 8, 484
camp meetings 35–38, 47, 240, 280, 304, 318, 330
Canada 56, 58, 59, 94, 125, 171, 321, 411, 413, 424, 428, 429, 472, 499
Candler, Asa 433, 437, 440, 458
Candler, Warren 322
candles 78
Cannon Jr., Bishop James 376
*Canons* 270, 271
capitalism 184–185, 204, 378
Capper, Joseph 331
Cardenal, Ernesto 186
Caribbean 70, 71, 74, 147
Carlyle, Thomas 6

Carr, Julian 458
Carroll, Henry K. 93
Carter, David 417
Carter, Henry 374, 378
Carter, Jimmy 307
Carter, Julia 415
Carter, R. Kelso 147
Carwardine, Richard 47, 48
Castro, Emilio 75, 125
Catholic Reformers 20
Catholicism
    Letter to a Roman Catholic (1745) 122
    Methodism and 20, 27, 76, 125, 126, 127–129, 260, 352–353, 414, 490, 491, 498
    in USA (mid 18th c.) 47
Caughey, James 304, 333
Cell, George Croft 20
Cennick, John 236, 298
census *see* statistics (religious)
Central America 134, 147
Central Jurisdiction 58, 67, 372–373, 494, 497
ceramics 400
Ceylon 421
Chadwick, Samuel 322, 333, 334, 336
Champness, Thomas 333
Chapel Aid Association 451
*Chapel and School Architecture* 395
*The Character of a Methodist* (1742) 219
charismatic worship 80, 147–148, 149, 150, 151, 152, 153, 285, 313, 323, 330, 332–333, 339, 349
charity 484–485
    see also wealth distribution
Charles Wesley Society 18, 79
*Charles Wesley and the Struggle for Methodist Identity* (2007) 19
Chartists 47, 331
Chilcote, Paul 163, 303, 485
children
    hymns for 247–248
    *Instructions for Children* 462
    John Wesley on nature of 408–409, 410
    National Children's Home 334
    in poverty 194
    sunday schools 242–243, 410–414, 425, 465, 490
    upbringing of 407–408
Chile 107, 141–142, 153

Chiles, Robert 321–322
China 66, 70, 95, 421
Chopp, Rebecca 179–180, 187, 341
Chown, Samuel Dwight 321
Christchurch, Pittsburgh 398
Christian Aid 73
*Christian Library* (John Wesley) 16, 296
Christian Methodist Episcopal (CME) 58, 67–68, 70, 76
*Christian Mission: How Christianity Became a World Religion* 61–62
Christian Perfection 47, 116, 142, 143, 147, 190, 302–304, 306, 320
*Christian Perfection* 462
*Christian's Pattern* 462
Christology 138–139
Chrysler, Walter 440, 458
Church of England
    attendance figures (18th century) 15
    image as dysfunctional 14
    image re-evaluated 14–15
    Methodist separation from 4, 24
    proposed unity with 24, 68, 75, 125–126
    relationship with Methodism 40, 129–130, 255, 260, 262, 414, 419
    Wesleys critical of 14, 272–273
*The Church of England, c.1689- c.1833* (1993) 15
Church of God 144, 145, 151
Church of God in Christ 153
'Church Methodist' party 19
Church of the Nazarene 144, 145, 264, 333
'Church', The (Methodist definition) 123
Churches Together in Britain and Ireland 75
*Circuit Rider* 472
'circuits' 400–401
City Temple, London 336
civil rights 82
Clapper, Gregory S. 23, 25
Clark, J.C.D. 14–15, 30
Clark, Sidney James Wells 89–90
Clarke, Adam 327, 328, 333
Clarke, Martin 239
class *see* middle class; occupational analysis; social change; working class
class meetings 19, 24, 37, 296, 318, 330, 401
class tickets 401
classicism 387, 389, 389–390
Claxton, Marshall 403–404

climate change/environment 385
Clowes, William 240, 330
Coca-Cola 433
cohabitation 82
Coke, Thomas 14, 18, 212, 252, 262–264, 312, 329, 330, 462
Cokebury 410
Coleman, James 421
Coles, George 159
Collier, Samuel 334
Collins, Kenneth J. 23
Colls, Robert 47
Colman, J. 412
colonialism 61–62, 71–73, 202, 381, 420
Colored Methodist Episcopal Church 372, 494
Comenius, John 408–409
*Commentary on the Bible* (1825) 328
Commission on Pan-Methodist Co-operation 68
'Committee for the Preservation of Methodism' 498
communism 184, 378, 384, 481, 498
*Companions to the Revised Common Lectionary* 340
*Compendium of Christian Theology* (1875) 317, 333
'Compton census' (1676) 88
*Concerning Isabel Carnaby* 471, 474
Cone, James 175, 178, 183, 187, 196, 341
conferences *see* general conferences
confirmation 78
congregational participation 78
Conkin, Paul 35
Connexional Temperance Movement 374
'connexionalism' 72, 122, 126, 257–268, 315, 349
Conservative Evangicals in Methodism 323
*Continuity and Change* 410
conversionism 109, 117, 118–119, 120, 210, 234, 291–293, 310, 311, 318, 333, 442
Cook, Thomas 333
Cooper, George 243
corporate worship 270, 272
Costa Rica 118
Couch, Harvey 458
Coulson, Charles 340, 378
Council of Bishops 254–255
Council of Evangelical Methodist Churches of Latin America (CIEMAL) 74

Covick, Owen 433
Coward, John 445
Cowdell, Thomas Daniel 472
Cowles, Gardner Jr (Mike) 458
Cowles, Gardner 458
Cowles, John 458
Cowper, William 464
Cox, Jeffrey 62
Coxford, Ronald 412
Cracknell, Kenneth 53, 137, 138, 253, 289, 297, 306, 420
Crane, Denis 433
Cranmer, Thomas 78
Crook, W. 93
Crosby, Fanny 247
Crosby, Richard 485
Crosby, Sarah 328, 465
'cross and flame' logo 390
Crowther, Jonathan 479, 484
crucicentrism 297–299, 311, 312, 317, 325
Cuba 182–183
Cullis, Charles 148
culture *see* architecture; art; baroque style; classicism; Gothic style; hymnody; music
*The Culture of Sensibility: Sex and Society in Eighteenth Century Britain* 473–474
Cunningham, Valentine 473
Curnock, Nehemiah 17
Currie, Robert 40, 87, 97, 107

dancing 374
Dandala, Mvume 190
*Daniel Quorm and his Religious Notions* 470
Darwinianism 320
*Daughters of Anowa: African Women and Patriarchy* 172
Davidoff, Leonore 167
Davie, Donald 235, 470
Davies, Rupert 203, 309, 338, 341, 407–408
Davis, Ellen 231
Dawes, Gil 176
Dawkins, Richard 340
day schools 414–420, 425, 491
Dayton, Donald 149, 154
Deacon, Thomas 270, 273
DeBardeleben, Henry Fairchild 458
Decalogue 280
*Deed of Union* 256, 309
democracy 40–42, 263, 313

diaconal ministry 77, 334
*Diary of an Oxford Methodist: Benjamin Ingham, 1733-1734* (1985) 18
diary-keeping 297
Dick, Malcolm 411
Dickins, John 330
dictionaries of business leaders 438–440
*Dictionary of Methodism* 401
'The Dignity of Human Nature' 368
disability provision 68
Disciples of Christ 313
*Discipline* (1798) 312
Dissenting Protestantism 15
divine healing 147–148, 150, 151
divine communication, dreams as 36
divorce 82
Dix, Gregory 284
Dixon, Dr James 332
'The Doctrine of Original Sin' 368
doctrine of sin 22, 179–185, 368
Dodd, C.H. 337
Doddridge, Philip 225, 463
Dolbey, George 388, 393–394, 401
*The Dominance of Evangelicalism* 316
Dorchester, Dr 93
Douglass, Frederick 43, 45
Dow, Lorenzo 35–36, 37–38
dreams, as Divine communcation 36
DuBose, Horace 322
Dubs, Homer 137
Dudley-Smith, Timothy 248
Duke, James Buchanan 458
Dunn, James D.G. 231
*The Duty of Giving Away a Stated Proportion of Income* 448
Dwight, Timothy 313
Dykes, John Bacchus 242, 243
Dymond, John 458

*Early Evangelicalism: A Global Intellectual History, 1670–1789* (2006) 310
*The Early Methodist Class Meeting* (1985) 24
East Asia Christian Conference 75
*Easter at Epworth* 472
Eayrs, George 478, 480
ecclesiology 260–262
Ecumenical Methodist Conferences 57, 93–94, 201–202
ecumenism 74–77, 121–126, 132–135, 260

Edinburgh World Missionary Conference (1910) 123, 137
education 27, 28, 54, 353, 407–429
Education Act (1902) 353, 418, 426
Edwards, Maldwyn 488
Edwards, Ronald 456
Edwards, Sir George 331
Egglestone, Edward 472
Egypt 70
Eldon, Lord 490
Eliot, George 239–240, 241, 473, 474
*Elmer Gantry* 497
Elmfield College, York 426–427
*The Elusive Mr Wesley* 110
Ely, Richard 497
*Eminent Methodist Women* 159, 162
empire
 Methodism as 64, 117–118
 see also imperialism
*Encountering Christ the Saviour: Church and Sacraments* (2011) 127–128
*England in 1815* (1913) 26–27
*England in the Eighteenth Century* 27
Englesea Brook Chapel and Museum 33
English, Donald 295, 339
*English Society, 1688-1832* (1985) 15
Enlightenment 19, 26, 294, 387
environment/climate change 385
Episcopalians 260
*episkopé* 253–256, 260, 262
Epworth Rectory fire 109, 116
eschatology 117, 118
*Essence of Education* 420
Estep, J. 407
Euro-centric bias 169
European Methodist Council 74, 76
Eusebius 237–239
Evangelical Alliance 39, 307, 316
Evangelical Association 379
Evangelical Lutheran Church 76
Evangelical Revival 16, 290, 292, 307–324, 330
Evangelical United Brethren Church 67, 227
evangelicalism 290
*Evangelicalism: Comparative Studies of Popular Protestantism in North America, the British Isles, and Beyond, 1700-1990* (1994) 310
*Evangelicalism in Modern Britain* 290, 311

Everett, James 403
Everett-Green, G.P. 403
existentialism 80

Fairbanks, Charles W. 437
Faith and Order Committee 228–230, 258, 284
Farley, Reuben 456
Farrar, Dr Dorothy 340
*The Farringdons* 471
Farrow, Leslie William 451
fasting 270–271, 297
'fear', gospel of 36
Fellowship of the Kingdom 321
*Female Ministry; or Women's Right to Preach the Gospel* 146
feminism
    affirmation of difference 159
    equal rights 158–159
    methodology of 160–161
    see also women
feminist theologies 179–180, 187
'feminist theology' 160
Fenwick, John 454
Ferens, Thomas 454
Fetter Lane Religious Society 237, 301, 313
Field, Clive 329
field meetings 35
field preaching 305
Field-Bibb, Jacqueline 168
Fiji 77, 359, 499
Findlay, J.A. 335, 337
*A Fine Picture of Enthusiasm* (1744) 237–239
Finney, Charles G. 147
First World War 378
Firth, Mark 454
Fisher, Geoffrey 75, 447
Flesher, John 241
Fletcher, John 7, 142–143, 144, 303, 304, 325, 328, 468
Fletcher, Mary 161, 162, 303, 465
Flew, Robert Newton 125
Foden, Edwin Richard 456
Foden, William 456
folk tunes 38
*The Fool of Quality* 464
Ford, Henry II 440, 458
Ford, John Batiste 458
Forsyth, P.T. 339
Forward, Martin 137

Forward Movement 333, 337, 397, 450, 495
*Foundation for Revival: Anthony Horneck, the Religious Societies, and the Construction of an Anglican Pietism* (2008) 16
'Foundery', London 392
Fowler, Ellen Thorneycroft 470, 471
France 94, 95
Free Methodists 70, 264
Freeman, Charles 396
Freeman, Thomas 422
Frink, Elisabeth 405
Frost, Stanley 337
Frykenberg, Robert E. 61
'full assurance of faith/hope' 23
Fumanti, Mattiah 172
fundamentalism 307, 308, 323
Furly, Dorothy 292
Furness, Christopher 445, 454
furnishings, church 399, 401
Furze, John 327

Gage, Lyman Judson 458
Gaitskell, Deborah 173
gambling 374, 384, 446–447, 452, 496
Gambold, John 235
Garrettson, Freeborn 262
Garrison, William Lloyd 45
Gartside, Thomas 456
Gary, Albert Henry 458
Gaskell, Elizabeth 473, 474
Gauntlett, Henry John 242, 243
gay, lesbian, bisexual, transgender communities 180
Gee, Henry Simpson 454
Gee, H.L. 472
General Commission on Religion and Race 373
general conferences
    1844 conference 45, 264
    dominated by United States 72
    lay members 55, 66, 265, 434–437
    occupations of delegates 434
*General Rules of the United Societies* (1743) 24–25, 44, 194, 295, 368
George, Raymond 338
Germany 57, 67, 76, 126, 338, 358–359, 498–499
Gerzina, Gretchen 370
Ghana 172–173, 197, 383, 422
Gibbs, Dr John M. 405, 417–418

Gibson, William 15
Gilbert, Alan 487
Gilbert, Anne Hart 472
Gilkes, Cheryl Townsend 153
Gill, Eric 405
Gill, F.C. 299, 473
girls
    Ayliff Industrial Institution for Girls 422
    education of 423–425, 427
    Lamplough Training Institution for Girls 422
Gladden, Washington 497
globalisation 34, 55, 71, 99–107, 114–115, 117, 199–213
glossalalia 146, 149, 150, 152, 153, 333
Gomme, Ebenezer 454
González, Justo 197
Good News movement 80, 323–324
*Good News to the Poor: John Wesley's Evangelical Economics* (1990) 22, 28
Gossett, Benjamin Brown 458
Gothic style 390, 395–398
grace 186–191
Graham, Billy 307, 323, 337
Graham, Dorothy 49, 426–427
Graham, William 423
Grant, Ulysses 47
Graves, Richard 473
Gray, Bowman 458
Gray, Bowman Junior 459
Gray, George Alexander 459
Gray, James Alexander Junior 459
*The Great Awakening: The Roots of Evangelical Christianity in Colonial America* (2007) 310
Green, Fred Pratt 248
Green, George 452
Gregory, Benjamin 122
Gregory, Jeremy 15
Gregory, T.S. 335
Grey Coat Charity School, Oxford 407
Grubb, Sir Kenneth 90
Guerra, Israel Batista 182
Gutiérrez, Gustavo 175, 195, 197

Habgood, Archbishop John 342
hagiography 109, 110, 115, 120
Halévy, Élie 26–27, 28, 350, 352
Hall, Catherine 167

Hamilton, Edith Henrietta 470
Hamilton, James 329
Hampson, John 483
happiness 303, 330
Hardy, Philip 36
Hargreaves, John 413–414
Harnack, Adolf 335
Harper Bros. 440
Harper, Fletcher 459
Harper, James 459
Harris, Elizabeth 137
Harris, Howell 4, 304, 484
Hartley, James 454
Hartley, William P. 432, 444, 445, 446, 448–449, 451, 454
Harvey, David 413
Hastings, Adrian 337
Hatch, Nathan 37
Hattersley, Richard 454
Hauerwas, Stanley 341, 381
Hay, Richard 231
Haydon, Colin 15
Headway 323
healing 147–148, 150, 151
'heart religion' 4, 19, 161, 228
*Heart Religion in the British Enlightenment* (2008) 26, 289
Heber, Reginald 243
Heck, Barbara 162
Heinz, H.J. 440, 459
Heitzenrater, Richard P. 13, 19, 110, 408, 409
Hempton, David 31, 34, 40–41, 64, 83, 84, 159, 160–161, 166, 341, 351–352, 388, 394, 411, 412, 414, 420, 421, 429–430, 488, 489
Henry, Carl 307
Hepburn, Tommy 46–47
Hepworth, Joseph 443, 445, 454
*Her Benny* 471, 472, 474
Herbert, George 234, 235, 462
*Heroines of Methodism* 159
Hervey, James 207–208, 470
Herzog, Frederick 175
Heslop, Joseph 46
Heylyn, John 225
Hickling, John 485
higher education 427–429
Higher Life movement 54, 148

Highland Park Methodist Church, U.S.A. 396
Hildebrandt, Franz 218
Hiles, Henry 242
Hill, George Washington 459
Hill, James Jerome 459
Hillman, Thomas Tennessee 459
Hindmarsh, D. Bruce 160, 163–164, 305
*A History of Wesleyan Methodism* 478
Hitler, Adolf 499
Hobsbawm, Eric 351
Hocking brothers 470, 471, 472
Holden, Edward 456
Holden, Isaac 433, 450, 454
Holiness Movement
    Keswick movement 147–148
    spread of 145–146
    United States 54
    Wesleyan branch 143–147
    see also Pentecostalism
*The Holiness-Pentecostal Tradition: Charismatic Movements in the Twentieth Century* 154
Holland, William 454
Holness, Lyn 173
Holy Club, Oxford 221, 233, 294
Holy Communion 276
*Holy Dying* (1651) 290, 462
*Holy Living* (1650) 290, 462
'holy love' 23
home mission societies 54
homosexuality 82, 268
Hook, James Clarke 403
Hooker, Morna 231
Hooker, Richard 228
Hoover, May 142, 147, 153
Hoover, Theressa 170–171
Hoover, Willis 142, 147, 152–153
Hopkins, E.J. 243
Hopper, Christopher 327
Hopson, Howard Colwell 459
Hornby, Frank 456
Horne, Melvill 327
Horneck, Anthony 16
Howard, W.F. 231
Hudson, Joseph Lowthian 459
Hudson, Winthrop 36
Hughes, Hugh Price 92–93, 199, 201, 305, 333–334, 366, 377, 385, 417, 418, 450, 495

Hughes, Katherine Price 334
Hughes, Maldwyn 335, 337
Hulbert, Charles 322, 334
Hulton, Mary 415
Huntingdon, Lady 3, 9, 293, 315, 390, 484
hymnody
    *A Collection of Hymns* (revised edition, 1876) 243
    after 1791 240–243
    of Bible Christians 241
    children's hymns 247–248
    *A Collection of Hymns for the Use of the People called Methodists* (1786) 239, 301
    *A Collection of Psalms and Hymns* 234, 253, 273
    *A Collection of Tunes. Set to Music.* (1742) 237
    'directions for singing' 238–239
    harmony used 237
    hymnals 399
    hymns of Charles Wesley 79, 127, 235–236, 239, 240, 292, 294, 298, 301, 312, 470
    *Hymns on God's Everlasting Love* (1741) 236
    *Hymns on the Great Festivals and Other Occasions* (1746) 239
    hymns of John Wesley 127, 209, 233–234, 236
    *Hymns on the Lord's Supper* (1745) 237, 299
    *Hymns and Psalms* (1983) 247–248
    *Hymns and Sacred Poems* (1739) 235, 236
    the 'large hymn book' 239, 241
    large number of 'Tune-Books' 241–242
    *The Methodist Hymn Book* (1904) 245
    Methodist hymn book (1933) 233, 245–247
    of Methodist New Connexion 240
    metre used 236
    music used in 78–79
    new hymn writing 248–249
    of Primitive Methodists 241, 243–244, 245
    of Protestant Methodists 241
    Psalms 271
    *Sacred Harmony* (1780) 239
    sanctification in 153–154
    singing encouraged by John Wesley 237

translation of hymns 114, 243
*The United Methodist Free Church Hymnal* (1889) 244–245
of Wesleyan Methodist Association 241
*The Wesleyan Psalmist* (1843) 242
of Wesleyan Reformers 241

Iball, Richard 309
identity, Methodist 9–10, 56
idolatry 182
Ilesanmi, Simeon 420, 421
Iliff, John Wesley 459
Im, Mi-Soon 173
*Imitation of Christ* 290
immigration 369–370, 496
imperialism 61–62, 117, 377, 378, 381, 388, 498
inclusiveness 68–69, 79
Independent Methodist Church 95
India 70, 71, 75, 95, 125, 135, 141, 146, 147, 284, 383, 421
Industrial Revolution 26, 48, 53
*The Infidel: A Story of the Great Revival* 473, 474
Ingham, Benjamin 315
Ingham, John 439
Inskip, John 145
*Instructions for Children* 462
Inter-Varsity Fellowship 323
interfaith relations 135–140
International Church of the Foursquare Gospel 148
International Missionary Council 75
internet technology 204–205, 248, 338, 467
*Interpretative Statistical Survey of the World Mission of the Christian Church* (1938) 89
intransitivity problem 134
*An Introduction to World Methodism* 53
Iona Community 249, 284
Iraq War 378
Ireland 57, 94, 95, 202, 211, 350–353, 384, 498
Irving, Henry 456
Israel-Palestine conflict 135–136
Italy 75
itinerant preachers 326–328, 330, 332, 334, 400, 426, 462–463, 473

Jabez Easterbrook 471

Jackson, George 317, 321, 334
Jackson, John 403
Jackson, Thomas 17, 317, 319, 328
Jacobites 29, 347
Jamaica 96
Jansenist Movement 16
Japan 57, 94
Jarratt, Devereux 313
Jarvis, John Wesley 403
Java 421
Jay, Elisabeth 206
Jennings, Theodore W. 22, 28, 180, 184, 191, 481
Jeremias, Joachim 337
Jessop, T.E. 339
Jobson, F.J. 395
*John Wesley* 110
*John Wesley and the Church of England* (1970) 24
*John Wesley and His World* 203
*John Wesley on Religious Affections: His Views on Experience and Emotion and Their Role in the Christian Life and Theology* (1989) 23
*John Wesley's Place in Church History: Determined with the Aid of Facts and Documents Unknown to, Or Unnoticed by, His Biographers* (1870) 20
*John Wesley's Social Ethics: Praxis and Principles* (1975) 28, 481
*John Wesley's Theology Today* (1960) 21
Johnson, Dr 211
Johnson, George Francis 459
Johnson, Simpson 442
Joint Declaration on the Doctrine of Justification 125
Jolly, James Hornby 455
Jones, E. Stanley 137
Jones, Richard 342
*Joshua Haggard's Daughter* 473
'Journal of a Connectional People' 261
*Journal of the Reverend John Wesley* 17–18, 206, 209, 273, 301, 305, 468
*The Journals of Dr Thomas Coke* (2005) 18
Joyce, Patrick 411
Judaism, Methodism and 27, 135–136

Kaan, Fred 248
Kairos document 193
Kang, Nam-Soon 173

Keble, John 243
Keeble, Samuel 447, 496
Keeling, Annie 159, 162
Kemp, Kathryn W. 433
Kempis, Thomas à 462
Ken, Thomas 243
Kennings, George 455
Kent, Alan 471
Kent, John 290, 310
Keswick movement 147–148
Keysor, Charles 324
Kidd, Thomas 310
Kidwell, Clara Sue 181
Kilham, Alexander 40, 240, 265, 328, 352, 356
Kingswood school 327, 395, 407, 409–410, 423, 428, 443, 461, 463, 484
Kisker, Scott Thomas 16
Knapp, Joseph Frederick 459
Knapp, Joseph Palmer 459
Knudsen, Albert C. 322
Kobia, Samuel 125
Korea 58, 69, 70, 71, 107, 118, 173, 176, 184, 202, 282, 286, 324, 398, 420, 498
Kresge, Sebastian Spering 459

Laister, Kay 415
Lambeth Conference 129–130
Lamont, Thomas William 459
Lampe, John Frederick 239
Lamplough Training Institution for Girls 422
Landman, Christina 172
Langford, Paul 205
Langford, Thomas 341
language 80
Lankford, Sarah Worrall 143
Laqueur, Walter 411
Larsen, Tim 311
Latin America 5, 7, 72, 74, 79, 153, 175, 198
Latin American liberation theology 181–183, 195
Law, William 290, 291, 302, 462
lay members 40, 55, 66, 67, 79, 265, 313, 434–437
Leaver, Robin A. 233
Lee, Ivy Ledbetter 459
Lee, Jesse 274, 379
Lee, Jung Young 180–181
Lee, Peter 331

Lee, Umphrey 25
Leeds Brunswick church 40
Lenton, John 165–166, 327, 328, 427, 428
Lerner, Gerda 165
*Letter to a Roman Catholic* (1745) 122
*The Letters of the Reverend John Wesley* (1931) 17
Lewis, Charles 445
Lewis, Sinclair 497
Leys School, Cambridge 430, 443
Liberal Protestantism 334–335, 337
liberation theology 175–198, 341
liberty 348–350
Lickes, Garfield 337
Lidgett, John Scott 318, 321, 334, 335, 417, 418, 419
*The Life of God in the Soul of Man* 290
*Life of the John Wesley, A.M.* (1793) 14
*The Life of Wesley; and the rise and progress of Methodism* 473
Lightwood, James T. 241, 244
Lilly, Josiah Kirby 459
Lincoln, Abraham 55
literature, Methodism in 461–475
Lithuania 383
Littlejohn, John 379
liturgical movement 284–285
liturgy
    18th century 270–274
    late 18th and 19th centuries 38, 273–282
    20th century 282–283
    changes in 78–79
    charismatic worship 80, 147–148, 149, 150, 151, 152, 153, 285, 313, 323, 330, 332–333, 339, 349
    collection of money 280
    corporate worship 270, 272
    days and seasons 283
    increasing sophistication of 281, 319
    liturgical movement 284–285
    in missions 282
    preaching 48–49, 146, 158, 165–166, 279, 305, 319, 325–342, 400, 426, 462–463, 473, 480–481, 485–486
    research methodology 269–270
    sharing of resources 283–284
    Sunday worship 279
    table 284–285
    see also band meetings; camp meetings; class meetings; field meetings;

hymnody; love feasts; music; prayer meetings; quarterly meetings; society meetings
Lloyd, Gareth 19
Lloyd, Jennifer 166, 167
Lloyd-Jones, Martyn 308
local preachers 329–331, 338, 339, 400
Lock Hospital, London 484
Locke, John 19, 25–26, 26, 407, 408, 462
*Locke, Wesley, and the Method of English Romanticism* (1984) 26
Lockhart, Grace 424
Lofthouse, W.F. 335
London, Wesleyan leaders concentrated in 444
London 'chapel' (1778) 393
Long, D. Stephen 358, 361, 381
Longacre, James Barton 403
Lonsdale, Marjorie 340
Lord's Prayer 280
Lord's Supper 272, 273, 277, 278, 280–281, 299, 330
Louden, Lois 425
love, God as 191–193
love feasts 37, 271, 280, 297, 301, 313, 318, 330
Ludlow, Mary 429
Lum, Clara E. 152
Luther, Martin 176
Lutherism 76, 125, 126, 130, 222, 224, 260
Lyerly, Cynthia 492, 493
Lyte, Henry Francis 243
Lyth, Mary 297

McArthur, William 433
McCaine, Alexander 42
McCarthy era 498
Mack, Phyllis 26, 31, 161, 163, 164, 289, 292, 298, 328
Mackintosh, Harold Vincent 455
Mackintosh, John 433, 434, 442, 444, 446–447, 455
McLeish, Alexander 90
McNeill, William 445–446
McPherson, Aimee Semple 148
Macquiban, Tim 164, 429
Madan, Martin 484
Maddox, Randy 22, 220
Magic Methodists of Delamere Forest 36
Mahan, Asa 147

*The Making of the English Working Class* (1963) 27, 33–34, 46
Malaysia 421, 422
Mallinson, Stuart Sidney 455
Mallinson, William J. 455
Maltby, William Russell 321, 335
Mandela, Nelson 382, 420
Manning, Bernard 239
Manson, T.W. 337
*The Manuscript Journal of the Reverend Charles Wesley* (2007-2008) 18
Maori Methodism 69
marginality/centrality 181
Marquardt, Manfred 28, 481
marriage 82, 276, 278
Marsh, Clive 340
Martineau, James 236
Martyr, Justin 271
*Marvels and Miracles* 150
Marxism 79, 351, 447
Mason, Hugh 456
'Master Narratives of Imperial Missions' 62
material environment of Methodism 399–401
Mathews, Donald 42, 491
Mathews, H.F. 490
Matthews, Antje 403
Matthews, Marjorie 69
Maurice, Frederic Denison 334
Mayson, Cedric 183–184
*Meditations and Contemplations* 470
Meeks, M. Douglas 184, 192, 194
meetings *see* band meetings; class meetings; field meetings; love feasts; prayer meetings; quarterly meetings; society meetings
'mega-churches' 398
Melle, Otto 384, 498–499
Melton, J. Gordon 42, 43–44
mergers *see* unions/mergers
Merritt, Timothy 143
*Methodism: Empire of the Spirit* 64, 83, 351
Methodism
    18th c. revival 142
    18th century context 14–16
    'authentic' 200
    authorised sources on 17
    communal spirituality of 295–297
    design used in 390–391
    development in Britain (1791-1865) 38

diversity within 217
emphasis on John Wesley 6–8
experiential basis of 157, 160, 163, 289, 314, 319–320
image of 82, 387, 405, 473–474
inter-Christian relations 121–135
lack of scholarly work 52, 59
loyalty to King 40, 349
material objects relating to 399–401
publishing of 401, 463
respectability of 33–38
*Methodism and the Common People of the Eighteenth Century* (1945) 27
*Methodism and Education* 414, 417
*Methodism and Literature* 465
*Methodism and Politics in British Society 1750-1850* 351
*Methodism and the Southern Mind 1770-1810* 492
*Methodism and the Working-Class Movements of England 1800-1850* 489
Methodist Church of Australasia 57
Methodist Church of Great Britain 58, 254–256, 283
Methodist Dogmatics 120
Methodist Episcopal Church (MEC) 252, 262–263, 273, 276–277, 281, 315, 371–372, 375–377, 411, 437, 496–497
Methodist Evangelicals Together 309
*The Methodist Experience in America* 319
Methodist League for Faith and Life 322
Methodist New Connexion 39, 40, 92, 95, 240, 245, 265, 329, 374, 397, 425, 435–437
Methodist Peace Fellowship 378
Methodist Pentecostal Church 153
*Methodist and Radical* 29, 191
*The Methodist Revolution* (1973) 28, 356
Methodist Society 305
Methodist Unitarians 39
Methodist Women in Britain 69
Methodist Youth Fellowship 380
*Methodists and the Crucible of Race 1930-1975* 494
Metropolitan Church, South Africa 396
Micklem, Caryl 248
middle class 5, 329, 330, 411–412
see also occupational analysis
Midgley, Alfred 475

Míguez Bonino, José 182, 183, 186, 188, 192–193, 195, 197–198, 339, 341–342
Míguez, Néstor 193
Milburn, Geoffrey 46
Miley, John 317, 321
Milman, Henry Hart 243
Milton, John 462
miners' strike (1849) 46
Minjung theology 176
mission schools 420–423
Mission Society for United Methodists 73, 80
missions
  global 70–73
  history of 52, 60–63
  International Review of Missions 89
  life-long service in 73
  liturgy used in 282
  Methodist Missionary Society 70, 267
  slave missions 493
  station farming 451
  United Methodist History of Mission series 113
  united training colleges 77
  World Missionary Atlas (1925) 89
*Missions and Empire* series 61
Mitchell, Dr Thomas 449
Mitchell, Henry 455
Model Deed 24
modernization 56–60
Monk, Robert 20
Monk, William Henry 242, 243
Moody, Dwight 447
Moody, William Lewis Junior 459
Moore, Basil 183, 197
Moore, Henry 14
Moore, Laurence 447
Moore, Mary Elizabeth 190
Moore, Robert 46
morality, personal 82
Moravian *Unitas Fratrum* 16
Moravianism 8, 20, 75, 209, 211, 212, 233, 237, 271, 291, 298, 408
More, Hannah 464
Morris, Colin 339, 378, 452
Morse, William Ewart 445
Mortimer, Elizabeth 162
Mosala, Itumeleng 196, 232
Mott, John R. 75, 123, 125
Moulton, James Hope 137, 231

Moulton, W.F. 429
Mount Sinai Holy Church of America 153–154
Mudimbe, V.Y. 420
Muelder, Walter 184–185
Mukti Mission revival 141–142, 150
Murray, Grace 327
Murray, Peter 494
Murray, Victor 335
Murry, John Middleton 378
Musgrave, John 455
music
    African 42, 78
    brass bands 495
    in charismatic worship 286
    choral singing 242–243, 280
    contemporary 78
    folk tunes 38
    Leeds organ dispute 40, 242
    local musical instruments 282
    'Methodism was born in song' 233
    metre used 236
    organ/piano become accepted 242, 280
    in Sunday Schools 242–243
    see also hymnody
Muslim-Methodist relations 136

National Children's Home 334
National Council of Churches of Christ (USA) 75
National Council of Negro Women 171
nationalism 498–499
Native Americans
    John Wesley's mission 209–210, 410
    theology of 181, 188
*The Nature and Mission of the Church* (2007) 125
*The Nature of Oversight* 265–267
Nazism 359, 378, 384, 498–499
Neale, John Mason 243, 244
Nelles, Samuel 428
Nelson, John 326, 327, 328
Nelson, Robert 270
Network organisation 69
networking 441, 442, 443, 444
*The New Creation: John Wesley's Theology Today* (1998) 22–23, 28
New Creation sermon 22
*A New History of Methodism* 478, 480
'New Room', Bristol 319–320, 397

New Testament *see* Bible
New Zealand 69, 70, 71, 129, 171–172, 397, 477
Newcomer, Mabel 439
Newton, John 164
Newton, Robert 332
Nicene Creed 78
Niebuhr, Reinhold 339
Noley, Homer 181, 188
Noll, Mark 35, 39, 45, 310, 314
'nonconformist conscience' 365–367, 369, 495
*North and South* 473, 474
Norway 76, 126, 141, 202
Norwich meeting-house 392
Nowell, Arthur Trevivian 404
nuclear weapons 82, 378, 381

Obama, Barack 341
Oberlin College 147
O'Bryan, William 240
occupational analysis 434–437, 440–441
Oconer, Luther 421
Oduyoye, Mercy Amba 172, 194–195, 197
Oecumenical Methodist Conference 74, 124
see also ecumenism
O'Kelly, James 41, 42, 263, 264
Oldham, J.H. 89
Oldstone-Moore, Christopher 495
*On Christian Perfection* (1726) 290
'On the Education of Children' 407
'On Obedience to Parents' 407
'Open Source Liturgy Project' 286–287
'orb and cross' logo 391
ordination
    of bishops 262
    litury 276
    of women 68–69, 75, 168
organisational structure
    centralization 56
    changes in 55–60, 266–268, 319
    connexionalism and 262–268
    of global mission 71–73
    indigenous leadership 72–73
    local autonomy 266
    Wesley's 315
    Wesley's US 252–256, 315
    see also bishops; lay members; unions/mergers
'Orphan House', Newcastle 392, 407, 484

Orthodox Church 76, 126, 131–132, 182, 260
Osborn, George 17
Osborn, J. 418–419
Otterbein, Phillip 57
Outler, Albert C. 22, 110, 177, 221, 223, 228
Owen, Christopher 492–493, 494
Owen, Owen 455
'The Oxford Edition of the Works of John Wesley' 17–18
Oxford Institute of Methodist Theological Studies 81, 83–84
Oxford Movement (1830s) 14, 15
Oxley, Dr Simon 90–91

pacifism 368–369, 374, 377–381, 383
Pakistan 125
Palestine-Israel conflict 135–136
Palladio, Andrea 389
Palmer, Phoebe 143, 144, 146, 304, 333
Palmer, Walter 146
Panama 147
parades (Sunday School) 413
Parham, Charles 151–152
Park, Andrew Sung 180–181, 187–188
Park, Jong Chun 184, 190, 196
Parnell, Charles 366
Parrinder, Geoffrey 137
patriotism (USA) 42
Pattison, Mark 92, 199
Paul (apostle) 176, 196, 198, 222
Pauline letters 222
Pawson, Frances 327
Pawson, John 328, 484, 485
Peace Award 74
Peake, Arthur Samuel 231, 317, 321, 335, 429, 449, 451
Pearse, Mark Guy 334, 470, 471, 472
Penfield Chapel, Australia 395
Pentecostalism 5, 84, 117, 126, 141–143, 146, 148–155, 341
perfection, Christian 47, 116, 142, 143, 147, 190, 302–304, 306, 320
Perkins Chapel of Southern Methodist University 396
Perks, Robert 433, 450, 455
*Personal Experience and the Christian Faith* (1939) 335
pews 399, 401
Philippines 324
Phillips, Frank 460

Pietism 15–16, 20, 209, 225
Piette, Maximin 20
piety 16, 191, 289
Pilgrim Holiness Church 144, 333
*Pilgrim's Progress* 207
Plumb, J.H. 27
Pocock, G. 332
*The Poetical Works of John and Charles Wesley* (1860s) 17
politics
    context of Methodism in USA (18th and 19th c.) 41–42, 47, 80, 353–356
    global 358–360
    impact of Methodism on 46–49, 55, 81–82, 350–353, 362–363, 447–448, 487–491, 495–499
    John Wesley and 27, 28–30, 211, 345–350, 357–358, 367–369, 481–485
    'nonconformist conscience' 365–367, 369, 495
    see also social change
*Politics in the Order of Salvation: Transforming Wesleyan Political Ethics* (2001) 29, 357
Pope, Liston 37
Pope, William Burt 317, 332, 333
*A portraiture of Methodism* 479
Portugal 71
Posnett, Robert Harold 455
Potter, Philip 75, 125
pottery 400
poverty
    children in 194
    evangelization by the poor 195, 196–197
    stewardship of the poor 27, 191–193, 479, 482–485
Pratt, Andrew 246
Pratt, E.J. 475
prayer 299–301
prayer meetings 25
pre-Raphaelites 390
preachers' plan 326
preaching 48–49, 146, 158, 165–166, 279, 305, 319, 325–342, 400, 426, 462–463, 473, 480–481, 485–486
preaching houses 271–272, 329, 391–395
Precisianism 16
predestination 314
    see also Calvinism
Premium Bonds 446–447

Presbyterians 260
Preston, Anne 173
Primitive Methodists 8, 33, 38, 39, 40, 46–47, 48–49, 57, 58, 67, 92, 95, 240–241, 265, 293, 319, 321, 330, 374, 397, 411, 412, 425–427, 434–437, 451, 452
prison reform 28
Pritchard, Frank 407
profit sharing schemes 445
*The Progress of Liberty among the People Called Methodists* (1795) 40
Prohibition 376–377, 496
see also alcohol
*The Protestant Evangelical Awakening* (1992) 16, 310
Protestant Methodists 39, 40, 42, 66, 241, 264, 265
Protestant Reformers 20
Puerto Rico 71
Pugin, A.W.N. 395
pulpits 399, 401
Punshon, William Morley 332
Purcell, Henry 388
Puritanism 20, 164, 290
Pusey, E.B. 319, 414
Pyer, John 332

'Quadrilateral, Wesleyan' 3, 21, 227–228, 230, 290, 311, 316–317, 325, 474
quarterly meetings 35
Queen's Foundation, Birmingham 77
Quietist Movement 16

Race
  African Americans sidelined in studies of Methodism 34
  African Methodist denominations established (1780s) 371
  Apostolic Faith Mission 152
  black people in USA Methodist movement 42–44, 58, 67, 79
  Black preaching 342
  Black theology 183, 187, 196, 341, 342
  delegation to South African government 74
  National Council of Negro Women 171
  racism 339, 369–370, 382
  segregation 371–372, 493, 494, 497
  theological reflections on sin 180

World Council of Churches' Programme to Combat Racism 73
see also apartheid; slavery
Rack, Henry D. 13, 18–19, 110, 200, 203, 290, 313, 408, 468, 486
Railton, George Scott 305
Ramabai, Pandita 141, 147
Ramsey, Paul 381
Rand, James Henry 460
Rand, James Henry Junior 460
Rank, Arthur J. 433, 442, 451–452, 455
Rank, James Voase 456
Rank, Joseph 433, 442, 443, 445, 446, 450, 451, 455
Rankin, Thomas 330
Rattenbury, J.E. 79, 334, 335
Rauschenbusch, Walter 497
Ray, Emma 148
reading
  encouraged by John Wesley 239, 314, 407, 461–464
  Methodists' practices 465–466
  'Reading Revolution' hypothesis 466–467
*Reasonable Enthusiast: John Wesley and the Rise of Methodism* 13, 18–19, 110
reconciliation 187, 188, 190
Reed, Albert 455, 456
Reformation 222, 224
Reformed Church 131
*Reforming the World: The Creation of America's Moral Empire* 60
relief work 73
*The Religion of the Heart* (1991) 16
*Religion and Political Culture in Britain and Ireland* 351
'Religious Camp Meeting' (painting) 35
Republican Methodists 39, 41
republicanism 42
research *see* statistics (religious); Wesley studies
respectability, of Methodism 33–38
*Responsible Grace: John Wesley's Practical Theology* (1994) 22
reunions *see* unions/mergers
Revival Fellowship 323
Revolution of 1688 14, 15, 29, 347
Reynolds, Joshua 389
Rhodes, Samuel 485
Richardson, Jonathan 389

Richardson, Kathleen 69
Richey, Russell 319, 353–354
Rigg, James H. 20, 417, 418
*The Rise of Evangelicalism* 310–311
Ritsbek, Heigo 384
Ritson, Alexander 443, 455
Rivers, Isabel 463
Robert, Dana L. 61–62
Roberts, Alfred 441
Roberts, B.T. 141
Roberts, Colin 322
Roberts Wesleyan University 141
Roberts, William 405
Robinson, Ida 153, 154
rococo 390
Rogers, Hester Anne 162
*The Romance of the Yorkshire Coast* 472
*The Romantic Movement and Methodism* 473
Romanticism 26
Romney, George 402
Roosevelt, Theodore 498
Rotuma 359–360
Rowe, Kenneth E. 319, 353–354
Rowntree 434
Royle, Edward 426–427, 427
Runciman, Walter 433, 455
Runyon, Theodore 22–23, 25, 28, 186, 341
Rupp, Gordon 337, 338, 339
Rushbrook, Frederick 455
Russell, John 403
Russell, William 403
Ruston, Joseph 456
Ruth, Lester 39, 304, 330
Ryle, Jacqueline 360

sacraments 40, 284
*The Sacred Flame of Love: Methodism and Society in Nineteenth-Century Georgia* 492
St George's Methodist Episcopal Church, Philadelphia 44
St. Paul's Cathedral 388
Salisbury, Frank 404
salvation 21, 22, 186–191, 302, 357
Salvation Army 8, 76, 126, 131–132, 146, 304, 305, 495
Samuel, Raphael 488
sanctification 142, 143, 144, 146, 147, 149, 153, 186, 220, 302, 303, 304, 320, 332, 333, 350

Sanders, E.P. 231
Sangster, W.E. 295, 322, 336–337, 338
Sankey, Ira D. 247
Sankey, John William 455
Sankey, Joseph 455
Saunders, Clarence 460
*The Saved Clergyman or the Story of John Wesley* 305
Saward, Michael 248
schism, American (1844) 39, 41, 45–46, 264, 371
Schleiermacher, Friedrich 334–335
Schmidt, Jean Miller 319, 354
Schmidt, Martin 20
schools *see* day schools; mission schools; sunday schools
scientific knowledge 71
Scotland 8, 75, 221, 255, 438
Scotland, Nigel 488
Scott, David 421
Scott, John 237, 416, 423, 429
Scott, Orange 371, 494
Scott, Percy 337
Scott, Sir George Gilbert 395
Scott, Sir Walter 326
Scougal, Henry 290
Scranton, William 421
*The Scriptural Doctrine of Christian Perfection* 147
Scripture *see* Bible
'Seasonable Address to the More Serious Part of the Inhabitants of Great Britain' 368
'Second Great Awakening' 35, 37
Second World War 338, 359, 378, 380, 383–384
secularisation 71, 79, 123
Selvanayagam, Israel 232
Semmel, Bernard 28, 29, 356
Semple, Neil 411, 424, 428
'sensibility' 390, 473–474
*A Serious Call to a Devout and Holy Life* (1728) 290, 462
*The Sermons of Charles Wesley* (2001) 18
*Sermons on Several Occasions* (1746) 220
sexuality 82, 324
Seymour, William J. 152
sharing agreements 75–76
*Sharing in God's Mission* 80
Sheffield businesses 444

Sheldrake, Philip 289
*Short Account of the Experience of Mrs Hester Ann Rogers* 469
*A Short Account of the Life and Death of the Reverend John Fletcher* 468
Shuler, Robert P. 'Fighting Bob' 322
'Sidmouth Bill' 41, 329
Sierra Leone 66–67, 107
Silva, Lynn de 137
Simon, John 424, 478
Simpson, A.B. 148, 153
Simpson, Matthew 55
sin 22, 179–185
Sinfield, H.M. 337
Singapore 118–119, 282
single-parent families 82
slavery
    abolition of 28, 47, 51, 367–368, 369, 371, 472, 486
    anti-abolitionists 45–46, 479
    Frederick Douglass 43, 45
    gospel used by slaves 196
    John Wesley on 44, 367–368
    Methodist stance on 44–46, 47, 51, 367–368, 369, 370–372, 481–482, 491–494
    offense against God 180, 192
    slave missions 493
*Slavery and Methodism: A Chapter in American Morality 1780-1845* 491
Sloan, Alfred P. 440, 460
Sloan, Harold P. 322
Smetham, James 403
Smith, Adam 88
Smith, Amanda Berry 145–146
Smith, Chris Hughes 413
Smith, George 478
Smith, Leonard 279
Smith, Prince 445, 455
Smith, Richard Mudie 89
Smith, Ryder 335
Smith, Sarah 145
Smith, William Cantwell 138
Snaith, Norman 337
Snell, Keith 412
social change 26–30, 39, 53–55, 385, 477–499
    see also working class
*Social Christianity* 495
Social Creed 496–497, 498
social holiness 350, 355–356, 477

Society for the Distribution of Religious Tracts Among the Poor 462
society meetings 19
*Some historical account of Guinea* 486
Somerset, Lady Henry 146
Soothill, W.E. 137
Soper, Donald 337, 338, 378, 451–452
South Africa 74, 75, 95, 107, 118, 147, 173, 183, 189, 282, 383, 422
South America 70, 71, 72, 134, 147
South Pacific 212, 359–360
Southern Methodist Church 66
Southey, Robert 473
Southlands College 429
Southport Convention 305, 322
Soviet Union 70
*Speaking for the Methodist Church* (2001) 256
speaking in tongues 146, 149, 150, 152, 153, 333
Spears, Anna 421
Spillman, Harry Collins 447
Spilsbury, Jonathan 402
Spinckes, Nathaniel 300
spires 397
*The Spiritual Principle of the Atonement* 318
*The Spiritual Quixote* 473, 474
spiritualism 80
Splicer, Reverend H. 46
Sri Lanka 71, 77
stained glass 401
Stamp, Josiah 433, 434, 451, 455
*The Standard Sermons* of John Wesley (1920) 17, 218
Stanley, Brian 61
'stationary' fasts 270, 271
'stationed' preachers 319
*Statistical Atlas of Christian Missions* (1910) 89
statistics (religious)
    1851 religious census 89, 412
    'adherents' problem 93–94, 96
    'Compton census' (1676) 88
    disputed figures 92–94, 199
    Ecumenical Methodist Conference figures (1891) 93–94
    EMC and WMC figures 97–101
    'General Statistics of Methodism' 95
    global church 87–91
    global methodist 70–71, 91–107, 200
    Handbook of Information 1956-1961 95

history of 88–91
Interpretative Statistical Survey of the World Mission of the Christian Church (1938) 89
John Wesley's records 91–92
London studies (1902, 1904) 89
National Methodist densities 104–106
occupational analysis 434–437, 440–441
Survey Application Trust 89
*World Christian Encyclopedia: A Comparative Survey of Churches and Religion in the Modern World* 91
*World Christian Handbook* 90, 96
World Council of Churches (WCC) data 90–91
*World Missionary Atlas* (1925) 89
*Yearbook of American Churches* 96
Stephen, James 316
Stephenson, Thomas Bowman 334
Stephenson, William Haswell 455
Stevens, Abel 159, 479, 480
Stewart, Charles 428
Stoddard, Solomon 310
Strawson, William 336
Streat, Edward Raymond 456
Strong, James 231
Stroudley, William 456
Stuart, Moses 376
Studebaker, Clement 440, 460
Sturdy, William Arthur 451
Sugden, E.H. 17
Sugirtharajah, R.S. 232
Sun Lane Methodist Sunday School 412
sunday schools 242–243, 410–414, 425, 465, 490
*The Sunday Service of the Methodists In North America* (1784) 24, 252–253, 273, 274–279, 281, 282
Sunderland, La Roy 494
supernaturalism 313
*Susanna Wesley: The Complete Writings* (1997) 18
Sutherland, Arthur M. 455
Sutherland, Graham 405
Sutherland, Stewart 207
Sweden 76, 126
Synan, Vinson 154

Taft, Zechariah 158
Taizé community 284

Tamez, Elsa 186, 196
Taylor, Ernest 340
Taylor, Frank 456
Taylor, Jeremy 223, 290, 302, 462
Taylor, Stephen 15
Taylor, Vincent 231, 337
Taylor, William 146–147
technology/internet 204–205, 248, 338, 467
Telford, John 17
Telford, Thomas 393
Temperance League 374
see also alcohol
Temple, William 335
Tennant, F.R. 337
Tent Methodists 39, 331–332
Thatcher, Margaret 441, 499
Theilen, Uta 173
*Theological Roots of Pentecostalism* 154
theologies, development of 176–178, 182
theology 20, 21–24, 79–81, 138, 160, 176–177, 181–183, 187, 188, 195, 196, 298, 341, 342
*The Theology of John Wesley: Holy Love and the Shape of Grace* (2007) 23
*Theology in the Wesleyan Spirit* 22
Thoburn, James 141
Thompson, Edward J. 472
Thompson, E.P. 27, 33–34, 37, 351, 488
Thompson, John Day 452
Thompson, Robert 455
Thompson, Robert Junior 455
Thompson, Thomas 329
Thorne, Serena 172
Thornton, William 331
'Thoughts on the Manner of Educating Children' 407, 410
'Thoughts upon the Present Scarcity of Provisions' 28, 368
'Thoughts Upon Slavery' 367, 486
Thwaites, Elizabeth Hart 472
Tidball, Derek 308
Tidmarsh, Henry 404
Tigert, John 261, 265
Tillich, Paul 80
Tinker, George 181
Titcomb, W.H.Y. 404
Todd, John Murray 20
Tolpuddle Martyrs 47, 478, 489
*Tongue of Fire* (1856) 333
Total Abstinence Society 374

Tottenham Court Road chapel 484
towers 397
Towns, Elmer 408
Townsend, William 478, 480
Tractarian Movement 14, 15
trade unionism 46–47, 445, 478, 496, 499
training 74, 77, 80, 416, 429
trances 150, 151
translations, of Wesleys' works 114
Tranter, Donald 408, 430
Trickett, David 297
Trollope, Anthony 473
*The True Principles of Pointed or Christian Architecture* 395
Truro College 443
Turberfield, Alan 417
Turner & Newall 446
Turner, John 455
Tyrrell, Ian 60

unions/mergers 57–60, 66–68, 75–76, 122, 283
Unitarianism 15
Unitarians, Methodist 39
United Brethren in Christ 379
United Holy Church of America 153
*United Methodist Book of Worship* (1992) 285
United Methodist Church (UMC) 58, 67, 76, 95, 194, 227–228, 253–256, 262, 266–268, 286, 373, 384, 385, 411, 477
United Methodist Committee on Relief 73
United Methodist Free Churches 92, 95, 241, 374, 425, 427, 435–437, 471
United Methodist History of Mission series 113
United Methodist Men 267
United Methodist Women 69, 170–171
United Nations 380, 397
United States
    American Revolution 347–348, 368–369, 379
    British conference representatives to (1891) 201
    church buildings in 396, 398–399
    conservative evangelism in 323
    different Methodist style from Britain 39
    education in (19th c.) 410
    evangelical developments (c.1900) 321–322
    growth in scholarly literature 111–112
    Holy Scripture in 227–228
    Methodism and class in 47
    Methodism as colonial Anglicanism 252, 261, 262
    Methodism expansion 35, 37, 38, 107
    Methodism splits (1844) 39, 41, 45–46, 264, 371
    Methodist bishops 41, 42, 252, 264–265
    Methodist Church formed (1939) 58, 283, 323
    political context of Methodism (18th and 19th c.) 41–42, 47, 80, 353–356
    prayer book revised for 273–274
    split with Holiness movement 143–144
    'Wesleyan heritage' 341
*The Unpublished Poetry of Charles Wesley* (1988-1992) 18
Urlin, Richard Denny 20
'The Use of Money' 443, 448

Valenze, Deborah 48, 164
Vennard, Iva Durham 142
*The Vicar of Bullhampton* 473
Vickers, Jason E. 29
Vickery, Amanda 164, 167
*A Victorian Class Conflict* 414, 415, 427
Vietnam War 380
Villa-Vicencio, Charles 189–190
Vincent, John 176, 184, 190, 191, 195, 339
visions 151
Voysey, C.F.A. 395

Wacker, Grant 148
Wainwright, Geoffrey 125, 341
Wakefield, Gordon 289
Wakelin, Michael 452
Walcott, Derek 475
Wales 8, 75, 150, 255, 438
Walker, Sarah Breedlove 460
Wall, Robert 225
Walmsley brothers 443, 455
Walsh, John 15, 312
Wan 447
Wanamaker, John 440, 460
Ward, Harry 497
Ward, Neville 338
Ward, Harry F. 447
Ward, W.R. 16, 34, 164, 310, 488
Warrick, Susan 170

*Was John Wesley A High Churchman? A Dialogue for the Times* (1882) 20
Wassenaer, Baroness van 482–483
watch nights 271
Waterhouse, E.S. 335
Watkins, Ruth 49
Watson, David Lowes 24, 296
Watson, Kevin M. 25, 31
Watson, Philip 337
Watson, Richard 332
Watts, Isaac 470
wealth accumulation 55, 443–445, 484
wealth distribution 448–452
*Wealth of Nations* (1776) 88
Wearing, Anne 49
Wearmouth, Robert F. 27, 478, 488, 499
Weatherhead, Leslie 336, 378
Webb, Pauline 159, 339
Weber, Max 37
Weber, Thomas R. 29, 349, 357–358
Wellings, Martin 8
Welsh revival 150
*Wesley: A Guide for the Perplexed* (2009) 29
Wesley Bible Union 322
Wesley, Charles
   at love feast (1739) 301
   brother John on hymns of 301
   Charles Wesley Society 18, 79
   conversion experience of 234, 291–292, 311
   founds Holy Club, Oxford 233
   on Frances Asbury 329–330
   hymns of 79, 127, 235–236, 239, 240, 292, 294, 298, 301, 312, 470
   influences on 290–291
   on itinerant preachers 327
   as a saint 116
   scholarly study of 110–111
   in shadow of brother John 7
   speaks about Christ on coaches 304
   works of 17, 18, 31
   see also Wesley Studies
Wesley Deaconess Institute 334
Wesley Guild 321
Wesley, John
   'A Word to A Drunkard' 368
   'Advice to a Soldier' 369
   'all the world is my parish' 207–208, 305
   Articles of Faith 227
   at Oxford 207, 209, 217, 270, 290, 389
   attitude towards Islam 341
   as author, editor and publisher 467–468
   biographies/works about 18–19, 20, 21, 23, 24, 28, 110, 203
   bullied at school 408
   *Calm Address to Our American Colonies* 354
   *The Character of a Methodist* (1742) 219
   character of 205–213, 327, 482–483, 484, 485
   childhood of 208
   church statistics by 91–92
   continental travels of 210–211
   conversion experience of 109, 118–119, 120, 210, 234, 291–293, 310, 311
   critical of Church of England 14, 272–273
   curacy of Wroote 206
   drinks alcohol in moderation 368
   on education of girls 423
   encourages reading 239, 314, 407, 461–464
   encourages singing 237
   encourages women leaders 305, 480–481
   in Georgia (Indian mission) 209–210, 410
   as 'high churchman' 20, 312, 483
   on hymns of brother Charles 301
   hymns of 127, 209, 233–234, 236
   idealisation of 6–7
   influences on 290–291
   *Instructions for Children* 462
   *Journal of the Reverend John Wesley* 17–18, 206, 209, 273, 301, 305, 468
   lack of memorial to 92, 199, 200
   *Letter to a Roman Catholic* (1745) 122
   library of 462
   'a man of one book' 223–224, 312, 325
   on nature of children 408–409
   New Creation sermon 22
   on non-Christian religions 136
   on novels 464
   'On the Education of Children' 407
   'On Obedience to Parents' 407
   peripatetic nature of 205–208, 212, 305, 392
   place in history books 200
   *Plain account of the Methodists* 484

and politics 27, 28–30, 211, 345–350, 357–358, 367–369, 481–485
preaching style 325–326
prison reform work 28
on purpose of education 409
reading of Scripture 217–225, 271, 294
reflects culture of Enlightenment 19
relationships with women 158, 207, 327, 485–486
rescued from Epworth Rectory fire 109, 116
as a saint 110n 6, 116
'Seasonable Address to the More Serious Part of the Inhabitants of Great Britain' 368
*Sermons on Several Occasions* (1746) 220
*A Short Account of the Life and Death of the Reverend John Fletcher* 468
*The Sunday Service of the Methodists In North America* (1784) 24, 252–253, 273, 274–279, 281, 282
'The Dignity of Human Nature' 368
'The Doctrine of Original Sin' 368
'The Use of Money' 443, 448
'The world is my parish' 70
theology of 20, 21–24, 81, 138, 176–177
'Thoughts on the Manner of Educating Children' 407, 410
'Thoughts upon the Present Scarcity of Provisions' 28, 368
'Thoughts Upon Slavery' 367, 486
visual depictions of 402, 403
'Wesleyana' 400
see also Wesley Studies
Wesley, Mary 327
Wesley Memorial Methodist Church 395–396
Wesley Monumental Methodist Church, Georgia, U.S.A. 396
*Wesley and the People Called Methodists* (1995) 19
Wesley, Samuel 239, 347
Wesley, Samuel Sebastian 243
Wesley studies
American Methodism 19, 111–112
authorised sources 17
British 19
critical works 110, 115, 119
future research 120
gaps in the literature 111, 113–114
history of 110–111, 115
Wesleys of history vs. Wesleys of faith 6–7, 119–120
Wesley, Susanna 18, 31, 162, 164, 347, 407, 423, 462
*Wesley and the Wesleyans* (2002) 290
Wesleyan Association 265
Wesleyan Methodism 24–25, 58, 241, 245, 264
Wesleyan Methodist Church 371
Wesleyan Methodist Connexion 278
Wesleyan Methodist Missionary Society's Ladies Committee 159
Wesleyan Methodists Association 92, 95
'Wesleyan Quadrilateral' 3, 21, 227–228, 230, 290, 311, 316–317, 325, 474
Wesleyan Reformers 95, 241, 245
Wesleyan Thanksgiving Fund 444, 450
'Wesleyana' 400
West Africa Central Conference 72
West, B.F. 421
Westminster Central Hall 334, 337, 397, 451
Westminster College (London) 395
Westminster Training College 416, 429
Weston, Willard Garfield 456
Wetherington, L.E. 7
Whaling, Frank 293
Whatcoat, Richard 262, 330
*Where Duty Lies* 471
Whiston, William 270, 271, 273
White, Charles 205
White, Susan 53, 253, 289, 297, 306, 420
White, William 263
Whitefield, George 3, 4, 9, 210, 211, 236, 291, 292, 293, 301, 304, 310, 314, 315, 325, 409, 484
Whitehead, Dr John 329
Whiteside, J. 422
Witham, A.E. 335, 336, 337
Wigger, John 313
Wilberforce, William 44, 368
Wilkes, John 347, 348
Wilkinson, J.T. 335
*The Will of God* 336
Willard, Frances 375
Williams, Colin W. 21–22
Willow Creek Community Church, Illinois 398
Willson, Edward 395
Wilson, Clarence True 376

Wilson, Kemmons 460
Wilson, Linda 167, 293
Winkler, Jim 385
Wiseman, Luke 334
Witherington III, Ben 232
Wolffe, John 167
womanist theology 160
women
    in American Methodism 169–171
    'angel in the house' ideology 167
    artists 403
    Australian studies 171–172
    Canadian studies 171
    correspondents with John Wesley 158, 300
    education of 424
    Female Ministry; or Women's Right to Preach the Gospel 146
    first deaconess 334
    Ghanaian studies 172–173
    history of Methodist 52
    in Holiness movement 144–145, 146
    home mission societies 54
    in John Wesley's lifetime 162–165
    Korean studies 173
    life-stories of 157–159, 160, 163
    Methodism and 157–174
    Methodist Women in Britain 69
    New Zealand studies 171–172
    ordination of 68–69, 75, 168
    in Pentecostal movement 153, 155
    preachers 48–49, 158, 165–166, 328, 331, 480–481, 485–486
    sidelined in studies of Methodism 34
    social context (19th c.) 167–168
    source material 161
    South African studies 173
    Southlands College 429
    in United Methodist Church 170–171
    women's liberation 79
    women's organisations 69
    World Federation of Methodist and Uniting Church Women 74
    see also feminism; girls
*Women of Methodism* 159
*Women of Mr. Wesley's Methodism* 480
Women's Christian Temperance Union 375
Women's Fellowship 69
Women's Work 69

Wood, Edward 456
Wood, Enoch 402
Woodhouse Grove 443
Woodsworth, James Shaver 499
Woodworth-Etter, Maria 149, 150–151
Woolworth, Charles Sumner 460
Woolworth, Frank Winfield 440, 460
'A Word to A Drunkard' 368
working class 5, 8, 27–30, 37–38, 46–47, 351, 374, 411–412, 416, 445–446, 446, 478–479, 495
Workman, George C. 317
Workman, Herbert Brook 25, 335, 478, 480
*Works of the Reverend John Wesley* 17
World Alliance of Reformed Churches 76
*World Christian Encyclopedia: A Comparative Survey of Churches and Religion in the Modern World* 91
*World Christian Handbook* 90, 96
World Council of Churches 75, 90–91, 124–125
World Federation of Methodist and Uniting Church Women 74
World Fellowship of Methodist and Uniting Church Men 74
World Methodist Council 74, 124–125, 201, 202, 382
World Methodist Historical Society 74
*World Missionary Atlas* (1925) 89
World Missionary Conference (1910) 89
'world society' 204
worship see liturgy
Wren, Brian 248
Wright, Frank Lloyd 393
writing
    literature (Methodism in) 461–475
    teaching of 412–413
Wycherley, Robert 456

Young, Carlton R. 234
Young, Dinsdale 322, 334
Young, Frances 231, 341
Young, Josiah 180
Youth for Christ 323
youth clubs 414

Zinzendorf, Nicholas Ludwig von 211, 212, 291, 295, 298
Zwingli, Ulrich 222, 224